# COMPUTER SYSTEM ARCHITECTURE

# COMPUTER SYSTEM ARCHITECTURE

M. MORRIS MANO

*Professor of Engineering*
*California State University, Los Angeles*

PRENTICE-HALL, INC., Englewood Cliffs, New Jersey

*Library of Congress Cataloging in Publication Data*

MANO, M MORRIS,
Computer system architecture.

Bibliography: p.
Includes index.
1. Electronic digital computers. I. Title.
QA76.5.M224 001.6'4'044 75-30545
ISBN 0-13-166363-1



10 9 8 7 6 5 4

Printed in the United States of America

PRENTICE-HALL INTERNATIONAL, INC., *London*
PRENTICE-HALL OF AUSTRALIA, PTY. LTD., *Sydney*
PRENTICE-HALL OF CANADA, LTD., *Toronto*
PRENTICE-HALL OF INDIA PRIVATE LIMITED, *New Delhi*
PRENTICE-HALL OF JAPAN, INC., *Tokyo*
PRENTICE-HALL OF SOUTHEAST ASIA (PTE.) LTD., *Singapore*

*To*

*Sandra, Susie, and Robin*

# CONTENTS

# PREFACE

*Computer Architecture* is a term commonly used to denote the *organization and design of digital computers.* This subject is of concern to Computer Engineers who deal with the hardware design of computer systems and Computer Scientists involved in the design of hardware dependent software systems. A computer *system* is a system that includes both hardware and software. The hardware part of the system consists of the physical components and all associated equipment. The software part of the system refers to a collection of operative programs whose purpose is to make the use of the computer more effective. This book is concerned mostly with the hardware aspects of computer systems, but the impact of software on the architecture of the computer has not been neglected.

Integrated circuits (ICs) are the building blocks upon which the architecture of computers is based. Medium scale integration (MSI) devices provide digital functions and large scale integration (LSI) devices provide complete computer modules. The most important property that these devices offer is the fact that they are enclosed in very small packages. With the advent of MSI and LSI functions, computer architecture has taken on a new dimension, giving the design engineer the freedom to create structures that were previously impractical or uneconomical. It is very important for the computer designer to be familiar with the various digital functions commonly encountered in integrated circuit packages. For this reason, over thirty different MSI and LSI functions are introduced throughout the book with an explanation of their internal and external characteristics.

The interconnection between IC digital functions is best described symbolically by means of a register transfer language. Such a language is developed in the book and its relation to the hardware organization and design of digital computers is fully explained. The register transfer language is used on many occasions to specify various computer operations in a concise and precise manner.

The most essential prerequisite to the subject matter covered here is a technical or scientific background and an interest in learning about the internal organization of digital computers. Basic knowledge of digital systems is necessary for grasping some of the hardware concepts presented. Some experience in programming, either in a machine-level or high-level language will enhance the understanding of the software concepts.

The plan of the book is to present the simpler material first and introduce the more advanced subjects later. The first six chapters cover material needed for the understanding of the organization, design, and programming of a simple digital computer. The last six chapters present the separate functional units of digital computers with an emphasis on more advanced topics not covered in the early part.

Chapter 1 introduces the fundamental knowledge needed for the design of digital systems when they are constructed with individual gates and flip-flops. It covers Boolean algebra, combinational circuits, and sequential circuits. In order to keep the book within reasonable bounds, it is necessary to limit the discussion of this subject to one introductory chapter. The justification for this approach is that the design of digital computers takes on a different dimension when integrated circuit functions are employed instead of individual gates and flip-flops. The material included in the first chapter provides the necessary background for understanding the digital systems being presented.

Chapter 2 starts by enumerating the general properties of integrated circuits. It covers in detail some of the most basic MSI functions such as registers, counters, decoders, multiplexers, RAMs, and ROMs. These digital functions are used as building blocks for the design of larger units in the chapters that follow. The last section contains a reference list of over twenty other MSI and LSI functions which are covered elsewhere in the book.

Chapter 3 presents the various data types found in digital computers and shows how they are represented in binary form in computer registers. The emphasis is on the representation of numbers employed in arithmetic computations and on the binary coding of symbols, such as the letters of the alphabet, used in data processing and other discrete symbols used for specific applications.

Chapter 4 defines a register transfer language and shows how it is used to express in symbolic form the micro-operation sequences among the registers of a digital computer. Symbols are defined for arithmetic, logic, and shift micro-operations as well as for control functions that initiate the micro-operations. The presentation goes to great lengths to show the hardware implications associated with the various symbols and register transfer statements.

Chapter 5 presents the organization and design of a basic digital computer. Although the basic computer is simple when compared with commercial computer systems, it nevertheless encompasses enough functional capabilities to demonstrate the power of a stored program, general purpose device. The register transfer language is used to define the internal operation of the computer and to specify the requirements for its design.

Chapter 6 utilizes the twenty-five instructions of the basic computer defined in Chapter 5 to illustrate many of the techniques commonly used to program a computer. Programming examples in symbolic code are presented for many elementary data processing tasks. The relationship between binary programs, symbolic code programs, and high-level language programs are explained by examples. This leads into the necessity for translation programs such as assemblers and compilers. The basic operations of an assembler is presented together with other system programs. The purpose of this chapter is to introduce the basic ideas of computer software without going deeply into detail. Knowledge of software principles coupled with the hardware presentation should give the reader an overview of a total computer system which includes both hardware and software.

Chapter 7 deals with the central processor unit (CPU) of digital computers. A bus organized CPU is presented and an arithmetic logic unit (ALU) is analyzed. Both binary and decimal arithmetic units are covered. Various instruction code formats are illustrated together with addressing techniques. The organization of a memory stack is explained with a demonstration of some of its applications. The last section introduces the microprocessor which is basically a CPU enclosed in one or several LSI packages. The development of microprocessors has revolutionized computer technology. Although this is not a book devoted to microprocessors, it nevertheless presents the basic concepts needed for understanding their operation, giving the reader the technical background with which particular microprocessors can be investigated using the manufacturers' reference manuals.

Chapter 8 introduces the concept of microprogramming. A specific microprogrammed control unit is developed to show by example how to generate the microcode for a typical set of computer instructions. The chapter discusses various methods for using a control memory to initiate control functions and for determining the sequence of microinstruction addresses. The last section discusses the advantages and applications of the principle of microprogramming.

Chapter 9 is devoted to the design of an arithmetic processor. It presents the algorithms for fixed-point binary addition, subtraction, multiplication, and division in signed-magnitude representation. The arithmetic processor is then designed using the register transfer language. The configuration ties the arithmetic processor to the computer designed in Chapter 5. A binary calculator is defined and used for demonstrating the method by which the arithmetic operations can be microprogrammed. This is compared with the hard-wired control implementation and the software implementation of the same operations.

Chapter 10 presents other basic arithmetic algorithms. Algorithms are developed for signed-2's complement binary data, for floating-point data and decimal data, as well as decimal-to-binary and binary-to-decimal conversion. The algorithms are presented by means of flow charts that use the register transfer language to specify the sequence of micro-operations and control decisions required for the implemention of the algorithms.

Chapter 11 explains the function of some commonly used input and output devices. The requirement of an interface between the processor and I/O devices is explained and the various configurations available for I/O control transfers are enumerated. Specific examples are employed to illustrate the interface requirements for asynchronous serial transfer and for direct memory access (DMA). Other topics covered are priority interrupt, I/O processors, and data communication processors.

Chapter 12 introduces the concept of memory hierarchy, composed of main memory and auxilliary memory devices such as magnetic disks, drums, and tapes. Various configurations for a memory bus organization are illustrated. The internal organization and external operation of associative memories is explained in detail. The concept of memory management is introduced through the presentation of the hardware requirements of a virtual memory system.

Every chapter includes a set of problems and a list of references. Some of the problems serve as exercises for the material covered in the chapter. Others are of more advanced nature and are intended to provide some practice in solving problems associated with the broad area of digital computers and systems. A solutions manual is available for the instructor from the publisher.

The book is suitable for a course in computer design in an Electrical or Computer Engineering department. It can be used in a Computer Science department for a course in computer organization. The book is also suitable for self-study by computer engineers and scientists who need to acquire knowledge of integrated circuit functions and basic as well as advanced concepts of computer architecture.

I wish to express my greatest thanks to my wife for editing the entire manuscript, for all the suggestions she made for improving the readability of the text, and for her encouragement and support during the entire project.

M. Morris Mano

# 1

# DIGITAL LOGIC CIRCUITS

## 1-1 LOGIC GATES

A digital computer, as the name implies, is a digital system that performs various computational tasks. The word *digital* implies that the information in the computer is represented by variables that take a limited number of *discrete* or *quantized* values. These values are processed internally by components that can maintain a limited number of discrete states. The decimal digits 0, 1, 2, . . . , 9, for example, provide ten discrete values. In practice, digital computers function more reliably if only two states are used. Because of the physical restriction of components, and because human logic tends to be binary (i.e., *true* or *false*, *yes* or *no* statements), digital components that are constrained to take discrete values are further constrained to take only two values and are said to be *binary*.

Digital computers use the binary number system, which has two digits: 0 and 1. A binary digit is called a *bit*. Information is represented in digital computers in groups of bits. By using various coding techniques groups of bits can be made to represent not only binary numbers but also any other discrete symbols such as decimal digits or letters of the alphabet. By judicious use of binary arrangements and by using various coding techniques, the binary digits or groups of bits may be used to develop complete sets of instructions for performing various types of computations.

In contrast to common decimal numbers that employ the base 10 system, binary numbers use a base 2 system. For example, the binary number 101101 represents a quantity which can be converted to a decimal number by multiplying each bit by the base 2 raised to an integer power as follows:

$$1 \times 2^5 + 0 \times 2^4 + 1 \times 2^3 + 1 \times 2^2 + 0 \times 2^1 + 1 \times 2^0 = 45$$

The six bits 101101 represent a binary number whose decimal equivalent is 45. However, the group of six bits could also represent a binary code for a letter of the alphabet or a control code for specifying some decision logic in a particular digital system. In other words, groups of bits in a digital computer are used to represent many different things. This is similar to the concept that the same letters of an alphabet are used to construct different languages, such as English and French.

Binary information is represented in a digital system by physical quantities called *signals*. Electrical signals such as voltages exist throughout a digital system in either one of two recognizable values and represent a binary variable equal to 1 or 0. For example, a particular digital system may employ a signal of 3 volts to represent a binary 1 and 0.5 volt for binary 0. As shown in Fig. 1-1, each binary value has an acceptable deviation from the nominal. The intermediate region between the two allowed regions is crossed only during state transition. The input terminals of digital circuits accept binary signals within the allowable tolerances and the circuits respond at the output terminals with binary signals that fall within the specified tolerances.

*Binary logic* deals with binary variables and with operations that assume a logical meaning. It is used to describe, in algebraic or tabular form, the manipulation and processing of binary information. The manipulation of binary information is done by logic circuits called *gates*. Gates are blocks of hardware that produce signals of binary 1 or 0 when input logic requirements are satisfied. Various logic gates are commonly found in digital computer

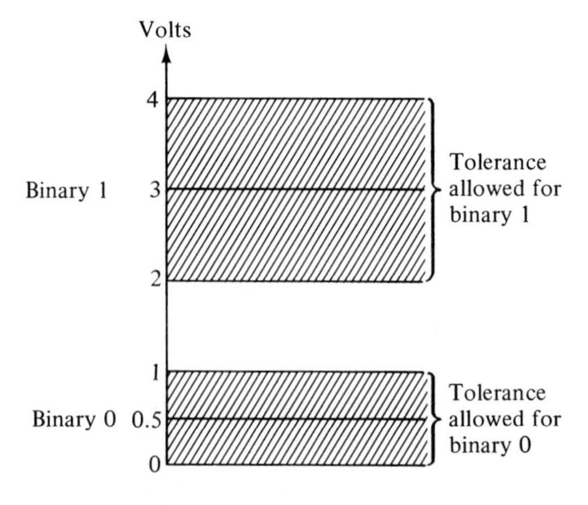


**Fig. 1-1** Example of a binary signal.

systems. Each gate has a distinct graphic symbol and its operation can be described by means of an algebraic function. The input-output relationship of the binary variables for each gate can be represented in tabular form in a *truth table.*

The names, graphic symbols, algebraic functions, and truth tables of eight logic gates are listed in Fig. 1-2. Each gate has one or two binary input variables designated by $A$ and $B$ and one binary output variable designated by $x$. The AND gate produces the AND logic function, i.e., the output is 1 if input $A$ *and* input $B$ are *both* binary 1; otherwise, the output is 0. These conditions are also specified in the truth table for the AND gate. The table shows that output $x$ is 1 only when both input $A$ and input $B$ are 1. The algebraic operation symbol of the AND function is the same as the multiplication symbol of ordinary arithmetic. We can either use a dot between the variables or concatenate the variables without an operation symbol between them. AND gates may have more than two inputs and by definition, the output is 1 if and only if *all* inputs are 1.

The OR gate produces the inclusive-OR function, i.e., the output is 1 if input $A$ or input $B$ or both inputs are 1; otherwise the output is 0. The algebraic symbol of the OR function is $+$, similar to arithmetic addition. OR gates may have more than two inputs and by definition, the output is 1 if *any* input is 1.

The inverter circuit inverts the logic sense of a binary signal. It produces the NOT, or *complement*, function. The algebraic symbol used for the logic complement is either a prime or a bar over the variable symbol. This book uses a prime for the logic complement of a binary variable while a bar over the letter is reserved for designating a complement micro-operation as defined in Chap. 4.

The small circle in the output of the graphic symbol of an inverter designates a logic complement. A triangle symbol by itself designates a buffer circuit. A buffer does not produce any particular logic function since the binary value of the output is the same as the binary value of the input. This circuit is used merely for signal amplification. For example, a buffer that uses 3 volts for binary 1 will produce an output of 3 volts when its input is 3 volts. However, the current supplied at the input is much smaller than the current produced at the output. This way, a buffer can drive many other gates requiring a large amount of current not otherwise available from the small amount of current applied to the buffer input.

The NAND function is the complement of the AND function as indicated by the graphic symbol which consists of an AND graphic symbol followed by a small circle. The designation NAND is derived from the abbreviation of NOT-AND. A more proper designation would have been AND-invert since it is the AND function that is inverted. The NOR gate is the complement of

| *Name* | *Graphic Symbol* | *Algebraic Function* | *Truth Table* |
|---|---|---|---|
| AND | 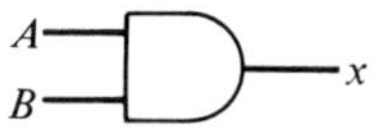 | $x = A \cdot B$ or $x = AB$ | $A$ $B$ \| $x$<br>0 0 \| 0<br>0 1 \| 0<br>1 0 \| 0<br>1 1 \| 1 |
| OR | 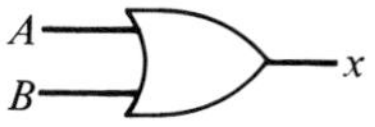 | $x = A + B$ | $A$ $B$ \| $x$<br>0 0 \| 0<br>0 1 \| 1<br>1 0 \| 1<br>1 1 \| 1 |
| inverter | 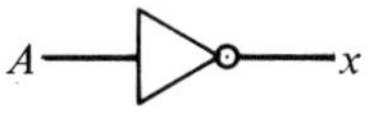 | $x = A'$ | $A$ \| $x$<br>0 \| 1<br>1 \| 0 |
| buffer | 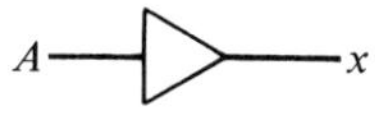 | $x = A$ | $A$ \| $x$<br>0 \| 0<br>1 \| 1 |
| NAND | 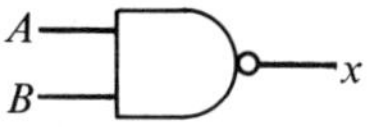 | $x = (AB)'$ | $A$ $B$ \| $x$<br>0 0 \| 1<br>0 1 \| 1<br>1 0 \| 1<br>1 1 \| 0 |

**Fig. 1-2** Digital logic gates.

the OR gate and uses an OR graphic symbol followed by a small circle. Both NAND and NOR gates may have more than two inputs and the output is always the complement of the AND or OR function, respectively.

The exclusive-OR gate has a graphic symbol similar to the OR gate except for the additional curved line on the input side. The output of this gate is 1 if any input is 1 but excludes the combination when both inputs are 1. The exclusive-OR function has its own algebraic symbol or can be expressed in terms of AND, OR, and complement operations as shown in Fig. 1-2. The exclusive-NOR is the complement of the exclusive-OR as indicated by the small circle in the graphic symbol. The output of this gate is 1 only if both inputs have the same binary value. We shall refer to the exclusive-NOR

| *Name* | *Graphic Symbol* | *Algebraic Function* | *Truth Table* |
|---|---|---|---|
| NOR | 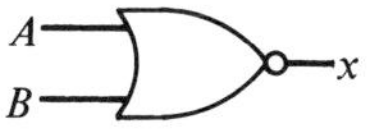 | $x = (A + B)'$ | A B \| x<br>0 0 \| 1<br>0 1 \| 0<br>1 0 \| 0<br>1 1 \| 0 |
| exclusive-OR (XOR) |  | $x = A \oplus B$<br>or<br>$x = A'B + AB'$ | A B \| x<br>0 0 \| 0<br>0 1 \| 1<br>1 0 \| 1<br>1 1 \| 0 |
| exclusive-NOR or equivalence | 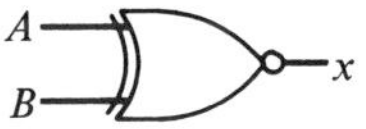 | $x = A \odot B$<br>or<br>$x = A'B' + AB$ | A B \| x<br>0 0 \| 1<br>0 1 \| 0<br>1 0 \| 0<br>1 1 \| 1 |

**Fig. 1-2** (Continued).

function as the *equivalence* function. This is because the exclusive-OR and equivalence functions are not always the complement of each other. A more fitting name for the exclusive-OR operation would be an *odd* function, i.e., its output is 1 if an odd number of inputs are 1. Thus in a three input exclusive-OR (odd) function, the output is 1 if only one input is 1 or if all three inputs are 1. The equivalence function is an *even* function, i.e., its output is 1 if an even number of inputs are 0. For a three input equivalence function, the output is 1 if none of the inputs are 0 (all inputs are 1) or if two of its inputs are 0 (one input is 1). Careful investigation will show that the exclusive-OR and equivalence functions are the complement of each other when the gates have an even number of inputs but the two functions are equal when the number of inputs is odd. These two gates are commonly available with two inputs and only seldom are they found with three or more inputs.

## 1-2 BOOLEAN ALGEBRA

Boolean algebra is an algebra that deals with binary variables and logic operations. The variables are designated by letters such as $A$, $B$, $x$, and $y$. The three basic logic operations are *AND*, *OR* and *complement*. A Boolean function is an algebraic expression formed with binary variables, the logic operation symbols, parentheses and equal sign. For a given value of the variables, the Boolean function can be either 1 or 0. Consider for example the Boolean function:

$$F = x + y'z$$

The function $F$ is equal to 1 if $x$ is 1 *or* if both $y'$ and $z$ are equal to 1; $F$ is equal to 0 otherwise. But saying that $y' = 1$ is equivalent to saying that $y = 0$ since $y'$ is the complement of $y$. Equivalently, we may say that $F$ is equal to 1 if $x = 1$ or $yz = 01$. The relationship between a function and its binary variables can be represented in a truth table. To represent a function in a truth table we need a list of the $2^n$ combinations with 1's and 0's of the $n$ binary variables. As shown in Fig. 1-3(a), there are eight possible distinct combinations for assigning bits to the three variables. The function $F$ is equal to 1 for those combinations where $x = 1$ or $yz = 01$; it is equal to 0 for all other combinations.

A Boolean function can be transformed from an algebraic expression into a *logic diagram* composed of AND, OR, and inverter gates. The logic diagram for $F$ is shown in Fig. 1-3(b). There is an inverter for input $y$ to generate its complement $y'$. There is an AND gate for the term $y'z$ and an OR gate is used to combine the two terms. In a logic diagram, the variables of the function are taken to be the inputs of the circuit and the variable symbol of the function is taken as the output of the circuit.

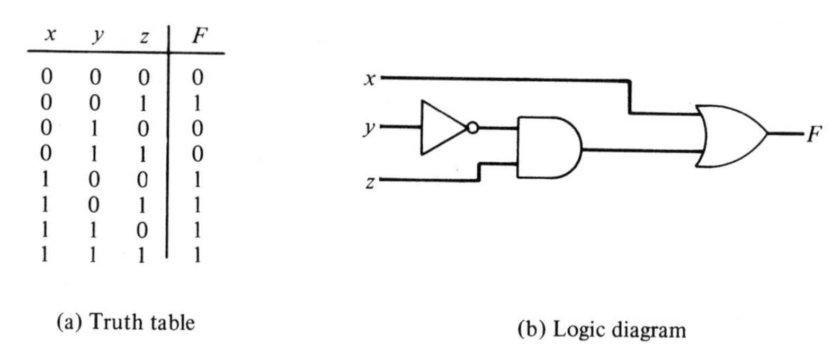

| $x$ | $y$ | $z$ | $F$ |
|---|---|---|---|
| 0 | 0 | 0 | 0 |
| 0 | 0 | 1 | 1 |
| 0 | 1 | 0 | 0 |
| 0 | 1 | 1 | 0 |
| 1 | 0 | 0 | 1 |
| 1 | 0 | 1 | 1 |
| 1 | 1 | 0 | 1 |
| 1 | 1 | 1 | 1 |



(a) Truth table

(b) Logic diagram

**Fig. 1-3** Truth table and logic diagram for $F = x + y'z$.

The purpose of Boolean algebra is to facilitate the analysis and design of digital circuits. It provides a convenient tool to:

(a) express in algebraic form a truth table relationship between variables,

(b) express in algebraic form the input-output relationship of logic diagrams and, most important,

(c) find simpler circuits for the same function.

A Boolean function specified by a truth table can be expressed algebraically in many different ways. By manipulating a Boolean expression according to Boolean algebra rules, one may obtain a simpler expression that will require fewer gates. To see how this is done, we must first study the manipulative capabilities of Boolean algebra.

Table 1-1 lists the most basic relations of Boolean algebra. All the relations can be proven by means of truth tables. The first eight in Table 1-1 show

**Table 1-1** *Basic relations of Boolean algebra*

| | |
|---|---|
| (1) $x + 0 = x$ | (2) $x \cdot 0 = 0$ |
| (3) $x + 1 = 1$ | (4) $x \cdot 1 = x$ |
| (5) $x + x = x$ | (6) $x \cdot x = x$ |
| (7) $x + x' = 1$ | (8) $x \cdot x' = 0$ |
| (9) $x + y = y + x$ | (10) $xy = yx$ |
| (11) $x + (y + z) = (x + y) + z$ | (12) $x(yz) = (xy)z$ |
| (13) $x(y + z) = xy + xz$ | (14) $x + yz = (x + y)(x + z)$ |
| (15) $(x + y)' = x'y'$ | (16) $(xy)' = x' + y'$ |
| (17) $(x')' = x$ | |

the basic relationship between a single variable and itself, or in conjunction with the binary constants of 1 and 0. The next five relations (9 to 13) are similar to ordinary algebra. Relation 14 does not apply in ordinary algebra but is very useful in manipulating Boolean expressions. Relations 15 and 16 are called *DeMorgan's theorems* and are discussed below. The last relation states that if a variable is complemented twice, one obtains the original value of the variable. The relations listed in the table apply to single variables $x$, $y$, and $z$ or to Boolean functions expressed by binary variables $x$, $y$, or $z$.

DeMorgan's theorem is very important in dealing with NOR and NAND gates. It states that a NOR gate that performs the $(x + y)'$ function is equivalent to the function $x'y'$. Similarly, a NAND function can be expressed by either $(xy)'$ or by $x' + y'$. For this reason, the NOR and NAND gates have two distinct graphic symbols as shown in Figs. 1-4 and 1-5. Instead of representing a NOR gate with an OR graphic symbol followed by a circle, we can represent it by an AND graphic symbol preceded by circles in all inputs. The invert-AND symbol for the NOR gate follows from DeMorgan's theorem and from the convention that small circles denote complementation. Similarly, the NAND gate has two distinct symbols as shown in Fig. 1-5.

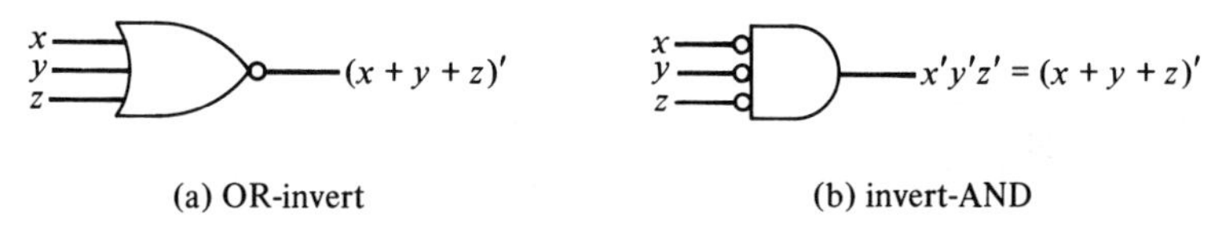


**Fig. 1-4** Two graphic symbols for NOR gate.

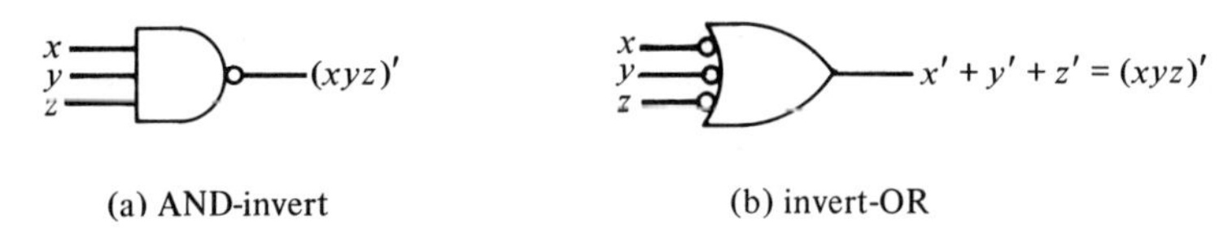


(a) AND-invert (b) invert-OR

**Fig. 1-5** Two graphic symbols for NAND gate.

To see how Boolean algebra manipulation is used to simplify digital circuits consider the logic diagram of Fig. 1-6(a). The output of the first NAND gate is, by DeMorgan's theorem, $(AB')' = A' + B$. The output of the circuit is the NAND operation of this term and $B'$:

$$x = [(A' + B) \cdot B']'$$

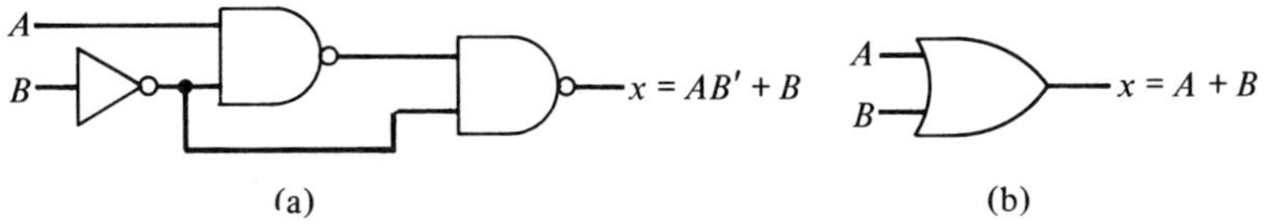

A
B
x = AB' + B
(a)

A
B
x = A + B
(b)

**Fig. 1-6** Two logic diagrams for the same Boolean function.

Using DeMorgan's theorem twice more we obtain:

$$x = (A' + B)' + B = AB' + B$$

Note that DeMorgan's theorem has been applied three times (to demonstrate its use) but could have been applied only once as follows:

$$x = [(AB')' \cdot B']' = AB' + B$$

The expression for $x$ can be simplified by application of the relations listed in Table 1-1.

$$\begin{aligned} x &= AB' + B && \textit{by relation} \\ &= B + AB' && (9) \\ &= (B + A)(B + B') && (14) \\ &= (B + A) \cdot 1 && (7) \\ &= B + A = A + B && (4), (9) \end{aligned}$$

The final result produces an OR function and can be implemented with a single OR gate as shown in Fig. 1-6(b). One can show that the two circuits produce identical input-output binary relationships by obtaining the truth table of each.

## 1-3 MAP SIMPLIFICATION

The complexity of the logic diagram that implements a Boolean function is directly related to the complexity of the algebraic expression from which the function is implemented. The truth table representation of a function is unique but the function can appear in many different forms when expressed algebraically. The expression may be simplified using the basic relations of Boolean algebra. This procedure, however, is sometimes difficult because it lacks specific rules for predicting each succeeding step in the manipulative process. The map method provides a simple, straightforward procedure for simplifying Boolean functions. This method may be regarded as a pictorial arrangement of the truth table which allows an easy interpretation for choosing the minimum number of variables needed to express the function algebraically. The map method is also known by the names *Karnaugh map* and *Veitch diagram.*

Each combination of the variables in a truth table is called a *minterm.* For example, the truth table of Fig. 1-3 contains eight minterms. A function of $n$ variables when expressed by means of a truth table will have $2^n$ minterms, equivalent to the $2^n$ binary numbers obtained from $n$ digits. A Boolean function will be equal to 1 for some minterms and to 0 for others. The information contained in a truth table may be expressed in compact form by listing the decimal equivalent of those minterms that produce a 1 for the function. For example, the truth table of Fig. 1-3 can be expressed as follows:

$$F(x, y, z) = \sum (1, 4, 5, 6, 7)$$

The letters in parentheses list the binary variables in the order that they appear in the truth table. The symbol $\sum$ stands for the sum of the minterms that follow in parentheses. The minterms that produce 1 for the function are listed in their decimal equivalent. The minterms missing from the list are the ones that produce 0 for the function.

The map is a diagram made up of squares, with each square representing one minterm. The squares corresponding to minterms that produce 1 for the function are marked by a 1 and the others are marked by a 0 or left empty. By recognizing various patterns and combining squares marked by 1's in the map, it is possible to derive alternate algebraic expressions for the function, from which the most convenient may be selected.

The maps for functions of two, three, and four variables are shown in Fig. 1-7. The number of squares in a map of $n$ variables is $2^n$. The $2^n$ minterms are listed by an equivalent decimal number for easy reference. The minterm numbers are assigned in an orderly arrangement such that adjacent squares represent minterms which differ by only one variable. The variable names are listed across both sides of the diagonal line in the corner of the map. The 0's

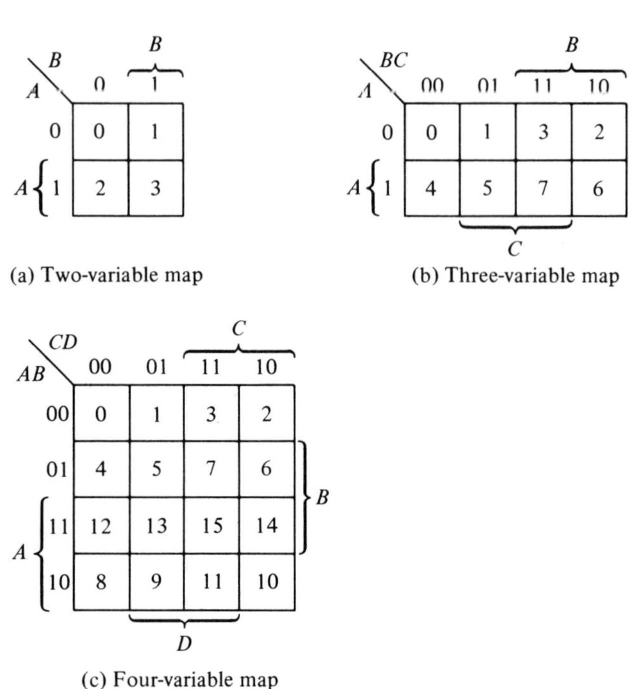


**Fig. 1-7** Maps for two, three, and four variable functions.

and 1's marked along each row and each column designate the value of the variables. Each variable under brackets contains half of the squares in the map where that variable appears unprimed. The variable appears with a prime (complemented) in the remaining half of the squares. All the information appearing in the maps of Fig. 1-7 is not always needed; it is shown here for explanation only.

The minterm represented by a square is determined from the binary assignments of the variables along the left and top edges in the map. For example, minterm 5 in the three-variable map is 101 in binary which may be obtained from the 1 in the second row concatanated with the 01 of the second column. This minterm represents a value for the binary variables $A$, $B$, and $C$, with $A$ and $C$ being unprimed and $B$ being primed, i.e., $AB'C$. On the other hand, minterm 5 in the four-variable map represents a minterm for four variables. The binary number contains the four digits 0101 and the corresponding term it represents is $A'BC'D$.

Minterms of adjacent squares in the map are identical except for one variable which appears complemented in one square and uncomplemented in the *adjacent* square. According to this definition of adjacency, the squares at the extreme ends of the same horizontal row are also to be considered adjacent. The same applies to the top and bottom squares of a column. As a result, the four corner squares of a map also must be considered to be adjacent.

A Boolean function represented by a truth table is entered into the map by inserting 1's in those squares where the function is 1. The squares containing 1's are combined in groups of adjacent squares. These groups must contain a number of squares which is an integral power of 2. Groups of combined adjacent squares may share one or more square with one or more group. Each group of squares represents an algebraic term, and the OR of those terms gives the simplified algebraic expression for the function. The following examples show the use of the map for simplifying Boolean functions.

***Example 1.*** Simplify the Boolean function

$$F(A, B, C) = \sum (3, 4, 6, 7)$$

The three-variable map for this function is shown in Fig. 1-8. There are four squares marked with 1's, one for each minterm that produces 1 for the function. These squares belong to minterms 3, 4, 6, and 7 and are recognized from Fig. 1-7(b). Two adjacent squares are combined in the third column. This column belongs to both $B$ and $C$ and produces the term $BC$. The remaining two squares with 1's in the two corners of the second row are adjacent and belong to row $A$ and the two columns of $C'$, so they produce the term $AC'$. The simplified algebraic expression for the function is the OR of the two terms:

$$F = BC + AC'$$

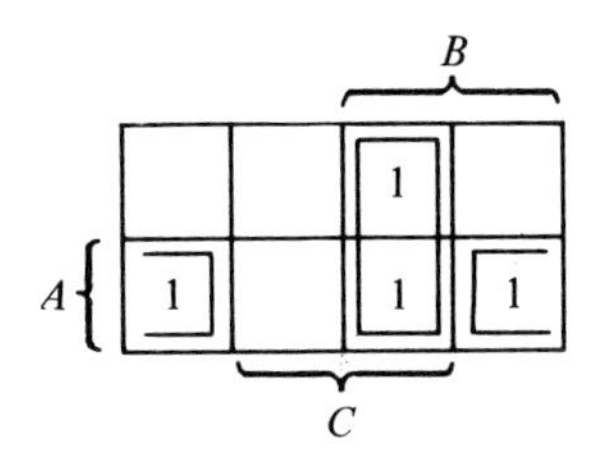


**Fig. 1-8** Map for $F = \sum(3, 4, 6, 7) = BC + AC'$

***Example 2.*** Simplify the Boolean function

$$F(A, B, C) = \sum (0, 2, 4, 5, 6)$$

The five minterms are marked by 1's in the corresponding squares of the three-variable map shown in Fig. 1-9. The four squares in the first and fourth columns are adjacent and represent the term $C'$. The remaining square marked with a 1 for minterm 5 is combined with the square of minterm 4 to produce the term $AB'$. The simplified function is:

$$F = C' + AB'$$

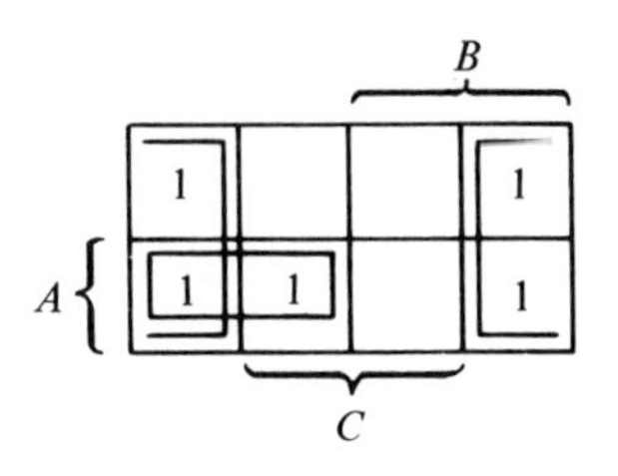


**Fig. 1-9** Map for $F = \sum(0, 2, 4, 5, 6) = C' + AB'$

*Example 3.* Simplify the Boolean function

$$F(A, B, C, D) = \sum (0, 1, 2, 6, 8, 9, 10)$$

The area in the map covered by this four-variable function consists of the squares marked with 1's in Fig. 1-10. The function contains 1's in the four corners that, when taken as a group, give the term $B'D'$. This is possible because these four squares are adjacent when the map is considered with top and bottom or left and right edges touching. The two 1's on the left of the top row are combined with the two 1's on the left of the bottom row to give the term $B'C'$. The remaining 1 in the square of minterm 6 is combined with minterm 2 to give the term $A'CD'$. The simplified function is

$$F = B'D' + B'C' + A'CD'$$

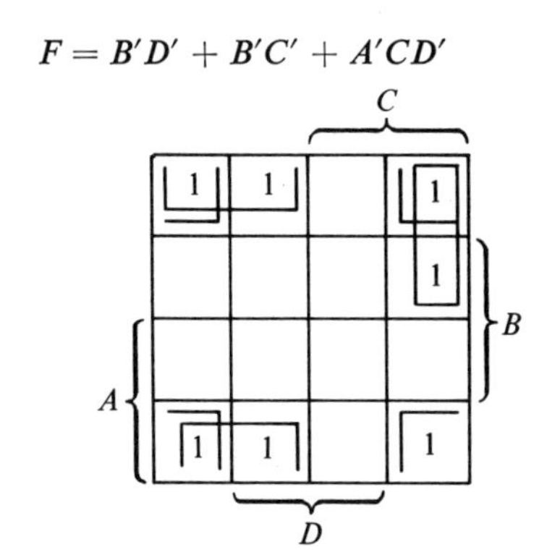


**Fig. 1-10** Map for $F = \sum(0, 1, 2, 6, 8, 9, 10) = B'D' + B'C' + A'CD'$

## *Product of Sums*

The Boolean functions derived from the maps in the previous examples were expressed in *sum of products* form. The product terms are AND terms and the sum denotes the ORing of these terms. It is sometimes convenient to obtain the algebraic expression for the function in a *product of sums* form. The sums are OR terms and the product denotes the ANDing of these terms. With a minor modification, a product of sums form can be obtained from a map.

The procedure for obtaining a product of sums expression follows from the basic properties of Boolean algebra. The 1's in the map represent the minterms that produce 1 for the function. The squares not marked by 1 represent the minterms that produce 0 for the function. If we mark the empty squares by 0's and combine them into groups of adjacent squares, we obtain the complement of the function, $F'$. Using DeMorgan's theorem, we take the complement of $F'$, i.e., $(F')' = F$ and the function so obtained is in product of sums form. The best way to show this is by example.

***Example 4.*** Simplify the following Boolean function in (a) sum of products form and (b) product of sums form.

$$F(A, B, C, D) = \sum (0, 1, 2, 5, 8, 9, 10)$$

The 1's marked in the map of Fig. 1-11 represent the minterms that produce a 1 for the function. The squares marked with 0's represent the minterms not included in $F$, and therefore, denote the complement of $F$. Combining the squares with 1's gives the simplified function in sum of products form:

$$F = B'D' + B'C' + A'C'D$$

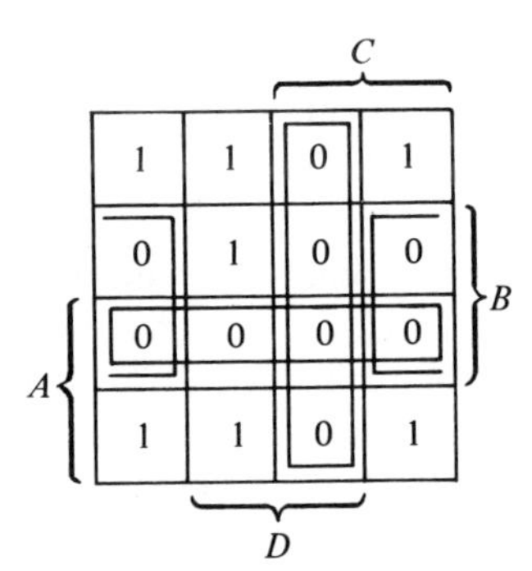


**Fig. 1-11** Map for Example 4.

If the squares marked with 0's are combined, as shown in the diagram, one obtains the simplified complemented function:

$$F' = AB + CD + BD'$$

Applying DeMorgan's theorem, we obtain the simplified function in product of sums form:

$$F = (A' + B')(C' + D')(B' + D)$$

The logic diagrams of the simplified expressions obtained in Example 4 are shown in Fig. 1-12. The sum of products expression is implemented in Fig. 1-12(a) with a group of AND gates, one for each AND term. The outputs of the AND gates are connected to the inputs of a single OR gate. The same function is implemented in Fig. 1-12(b) in its product of sums form with a group of OR gates, one for each OR term. The outputs of the OR gates are connected to the inputs of a single AND gate. In each case it is assumed that

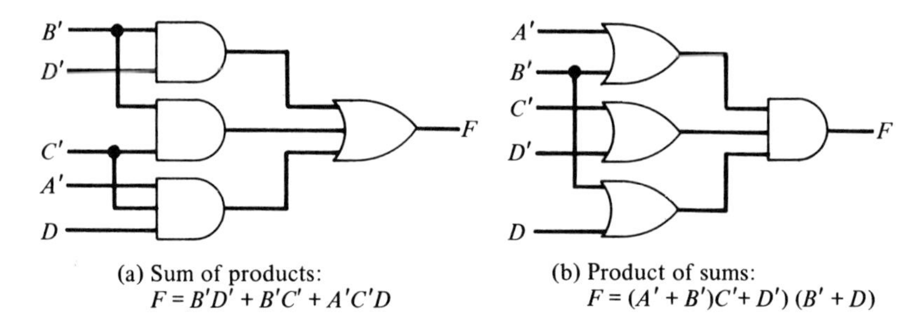


(a) Sum of products:
$F = B'D' + B'C' + A'C'D$

(b) Product of sums:
$F = (A' + B'C' + D')(B' + D)$

**Fig. 1-12** Logic diagrams for the function of Example 4.

the input variables are directly available in their complement so inverters are not included. The pattern established in Fig. 1-12 is the general form by which any Boolean function is implemented when expressed in one of the standard forms. AND gates are connected to a single OR gate when in sum of products form. OR gates are connected to a single AND gate when in product of sums form.

A sum of products expression can be implemented with NAND gates as shown in Fig. 1-13(a). Note that the second NAND gate is drawn with the graphic symbol of Fig. 1-5(b). There are three lines in the diagram with small circles at both ends. Two circles in the same line designate double complementation and since $(x')' = x$, the two circles can be removed and the resulting diagram is equivalent to the one shown in Fig. 1-12(a). Similarly, a product of sums expression can be implemented with NOR gates as shown in Fig. 1-13(b). The second NOR gate is drawn with the graphic symbol of Fig. 1-4(b). Again the two circles on both sides of each line may be removed and the diagram so obtained is equivalent to the one shown in Fig. 1-12(b).

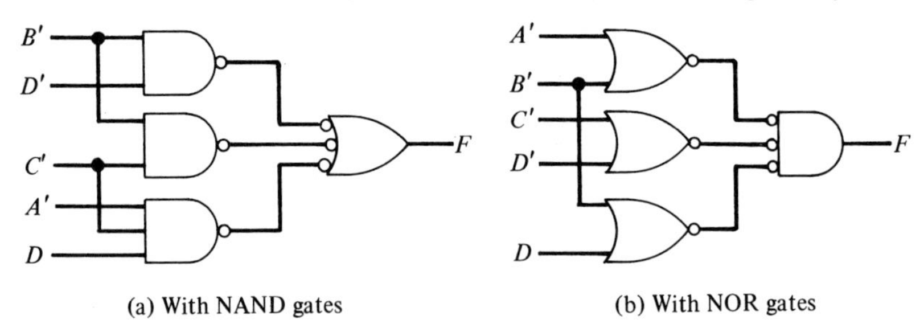


(a) With NAND gates

(b) With NOR gates

**Fig. 1-13** Logic diagrams for the function of Example 4.

### *Don't-Care Conditions*

The 1's and 0's in the map represent the minterms that make the function equal to 1 or 0. There are occasions when it does not matter if the function produces 0 or 1 for a given minterm. Since the function may be either 0 or 1, we say that we don't-care what the function output is to be for this minterm. Minterms that may produce either 0 or 1 for the function are said to be *don't-care conditions* and are marked by an $X$ in the map. These don't-care conditions can be used to provide further simplification of the algebraic expression.

When choosing adjacent squares for the function in the map, the $X$'s may be assumed to be either 0 or 1, whichever gives the simplest expression. In addition, an $X$ need not be used at all if it does not contribute to the simplification of the function. In each case, the choice depends only on the simplification that can be achieved.

***Example 5.*** Simplify the Boolean function

$$F(A, B, C) = \sum (0, 2, 6)$$

having the don't-care conditions

$$d(A, B, C) = \sum (1, 3, 5)$$

The minterms listed with $F$ produce a 1 for the function. The minterms of $d$ may produce either a 0 or a 1 for the function. The remaining minterms, i.e., 4 and 7, produce a 0 for the function. The map is shown in Fig. 1-14. The minterms of $F$ are marked with 1's, those of $d$ are marked by $X$'s, and the remaining squares may be marked by 0's or left empty. The 1's and $X$'s are combined in any convenient manner so as to enclose the maximum number of adjacent squares. It is not necessary to include all or any of the $X$'s but all the 1's must be included. By including the don't-care minterms 1 and 3 with the 1's in the first row we obtain the term $A'$. The remaining 1 for minterm 6 is combined with minterm 2 to obtain the term $BC'$. The simplified expression is

$$F = A' + BC'$$

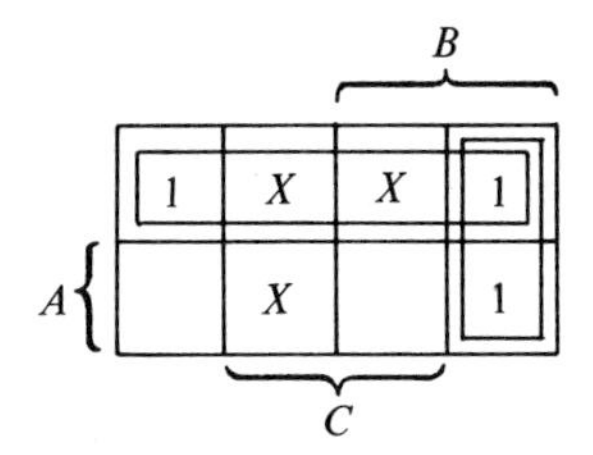


**Fig. 1-14** Example of map with don't-care conditions.

Note that don't-care minterm 5 was not included because it does not contribute to the simplification of the expression. Note also that if don't-care minterms 1 and 3 were not included with the 1's, the simplified expression for $F$ would have been

$$F = A'C' + BC'$$

This would require two AND gates and an OR gate, as opposed to the expression obtained previously which requires only one AND and one OR gate.

The function is completely determined once the $X$'s are assigned to the 1's or 0's in the map. Thus, the expression

$$F = A' + BC'$$

when transferred to a truth table will have minterms 0, 1, 2, 3, and 6 produce a 1 for the function and minterms 4, 5, and 7 produce a 0. Since minterms 1, 3, and 5 were specified as being don't-care conditions, i.e., they can produce either a 0 or a 1 for the function, we have chosen minterms 1 and 3 to produce a binary 1 and minterm 5 to produce a 0 because this combination gives the simplest Boolean expression.

## 1-4 COMBINATIONAL CIRCUITS

A combinational circuit is a connected arrangement of logic gates with a set of inputs and outputs. At any given time, the binary values of the outputs are a function of the combination of 1's and 0's presented at the inputs. By contrast, a sequential circuit contains not only gates but also storage circuits called *flip-flops.* The binary values of the outputs in a sequential circuit are a function of both the input combinations and the state of the flip-flops. Flip-flops are presented in Sec. 1-5 and sequential circuits are discussed in Sec. 1-6.

A combinational circuit can be described by a truth table showing the binary relations between $n$ inputs and $m$ outputs. For $n$ input variables, there are $2^n$ possible combinations of binary input values. For each of the $2^n$ possible input combinations in the truth table, there is one and only one output combination.

A combinational circuit is also specified by $m$ Boolean functions, one for each output variable. Each output function is expressed in terms of the $n$ input variables.

Combinational circuits are employed in digital systems for (a) generating binary control decisions and (b) generating digital functions required in data processing. The following examples demonstrate the use of combinational circuits in the design of digital systems.

### *Binary Decision Logic*

Digital computers have internal hardware that generates various data processing tasks. Each task is generated by a combinational circuit and controlled by binary decision logic. An example that may clarify this concept is presented in the block diagram of Fig. 1-15. Here we have two digital function modules that perform two data processing tasks. For example, digital function I may generate the arithmetic sum of two numbers available in its data inputs and digital function II may add a constant to its data input

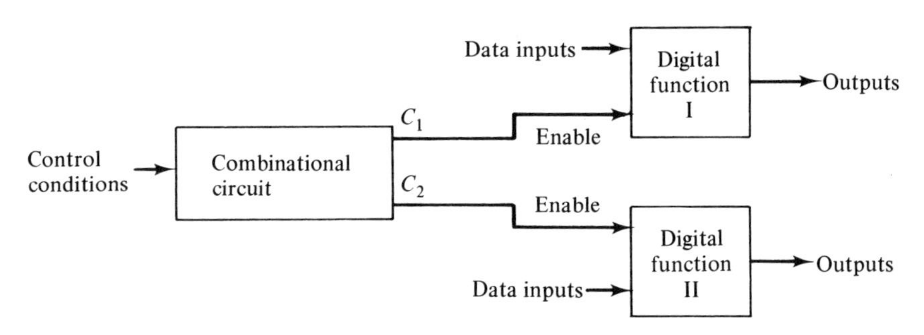


**Fig. 1-15** Example showing binary decision logic.

value. These functions must be generated at a given time and under conditions dictated by control inputs $C_1$ and $C_2$ respectively. In other words, if $C_1 = 0$ the output of digital function I does not change. If $C_1 = 1$, the function is said to be *enabled* and the output generates the required function.

Let us assume that the control conditions are dictated by three timing sequences, $T_1$, $T_2$, and $T_3$, and by the values of two binary variables generated within the system, $x$ and $y$. The timing sequences are binary signals that occur in time sequence one after the other. Thus, at a given time, signal $T_1 = 1$ while $T_2 = T_3 = 0$. During the next time period $T_1 = 0$, $T_2 = 1$, and $T_3 = 0$, etc. The internal variables are results of previous operations that are sometimes used to condition succeeding operations. For example, binary variable $x$ may be used to indicate that two numbers are equal ($x = 1$) or unequal ($x = 0$).

The conditions that control variables $C_1$ and $C_2$ to enable the digital functions may be specified by a set of Boolean functions. Let us assume that these functions are as follows:

$$C_1 = xT_1 + T_2 + yT_3$$

$$C_2 = y'T_3$$

The interpretation of these functions is that $C_1 = 1$ if $x = 1$ when timing variable $T_1 = 1$ *or* if timing variable $T_2 = 1$ *or* if $y = 1$ when timing variable $T_3 = 1$; otherwise, $C_1 = 0$. Similarly, $C_2 = 1$ if $y = 0$ and timing variable $T_3 = 1$. The two Boolean functions for $C_1$ and $C_2$ specify a combinational circuit. The logic diagram for this circuit is shown in Fig. 1-16. It consists of three AND gates for the three AND terms, an inverter to generate $y'$ and an OR gate for the three terms of $C_1$.

Binary control decisions in digital computers are generated in combinational or sequential circuits. The input variables for these circuits are internal timing sequences and binary variables from various parts of the system. The digital functions being controlled are circuits that implement various data processing tasks. Examples of digital functions are circuits that perform

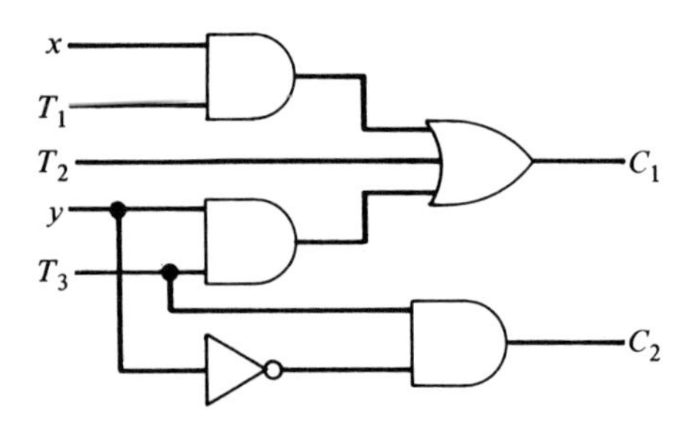


**Fig. 1-16** Combinational circuit for control logic.

arithmetic operations, circuits for decoding binary codes, and circuits for storing binary information. Many digital functions are available commercially in small packages called *integrated circuits.* Chapter 2 introduces integrated circuits and a number of digital functions commonly found in integrated circuit packages.

To demonstrate the design of combination circuits we will present a few simple circuits that serve as building blocks for the construction of more complicated arithmetic digital functions.

### Half-Adder

The most basic digital arithmetic function is the addition of two binary digits. A combinational circuit that performs the arithmetic addition of two bits is called a *half-adder*. One that performs the addition of three bits (two significant bits and a previous carry) is called a *full-adder*. The name of the former stems from the fact that two half-adders can be employed to implement a full-adder.

The input variables of a half-adder are called the *augend* and *addend* bits. The output variables are called the *sum* and *carry*. It is necessary to specify two output variables because the sum of $1 + 1$ is binary 10, which has two digits. We assign symbols $x$ and $y$ to the two input variables, and $S$ (for sum) and $C$ (for carry) to the two output variables. The truth table for the half-adder is shown in Fig. 1-17(a). The $C$ output is 0 unless both inputs are 1.

| $x$ | $y$ | $C$ | $S$ |
|---|---|---|---|
| 0 | 0 | 0 | 0 |
| 0 | 1 | 0 | 1 |
| 1 | 0 | 0 | 1 |
| 1 | 1 | 1 | 0 |

(a) Truth table

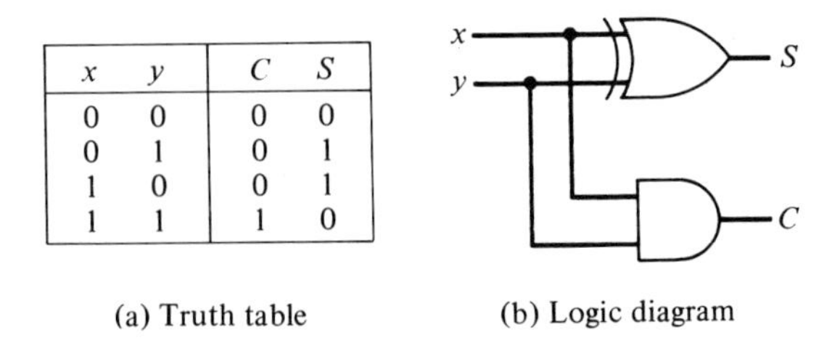


(b) Logic diagram

**Fig. 1-17** Half-adder.

The $S$ output represents the least significant bit of the sum. The Boolean functions for the two outputs can be obtained directly from the truth table:

$$S = x'y + xy' = x \oplus y$$
$$C = xy$$

The logic diagram is shown in Fig. 1-17(b). It consists of an exclusive-OR gate and an AND gate.

### *Full-Adder*

A full-adder is a combinational circuit that forms the arithmetic sum of three input bits. It consists of three inputs and two outputs. Two of the input variables, denoted by $x$ and $y$, represent the two significant bits to be added. The third input, $z$, represents the carry from the previous lower significant position. Two outputs are necessary because the arithmetic sum of three binary digits ranges in value from 0 to 3, and binary 2 or 3 needs two digits. The two outputs are designated by the symbols $S$ (for sum) and $C$ (for carry). The binary variable $S$ gives the value of the least significant bit of the sum. The binary variable $C$ gives the output carry. The truth table of the full-adder is shown in Table 1-2.

**Table 1-2** *Truth table for full-adder*

| *Inputs* | | | *Outputs* | |
|---|---|---|---|---|
| $x$ | $y$ | $z$ | $C$ | $S$ |
| 0 | 0 | 0 | 0 | 0 |
| 0 | 0 | 1 | 0 | 1 |
| 0 | 1 | 0 | 0 | 1 |
| 0 | 1 | 1 | 1 | 0 |
| 1 | 0 | 0 | 0 | 1 |
| 1 | 0 | 1 | 1 | 0 |
| 1 | 1 | 0 | 1 | 0 |
| 1 | 1 | 1 | 1 | 1 |

The eight rows under the input variables designate all possible combinations of 1's and 0's that these variables may have. The 1's and 0's for the output variables are determined from the arithmetic sum of the input bits. When all input bits are 0's the output is 0. The $S$ output is equal to 1 when only one input is equal to 1 or when all three inputs are equal to 1. The $C$ output has a carry of 1 if two or three inputs are equal to 1.

The maps of Fig. 1-18 are used to find algebraic expressions for each of the output variables. The 1's in the squares for the maps of $S$ and $C$ are determined directly from the minterms in the truth table. The squares with 1's for the $S$ output do not combine in groups of adjacent squares. But since the output is 1 when an odd number of inputs are 1, $S$ is an odd function, and represents the exclusive-OR relation of the variables (see discussion at the end of Sec. 1-1). The squares with 1's for the $C$ output may be combined in a variety of ways. One possible expression for $C$ is:

$$C = xy + (x'y + xy')z$$

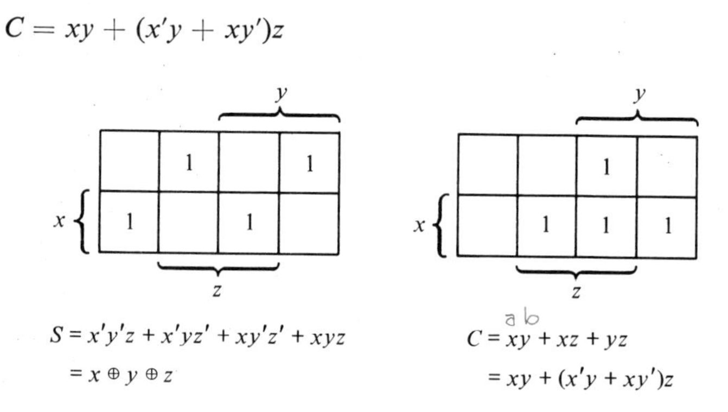


**Fig. 1-18** Maps for full-adder.

Realizing that $x'y + xy' = x \oplus y$, and including the expression for output $S$, we obtain the two functions for the full-adder:

$$S = x \oplus y \oplus z$$
$$C = xy + (x \oplus y)z$$

The logic diagram for the full-adder is drawn in Fig. 1-19(a). Note that the full-adder circuit consists of two half-adders and an OR gate.

The full-adder circuit is the most basic digital function for generating arithmetic operations in digital computers. When used in subsequent chap-

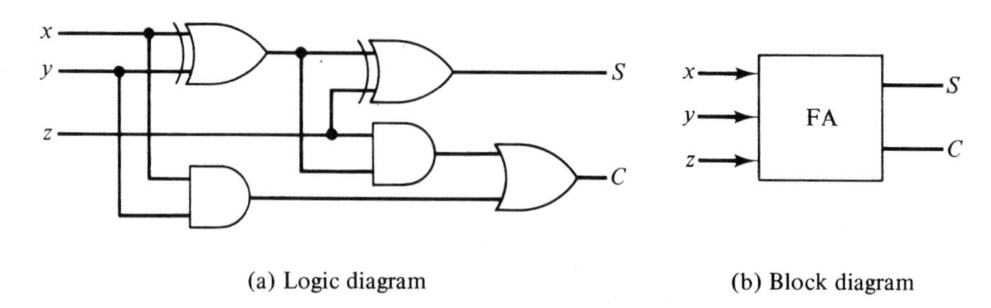


(a) Logic diagram (b) Block diagram

**Fig. 1-19** Full-adder circuit.

ters, the full-adder circuit will be designated by a block diagram symbol as shown in Fig. 1-19(b).

### *Full-Subtractor*

A full-subtractor is a combinational circuit that performs a subtraction between two bits while taking into account the fact that a 1 may have been borrowed by a lower significant position. This circuit consists of three inputs and two outputs. The three inputs $x$, $y$, and $z$ denote the minuend, subtrahend, and previous borrow, respectively. The two outputs $D$ and $K$ represent the difference and next borrow, respectively. The truth table for the circuit is shown in Table 1-3.

**Table 1-3** *Truth table for full-subtractor*

| *Inputs* | | | *Outputs* | |
|---|---|---|---|---|
| $x$ | $y$ | $z$ | $K$ | $D$ |
| 0 | 0 | 0 | 0 | 0 |
| 0 | 0 | 1 | 1 | 1 |
| 0 | 1 | 0 | 1 | 1 |
| 0 | 1 | 1 | 1 | 0 |
| 1 | 0 | 0 | 0 | 1 |
| 1 | 0 | 1 | 0 | 0 |
| 1 | 1 | 0 | 0 | 0 |
| 1 | 1 | 1 | 1 | 1 |

The eight rows under the input variables designate all possible combinations of 1's and 0's that the binary variables may take. The 1's and 0's for the output variables are determined from the subtraction of $x - y$, taking into account that when $z = 1$, it signifies that a bit has been borrowed by the previous lower significant position. This borrow must be subtracted from the minuend bit $x$. For example, with $x = 0$, $y = 0$, and $z = 1$, we have to borrow a 1 from the next stage, which makes $K = 1$ and adds 2 to $x$. Since $z = 1$ signifies a previous borrow we must subtract a 1 from $x$ so that $2 - 1 = 1$. The value of $y$ is then subtracted from $x$ to give for the difference $D = 1 - 0 = 1$.

The simplified Boolean functions for the two outputs of the full-subtractor can be derived by means of maps. The output functions are:

$$D = x \oplus y \oplus z$$

$$K = x'y + x'z + yz$$

We note that the logic function for output $D$ in the full-subtractor is exactly the same as output $S$ in the full-adder. Moreover, the output $K$ resembles the function for $C$ in the full-adder except that the input variable $x$ is complemented. Because of these similarities, it is possible to convert a full-adder into a full-subtractor merely by complementing input $x$ (the minuend) prior to its application to the gates that form the carry output. Subtractors are very seldom used as digital functions because, as we shall see in Chap. 3, a subtraction operation may be achieved by complementing the subtrahend and adding it to the minuend.

## 1-5 FLIP-FLOPS

There are two types of sequential circuits and their classification depends on the timing of their signals. A *synchronous* sequential circuit employs storage elements called *flip-flops* that are allowed to change their binary value only at discrete instants of time. An *asynchronous* sequential circuit is a system whose outputs depend upon the order in which its input variables change and can be affected at any instant of time. Gate-type asynchronous systems are basically combinational circuits with feedback paths. Because of the feedback among logic gates the system may, at times, become unstable. The instability problems encountered in asynchronous systems impose many difficulties and for this reason, they are very seldom used in the design of digital computer systems.

Synchronous sequential logic systems use logic gates and flip-flop storage devices. Synchronization is achieved by a timing device called a *clock pulse* generator. The clock pulses from the generator are distributed throughout the system in such a way that flip-flops are affected only with the arrival of the synchronization pulse. Clocked synchronous sequential circuits do not manifest instability problems and their timing is easily broken down into independent discrete steps, each of which may be considered separately. The sequential circuits discussed in this book are exclusively of the clocked synchronous type.

A flip-flop is a binary cell capable of storing one bit of information. It has two outputs, one for the normal value and one for the complement value of the bit stored in it. A flip-flop maintains a binary state until directed by a clock pulse to switch states. The difference among various types of flip-flops is in the number of inputs they possess and in the manner in which the inputs affect the binary state. The most common types of flip-flops are discussed below.

### *Basic Flip-Flop or Latch*

An asynchronous flip-flop is constructed from two NAND gates or two NOR gates connected back to back. The circuit for the NAND version is shown in Fig. 1-20. The cross-coupled connections from the output of one gate to the input of the other gate constitutes a feedback path. For this reason, the circuit is classified as asychronous. Each flip-flop has two outputs, $Q$ and $Q'$, and two inputs, *set* and *reset*. This type of flip-flop is called a *direct-coupled RS* flip-flop, the $R$ and $S$ being the first letters of the two input names. Another more popular name for this type of flip-flop is a *latch*. The latch forms a basic circuit upon which more complicated flip-flop types can be constructed.

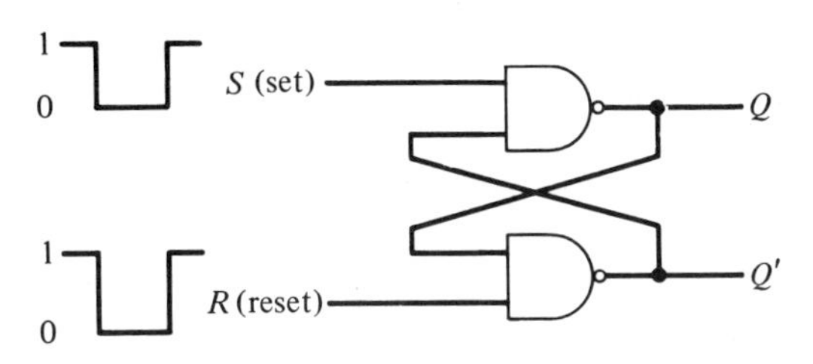


**Fig. 1-20** Basic flip-flop (latch).

The NAND latch operates with both inputs normally at 1, unless the state of the circuit has to be changed. The application of a momentary 0 to the set input causes output $Q$ to go to 1 and $Q'$ to go to 0. The outputs of the circuit do not change when the set input returns to 1. A momentary 0 applied to the reset input causes an output of $Q = 0$ and $Q' = 1$. The state of the flip-flop is always taken from the value of its normal output $Q$. When $Q = 1$, we say that the flip-flop stores a 1 and is in the *set* state. When $Q = 0$, we say that the flip-flop stores a 0 and is in the *clear* state.

The latch circuit manifests an undesirable condition if *both* inputs go to 0 simultaneously. Investigation of the circuit will show that when both inputs are 0, outputs $Q$ and $Q'$ will go to 1, a condition which is normally meaningless in flip-flop operation. If both inputs are then returned to 1, the state of the flip-flop is unpredictable; either state may result, depending on which input remains in the 0 state for a longer period of time before the transition to 1.

### *RS Flip-Flop*

By adding gates to the inputs of the latch, the flip-flop can be made to respond only during the occurrence of a clock pulse. The clocked $RS$ flip-flop, shown in Fig. 1-21, consists of the basic latch and two other NAND gates. The outputs of gates 3 and 4 remain at 1 as long as the clock pulse (abbreviated $CP$) is 0, regardless of the $S$ and $R$ input values. When the clock pulse goes to 1, information from the $S$ and $R$ inputs is allowed to reach the latch in gates 1 and 2. The set state is reached with $S = 1$, $R = 0$, and $CP = 1$. To change to the clear state, the inputs must be $S = 0$, $R = 1$, and $CP = 1$.

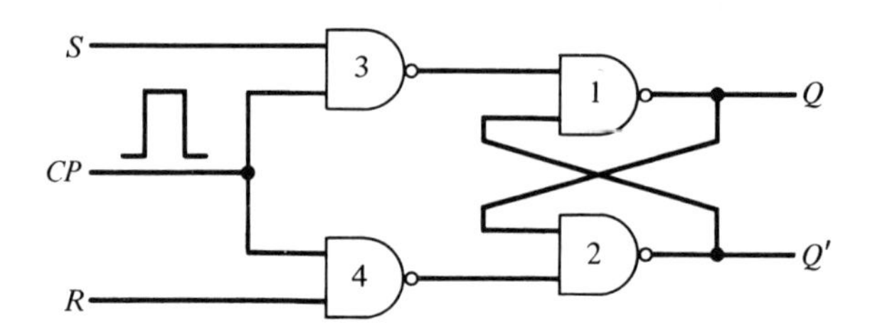


**Fig. 1-21** Logic diagram of a clocked *RS* flip-flop.

With both $S = 0$ and $R = 0$, a *CP* of 1 does not affect the state of the flip-flop. *S* and *R* cannot be 1 during the occurrence of a clock pulse because the next state of the flip-flop is indeterminate.

The graphic symbol of the *RS* flip-flop is shown in Fig. 1-22. It has three inputs: *S*, *R*, and *CP*. The *CP* input is marked with a small triangle. The triangle is a symbol for a *dynamic indicator* and denotes the fact that the circuit responds to an input *transition* from 0 to 1.† The outputs of the flip-flop are given a variable name such as *Q* or any other convenient letter designation. The small right-angle triangle is a graphic symbol for a *polarity indicator*. It designates the complement output of the flip-flop which in this case is $Q'$.

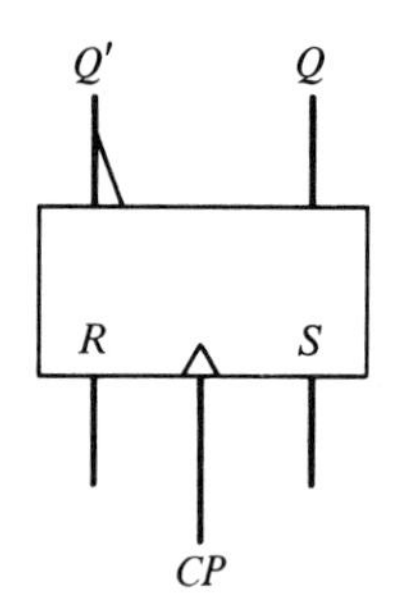


(a) Graphic symbol

| *S* | *R* | $Q(t + 1)$ | Comments |
|---|---|---|---|
| 0 | 0 | $Q(t)$ | No change |
| 0 | 1 | 0 | Clear |
| 1 | 0 | 1 | Set |
| 1 | 1 | ? | Not allowed |

(b) Characteristic table

**Fig. 1-22** *RS* flip-flop.

The characteristic table shown in Fig. 1-22(b) summarizes the operation of the *RS* flip-flop in tabular form. $Q(t)$ is the binary state of the flip-flop at a given time (referred to as *present state*). The *S* and *R* columns give the binary values of the inputs. $Q(t + 1)$ is the state of the flip-flop after the occurrence of a clock pulse (referred to as *next state*). If $S = R = 0$, a pulse produces no change of state, i.e., $Q(t + 1) = Q(t)$. If $S = 0$ and $R = 1$ the flip-flop goes

†This graphic symbol and all other logic symbols in this book follow the recommendation of the American National Standard Institute *graphic symbols for logic diagrams* as specified in ANSI Y32.14–1973.

to the 0 (clear) state. If $S = 1$ and $R = 0$ the flip-flop goes to the 1 (set) state. An *RS* flip-flop should not be pulsed when $S = R = 1$ since it produces an indeterminate next state.

### *D Flip-Flop*

The *D* (data) flip-flop is a slight modification of the *RS* flip-flop. An *RS* flip-flop is converted to a *D* flip-flop by inserting an inverter between *S* and *R* and assigning the symbol *D* to the *S* input. The *D* input is sampled during the occurrence of a clock pulse and if it is 1, the flip-flop goes to the 1 state (because $S = 1$ and $R = 0$). If it is 0, a pulse changes the state of the flip-flop to 0 (because $S = 0$ and $R = 1$). The graphic symbol and characteristic table of the *D* flip-flop are shown in Fig. 1-23. Note that no input condition exists that will leave the state of the flip-flop unchanged. Although a *D* flip-flop has the advantage of having only one input (excluding the *CP*), it has the disadvantage that its characteristic table does not have a "no change" condition $Q(t + 1) = Q(t)$. The "no change" condition can be accomplished either by disabling the clock pulses with an external AND gate or by feeding the output back into the input so clock pulses keep the state of the flip-flop unchanged.

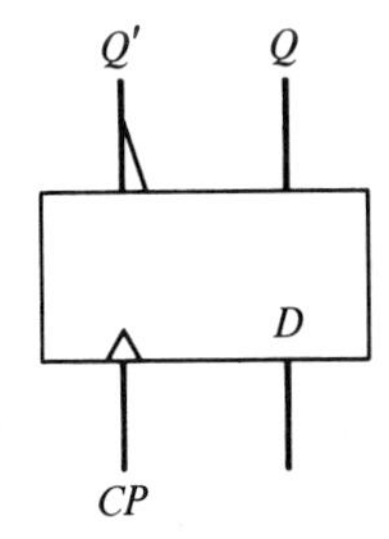


(a) Graphic symbol

| $D$ | $Q(t + 1)$ | Comments |
|---|---|---|
| 0 | 0 | Clear |
| 1 | 1 | Set |

(b) Characteristic table

**Fig. 1-23** *D* flip-flop.

### *JK and T Flip-Flops*

A *JK* flip-flop is a refinement of the *RS* flip-flop in that the indeterminate condition of the *RS* type is defined in the *JK* type. Inputs *J* and *K* behave like input *S* and *R* to set and clear the flip-flop, respectively. When inputs *J* and *K* are both equal to 1, a clock pulse switches the outputs of the flip-flop to its complement state, $Q(t + 1) = Q'(t)$. The graphic symbol and characteristic table of the *JK* flip-flop are shown in Fig. 1-24. Note that the *J* input is equivalent to the *set* condition while the *K* input produces the *clear* condition. In addition there are both *no change* and *complement* conditions in this type of flip-flop.

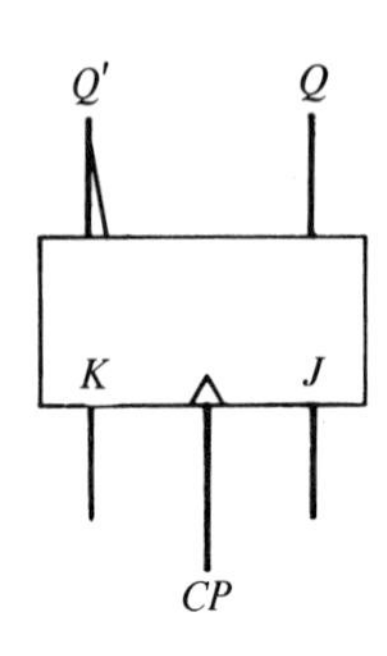


| J | K | Q(t + 1) | Comments |
|---|---|---|---|
| 0 | 0 | $Q(t)$ | No change |
| 0 | 1 | 0 | Clear |
| 1 | 0 | 1 | Set |
| 1 | 1 | $Q'(t)$ | Complement |

(a) Graphic symbol (b) Characteristic table

**Fig. 1-24** *JK* flip-flop.

Another type of flip-flop found in textbooks is the *T* (toggle) flip-flop. This flip-flop, shown in Fig. 1-25, is obtained from a *JK* type when inputs *J* and *K* are tied together. The *T* flip-flop, therefore, has only two conditions. When $T = 0$ ($J = K = 0$) a clock pulse does not change the state of the flip-flop. When $T = 1$ ($J = K = 1$) a clock pulse complements the state of the flip-flop.

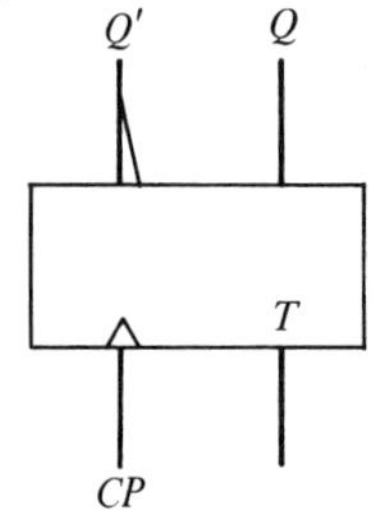


| T | Q(t + 1) | Comments |
|---|---|---|
| 0 | $Q(t)$ | No change |
| 1 | $Q'(t)$ | Complement |

(a) Graphic symbol (b) Characteristic table

**Fig. 1-25** *T* flip-flop.

### *Excitation Tables*

The characteristic tables of flip-flops specify the next state when the inputs and the present state are known. During the design process we usually know the required transition from present state to next state and wish to find the flip-flop input conditions that will cause the required transition. For this reason we need a table that lists the required input combinations for a given change of state. Such a table is called a *flip-flop excitation table.*

Table 1-4 lists the excitation tables for the four types of flip-flops. Each table consists of two columns, $Q(t)$ and $Q(t + 1)$, and a column for each input to show how the required transition is achieved. There are four possible transitions from present state $Q(t)$ to next state $Q(t + 1)$. The required input conditions for each of these transitions are derived from the information

**Table 1-4** *The excitation tables for the four types of flip-flops.*

| $Q(t)$ | $Q(t+1)$ | $S$ | $R$ |
|---|---|---|---|
| 0 | 0 | 0 | $X$ |
| 0 | 1 | 1 | 0 |
| 1 | 0 | 0 | 1 |
| 1 | 1 | $X$ | 0 |

(a) *RS* flip-flop

| $Q(t)$ | $Q(t+1)$ | $J$ | $K$ |
|---|---|---|---|
| 0 | 0 | 0 | $X$ |
| 0 | 1 | 1 | $X$ |
| 1 | 0 | $X$ | 1 |
| 1 | 1 | $X$ | 0 |

(b) *JK* flip-flop

| $Q(t)$ | $Q(t+1)$ | $D$ |
|---|---|---|
| 0 | 0 | 0 |
| 0 | 1 | 1 |
| 1 | 0 | 0 |
| 1 | 1 | 1 |

(c) *D* flip-flop

| $Q(t)$ | $Q(t+1)$ | $T$ |
|---|---|---|
| 0 | 0 | 0 |
| 0 | 1 | 1 |
| 1 | 0 | 1 |
| 1 | 1 | 0 |

(d) *T* flip-flop

available in the characteristic tables. The symbol $X$ in the tables represents a don't-care condition; that is, it does not matter whether the input to the flip-flop is 0 or 1.

The reason for the don't-care conditions in the excitation tables is that there are two ways of achieving the required transition. For example, in an *RS* flip-flop, a transition from present state of 0 to a next state of 0 can be achieved by having inputs $S$ and $R$ equal to 0 (to obtain *no change* when the clock pulse is applied), or by letting $S = 0$ and $R = 1$ to *clear* the flip-flop (although it is already cleared). In both cases $S$ must be 0, but $R$ is 0 in the first case and 1 in the second. Since the required transition will occur in either case, we mark the $R$ input with an $X$ and let the designer choose either 0 or 1 for the $R$ input, whichever is more convenient.

## 1-6 SEQUENTIAL CIRCUITS

A sequential circuit is an interconnection of flip-flops and gates. The gates by themselves constitute a combinational circuit but when included with the flip-flops, the overall circuit is classified as a sequential circuit. A block diagram of a clocked sequential circuit is shown in Fig. 1-26. It consists of a combinational circuit and two *JK* clocked flip-flops. In general, any number or type of flip-flops may be encountered. The combinational circuit part receives binary signals from external inputs and from the outputs of flip-flops. It generates binary signals to external outputs and to inputs of flip-flops.

The gates in the combinational circuit determine not only the value of external outputs but also the binary value to be stored in the flip-flops after each clock pulse. The outputs of flip-flops, in turn, are applied to the combina-

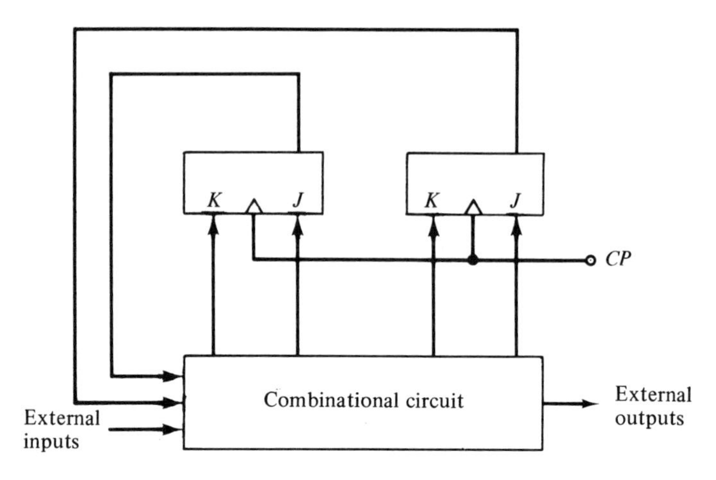


**Fig. 1-26** Block diagram of a sequential circuit.

tional circuit inputs and determine the circuit's behavior. This process clearly demonstrates that the external outputs of a sequential circuit are functions of both external inputs and the present state of the flip-flops. Moreover, the next state of flip-flops is also a function of their present state and external inputs. Thus, a sequential circuit is specified by a time sequence of external inputs, external outputs, and internal flip-flop binary states.

### *Flip-Flop Input Functions*

An example of a sequential circuit is shown in Fig. 1-27. It has one input variable $x$, one output variable $y$, and two clocked $RS$ flip-flops. The AND gates and inverter form the combinational logic part of the circuit. The interconnections among the gates in the combinational circuit can be specified by a set of Boolean functions. The part of the combinational circuit that generates the inputs to flip-flops are described by a set of Boolean functions called flip-flop *input functions* or *input equations.* We adopt the convention of using two letters to designate the binary variable of an input function. The first letter designates the type of flip-flop input and the second, the name of the flip-flop. Thus, in Fig. 1-27, we have four input functions designated by $RA$, $SA$, $RB$, $SB$. The first letter in each symbol denotes the $R$ or $S$ input of an $RS$ flip-flop. The second letter is the symbol name of the flip-flop.

The input functions are Boolean functions for flip-flop input variables. They can be derived by inspection of the circuit. The output of the AND gate marked $RA$ has inputs from $B'$ and $x$. Since this output goes to the $R$ input of flip-flop $A$, we write the input function as:

$$RA = B'x$$

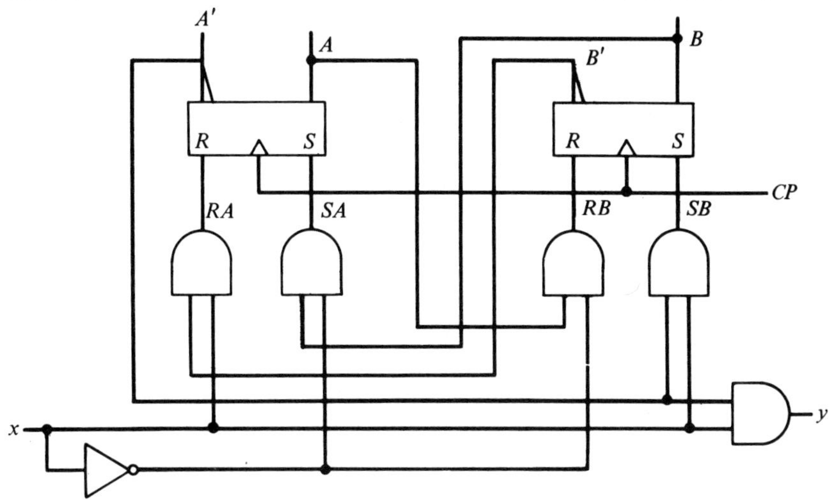


**Fig. 1-27** Example of a sequential circuit.

where $RA$ is a binary variable having a two letter symbol. Similarly, the other input functions are:

$$SA = Bx'$$

$$RB = Ax'$$

$$SB = A'x$$

The sequential circuit also has an external output which is a function of the input variable and the state of one of its flip-flops. This output can be specified algebraically by the expression

$$y = A'x$$

From this example, we note that a flip-flop input function is a Boolean function for a combinational circuit. The two-letter designation is a binary variable name for an output of the combinational circuit. This output is always connected to a flip-flop input terminal.

### *State Table*

The behavior of a sequential circuit is determined from the inputs, the outputs, and the state of its flip-flops. Both the outputs and next state are a function of the inputs and the present state. A sequential circuit is specified by a *state table* which relates outputs and next states as a function of inputs and present states. In clocked sequential circuits, the transition from present state to next state is activated by the presence of a clock pulse.

The state table for the sequential circuit of Fig. 1-27 is shown in Table 1-5.

**Table 1-5** *State table for circuit of Fig. 1-27*

| *Present State* | | *Input* | *Next State* | | *Output* |
|---|---|---|---|---|---|
| $A$ | $B$ | $x$ | $A$ | $B$ | $y$ |
| 0 | 0 | 0 | 0 | 0 | 0 |
| 0 | 0 | 1 | 0 | 1 | 1 |
| 0 | 1 | 0 | 1 | 1 | 0 |
| 0 | 1 | 1 | 0 | 1 | 1 |
| 1 | 0 | 0 | 1 | 0 | 0 |
| 1 | 0 | 1 | 0 | 0 | 0 |
| 1 | 1 | 0 | 1 | 0 | 0 |
| 1 | 1 | 1 | 1 | 1 | 0 |

The present state designates the state of flip-flops before the occurrence of a clock pulse. At any given time, the present state of flip-flops $A$ and $B$ together with the input can be in one of eight possible binary values. These binary values are listed under the columns labeled present state and input. The next state lists the state of the flip-flops after the application of a clock pulse. The output column lists the value of the output variable.

The derivation of the state table is facilitated if the input functions of the flip-flops are obtained first. The input functions for the circuit have already been derived and are repeated again for convenience.

$$RA = B'x \qquad SA = Bx'$$

$$RB = Ax' \qquad SB = A'x$$

From these functions we note that flip-flop $A$ is cleared if $Bx = 01$, it is set if $Bx = 10$, and remains unchanged otherwise. Going down column $A$ in the next state, we write a 0 when $Bx = 01$, a 1 when $Bx = 10$ and transfer the value of $A$ from the present state column to the next state column in the other rows. Similarly, from the input functions we note that flip-flop $B$ is cleared if $Ax = 10$, set if $Ax = 01$, and unchanged otherwise. The binary values in the $B$ column of the next state are derived from these conditions in a similar manner. By this procedure we can determine the next state values from knowledge of the present state and input values.

The entries for the output column are also a function of the present state and input. The output can be expressed by the Boolean function

$$y = A'x$$

which means that the output is equal to 1 if the present state of flip-flop $A$ is

0 and if the input is 1. Output $y$ is 0 otherwise. Therefore, $y$ has a 1 in the two rows where $Ax = 01$ and a 0 in all other entries.

The state table of any sequential circuit is obtained by the procedure used in this example. In general, a sequential circuit with $m$ flip-flops, $n$ input variables and $p$ output variables will contain $m$ columns for present state, $n$ columns for inputs, $m$ columns for next state and $p$ columns for outputs. The present state and input columns are combined and under them we list all the $2^{m+n}$ binary combinations of 1's and 0's. The next state and output columns are functions of the present state and input values and are derived directly from the circuit.

### *State Diagram*

The information available in a state table may be represented graphically in a *state diagram.* In this diagram, a state is represented by a circle and the transition between states is indicated by directed lines connecting the circles. The state diagram of the sequential circuit of Fig. 1-27 is shown in Fig. 1-28. The binary number inside each circle identifies the state of flip-flops $A$ and $B$. The directed lines are labeled with two binary numbers separated by a slash. The input value that causes the state transition is labeled first; the number after the slash gives the value of the output during the present state. For example, the directed line from state 00 to 01 is labeled 1/1, meaning that the sequential circuit is in a present state 00 while $x = 1$ and $y = 1$. On the application of the next clock pulse, the circuit goes to next state 01. A directed line connecting a circle with itself indicates that no change of state occurs. The state diagram provides the same information as the state table and is obtained directly from Table 1-5.

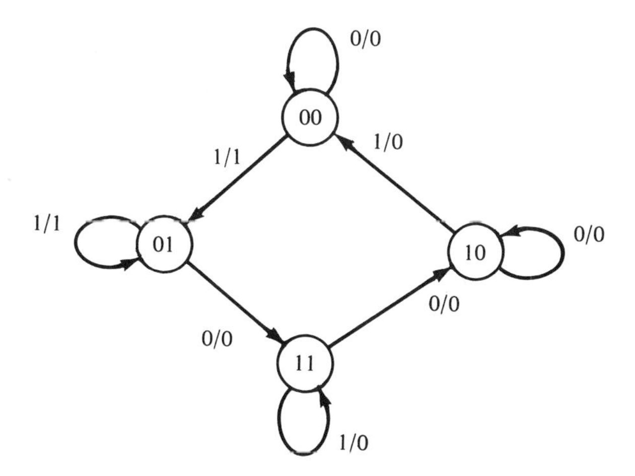


**Fig. 1-28** State diagram for circuit of Fig. 1-27.

There is no difference between a state table and a state diagram except in the manner of representation. The state table is easier to derive from the circuit diagram and the state diagram follows directly from the state table. The state diagram gives a pictorial view of state transitions and is in a form suitable for human interpretation of the circuit operation. The state diagram is often used as the initial design specification of a sequential circuit.

### *Design Example*

The procedure for designing sequential circuits will be demonstrated by a specific example. The design procedure consists of first translating the circuit specifications into a state diagram. The state diagram is then converted into a state table. From the state table we obtain the information for obtaining the circuit diagram.

We wish to design a clocked sequential circuit that goes through a sequence of repeated binary states 00, 01, 10, and 11 when an external input $x$ is equal to 1. The state of the circuit remains unchanged when $x = 0$. This type of circuit is called a two-bit *binary counter* because the state sequence is identical to the count sequence of two binary digits. Input $x$ is the control variable that specifies when the count should proceed.

The binary counter needs two flip-flops because two bits are specified for each state. The state diagram for the circuit is shown in Fig. 1-29. The diagram is drawn to show that the states of the circuit follow the binary count as long as $x = 1$. The state following 11 is 00 which causes the count to be repeated. If $x = 0$, the state of the circuit remains unchanged. This sequential circuit has no external outputs and therefore, only the input value is labeled in the diagram. The state of the flip-flops may be considered as the outputs of the circuit.

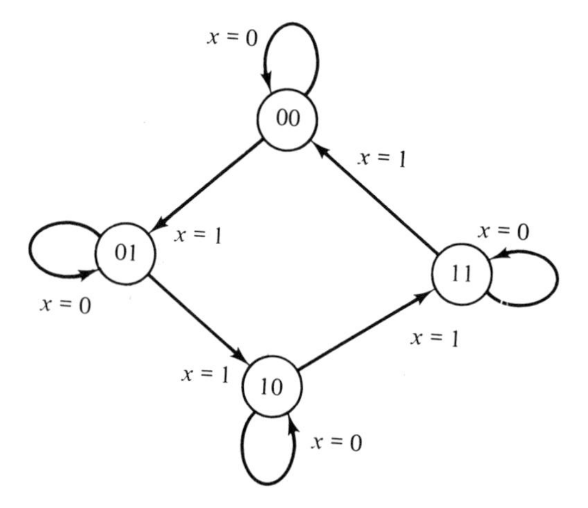


**Fig. 1-29** State diagram for binary counter.

We have already assigned the symbol $x$ to the input variable. Let us now assign the symbols $A$ and $B$ to the two flip-flops. The next state of $A$ and $B$ as a function of their present state and input $x$ can be transferred from the state diagram into a state table. The first five columns of Table 1-6 constitute the state table. The entries for this table are obtained directly from the state diagram.

**Table 1-6** *Excitation table for binary counter*

| State table | | | | | | | | |
|---|---|---|---|---|---|---|---|---|
| *Present State* | | *Input* | *Next State* | | *Flip-Flop Input Conditions* | | | |
| *A* | *B* | *x* | *A* | *B* | *JA* | *KA* | *JB* | *KB* |
| 0 | 0 | 0 | 0 | 0 | 0 | *X* | 0 | *X* |
| 0 | 0 | 1 | 0 | 1 | 0 | *X* | 1 | *X* |
| 0 | 1 | 0 | 0 | 1 | 0 | *X* | *X* | 0 |
| 0 | 1 | 1 | 1 | 0 | 1 | *X* | *X* | 1 |
| 1 | 0 | 0 | 1 | 0 | *X* | 0 | 0 | *X* |
| 1 | 0 | 1 | 1 | 1 | *X* | 0 | 1 | *X* |
| 1 | 1 | 0 | 1 | 1 | *X* | 0 | *X* | 0 |
| 1 | 1 | 1 | 0 | 0 | *X* | 1 | *X* | 1 |
| Inputs of combinational circuit | | | | | Outputs of combinational circuit | | | |

The *excitation table* of a sequential circuit is an extension of the state table. This extension consists of a list of flip-flop input excitations that will cause the required state transitions. The flip-flop input conditions are a function of the type of flip-flop used. If we employ *JK* flip-flops we need columns for the $J$ and $K$ inputs of each flip-flop. We denote the inputs of flip-flop $A$ by $JA$ and $KA$, and those of flip-flop $B$ by $JB$ and $KB$.

The excitation table for the *JK* flip-flop specified in Table 1-4(b) is now used to derive the excitation table of the sequential circuit. For example, in the first row of Table 1-6, we have a transition for flip-flop $A$ from 0 in the present state to 0 in the next state. In Table 1-4(b), we find that a transition of states from 0 to 0 requires that input $J = 0$ and input $K = X$. So 0 and $X$ are copied in the first row under $JA$ and $KA$, respectively. Since the first row also shows a transition for flip-flop $B$ from 0 in the present state to 0 in the next state, 0 and $X$ are copied in the first row under $JB$ and $KB$. The second row of Table 1-6 shows a transition for flip-flop $B$ from 0 in the present state to 1 in the next state. From Table 1-4(b) we find that a transition from 0 to 1 requires that input $J = 1$ and input $K = X$. So 1 and $X$ are copied in the second row under $JB$ and $KB$, respectively. This process is continued for each row of the table and for each flip-flop, with the input conditions as specified in Table 1-4(b) being copied into the proper row of the particular flip-flop being considered.

Let us now pause and consider the information available in an excitation table such as Table 1-6. We know that a sequential circuit consists of a number of flip-flops and a combinational circuit. Figure 1-26 shows two *JK* flip-flops and a box to represent the combinational circuit. From the block diagram, it is clear that the outputs of the combinational circuit go to flip-flop inputs. The inputs to the combinational circuit are the external inputs and the present state values of the flip-flops. Moreover, the Boolean functions that specify a combinational circuit are derived from a truth table that shows the input-output relations of the circuit. The entries that list the combinational circuit *inputs* are specified under the present state and input columns and the combinational circuit *outputs* are specified under the flip-flop input columns. Thus, as shown in Table 1-6, an excitation table transforms a state diagram to a truth table needed for the design of the combinational circuit part of the sequential circuit.

The simplified Boolean functions for the combinational circuit can now be derived. The inputs are the variables $A$, $B$, and $x$; the outputs are the variables $JA$, $KA$, $JB$, and $KB$. The information from the excitation table is transferred into the maps of Fig. 1-30, where the four simplified flip-flop input functions are derived:

$$JA = Bx \qquad KA = BX$$

$$JB = x \qquad KB = x$$

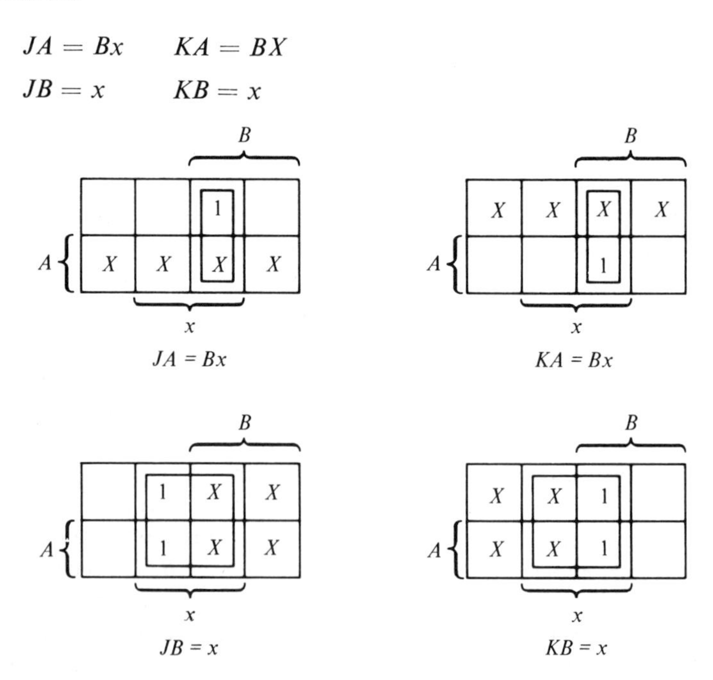


**Fig. 1-30** Maps for combinational circuit of counter.

The logic diagram is drawn in Fig. 1-31 and consists of two flip-flops and an AND gate. Note that inputs $J$ and $K$ determine the transition that will occur when a clock pulse ($CP$) arrives. If both $J$ and $K$ are equal to 0, a clock pulse will have no effect, i.e., the state of the flip-flops will not change. Thus, when $x = 0$, the state of the flip-flops remains unchanged even though clock pulses are continuously applied.

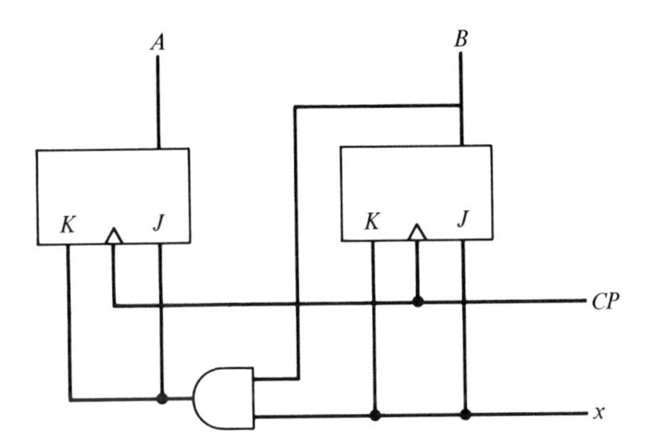


**Fig. 1-31** Logic diagram of binary counter.

*Design Procedure*

The design of sequential circuits follows the outline described in the previous example. The behavior of the circuit is first formulated in a state diagram. The number of flip-flops needed for the circuit is determined from the number of bits listed within the circles of the state diagram. The number of inputs for the circuit is specified along the directed lines between the circles. We then assign letters to designate all flip-flops and input variables and proceed to obtain the state table.

For $m$ flip-flops and $n$ inputs, the state table will consist of $m$ columns for the present state, $n$ columns for the inputs and $m$ columns for the next state. The number of rows in the table will be up to $2^{m+n}$, one row for each binary combination of present state and inputs. For each row we list the next state as specified by the state diagram.

Next, the flip-flop type to be used in the circuit is chosen. A two letter symbol for flip-flop inputs may be used to designate the outputs of the combinational circuit part of the circuit. By this convention, the first letter designates the type of input and the second letter the name of the flip-flop.

The state table is then extended into an excitation table by including columns for each input of each flip-flop. The excitation table for the type of flip-flop in use can be found in Table 1-4. From the information available in this table and by inspecting present to next state transitions in the state table, we obtain the information for the flip-flop input conditions in the excitation table.

The truth table for the combinational circuit part of the sequential circuit is available in the excitation table. The present state and input columns constitute the *inputs* in the truth table. The flip-flop input conditions constitute the *outputs* in the truth table. By means of map simplification techniques, we obtain a set of flip-flop input functions for the combinational circuit. Each flip-flop input function specifies a logic diagram whose output must be connected to one of the flip-flop inputs. The combinational circuit so obtained together with the flip-flops constitute the sequential circuit.

The outputs of flip-flops are often considered to be also the outputs of the sequential circuit. However, the combinational circuit may also contain external outputs. In such a case, the Boolean functions for the external outputs are derived from the state table by combinational circuit design techniques.

A set of flip-flop input functions specifies a sequential circuit in algebraic form. The procedure for obtaining the logic diagram from a set of flip-flop input functions is a straightforward process. First draw the flip-flops (specified by the second letter of the two letter symbols) and label all their inputs and outputs. Then draw the combinational circuit from the Boolean functions given by the flip-flop input functions. Finally, connect outputs of flip-flops to inputs in the combinational circuit and outputs of the combinational circuit to flip-flop inputs.

## 1-7 CONCLUDING REMARKS

This chapter introduces the basic digital circuits that serve as building blocks for the construction of digital computers or any digital system. The chapter also presents the fundamental concepts needed for the design of digital systems, especially when they are constructed with individual gates and flip-flops.

In order to keep the book within reasonable bounds, it was necessary to limit the discussion of digital system design to one introductory chapter. The justification for this approach is that the design of digital computers takes on a different dimension when integrated circuits are employed instead of individual gates and flip-flops. Integrated circuits provide entire digital functions in small packages so the designer does not have to deal with individual gates and flip-flops but instead with the interaction between integrated circuit functions. The next chapter presents a number of useful digital functions available in integrated circuit packages. The rest of the book uses these functions to investigate the organization and design of digital computers.

The basic concepts presented in this chapter are, nevertheless, important for the understanding of the functions that integrated circuits provide. Moreover, a computer designer with the responsibility of making hardware work must have extensive knowledge of digital system design concepts.

Although the material presented in this chapter is sufficient for the understanding of the subject matter in this book, the reader interested in digital system design is advised to acquire more information from any of the books listed in the reference section.

## REFERENCES

1. MANO, M. M., *Computer Logic Design*, Chaps. 1-7. Englewood Cliffs, N.J.: Prentice-Hall, Inc., 1972.
2. RHYNE, V. T., *Fundamentals of Digital System Design*, Englewood Cliffs, N.J.: Prentice-Hall, Inc., 1973.
3. DIETMEYER, D. L., *Logic Design of Digital Systems*, Boston, Mass.: Allyn and Bacon, Inc., 1971.
4. PEATMAN, J. P., *The Design of Digital Systems*, New York: McGraw-Hill Book Co., 1972.
5. HILL, F. J., and G. P. PETERSON, *Switching Theory and Logical Design* (2nd ed.), New-York: John Wiley & Sons, Inc., 1974.
6. MARCOVITZ. A. B., and J. H. PUGSLEY, *An Introduction to Switching System Design*, New York: John Wiley & Sons, Inc., 1971.
7. MALEY, G. A., and J. EARLE, *The Logic Design of Transistor Digital Computers*, Englewood Cliffs, N.J.: Prentice-Hall, Inc., 1963.

## PROBLEMS

1-1 Obtain the truth tables for the logic diagrams of Fig. 1-6 and show that the two truth tables are identical.

1-2 Verify the two DeMorgan's theorems by means of truth tables.

1-3 (a) Show that the following circuit of NAND gates produces the exclusive-OR function. (b) Replace the NAND gates by NOR gates and show that the exclusive-NOR function (equivalence) is obtained.

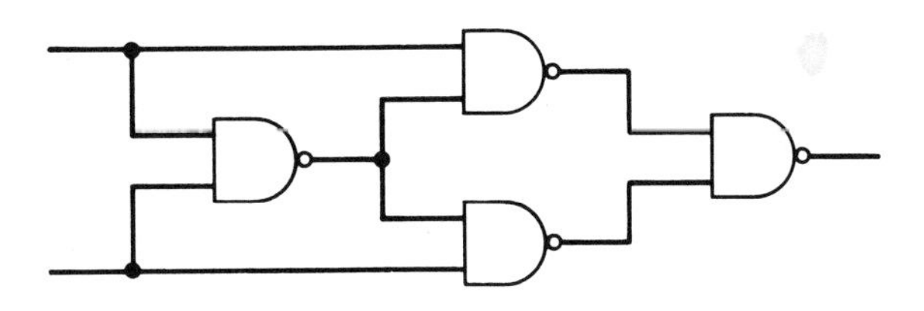

**Fig. P1-3**

1-4 Using the Boolean algebra relations of Table 1-1 show that

$$x + xy = x$$

List the relation used in each step.

1-5 Simplify the following Boolean functions algebraically.

| | *Answers* |
|---|---|
| (a) $xy + xy'$ | $x$ |
| (b) $(x + y)(x + y')$ | $x$ |
| (c) $xz + xyz'$ | $x(y + z)$ |
| (d) $(A + B)'(A' + B')'$ | 0 |
| (e) $A + A'B + A'B'$ | 1 |

1-6 Obtain the truth table for the function $F = AB' + B'C + A'C$.

1-7 Simplify the following Boolean function in sum of products form by means of a four variable map. Draw the logic diagram with: (a) AND-OR gates and (b) NAND gates.

$$F(w, x, y, z) = \Sigma\,(0, 2, 8, 9, 10, 11, 14, 15)$$

1-8 Simplify the following Boolean function in product of sums form by means of a four variable map. Draw the logic diagram with (a) OR-AND gates, and (b) NOR gates.

$$F(A, B, C, D) = \Sigma\,(2, 3, 4, 5, 6, 7, 11, 14, 15)$$

1-9 Simplify $F$ together with its don't-care condition $d$ in (a) sum of products form and (b) product of sums form.

$$F(A, B, C, D) = \Sigma\,(0, 1, 2, 8, 9, 12, 13)$$
$$d(A, B, C, D) = \Sigma\,(10, 11, 14, 15)$$

1-10 Implement the following Boolean function with NAND gates. Use inverters to complement inputs.

$$F(x, y, z) = \Sigma\,(0, 2, 4, 5)$$

1-11 By algebraic manipulation show that the $S$ output of a full-adder is the exclusive-OR (odd function) of its three inputs.

1-12 A majority function is a digital circuit whose output is 1 if and only if the majority of the inputs are 1. The output is 0 otherwise.
(a) Obtain the truth table of a three-input majority function.
(b) Show that the circuit of a majority function can be obtained with four NAND gates.
(c) Show that a full-adder circuit consists of a three-input exclusive-OR and a three-input majority function.

1-13 Two digital functions are enabled by control variables $C_1$ and $C_2$. The Boolean functions for the control signals are:

$$C_1 = ABT_1 + A'B'T_2$$
$$C_2 = AT_1 + B'T_2$$

Under what conditions of input variables $A$, $B$ and timing variables $T_1$, $T_2$ will the two digital functions be enabled at the same time.

1-14 Obtain the simplified Boolean functions of the full-adder in sum of products form and draw the logic diagram using NAND gates.

1-15 Design a combinational circuit that accepts a three-bit number and generates an output binary number equal to the square of the input number.

1-16 The difference between a full-adder and a full-subtractor is in the Boolean function that generates the carry or borrow. Use a control variable $w$ and obtain the logic diagram of a circuit that functions as a full-adder when $w = 0$ and as a full-subtractor when $w = 1$.

1-17 A set-dominate flip-flop has set ($S$) and reset ($R$) inputs. It differs from a conventional $RS$ flip-flop in that an input of $S = R = 1$ results in setting the flip-flop. Obtain the characteristic table and excitation table of the set-dominate flip-flop.

1-18 Show that a $JK$ flip-flop can be converted to a $D$ flip-flop with an inverter between the $J$ and $K$ inputs.

1-19 Design a two-bit countdown counter. This is a sequential circuit with two flip-flops and one input $x$. When $x = 0$, the state of the flip-flops does not change. When $x = 1$, the state sequence is 11, 10, 01, 00, 11, etc.

1-20 Design the circuit and draw the logic diagram of the sequential circuit specified by the following state diagram. Use an $RS$ flip-flop.

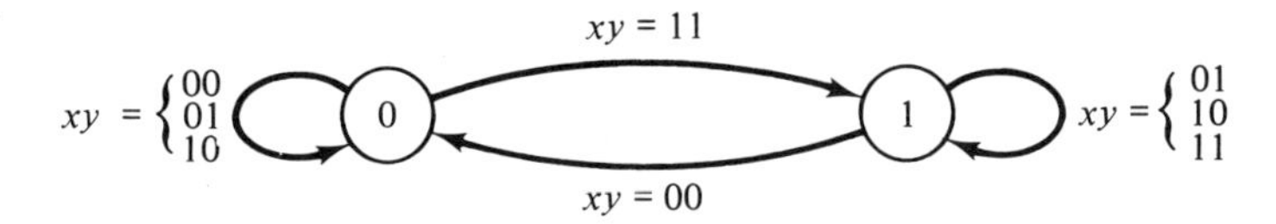


**Fig. P1-20**

1-21 A sequential circuit is specified by the following flip-flop input functions. Draw the logic diagram of the circuit.

$$JA = Bx' \qquad KA = Bx$$

$$JB = x \qquad KB = A \oplus x$$

# 2

# INTEGRATED CIRCUITS AND DIGITAL FUNCTIONS

## 2-1 DIGITAL INTEGRATED CIRCUITS

An integrated circuit (IC) is a small silicon semiconductor crystal called a *chip* containing electrical components such as transistors, diodes, resistors and capacitors. The various components are interconnected inside the chip to form an electronic circuit. The chip is mounted in a metal or plastic package and connections are welded to external pins to form the IC. Integrated circuits differ from conventional discrete component circuits in that individual components cannot be separated or disconnected and the circuit inside the IC package is accessed only through its external pins. The benefits derived from ICs as compared to circuits with discrete components are: (1) a substantial reduction in size; (2) a substantial reduction in cost; (3) a reduction in power requirements; (4) a higher reliability against failures; (5) an increase in operating speed; and (6) a reduction of externally wired connections.

Integrated circuits are classified as being in one of two general categories, *linear* or *digital*. Linear integrated circuits operate with continuous waveforms to provide electronic functions such as operational amplifiers, voltage comparators, and voltage regulators. Digital integrated circuits operate with binary signals and provide such digital functions as gates, flip-flops, registers, counters, adders, memories, and arithmetic calculators. Here we will be concerned only with digital integrated circuits.

Because of their many advantages, integrated circuits are used exclusively to provide various digital functions needed in the design of computer systems. In order to understand the architecture of computer systems it is very important that one should be familiar with the different digital functions commonly encountered in integrated circuit packages. For this reason, the most basic functions are introduced in this chapter and many other IC digital functions are explained in succeeding chapters.

### *Logic Circuit Families*

Digital integrated circuits are classified not only by their function but also by their being members of a specific logic circuit family. Each logic family has its own basic electronic circuit upon which more complex circuits and functions are developed. The basic circuit in each family is either a NOR or a NAND gate. The topology of this basic circuit, i.e., the electronic components employed and their interconnection, is usually used to derive the name of the family. Many different logic families of digital integrated circuits have been introduced commercially. The ones that have achieved widespread popularity are listed below.

| | |
|---|---|
| RTL | Resistor transistor logic |
| DTL | Diode transistor logic |
| TTL | Transistor transistor logic |
| ECL | Emitter coupled logic |
| MOS | Metal oxide semiconductor |
| CMOS | Complementary metal oxide semiconductor |

The first two, RTL and DTL, have only historical significance since they are seldom used in new designs. TTL has an extensive list of digital functions and is the most popular logic family at the time of this writing. ECL is used for systems requiring high-speed operation. MOS is used in circuits requiring high component density and CMOS is used in systems requiring low power consumption.

The characteristics of digital logic families are usually compared by analyzing the circuit of the basic gate in each family. The most important parameters that are evaluated and compared are listed below.

1. *Fan-out* specifies the number of standard loads that the output of a standard gate can drive without impairing its normal operation. A standard load is usually defined to be the load (the amount of current) needed by an input of another similar standard gate.
2. *Power dissipation* is the power consumed by the gate which must be available from the power supply.
3. *Propagation delay* is the average transition delay time for the signal to

propagate from input to output when the binary signals change in value. The operating speed is inversely proportional to the propagation delay.

4. *Noise margin* is the minimum noise voltage that causes an undesirable change in the circuit output.

### *Transistor Transistor Logic—TTL*

The basic circuit for the TTL logic family is the NAND gate. There are many versions (sometimes referred to as *series*) of the TTL gate. The names of five versions are listed in Table 2-1 together with their respective propagation delay and power dissipation. The standard TTL gate was the first version of the TTL family. Additional improvements were added as TTL technology progressed. In the low-power version, the propagation delay is sacrificed to provide a reduced power dissipation. In the high-speed version, the power dissipation is increased to reduce the propagation delay. The Schottky TTL is a later improvement that increases the speed of operation without excessive increases in dissipated power. Finally, the low-power Schottky version sacrifices some speed for reduced power dissipation. It compares favorably with the standard TTL in speed and requires considerably less power. The fan-out of TTL gates is 10 when the standard loads are of the same circuit version. The noise margin is better than 0.4 volt with a typical value of 1 volt.

**Table 2-1** *Characteristics of five TTL versions*

| *Name of Version* | *Abbreviation* | *Propagation Delay* (ns) | *Power Dissipation* (mW) | *Speed-Power Product* (pJ) |
|---|---|---|---|---|
| Standard | TTL | 10 | 10 | 100 |
| Low-power | LTTL | 33 | 1 | 33 |
| High-speed | HTTL | 6 | 22 | 132 |
| Schottky | STTL | 3 | 19 | 57 |
| Low-power Schottky | LSTTL | 9.5 | 2 | 19 |

Each of the five TTL versions come in one of three output circuit configurations commonly referred to as:

1. Open collector output.
2. Totem pole output.
3. Tri-state output.

The open collector gate needs an external resistor for proper operation.

This resistor is connected to the IC package externally. Outputs of two or more collector gates can be connected to a common resistor to achieve an external AND function. This is shown in Fig. 2-1 for two open collector NAND gates. The AND gate formed by connecting together the two outputs is called a *wire-AND* function. The AND gate is drawn with the lines going through the center of the gate to distinguish it from a conventional gate. The wire-AND gate is not a physical gate but only a symbol to designate the function obtained from the indicated connection. Note that two open collector gates connected to a common resistor produce the so-called AND-OR-INVERT function $(AB + CD)'$.

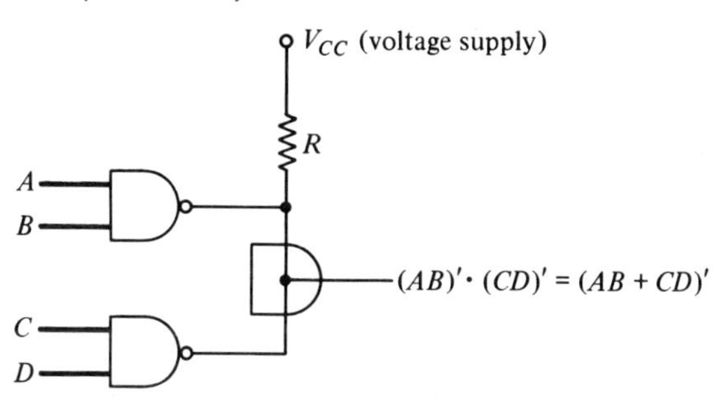


**Fig. 2-1** Wire-AND connection of two open collector TTL NAND gates.

The totem-pole output is the standard output of a TTL gate and is specifically designed to reduce the propagation delay in the circuit and to provide sufficient output power for a high fan-out. Totem-pole outputs cannot be connected together to form an AND function as in open collector outputs.

The tri-state output exhibits three output state conditions. Two of the states are signals equivalent to binary 1 and 0, similar to a conventional gate. The third state is a high impedance state. This means, for all practical purposes, that the circuit behaves as if the output is disabled. As a consequence, the output cannot affect or be affected by any external signal at its terminals. The third state is controlled by a separate input as shown in Fig. 2-2. When the control input $C$ is 1, the gate behaves like a normal NAND gate providing states of 0 and 1. When the control input is 0, the output is disabled irrespective of the values of the normal inputs. Tri-state gates are also available with the control input having a complementary effect, i.e., disabling the gate when

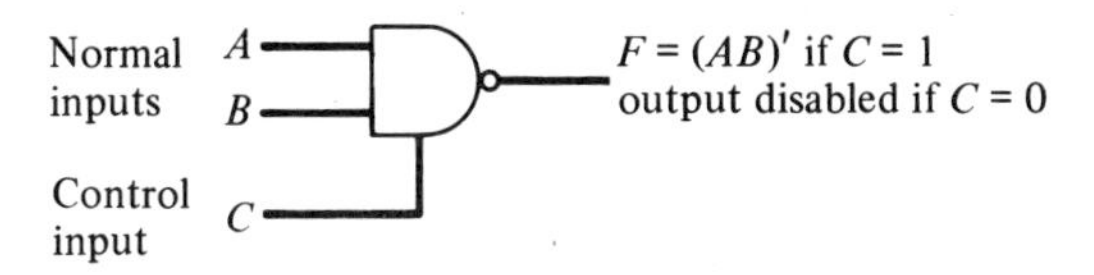


**Fig. 2-2** Symbol for tri-state NAND gate.

the control input is 1 and enabling it when it is 0. The high impedance state of a tri-state gate allows the possibility of making direct wire connection from many outputs to a common bus line with only one output having access to the bus at any given time. The gate having access to the common output line will be the one whose control input is enabled while all other outputs are disabled by their respective control inputs.

### *Emitter Coupled Logic—ECL*

The transistors in the ECL gates operate in a so-called *non-saturation state*, a condition that allows the achievement of propagation delays of 1 to 2 nsec. This logic family has the lowest propagation delay compared with any other logic family and is used mostly in systems requiring very high-speed operation.

The basic circuit of the ECL logic family is a NOR gate but many ECL ICs provide an output for the OR function as well. The symbol for the ECL gate is shown in Fig. 2-3. Two outputs are available, one for the NOR func-

$A$, $B$ → $(A+B)'$ (NOR), $A+B$ (OR)

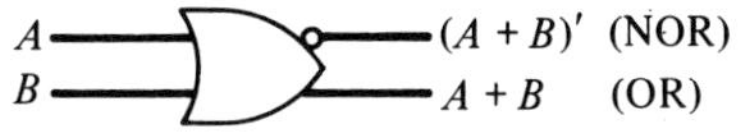

**Fig. 2-3** Graphic symbol for ECL gate.

tion and the other for the OR function. The outputs of two or more ECL gates can be connected externally (with or without a resistor) to form a *wire-OR* function. This property may be utilized to form other logic functions by connecting the outputs of gates. Outputs of ECL gates are sometimes connected *internally* within the IC to form a *dot-AND* function. As shown in Fig. 2-4, the wire-OR connection of two NOR gates produces an OR-AND-INVERT function. The internal dot-AND connection of two OR gates produces an OR-AND function.

The ECL logic family has a variety of versions. The propagation delay of a typical gate is between 1 and 2 nsec, depending on the version used. The power dissipation is about 25 mW; the fan-out is greater than 25. The noise margin is the lowest of all families and is about 0.2 volt.

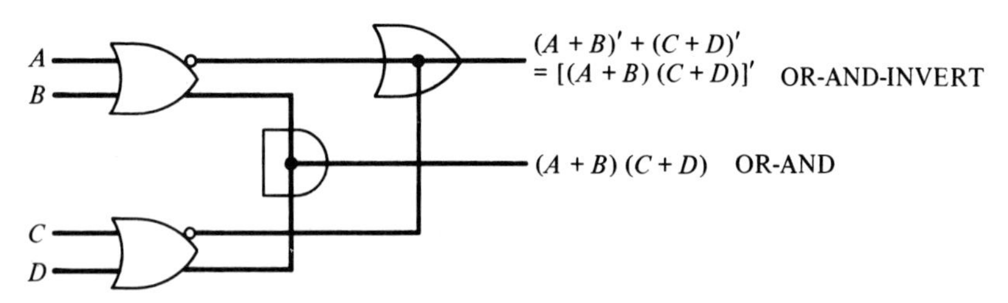


**Fig. 2-4** Wired combinations in ECL gates.

### *Metal Oxide Semiconductor—MOS*

MOS is a unipolar transistor that depends upon the flow of only one type of electronic carrier which may be electrons (N-channel) or holes (P-channel). This is in contrast to the bipolar transistor used in TTL and ECL gates where both carriers exist during normal operation. A P-channel MOS, referred to as PMOS, requires negative voltages for its operation. An N-channel MOS, referred to as NMOS, requires positive voltages for its operation. Complementary MOS, or CMOS, uses one PMOS and one NMOS transistor, connected in a complementary fashion. CMOS requires positive voltages for its operation.

The one major disadvantage of MOS over bipolar circuits is that propagation delays are much higher in MOS circuits. This means that they are not practical for use in systems requiring high-speed operations. Nevertheless, the speed of MOS devices has been improved gradually by advancements in technology. The three most important advantages of MOS over bipolar are as follows.

1. High packing density that allows more circuits to be placed in a given chip area.
2. Simpler processing techniques when fabricated in integrated circuits and therefore more economical to manufacture.
3. MOS gate power consumption is much less than the bipolar gate. This makes MOS circuits more economical to operate.

PMOS and NMOS ICs do not come with individual gates; they are mostly used in ICs that provide digital functions such as memories and calculators. CMOS ICs come in a variety of functions similar to TTL and ECL. The fan-out of CMOS gates is over 50. The power dissipation is extremely low, usually in the order of 10nW. The propagation delay varies with power supply voltage and is typically 25nsec. The noise margin is greater than 2 volts and is better than bipolar logic families.

### *Gate Complexity*

Each digital logic family is recognized by its basic NOR or NAND gate. The basic gate is the building block from which more complex functions are constructed. For example, a latch circuit is constructed from two NAND gates or two NOR gates connected back to back. A master-slave flip-flop is obtained from the interconnection of nine basic gates. A register is obtained from the interconnection of flip-flops and NAND gates. Each logic family has a catalog of integrated circuit packages that lists thc digital functions available in the logic family. It is customary to classify the gate complexity of an IC in one of the three following categories.

1. An SSI (small scale integration) device has a complexity of less than 10 gates. These are ICs that contain several gates or flip-flops in one package.
2. An MSI (medium scale integration) device has a complexity of 10 to 100 gates. These are ICs that provide elementary logic functions such as registers, counters, and decoders.
3. An LSI (large scale integration) device has a complexity of more than 100 gates. Examples of LSI ICs are large memories, microprocessors, and calculator chips.

Three logic families, TTL, ECL, and CMOS, have a large number of SSI and MSI packages. SSI ICs are those that contain a small number of NAND, NOR, flip-flops, or other type gates, in one package. The limit on the number of digital circuits in SSI devices is the number of pins in the package. A 14 pin package for example, can accomodate only four two-input NAND gates. This is because each gate requires three external pins (two for inputs and one for output), for a total of $4 \times 3 = 12$ pins. The remaining two pins are needed for supplying power to the circuits.

One will appreciate the variety of MSI functions available in IC packages by looking at a data book or catalog provided by a vendor. A typical data book may list over 100 different MSI functions. When these functions are divided into categories, one may find about 15 different arithmetic elements, over 20 types of registers, about 10 types of memories, 10 decoders, 5 multiplexers, 20 counters and other assorted functions. The succeeding sections of this chapter present the most common digital functions encountered in IC packages. Other digital functions are explained in succeeding chapters.

TTL, ECL, and CMOS have many SSI and MSI functions and some LSI functions as well. On the other hand, MOS ICs very seldom come as SSI or even as MSI. Because of the high density of transistors that can be fabricated on a given area of silicon, MOS is mostly used to supply a variety of LSI functions. LSI functions available in MOS are shift-registers, memory units, microprocessors, and electronic calculator chips.

### *IC Packages*

Digital integrated circuits come in two types of packages, the *flat* package and the *dual-in-line* (DIP) package. The latter is the most widespread type used for digital ICs because of its low price and easy installation on printed circuit boards. The envelope of the IC package is usually made of plastic or ceramic. Most packages have standard sizes and the number of pins range from 14 to 40. Each IC has a numerical designation number which is printed on the surface of the package for identification. The numbers are assigned by the semiconductor manufacturer. Each vendor publishes a data book or catalog that provides the necessary information concerning the various products.

TTL ICs are usually distinguished by their numerical designation as the 5400 and 7400 series. The former has a wide operating temperature range, suitable for military use, and the latter has a narrower temperature range, suitable for industrial use. The numerical designation of 7400 series, for example, means that IC packages are numbered as 7400, 7401, 7402, . . . , 74181, etc. Some vendors make available TTL ICs with different numerical designation such as 9000 or 8000 series.

The most common ECL version is designated by the 10000 series. That of CMOS is the 4000 series (also known as COS/MOS, or complementary symmetry MOS). Other versions of CMOS ICs are the 54C00 and 74C00 series. The ICs in these series are compatible with the TTL series and are pin-to-pin replaceable with their TTL counterpart 5400 and 7400 numbers.

In summary, a digital integrated circuit is identified by all of the following designations:

1. The logic circuit family type.
2. The circuit function name, such as register, memory, etc.
3. The circuit complexity, i.e., SSI, MSI, or LSI.
4. The type of package and number of pins.
5. The IC identification number and the name of the vendor.

## 2-2 IC FLIP-FLOPS AND REGISTER

The digital function commonly used for holding binary information in a digital computer is called a *register*. A register is a group of binary storage cells. A group of flip-flops constitutes a register since a flip-flop is a binary cell capable of storing one bit of information. In addition to the flip-flops, a register may have combinational gates that perform certain data processing tasks. In its broadest definition, a register consists of a group of flip-flops and the gates that effect their transition. The flip-flops hold binary information while the gates control when and how the information is transferred into the register.

### *Master-Slave Flip-Flop*

The flip-flops in integrated circuit registers are usually constructed internally from two separate flip-flop circuits. One circuit serves as a master and the other as a slave and the overall circuit is referred to as a *master-slave* flip-flop. The logic diagram of an *RS* master-slave flip-flop is shown in Fig. 2-5. It consists of a master flip-flop, a slave flip-flop and an inverter. When the clock pulse *CP* is 0, the output of the inverter is 1. Since the clock input of the slave (the terminal marked with a small triangle) is 1, the flip-flop is enabled and output $Q$ is equal to $Y$ while $Q'$ is equal to $Y'$. The master flip-flop is disabled because $CP = 0$. When the pulse becomes 1, the information then at the external $R$ and $S$ inputs is transmitted to the master flip-flop. The slave flip-flop however is isolated as long as the pulse is at its 1 level because the output of the inverter is 0. When the pulse returns to 0, the master flip-flop is isolated, preventing the external inputs from affecting it. The slave flip-flop then goes to the same state as the master flip-flop.

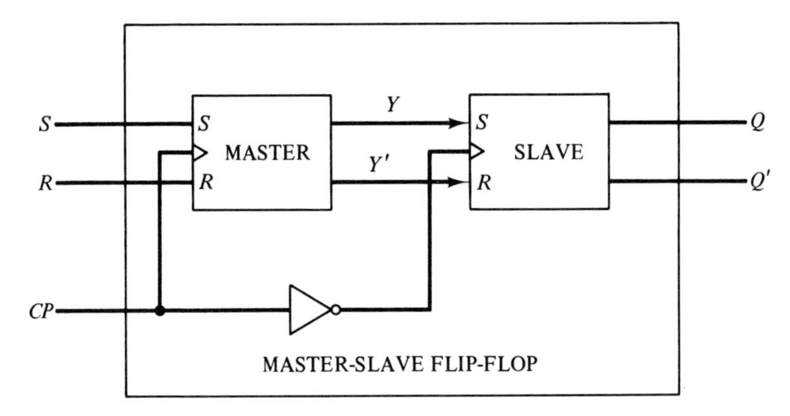


**Fig. 2-5** Logic diagram of a master-slave flip-flop.

The timing relations shown in Fig. 2-6 illustrate the sequence of events that occur in a master-slave flip-flop. Assume that the flip-flop is in the clear state prior to the occurrence of a pulse so that $Y = 0$ and $Q = 0$. The input conditions are $S = 1$, $R = 0$, and the next clock pulse should change the flip-flop to the set state with $Q = 1$. During the pulse transition from 0 to 1, the master flip-flop is set and changes $Y$ to 1. The slave flip-flop is not affected because its *CP* input is 0. Since the master flip-flop is an internal circuit, its change of state is not noticeable in the outputs $Q$ and $Q'$. When the pulse returns to 0, the information from the master is allowed to pass through to the slave making the external output $Q = 1$. Note that the external $S$ input can be changed at the same time that the pulse goes to 0. This is because once the *CP* reaches 0, the master is disabled and its $R$ and $S$ inputs have no influence until the next clock pulse occurs. Thus, in a master-slave flip-flop, it is possible to switch the output of the flip-flop and its input information with the same clock pulse.

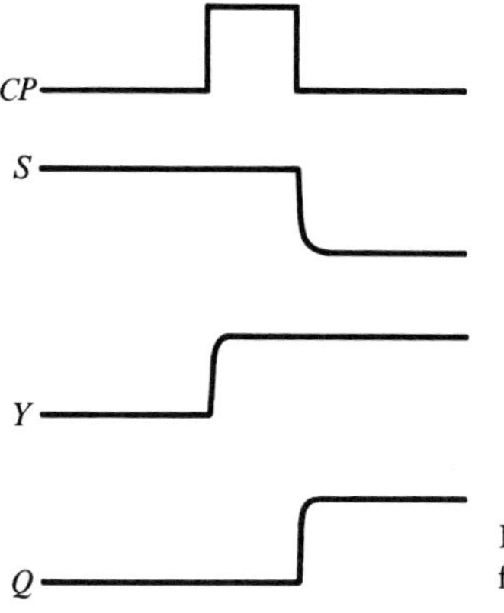


**Fig. 2-6** Timing relations in a master-slave flip-flop.

Now consider a digital system containing many master-slave flip-flops with outputs of some flip-flops going to inputs of other flip-flops. Assume that clock pulse inputs to all flip-flops are synchronized and occur at the same time. At the beginning of each clock pulse, some of the master elements will change state, but all flip-flop outputs will remain at their previous values. After the clock pulse returns to 0, some of the outputs will change state and none of these new states will have an effect on any of the master elements until the next clock pulse. Thus the state of flip-flops in the system can be changed simultaneously during the same clock pulse even though outputs of flip-flops are connected to inputs of flip-flops. This is possible because the new state appears at the output terminals only after the clock pulse has returned to 0. Therefore, the binary content of one register can be transferred to a second register and the content of the second register transferred to the first, and both transfers can occur during the same clock pulse.

The behavior of the master-slave flip-flops just described dictates that state changes in all registers coincide with the 1 to 0 transition of clock pulses. However, some IC master-slave flip-flops change state on the 0 to 1 transition of clock pulses. This happens in registers whose master-slave flip-flops receive the complement of the clock pulse (through a second inverter) so that a 1 to 0 pulse transition affects the master and a 0 to 1 transition affects the slave.

### *Other IC Flip-Flops*

Another type of flip-flop that synchronizes the state change during a clock pulse transition is the *edge-triggered* flip-flop. In this type of flip-flop, output transitions occur at a specific level of the clock pulse. When the pulse input level exceeds this threshold level, the inputs are locked out so that the flip-flop is unresponsive to further changes in inputs until the clock pulse returns to 0 and another pulse occurs. Some edge-triggered flip-flops cause a transition on the rising edge of the clock pulse (0 to 1 transition) and others cause a transition on the falling edge (1 to 0 transition). Flip-flops commonly available in IC form are of the above four varieties. Most digital systems are constructed using master-slave and edge-triggered flip-flops having one type of transition so complete synchronization is achieved. For the sake of uniformity, this book assumes that all flip-flops are of the master-slave type with output transitions during the falling edge of the clock pulse.

Flip-flops available in IC packages will sometimes provide special input terminals for setting or clearing the flip-flop asynchronously. These inputs are usually called "preset" and "clear." They affect the flip-flop on a positive (or negative) swing of the input signal without the need of a clock pulse. These inputs are useful for bringing the flip-flops to an initial state prior to its clocked operation.

### *Register with Parallel Load*

It was mentioned previously that a register is a group of flip-flops together with gates that effect the flip-flop transitions. The number of flip-flops in the register dictates the number of bits stored in it. An $n$-bit register consists of $n$ flip-flops and can store any binary information containing $n$ bits. An example of a four-bit register is shown in Fig. 2-7. It consists of four flip-flops and a variety of gates. When included in an IC package it will have four outputs $A_1$ to $A_4$, four inputs $I_1$ to $I_4$ and three common control inputs. Each control input has a buffer (a non-inverting amplifier) whose purpose is to reduce the loading of the input control signal. This is because each control input is connected to only one buffer input instead of to the four gate inputs that would have been required if the buffer gate were not present.

The *clear* input goes to a special terminal in each flip-flop (marked with a circle). When this terminal goes to 0, the flip-flop is cleared asynchronously, i.e., without the requirement of a clock pulse. This input is useful for bringing all flip-flops in the register to an initial cleared state prior to its clocked operation. The clear input must go to the 1 state during normal clocked operations.

The clock pulse input of the register receives continuous synchronized pulses which are applied to all flip-flops. The CP input in each flip-flop is marked by a small triangle. The small circle below the triangle indicates that flip-flop output transitions occur during the falling edge of the clock pulse (1 to 0 transition). However, whether an output transition occurs or not is dictated by the *load* input and the state of inputs $I_1$ through $I_4$.

The two AND gates and inverter in each flip-flop determine the values of the $R$ and $S$ inputs. If the *load* input is 0, both $R$ and $S$ are 0 and no change of state can occur with any clock pulse. Thus the *load* input is a control

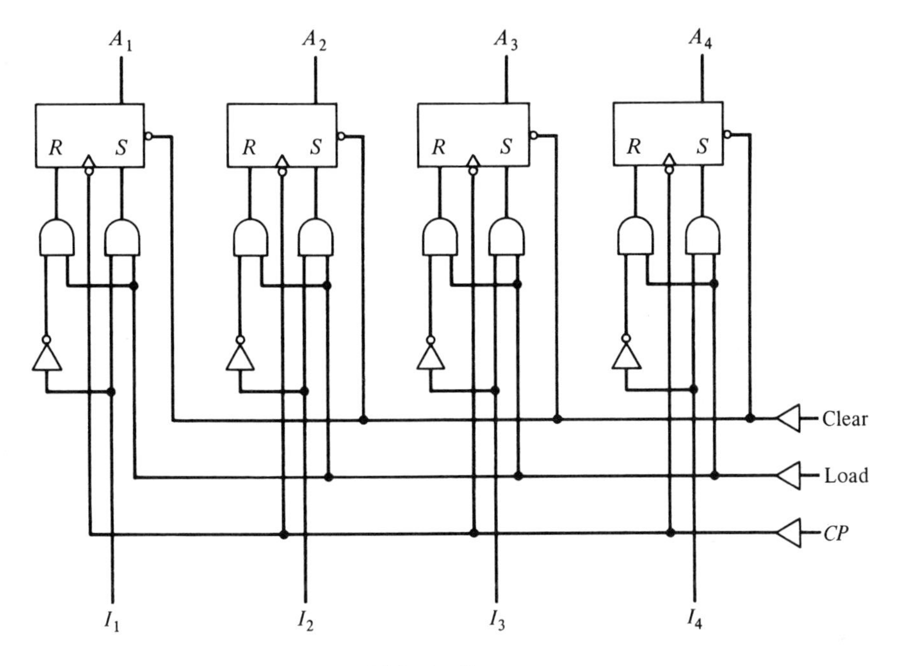


(a) Logic diagram

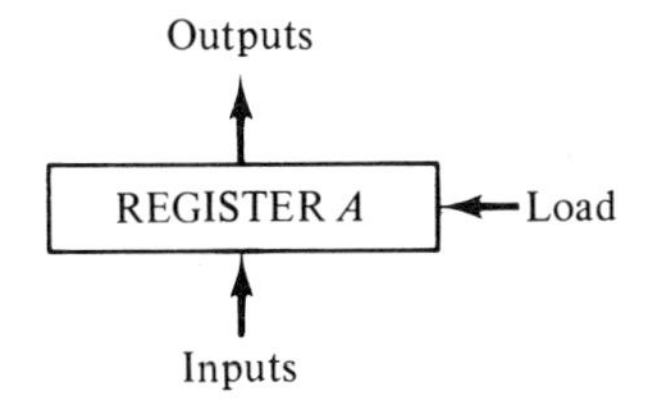


(b) Block diagram

**Fig. 2-7** Four-bit register with parallel load.

variable which can prevent any information change in the register as long as its input is 0. When the *load* input goes to 1, the inputs $I_1$–$I_4$ determine what binary information will be transferred into the register on the next clock pulse. For each $I$ that is equal to 1, the corresponding flip-flop inputs are maintained at $S = 1$ and $R = 0$. For each $I$ that is equal to 0, the corresponding flip-flop inputs are $R = 1$ and $S = 0$. This information is transferred into the register, provided the *load* input is 1, the *clear* input is 1, and a clock pulse occurs. This type of transfer is designated as a *parallel load* transfer because all bits of the register are loaded simultaneously.

When this register is enclosed inside an IC package it will have four output terminals, four input terminals, three control terminals and two or three power supply terminals. It can, therefore, be enclosed in a standard 14-pin package. The register can be expanded to five bits in a 16-pin package or to 9 bits in a 24-pin package. If more than four bits are needed for the register, two or more 14-pin ICs will have to be used. Thus an eight-bit register requires two ICs and a 16-bit register requires four ICs.

Digital computers use a considerable number of registers with parallel load capabilities. To avoid drawing the logic diagram of the register every time it is encountered, we will adopt the convention of drawing its block diagram instead. As shown in Fig. 2-7(b), the block diagram consists of a rectangular box with the name of the register written inside. One line is used to designate the inputs and one line to designate the outputs. The number of bits of the register will be evident from its function within the computer. The CP and clear terminals are not shown in the block diagram but they will be assumed to be included in all registers requiring clocked operations and an initial cleared state. The *load* input is included in the diagram to specify the type of control available in this particular register. It will be shown subsequently that it is possible to have registers with more or different types of control inputs.

## 2-3 DECODERS AND MULTIPLEXERS

A *decoder* is a digital function that converts binary information from one coded form to another. For example, a BCD-to-seven-segment decoder converts a decimal digit in BCD (binary-coded decimal) into seven outputs for the selection of the set of segments needed to display a decimal digit. The decoders presented in this section are called $n$-to-$2^n$ line decoders and their purpose is to generate the $2^n$ minterms of $n$ input variables. These decoders form a combinational circuit with $n$ input variables and $2^n$ output variables. For each binary input combination of 1's and 0's there is one, and only one, output line that assumes the value of 1. This type of decoder is found in many applications and is used extensively in the design of digital systems.

### *Decoders*

An example of a 2 by 4 decoder is shown in Fig. 2-8. It consists of four AND gates and two inverters. A decoder has as many outputs as there are possible binary input combinations. In this particular example, the two inputs $x$ and $y$ can be in one of four possible binary values, as shown in the truth table accompanying the diagram. Observe that the output variables are mutually exclusive and that only one output can be equal to 1 at any one time.

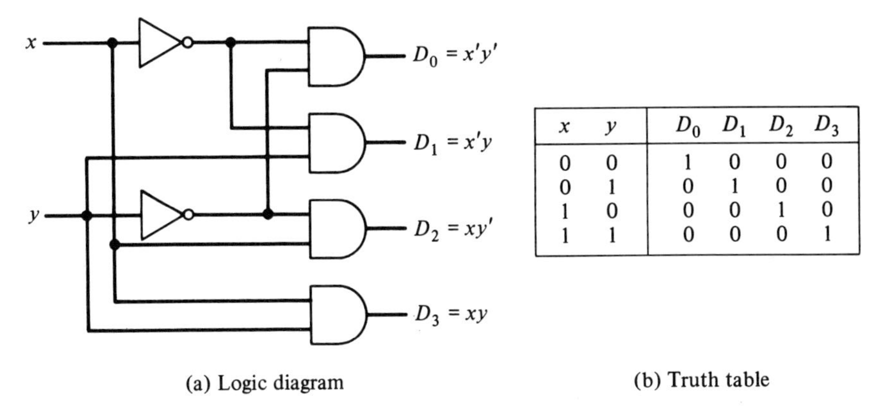


| $x$ | $y$ | $D_0$ | $D_1$ | $D_2$ | $D_3$ |
|---|---|---|---|---|---|
| 0 | 0 | 1 | 0 | 0 | 0 |
| 0 | 1 | 0 | 1 | 0 | 0 |
| 1 | 0 | 0 | 0 | 1 | 0 |
| 1 | 1 | 0 | 0 | 0 | 1 |

(a) Logic diagram (b) Truth table

**Fig. 2-8** 2 by 4 decoder.

The output whose value is equal to 1 represents the minterm combination in the input lines.

Integrated circuit decoders may use NAND or NOR gates instead of AND gates. In such a case, the outputs are the complement of the values listed in the truth table. The minterm combination of the input variables is then distinguished by the output whose value is 0 while all other outputs are equal to 1.

It is sometimes convenient to include an enable input with a decoder to control the circuit operation. For example, a 3 by 8 decoder with an enable input is shown in Fig. 2-9. All outputs will be equal to 0 if the enable input is 0. This occurs because a 0 input to an AND gate produces a 0 output, no matter what the other input values are. When the enable input is 1, the circuit operates as a conventional decoder. Decoders will be used extensively in subsequent discussions. In order to avoid drawing the logic diagram every time a decoder is needed, we will draw its block diagram instead, as shown in Fig. 2-9(b). The enable input may or may not be included in the block diagram, depending on the particular application.

The size of a decoder in an IC package is usually dependent on the number of external pins in the package. For example, two 2 by 4 decoders can be inserted in a 14-pin package. One 3 by 8 decoder with an enable input can be inserted in a 14-pin package (eight outputs, three inputs, one enable and two pins for power supply). It is possible to provide three enable inputs if the package contains 16 pins.

Binary information stored in a register is said to be decoded if there exist $2^n$ distinct output lines, one for each of the states that the register can assume. The binary information held in a four-bit register can be decoded with a 4 by 16 decoder. It is also possible to employ two 3 by 8 decoders with

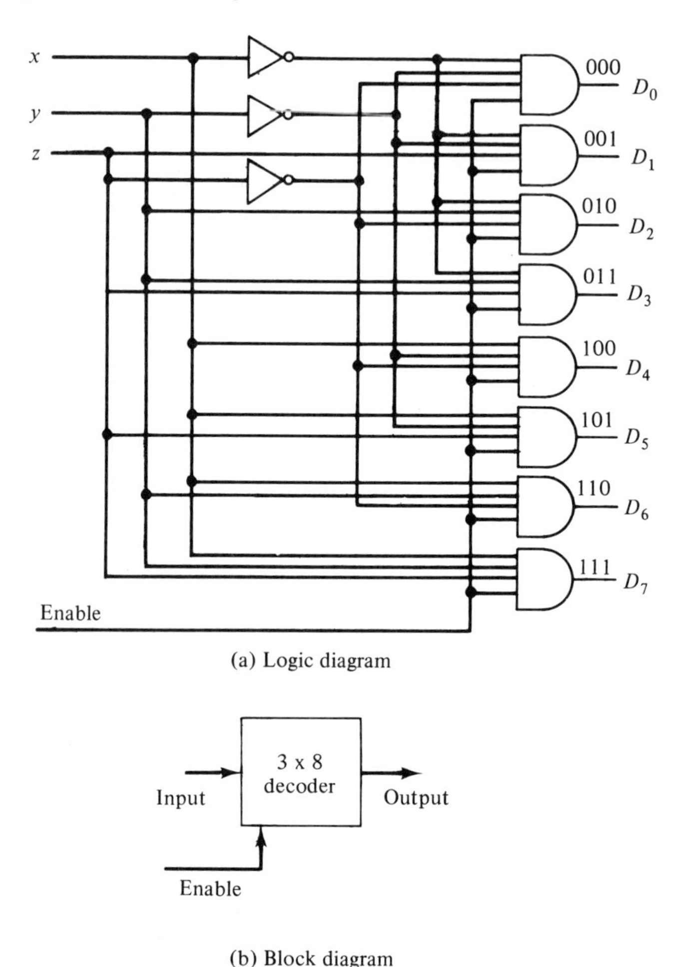


(a) Logic diagram



(b) Block diagram

**Fig. 2-9** 3 by 8 decoder with enable input.

enable inputs and connect them to the register as shown in Fig. 2-10. The register has four outputs labeled $A_0$ to $A_3$, with $A_3$ holding the high-order bit. When $A_3 = 0$, the enable input of the bottom decoder is 0 and the top is 1. This condition enables the outputs of the top decoder but produces 0's in the outputs of the bottom decoder. The top eight outputs then generate minterms 0000 to 0111. When $A_3 = 1$, the enable conditions are reversed and the bottom decoder outputs generate minterms 1000 to 1111. Thus, two 3 by 8 decoders with enable inputs can be used to generate a 4 by 16 decoder function. This example demonstrates the usefulness of the enable inputs in ICs. In general, the enable lines are convenient for expanding two or more IC packages into a digital function of larger capacity.

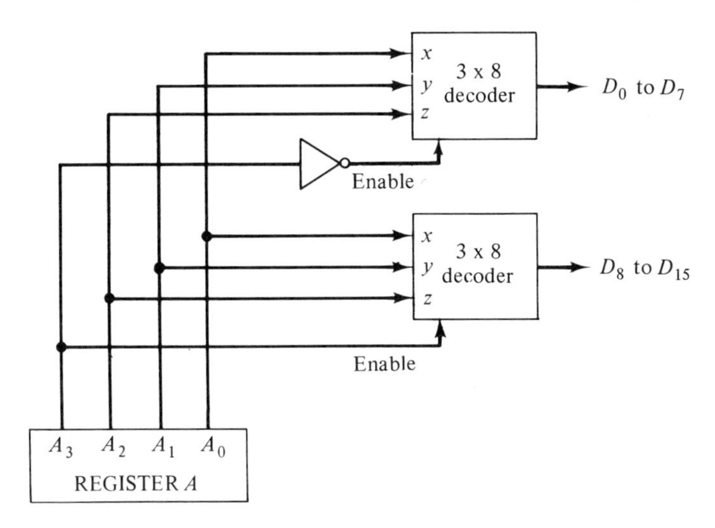


**Fig. 2-10** A 4 by 16 decoder constructed with two 3 by 8 decoders.

### *Demultiplexers*

A decoder with one or more enable inputs can function as a demultiplexer. A *demultiplexer* is a digital function that receives information on a single line and transmits this information in one of $2^n$ possible output lines. The output line being selected is determined from the bit combination of $n$ selection lines. The decoder of Fig. 2-9 will function as a demultiplexer if the enable line is taken as the data input and the decoder inputs $x$, $y$, and $z$ are taken as the selection lines. The single input variable (available in the enable line) has a path to all eight outputs, but the input information is directed to only one of the output lines as specified by the binary combination of the three selection lines. For example, if the selection lines $xyz = 000$, output $D_0$ will be the same as the input information in the enable line while all other outputs will be maintained at 0. Because of the similarity of decoders and demultiplexers, these circuits are usually referred to as *decoder/demultiplexer* circuits.

### *Multiplexers*

The function of a demultiplexer is to receive binary information from a single source and steer it to any of $2^n$ outputs under control of the selection lines. A digital multiplexer performs the reverse operation. A *multiplexer* is a digital function that receives binary information from $2^n$ lines and transmits information on a single output line. The one input line being selected is determined from the bit combination of $n$ selection lines. An example of a 4 by 1 multiplexer is shown in Fig. 2-11. The four input lines are applied to four AND gates whose outputs go to a single OR gate. Only one input line has a path to the output at any particular time. The selection lines $S_1$ and $S_0$ determine which input is selected to have a direct path to the output. Thus, with $S_1S_0 = 10$, the AND gate associated with input $I_2$ has two of its inputs equal to 1. If $I_2 = 1$ the output of the gate is also 1; if $I_2 = 0$, the output is 0. All other AND gates have an output of 0. The output of the OR gate will be equal to the output value of the AND gate associated with input $I_2$. A multiplexer is also called a *data selector* since it selects one of multiple input data lines and steers the binary information to the output line.

The AND gates in a multiplexer resemble a decoder circuit and indeed, they decode the input selection lines. In general, a multiplexer circuit is constructed from an $n$ by $2^n$ decoder by adding one input line to each AND gate and applying all AND gate outputs to a single OR gate. The size of a multiplexer is specified by the number of its inputs, $2^n$. It is then implied that it also contains one output line and $n$ selection lines. A multiplexer may have one or more enable lines, as in a decoder. The enable lines can then be used to expand two or more multiplexer ICs to a digital multiplexer with a larger number of inputs.

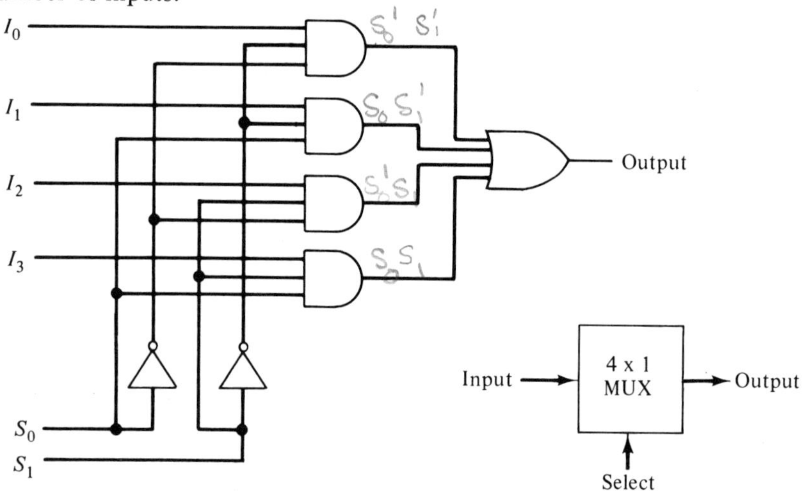


(a) Logic diagram

(b) Block diagram

**Fig. 2-11** 4 by 1 multiplexer.

## 2-4 BINARY COUNTERS

A register that goes through a predetermined sequence of states upon the application of input pulses is called a *counter*. The input pulses may be clock pulses or may originate from an external source. They may occur at uniform intervals of time or at random. Counters are found in almost all equipment containing digital logic. They are used for counting the number of occurrences of an event and are useful for generating timing signals to control the sequence of operations in digital computers. The sequence of states of a counter may follow a binary count or any other sequence. A wide variety of different types of counters are available in integrated circuit packages.

Counters may be operated synchronously or asynchronously. The signals that affect the flip-flops in an asynchronous counter are generated in output transitions of other flip-flops. Asynchronous counters are sometimes called *ripple* counters. This is because flip-flop transitions ripple through from one flip-flop to the next in sequence until all flip-flops reach a new state. In a synchronous counter, all the flip-flops receive the same clock pulse and as a consequence, all flip-flops change state synchronously with the pulse. We will consider here synchronous counters only.

### *Binary Counter Sequence*

Of the various sequences a counter may follow, the straight binary sequence is the simplest and most straightforward. A counter that follows the binary number sequence is called a *binary counter*. An $n$-bit binary counter is a register of $n$ flip-flops and associated gates that follows a sequence of states according to the binary count of $n$ bits, from 0 to $2^n - 1$. The design of binary counters can be carried out by the procedure outlined in Sec. 1-6. A simpler alternate design procedure may be carried out from a direct inspection of the sequence of states that the register must undergo in order to achieve a straight binary count. Going through a sequence of binary numbers, as shown in Table 2-2, we note that the lower-order bit is complemented after every count and every other bit is complemented from one count to the next if and only if all its lower-order bits are equal to 1. If the table is extended to four-bit numbers we will find that the binary number 1000 is

**Table 2-2** *Complement conditions for binary counter*

| *Count Sequence* $A_2\ A_1\ A_0$ | *Flip-Flops to Be Complemented for Next Count* |
|---|---|
| 0 0 0 | $A_0$ |
| 0 0 1 | $A_0$, $A_1$ because $A_0 = 1$ |
| 0 1 0 | $A_0$ |
| 0 1 1 | $A_0$, $A_1$ because $A_0 = 1$, $A_2$ because $A_1A_0 = 11$ |
| 1 0 0 | $A_0$ |
| 1 0 1 | $A_0$, $A_1$ because $A_0 = 1$ |
| 1 1 0 | $A_0$ |
| 1 1 1 | $A_0$, $A_1$ because $A_0 = 1$, $A_2$ because $A_1A_0 = 11$ |

obtained from its preceeding number 0111 by: (a) complementing the low-order bit; (b) complementing the second-order bit (because the first bit is 1); (c) complementing the third bit (because the first two are 1's); and (d) complementing the fourth bit (because the first three bits are all 1's).

A counter circuit will usually employ flip-flops with complementing capabilities. Both $T$-type and $JK$-type flip-flops have this property. The flip-flop in a binary counter that holds the low-order bit is complemented with every clock pulse. Every other flip-flop in the register is complemented if and only if all its lower order flip-flops contain 1's.

The logic diagram of a four-bit binary counter using $T$-type flip-flops is shown in Fig. 2-12. Flip-flop $A_0$ (holding the low-order bit) is complemented with each pulse arriving in the $CP$ terminal. This occurs because the $T$ input of the flip-flop is maintained at 1 permanently. $A_1$ is complemented with a pulse if $A_0 = 1$. $A_2$ is complemented if $A_1A_0 = 11$ and $A_3$ is complemented if $A_2A_1A_0 = 111$. For every clock pulse, the state of the register goes to a next state dictated by the binary count sequence from 0000 to 1111. The next state after 1111 is 0000 because all flip-flops will be complemented after the 1111 state. A binary counter can be expanded to any number of bits by providing one flip-flop and one AND gate for each additional bit and connecting them in cascade according to the pattern shown in the diagram.

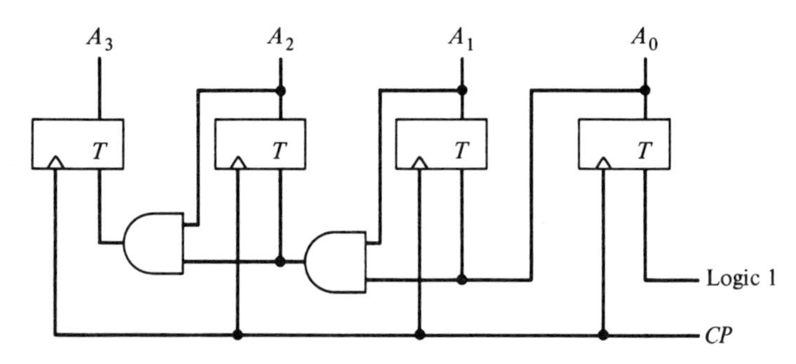


**Fig. 2-12** Four-bit binary counter.

### *Binary Down-Counter*

A binary counter with a reverse count is called a binary *down-counter*. In a down-counter the binary count is reduced by one with every input pulse. The state of the flip-flops in a four-bit down-counter starts from binary 15 and continues to binary states 14, 13, 12, . . . , 0 and then back to 15. Going through a descending sequence of binary numbers, one will find that the low-order bit is complemented with each down-count and every other bit is complemented if and only if all of its lower order bits are equal to 0. This means that a register will operate as a binary down-counter if each flip-flop in the register is complemented when its lower-order flip-flops are equal to 0, except for the first, which is complemented with every pulse. The logic diagram of a four-bit binary down-counter is shown in Fig. 2-13. It is similar to the *up* counter of Fig. 2-12 except that the AND gates receive inputs from the complement outputs of flip-flops.

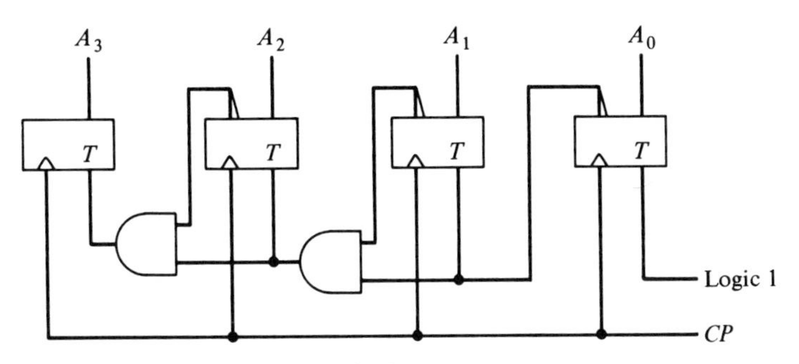


**Fig. 2-13** Four-bit binary down-counter.

*Binary Counter with Parallel Load*

The counters just described will count the input pulses arriving in the CP terminal every time a pulse occurs. It is sometimes necessary to control the count sequence by a control signal so that clock pulses affect the counter only if the control signal is enabled. This was done in the two-bit counter designed in Sec. 1-6. If we refer back to Fig. 1-29 we will find that the input control designated by $x$ determines whether the counter goes to the next state (when $x = 1$) or remains in its present state (when $x = 0$). Furthermore, counters employed in digital computers quite often require a parallel load capability for transferring an initial binary number into the register prior to its operation as a counter. Figure 2-14 shows the logic diagram of a register that has a parallel load capability and can also operate as a counter when enabled by a control input. This is a very useful register and will be used extensively in succeeding chapters. The input *load* control, when equal to 1, disables the count sequence and causes a transfer of data from inputs $I_0$ to $I_3$ into flip-flops $A_0$ to $A_3$, respectively. If the load input is 0 and the increment input control is 1, the register operates as a counter and the next clock pulse causes the state of the flip-flops to go to the next binary count sequence. If both control inputs are 0, clock pulses do not change the state of the register.

The operation of the register is summarized in Table 2-3. The four control inputs *clear*, *CP*, *load*, and *increment* determine the next output state. The clear input is asynchronous and, when equal to 0, causes the register to be cleared irrespective of the presence of clock pulses or other inputs. This is indicated in the table by the $X$ entries, which symbolize don't-care conditions

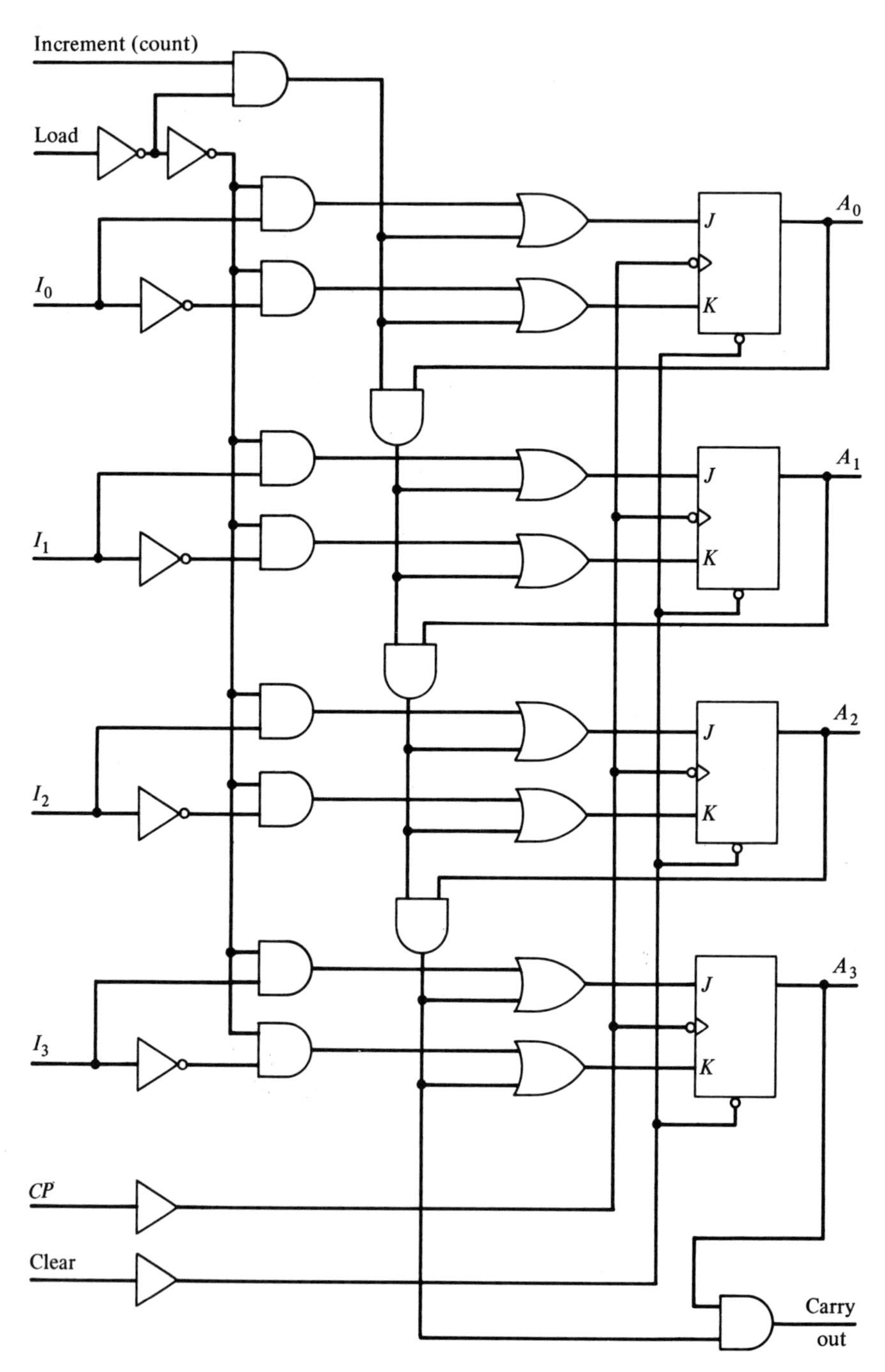


**Fig. 2-14** Binary counter with parallel load.

**Table 2-3** *Control functions in register of Fig. 2-14*

| *Clear* | *CP* | *Load* | *Increment* | *Outputs* $A_0$–$A_3$ |
|---|---|---|---|---|
| 0 | $X$ | $X$ | $X$ | All 0's |
| 1 | $X$ | 0 | 0 | No change |
| 1 | $\downarrow$ | 1 | $X$ | Receive inputs $I_0$–$I_3$ |
| 1 | $\downarrow$ | 0 | 1 | Count to next value |

for the other control inputs, so their values may be either 0 or 1. The clear input must go to the 1 state for clocked operations. With both the load and increment inputs at 0, the outputs of the register will not change, whether a pulse is applied or not. A load input of 1 causes a transfer from inputs $I_0$–$I_3$ into the register during the falling edge of an input pulse. The input information is transferred into the register when the load input is 1 irrespective of the value of the increment input. If the load input is maintained at 0, the increment input controls the count sequence. A count occurs with every clock pulse if the increment input is 1 and no change of state occurs if the increment input is 0.

The carry-out terminal in the register will be 1 if all flip-flops are equal to 1. This is the condition for complementing the flip-flop holding the next higher-order bit. This output is useful for expanding the counter to more than four bits. The speed of the counter can be increased if the two-input AND gates that propagate the carry are replaced with AND gates whose inputs are connected directly to all previous flip-flop outputs. Thus, the AND gate associated with flip-flops $A_1$, $A_2$, and $A_3$ will have two, three, and four inputs respectively. The AND gate associated with the carry output will have five inputs, one from the increment control and one from each of the flip-flop outputs. This type of arrangement is called a *look-ahead* carry.

The four-bit register shown in Fig. 2-14 can be enclosed in a 16-pin IC package. Two ICs are necessary for the construction of an eight-bit register, four ICs for a 16-bit register, etc. The carry output of one IC must be connected to the increment input of the IC holding the four next higher-order bits of the register.

Counters with parallel load capability having a specified number of bits will be used in succeeding chapters to design digital computers. We will refer to them by means of the block diagram shown in Fig. 2-15. The clear and *CP* inputs are not included in the block diagram since their presence will be implied in all registers. The data input variables are represented by a single line and so are the data output lines. The two control inputs *load* and *increment* and the carry output are labeled along horizontal lines with arrows going into or out of the register.

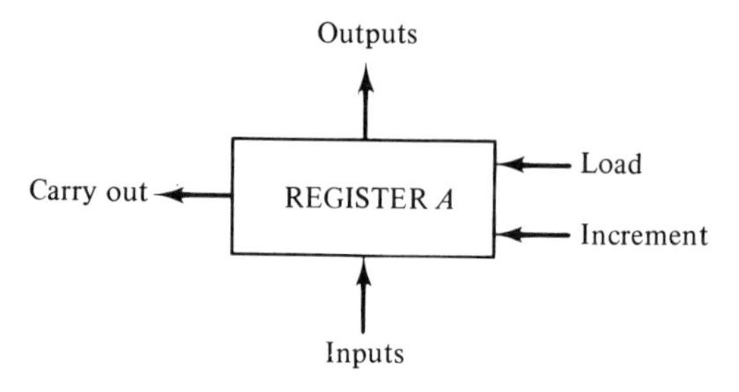


**Fig. 2-15** Block diagram of a register with increment and parallel load capabilities.

## 2-5 SHIFT-REGISTERS

A register capable of shifting its binary information either to the right or to the left is called a *shift-register.* An $n$-bit shift register consists of $n$ flip-flops and the gates that control the shift operation. A block diagram of a shift-right register is shown in Fig. 2-16. It has a *shift-right* control input whose purpose is to enable the shift operation. The *serial input* is a single line going to the input of the left-most flip-flop of the register. The *serial-output* is a single line from the output of the right-most flip-flop of the register. The parallel output consists of $n$ lines, one for each of the flip-flops in the register.

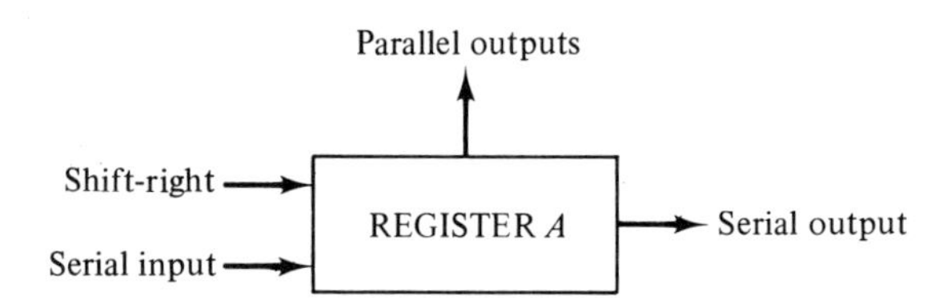


**Fig. 2-16** Block diagram of a shift-right register.

The reason for calling some lines *serial* and others *parallel* will become evident from the operation of a four-bit shift-right register as depicted in Table 2-4. The initial binary information stored in the register is 0111. The parallel outputs have one line for each flip-flop so the information stored in the register can be inspected through these lines all at once. The serial output is a single line coming from the output of the right-most flip-flop, so that the four bits stored in the register can come out through this line one at a time. Similarly, the serial input is a single line and new binary information can enter the register one bit at a time during four consecutive clock pulses. Information is transferred serially in and out when the register is shifted to the right.

**Table 2-4** *Serial input and output in a four-bit shift-right register*

| *Clock Pulse* | *Serial Input Bit* | *State of Register (parallel outputs)* | | | | *Serial Output Bit* |
|---|---|---|---|---|---|---|
| Initial | 1 | 0 | 1 | 1 | 1 | 1 |
| 1 | 1 | 1 | 0 | 1 | 1 | 1 |
| 2 | 0 | 1 | 1 | 0 | 1 | 1 |
| 3 | 1 | 0 | 1 | 1 | 0 | 0 |
| 4 | $X$ | 1 | 0 | 1 | 1 | 1 |

Suppose that we want to transfer the binary number 1011 into the register in a serial fashion and, at the same time, in serial fashion extract the stored 0111 information. Since there is only one serial input line, the binary information must be applied at this input one bit at a time. The least significant bit of the input information is brought into the serial input line prior to the arrival of the clock pulse that causes the shift. At the same time, the bit in the right-most flip-flop of the register is extracted from the serial output line. As the input bit is transferred into the left-most flip-flop (with a clock pulse), the other bits of the register are shifted to the right, bringing the second bit into the serial output line. The other three input bits are shifted in a similar fashion. After four shift pulses, the input number 1011 is shifted into the register (lower-order bit first) and the previously stored number 0111 is shifted out, one bit at a time. At the same time, the parallel output lines give the state of the register after each shift. However, a shift register may or may not have external pins for the parallel output lines, and their use depends on the particular application.

Computers may operate in a serial mode, a parallel mode, or in a combination of both. The parallel outputs of registers are not needed if the computer operates in a serial mode only. Information is transferred into shift-registers through their serial input lines and information is taken out of registers through their serial output lines. Serial operations are slower than parallel operations because of the time it takes to transfer information in and out of shift-registers. Serial computers, however, require less hardware to perform other operations because one common circuit can be used over and over again to manipulate the bits coming out of shift-registers in a sequential manner.

Most computers operate in a parallel mode because this is a faster mode of operation. But even parallel computers need to perform shift operations. For example, the multiplication of two numbers is implemented in digital computers by successive additions and shifts. Division is done by successive subtractions and shifts. When shift-registers are used in parallel computers, the output is taken from the parallel output lines. The serial input and serial output lines are needed for cascading IC registers into shift-registers with more bits and for entering data into the extreme flip-flops of the register.

Registers may have either shift-right or shift-left capabilities, or both. Some shift-registers may also provide parallel input lines for parallel loading of information into the register. The most general shift register will have all the capabilities listed below. Others may have only some of these capabilities with at least one shift operation.

1. A *clear* control to clear the register to 0.
2. A *CP* input for clock pulses to synchronize all operations.

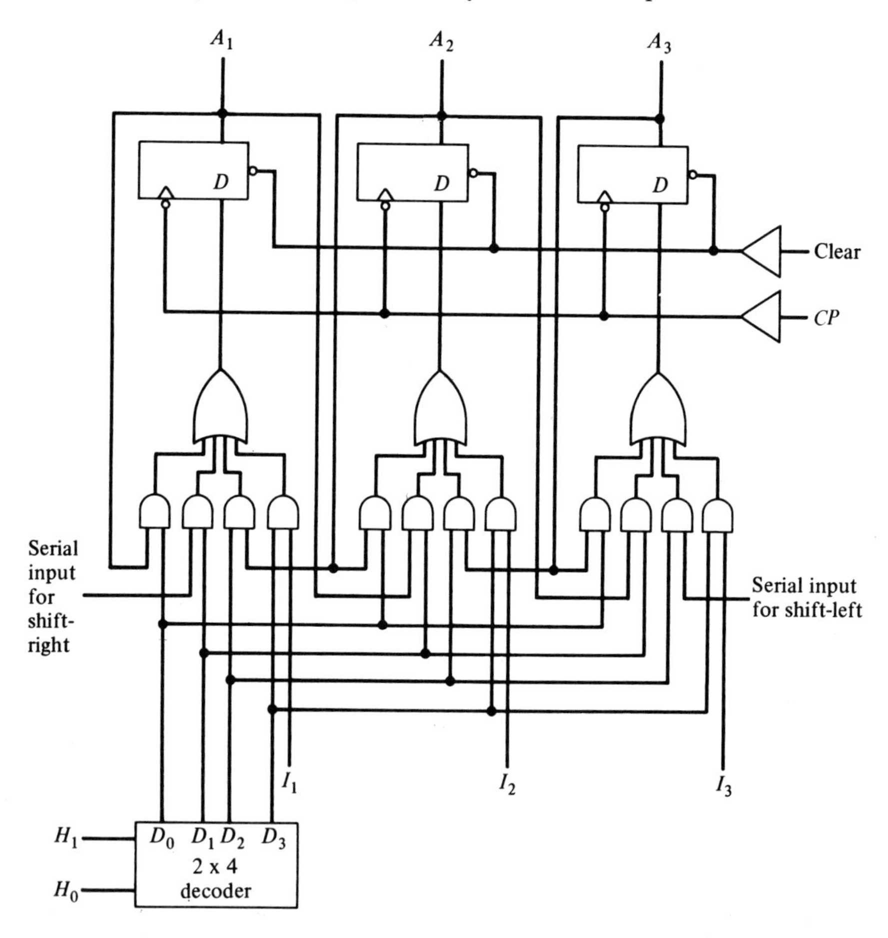


**Fig. 2-17** Three-bit bidirectional shift-register with parallel input and output.

3. A *shift-right* control to enable the shift-right operation and the *serial input* and *output* lines associated with the shift-right operation.
4. A *shift-left* control to enable the shift-left operation and the *serial input* and *output* lines associated with the shift-left operation.
5. A *parallel-load* control to enable the parallel transfer of $n$ *input* lines.
6. $n$ parallel output lines.

In addition, there may be a control state that leaves the information in the register unchanged even though clock pulses are continuously applied to the inputs of the flip-flops.

The logic diagram of a three-bit shift-register with all the capabilities mentioned above is shown in Fig. 2-17. It consists of three $D$-type flip-flops, a number of gates for controlling the various operations, and a 2 by 4 decoder. The two-mode control lines $H_1$ and $H_0$ determine the operation that occurs in the register during the falling edge of a clock pulse. When $H_1H_0 = 00$, output $D_0$ of the decoder is equal to 1 and the other three decoder outputs are equal to 0. This condition forms a path from the output of each flip-flop, through the left-most gate, and into the input of the flip-flop. The next clock pulse will transfer into each flip-flop the binary value it held previously and no change of state will result. When $H_1H_0 = 01$, output $D_1$ causes a shift-right operation. When $H_1H_0 = 10$, output $D_2$ causes a shift-left operation. Finally, when $H_1H_0 = 11$, the binary information in the parallel input lines $I_1$, $I_2$, $I_3$ is transferred into the flip-flops in parallel. Table 2-5 summarizes the effect of the mode control lines on the operation of the register.

**Table 2-5** *Effect of mode control on the shift register of Fig. 2-17*

| *Mode Control* $H_1\ H_0$ | *Decoder Output* | *Register Operation* |
|---|---|---|
| 0 0 | $D_0$ | No change in register |
| 0 1 | $D_1$ | Shift-right |
| 1 0 | $D_2$ | Shift-left |
| 1 1 | $D_3$ | Parallel-load $I_1$–$I_3$ |

## 2-6 RANDOM-ACCESS MEMORIES (RAM)

A memory unit is a collection of storage registers, together with the associated circuits needed to transfer information in and out of the registers. Memory registers can be accessed for information transfer as required and hence the name *random-access memory*, abreviated RAM.

A memory unit stores binary information in groups of bits called *words*. Each word is stored in one memory register. A word in memory is an entity of $n$ bits that move in and out of the memory unit. A word of eight bits is sometimes called a *byte*. A memory word is a group of 0's and 1's and may represent a number, an instruction code, alphanumeric characters, or any other binary coded information.

The communication between a memory unit and its environment is achieved through control lines, address selection lines, and data input and output lines. The control signals specify the direction of transfer required, that is, whether a word is to be stored in a memory register or whether a word previously stored is to be transferred out of a memory register. The address lines specify the particular word chosen out of hundreds or thousands available. The input lines provide the information to be stored in memory and the output lines supply the information coming out of memory. A block diagram of a memory unit is shown in Fig. 2-18.

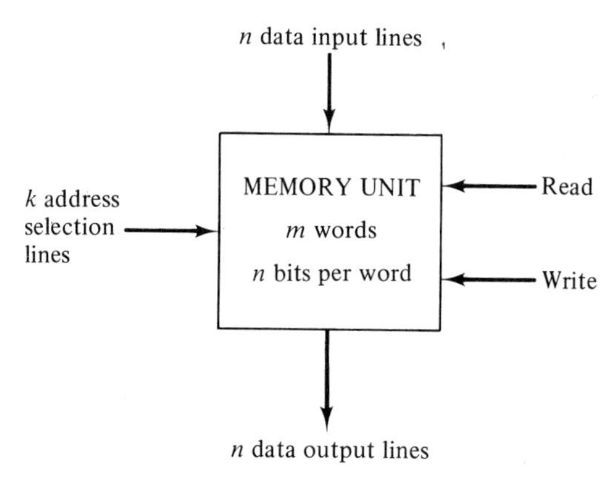


**Fig. 2-18** Block diagram of a memory unit.

A memory unit is specified by the number of words it contains and the number of bits in each word. The address selection lines select one particular memory word out of the $m$ words available. Each word in a memory is assigned an identification number, called an *address*, starting from 0 and continuing with 1, 2, 3, and up to $m - 1$. The selection of a specific word inside the memory is done by inserting its binary address value into the selection lines. A decoder inside the memory unit accepts this address and opens the paths needed to select the word specified. Thus, $k$ address bits can select any one of $2^k = m$ words. Computer memories may range from 1024 words, requiring an address of 10 bits, to $1{,}048{,}576 = 2^{20}$ words, requiring 20 address bits. It is customary to refer to the number of words in a memory unit with the unit $K$. $K$ refers to $1024 = 2^{10}$ words; thus $1K = 1024$ words, $4K = 4096$ words and $64K = 2^{16}$ words.

The two control signals are called *read* and *write*. A write signal specifies a transfer-in operation; a read signal specifies a transfer-out operation. On accepting one of the control signals, the internal control circuits inside the memory unit provide the desired function. When the memory unit receives a *write* control signal, the internal control transfers the $n$ data input bits into the word specified by the address lines. With a *read* control signal, the word selected by the address lines appears in the $n$ data output lines.

### *IC RAM*

Integrated circuit memories sometimes have a single line for the read/write control. One binary state, say 1, specifies a read operation and the other binary state specifies a write operation. In addition, one or more enable lines may be included in each IC package to provide means for expanding several packages into a memory unit with a larger number of words.

The internal construction of a random-access memory of $m$ words with $n$ bits per word consists of $m \times n$ binary storage cells and the associated logic needed to select a word for writing or reading. The binary storage cell is the basic building block of a memory unit. The logic diagram of a binary cell that stores one bit of information is shown in Fig. 2-19. Although the cell is shown to include five gates and a flip-flop, internally it is constructed with a two-transistor flip-flop having multiple inputs. The binary cell of a memory unit must be very small in order to be able to pack as many cells as possible in the semiconductor area available in the chip. The binary cell is shown to have three input lines and one output line. The purpose of the select input is

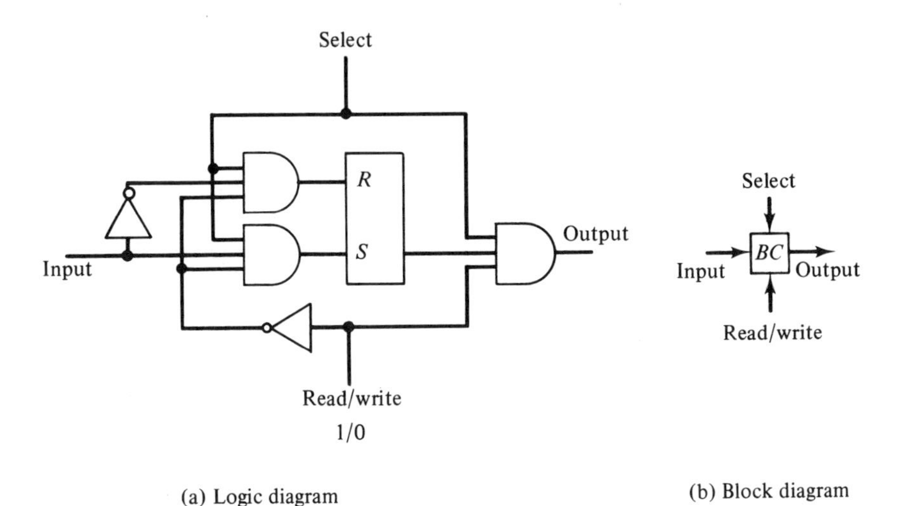


(a) Logic diagram (b) Block diagram

**Fig. 2-19** Memory Cell.

to select one cell out of the many available. With the select line at 1, a 1 in the read/write terminal forms a path from the output of the flip-flop to the output terminal. With the read/write terminal at 0, the bit in the input line is transferred into the flip-flop. Both the input and output are disabled when the select line is 0. Note that the flip-flop operates without a clock pulse and that its purpose is to store the information bit in the binary cell.

The configuration of a 4 by 3 RAM is shown in Fig. 2-20. It consists of four words of three bits each for a total of 12 binary storage cells. Each small box labeled *BC* in the diagram includes within it the circuit of a binary cell. The four lines included with each *BC* box designate the three inputs and one output as specified in the diagram of Fig. 2-19.

The two address lines go through a 2 by 4 decoder with an enable input.

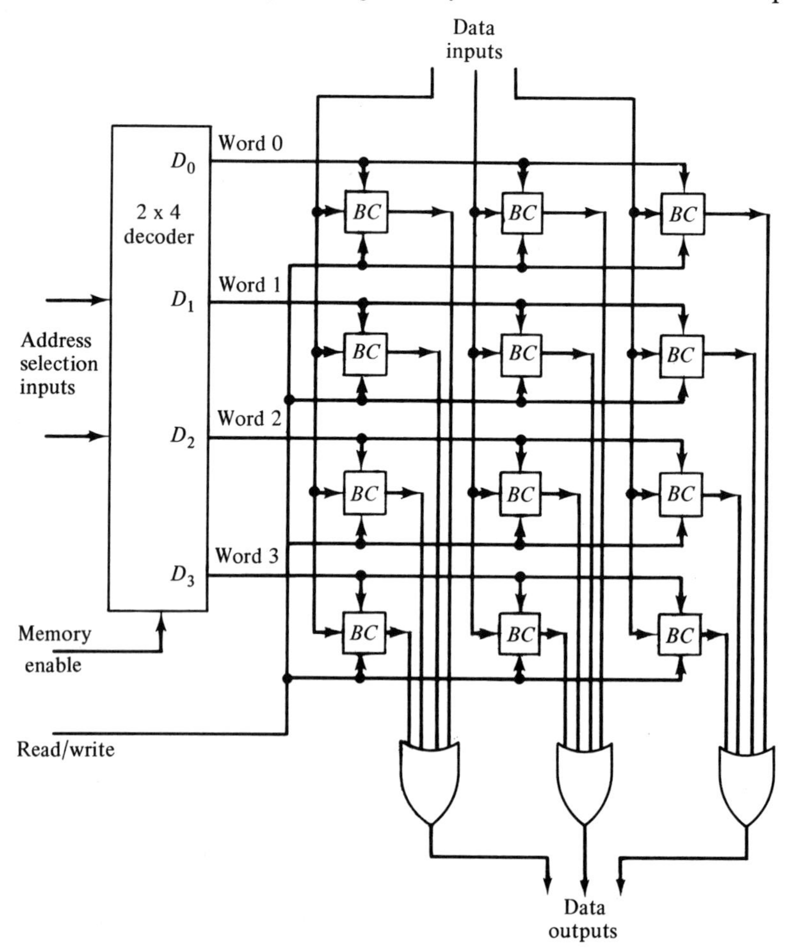


**Fig. 2-20** 4 by 3 IC RAM (BC is the binary cell of Fig. 2-19).

When the memory enable is 0, all the outputs of the decoder are 0 and none of the memory words are selected. With the memory enable input at 1, one of the four words is selected, depending on the bit combination of the two address lines. Now, with the read/write control at 1, the bits of the selected word go through the three OR gates to the output terminals. The non-selected binary cells produce 0's in the inputs of the OR gate and have no effect on the outputs. With the read/write control at 0, the information available in the input lines is transferred into the flip-flops of the selected word. The non-selected binary cells in the other words are disabled by their selection line so their previous values remain unchanged. Thus, with the memory enable at 1, the read/write control initiates the required read and write operations for the memory unit. An inhibit operation is obtained by maintaining the memory enable at 0. This condition leaves the contents of all words in memory as they were, irrespective of the value of the read/write control.

IC RAMs sometimes employ binary cells whose outputs can be tied to form a wire-OR or a wire-AND function. Other IC RAMs provide tri-state outputs. These outputs are convenient when two or more ICs are connected to form a memory unit with a larger number of words since they eliminate the need for external OR gates that would otherwise be needed.

### *Magnetic Core Memory*

IC memories retain the binary information when a word is read from memory. This type of memory is said to have a *non-destructive-read* property because the content of the word in memory is not destroyed during the reading process. Another component commonly used as a binary storage cell in memory units is the *magnetic core*. A magnetic core is a very small toroid made of ferromagnetic material. The physical quantity that makes the magnetic core suitable for binary storage is its magnetic property. One direction of magnetization is used to represent a 0 and the other to represent a 1. Reading out the binary information stored in a core requires that its direction of magnetization be forced into the 0 state. Therefore, a magnetic core memory has a *destructive-read* property; it loses the previously stored information after the reading process. Because of its destructive-read property, a magnetic core memory must provide additional control functions to restore the original contents of the word just read. A *read* control signal applied to a magnetic core memory transfers the contents of the addressed word into an *external register* and, at the same time, the memory register is automatically cleared. The sequence of internal control in a magnetic core memory then provides appropriate signals to cause the restoration of the word into the memory register. This is done by writing back the information from the external register into the same word in memory. Similarly, in order to write new information into a word in a magnetic core memory, the bits of the selected word are first cleared to 0's. The binary information from the input lines is then transferred into the selected word by setting those bits that need 1 and not changing the bits that need 0. Again, this double operation is automatically taken care of by the internal control inside the memory unit.

### *Memory Operations*

The internal control sequence of a memory unit is a function of its components and the type of control lines provided with the unit. Moreover, address and input information may come from many sources and output information may go to many destinations. The operation of a memory unit is simplified if we associate with it two external registers and assume the availability of two control signals as shown in Fig. 2-21. The address lines of the memory unit are permanently connected to the outputs of a single external register called the Memory Address Register, abreviated *MAR*. Binary information is transferred between words of memory and the external environment through one common external register called the Memory Buffer Register, abbreviated *MBR* (other names are: *information register*, *storage register*, and *data register*.) Input information is always transferred to *MBR*, and output information is always taken from *MBR*. When the memory receives a *write* command, the internal control interprets the contents of the buffer register as the information bits of the word to be stored. With a *read* command, the internal control transfers the word from memory into the buffer register. In each case, the contents of the address register specify the particular word in memory referenced for writing or reading. If a magnetic core memory is used, its internal control sequence *automatically* restores the word into memory after a read operation.

The sequence of *external* operations needed to communicate with the

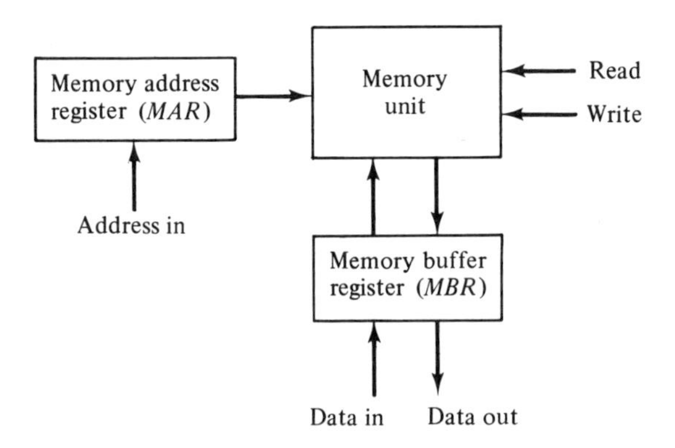


**Fig. 2-21** Block diagram of memory and associated registers.

memory unit for the purpose of transferring a word out to the external environment are as follows:

1. Transfer the address bits of the required word into *MAR*.
2. Activate the *read* control input.

The binary information stored in the memory word specified by *MAR* will then be found in *MBR*. The content of the word read from the memory will not be destroyed.

The sequence of *external* operations needed to store a word into memory are:

1. Transfer the address bits of the required word into *MAR*.
2. Transfer the data bits of the word into the *MBR*.
3. Activate the write signal.

The information from *MBR* is then stored in the memory word specified by *MAR*. The previous contents of the word are, obviously, destroyed.

### *Special Characteristics*

*Access time* is defined as the time differential between the time a memory unit receives a read signal and the time when the information read from memory is available in its outputs. In a destructive read memory, such as magnetic core, information read out is physically destroyed by the reading process. It is, however, automatically restored; but this requires an additional time. The sum of access time and restoration time is called *cycle* time. In a non-destructive read memory, the cycle time is equal to the access time because no restoration is necessary. Typical cycle times of memory units range from about 100 nsec to 1 $\mu$sec.

The mode of access of a memory unit is determined by the type of components used. In a *random-access* memory, the memory registers may be thought of as being separated in space, with each register occupying one particular spatial location as in an IC RAM or magnetic core memory. In a *sequential-access* memory, the information stored in some medium is not immediately accessible but is available only at certain intervals of time. A shift-register memory is of this type. Shift-registers are used as serial memories and are available in MOS/LSI packages. The contents of the memory are recirculated via a feedback loop from the output to the input. An *m* words by *n* bits sequential access memory is obtained from *n* shift-registers in synchronization, with each shift-register representing one bit of the word. The length of the shift-register determines the number of words. Recirculating shift-registers used as memories derive their address from an auxiliary counter which determines the word just emerging from the output terminals. Each word passes the output terminals in turn and the information is read out when the requested word is available in the output terminals.

In a random-access memory, the access time is always the same regardless of the word's particular location in space. In a sequential memory, the access time depends on the position of the word at the time of the request. If the word is just emerging from storage at the time it is requested, the access time is the time necessary to read it. If the word happened to be in a different position, the access time also includes the time required for all the other words to move past the output terminals. Thus, access time in a sequential memory is variable.

Memory units whose components lose stored information with time or when the power is turned off are said to be *volatile*. IC memories are volatile since their binary cells require external power to maintain the stored information. By contrast, a *nonvolatile* memory unit such as magnetic core or magnetic disk retains its stored information after power is removed. This is because the stored information in magnetic components is manifested by the direction of magnetization, which is retained when power is turned off. A nonvolatile property is desirable in digital computers because many useful programs are left permanently in the memory unit. When power is turned off and then on again, the previously stored programs and other information are not lost but continue to reside in memory. Computers with volatile memories may solve the problem of power failure by using backup batteries or special power supplies that continue to deliver power for some time after a power interruption occurs.

## 2-7 READ-ONLY MEMORIES (ROM)

A read-only memory (ROM), as the name implies, is a memory unit that performs the read operation only; it does not have a write capability. This implies that the binary information stored in a ROM is made permanent during the hardware production of the unit and cannot be altered by writing different words into it. While a RAM is a general-purpose device whose contents can be altered during the computational process, a ROM is restricted to reading words that are permanently stored within the unit.

An $m$ by $n$ ROM is an array of binary cells organized into $m$ words of $n$ bits each. As shown in the block diagram of Fig. 2-22, a ROM has $k$ address lines to select one of $2^k = m$ words of memory, and $n$ output lines, one for each bit of the word. An IC ROM may also have one or more enable lines for expanding a number of IC packages into a ROM with larger capacity.

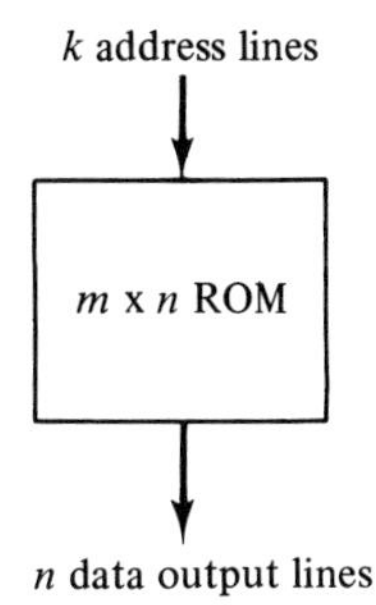


**Fig. 2-22** Block diagram of a read-only memory (ROM).

The ROM does not need a read-control line since at any given time, the output lines automatically provide the 1's and 0's of the $n$ bits of the word selected by the address value. Because the outputs are a function of only the present inputs (the address lines) a ROM is classified as a combinational circuit. In fact, a ROM is constructed internally with decoders and a set of OR gates. There is no need for providing storage capabilities as in a RAM, since the values of the bits in the ROM are permanently fixed.

Consider the logic diagram of a 4 by 3 ROM as depicted in Fig. 2-23. The unit contains a 2 by 4 decoder to decode the two address lines. The OR gates provide the three outputs. If each minterm output of the decoder is connected to the input of each OR gate, the circuit outputs will all be 1 no matter what word is selected by the address lines. Suppose we want the ROM to contain the bit combinations listed in the truth table accompanying the diagram. The truth table specifies a bit combination of 010 for word 0. This bit combination is obtained by breaking two wires (marked with a cross) between word 0 and the left-most inputs of the OR gates. In other words, when the input address is 00, the $D_0$ output of the decoder is equal to 1 and all other outputs of the decoder are equal to 0. Only the OR gate associated with output $A_2$ receives an input of 1 because the other two wires are broken. Therefore, the output lines will provide an output $A_1A_2A_3 = 010$ (assuming that an open wire to the OR gate behaves as a 0 input). Similarly, all other wires marked with crosses indicate broken wires and when these wires are removed from the diagram, the logic diagram so obtained will implement the truth table listed for the ROM.

An IC ROM is fabricated first with outputs all being 1 (or all 0, depending on the particular IC). The particular pattern of 1's and 0's is then obtained by providing a *mask* in the last fabrication step. Each cell in a ROM incorporates a link (in the position of the cross in the diagram of Fig. 2-23) that can be fused during the last fabrication process. A broken link in a cell defines one binary state and an unbroken link represents the other state. The procedure involved in fabricating a ROM requires that the customer fill out the truth table he wishes the ROM to satisfy. The manufacturer then makes the corresponding mask for the links to produce the 1's and 0's of each word

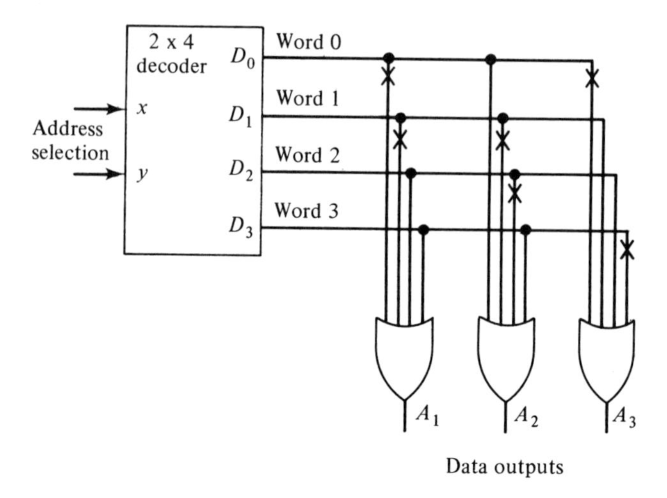


(a) Logic diagram

| Address | | Outputs | | |
|---|---|---|---|---|
| $x$ | $y$ | $A_1$ | $A_2$ | $A_3$ |
| 0 | 0 | 0 | 1 | 0 |
| 0 | 1 | 0 | 0 | 1 |
| 1 | 0 | 1 | 0 | 1 |
| 1 | 1 | 1 | 1 | 0 |

(b) Truth table

**Fig. 2-23** An example of a 4 by 3 ROM.

desired. This process is called *custom* or *mask programming*. It is a hardware procedure even though the word *programming* is used.

For small quantities it is more convenient to use a *programmable* ROM, referred to as PROM. When ordered, PROMs contain all 0's (or all 1's) in every word. Each cell in a PROM incorporates a link that can be fused by application of a high current pulse. A broken link in a cell defines one binary state and an unbroken link represents the other state. The procedure is usually irreversible and, once fused, the output for that bit is permanent. This allows the user to program the unit in his own laboratory by fusing those links which must be opened to achieve the desired relationship between input address and output data. Erasable PROMs are also available. Such ROMs have special procedures for restructuring the links back to their initial value (all 0's or all 1's) even though they have been programmed previously. In any case, all procedures for programming or erasing ROMs are *hardware* procedures. Digital applications that use ROMs specify a fixed-word pattern. The programming aspect of ROMs is concerned with the procedures for obtaining the desired fixed pattern.

ROMs find a wide range of applications in the design of digital systems. Basically, a ROM generates an input-output relation specified by a truth table. As such, it can implement any combinational circuit with $k$ inputs and $n$ outputs. A ROM can also be used in the design of sequential circuits. This is because a sequential circuit can be subdivided into a group of flip-flops and a combinational circuit (see Sec. 1-6). A register can be used for the group of flip-flops and a ROM for the combinational circuit.

Another type of LSI circuit that implements a complex combinational circuit is the *Programmable Logic Array* (PLA). A PLA is similar to a ROM in concept except that it does not provide full decoding of the input lines. Thus, in a PLA, the decoder in Fig. 2-23 is replaced by a group of AND gates each of which can be programmed to produce an AND term of the input variables. The AND and OR gates inside the PLA are initially fabricated without interconnections. The specific functions desired are implemented in the last processing step and involve a mask for linking the input lines to the AND gates and the outputs of the AND gates to the inputs of the OR gates.

ROMs are widely used for converting one binary code to another, for look-up tables needed in mathematical functions, for the display of characters, and in many other applications requiring a large number of inputs and outputs. They are also employed in the design of control units for digital computers. As such they are used to store coded information that represents the sequence of internal control variables needed for enabling the various operations in the computer. A control unit that utilizes a ROM to store binary control information is called a microprogrammed control unit. Chapter 8 discusses this subject in more detail.

## 2-8 REFERENCE LIST OF IC DIGITAL FUNCTIONS

The IC digital functions introduced in this chapter will be used in subsequent chapters to describe the organization and design of digital computers. Knowledge of these functions is necessary to understand the topics discussed later in the book. The following list provides a cumulative reference to the digital functions found in this chapter. The list is for the reader who wants to review a digital function when he encounters it elsewhere.

| | |
|---|---|
| Master-slave flip-flop | Fig. 2-5 |
| Register with parallel load | Fig. 2-7 |
| Decoder/demultiplexer | Fig. 2-9 |

| | |
|---|---|
| Multiplexer/data selector | Fig. 2-11 |
| Binary counter | Fig. 2-12 |
| Binary down counter | Fig. 2-13 |
| Binary counter with parallel load | Figs. 2-14, 2-15, Table 2-3 |
| Shift-register | Figs. 2-16, 2-17, Table 2-5 |
| IC RAM | Figs. 2-19, 2-20, Table 2-6 |
| Read-only memory (ROM) | Figs. 2-22, 2-23 |

Other digital functions available in IC packages are introduced later in conjunction with their particular application. For convenience, these digital functions are listed below together with the section or figure in which they appear.

| | |
|---|---|
| Full-adder | Fig. 1-19 |
| Parity generator/checker | Fig. 3-3 |
| Common bus system | Figs. 4-6, 4-7, 7-1 |
| Binary parallel-adder | Fig. 4-9 |
| 2's complementer | Fig. 4-11 |
| Accumulator register | Figs 5-10, 5-11 |
| Arithmetic-logic unit (ALU) | Sec. 7-2 |
| Combinational circuit shifter | Fig. 7-5 |
| Look-ahead carry generator | Fig. 7-8 |
| BCD adder | Fig. 7-11 |
| Decimal arithmetic unit | Fig. 7-12 |
| Memory stack | Sec. 7-6 |
| LSI microprocessor | Sec. 7-7 |
| Bidirectional data bus | Fig. 7-20 |
| Control and read-only memory | Fig. 8-2 |
| Magnitude comparator | Fig. 9-1 |
| Complementer | Figs. 9-2, 9-3 |
| Arithmetic calculator | Sec. 9-8 |
| Parallel binary multiplier | Fig. 10-3 |
| BCD-to-binary converter | Sec. 10-6 |
| Binary-to-BCD converter | Sec. 10-6 |

| | |
|---|---|
| Asynchronous data interface | Figs. 11-6, 11-7 |
| Priority encoder | Figs. 11-12, 11-13 |
| Content-addressable memory (CAM) | Sec. 12-4 |

## REFERENCES


1. GARRETT, L. S., "Integrated-Circuit Digital Logic Families," *IEEE Spectrum* (October, November, December), 1970. (In three parts.)
2. MILLMAN, J., and C. C. HALKIAS, *Integrated Electronics: Analog and Digital Circuits and Systems*, Chaps. 6 and 17. New York: McGraw-Hill Book Co., 1972.
3. BARNA, A., and D. I. PORAT, *Integrated Circuits in Digital Electronics*, New York: John Wiley & Sons, Inc., 1973.
4. *The TTL Data Book for Design Engineers*, Dallas, Texas: Texas Instruments, Inc., 1973.
5. *The Fairchild Semiconductor TTL Data Book*, Mountain View, Calif.: Fairchild Semiconductor, 1972.
6. MORRIS, R. L., and J. R. MILLER, eds., *Designing with TTL Integrated Circuits*, New York: McGraw-Hill Book Co., 1971.
7. *Signetics Digital, Linear, MOS* (Data Book), Sunnyvale, Calif.: Signetics, 1972.
8. *MECL Integrated Circuits Data Book*, Phoenix, Ariz.: Motorola Semiconductor Products, Inc., 1972.
9. *Digital Integrated Circuits*, Santa Clara, Calif.: National Semiconductor Corp., 1973.
10. *RCA Solid State, '74 Data Book Series SSD-203B: COS/MOS Digital Integrated Circuits*, Somerville, N.J.: RCA Solid State Div., 1974.


## PROBLEMS

2-1 TTL SSI come mostly in 14-pin IC packages. Two pins are reserved for power supply and the other pins are used for input and output terminals. How many circuits are included in one such package if it contains the following type of circuits: (a) inverters; (b) 2-input exclusive-OR gates; (c) 3-input OR gates; (d) 4-input AND gates; (e) 5-input NOR gates; (f) 8-input NAND gates; (g) clocked *JK* flip-flops with asynchronous clear.

2-2 ECL SSI gates come in 16-pin packages. Three pins are reserved for power supply and the other pins are used for input and output terminals. (a) Draw four ECL gates (Fig. 2-3) and include them in an IC package. How would you resolve the problem that the package has a smaller number of pins than gate terminals? (b) Repeat (a) with each pair of gates connected internally as shown in Fig. 2-4.

2-3 List in tabular form the fan-out, power dissipation, propagation delay, and noise margin for the following digital IC logic families: TTL, STTL, ECL, CMOS.

2-4 Consider two master-slave *JK* flip-flops $Q_1$ and $Q_2$. The output of $Q_1$ is connected to both the *J* and *K* inputs of $Q_2$ and the output of $Q_2$ is connected to both the *J* and *K* inputs of $Q_1$. Prior to the occurrence of a pulse $Q_1 = 1$ and $Q_2 = 1$. Draw the timing relations of the master and slave elements of each flip-flop during the clock pulse. What is the advantage of using master-slave flip-flops for this type of application?

2-5 What modifications should be made to the register of Fig. 2-7 so the outputs of the master-slave flip-flops change state during the *rising edge* of the input clock pulse from the *CP* terminal? The change of state should occur only if the *load* input is 0.

2-6 Redraw the register of Fig. 2-7 with NOR gates instead of the AND gates and show that the number of gates does not change.

2-7 For the following MSI registers, draw the logic diagram and assign pins to the IC package. (a) A 6-bit register with *D*-type flip-flops with six inputs, six outputs, one common *CP* terminal and one common asynchronous clear terminal. (b) A 4-bit register with *D*-type flip-flops having a parallel-load capability and tri-state gates in the four outputs. Use a common *CP* and a common clear terminal.

2-8 Draw the logic diagram of a 2 by 4 decoder with an enable input using (a) NAND gates and (b) NOR gates. Show that with NAND gates it is more convenient to distinguish the selected output with a value of 0.

2-9 Show the circuit of a 5 by 32 decoder constructed with four 3 by 8 decoders (with enable inputs) and one 2 by 4 decoder.

2-10 (a) Draw the logic diagram of a 4 by 1 multiplexer with an enable input. (b) Show how two 4 by 1 multiplexers with enable inputs can be connected to provide an 8 by 1 multiplexer. Would it be advantageous to provide a wire-OR capability to the outputs of the multiplexers?

2-11 Draw the logic diagram of a 4-bit up-down binary counter with an enable input terminal and up-down control terminals. Provide carry outputs for both the up and down count.

2-12 Show the external connections of four IC binary counters with parallel load (Fig. 2-14) to produce a 16-bit register with increment and load capabilities. Use a block diagram for each IC.

2-13 Show how the binary counter with parallel load of Fig. 2-14 can be made to operate as a divide-by-*N* counter, i.e., a counter that counts from 0000 to $N - 1$ and back to 0000. Specifically show the circuit for a divide-by-ten counter. Use an external AND gate.

2-14 Expand the bidirectional shift-register of Fig. 2-17 into four bits. Remove the decoder shown in the diagram and include the decoding function within the AND gates by providing three inputs for each.

2-15 Show the external connections of four IC bidirectional shift registers (Fig. 2-17) to produce a 12-bit bidirectional shift-register. Use a block diagram for each IC and neglect the parallel inputs.

2-16 Obtain a table similar to Table 2-4 to show the timing sequence for serial input of 1110 and serial output of 0110.

2-17 Show how a shift register with parallel load can be used to convert serial input to parallel output and parallel input to serial outputs.

2-18 (a) Show how the read and write signals of Fig. 2-21 must be connected to the enable and read/write control inputs of the RAM in Fig. 2-20.
(b) Show how the *MBR* of Fig. 2-21 can be included with the RAM of Fig. 2-20. Use a register with parallel load and a multiplexer.

2-19 When the number of words in a memory is too large it is convenient to use binary storage cells with two select inputs: one $X$ (horizontal) and one $Y$ (vertical) select input.
(a) Draw a binary storage cell similar to Fig. 2-19 with an $X$ and a $Y$ select input.
(b) Show how the select inputs are to be connected internally in a 256 by 1 RAM. Use two 4 by 16 decoders.

2-20 A TTL 64-bit RAM is organized as 16 words with 4 bits per word and open collector outputs. The function table for the memory is given below.
(a) Draw a block diagram of the RAM listing the number of data input lines, data output lines, address selection lines, and control inputs.
(b) Show the external connections of two ICs that will produce a 16 by 8 RAM.
(c) Show the external connections of two ICs that will produce a 32 by 4 RAM.
(d) Show the external connections of eight ICs that will produce a 64 by 8 RAM. Use a 2 by 4 decoder constructed with NAND gates.

| *Enable Control* | *Read/ Write* | *Operation* | *Condition of Outputs* |
|---|---|---|---|
| 0 | 0 | Write | All 1's |
| 0 | 1 | Read | Value of selected word |
| 1 | $X$ | Inhibit | All 1's |

2-21 (a) A magnetic core memory has a capacity of 8,192 words of 24 bits each. How many flip-flops are needed for the *MAR* and *MBR* (Fig. 2-21)?
(b) How many words would a memory unit contain if it has an *MAR* of 15 bits?

2-22 Draw the logic diagram of an 8 by 2 ROM that produces the full-adder function (see Table 1-2). Indicate with crosses the links that must be broken.

2-23 (a) Draw the block diagram of a 32 by 8 ROM with an *enable* input. How many address lines and output lines are needed?

(b) Show the external connections of two such ROMs in order to produce a 64 by 8 ROM.

2-24 List the truth table of a 16 by 4 ROM that multiplies two binary numbers, each two bits long, and forms a four-bit product.

# 3

# DATA REPRESENTATION

## 3-1 DATA TYPES

Binary information in digital computers is stored in memory or processor registers. Registers contain either data or control information. Control information is a bit or a group of bits used to specify the sequence of command signals needed for manipulation of the data in other registers. Data are numbers and other binary-coded information that are operated on to achieve required computational results. This chapter presents the most common types of data found in digital computers and shows how the various data types are represented in binary-coded form in computer registers.

The data types found in the registers of digital computers may be classified as being one of the following categories: (a) numbers used in arithmetic computations; (b) letters of the alphabet used in data processing; and (c) other discrete symbols used for specific purposes. All types of data, except binary numbers, are represented in computer registers in binary-coded form. This is because registers are made up of flip-flops and flip-flops are two-state devices that can store only 1's and 0's. The binary number system is the most natural system to use in a digital computer. But sometimes it is convenient to employ different number systems, especially the decimal number system, since it is used by people to perform arithmetic computations.

### *Number Systems*

A number system of *base*, or *radix*, $r$ is a system that uses distinct symbols for $r$ digits. Numbers are represented by a string of digit symbols. To determine the quantity that the number represents, it is necessary to multiply each digit by an integer power of $r$, and then form the sum of all weighed digits. For example, the decimal number system in everyday use employs the radix 10 system. The 10 symbols are: 0, 1, 2, 3, 4, 5, 6, 7, 8, and 9. The string of digits 724.5 is interpreted to represent the quantity

$$7 \times 10^2 + 2 \times 10^1 + 4 \times 10^0 + 5 \times 10^{-1}$$

That is: 7 hundreds, plus 2 tens, plus 4 units, plus 5 tenths. Every decimal number can be similarly interpreted to find the quantity it represents.

The *binary* number system uses the radix 2. The two digit symbols used are 0 and 1. The string of digits 101101 is interpreted to represent the quantity

$$1 \times 2^5 + 0 \times 2^4 + 1 \times 2^3 + 1 \times 2^2 + 0 \times 2^1 + 1 \times 2^0 = 45$$

In order to distinguish between different radix numbers, the digits will be enclosed in parentheses and the radix of the number inserted as a subscript. For example, to show the equality between decimal and binary forty-five we will write $(101101)_2 = (45)_{10}$.

Besides the decimal and binary number systems, the *octal* (radix 8) and *hexadecimal* (radix 16) are important in digital computer work. The eight symbols of the octal system are 0, 1, 2, 3, 4, 5, 6, and 7. The sixteen symbols of the hexadecimal system are 0, 1, 2, 3, 4, 5, 6, 7, 8, 9, A, B, C, D, E, and F. The last six symbols are, unfortunately, identical to the letters of the alphabet and can cause confusion at times. However, this is the adopted convention and the symbols A, B, C, D, E, F, when used to represent hexadecimal digits, correspond to the decimal numbers 10, 11, 12, 13, 14, 15, respectively.

A number in radix $r$ can be converted to the familiar decimal system by forming the sum of the weighted digits. For example, octal 736.4 is converted to decimal as follows:

$$\begin{aligned}(736.4)_8 &= 7 \times 8^2 + 3 \times 8^1 + 6 \times 8^0 + 4 \times 8^{-1} \\ &= 7 \times 64 + 3 \times 8 + 6 \times 1 + 4/8 = (478.5)_{10}\end{aligned}$$

The equivalent decimal number of hexadecimal F3 is obtained from the following calculation:

$$(\text{F3})_{16} = \text{F} \times 16 + 3 = 15 \times 16 + 3 = (243)_{10}$$

The conversion from decimal to its equivalent representation in radix $r$ system is carried out by separating the number into its *integer* and *fraction* parts and converting each part separately. The conversion of a decimal integer into a base $r$ representation is done by successive divisions by $r$ and accumulation of the remainders. The conversion of a decimal fraction to radix $r$ representation is accomplished by successive multiplications by $r$ and accumulation of the integer digits so obtained. Figure 3-1 demonstrates these procedures.

The conversion of decimal 41.6875 into binary is done by first separating the number into its integer part 41 and fraction part .6875. The integer part

Integer = 41

| 41 | |
|---|---|
| 20 | 1 |
| 10 | 0 |
| 5 | 0 |
| 2 | 1 |
| 1 | 0 |
| 0 | 1 |

$(41)_{10} = (101001)_2$

Fraction = 0.6875

$$\begin{array}{r} 0.6875 \\ 2 \\ \hline 1.3750 \\ \text{x } 2 \\ \hline 0.7500 \\ \text{x } 2 \\ \hline 1.5000 \\ \text{x } 2 \\ \hline 1.0000 \end{array}$$

$(0.6875)_{10} = (0.1011)_2$

$$(41.6875)_{10} = (101001.1011)_2$$

**Fig. 3-1** Conversion of decimal 41.6875 into binary.

is converted by dividing 41 by $r = 2$ to give an integer quotient of 20 and a remainder of 1. The quotient is again divided by 2 to give a new quotient and remainder. This process is repeated until the integer quotient becomes 0. The coefficients of the binary number are obtained from the remainders with the first remainder giving the low-order bit of the converted binary number.

The fraction part is converted by multiplying it by $r = 2$ to give an integer and a fraction. The new fraction (*without* the integer) is multiplied again by 2 to give a new integer and a new fraction. This process is repeated until the fraction part becomes zero or until the number of digits obtained gives the required accuracy. The coefficients of the binary fraction are obtained from the integer digits with the first integer computed being the digit to be placed next to the binary point. Finally, the two parts are combined together to give the total required conversion.

### *Binary, Octal, and Hexadecimal Representation*

The conversion from and to binary, octal, and hexadecimal representation plays an important part in digital computers. Since $2^3 = 8$ and $2^4 = 16$, each octal digit corresponds to three binary digits and each hexadecimal digit corresponds to four binary digits. The conversion from binary to octal is easily accomplished by partitioning the binary number into groups of three bits each. The corresponding octal digit is then assigned to each group of bits and the string of digits so obtained gives the octal equivalent of the binary number. Consider for example a 16-bit register. Physically, one may think of the register as composed of 16 binary storage cells, with each cell capable of holding either a 1 or a 0. Suppose that the bit configuration stored in the register is as shown in Fig. 3-2. Since a binary number consists of a string of 1's and 0's, the 16-bit register can be used to store any binary number from 0 to $2^{16} - 1$. For the particular example shown, the binary number stored in the register is the equivalent of decimal 44899. Starting from the low-order bit, we partition the register into groups of three bits each (the sixteenth bit remains in a group by itself). Each group of three bits is assigned its octal equivalent and placed on top of the register. The string of octal digits so obtained represents the octal equivalent of the binary number.

| | |
|---|---|
| 1 2 7 5 4 3 | Octal |
| 1 010 111 101 100 011 → 1 0 1 0 1 1 1 1 0 1 1 0 0 0 1 1 | Binary |
| A F 6 3 | Hexadecimal |

**Fig. 3-2** Binary, octal, and hexadecimal conversion.

Conversion from binary to hexadecimal is similar except that the bits are divided into groups of four. The corresponding hexadecimal digit for each group of four bits is written as shown below the register of Fig. 3-2. The string of hexadecimal digits so obtained represents the hexadecimal equivalent of the binary number. The corresponding octal digit for each group of three bits is easily remembered after studying the first eight entries listed in Table 3-1. The correspondence between a hexadecimal digit and its equivalent four-bit code can be found in the first 16 entries of Table 3-2.

Table 3-1 lists a few octal numbers and their representation in registers in binary-coded form. The binary code is obtained by the procedure explained above. Each octal digit is assigned a three-bit code as specified by the entries of the first eight digits in the table. Similarly, Table 3-2 lists a few hexadecimal numbers and their representation in registers in binary-coded form. Here the binary code is obtained by assigning to each hexadecimal digit the four-bit code listed in the first 16 entries of the table.

Comparing the binary-coded octal and hexadecimal numbers with their binary number equivalent we find that the bit combination in all three representations is exactly the same. For example, decimal 99, when converted to binary, becomes 1100011. The binary-coded octal equivalent of decimal 99 is 001 100 011 and the binary-coded hexadecimal of decimal 99 is 0110 0011. If we neglect the leading zeros in these three binary representations we find that their bit combination is identical. This should be so because of the straightforward conversion that exists between binary numbers and octal or hexadecimal. The point of all this is that a string of 1's and 0's stored in a register could represent a binary number, but this same string of bits may

**Table 3-1** *Binary-coded octal numbers*

| *Octal Number* | *Binary-Coded Octal* | *Decimal Equivalent* | |
|---|---|---|---|
| 0 | 000 | 0 | ↑ |
| 1 | 001 | 1 | |
| 2 | 010 | 2 | Code |
| 3 | 011 | 3 | for one |
| 4 | 100 | 4 | octal |
| 5 | 101 | 5 | digit |
| 6 | 110 | 6 | |
| 7 | 111 | 7 | ↓ |
| 10 | 001 000 | 8 | |
| 11 | 001 001 | 9 | |
| 12 | 001 010 | 10 | |
| 24 | 010 100 | 20 | |
| 62 | 110 010 | 50 | |
| 143 | 001 100 011 | 99 | |
| 370 | 011 111 000 | 248 | |

**Table 3-2** *Binary-coded hexadecimal numbers*

| *Hexadecimal Number* | *Binary-Coded Hexadecimal* | *Decimal Equivalent* | |
|---|---|---|---|
| 0 | 0000 | 0 | ↑ |
| 1 | 0001 | 1 | |
| 2 | 0010 | 2 | |
| 3 | 0011 | 3 | |
| 4 | 0100 | 4 | |
| 5 | 0101 | 5 | |
| 6 | 0110 | 6 | Code |
| 7 | 0111 | 7 | for one |
| 8 | 1000 | 8 | hexadecimal |
| 9 | 1001 | 9 | digit |
| A | 1010 | 10 | |
| B | 1011 | 11 | |
| C | 1100 | 12 | |
| D | 1101 | 13 | |
| E | 1110 | 14 | |
| F | 1111 | 15 | ↓ |
| 14 | 0001 0100 | 20 | |
| 32 | 0011 0010 | 50 | |
| 63 | 0110 0011 | 99 | |
| F8 | 1111 1000 | 248 | |

be interpreted as holding an octal number in binary-coded form (if we divide the bits in groups of three) or as holding a hexadecimal number in binary-coded form (if we divide the bits in groups of four).

The registers in a digital computer contain many bits. Specifying the content of registers by their binary values will require a long string of binary digits. It is more convenient to specify content of registers by their octal or hexadecimal equivalent. The number of digits is reduced by one third in the octal designation and by one fourth in the hexadecimal designation. For example, the binary number 1111 1111 1111 has 12 digits. It can be expressed in octal as 7777 (four digits) or in hexadecimal as FFF (three digits). Computer manuals invariably choose either the octal or the hexadecimal designation for specifying contents of registers.

### *Decimal Representation*

The binary number system is the most natural system for a computer, but people are accustomed to the decimal system. One way to solve this conflict is to convert all input decimal numbers into binary numbers, let the computer perform all arithmetic operations in binary and then convert the binary results back to decimal for the human user to understand. However, it is also possible for the computer to perform arithmetic operations directly with decimal numbers provided they are placed in registers in a coded form. Decimal numbers enter the computer usually as binary-coded alphanumeric characters. These codes, introduced later, may contain from six to eight bits for each decimal digit. When decimal numbers are used for internal arithmetic computations, they are converted to a binary code with four bits per digit.

A binary code is a group of $n$ bits that assume up to $2^n$ distinct combinations of 1's and 0's with each combination representing one element of the set that is being coded. For example, a set of four elements can be coded by a two-bit code with each element assigned one of the following bit combinations: 00, 01, 10, or 11. A set of eight elements requires a three-bit code, a set of 16 elements requires a four-bit code, etc. A binary code will have some unassigned bit combinations if the number of elements in the set is not a multiple power of 2. The 10 decimal digits form such a set. A binary code that distinguishes among 10 elements must contain at least four bits, but six combinations will remain unassigned. Numerous different codes can be obtained by arranging four bits in 10 distinct combinations. The bit assignment most commonly used for the decimal digits is the straight binary assignment listed in the first 10 entries of Table 3-3. This particular code is called *binary-coded decimal* and is commonly referred to by its abbreviation BCD. Other decimal codes are sometimes used and a few of them will be given in Sec. 3-4.

**Table 3-3** *Binary-coded decimal (BCD) numbers*

| *Decimal Number* | *Binary-Coded Decimal* (BCD) *Number* | |
|---|---|---|
| 0 | 0000 | ↑ |
| 1 | 0001 | |
| 2 | 0010 | |
| 3 | 0011 | Code |
| 4 | 0100 | for one |
| 5 | 0101 | decimal |
| 6 | 0110 | digit |
| 7 | 0111 | |
| 8 | 1000 | |
| 9 | 1001 | ↓ |
| 10 | 0001 0000 | |
| 20 | 0010 0000 | |
| 50 | 0101 0000 | |
| 99 | 1001 1001 | |
| 248 | 0010 0100 1000 | |

It is very important to understand the difference between the *conversion* of decimal numbers into binary and the *binary coding* of decimal numbers. For example, the decimal number 99, when *converted* to a binary number, is represented by the string of bits 1100011, but when represented in BCD, it becomes 1001 1001. The *only* difference between a decimal number represented by the familiar digit symbols 0, 1, 2, . . . , 9 and the BCD symbols 0001, 0010, . . . , 1001 is in the symbols used to represent the digits—the number itself is exactly the same. A few decimal numbers and their representation in BCD are listed in Table 3-3.

### *Alphanumeric Representation*

Many applications of digital computers require the handling of data that consist not only of numbers, but also of the letters of the alphabet and certain special characters. An *alphanumeric character set* is a set of elements that includes the 10 decimal digits, the 26 letters of the alphabet and a number of special characters such as \$, +, =, etc. Such a set contains between 32 and 64 elements (if only upper-case letters are included) or between 64 and 128 (if both upper-case and lower-case letters are included). In the first case, the binary code will require six bits and in the second case, seven bits. The standard alphanumeric binary code is the ASCII (American National Standard Code for Information Interchange) which uses seven bits to code 128 characters. The binary code for the upper-case letters, the decimal digits,

**Table 3-4** *American National Standard Code for Information Interchange (ASCII)*

| *Character* | *Binary Code* | *Character* | *Binary Code* |
|---|---|---|---|
| A | 100 0001 | 0 | 011 0000 |
| B | 100 0010 | 1 | 011 0001 |
| C | 100 0011 | 2 | 011 0010 |
| D | 100 0100 | 3 | 011 0011 |
| E | 100 0101 | 4 | 011 0100 |
| F | 100 0110 | 5 | 011 0101 |
| G | 100 0111 | 6 | 011 0110 |
| H | 100 1000 | 7 | 011 0111 |
| I | 100 1001 | 8 | 011 1000 |
| J | 100 1010 | 9 | 011 1001 |
| K | 100 1011 | | |
| L | 100 1100 | | |
| M | 100 1101 | blank | 010 0000 |
| N | 100 1110 | . | 010 1110 |
| O | 100 1111 | ( | 010 1000 |
| P | 101 0000 | + | 010 1011 |
| Q | 101 0001 | $ | 010 0100 |
| R | 101 0010 | * | 010 1010 |
| S | 101 0011 | ) | 010 1001 |
| T | 101 0100 | — | 010 1101 |
| U | 101 0101 | / | 010 1111 |
| V | 101 0110 | , | 010 1100 |
| W | 101 0111 | = | 011 1101 |
| X | 101 1000 | | |
| Y | 101 1001 | | |
| Z | 101 1010 | | |

and a few special characters is listed in Table 3-4. Note that the decimal digits in ASCII can be converted to BCD by removing the three high-order bits, 011.

Binary codes play an important part in digital computer operations. The codes must be in binary because registers can only hold binary information. One must realize that binary codes merely change the symbols, not the meaning of the discrete elements they represent. The operations specified for digital computers must take into consideration the meaning of the bits stored in registers so that operations are performed on operands of the same type. In inspecting the bits of a computer register at random, one is likely to find that it represents some type of coded information rather than a binary number.

Binary codes can be formulated for any set of discrete elements: the colors of the spectrum, musical notes, and chess pieces and their positions on the chess board. Binary codes are also used to formulate instructions that specify control information for the computer. This chapter is concerned with *data* representation. Instruction codes will be discussed in Chap. 5.

## 3-2 FIXED-POINT REPRESENTATION

Numbers used in scientific calculations are designated by a sign, the magnitude of the number and sometimes a decimal point. The sign is needed for arithmetic operations as it shows whether the number is positive or negative. The position of the decimal (or binary) point is needed to represent fractions or mixed integer-fraction numbers.

The sign of a number may be considered as a set of two elements, *plus* and *minus*. This two-element set can be assigned a binary code of one bit. The convention is to represent a plus with a 0 and a minus with a 1. To represent a signed binary number in a register we need $n + 1$ bits; $n$ bits for the number and one bit for the sign. The sign bit is customarily placed in the leftmost position of the register.

The representation of the decimal (or binary) point in a register is complicated by the fact that it is characterized by a *position* between two flip-flops in the register. There are two ways of specifying the position of the decimal point in a register: by giving it a *fixed* position or by employing a *floating-point* representation. The fixed-point method assumes that the decimal point is always fixed in one position. The two positions most widely used are: (a) a decimal point in the extreme left of the register to make the stored number a fraction, and (b) a decimal point in the extreme right of the register to make the stored number an integer. In either case, the decimal point is not actually present but its presence is assumed from the fact that the number stored in the register is treated as a fraction or as an integer. The floating-point representation uses a second register to store a number that designates the position of the decimal point in the first register. Floating-point representation is discussed further in the next section.

Before proceeding to show how fixed-point numbers are represented in registers, it is necessary to define the *complement* of a number. Complements are used in digital computers to represent negative numbers because this representation facilitates arithmetic manipulations. There are two types of complements for each radix $r$ number system: (a) the $r$'s complement and (b) the $(r - 1)$'s complement. When the radix number is substituted for $r$, the two types receive the names 2's and 1's complement for binary numbers, or 10's and 9's complement for decimal numbers.

### The $(r - 1)$'s Complement

The $(r - 1)$'s complement of a number in radix $r$ is obtained by subtracting each digit of the number from $(r - 1)$. For decimal numbers, $(r - 1) = 9$ and for binary numbers, $(r - 1) = 1$. Thus, the 9's complement of decimal 835 is 164 and is obtained by subtracting each digit from 9. The 1's complement of the binary number 1010 is 0101 and is obtained by subtracting each digit from 1. However, when subtracting binary digits from 1, we can have either $1 - 0 = 1$ or $1 - 1 = 0$. In either case, the digit obtained by subtracting it from 1 is the complement of its original value. In other words, the 1's complement of a binary number is identical to the bit-by-bit logic complement operation. An easier way to obtain the 1's complement is to change all 1's to 0's and all 0's to 1's. Since the logic complement and 1's complement are identical operations for binary digits, we will sometimes drop the designation 1's and call it just *complement.*

The $(r - 1)$'s complement of octal or hexadecimal numbers are obtained by subtracting each digit from 7 or F (decimal 15), respectively. When these numbers are binary coded, the complement is obtained by changing 1's to 0's and 0's to 1's.

### The $r$'s Complement

The $r$'s complement of a number in radix $r$ is obtained by adding 1 to the low-order digit of its $(r - 1)$'s complement. Thus, the 10's complement of the decimal 835 is $164 + 1 = 165$ and is obtained by adding 1 to its 9's complement value. The 2's complement of binary 1010 is $0101 + 1 = 0110$ and is obtained by complementing each bit and adding 1.

The 2's complement can be formed also by leaving all least significant 0's and the first 1 unchanged, and then complementing the remaining digits. For example, the 2's complement of 10100 is 01100 and is obtained by leaving the two low-order 0's and the first 1 unchanged, and then complementing the two most significant bits.

### Binary Fixed-Point Representation

When a fixed-point binary number is positive, the sign is represented by 0 and the magnitude by a positive binary number. When the number is negative, the sign is represented by 1 but the rest of the number may be represented in one of three possible ways. These are:

1. Signed-magnitude representation, or
2. Signed-1's complement representation, or
3. Signed-2's complement representation.

In the signed-magnitude representation of a negative number the magnitude of the number is inserted next to its negative sign. In the other two representations, the negative number is represented as either the 1's or 2's complement of its position value designation. As an example, consider the number 9 stored in a seven-bit register. +9 is represented by a sign bit of 0 in the left-most position followed by the binary equivalent of 9: 0 001001. Note that each of the seven bits of the register must have a value and therefore, 0's must be inserted in the two most significant positions following the sign bit. Although there is only one way to represent +9, there are three different ways to represent −9. These representations are shown below:

| | |
|---|---|
| In signed-magnitude representation | 1 001001 |
| In signed-1's complement representation | 1 110110 |
| In signed-2's complement representation | 1 110111 |

The signed-magnitude representation of −9 is obtained from +9 (0 001001) by complementing *only* the sign bit. The signed-1's complement representation of −9 is obtained by complementing *all* the bits of 0 001001 (+9), including the sign bit. The signed-2's complement designation is obtained by taking the 2's complement of the positive number, *including* its sign bit.

### *Arithmetic Addition*

The reason for using the signed-complement representation for negative numbers will become apparent after we consider the steps involved in forming the sum of two signed numbers. The signed-magnitude representation is the one used in everyday calculations. For example, +23 and −35 are represented with a sign, followed by the magnitude of the number. To add these two numbers, it is necessary to subtract the smaller magnitude from the larger and to use the sign of the larger number for the sign of the result, that is: $(+23) + (-35) = -(35 - 23) = -12$. The process of adding two signed numbers when negative numbers are represented in signed-magnitude form requires that we compare their signs. If the two signs are the same, we add the two magnitudes. If the signs are not the same, we compare the relative magnitudes of the numbers and then subtract the smaller from the larger. It is necessary also to determine the sign of the result. This is a process that, when implemented with digital hardware, requires a long sequence of control decisions as well as circuits that can compare, add, and subtract numbers.

Now compare the above procedure with the procedure that forms the sum of two signed binary numbers when negative numbers are in signed-2's complement representation. This procedure is very simple and can be stated as follows:

> *Add the two numbers, including their sign bit, and discard any carry out of the left-most (sign) bit.*

Numerical examples for addition of two binary numbers with negative numbers in their signed-2's complement representation are shown below. Note that negative numbers must be initially in signed-2's complement representation and the sum obtained after the addition, if negative, is also in its signed-2's complement representation. The two numbers in the four examples are added, including their sign bit, and any carry out of the sign bit is discarded.

| | | | |
|---|---|---|---|
| +6 | 0 000110 | −6 | 1 111010 |
| | + | | + |
| +9 | 0 001001 | +9 | 0 001001 |
| +15 | 0 001111 | +3 | 0 000011 |

| | | | |
|---|---|---|---|
| +6 | 0 000110 | −9 | 1 110111 |
| | + | | + |
| −9 | 1 110111 | −9 | 1 110111 |
| −3 | 1 111101 | −18 | 1 101110 |

This procedure is much simpler than the one used for signed-magnitude numbers. It requires only one control decision and a circuit for adding two numbers. The procedure requires that negative numbers be initially stored in registers in their 2's complement form. This can be easily accomplished by complementing and then incrementing the positive number.

The procedure that forms the sum of two binary numbers when negative numbers are in signed-1's complement form is similar and can be stated as follows:

*Add the two numbers, including their sign bit. If there is a carry out of the most significant (sign) bit, the result is incremented by 1 and the carry discarded.*

The two examples shown below demonstrate this procedure. Note that all negative numbers, including results, are in their signed-1's complement form. The carry out of the sign bit, when 1, is returned and added to the least significant bit. This is referred to as *end around carry.*

| | | | |
|---|---|---|---|
| +6 | 0 000110 | −6 | 1 111001 |
| | + | | + |
| −9 | 1 110110 | +9 | 0 001001 |
| −3 | 1 111100 | | 1 0 000010 |
| | | | + |
| | | | 1 |
| | | +3 | 0 000011 |

The advantage of the signed-2's complement representation over the signed-1's complement form (and the signed-magnitude form) is that it contains only one type of zero. The other two representations have both a positive zero and a negative zero. For example, adding (+9) to (−9) in the 1's complement representation, one obtains:

| | |
|---|---|
| +9 | 0 001001 |
| −9 | 1 110110 |
| −0 | 1 111111 |

and the result is a negative zero, i.e., the complement of 0 000000 (positive zero).

A zero with an associated sign bit will appear in a register in one of the following forms, depending on the representation used for negative numbers:

| | +0 | −0 |
|---|---|---|
| In signed-magnitude | 0 0000000 | 1 0000000 |
| In signed-1's complement | 0 0000000 | 1 1111111 |
| In signed-2's complement | 0 0000000 | none |

Both the signed-magnitude and the 1's complement representations have associated with them the possibility of a negative zero. The signed-2's complement representation has only a positive zero. This occurs because the 2's complement of 0 000000 (positive zero) is 0 000000 and may be obtained from the 1's complement plus 1 (i.e., 1 111111 + 1) provided the end-carry is discarded.

### *Arithmetic Subtraction*

Subtraction of two signed binary numbers when negative numbers are in the 2's complement form is very simple and can be stated as follows:

*Take the 2's complement of the subtrahend* (*including the sign bit*) *and add it to the minuend* (*including sign bit*).

This procedure utilizes the fact that a subtraction operation can be changed to an addition operation if the sign of the subtrahend is changed. This is demonstrated by the following relations ($B$ is the subtrahend):

$$(\pm A) - (-B) = (\pm A) + (+B)$$

$$(\pm A) - (+B) = (\pm A) + (-B)$$

But changing a positive number to a negative number is easily done by taking its 2's complement (including the sign bit). The reverse is also true because the complement of the complement restores the number to its original value.

The subtraction with 1's complement numbers is similar except for the end around carry. Subtraction with signed-magnitude numbers is more complicated and is covered in detail in Sec. 9-3.

Because of the availability of simple procedures for adding and subtracting numbers when negative numbers are in the signed-2's complement form, many computers adopt this representation over the more familiar signed-magnitude form. The reason 2's complement is usually chosen over 1's complement is to avoid the occurrence of a negative zero.

### *Decimal Fixed-Point Representation*

The representation of decimal numbers in registers is a function of the binary code used to represent a decimal digit. A 4-bit decimal code requires four flip-flops for each decimal digit. The representation of +4385 in BCD requires at least 17 flip-flops, one flip-flop for the sign and four for each digit. This number will be represented in a register with 25 flip-flops as follows:

| + | 0 | 0 | 4 | 3 | 8 | 5 |
|---|---|---|---|---|---|---|
| 0 | 0 0 0 0 | 0 0 0 0 | 0 1 0 0 | 0 0 1 1 | 1 0 0 0 | 0 1 0 1 |

By representing numbers in decimal we are wasting a considerable amount of storage space since the number of flip-flops needed to store a decimal number in a binary code is greater than the number of flip-flops needed for its equivalent binary representation. Also, the circuits required to perform decimal arithmetic are more complex. However, there are some advantages in the use of decimal representation because computer input and output data are generated by people who use the decimal system. Some applications such as electronic calculators or business data processing require small amounts of arithmetic computations compared to the amount required for input and output of data. For this reason, some computers and all calculators will perform arithmetic computations directly on decimal data (in binary code) and thus eliminate the need for conversion to binary and back to decimal. Large scale computer systems usually have hardware for arithmetic calculations with both binary and decimal data. The user can specify by programmed instructions whether he wants the computer to perform calculations on binary or decimal data.

There are three ways to represent negative fixed-point decimal numbers. They are similar to the three representations of a negative binary number except for the radix change:

1. Signed-magnitude representation, or
2. Signed-9's complement representation, or
3. Signed-10's complement representation.

For all three representations, a positive decimal number is represented by 0 for plus followed by the magnitude of the number. It is in regard to negative numbers that the representations differ. The sign of a negative number is represented by 1 and the magnitude of the number is positive in signed-magnitude representation. In the other two representations the number is represented by the 9's or 10's complement form. The sign of the decimal number is sometimes represented by a four-bit code to conform with the four-bit representation of digits. For example, the code 1100 (not assigned to a BCD digit) may be used to represent a plus and 1101 to represent a minus.

Arithmetic addition and subtraction of decimal numbers employs the same procedures as binary numbers except for the difference in the radix. The 2's complement procedures of binary numbers, described previously, apply also to decimals when negative numbers are represented in their signed-10's complement form. The sign is represented by 0 or 1 and placed in the left-most position of the number. The sign bit is added together with the other digits. A corresponding similarity exists with the other two representations.

## 3-3 FLOATING-POINT REPRESENTATION

The floating-point representation of a number needs two parts. The first part represents a signed, fixed-point number called the *mantissa*. The second part designates the position of the decimal (or binary) point and is called the *exponent*. The fixed-point mantissa may be a fraction or an integer. For example, the decimal number +6132.789 is represented in floating point as follows:

| *sign* | | *sign* | |
|---|---|---|---|
| 0 | .6132789 | 0 | 04 |
| mantissa | | exponent | |

The mantissa has a 0 in the left-most position to denote a plus. The mantissa here is considered to be a fixed-point *fraction*, so the decimal point is assumed to be at the left of the most significant digit. The decimal mantissa, when stored in a register, requires at least 29 flip-flops: four flip-flops for each BCD digit and one for the sign. The decimal point is not physically indicated in the register; it is only assumed to be there. The exponent contains the decimal number +04 (in BCD) to indicate that the *actual* position of the decimal point is four decimal positions to the right of the *assumed* decimal point. This representation is equivalent to the number expressed as a fraction times 10 to an exponent, that is, $+.6132789 \times 10^{+04}$. Because of this analogy, the mantissa is sometimes called the *fraction part*.

In the previous example, we have assumed that the mantissa is a fixed-point fraction and that the exponent is associated with a radix of 10. Some computers assume a fixed-point integer for the mantissa. Moreover, the assumed radix for the exponent is a function of the number system that is being represented in the register. Consider, for example, a computer that assumes integer representation for the mantissa and radix 8 for the numbers. The octal number $+36.754 = 36754 \times 8^{-3}$, in its floating-point representation, will look like this:

$$\underbrace{\overset{sign}{0} \quad 36754.}_{\text{mantissa}} \qquad \underbrace{\overset{sign}{1} \quad 03}_{\text{exponent}}$$

When this number is represented in a register, in its binary coded form, the actual value of the register becomes:

0 011 110 111 101 100    1 000 011

The register needs 23 flip-flops. The circuits that operate on such data must recognize the flip-flops assigned to the bits of the mantissa and exponent and their associated signs. Note that if the exponent is increased by one (to $-2$) the *actual* point of the mantissa is shifted to the right by three bits (one octal digit).

Floating-point is always interpreted to represent a number in the following form:

$$m \times r^e$$

Only the mantissa $m$ and the exponent $e$ are physically represented in the register (including their signs). The radix $r$ and the radix-point position of the mantissa are always *assumed.* The circuits that manipulate the floating-point numbers in registers must conform with these two assumptions if correct computational results are to be achieved. A floating-point binary number is represented in a similar manner except that the radix assumed is 2. For example, the number $+1001.11$ is represented in a 16-bit register as follows:

$$\underbrace{\overset{sign}{0} \quad 100111000}_{\text{mantissa}} \qquad \underbrace{\overset{sign}{0} \quad 00100}_{\text{exponent}}$$

with the mantissa occupying ten bits and the exponent six bits. The mantissa is assumed to be a fixed-point fraction. If the mantissa is assumed to be an integer, the exponent will be 1 00101 ($-5$).

A floating-point number is said to be *normalized* if the most significant position of the mantissa contains a non-zero digit. For example, the mantissa 035 is not normalized but 350 is. When 350 is represented in BCD, it becomes

0011 0101 0000 and although two 0's seem to be present in the two most significant positions, the mantissa *is* normalized. Because the bits represent a *decimal* number, not a binary number, and decimal numbers in BCD must be taken in groups of four bits, the first digit is 3 and is non-zero.

When the mantissa is normalized, it has no leading zeros and therefore contains the maximum possible number of significant digits. Consider, for example, a register that can accommodate a mantissa of five decimal digits and a sign. The number $+.35746 \times 10^2 = 35.746$ is normalized because the mantissa has a non-zero digit 3 in its most significant position. The number can be represented in an unnormalized form as $+.00357 \times 10^4 = 35.7$. This unnormalized number contains two most significant zeros and therefore the mantissa can accommodate only three significant digits. The two least significant digits, 4 and 6, that were accommodated in the normalized form, have no room in the unnormalized form because the register can only accommodate five digits.

A zero cannot be normalized because it does not contain a non-zero digit. A zero is represented in floating-point by all 0's in the mantissa and exponent, including their signs. It is then necessary to check for an all 0 quantity before deciding whether the number can be normalized.

Arithmetic operations with floating-point numbers are more complicated than arithmetic operations with fixed-point numbers and their execution takes longer and requires more complex hardware. However, floating-point representation is a must for scientific computations because of the scaling problems involved with fixed-point computations. Many computers and all electronic calculators have the built-in capability of performing floating-point arithmetic operations. Computers that do not have hardware for floating-point computations have a set of subroutines to help the user program his scientific problems with floating-point numbers. Floating-point numbers are called *real* numbers when specified in a FORTRAN program. Arithmetic operations with floating-point numbers are discussed in Sec. 10-4.

## 3-4 OTHER BINARY CODES

The previous sections introduced the most common types of binary-coded data found in digital computers. Other binary codes for decimal numbers and alphanumeric characters are sometimes used. Digital computers also employ other binary codes for special applications. A few additional binary codes encountered in digital computers are presented in this section.

### *Gray Code*

Digital systems can process data in discrete form only. Many physical systems supply continuous output data. The data must be converted into digital form before it can be used by a digital computer. Continuous, or analog, information is converted into digital form by means of an analog-to-digital converter. The reflected binary or *Gray* code, shown in Table 3-5, is

**Table 3-5** *4-bit Gray code*

| *Binary Code* | *Decimal Equivalent* | *Binary Code* | *Decimal Equivalent* |
|---|---|---|---|
| 0000 | 0 | 1100 | 8 |
| 0001 | 1 | 1101 | 9 |
| 0011 | 2 | 1111 | 10 |
| 0010 | 3 | 1110 | 11 |
| 0110 | 4 | 1010 | 12 |
| 0111 | 5 | 1011 | 13 |
| 0101 | 6 | 1001 | 14 |
| 0100 | 7 | 1000 | 15 |

sometimes used for the converted digital data. The advantage of the Gray code over straight binary numbers is that the Gray code changes by only one bit as it sequences from one number to the next. In other words, the change from any number to the next in sequence is recognized by a change of only one bit from 0 to 1 or from 1 to 0. A typical application of the Gray code occurs when the analog data is represented by the continuous change of a shaft position. The shaft is partitioned into segments with each segment assigned a number. If adjacent segments are made to correspond to adjacent Gray code numbers, ambiguity is reduced when the shaft position is in the line that separates any two segments.

Gray code counters are sometimes used to provide the timing sequences that control the operations in a digital system. A Gray code counter is a counter whose flip-flops go through a sequence of states as specified in Table 3-5. Gray code counters remove the ambiguity during the change from one state of the counter to the next because only one bit can change during the state transition.

### *Other Decimal Codes*

Binary codes for decimal digits require a minimum of four bits. Numerous different codes can be formulated by arranging four or more bits in 10 distinct possible combinations. A few possibilities are shown in Table 3-6.

The BCD (Binary-Coded Decimal) has been introduced before. It uses a straight assignment of the binary equivalent of the digit. The six unused bit combinations listed have no meaning when BCD is used, just as the letter H

**Table 3-6** *Four different binary codes for the decimal digit*

| *Decimal Digit* | BCD 8421 | 2421 | *Excess*-3 | *Excess*-3 *Gray* |
|---|---|---|---|---|
| 0 | 0000 | 0000 | 0011 | 0010 |
| 1 | 0001 | 0001 | 0100 | 0110 |
| 2 | 0010 | 0010 | 0101 | 0111 |
| 3 | 0011 | 0011 | 0110 | 0101 |
| 4 | 0100 | 0100 | 0111 | 0100 |
| 5 | 0101 | 1011 | 1000 | 1100 |
| 6 | 0110 | 1100 | 1001 | 1101 |
| 7 | 0111 | 1101 | 1010 | 1111 |
| 8 | 1000 | 1110 | 1011 | 1110 |
| 9 | 1001 | 1111 | 1100 | 1010 |
| Unused bit combi- nations | 1010 | 0101 | 0000 | 0000 |
| | 1011 | 0110 | 0001 | 0001 |
| | 1100 | 0111 | 0010 | 0011 |
| | 1101 | 1000 | 1101 | 1000 |
| | 1110 | 1001 | 1110 | 1001 |
| | 1111 | 1010 | 1111 | 1011 |

has no meaning when decimal digit symbols are written down. For example, saying that 1001 1110 is a decimal number in BCD is like saying that 9H is a decimal number in the conventional symbol designation. Both cases contain an invalid symbol and, therefore, designate a meaningless number.

One disadvantage of using BCD is the difficulty encountered when the 9's complement of the number is to be computed. On the other hand, the 9's complement is easily obtained with the 2421 and the excess-3 codes listed in Table 3-6. These two codes have a self-complementing property which means that the 9's complement of a decimal number, when represented in one of these codes, is easily obtained by changing 1's to 0's and 0's to 1's. This property is useful when arithmetic operations are done in signed-complement representation.

The 2421 is an example of a *weighted* code. In a weighted code, the bits are multiplied by the weights indicated and the sum of the weighted bits gives the decimal digit. For example, the bit combination 1101, when weighted by the respective digits 2421, gives the decimal equivalent of $2 \times 1 + 4 \times 1 + 2 \times 0 + 1 \times 1 = 7$. The BCD code can be assigned the weights 8421 and for this reason it is sometimes called the 8421 code.

The excess-3 code is a decimal code that has been used in older computers. This is an unweighted code. Its binary code assignment is obtained from the corresponding BCD equivalent binary number after the addition of binary 3 (0011).

From Table 3-5 we note that the Gray code is not suited for a decimal code if we were to choose the first 10 entries in the table. This is because the transition from 9 back to 0 involves a change of three bits (from 1101 to 0000). To overcome this difficulty, we choose the 10 numbers starting from the third entry 0010 up to the twelfth entry 1010. Now the transition from 1010 to 0010 involves a change of only one bit. Since the code has been shifted up three numbers, it is called the excess-3 Gray. This code is listed with the other decimal codes in Table 3-6.

### *Other Alphanumeric Codes*

The ASCII code (Table 3-4) is the standard code commonly used for the transmission of binary information. Each character is represented by a 7-bit code and usually an eighth bit is inserted for parity (see Sec. 3-5). The code consists of 128 characters. 95 characters represent *graphic symbols* that include upper and lower case letters, numerals zero to nine, punctuation marks and special symbols. Twenty-three characters represent *format effectors* which are functional characters for controlling the layout of printing or display devices such as carriage return, line feed, horizontal tabulation, and back space. The other 10 characters are used to direct the data communication flow and report its status.

Another alphanumeric (sometimes called *alphameric*) code used in IBM equipment is the EBCDIC (Extended BCD Interchange Code). It uses eight bits for each character (and a ninth bit for parity). EBCDIC has the same character symbols as ASCII but the bit assignment to characters is different.

When alphanumeric characters are used internally in a computer for data processing (not for transmission purposes) it is more convenient to use a 6-bit code to represent 64 characters. A 6-bit code can specify the 26 uppercase letters of the alphabet, numerals zero to nine, and up to 28 special characters. This set of characters is usually sufficient for data processing purposes. Using fewer bits to code characters has the advantage of reducing the memory space needed to store large quantities of alphanumeric data.

When alphanumeric information is transferred to the computer via punched cards, the alphanumeric characters use a 12-bit code. Programs and data are often prepared on punched cards for input to a computer. Of the different cards that are in use, the *Hollerith* card is the most common. A punched card consists of 80 columns and 12 rows. Each column represents an alphanumeric character of 12 bits by punching holes in the appropriate rows. A hole is sensed as a 1 and the absence of a hole is sensed as a 0. The 12 rows are marked, starting from the top, as 12, 11, 0, 1, 2, . . . , 9 punch. The first three are called the *zone* punch and the last nine are called the *numeric* punch. The decimal digits are represented by a single hole in a numeric punch. The letters of the alphabet are represented by two holes, one in a zone and the other in a numeric punch. Special characters are represented by one, two or three holes; the zone is always used, and the other two holes, if used, are in a numeric punch with the 8 punch most commonly used. The 12-bit card code is inefficient with respect to the number of bits used. Most computers convert the input 12-bit card code into an internal 6-bit code to conserve bits of memory.

## 3-5 ERROR DETECTION CODES

Binary information transmitted through some form of communication medium is subject to external noise that could change bits from 1 to 0 and vice versa. An error detection code is a binary code that detects digital errors during transmission. The detected errors cannot be corrected but their presence is indicated. The usual procedure is to observe the frequency of errors. If errors occur infrequently at random, the particular erroneous information is transmitted again. If the error occurs too often, the system is checked for malfunction.

The most common error detection code used is the *parity* bit. A parity bit is an extra bit included with a binary message to make the total number of 1's either odd or even. A message of three bits and two possible parity bits is shown in Table 3-7. The $P$(odd) bit is chosen in such a way as to make

**Table 3-7** *Parity bit generation*

| *Message* *xyz* | *P(odd)* | *P(even)* |
|---|---|---|
| 000 | 1 | 0 |
| 001 | 0 | 1 |
| 010 | 0 | 1 |
| 011 | 1 | 0 |
| 100 | 0 | 1 |
| 101 | 1 | 0 |
| 110 | 1 | 0 |
| 111 | 0 | 1 |

the sum of 1's (in all four bits) odd. The $P$(even) bit is chosen to make the sum of all 1's even. In either case, the sum is taken over the message and the $P$ bit. In any particular application, one or the other type of parity will be adopted. The even parity scheme has the disadvantage of having a bit combination of all 0's, while in the odd parity there is always one bit (of the four bits that constitute the message and $P$) that is 1. Note that the $P$(odd) is the complement of the $P$(even).

During transfer of information from one location to another, the parity bit is handled as follows. At the sending end, the message (in this case three bits) is applied to a *parity generator*, where the required parity bit is generated. The message, including the parity bit, is transmitted to its destination. At the receiving end, all the incoming bits (in this case, four) are applied to a *parity checker* that checks the proper parity adopted (odd or even). An error is detected if the checked parity does not conform to the adopted parity. The parity method detects the presence of one, three, or any odd number of errors. An even number of errors is not detected.

Parity generator and checker networks are logic circuits constructed with exclusive-OR functions. This is because, as mentioned in Sec. 1-1, the exclusive-OR function of three or more variables is by definition an odd function. An odd function is a logic function whose value is binary 1 if, and only if, an odd number of variables are equal to 1. According to this definition, the $P$(even) function is the exclusive-OR of $x$, $y$, and $z$ because it is equal to 1 when either one or all three of the variables are equal to 1 (Table 3-7). The $P$(odd) function is the complement of the $P$(even) function.

As an example, consider a three-bit message to be transmitted with an odd parity bit. At the sending end, the odd parity bit is generated by a parity generator circuit. As shown in Fig. 3-3, this circuit consists of one exclusive-OR and one exclusive-NOR gate. Since $P$(even) is the exclusive-OR of $x$, $y$, $z$, and $P$(odd) is the complement of $P$(even), it is necessary to employ an exclusive-NOR gate for the needed complementation. The message and the odd parity bit are transmitted to their destination where they are applied to a parity checker. An error has occurred during transmission if the parity of

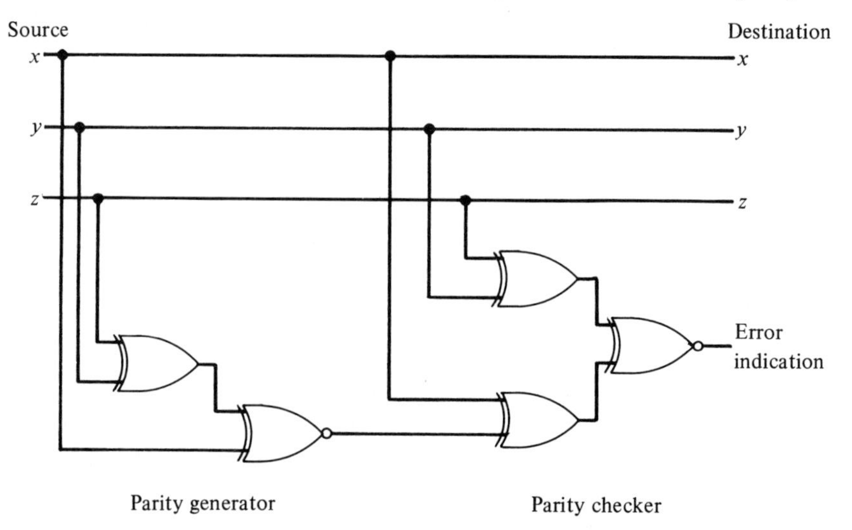


**Fig. 3-3** Error detection with odd parity bit.

the four bits received is even, since the binary information transmitted was originally odd. The output of the parity checker would be 1 when an error occurs, i.e., when the number of 1's in the four inputs is even. Since the exclusive-OR function of the four inputs is an odd function, we again need to complement the output by using an exclusive-NOR gate.

It is worth noting that the parity generator can use the same circuit as the parity checker if the fourth input is permanently held at a logic-0 value. The advantage of this is that the same circuit can be used for both parity generation and parity checking.

It is evident from the above example that even parity generators and checkers can be implemented with exclusive-OR functions. Odd parity networks need an exclusive-NOR at the output to complement the function. Parity generator/checker circuits are available in IC packages.

## REFERENCES

1. MANO, M. M., *Computer Logic Design*, Englewood Cliffs, N.J.: Prentice-Hall, Inc., 1972.
2. CHU, Y., *Digital Computer Design Fundamentals*, Chaps. 1 and 2. New York: McGraw-Hill Book Co., 1962.
3. GSCHWIND, H. W., *Design of Digital Computers*, Chap. 8. New York: Springer-Verlag, 1967.

## PROBLEMS

3-1 Give the decimal equivalent of $(11010.111)_2$, $(736.5)_8$, and $(3FA.8)_{16}$.

3-2 Convert the following decimal numbers to binary: 12.0625, $10^4$, 673.23, and 1998.

3-3 Convert decimal 225.225 to octal and hexadecimal.

3-4 Show the value of all cells of a 12-bit register that hold the number equivalent to $(215)_{10}$ in (a) binary, (b) binary-coded octal, (c) binary-coded hexadecimal and (d) BCD.

3-5 Represent your first name, middle initial, and last name in binary using ASCII (Table 3-4). Include blanks between names and a period after the middle initial.

3-6 Why do you suppose people adopted the decimal number system for everyday use? If you had to propose another number system so as to facilitate arithmetic computations, what radix would you choose? As a computer architect, what radix would you recommend?

3-7 A computer has been proposed based on the radix 3 system. (a) What type of storage cells are needed for memory and registers? (b) What type of logic system is needed to replace the two-valued Boolean algebra? (c) How many combinations will be unassigned in a radix 3 code for the ten decimal digits?

3-8 Show the bit configuration of a 24-bit register when its content represents the decimal equivalent of 295: (a) in binary, (b) in BCD, and (c) in ASCII.

3-9 Assign a binary code in some orderly manner to the 52 playing cards.

3-10 Obtain the 1's and 2's complement of the following binary numbers: 1010101, 0111000, 0000001, 10000, and 0000.

3-11 Obtain the 9's and 10's complement of the following decimal numbers: 13579, 09900, 90090, 10000, and 0000. Show their representation in BCD.

3-12 Obtain the 7's and 8's complement of the following octal numbers: 770, 1263, 00010, and 0000. Show their representation in binary-coded form.

3-13 Obtain the 15's and 16's complement of the following hexadecimal numbers: FF0, 1234, ABCD, and 0000. Show their representation in binary-coded form.

3-14 Represent the binary equivalent of −86 in three different ways using a register of 10 bits.

3-15 Represent −8620 in BCD in three different ways.

3-16 The binary numbers listed below have a sign bit in the left-most position. Negative numbers are in their signed-2's complement form. Perform the arithmetic operations indicated and leave results, if negative, in the signed-2's complement form. Verify your results.

| | |
|---|---|
| 001110 + 110010 | 010101 − 000111 |
| 010101 + 000011 | 001010 − 111001 |
| 111001 + 001010 | 111001 − 001010 |
| 101011 + 111000 | 101011 − 100110 |

3-17 Repeat Prob. 3-16 assuming that negative numbers are in signed-1's complement representation.

3-18 The procedure stated in Sec. 3-2 for addition and subtraction of binary numbers with negative numbers in signed-2's complement form neglects the effect of overflow. Using seven bits for the fixed-point numbers, perform (+35) + (+40) and (−35) + (−40) in binary and show that a 7-bit answer will be incorrect because of an overflow. Show that when two numbers of the same sign are added, an overflow exists if the sign of the result is different from the original signs of the numbers.

3-19 What is the difference (if any) between fixed-point numbers (in any representation) and binary-coded octal or binary-coded hexadecimal numbers? Would arithmetic calculations give the same results? From your answer to the above, how could you explain a statement from a computer manufacturer who says that his computer is an octal machine rather than a binary machine?

3-20 The procedure for adding and subtracting decimal numbers when negative numbers are in signed-10's complement form is similar to the procedure used for binary numbers when negative numbers are in signed-2's complement representation. Formulate this procedure and apply it to the following decimal computations: $(-638) + (+785)$ and $(-638) - (+185)$.

3-21 A 36-bit floating-point binary number has 8 bits plus a sign for the exponent. The mantissa is assumed to be a normalized fraction. Negative numbers in the mantissa and exponent are in signed-magnitude representation. What are the largest and smallest positive quantities that can be represented, excluding zero?

3-22 A 30-bit register holds a decimal floating-point number represented in BCD. The mantissa occupies 21 bits of the register and is assumed to be a normalized integer. Negative numbers in the mantissa and exponent are in signed-10's complement representation. What are the largest and smallest quantities which can be represented, excluding zero?

3-23 Represent the number $(+47.5)_{10}$ with a normalized integer mantissa of 13 bits and an exponent of 7 bits.
(a) As a binary number (assumed radix of 2).
(b) As a binary-coded octal (assumed radix of 8).
(c) As a binary-coded hexadecimal (assumed radix of 16).
Show that the mantissa is the same in all three cases but that the value of the exponent changes. Determine the largest positive number that the 20-bit register can hold in each of the three representations. What is the advantage of using radix 8 (or 16) over radix 2 for floating-point numbers in registers?

3-24 Show that a decimal digit in BCD has the corresponding weights of 8421.

3-25 The Gray code is sometimes called a *reflected* code because the bit values are reflected on both sides of any $2^n$ value. For example, as shown in Table 3-5, the values of the three low-order bits are reflected over a line drawn between 7 and 8 ($8 = 2^3$). Using this property of the Gray code obtain:
(a) The Gray code numbers for 16 to 31 as a continuation of Table 3-5.
(b) The excess-3 Gray code for decimals 10 to 19 as a continuation of Table 3-6, column 5.

3-26 Obtain the 9's complement of 1763 in BCD. Add it to BCD 8391 and interpret the result obtained.

3-27 Represent decimal +3984 in the 2421 code of Table 3-6. Complement all bits and show that the result is −3985 in signed-9's complement representation with the 2421 code.

3-28 Generate an even parity bit for all ASCII characters listed in Table 3-4 and place it in the most significant position. List the 8-bit code obtained for each character as a two-digit hexadecimal.

3-29 Look at the special characters of a typewriter and find about ten more special characters that are not included in Table 3-4.

3-30 How would you convert the 7-bit code of the characters listed in Table 3-4 to a 6-bit code?

3-31 Hollerith cards with a 12-bit code are inefficient with respect to the number of bits used. (a) Why do you suppose that it is the most widely used? (b) How would you formulate a more efficient card code?

3-32 Show that the exclusive-OR function $x = A \oplus B \oplus C \oplus D$ is an odd function. One way to show this is to obtain the truth table for $y = A \oplus B$ and for $z = C \oplus D$ and then formulate the truth table for $x = y \oplus z$.

3-33 Prove that the generation of P(even) for any number of message bits is obtained by the exclusive-OR function of all message bits. Prove that P(odd) is always the complement of P(even).

3-34 Draw the circuit of an 8-bit parity generator/checker having eight inputs and two outputs, one for even and the other for odd parity. What should be the value of the eighth input when the circuit is used to generate an even parity bit for seven message bits?

# 4

# REGISTER TRANSFER AND MICRO-OPERATIONS

## 4-1 REGISTER TRANSFER LANGUAGE

A digital system is an interconnection of digital hardware modules that accomplish a specific information processing task. Digital systems vary in size and complexity from a few integrated circuits to a complex of interconnected and interacting digital computers. Digital computer design invariably uses a modular approach. The modules are constructed from such digital functions as registers, decoders, arithmetic elements, and control logic. The various modules are interconnected with common data and control paths to form a digital computer system.

Each digital module is best defined by the registers it contains and the operations that are performed on the data stored in them. The operations executed on data stored in registers are called *micro-operations.* A micro-operation is an elementary operation, performed during one clock pulse, on the information stored in one or more registers. The result of the operation may replace the previous binary information of a register or may be transferred to another register. Examples of micro-operations are shift, count, clear, and load. Some of the IC digital functions introduced in Chap. 2 are registers that implement micro-operations. For example, a counter with parallel load is capable of performing the micro-operations increment and load. A bidirectional shift-register is capable of performing the shift-right and shift-left micro-operations.

The organization of a digital computer is best defined by specifying:

1. The set of registers it contains and their function.

2. The sequence of micro-operations performed on the binary information stored in the registers.

3. The control functions that initiate the sequence of micro-operations.

It is possible to specify the sequence of micro-operations in a computer by explaining every operation in words, and though sometimes done, this procedure usually involves a lengthy explanation. It is more convenient to adopt a suitable symbology to describe the sequence of transfers between registers and the various arithmetic and logic micro-operations associated with the transfers. The use of symbols, instead of a narrative explanation, provides an organized and concise manner for listing the micro-operation sequences in registers and the control functions that initiate them.

The symbolic notation used to describe the micro-operation transfers among registers is called a *register transfer language.* The term *register transfer* implies the availability of hardware logic circuits that can perform a stated micro-operation and transfer the result of the operation to the same or another register. The word *language* is borrowed from programmers who apply this term to programming languages. A programming language is a procedure for writing symbols to specify a given computational process. Similarly, a natural language such as English is a system for writing symbols and combining them into words and sentences for the purpose of communication between people. A register transfer language is a system for expressing in symbolic form the micro-operation sequences among the registers of a digital module. It is a convenient tool for describing the internal organization of digital computers in concise and precise manner. It can also be used to facilitate the design process of digital systems.

At this time no standard symbology exists for a register transfer language since different sources adopt different conventions. The register transfer language adopted here is believed to be as simple as possible, so it should not take very long to memorize. We will proceed to define symbols for various types of micro-operations, and at the same time, describe associated hardware that can implement the stated micro-operations. Unlike a programming language, a register-transfer language is directly related to and cannot be separated from the registers and other hardware that it defines.

The symbolic designation introduced in this chapter will be utilized in subsequent chapters to specify the register transfers, the micro-operations and the control functions that describe the architecture of digital computers. Other symbology in use can be easily learned once this language has become familiar, for most of the differences between register transfer languages consist of variations in detail rather than in over-all purpose.

## 4-2 INTER-REGISTER TRANSFER

Computer registers are designated by capital letters (sometimes followed by numerals) usually chosen so as to denote the function of the register. For example, the register that holds the address of a memory unit is usually called the *memory address register* and is designated by the capital letters *MAR*. Other designations for registers are: *A*, *AC*, *R*3, and *MBR*. The cells (flip-flops) of an $n$-bit register are numbered in sequence from 1 to $n$ (or from 0 to $n - 1$) starting either from the left or from the right. Figure 4-1 shows

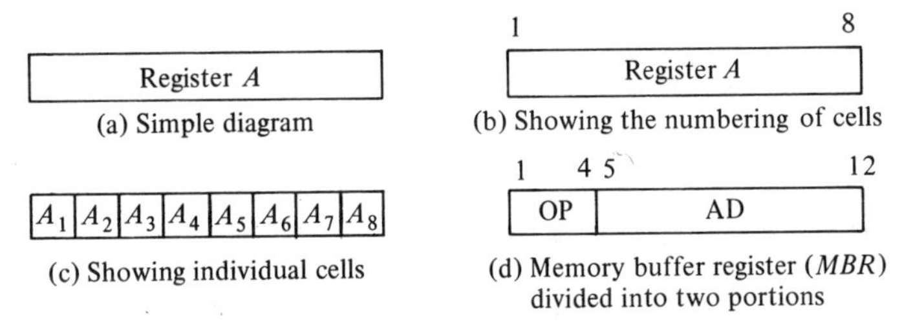


**Fig. 4-1** Block diagrams for registers.

four ways of drawing the block diagram of a register. In (a) we use a rectangular box with the name of the register inside the box. The numbering of cells from left to right in an eight-bit register is indicated in (b). The individual cells are shown in (c) with each cell assigned a subscript number under *A*—the letter that designates the name of the register. A 12-bit register is partitioned into two parts in (d). Bits 1 to 4 of the register are assigned the function name *OP* (for *operation*) and bits 5 to 12 are assigned the function name *AD* (for *address*). The symbol *MBR* refers to the 12-bit register. The symbol *MBR*(*OP*) or *MBR* (1–4) refers to the first four bits of the register while *MBR*(*AD*) or *MBR* (5–12) refers to bits 5 to 12 of the register.

Data transfer among registers is accomplished by means of *inter-register transfer* micro-operations. These micro-operations perform a direct transfer of binary information from one register to another. The destination register that receives the information assumes the previous value of the source register. The value of the source register does not change because of the transfer.

### *Parallel Transfer*

Information transfer from one register to another can be performed either in parallel or in serial. Parallel transfer is a simultaneous transfer of all bits from the source register to the destination register and is accomplished during one clock pulse. This micro-operation is designated in symbolic form as follows:

$$A \leftarrow B$$

and denotes a transfer of the *content* of register $B$ into register $A$.

The statement of the transfer $A \leftarrow B$ implies that circuits are available from the outputs of register $B$ to the cell inputs of register $A$. Normally we do not want this transfer to occur with every clock pulse but only under a predetermined condition. The binary condition that determines when the transfer is to occur is called a *control function*. A control function is a binary function. This means that it can be equal to either 0 or 1. The control function is included with the transfer micro-operation by modifying the symbology as follows:

$$P: \quad A \leftarrow B$$

The control function $P$ (followed by a colon) symbolizes the fact that the stated micro-operation is executed by the hardware only if $P = 1$.

Figure 4-2 shows the hardware for implementing the micro-operation $P: \ A \leftarrow B$. The outputs of register $B$ are connected to the inputs of register $A$. Register $A$ has a parallel load capability, i.e., the transfer occurs only if the load input is equal to 1. Although not shown, it is assumed that register $A$ has an additional input that accepts continuous synchronized clock pulses (see Fig. 2-7). The control function $P$ is generated in a control

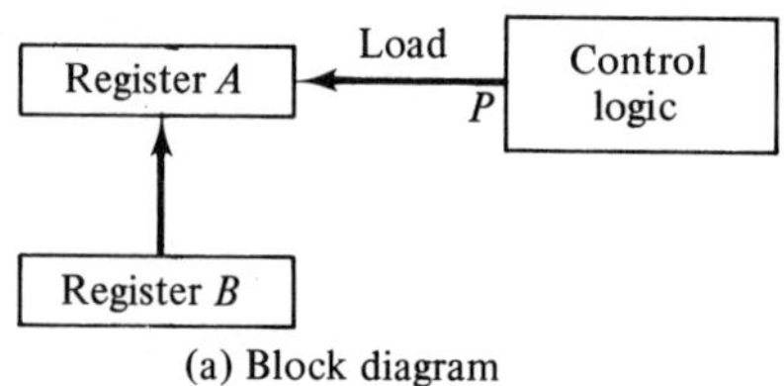


(a) Block diagram

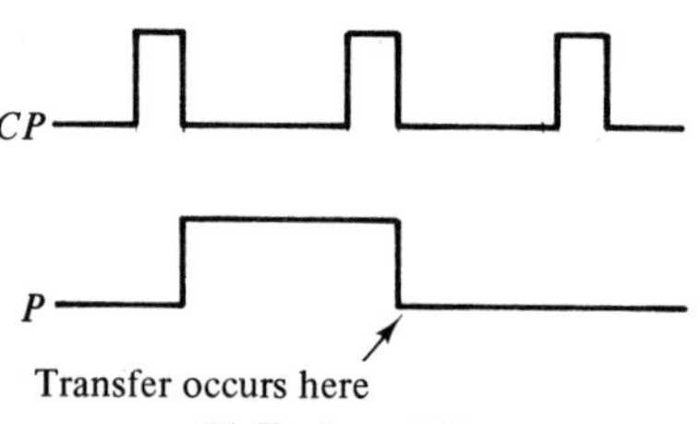


(b) Timing relation

**Fig. 4-2** Hardware implementation of the statement $P: \ A \leftarrow B$.

logic network and applied to the load input of the register. It is assumed that the control logic is also synchronized by the clock pulses so output $P$ becomes 1 right after the falling edge of a clock pulse. During the next clock pulse, the load input is in the 1 state and the transfer from $B$ to $A$ occurs right after the falling edge of this clock pulse. The timing relations conform with the state transition adopted in Sec. 2-2 for master-slave flip-flops.

The basic symbols for the register transfer language are listed in Table 4-1. As mentioned before, capital letters are used to denote registers and subscripts denote individual cells of the register. Parentheses are used to define a

**Table 4-1** *Basic symbols for register transfer language.*

| *Symbol* | *Description* | *Examples* |
|---|---|---|
| capital letters and numerals | denotes a register | $A$, $MBR$, $R3$ |
| subscript | denotes a bit of a register | $A_2$, $B_i$ |
| parentheses ( ) | denotes portion of a register | $I(1\text{-}5)$, $MBR(AD)$ |
| arrow ← | denotes transfer of information | $A \leftarrow B$ |
| colon : | denotes termination of control function | $P$: |
| comma , | separates two micro-operations | $A \leftarrow B$, $B \leftarrow A$ |

portion of a register. The arrow must be present in every micro-operation statement and denotes a transfer of the *content* of the register listed on the right side of the arrow into the register listed on the left side of the arrow. The colon denotes a control function and the comma is used to separate two or more micro-operations when executed at the same time. For example,

$$E: \quad A \leftarrow B, \quad C \leftarrow B$$

specifies two transfers that occur simultaneously provided $E = 1$. It is also possible to swap the contents of two registers during one clock pulse. This is designated in symbolic form by the statement:

$$F: \quad A \leftarrow B, \quad B \leftarrow A$$

This simultaneous operation is possible if the registers contain master-slave or edge-triggered flip-flops.

### *Serial Transfer*

For serial transfer, both the source and destination registers are shift-registers. The information is transferred one bit at a time by shifting the bits out of the source register into the destination register. In order not to lose the information stored in the source register it is necessary that thc information shifted out of the source register be circulated and shifted back at the same time.

The serial transfer of information from register $B$ to register $A$ is done with shift registers as shown in the block diagram of Fig. 4-3. Each register

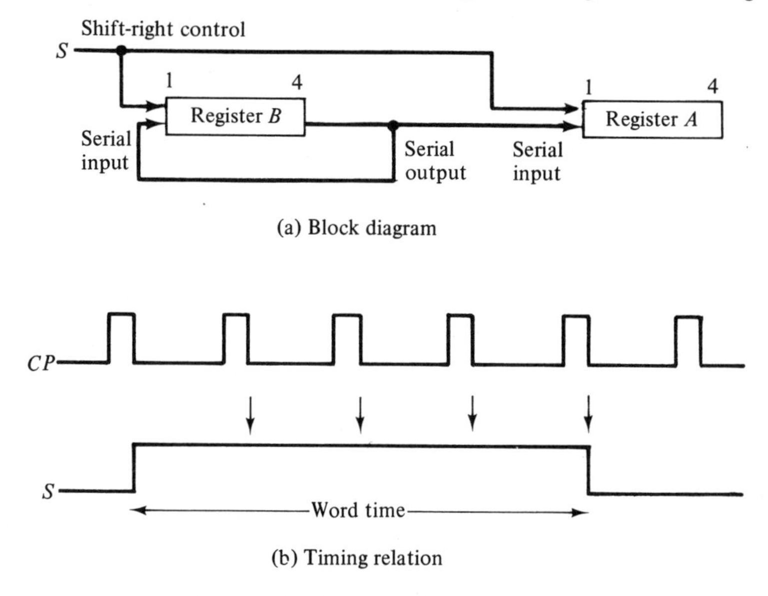


**Fig. 4-3** Serial transfer with shift registers.

contains four cells as indicated by the numbers on top of the box. The serial output of register $B$ comes from the output of the right-most flip-flop $B_4$. The serial input of register $A$ goes into the left-most flip-flop $A_1$. When the shift-right control $S$ is 1, and a clock pulse occurs, the contents of registers $A$ and $B$ are shifted once to the right and the value of $B_4$ transferred to flip-flops $A_1$ and $B_1$. This causes the transfer of one bit of information from register $B$ to negister $A$ and, at the same time, one bit is circulated back in register $B$. This transfer can be expressed by means of symbolic notation as follows:

$$S\colon \quad A_1 \leftarrow B_4,\ B_1 \leftarrow B_4,\ A_i \leftarrow A_{i-1},\ B_i \leftarrow B_{i-1} \qquad i = 2, 3, 4$$

The control function $S$ is terminated by a colon and designates a Boolean condition; i.e., the register micro-operations listed after the colon are performed only if $S = 1$. The micro-operations are separated by a comma and are performed simultaneously during one clock pulse. The subscript $i$ denotes the individual cells of the register. Note that a micro-operation, by definition, is executed during one clock pulse. Therefore, the above symbolic statement designates a transfer of one bit only. For a complete transfer of four bits, the control function $S$ must remain 1 for a period of four clock pulses. This time period is called a *word-time* and is depicted in the timing diagram of Fig. 4-3.

The above statement for serial transfer is cumbersome to write because it mentions each bit of each register. For serial computers, it may be convenient to redefine a mirco-operation as an operation that takes a word-time for execution (instead of a bit-time). If this convention is adopted, the serial transfer can be stated as:

$$S: \quad A \leftarrow B, \quad B \leftarrow B$$

A third symbolic designation for serial transfer uses the *shift* micro-operation (to be introduced in Sec. 4-5).

The registers in serial digital systems are shift-registers. The external circuits that perform micro-operations receive the bits from registers sequentially. The time interval between adjacent bits is called the *bit-time*, and the time required to shift the entire content of registers is called the *word-time*. These timing sequences are generated by the control section of the system. In a parallel computer, a control function is enabled during one clock pulse interval. Transfers into registers are in parallel and occur upon the application of a single clock pulse. In a serial computer, the control function must be enabled during one word-time period. The pulse applied every bit-time transfers the results of micro-operations one at a time into a shift register.

### *Bus Transfer*

In a system with many registers, the transfer from each register to another requires that lines be connected from the output of each flip-flop in one register to the input of each flip-flop in all the other registers. Consider for example, the requirement for transfer among three registers as shown in Fig. 4-4. There are six data paths between registers. If each register consists of $n$ flip-flops, there is a need for $6n$ lines for parallel transfer from each register to each other register. As the number of registers increases, the number of

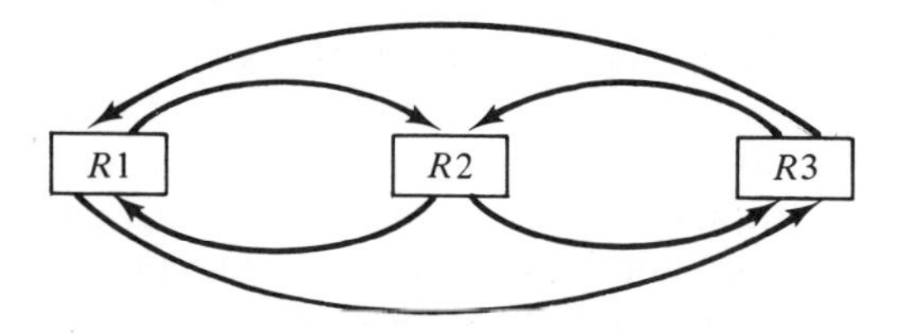


**Fig. 4-4** Transfer among three registers.

lines increases considerably. However, if we restrict the transmission of data between registers to one at a time, the number of paths among all registers can be reduced to just one per flip-flop for a total of $n$ lines. This is shown in Fig. 4-5, where the output and input of each flip-flop are connected to a

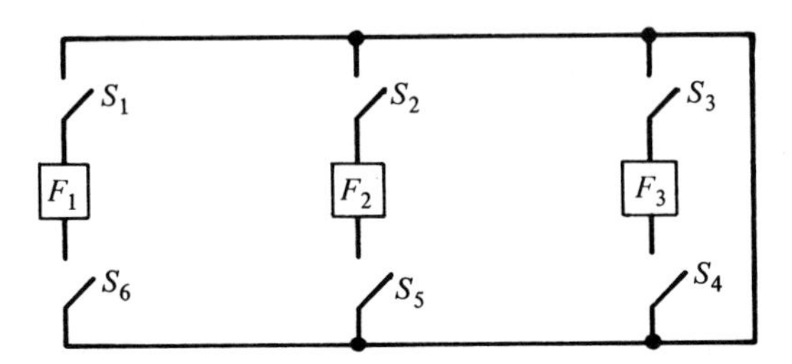


**Fig. 4-5** Transfer through one common line.

common line through an electronic circuit that acts like a switch. All the switches are normally open until a transfer is required. For a transfer from $F_1$ to $F_3$, for example, switches $S_1$ and $S_4$ are closed to form the required path. This scheme can be extended to registers with $n$ flip-flops and requires $n$ common lines since each flip-flop of the register must be connected to one common line.

A group of wires through which binary information is transferred among registers is called a *bus*. For a parallel transfer, the number of wires in the bus is equal to the number of flip-flops in the register. The idea of a bus transfer is analogous to a central transportation system used to bring commuters from one point to another. Instead of each commuter using his own private car to go from one location to another, a bus system is used with each commuter waiting in line until transportation is available.

A bus system is formed with multiplexer circuits. A digital multiplexer selects data from many lines and directs it to a single output line. Figure 4-6 shows how four registers are connected through multiplexers to form one set of common bus lines. Each register has four bits. Each 4 by 1 multiplexer (see Fig. 2-11) has four data input lines, two selection lines, and one output line. The first cell in each register is connected to one of the inputs of the left-most multiplexer, the second cell to the second multiplexer and so on. The selection lines are connected in parallel to input selection variables $x$ and $y$. With $xy = 00$, multiplexer inputs $I_0$ are selected and applied to the outputs that form the bus. The bus lines receive the contents of register $A$ since this register is connected to the $I_0$ inputs of the multiplexers. Similarly, register $B$ is selected if $xy = 01$, and so on. To simplify the diagram, the lines from registers $B$, $C$, and $D$ are not drawn, but their connections are indicated by labels at the multiplexer inputs. It is sometimes necessary to simplify the block diagram shown in Fig. 4-6(a) into the one shown in Fig. 4-6(b). The

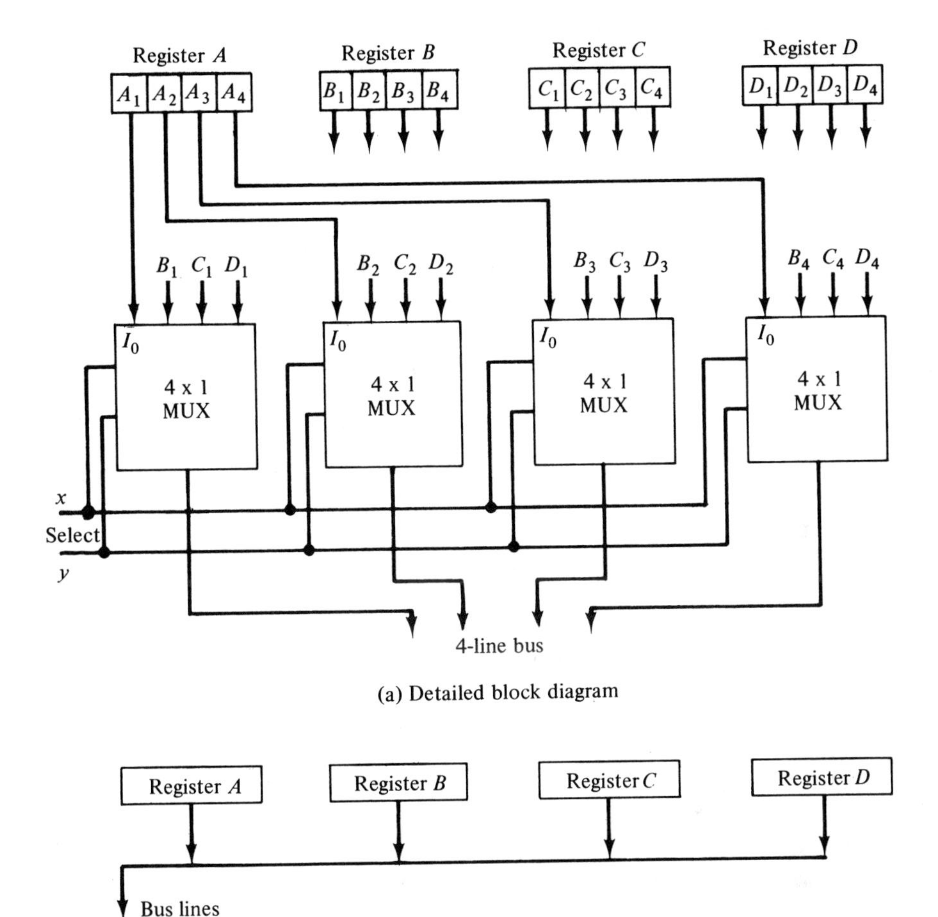


(a) Detailed block diagram



(b) Simplified block diagram

**Fig. 4-6** A bus system for four registers.

multiplexers are assumed to be part of the bus system although they are not drawn in the block diagram of part (b). The multiplexers may sometimes have an enable line to prevent any register from communicating with the bus.

A bus system can be constructed without multiplexers if the outputs of the registers have tri-state outputs. Outputs of tri-state gates can be connected directly without affecting each other (see Fig. 2-2). The register that communicates with the bus is selected by enabling the control input associated with its tri-state gates. The selection can be controlled by activating the individual tri-state control lines in each register.

The transfer of information from a bus into one of many destination registers can be accomplished by connecting the bus lines to the inputs of all registers and activating the *load* control of the particular destination register

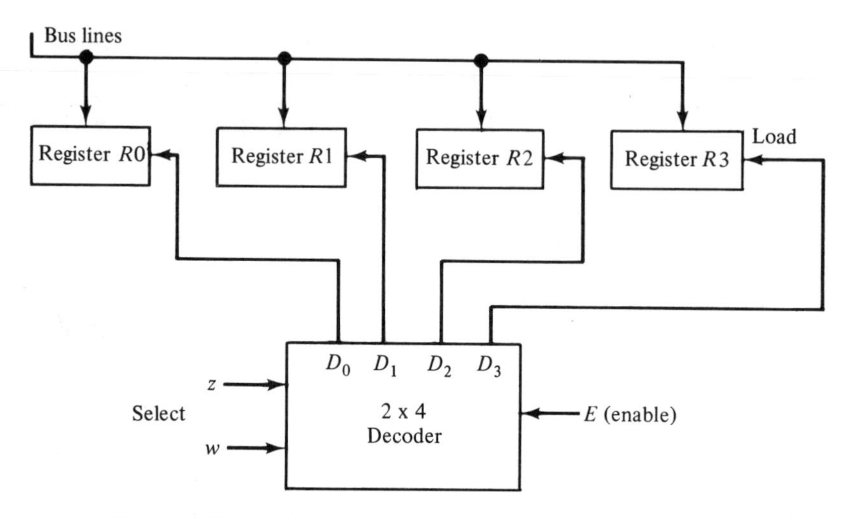


**Fig. 4-7** Transfer of information from bus to one of multiple registers.

selected. As shown in Fig. 4-7, the bus lines are connected to the data inputs of all registers. Activating the load input of a particular register will cause a transfer of information from the bus into the register. The load inputs of the registers can be decoded to reduce the number of selection lines from four to two.

Transfer through a bus is limited to one transmission at a time. If two transfers are required at the same time, two busses must be used. A large digital system will normally employ a number of busses with each of its registers being connected to one or more busses to form the various paths needed for the transfer of information.

The symbolic statement for a bus transfer may mention the bus and the control functions, or their presence may be implied in the statement. When the bus and control functions are included in the statement, the register transfer is symbolized as follows:

$$xy': \quad BUS \leftarrow C$$

$$z'wE: \quad R1 \leftarrow BUS$$

where $x$ and $y$ are the control selection lines for the source register (see Fig. 4-6) and $z$, $w$, and $E$ (enable) are the control lines for the destination register (see Fig. 4-7). When selection lines $xy = 10$, register $C$ is selected to communicate with the bus. When selection lines $zw = 01$ and $E = 1$, register $R1$ is selected to accept the information from the bus.

The transfer from register $C$, through the bus, to register $R1$ can be executed during one clock pulse. To indicate the fact that the two micro-operations are done simultaneously we separate them by a comma as follows:

$$BUS \leftarrow C, \qquad R1 \leftarrow BUS$$

with the control functions being implied or, if necessary, included in the statement.

If the bus is known to exist in the system, it may be convenient to just state one transfer

$$R1 \leftarrow C$$

and from that, the designer knows the values to be inserted for $x$, $y$, $z$, $w$, and $E$. This is convenient when the control functions are generated in a control memory as explained in Chap. 8.

### *Memory Transfer*

The words of a memory unit may be considered as stored in registers with each memory register holding one word. It is convenient to associate two other external registers with a memory unit: *MAR* (memory address register) and *MBR* (memory buffer register).† To simplify the symbology associated with memory transfer operations, we will use the letter $M$ to designate the memory word specified by the content of *MAR*. A *read* micro-operation is a transfer from the selected word $M$ into *MBR*. This is designated symbolically as follows:

$$R: \qquad MBR \leftarrow M$$

$R$ is the control function that initiates the memory-read micro-operation. This causes a transfer of information from the selected memory word $M$ into *MBR*.

A *write* micro-operation is a transfer from *MBR* to the selected memory word $M$. This is designated by the statement:

$$W: \qquad M \leftarrow MBR$$

$W$ is the control function that initiates the memory-write micro-operation. This causes a transfer of information from *MBR* into the memory register $M$ selected by the address presently available in *MAR*.

The memory unit of a digital computer is used for storing large quantities of programs and data. The processor unit of a computer usually has a small number of registers (between 4 and 32) which are used for holding the binary information while it is being processed. These registers are usually connected

†See Sec. 2-6

to a bus system. Processor registers are sometimes organized as a small memory unit referred to as a *scratch-pad* memory. The use of a scratch-pad memory is a cheaper alternative to connecting processor registers through a bus system. The difference between the two systems is in the manner in which information is transferred from one register to another. In a bus system, any register can transfer information to any other register. On the other hand, a group of registers organized as a small memory cannot communicate directly with other registers in the same memory. The communication is done through one common external register which we call the *MBR* (memory buffer register).

### *Summary of Inter-Register Micro-Operations*

Table 4-2 summarizes the symbols to be used for the various inter-register transfers. Note the notation used for transferring parts of registers such as *MBR*(*AD*). The transfer of a constant value into a register is symbolized by specifying the constant in binary, octal, decimal, or hexadecimal. If there is more than one bus in the system, it is necessary to give each bus a different symbol name such as *ABUS* or *RBUS*. If there is more than one memory in the system, it is necessary to specify different names for the memory registers and use a different symbol to denote the memory word specified by the address value.

**Table 4-2** *Inter-register micro-operations*

| *Symbolic Designation* | *Description* |
|---|---|
| $A \leftarrow B$ | Transfer content of register *B* into register *A* |
| $MAR \leftarrow MBR(AD)$ | Transfer content of *AD* portion of register *MBR* into register *MAR* |
| $A \leftarrow$ constant | Transfer binary (code) constant into register *A* |
| $ABUS \leftarrow R1$, $R2 \leftarrow ABUS$ | Transfer content of *R*1 into bus *A* and, at the same time, transfer content of bus *A* into *R*2 |
| *MAR* | Memory address register: holds the address of the memory unit |
| *MBR* | Memory buffer register: holds the data transferred in or out of the memory unit |
| *M* | Denotes the memory word specified by *MAR* |
| $MBR \leftarrow M$ | Memory *read* operation: transfers content of memory word specified by *MAR* into *MBR* |
| $M \leftarrow MBR$ | Memory *write* operation: transfers content of *MBR* into memory word specified by *MAR* |

## 4-3 ARITHMETIC MICRO-OPERATIONS

The inter-register transfer micro-operations discussed thus far do not change the information content when the binary information moves from the source register to the destination register. All other micro-operations change the information content during the transfer. For example, the arithmetic micro-operation defined by the statement:

$$R3 \leftarrow R1 + R2$$

specifies an *add* micro-operation. It states that the content of register $R1$ is to be added to the content of $R2$ and the sum transferred to $R3$. This is an operational statement and requires for its implementation not only the three registers, but also the logic circuits that perform the stated arithmetic function.

The logic circuit that forms the arithmetic sum of two bits and a previous carry is called a *full-adder* (see Fig. 1-19). Two binary numbers can be added serially by shifting pairs of significant bits sequentially through a full-adder. The sum bit out of the full-adder is shifted into the register that holds the sum. The carry out of the full-adder is stored in a special flip-flop. This flip-flop then provides the carry for the next pair of significant bits coming out of the shift registers that hold the augend and addend.

A *binary parallel-adder* is a digital function that produces the arithmetic sum of two binary numbers in parallel. It consists of full-adders connected in cascade, with the output-carry from one full-adder connected to the input-carry of the next full-adder.

Figure 4-8 shows the interconnections of four full-adders (FA) to provide a four-bit parallel adder. The augend bits of $A$ and the addend bits of $B$ are designated by subscript numbers from right to left with subscript 1 denoting the low-order bit. The carries are connected in a chain through the full-adders. The $S$ outputs of the full-adders generate the required sum bits. When the 4-bit full-adders circuit is enclosed within an IC package, it has

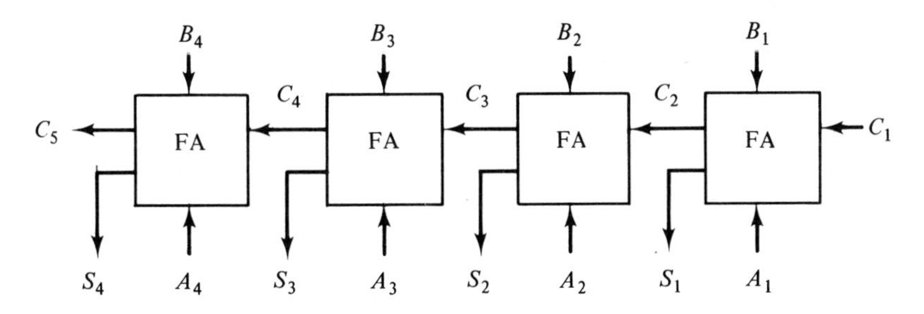


**Fig. 4-8** Four-bit full-adders.

four terminals for the augend bits, four terminals for the addend bits, four terminals for the sum bits and two terminals for the input- and output-carries $C_1$ and $C_5$.

An $n$-bit binary parallel-adder requires $n$ full-adders. It can be constructed from 4-bit full-adders ICs by cascading several packages. The output-carry from one package must be connected to the input-carry of the one with the next higher-order bits. The block diagram of an $n$-bit binary parallel-adder is shown in Fig. 4-9.

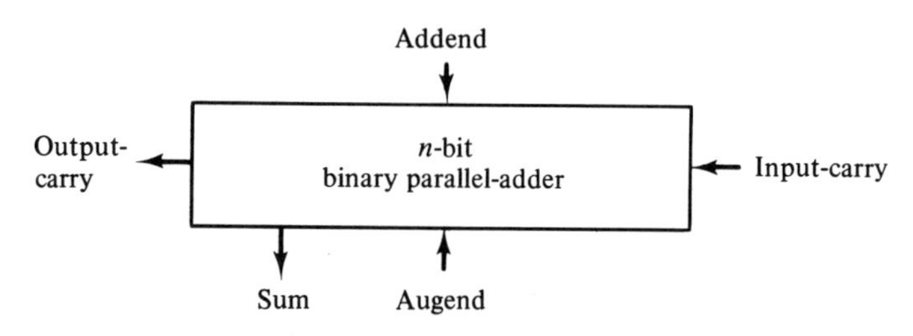


**Fig. 4-9** Binary parallal-adder block diagram.

The following numerical example demonstrates the operation of the parallel-adder:

| *Subscript i* | 4 | 3 | 2 | 1 | |
|---|---|---|---|---|---|
| Input carry | 0 | 1 | 1 | 0 | $C_i$ |
| Augend | 1 | 0 | 1 | 1 | $A_i$ |
| Addend | 0 | 0 | 1 | 1 | $B_i$ |
| Sum | 1 | 1 | 1 | 0 | $S_i$ |
| Output carry | 0 | 0 | 1 | 1 | $C_i + 1$ |

The bits are added starting from the least significant position (subscript 1) to form the sum bit and carry bit. The input-carry $C_1$ in the least significant position must be 0. The value of $C_i + 1$ in a given significant position is the output-carry of the full-adder. This value is transferred into $C_i$ (input-carry of full-adder) one higher significant position to the left. The sum bits are thus generated starting from the right-most position and are available as soon as the corresponding previous carry bits are generated.

An *add* micro-operation may employ two or three different registers. The micro-operation symbolized by the statement:

$$P: \quad A \leftarrow A + B$$

specifies two registers, $A$ and $B$. It also specifies a parallel-adder needed for obtaining the arithmetic sum, and the paths for loading the sum back into

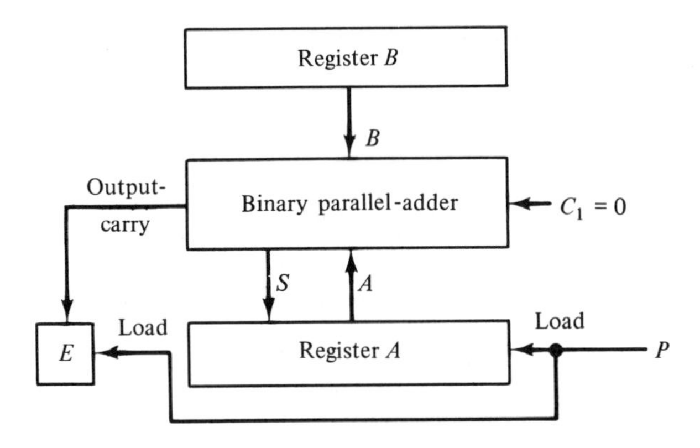


**Fig. 4-10** Block diagram for $P$: $EA \leftarrow A + B$.

register $A$. This implementation is shown in Fig. 4-10. The diagram also includes a flip-flop, labeled $E$, that accepts the output-carry from the parallel-adder. If we use the symbol $EA$ to designate the combined register formed by cascading $E$ and $A$, we can modify the micro-operation statement by writing:

$$P: \quad EA \leftarrow A + B$$

which takes care of the output-carry transfer.

Note that the sum bits and the output-carry are available at the output terminals of the parallel-adder at all times, since the parallel-adder is a combinational circuit. The micro-operation is executed by control function $P$, and only after $P = 1$ do we see a change in the contents of register $A$. When $P = 1$, the load control of the $EA$ register is activated, so on the next clock pulse, the outputs of the parallel-adder are transferred into the destination register. As long as $P = 0$, register $A$ holds the augend and although the sum is available in the $S$ outputs of the parallel-adder, the sum is not transferred into register $A$.

### *Other Arithmetic Micro-Operations*

The most basic arithmetic micro-operations are listed in Table 4-3. Arithmetic addition has been defined. Arithmetic subtraction implies the availability of a binary parallel-subtractor composed of full-subtractor circuits connected in cascade. Subtraction is most often implemented through complementation and addition as explained below.

The increment and decrement micro-operations are specified symbolically by a *plus one* or *minus one* operation executed on the contents of the register. These micro-operations are implemented with hardware by providing a count-up or count-down control to the register (see Sec. 2-4). The symbol for the

**Table 4-3** *Arithmetic micro-operations*

| *Symbolic Designation* | *Description* |
|---|---|
| $A \leftarrow A + B$ | Addition: content of $A$ plus $B$ transferred to $A$ |
| $A \leftarrow A - B$ | Subtraction: content of $A$ minus $B$ transferred to $A$ |
| $A \leftarrow A + 1$ | Increment the content of $A$ by one (count-up) |
| $A \leftarrow A - 1$ | Decrement the content of $A$ by one (count-down) |
| $A \leftarrow \bar{A}$ | Complement register $A$ (1's complement) |
| $A \leftarrow \bar{A} + 1$ | Form the 2's complement of register $A$ |
| $A \leftarrow A + \bar{B}$ | Transfer the content of $A$ plus the 1's complement of $B$ into register $A$ |
| $A \leftarrow A + \bar{B} + 1$ | Transfer the content of $A$ plus the 2's complement of $B$ into register $A$ (equivalent to subtraction) |

complement micro-operation is a bar over the letter (or letters) that symbolize the register. It denotes the complementation of *all* bits of the register. This is in contrast to the complement operation used in expressing Boolean functions, where the prime symbol is used to denote the complementation of a *single* binary variable. The complement micro-operation is implemented with hardware by providing a complement control to the register.

The 2's complement of a binary number is obtained by complementing each bit of the number and adding 1 to the least significant position. However, the statement:

$$P: \quad A \leftarrow \bar{A} + 1$$

implies that the 2's complement of the number stored in register $A$ is executed during one clock pulse period. The control gates associated with the register that has such a capability are shown in Fig. 4-11. The gates are derived from the alternate procedure for obtaining the 2's complement. By this procedure we leave any least significant zeros and the first one unchanged, and then complement all other bits. The first low-order bit $A_1$ is never complemented because it is either a 0 or the first 1 so a 0 is applied to the $T$ input of the flip-flop holding this bit (by connecting the input carry to 0). Each other flip-flop is complemented provided $P = 1$ and one of the previous flip-flops is 1. The four-bit register can be expanded to more bits by connecting the carry out of $A_4$ to the carry-in of the next stage.

The 2's complement micro-operation can be executed during two clock pulses provided the register has a complement and increment capability. When such a register is available, we can save the gates of Fig. 4-11 and specify the 2's complement operation by two consecutive micro-operation statements:

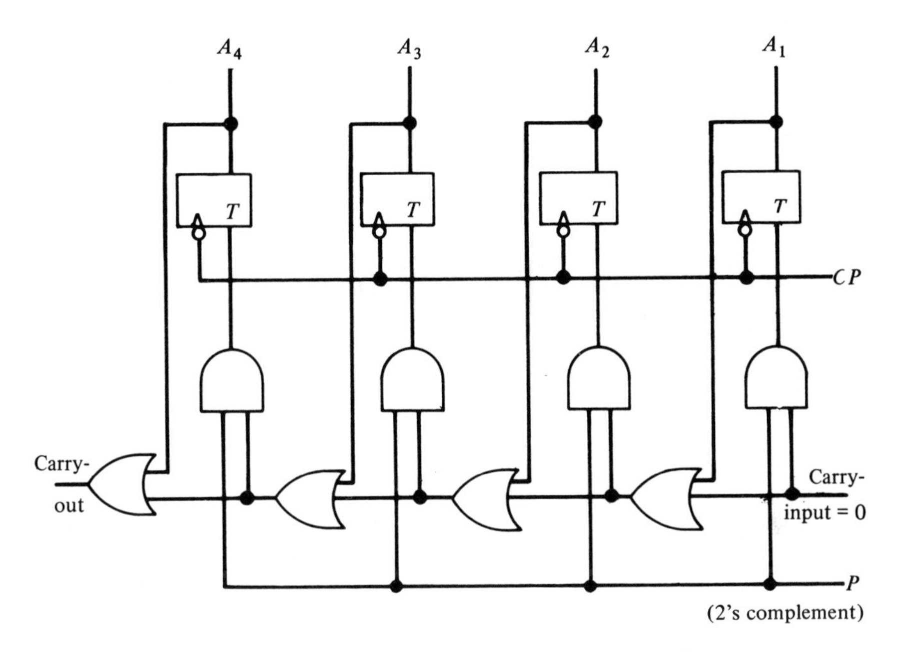


**Fig. 4-11** A four-bit register with 2's complement capability.

$$T_1: \quad A \leftarrow \bar{A}$$
$$T_2: \quad A \leftarrow A + 1$$

where $T_1$ and $T_2$ are two consecutive control functions. When $T_1 = 1$ the register is complemented, forming the 1's complement of the number stored in it. When $T_2 = 1$, the register is incremented to form the 2's complement.

It was stated in Sec. 3-2 that two binary numbers can be subtracted by adding the minuend to the 2's complement of the subtrahend. This micro-operation can be stated as follows:

$$A \leftarrow A + \bar{B} + 1$$

and implies that the hardware forms the 2's complement of $B$ and loads the sum into register $A$, all during one clock pulse period. If circuits are not available to do all these operations simultaneously, it is possible to break the statement into three individual micro-operations. For example, the three consecutive micro-operations:

$$T_1: \quad B \leftarrow \bar{B}$$
$$T_2: \quad B \leftarrow B + 1$$
$$T_3: \quad A \leftarrow A + B$$

will accomplish a subtraction of $B$ from $A$. The statements imply that register $B$ has the capability of executing the complement and increment micro-operations, that a parallel-adder is available between $A$ and $B$ and that register $A$ has a parallel-load capability.

## 4-4 LOGIC MICRO-OPERATIONS

Logic micro-operations specify binary operations for strings of bits stored in registers. These operations consider each bit of the register separately and treat them as binary variables. For example, the exclusive-OR micro-operation between the contents of two registers $A$ and $B$ is symbolized by the statement:

$$P: \quad A \leftarrow A \oplus B$$

and it specifies a logic micro-operation to be executed on the individual bits of the registers.

As a numerical illustration, assume that each register has four cells. Let the content of $A$ be 1010 and the content of $B$ be 1100. The exclusive-OR micro-operation stated above symbolizes the following logic computation:

| | |
|---|---|
| 1010 | content of $A$ |
| 1100 | content of $B$ |
| 0110 | content of $A$ after $P = 1$. |

The content of $A$, after the execution of the micro-operation, is equal to the bit-by-bit exclusive-OR operation on pairs of bits in $B$ and previous values of $A$.

When the bits of the registers are designated by a subscript number, the above micro-operation can be stated as:

$$P: \quad A_i \leftarrow A_i \oplus B_i \qquad i = 1, 2, 3, \ldots, n$$

which emphasizes the fact that the logic operation is done on pairs of bits treated as binary variables.

Special symbols will be adopted for the logic micro-operations OR, AND, and complement, in order to distinguish them from the corresponding symbols used to express Boolean functions. The symbol $\vee$ will be used to denote an OR micro-operation and the symbol $\wedge$ to denote an AND micro-operation. The complement micro-operation is the same as the 1's complement and uses a bar on top of the letter (or letters) that denotes the register. By using different symbols, it will be possible to differentiate between a logic micro-operation and a control (or Boolean) function. Another reason for adopting two sets of symbols is to be able to distinguish the symbol +, when used to symbolize an arithmetic plus, from a logic OR operation. Although the + symbol has two meanings, it will be possible to distinguish between them by noting where the symbol occurs. When the symbol + occurs in a micro-operation, it will denote an arithmetic plus. When it occurs in a control (or Boolean) function, it will denote a binary OR operation. We will never use it to symbolize an OR micro-operation. For example, in the statement:

$$T_1 + T_2: \qquad A \leftarrow A + B, \qquad C \leftarrow D \vee F$$

the + between $T_1$ and $T_2$ is an OR operation between two binary variables of a control function. The + between $A$ and $B$ specifies an *add* micro-operation. The OR micro-operation is designated by the symbol $\vee$ between registers $D$ and $F$.

Logic micro-operations are seldom used in scientific computations, but they are very useful for bit manipulation of binary data and for making logical decisions. By having bits of registers perform logic operations, it is possible to program logical functions that are not otherwise built in the hardware. As an extreme case, consider a hypothetical computer that has logic micro-operations but no arithmetic micro-operations. We can nevertheless program the computer to simulate the truth table of a full-adder by means of logic micro-operations. This simulation will provide a capability for performing arithmetic operations through a long sequence of logic micro-operations.

### *A List of Logic Micro-Operations*

There are 16 different logic operations that can be performed with two binary variables. They can be determined from all possible truth tables obtained with two binary variables. The 16 truth tables are derived in Table 4-4. In this table, each of the 16 columns, $F_0$ to $F_{15}$, represents a truth table of one possible Boolean function for the two variables $x$ and $y$. Note that the

**Table 4-4** *Truth tables for 16 functions of two variables*

| $x$ $y$ | $F_0$ | $F_1$ | $F_2$ | $F_3$ | $F_4$ | $F_5$ | $F_6$ | $F_7$ | $F_8$ | $F_9$ | $F_{10}$ | $F_{11}$ | $F_{12}$ | $F_{13}$ | $F_{14}$ | $F_{15}$ |
|---|---|---|---|---|---|---|---|---|---|---|---|---|---|---|---|---|
| 0 0 | 0 | 0 | 0 | 0 | 0 | 0 | 0 | 0 | 1 | 1 | 1 | 1 | 1 | 1 | 1 | 1 |
| 0 1 | 0 | 0 | 0 | 0 | 1 | 1 | 1 | 1 | 0 | 0 | 0 | 0 | 1 | 1 | 1 | 1 |
| 1 0 | 0 | 0 | 1 | 1 | 0 | 0 | 1 | 1 | 0 | 0 | 1 | 1 | 0 | 0 | 1 | 1 |
| 1 1 | 0 | 1 | 0 | 1 | 0 | 1 | 0 | 1 | 0 | 1 | 0 | 1 | 0 | 1 | 0 | 1 |

functions are determined from the 16 binary combinations that can be assigned to $F$.

The 16 Boolean functions of two variables $x$ and $y$ are expressed in algebraic form in the first column of Table 4-5. The 16 logic micro-operations are

**Table 4-5** *Sixteen logic micro-operations*

| *Boolean Function* | *Micro-Operation* | *Name* |
|---|---|---|
| $F_0 = 0$ | $F \leftarrow 0$ | Clear |
| $F_1 = xy$ | $F \leftarrow A \wedge B$ | AND |
| $F_2 = xy'$ | $F \leftarrow A \wedge \bar{B}$ | |
| $F_3 = x$ | $F \leftarrow A$ | Transfer $A$ |
| $F_4 = x'y$ | $F \leftarrow \bar{A} \wedge B$ | |
| $F_5 = y$ | $F \leftarrow B$ | Transfer $B$ |
| $F_6 = x \oplus y$ | $F \leftarrow A \oplus B$ | Exclusive-OR |
| $F_7 = x + y$ | $F \leftarrow A \vee B$ | OR |
| $F_8 = (x + y)'$ | $F \leftarrow \overline{A \vee B}$ | NOR |
| $F_9 = (x \oplus y)'$ | $F \leftarrow \overline{A \oplus B}$ | Exclusive-NOR |
| $F_{10} = y'$ | $F \leftarrow \bar{B}$ | Complement $B$ |
| $F_{11} = x + y'$ | $F \leftarrow A \vee \bar{B}$ | |
| $F_{12} = x'$ | $F \leftarrow \bar{A}$ | Complement $A$ |
| $F_{13} = x' + y$ | $F \leftarrow \bar{A} \vee B$ | |
| $F_{14} = (xy)'$ | $F \leftarrow \overline{A \wedge B}$ | NAND |
| $F_{15} = 1$ | $F \leftarrow$ all 1's | Set to all 1's |

derived from these functions by replacing the single variable $x$ by the binary content of register $A$ and that of $y$ by the binary content of regiester $B$. Table 4-5 lists all 16 micro-operations and also names some of them. The destination register chosen for the micro-operations is a register denoted by the letter $F$, but either $A$ or $B$ or any other register could be designated. Note that the symbols used for OR, AND, and complement in micro-operations are $\vee$, $\wedge$, and a bar, respectively.

It is important to realize that the Boolean functions listed in the first column of Table 4-5 represent a relation between two binary variables $x$ and $y$. The logic micro-operations listed in the second column represent a relation between the binary content of two registers $A$ and $B$. Each bit of the register is treated as a binary variable and the micro-operation is performed on the string of bits stored in the registers.

### *Hardware Implementation*

The hardware implementation of logic micro-operations requires that logic gates be inserted for each bit or pair of bits in the registers to perform the required logic function. To illustrate this procedure, the gates for five logic micro-operations are shown in Fig. 4-12. The diagram shows one typical stage designated by subscript $i$. This diagram must be repeated $n$ times for $i = 1, 2, 3, \ldots, n$, where $n$ is the number of bits of the registers. The source registers are $A$ and $B$ and the destination register is $F$. The clear micro-operation inserts 0's into register $F$; the complement micro-operation complements the bits of $A$ and transfers them to register $F$. The AND, OR, and XOR (exclusive-OR) micro-operations perform the required function through the corresponding gates.

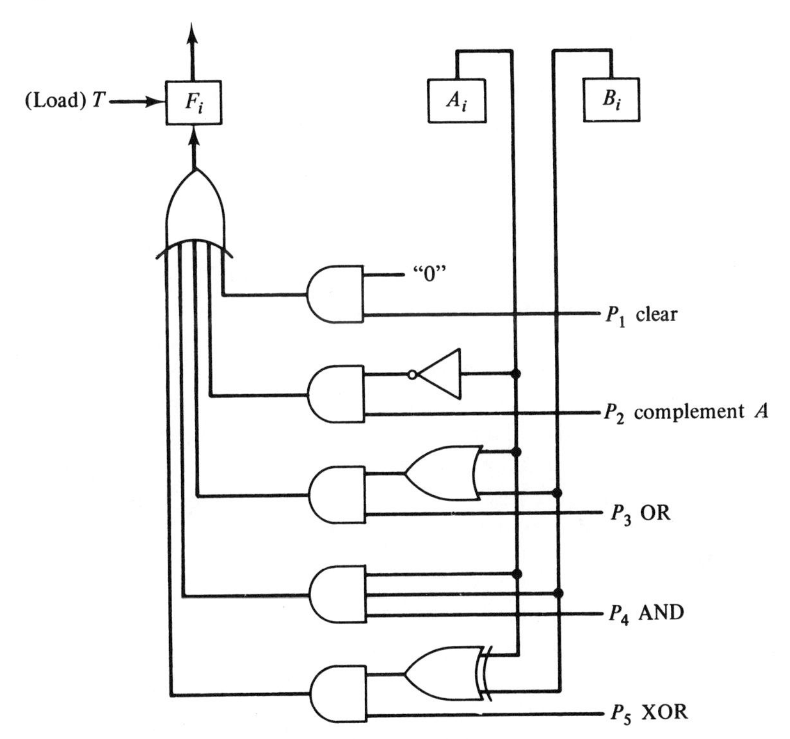


**Fig. 4-12** Hardware for five logic micro-operations.

A micro-operation is executed by making its $P$ control 1 and enabling the $F$ register through its load control $T$. For example, the OR micro-operation is specified by the statement:

$$TP_3: \quad F \leftarrow A \lor B$$

The control function is a Boolean function and the absence of an operator between $T$ and $P_3$ signifies a Boolean AND operation. Both $T$ and $P_3$ must be equal to 1 for the hardware execution of the micro-operation. The micro-operation is done on individual bits of the registers. To emphasize this fact, we could symbolize the OR micro-operation by the alternate statement:

$$TP_3: \quad F_i \leftarrow A_i \vee B_i \qquad i = 1, 2, 3, \ldots, n$$

The gates shown in Fig. 4-12 are for one stage only and they must be repeated $n$ times.

The hardware implementation can be simplified if the destination register is one of the source registers. For example, the clear micro-operation:

$$P_1: \quad A \leftarrow 0$$

can be implemented with $JK$ flip-flops for the $A$ registers by applying control function $P_1$ directly to all the $K$ inputs of the flip-flops. The complement micro-operation

$$P_2: \quad A \leftarrow \bar{A}$$

can be implemented by applying $P_2$ to both the $J$ and $K$ inputs. The gates for the other three logic micro-operations can be derived by means of sequential circuit theory (see Sec. 1-6).

When the destination register is also one of the source registers, the digital system can be considered as a sequential circuit and its behavior tabulated in a state or excitation table. The bit content of the source register corresponds to the present state values in the excitation table. The content of the same register after the micro-operation is executed corresponds to the next state values in the table. For example, the micro-operation:

$$P_3: \quad A \leftarrow A \vee B$$

uses register $A$ as both a source and a destination. The bits of $A$ prior to the execution of the micro-operation are the present state values. The bits of $A$ after the execution are the next state values.

Figure 4-13 lists the excitation tables for one typical state $i$ for the logic micro-operations OR, AND, and XOR. The source registers are $A$ and $B$; the destination register is $A$. The value of bit $A_i$ is listed in both the present and next state columns. The bit of $B_i$ is considered as an input to the sequential circuit. From the change of present to next state, we obtain the flip-flop input values. These values are obtained from the $JK$ flip-flop excitations listed in Table 1-4(b). The maps accompanying each table derive the simplified Boolean functions for $JA_i$ ($J$ input of flip-flop $A_i$) and $KA_i$ ($K$ input of flip-flop $A_i$).

Using the results obtained from the excitation tables, we draw the logic diagram of Fig. 4-14. Each control function $P_j$ must be ANDed with the

| Present State | Input | Next State | Flip-flop Inputs | |
|---|---|---|---|---|
| $A_i$ | $B_i$ | $A_i$ | $JA_i$ | $KA_i$ |
| 0 | 0 | 0 | 0 | X |
| 0 | 1 | 1 | 1 | X |
| 1 | 0 | 1 | X | 0 |
| 1 | 1 | 1 | X | 0 |

$JA_i = B_i$ $KA_i = 0$

(a) Logic OR

| Present State | Input | Next State | Flip-flop Inputs | |
|---|---|---|---|---|
| $A_i$ | $B_i$ | $A_i$ | $JA_i$ | $KA_i$ |
| 0 | 0 | 0 | 0 | X |
| 0 | 1 | 0 | 0 | X |
| 1 | 0 | 0 | X | 1 |
| 1 | 1 | 1 | X | 0 |

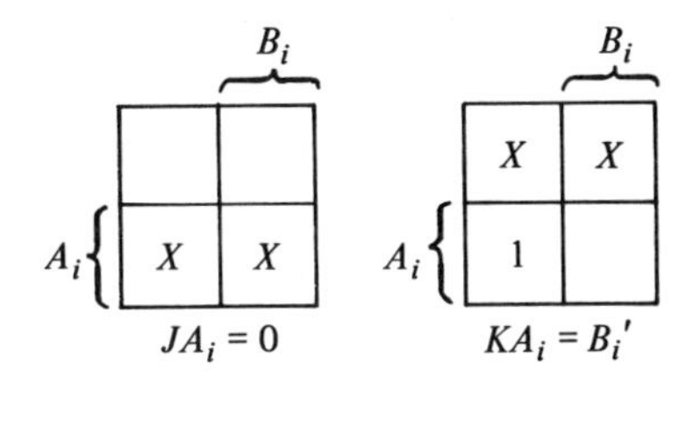


(b) Logic AND

| Present State | Input | Next State | Flip-flop Inputs | |
|---|---|---|---|---|
| $A_i$ | $B_i$ | $A_i$ | $JA_i$ | $KA_i$ |
| 0 | 0 | 0 | 0 | X |
| 0 | 1 | 1 | 1 | X |
| 1 | 0 | 1 | X | 0 |
| 1 | 1 | 0 | X | 1 |

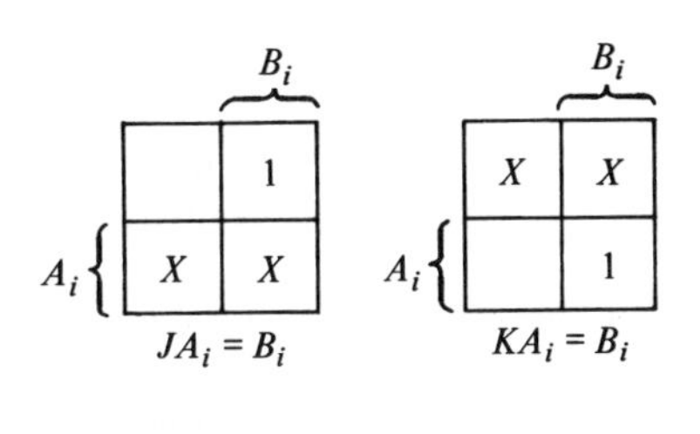


(c) Logic exclusive-OR (XOR)

**Fig. 4-13** Excitation tables for the micro-operations.

condition derived in the maps of Fig. 4-13. For example, the OR micro-operation requires that the $J$ input of $A_i$ be excited if $B_i = 1$ and the $K$ input be left at binary value 0. This function is controlled by $P_3$ so when $P_3 = 1$ and $B_i = 1$, the $J$ input receives a 1 and the $K$ input is maintained at 0 because all other $P$'s are equal to 0.

### *Some Applications*

Logic micro-operations are very useful for manipulating individual bits or a portion of a word stored in a register. They can be used to change bit values, delete a group of bits or insert new bit values into a register. The

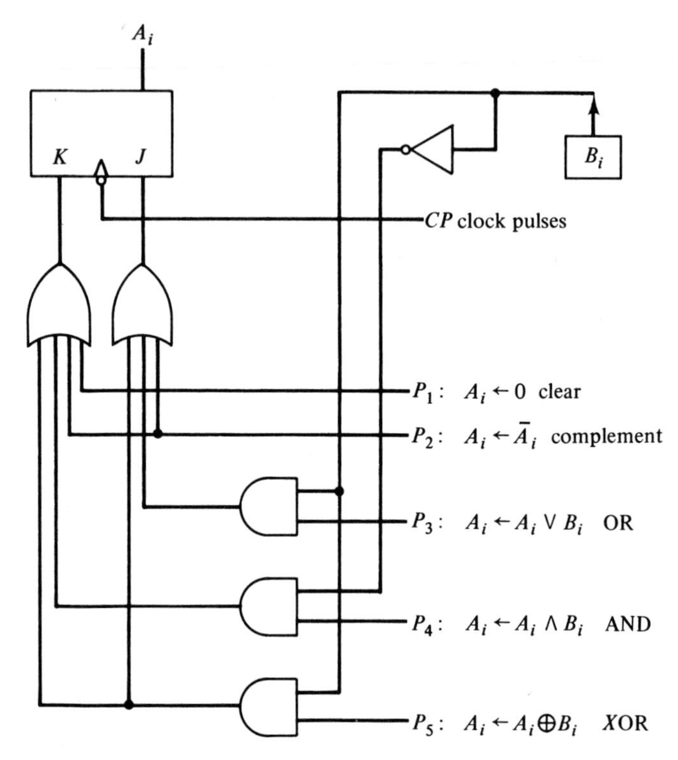


**Fig. 4-14** Hardware implementation of logic operations when the destination register is also a source register.

following examples show how the bits of one register (designated by $A$) are manipulated by logic micro-operations as a function of the bits of another register (designated by $B$). In a typical application, register $A$ is a processor register and the bits of register $B$ constitute a logic operand extracted from the memory unit and placed in register $B$.

The *selective-set* operation sets the bits in register $A$ where there are corresponding 1's in register $B$. It does not affect bit positions which have 0's in $B$. The following numerical example clarifies this operation.

| | |
|---|---|
| 1010 | $A$ before |
| 1100 | $B$ |
| 1110 | $A$ after |

The two left-most bits of $B$ are 1's and so the corresponding bits of $A$ are set. One of these two bits was already set and the other has been changed from 0 to 1. The two bits of $A$ with corresponding 0's in $B$ remain unchanged. The above example serves as a truth table since it has all four possible combinations of two binary variables. From the truth table we note that the bits of $A$ after the operation are obtained from the logic-OR operation of bits in $B$ and previous values of $A$. Therefore, the OR micro-operation can be used to selectively set bits of a register.

The *selective-complement* operation complements bits in $A$ where there are corresponding 1's in $B$. It does not affect bit positions which have 0's in $B$. For example:

| | |
|---|---|
| 1010 | $A$ before |
| 1100 | $B$ |
| 0110 | $A$ after |

Again the two left-most bits of $B$ are 1's and so the corresponding bits of $A$ are complemented. This example again can serve as a truth table from which one can deduce that the selective-complement operation is just an exclusive-OR micro-operation. Therefore, the exclusive-OR micro-operation can be used to selectively complement bits of a register.

The *selective-clear* operation clears the bits in $A$ only where there are corresponding 1's in $B$. For example:

| | |
|---|---|
| 1010 | $A$ before |
| 1100 | $B$ |
| 0010 | $A$ after |

Again the two left-most bits of $B$ are 1's and so the corresponding bits of $A$ are cleared to 0. One can deduce that the logic operation performed on the individual bits is $A_i B_i'$. The corresponding logic micro-operation is:

$$A \leftarrow A \wedge \bar{B}$$

The *mask* operation is similar to the selective-clear operation except that the bits of $A$ are cleared only where there are corresponding 0's in $B$. The mask operation is an AND micro-operation as seen from the following numerical example:

| | |
|---|---|
| 1010 | $A$ before |
| 1100 | $B$ |
| 1000 | $A$ after masking |

The two right-most bits of $A$ are cleared because the corresponding bits of $B$ are 0's. The two left-most bits are left unchanged because the corresponding bits of $B$ are 1's.

The mask operation is more convenient to use than the selective-clear operation because most computers provide an AND instruction and only few provide an instruction that executes the micro-operation for selective-clear. The mask operation can be considered as a *delete* operation. Theoretically, a delete operation will delete selected bits of a word stored in a register. However, because register cells are binary, they can be either 0 or 1 and nothing else. There is really no way of making "deletions" from registers, but by changing a group of bits to all 0's we can assume that the previous content of the bits has been "deleted."

The *insert* operation inserts a new value into a group of bits. This is done by first masking (deleting) the bits and then ORing them with the required value. For example, suppose an $A$ register contains eight bits, 0110 1010. To replace the four left-most bits by the value 1001 we first mask the four unwanted bits:

| | |
|---|---|
| 0110 1010 | $A$ before |
| 0000 1111 | $B$ (mask) |
| 0000 1010 | $A$ after masking |

and then insert the new value

| | |
|---|---|
| 0000 1010 | $A$ before |
| 1001 0000 | $B$ (insert) |
| 1001 1010 | $A$ after insertion |

The mask operation is an AND micro-operation and the insert operation is an OR micro-operation.

The *compare* operation compares the words in $A$ and $B$ and produces all 0's in $A$ if the two words are equal. This operation is achieved by an exclusive-OR micro-operation as shown by the following example:

| | |
|---|---|
| 1010 | $A$ |
| 1010 | $B$ |
| 0000 | $A \leftarrow A \oplus B$ |

When both $A$ and $B$ are equal, the two corresponding bits are either both 0 or both 1. In either case the exclusive-OR function produces a 0. The all 0's result is then checked to determine if the words were equal.

The *packing* of binary coded information such as characters is an operation that groups two or more characters in one word. For example, three binary-coded characters that occupy seven bits each in ASCII (Table 3-4) can be packed into one 21-bit word. To pack the three characters "MAY" into a 21-bit processor register $A$, we read the characters from memory one at a time and perform the following logic micro-operations:

| *Micro-Operation* | *Register A* |
|---|---|
| Clear *A* | 0000000 0000000 0000000 |
| OR with "*M*" = 100 1101 | 0000000 0000000 1001101 |
| Shift-left seven times | 0000000 1001101 0000000 |
| OR with "*A*" = 100 0001 | 0000000 1001101 1000001 |
| Shift-left seven times | 1001101 1000001 0000000 |
| OR with "*Y*" = 101 1001 | 1001101 1000001 1011001 |

It is assumed that the binary-coded characters are stored in a 21-bit memory word with the 14 high-order bits all 0's. The words are read from memory into *MBR* and the contents of *A* are ORed with *MBR*. A shift with 0's inserted in the empty spaces is considered as a logical shift (see next section). The final packed word of three characters can be stored in a single memory word.

The *unpacking* of binary-coded information is a reverse operation from packing. It separates two or more characters stored in one word into three separate characters. The unpacking is accomplished by masking the unwanted characters in the register.

Logic micro-operations are very useful for data processing of alphanumeric data. They can change, remove, delete, and modify characters. *Editing* operations are performed by a sequence of logical operations such as masking, insertion, and shift. An example of a financial edit of alphanumeric characters is one that provides output data in a special format. Such a format may require the insertion of a leading dollar sign, the deletion of leading zeros, the insertion of commas and period and the conversion of the algebraic sign to special symbols. For example, a financial edit on the string of characters +00023598 might yield as output $23,598.00 CREDIT, but on −00023598 might yield $23,598.00 DEBIT.

## 4-5 SHIFT MICRO-OPERATIONS

Shift micro-operations transfer binary information between registers in serial computers. They are also used in parallel computers for arithmetic, logic, and other data processing operations. While the bits of a register are shifted, the extreme flip-flop receives information from the serial input of the register. The extreme flip-flop is in the left-most position of the register during a right-shift micro-operation and in the right-most position during a left-shift micro-operation. The information transferred into the extreme flip-flop determines the type of shift implemented. There are four types of shifts: serial transfer shift, logical shift, circular shift and arithmetic shift.

*Serial transfer* was discussed in Sec. 4-2. The serial input in the destination register receives the bit from the source register. The source register is circulated to restore the information being shifted out. We adopt the symbols *shl* and *shr* to indicate a shift-left and a shift-right micro-operation, respectively. The symbols *cil* and *cir* will be used for circular left-shift and circular right-shift, respectively. A serial transfer from register $B$ into register $A$ can be symbolized by the following statement (see Fig. 4-3):

$$S: \quad \text{shr } A, \quad \text{cir } B, \quad A_1 \leftarrow B_n$$

where $n$ denotes the number of bits in the registers. $B_n$ is the right-most cell of $B$, and $A_1$ the left-most cell of $A$.

A *logical shift* is one that inserts a 0 into the extreme flip-flop. Therefore, the serial input of the shift-register must contain a 0 during a logical shift micro-operation. The symbols *shl* and *shr* can be used to indicate a logical shift when the information inserted into the extreme flip-flop is not specified explicitly. Thus, the statement:

$$L: \quad \text{shl } A$$

specifies a logical shift-left micro-operation for register $A$, and the statement

$$S: \quad \text{shr } A$$

specifies a logical shift-right micro-operation. Note that the first statement does not specify what goes into the right-most flip-flop $A_n$, nor does the second statement specify what goes into $A_1$. Therefore, we conclude that these extreme flip-flops receive a 0.

A *circular shift* circulates the bits of the register around the two ends. This is accomplished by connecting the serial output of the shift register into its serial input. The statement

$$P: \quad \text{cil } A, \quad \text{cir } B$$

specifies that register $A$ is to be circulated to the left and register $B$ circulated to the right.

An *arithmetic shift* is a micro-operation that shifts a *signed* number to the left or the right. This type of shift is also called *scaling* or *shift with sign extention*. The binary information in the register during an arithmetic shift is considered to be an arithmetic operand holding a fixed-point number or the exponent of a floating-point number. An arithmetic left-shift multiplies a signed binary number by two, and an arithmetic right shift divides it by two. Remember that the left-most flip-flop in the register holds the sign bit and that negative numbers may be represented in one of three different ways.

Arithmetic shifts must leave the sign bit unchanged because the sign of the number remains the same when it is multiplied or divided by 2. For positive numbers and negative numbers in signed-magnitude representation, the added bits during the shift are 0's. This is equivalent to a logical shift among the $n - 1$ bits that represent the number, excluding the sign bit which remains unchanged. When a negative number in 2's complement representation is shifted left, the added bits from the right are 0's but the sign bit is not shifted out. During a right shift, the sign bit is shifted into the high-order bit position of the number. For negative numbers in signed-1's complement representation, all bits shifted into the extreme flip-flops that represent the number (excluding the sign bit) are 1's. The rules for arithmetic shifts are summarized in Table 4-6.

The symbols for six shift micro-operations are listed in Table 4-7. Note that arithmetic shifts are symbolized by *ashl* and *ashr*. The hardware imple-

**Table 4-6** *Arithmetic shifts for signed binary numbers*

| *Representation* | *Sign Bit* | *Number Bits* |
|---|---|---|
| Positive number | Unchanged | All added bits are 0's |
| Negative number in signed-magnitude | Unchanged | All added bits are 0's |
| Negative number in signed-2's complement | Unchanged | Added bits are 0's for left-shift<br>Added bits are 1's for right-shift |
| Negative number in signed-1's complement | Unchanged | All added bits are 1's |

**Table 4-7** *Shift micro-operations*

| *Symbolic Designation* | *Description* |
|---|---|
| shl *A* | Shift-left register *A*, content of right-most flip-flop becomes 0 unless specified otherwise |
| shr *A* | Shift-right register *A*, content of left-most flip-flop becomes 0 unless specified otherwise |
| cil *A* | Circulate left contents of register *A* |
| cir *A* | Circulate right contents of register *A* |
| ashl *A* | Arithmetic shift-left contents of register *A* |
| ashr *A* | Arithmetic shift-right contents of register *A* |

mentation of these micro-operations depends on the type of data stored in the register and the type of representation adopted for negative numbers.

## 4-6 CONTROL FUNCTIONS

The timing for all registers in a synchronous digital system is controlled by a master clock generator, whose clock pulses are applied to all flip-flops in the system. The continuous clock pulses applied to a register do not change the state of the register unless its specific function is enabled. The binary variables that control the enable inputs of registers are called *control functions.* We have used control functions in previous examples. This section defines them more precisely and considers their hardware inplementation.

The hardware control network that generates control functions can be organized in one of three different ways: (a) as a sequential circuit, (b) as a sequence of timing signals coupled with control conditions, or (c) as a control memory.

A control logic network designed as a sequential circuit requires that it be specified by a state diagram or a state table and designed by sequential circuit theory methods. The disadvantages of this method are threefold: (a) The number of states in a control logic network for a typical digital computer is very large. Design methods that use state and excitation tables can be used in theory, but in practice they are cumbersome and difficult to manage. (b) The final control circuit obtained by this method is irregular and requires an excessive number of SSI gates and flip-flops. Constructing digital circuits with SSI integrated circuits is inefficient with respect to the number of packages used and the number of wires that must be interconnected. (c) It is difficult for a person to familiarize himself with the sequence of events that the control logic undergoes and as a consequence, it is difficult to service and maintain the equipment. For these reasons, the method is seldom used for controlling the operations of digital computers and therefore, this method is not discussed any further here. The interested reader can find more information in the references listed at the end of Chap. 1.

The second method provides a sequence of timing signals. These signals are combined with various other control conditions to generate the required control functions. This method solves the first and third difficulties listed above but the second difficulty is improved only slightly since this method also requires a large number of SSI gates. The hardware that generates timing signals and the control functions obtained by this method are discussed in this section.

The third method uses a special memory unit, usually a ROM, to store the 1's and 0's of the control functions for all registers. By reading words from control memory in a prescribed sequence, it is possible to activate the necessary registers and execute the micro-operations for the system. This is the most efficient method of control organization for a digital system. Assigning the 1's and 0's for the words in a control memory is called *micro-programming*. Because of its importance, all of Chap. 8 is devoted to this topic.

*Timing Sequences*

Timing signals that control the sequence of operations in a digital computer can be generated with a ring-counter or a binary counter and a decoder. A *ring-counter* is a circular shift-register with only one flip-flop being set at any particular time; all others are cleared. The single bit is shifted from one flip-flop to the other to produce the sequence of timing signals. Figure 4-15(a) shows the block diagram of a ring-counter that produces four

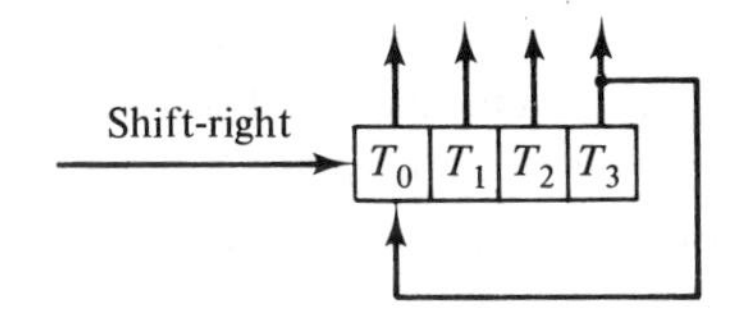


(a) Four-bit ring-counter (initial value of $T = 1000$)

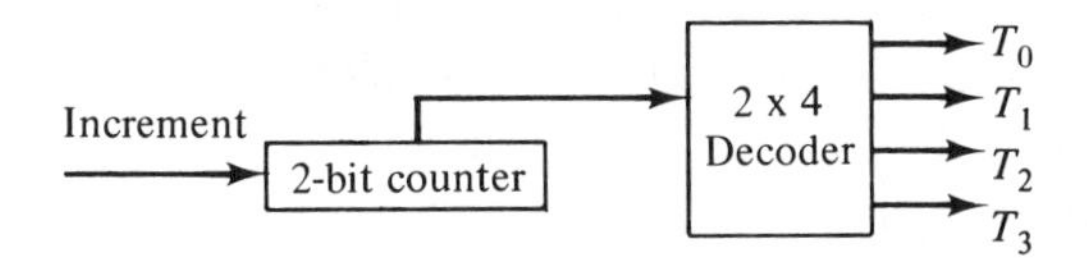


(b) Counter decoder block diagram

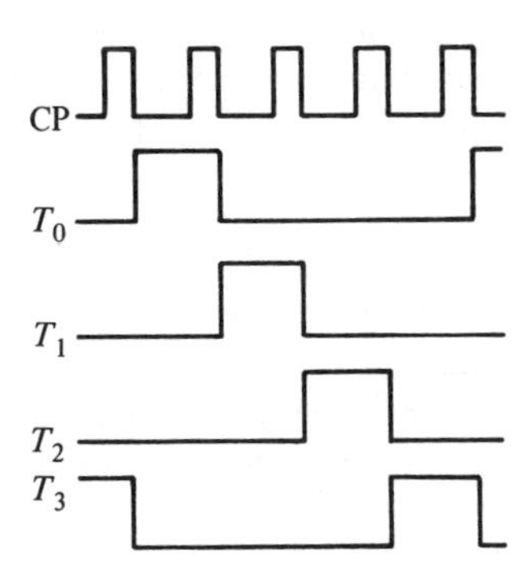


(c) A sequence of four timing signals

**Fig. 4-15** Generation of four consecutive timing signals.

timing signals. The initial value of the shift-register $T$ is 1000. The single bit is shifted right with every clock pulse and circulated back from $T_3$ to $T_0$. Each flip-flop is in the 1 state once every four clock pulses and produces one of the four timing signals shown in Fig. 4-15(c). Each output becomes 1 at the falling edge of a clock pulse and remains 1 during the next pulse. Thus, each clock pulse is associated with one of the timing variables. The timing signals can be generated also by continuously incrementing a binary counter and applying its outputs to a decoder as shown in Fig. 4-15(b). This type of circuit will also generate the required timing signals.

Small digital computers provide a timing sequence of 8 to 16 repetitive timing signals. The time of one repetitive sequence is called a *computer cycle*. Each computer cycle is synchronized with the memory cycle and initiates the control functions for the micro-operations associated with each access to memory. Large computer systems have multiple timing sequences with each sequence providing control to a different module in the system. Timing sequences in a synchronous system are synchronized with the master clock generator. In an asynchronous system each timing signal is generated after the completion of the previous micro-operation.

The timing signals shown in Fig. 4-15, when enabled by the clock pulses, will provide multiple phase clock pulses. For example, if $T_0$ is ANDed with $CP$, the output of the AND gate will generate clock pulses at one-fourth the frequency of the master clock pulses. Multiple phase clock pulses can be used for controlling different registers with different time scales.

### *Generation of Control Functions*

Each computer cycle is associated with a sequence of micro-operations. These micro-operations are controlled by the timing signals and other binary conditions in the system. The Boolean functions that generate the control decisions are the control functions that we have been using. For example, a digital computer may require that a word be read from memory during time $T_1$ of every computer cycle. This is symbolized by the statement:

$$T_1: \quad MBR \leftarrow M$$

In other words, timing variable $T_1$ serves as a read-control input for the memory unit. As another illustration, suppose that the content of register $B$ is to be transferred to register $A$ every time a signal $F$ is 1 during time $T_1$ or if another signal $R$ is 0 during time $T_3$. This is symbolized by the statement:

$$FT_1 + R'T_3: \quad A \leftarrow B$$

The control function, being a Boolean function, can be generated with logic gates as shown in Fig. 4-16. The gates that generate the control function go to

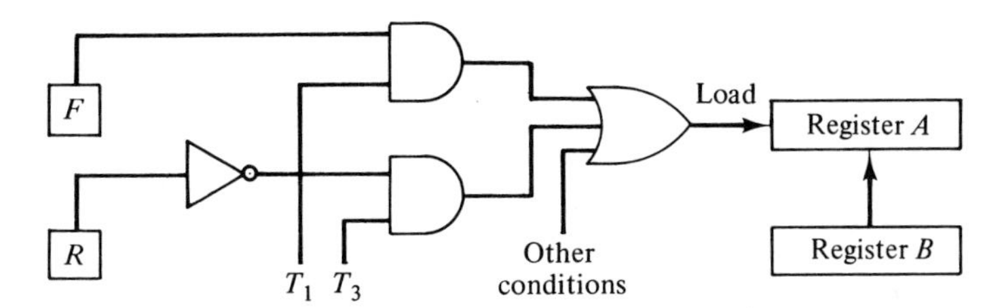


**Fig. 4-16** Hardware for the symbolic statement $FT_1 + R'T_3$: $A \leftarrow B$

the *load* input of register $A$ to initiate the transfer. Other conditions from other statements may also require the same transfer. Moreover, flip-flops $F$ and $R$ themselves are set or reset according to other conditions dictated by other control functions.

### *Conditional Control Statements*

It is sometimes convenient to specify a control function by a conditional statement. *A conditional control* statement is symbolized by an *if–then* statement in the following way:

$P$: If (condition) then (micro-operation(s))

and is interpreted to mean that if the condition stated within the parentheses after the word *if* is met, then the micro-operation, or micro-operations, enclosed within the parentheses after the word *then* are executed. In addition, the control function $P$ must be 1. If the condition is not met, or if $P = 0$, the micro-operation is not executed.

As an example, consider a 4-bit binary counter, denoted by the symbol $C$, which is initially set to all 1's. The counter is decremented with timing signal $T_7$. During the next time sequence, at $T_8$, we want to check the content of the counter, and if it is 0, set a flip-flop labelled $F$. Since $C$ is initially set to all 1's (binary 15) it is necessary that $T_7$ appears 15 times for the binary down-counter to reach the value of 0. The two micro-operations just described are stated symbolically below. The second statement is a conditional control statement.

$T_7$: $C \leftarrow C - 1$

$T_8$: If $(C = 0)$ then $(F \leftarrow 1)$

During $T_7$, the counter is decremented and during $T_8$, its content is checked for 0. If the value stored in $C$ is 0, $F$ is set to 1 during $T_8$; if not, $F$ is not changed. The hardware inplementation of the above statements is shown in

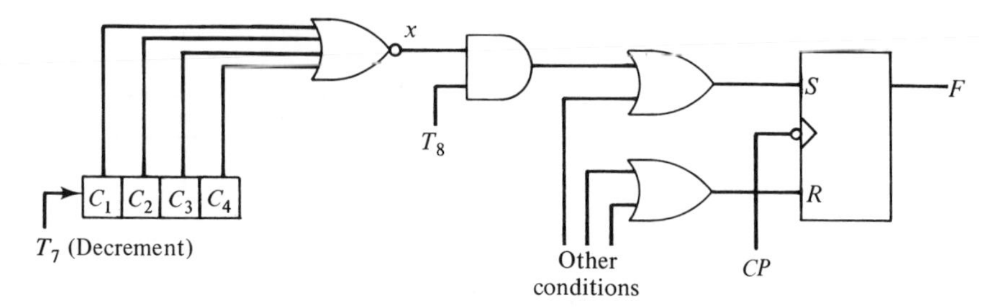


**Fig. 4-17** Hardware for conditional control statement $T_8$: If $(C = 0)$ then $(F \leftarrow 1)$.

Fig. 4-17. $T_7$ decrements the counter and $T_8$ sets flip-flop $F$ if $x = 1$. The Boolean function for $x$ is derived from the condition $(C = 0)$. This condition is met if all four flip-flops of $C$ are 0. The condition is expressed by the Boolean function:

$$x = C'_1C'_2C'_3C'_4 = (C_1 + C_2 + C_3 + C_4)'$$

The second form is derived from DeMorgan's theorem. Therefore, signal $x$ can be generated by a NOR gate with all cells of the register as inputs. The above conditional control statement can be stated without the *if–then* statement as follows:

$$xT_8: \quad F \leftarrow 1$$

provided we define the binary variable $x$ by the above Boolean function.

When using a conditional control statement one must realize that the condition specified in the statement is a control condition that must be generated with hardware and incorporated with the associated control function. The necessary hardware must be deduced from the stated control condition after the word *if*.

### *Tabular Summary of Control Functions*

Table 4-8 lists the symbols used to specify control functions. The Boolean operators AND, OR and complement are used to express control functions. This is in contrast to the symbols used to express logic micro-operations of the same type. A control function is terminated by a colon ( : ) and is implemented by a digital circuit composed of logic gates. Control information can be specified by control functions or conditional control statements. Although not shown here, a control network constructed around a control memory is specified by a *microprogram* instead of control functions. This procedure is discussed in Chap. 8.

**Table 4-8** *Control functions*

| *Symbolic Designation* | *Description* |
|---|---|
| $+$ | Denotes logic OR in a control function |
| $\cdot$ | (or absence of operator) denotes logic AND in a control function |
| $'$ (prime) | Denotes logic complement in a control function |
| $xT_1 + y'T_2$: | Denotes control function terminated by a colon |
| If $(SC = 0)$ then $(A \leftarrow B)$ | Conditional control statement with control condition specified in parentheses after the word *If* |

## 4-7 CONCLUDING REMARKS

A register transfer language is very useful in dealing with the architecture of digital computers. It can be used to describe the internal organization of digital systems and, if used properly, can be very helpful in the design of digital systems. In this chapter we have gone to great lengths to show the hardware associated with each statement written in a register transfer language. This was done for two reasons: the first is to avoid redrawing block diagrams of circuits every time a statement is mentioned in succeeding chapters; the second is to make the reader aware of the fact that a register transfer statement should not be written without considering the hardware implications associated with the statement. This is important when one is specifying the architecture of digital systems by means of register transfer methods.

There is a fundamental difference between a statement in a programming language and a statement in a register transfer language. For example, a Fortran statement such as

$$A = A + B$$

specifies that the value of variable $A$ should be replaced by the sum of the present values of $A$ and $B$. The programmer does not have to be concerned with how this statement is executed in the computer as long as the indicated computation is carried out correctly. On the other hand, the register transfer statement

$$A \leftarrow A + B$$

carries with it the hardware implication that two registers are available in the system, that there is a parallel-adder circuit, and that paths exist between the registers and the parallel-adder.

The register transfer language introduced in this chapter will save drawing detailed logic diagrams when we discuss the architecture of digital computers in succeeding chapters. Specifying a set of micro-operations and their control functions is equivalent to specifying the hardware of the system. In this chapter we have shown the relation between a symbolic statement and the hardware block diagram it represents. In Chap. 2 we have shown in detail the digital functions represented by the block diagrams. In Chap. 1 we explained the operation of the gates and flip-flops from which the digital functions are constructed. From the study of these three chapters, it is expected that the reader will be able to produce the hardware, once the micro-operation statements of a system are specified.

The symbols for the register transfer language adopted here are summarized in six tables (Tables 4-1, 4-2, 4-3, 4-5, 4-7, and 4-8). They should be used as a reference when an unfamiliar statement is encountered in other chapters. The symbols for the arithmetic and shift micro-operations apply mostly to binary data. These symbols may need some modification when the stored data in registers represents decimal or other binary-coded information. In fact, the symbols presented in this chapter constitute a minimum set for a register transfer language. New symbols may have to be adopted when necessary.

## REFERENCES


1. Reed, I. S., "Symbolic Design Techniques Applied to a Generalized Computer," M.I.T. Lincoln Lab. Tech. Rept. 141, January, 1957.
2. Schorr, H. "A Register Transfer Language to Describe Digital Systems," Princeton Univ. Dept. of Electrical Engineering, Digital Systems Lab. Tech. Rept. 30, September, 1962.
3. Schorr, H., "Computer-Aided Digital System Design and Analysis Using a Register Transfer Language," *IEEE Trans. on Electronic Computers*, Vol. EC-13 (December, 1964), pp. 730–737.
4. Iverson, K. E., "A Common Language for Hardware, Software, and Applications," 1962 Fall Joint Computer Conference, *AFIPS Proc.*, Vol. 22, Washington, D.C.: Spartan, pp. 121–129.
5. Proctor, R. M., "A Logic Design Translator Experiment Demonstrating Relationship of Language to Systems and Logic Design," *IEEE Trans. on Electronic Computers*, Vol. EC-13 (August, 1964), pp. 442–430.
6. Bartee, T. C., I. L. Lebow, and I. S. Reed, *Theory and Design of Digital Machines*, New York: McGraw-Hill Book Co., 1962.
7. Parnas, D. L., "A Language for Describing the Functions of Synchronous Systems," *Comm. of the ACM*, Vol. 9 (February, 1966), pp. 72–76.
8. Duley, J. R., and D. L. Dietmeyer, "A Digital System Design Language (DDL)," *IEEE Trans. on Computers*, Vol. C-18 (September, 1968), pp. 850–861.

9. BELL, C. G., J. L. EGGERT, J. GRASON, and P. WILLIAMS, "The Description and Use of Register Transfer Modules," *IEEE Trans. on Computers*, Vol. C-21 (May, 1972), pp. 495–500.

10. CHU, Y., *Computer Organization and Micro-Programming*, Englewood Cliffs, N.J.: Prentice-Hall, Inc., 1972.

11. SU, S. Y. H., "A Survey of Computer Hardware Description Languages," *Computer*, Vol. 7 (December, 1974), pp. 45–51.

12. BARBACCI, M. R., "A Comparison of Register Transfer Languages for Describing Computers and Digital Systems," *IEEE Trans on Computers*, Vol. C-24 (February, 1975), pp. 137–150.

## PROBLEMS

4-1 List the micro-operations that transfer bits 1–8 of register $A$ to bits 9–16 of register $B$ and bits 1–8 of register $B$ to bits 9–16 of register $A$. Draw a block diagram of the hardware.

4-2 Show the block diagram that executes the statement

$$T: \quad A \leftarrow B, B \leftarrow A$$

4-3 Show the hardware for transferring the binary-coded hexadecimal F3 into register $A$. This is stated symbolically as:

$$P: \quad A \leftarrow (\mathrm{F3})_{16}$$

4-4 An 8-bit register $A$ has one binary input $x$. The register operation can be described symbolically as follows

$$P: \quad A_8 \leftarrow x, A_i \leftarrow A_{i+1} \qquad i = 1, 2, \ldots, 7$$

What is the function of the register? The cells are numbered from left to right.

4-5 A serial computer employs 32-bit registers and clock pulses at a rate of one million per second. What is the bit-time and the word-time of the computer?

4-6 (a) Show the block diagram of a 4-bit register with tri-state inverters at each cell output. The register should have one common control input to enable all tri-state gates.

(b) Show the block diagram of four such registers connected to a common bus. Include a decoder for selecting the register that communicates with the bus.

4-7 Draw a block diagram of a bus system connected to four registers with information transferred *serially* from any register to any other register. Use a decoder and a multiplexer to select the source register and a decoder to select the destination register.

4-8 What should be the values of $x$ and $y$ in Fig. 4-6 and $z$, $w$, and $E$ in Fig. 4-7 to initiate the transfers:
(a) $R3 \leftarrow D$
(b) $R0 \leftarrow B$
(c) $R2 \leftarrow C$
(d) $R1 \leftarrow A$

4-9 Draw the block diagram of a bus system connected to 8 registers with 8 bits in each register.

4-10 A digital system has 16 registers, each with 32 bits. It is necessary to provide parallel data transfer from each register to each other register. (a) How many lines are needed for direct parallel transfer? (b) How many lines are needed for transfer along a common bus? (c) If the registers form a scratch-pad memory, how is information transferred from one register to another? Let the registers in the memory be designated by $R0$ to $R15$. List the sequence of micro-operations for a transfer of the content of $R6$ into $R13$.

4-11 Draw a block diagram for the *add* micro-operation when implemented in a serial computer. Include two shift-registers, one full-adder and a flip-flop to store the carry. Assume that the carry flip-flop is initially cleared.

4-12 Register $A$ in Fig. 4-10 holds the number 1011 and register $B$ holds 0111.
(a) Determine the values of each $S$ and $C$ output of the four full-adders in the binary parallel adder.
(b) Repeat part (a) after register $A$ is enabled by the control function $P$.

4-13 (a) Draw the logic diagram of a full-subtractor from the Boolean functions derived in Sec. 1-4.
(b) Draw a block diagram of a binary parallel-subtractor composed of four full-subtractors. Let $A$ be the minuend and $B$ the subtrahend.
(c) If the minuend $A$ is 1010 and the subtrahend $B$ is 0111, determine the values of each $D$ (difference) and each $K$ (borrow) output of the four full-subtractors.

4-14 Draw the logic diagram of a 4-bit register with clocked $JK$ flip-flops having control inputs for the increment, complement, and parallel transfer micro-operations. Show how the 2's complement can be implemented in this register.

4-15 (a) Modify the circuit of Fig. 4-11 by using $JK$ flip-flops and including control inputs for a parallel transfer as well as the 2's complement micro-operation.
(b) Let this register be register $B$ in Fig. 4-10. List the micro-operation sequence that subtracts the content of $B$ from the content of $A$ and places the difference in register $A$.

4-16 The content of register $A$ is 1101 and that of $B$ is 0110. Show that either one of the micro-operation sequences listed below produce the difference 0111.

| (a) | | (b) | |
|---|---|---|---|
| $T_1$: | $B \leftarrow \bar{B}$ | $T_1$: | $B \leftarrow \bar{B}$ |
| $T_2$: | $B \leftarrow B + 1$ | $T_2$: | $EA \leftarrow A + B$ |
| $T_3$: | $A \leftarrow A + B$ | $ET_3$: | $A \leftarrow A + 1$ |

4-17 Derive a combinational circuit that selects and generates any one of the 16 functions listed in Table 4-4.

4-18 Design a typical stage (similar to Fig. 4-14) that implements the following logic micro-operations.

$$P_6: \quad A \leftarrow A \vee \bar{B} \qquad P_8: \quad A \leftarrow \overline{A \vee B}$$
$$P_7: \quad A \leftarrow \bar{A} \wedge B \qquad P_9: \quad A \leftarrow \overline{A \wedge B}$$

4-19 List the sequence of logic micro-operations required for packing the six alphanumeric characters "HI-LO." into a 48-bit register. Use 8 bits per character, obtained from the 7 ASCII bits (Table 3-4) and an even parity bit in the most significant position.

4-20 How would you convert decimal digits represented by a 7-bit ASCII into a 4-bit BCD and pack the BCD digits in one register?

4-21 Show that the statement

$$A \leftarrow A + A$$

symbolizes a shift-left micro-operation.

4-22 (a) Show the representation of +12 in binary in a 7-bit register. Divide and multiply this number by 2 and show how it can be done by means of arithmetic shift micro-operations.
(b) Repeat (a) for −12 when it is in (1) signed-magnitude representation; (2) signed-1's complement representation; and (3) signed-2's complement representation.
(c) From the above results, justify the entries of Table 4-6.

4-23 Show that an $n$-bit binary counter connected to an $n$ by $2^n$ decoder is equivalent to a ring-counter with $2^n$ flip-flops. Show the block diagram of both circuits for $n = 3$. How many timing signals are generated?

4-24 Include an enable input to the decoder of Fig. 4-15(b) and connect it to the master clock pulse generator. Draw the sequence of timing signals (similar to Fig. 4-15(c)) that are now generated at the outputs of the decoder.

4-25 Show the hardware, including the logic gates for the control function, that implements the statement

$$xy'T_0 + T_1 + x'yT_2: \qquad A \leftarrow A + 1$$

4-26 Prove that the following conditional control statement:

$$P: \quad \text{If } (C = 1001) \text{ then } (C \leftarrow 0), \text{ If } (C \neq 1001) \text{ then } (C \leftarrow C + 1)$$

symbolizes a one-decade BCD counter.

4-27 A computer has three timing signals that repeat in sequence, $T_0$, $T_1$, $T_2$, $T_0$, $T_1$, $T_2$. There are three registers, $A$, $B$, and $SC$, and two flip-flops, $R$ and $F$.

Initially, $R = 0$ and $F = 0$, so none of the micro-operations listed below are executed. Show that if $R$ is set to 1, the sequence of micro-operations will form the product of $A$ and $B$ and then disable itself.

$$T_0R: \quad SC \leftarrow A, \; A \leftarrow 0, \; R \leftarrow 0, \; F \leftarrow 1$$

$$T_1F: \quad A \leftarrow A + B, \; SC \leftarrow SC - 1$$

$$T_2F: \quad \text{If } (SC = 0) \text{ then } (F \leftarrow 0)$$

# 5

# BASIC COMPUTER ORGANIZATION AND DESIGN

## 5-1 INSTRUCTION CODES

The internal organization of a digital system is defined by the sequence of micro-operations it performs on data stored in its registers. In a *special purpose* digital system, the sequence of micro-operations is fixed by the hardware and the system performs the same specific task over and over again. Once a special purpose system is built, its sequence of micro-operations is not subject to alterations. Examples of special purpose digital systems can be found in numerous peripheral control units, one of which is a magnetic tape controller. Such a unit controls the movement of a magnetic tape transport and the transfer of binary information between the tape and its external environment. The unit cannot perform any operations other than the special task for which it was designed.

A digital computer is a *general purpose* digital system. A general purpose digital computer is capable of executing various micro-operations and, in addition, can be instructed as to what specific sequence of operations it must perform. The user of such a system can control the process by means of a *program*, i.e., a set of instructions that specify the operations, operands and the sequence by which processing has to occur. The data processing task may be altered simply by specifying a new program with different instructions or specifying the same instructions with different data. A computer instruction is a binary code that specifies a sequence of micro-operations for the computer. Instruction codes together with data are stored in memory. The control reads each instruction from memory and places it in a control register. The control then interprets the binary code of the instruction and proceeds to execute the instruction by issuing a sequence of control functions. Every general purpose computer has its own unique instruction repertoire. The ability to store and execute instructions, the stored program concept, is the most important property of a general purpose computer.

An *instruction code* is a group of bits that tell the computer to perform a specific operation. It is usually divided in parts, each having its own particular interpretation. The most basic part of an instruction code is its operation part. The *operation code* of an instruction is a group of bits that define such operations as add, subtract, multiply, shift, and complement. The set of operations formulated for a computer depends on the processing it is intended to carry out. The total number of operations thus obtained determines the set of machine operations. The number of bits required for the operation part of an instruction code is a function of the total number of operations used. It must consist of at least $n$ bits for a given $2^n$ (or less) distinct operations. As an illustration, consider a computer with 32 distinct operations, one of them being an ADD operation. The operation code consists of five bits, with a bit configuration 10010 assigned to the ADD operation. When this operation code is received by the control unit, it issues control functions which read an operand from memory and add the operand to a processor register.

At this point we must recognize the relation between an operation and a micro-operation. An operation is part of an instruction stored in computer memory. It is a binary code that tells the computer to perform a specific operation. The control unit receives the instruction from memory and interprets the operation code bits. It then issues a sequence of control functions that perform micro-operations in internal computer registers. For every operation code, the control issues a sequence of micro-operations needed for the hardware implementation of the specified operation. For this reason, an operation code is sometimes called a *macro-operation* because it specifies a set of micro-operations.

The operation part of an instruction code specifies the operation to be performed. This operation must be executed on some data stored in memory and/or processor registers. An instruction code, therefore, must specify not only the operation, but also the registers and/or the memory words where the operands are to be found, as well as the register or memory word where the result is to be stored. Memory words can be specified in instruction codes by their address. Processor registers can be specified by assigning to the instruction another binary code of $k$ bits that specifies one of $2^k$ registers. There are many variations for arranging the binary code of instructions and each computer has its own particular instruction code format. Instruction code formats are conceived by computer designers who specify the architecture of the computer. There are as many instruction code formats as there are computers on the market. In this chapter we choose a particular instruction code to explain the basic organization of digital computers.

The simplest way to organize a computer is to have one processor register and an instruction code format with two parts. The first part specifies the operation to be performed and the second specifies an address. The address tells the control where to find an operand in memory. This operand is read from memory and used as the data to be operated on together with the data stored in the processor register.

Figure 5-1 depicts this type of organization. Instructions are stored in one section of memory and data in another. For a memory unit with 4096 words

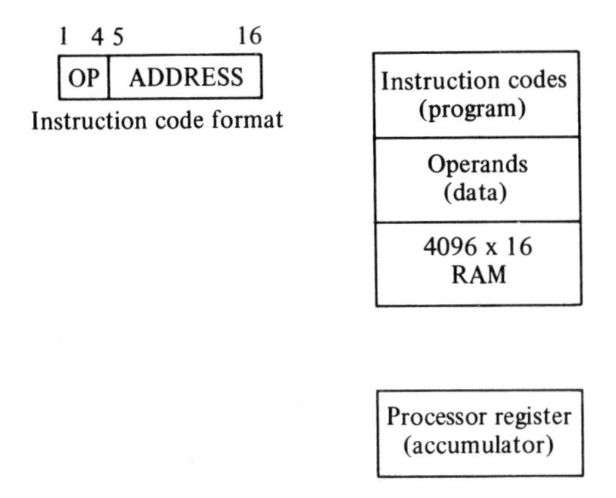


**Fig. 5-1** Stored program organization.

we need 12 bits to specify an address since $2^{12} = 4096$. If we store each instruction code in one 16-bit memory word, we have available four bits to specify one out of 16 possible operations and 12 bits to specify the address of an operand. The control reads a 16-bit instruction from the program portion of memory. It uses the 12-bit address part of the instruction to read an operand from the data portion of memory. It then executes the operation by means of micro-operations between the operand and the processor register. Computers that have a single processor register usually assign to it the name *accumulator* and label it *AC*.

If an operation in an instruction code does not need an operand from memory, the rest of the bits in the instruction can be used for other purposes. For example, operations such as clear *AC*, complement *AC*, and increment *AC* operate on data stored in the *AC* register. They do not need an operand from memory. For these types of operations, the second part of the instruction code (bits 5 to 16) is not needed for specifying a memory address and can be used to specify other operations for the computer.

It is sometimes convenient to use the address bits of an instruction code not as an address but as the actual operand. When the second part of an instruction code specifies an operand, the instruction is said to have an *immediate* operand. When the second part specifies the address of an operand, the instruction is said to have a *direct* address. This is in contrast to a third possibility called *indirect* address, where the bits in the second part of the instruction designate an address of a memory word in which the *address of the operand* is found. It is customary to use one bit in the instruction code to distinguish between a direct and an indirect address.

As an illustration of this concept, consider the instruction code format shown in Fig. 5-2(a). It consists of a three-bit operation code designated by OP, a six-bit address part designated by $AD$, and an indirect-address mode bit designated by $I$. The mode bit is 0 for a direct address and 1 for an indirect address. A direct address instruction is shown in Fig. 5-2(b). It is

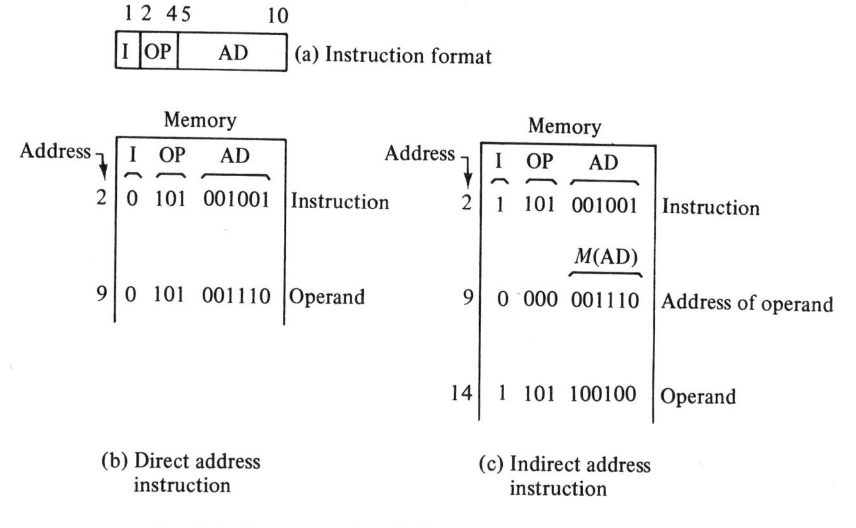


**Fig. 5-2** Demonstration of direct and indirect instructions.

placed in address 2 in memory. The $I$ bit is 0 so the instruction is recognized (by the control) as a direct address instruction. Since the address part $AD$ is equal to the binary equivalent of 9 (001001), the control finds the operand in memory at address 9. The instruction in address 2 shown in Fig. 5-2(c) has a mode bit $I = 1$. Therefore, it is recognized as an indirect address instruction. The address part is the binary equivalent of 9. The control goes to address 9 to find the *address of the operand.* This address is in the address portion of the word and is designated by $M(AD)$. Since $M(AD)$ contains 14 (binary 001110), the control finds the operand in memory at address 14. The indirect address instruction needs two references to memory to fetch an operand. The first reference is needed to read the address of the operand; the second is for the operand itself.

## 5-2 COMPUTER INSTRUCTIONS

Computer instructions are normally stored in consecutive memory locations and are executed sequentially one at a time. The control reads an instruction from a specific address in memory and executes it. It then continues by reading the next instruction in sequence and executes it, and so on. This type of instruction sequencing needs a counter to calculate the address of the next instruction after the execution of the current instruction is completed. Moreover, memory words cannot communicate with processor registers directly without going through an address and buffer register. It is also necessary to provide a register in the control unit for storing operation codes after they are read from memory. These requirements dictate the register configuration shown in Fig. 5-3. This register configuration will be used to describe the internal organization of a basic digital computer.

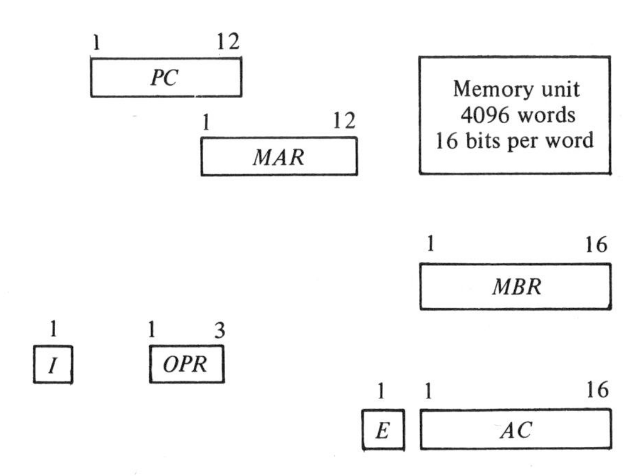


**Fig. 5-3** Basic computer registers.

The memory unit has a capacity of 4096 words and each word contains 16 bits. Twelve bits of an instruction word are needed to specify the address of an operand. This leaves four bits for the operation part of the instruction. However, only three bits are used to specify an operation code. The fourth bit is used to specify a direct or indirect addressing mode. The memory buffer register (*MBR*) consists of 16 bits, as does the *AC* (accumulator) register. The *E* flip-flop is an extension of the *AC*. It is used during shifting operations, it receives the end-carry during addition, and otherwise is a useful flip-flop that can simplify the data processing capabilities of the computer. The *I* register has a single cell for storing the mode bit and the operation register (*OPR*) stores the three-bit operation code read from memory.

The memory address register *MAR* has 12 bits since this is the length of a memory address. The program counter (*PC*) also has 12 bits and it holds the address of the next instruction to be read from memory after the current instruction is executed. This register goes through a counting sequence and causes the computer to read sequential instructions previously stored in memory. Instruction words are read and executed in sequence unless a branch instruction is encountered. A branch instruction has an operation part that calls for a transfer to a nonconsecutive instruction in memory. The address part of a branch instruction is transferred to *PC* to become the address of the next instruction. To read an instruction, the content of *PC* is transferred to *MAR*, a memory read cycle initiated, and *PC* is incremented by one. This places the instruction code into *MBR* and prepares *PC* for the address of the next instruction. The operation code is transferred to *OPR*, the mode bit into *I* and the address part into *MAR*. A memory read operation places the operand (if $I = 0$) into *MBR*. The *AC* and the *MBR* are used as the source registers for the micro-operations specified by the operation code. The result of the operation is stored in the *AC*.

However, an instruction may have an indirect bit *I* equal to 1, or may not require an operand from memory, or may be a branch instruction. In each of these cases, the control must issue a different set of control functions to execute different types of register transfers. In order to investigate the role that the control unit plays in executing instructions it is necessary to define the computer instructions and their code formats.

The basic computer has three different instruction code formats, as shown in Fig. 5-4. The operation part of the instruction contains three bits; the meaning of the remaining thirteen bits depends on the operation code encountered. A *memory-reference* instruction uses the last 12 bits to specify an address and the first bit to specify the mode *I*. A *register-reference*

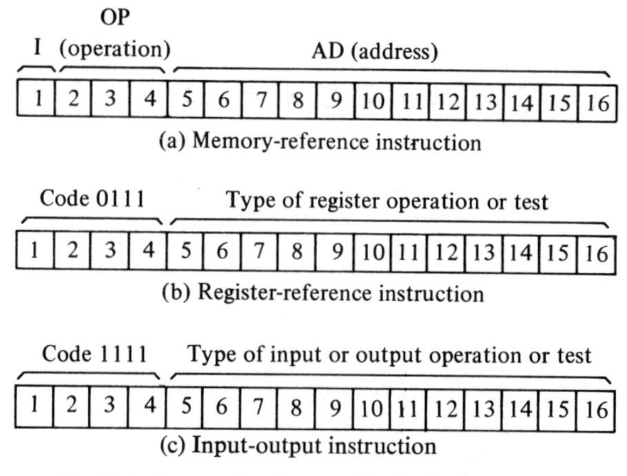


**Fig. 5-4** Instruction formats for the basic computer.

instruction specifies an operation on or a test of the *AC* or *E* register. An operand from memory is not needed; therefore, the last 12 bits are used to specify the operation or test to be executed. A register-reference instruction is recognized by the operation code 111 with a 0 in the first bit of the instruction. Similarly, an input-output instruction does not need a reference to memory and is recognized by the operation code 111 with a 1 in the first bit of the instruction. The remaining 12 bits are used to specify the type of input-output operation or test performed. Note that the first bit of the instruction code is not used as a mode bit when the last 12 bits are not used to designate an address.

Only three bits of the instruction are used for the operation code. It may seem that the computer is restricted to a maximum of eight distinct operations. However, since register-reference and input-output instructions use the remaining 12 bits as part of the operation code, the total number of instructions can exceed eight. In fact, the total number of instructions chosen for the basic computer is equal to 25.

The instructions for the computer are listed in Table 5-1. The symbol designation is a three-letter word and represents an abbreviation intended for

**Table 5-1** *Computer instructions*

| | *Hexadecimal Code* | | | |
|---|---|---|---|---|
| *Symbol* | $I = 0$ | $I = 1$ | *Address* | *Description* |
| AND | 0 | 8 | *AD* | AND memory word to *AC* |
| ADD | 1 | 9 | *AD* | Add memory word to *AC* |
| LDA | 2 | A | *AD* | Load *AC* from memory |
| STA | 3 | B | *AD* | Store *AC* into memory |
| BUN | 4 | C | *AD* | Branch unconditionally |
| BSA | 5 | D | *AD* | Branch and save return address |
| ISZ | 6 | E | *AD* | Increment and skip if zero |
| CLA | 7800 | | | Clear *AC* |
| CLE | 7400 | | | Clear *E* |
| CMA | 7200 | | | Complement *AC* |
| CME | 7100 | | | Complement *E* |
| CIR | 7080 | | | Circulate right *E* and *AC* |
| CIL | 7040 | | | Circulate left *E* and *AC* |
| INC | 7020 | | | Increment *AC* |
| SPA | 7010 | | | Skip if *AC* is positive |
| SNA | 7008 | | | Skip if *AC* is negative |
| SZA | 7004 | | | Skip if *AC* is zero |
| SZE | 7002 | | | Skip if *E* is zero |
| HLT | 7001 | | | Halt computer |
| I/O | FXXX | | | Input-output instructions (see Table 5-5) |

programmers and users. The hexadecimal code is equal to the equivalent hexadecimal number of the binary code used for the instruction. By using the hexadecimal equivalent we reduced the 16 bits of an instruction code to four digits with each hexadecimal digit being equivalent to four bits. A memory-reference instruction has an address part of 12 bits. The address part is denoted by the symbol $AD$ and must be specified by three hexadecimal digits. The first bit of the instruction is designated by the symbol $I$. When $I = 0$, $AD$ is the address of the operand. In this case, the first four bits of an instruction have a hexadecimal designation from 0 to 6 since the first bit is 0. When $I = 1$, $AD$ is an address where the address of the operand is to be found in memory. The hexadecimal digit equivalent of the first four bits of the instruction ranges from 8 to E since the first bit is 1.

Register-reference instructions use 16 bits to specify an operation. The first four bits are always 0111, which is equivalent to hexadecimal 7. The other three hexadecimal digits give the binary equivalent of the remaining 12 bits. The input-output instructions also use all 16 bits to specify an operation. The first four bits are always 1111 which is equivalent to hexadecimal F. The three $X$'s following the F for an input-output instruction are digits that distinguish between the different $I$/O instructions. These digits are specified later in Table 5-5.

Before investigating the operations performed by the instructions, let us discuss the type of instructions that must be included in a practical computer. A computer should have a set of instructions that allows the user to formulate any conceivable data processing task. To insure this, the computer must include a sufficient number of instructions in each of the following categories:

1. Arithmetic, logic, and shift instructions.
2. Instructions for moving information to and from memory and processor registers.
3. Instructions that check status information to provide decision making capabilities.
4. Input and output instructions.
5. The capability of stopping the computer.

Arithmetic, logic, and shift instructions provide computational capabilities for processing the type of data that the user may wish to employ. The bulk of the binary information in a digital computer is stored in memory but all computations are done in processor registers. Therefore, the user must have the capability of moving information between these two units. Decision-making capabilities are an important aspect of digital computers. For example, two numbers can be compared; however, if the first is greater than the second, it may be necessary to proceed differently than if the second is greater than the first. Logical decisions are provided in computers by instructions that check status conditions after a computation. The branch instructions are then used to branch to a different set of instructions depending on the status condition encountered. Input and output instructions are needed for communication between the computer and the user. Programs and data must be transferred into memory and results of computations must be transferred back to the user. Finally, there must be an instruction that will halt further computer operations when necessary.

The instructions listed in Table 5-1 constitute a minimum set that provides all the capabilities mentioned above. There are three arithmetic instructions: ADD, complement $AC$ (CMA), and increment $AC$ (INC). With these three instructions we can add and subtract binary numbers when negative numbers are in signed-2's complement representation. The circulate instructions, CIR and CIL, can be used for arithmetic shifts to provide multiplication and division operations as well as any other type of shifts desired. There are three logic operations: AND, complement $AC$ (CMA), and clear $AC$ (CLA). With these operations, it is possible to obtain all 16 other logic operations.

Moving information from memory to $AC$ is accomplished by the load $AC$ (LDA) instruction. Storing information from $AC$ into memory is done by the store $AC$ (STA) instruction. The branch instructions BUN and BSA, the ISZ instruction, the four skip instructions, and the instructions associated with the $E$ register provide capabilities for making logical decisions. These instructions will be explained further in Sec. 5-4 and their capabilities will be demonstrated in the programming examples of Chap. 6. The input-output instructions are explained in Sec. 5-5. Finally, the halt (HLT) instruction is provided to stop the computer by programming means.

The detailed function of each instruction and the micro-operations needed for their execution are presented in Sec. 5-4. We delay this discussion because we must first consider the control unit and understand its internal organization.

## 5-3 TIMING AND CONTROL

The digital computer operates in discrete steps. Micro-operations are performed during each step. Instructions are read from memory and executed in registers by a sequence of micro-operations. Once a start switch is activated, the computer sequence follows a basic pattern. An instruction whose address is in the $PC$ register is read from memory into $MBR$. Its operation part is transferred into $OPR$ and the mode bit into the $I$ register. The operation part is decoded in the control unit. If it is a memory reference type that needs an operand from memory, control checks the bit in $I$. If $I = 0$, the memory is accessed again to read the operand. If $I = 1$, the memory is accessed to read the address of the operand and again to read the operand. Thus a word read from memory into *MBR* may be an insruction, an operand, or an address of an operand. When an instruction is read from memory, the computer is said to be in an instruction *fetch* cycle. When the word read from memory is an address of an operand the computer is in an *indirect* cycle. When the word read from memory is an operand, the computer is in a data *execute* cycle. It is the function of the control to keep track of the various cycles.

The control unit uses two flip-flops to distinguish between the three cycles. These flip-flops are denoted by the letters $F$ and $R$. A 2 by 4 decoder associated with these flip-flops provides four outputs, three of which can be used to differentiate between the above-mentioned cycles. The computer has a fourth cycle to be introduced in Sec. 5-5. Table 5-2 lists the binary values of $F$ and $R$ and the decoder variable $c_i$ that is equal to 1 for each of the four cycles.

**Table 5-2** *Computer cycle control*

| *Flip-Flops* $F$ | $R$ | *Decoder Output* | *Computer Cycle* |
|---|---|---|---|
| 0 | 0 | $c_0$ | Fetch cycle (read instruction) |
| 0 | 1 | $c_1$ | Indirect cycle (read address of operand) |
| 1 | 0 | $c_2$ | Execute cycle (read operand) |
| 1 | 1 | $c_3$ | Interrupt cycle (see Sec. 5-5) |

The block diagram of the control unit for the basic computer is shown in Fig. 5-5. The timing in the computer is generated by a 2-bit sequence counter (*SC*) and a 2 by 4 decoder. The timing signals out of the decoder are designated by $t_0$, $t_1$, $t_2$ and $t_3$. We will assume that the memory cycle is shorter than the time interval between two clock pulses. According to this assumption, a memory read or write cycle initiated by the falling edge of one timing variable will be completed by the time the next clock pulse arrives (see Fig. 4-15(c)). This is not common in most computers because a memory cycle is usually longer than the interval between two clock pulses. We make this assumption here to facilitate the presentation. The four timing variables employed in this computer are sufficient for the execution of any instruction during two or three cycles.

The operation code part of the instruction in *OPR* is decoded into eight outputs $q_0$–$q_7$, the subscript number being equal to the binary equivalent of the operation code. The cycle control flip-flops $F$ and $R$ are decoded into four outputs $c_0$–$c_3$ as specified in Table 5-2. The control logic gates generate the various control functions for the micro-operations in the computer. Each

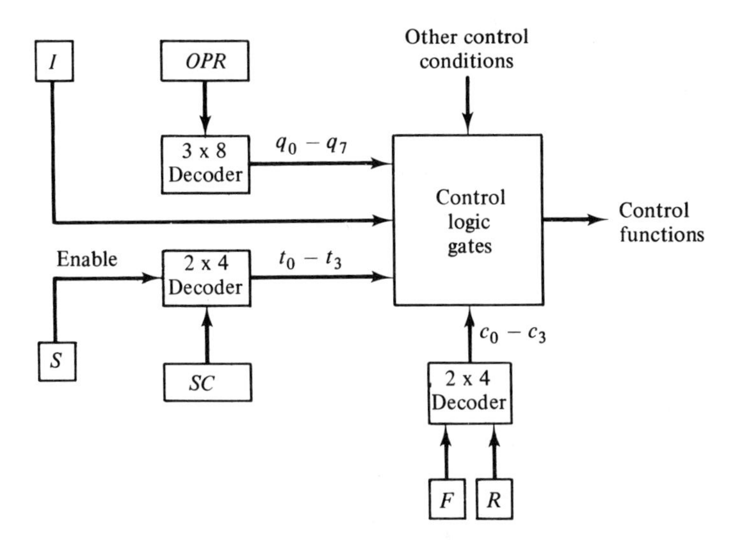


**Fig. 5-5** Block diagram of control unit.

control function includes with it a timing variable $t_i$ and a cycle designation $c_i$. During the execute cycle, the control function will also include a $q_i$ variable. The $I$ variable and other control conditions are also needed for the generation of control functions.

The control block diagram shows a start-stop flip-flop $S$ connected to the enable input of the timing decoder. All micro-operations are conditioned on the timing signals. The timing signals are generated only when $S = 1$. When $S = 0$, none of the variables $t_0$–$t_3$ are equal to 1 and therefore the control sequence stops and the computer halts. The $S$ flip-flop can be set or cleared from switches in the computer console, or cleared by the HLT (halt) instruction. It is necessary to insure that when $S$ is set by a start switch, signal $t_0$ is the first to occur; and when $S$ is cleared by a stop switch, the current instruction is completed before the computer halts.

We are now ready to specify in symbolic notation the sequence of control functions and micro-operations for the computer. Each symbolic statement consists of a control function followed by a colon, followed by one or more micro-operations. All statements are to be interpreted in accordance with the symbolic notation defined in Chap. 4.

### *Fetch Cycle*

An instruction is read from memory during the instruction fetch cycle. The register transfer relations that specify this process are:

| | | |
|---|---|---|
| $c_0t_0$: | $MAR \leftarrow PC$ | Transfer instruction address |
| $c_0t_1$: | $MBR \leftarrow M$, $PC \leftarrow PC + 1$ | Read instruction and increment $PC$ |
| $c_0t_2$: | $OPR \leftarrow MBR(OP), I \leftarrow MBR(I)$ | Transfer OP code and mode bit |
| $q'_7Ic_0t_3$: | $R \leftarrow 1$ | Go to indirect cycle |
| $(q_7 + I')c_0t_3$: | $F \leftarrow 1$ | Go to execute cycle |

The fetch cycle is recognized by variable $c_0$. The four timing signals that occur during this cycle initiate the sequence of micro-operations for the fetch cycle. The address, which is in $PC$, is transferred into $MAR$. The memory reads the instruction and places it in $MBR$. At the same time, the program counter is incremented by one to prepare it for the address of the next instruction. The operation part and the mode bit of the instruction are transferred from $MBR$ into $OPR$ and $I$, respectively. Note that the address part of the instruction remains in $MBR$.

At time $t_3$ control makes a decision as to what should be the next computer cycle. If the operation code contains 111, the instruction is either a register-reference or input-output instruction. Therefore, if $q_7 = 1$, the $F$ flip-flop is set and control goes to the execute cycle. If $q_7 = 0$, the instruction is a memory-reference instruction. Now, if $I = 0$, it signifies that the instruction is a direct instruction so control goes to the execute cycle by setting $F$ to 1. If $I = 1$, it is an indirect instruction. Control goes to the indirect cycle by setting $R$ to 1. Note that the condition for going to the execute cycle is the complement of the condition for going to the indirect cycle, i.e., $(q'_7I)' = q_7 + I'$.

Remember that $F$ and $R$ are 0 during the fetch cycle. Setting $R$ to 1 results in $FR = 01$. Setting $F$ to one results in $FR = 10$. The timing variable that becomes 1 after $t_3$ is $t_0$. When the next $t_0$ becomes 1 the computer may be either in the execute or in the indirect cycle.

### *Indirect Cycle*

The indirect cycle is recognized by variable $c_1$. During this cycle, control reads the memory word where the address of the operand is to be found. The register transfer micro-operations for the indirect cycle are:

| | | |
|---|---|---|
| $c_1t_0$: | $MAR \leftarrow MBR(AD)$ | Transfer address part of instruction |
| $c_1t_1$: | $MBR \leftarrow M$ | Read address of operand |
| $c_1t_2$: | | Nothing |
| $c_1t_3$: | $F \leftarrow 1$, $R \leftarrow 0$ | Go to execute cycle |

The address part of the instruction is in *MBR*(5–16). These 12 bits are symbolized by *MBR*(*AD*). They are transferred into *MAR* and a memory cycle is initiated. Bits 5–12 of the word just read from memory contain the address of the operand. Now that the address of the operand is in *MBR*(*AD*), control goes to the execute cycle by setting *F* and clearing *R*. Note that nothing is done during time $t_2$. Changing *F* and *R* should be avoided during this time because timing variable $t_3$ that follows $t_2$ will find the computer in a different cycle. Changes from one cycle to another must be done at time $t_3$ so the next cycle can start with timing variable $t_0$.

### *Control Flow Chart*

Control reaches the execute cycle from two different paths, after the fetch cycle or after the indirect cycle. The flow chart of Fig. 5-6 illustrates the various paths available in the control unit. It summarizes the discussion up to this point and indicates the paths that the control takes during the execute cycle. A flow chart is a block diagram connected by directed lines. The directed lines between blocks designate the path to be taken from one step to the other. The two major types of blocks are (a) function blocks that show the operations to be performed (rectangular boxes), and (b) decision blocks that have two or more alternate paths dependent on the status of the condition indicated within a diamond-shaped box.

As shown in the flow chart, the start switch clears the cycle control flip-flops. This puts the computer in the fetch cycle. An instruction is read from memory and its operation and mode bits placed in control registers. If $q_7 = 1$, or if $q_7 = 0$ and $I = 0$, control goes to the execute cycle by setting *F* to 1. If $q_7 = 0$ and $I = 1$, it goes to the indirect cycle by setting *R* to 1. During the indirect cycle, control reads the address of the operand and moves to the execute cycle.

At the beginning of the execute cycle, the operation code of the instruction is in *OPR*, the first bit of the instruction is in *I*, and *MBR*(5–16) holds the rest of the instruction. If $q_7 = 0$, *MBR*(5–16) contains the *effective address*. This is the actual address of the operand and may have come from either the address part of the instruction (when $I = 0$) or from the indirect cycle (when $I = 1$). In either case, this address part in *MBR* is designated by *MBR*(*AD*). Control reads the operand found in the effective address and executes the memory reference instruction. If $q_7 = 1$, the bits in *MBR*(5–16) are part of the operation code. Control checks the bit in *I* to determine whether the instruction is a register-reference or an input-output type. It then checks the bits of *MBR*(5–16) to decide which specific instruction to execute. Cycle control flip-flop *F* is cleared after the execution of the instruction. This causes a return to the fetch cycle to start all over again to read and execute the next instruction.

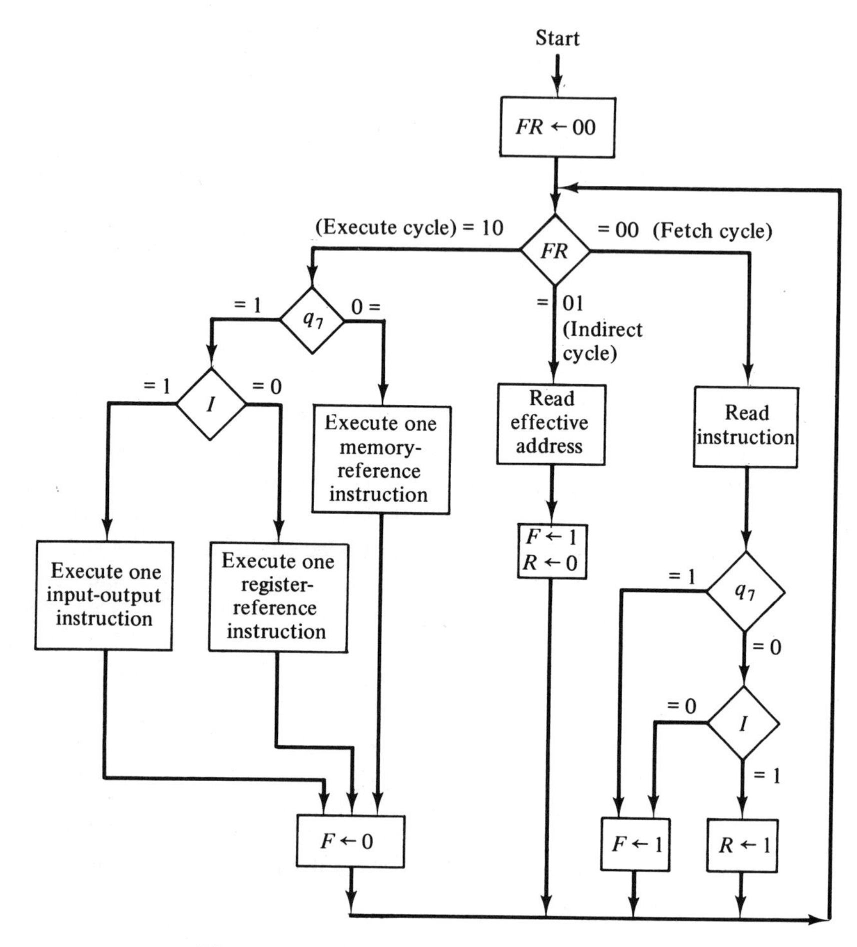


**Fig. 5-6** Flow chart for computer cycle control.

## 5-4 EXECUTION OF INSTRUCTIONS

In order to specify the micro-operations needed for the execution of each instruction, it is necessary that the function that they are intended to perform be defined precisely. Looking back to Table 5-1, where the instructions are listed, we find that some instructions have an ambiguous description. This is because the explanation of an instruction in words is usually lengthy, and not enough space is available in the table for such a lengthy explanation. We will now show that the function of computer instructions can be defined precisely by means of symbolic notation.

Table 5-3 lists the seven memory-reference instructions and their func-

**Table 5-3** *Memory reference instructions*

| *Symbol* | *Operation Decoder* | *Effective Address* | *Memory Word* | *Symbolic Designation* |
|---|---|---|---|---|
| AND | $q_0$ | $m$ | $M$ | $AC \leftarrow AC \wedge M$ |
| ADD | $q_1$ | $m$ | $M$ | $EAC \leftarrow AC + M$ |
| LDA | $q_2$ | $m$ | $M$ | $AC \leftarrow M$ |
| STA | $q_3$ | $m$ | $M$ | $M \leftarrow AC$ |
| BUN | $q_4$ | $m$ | — | $PC \leftarrow m$ |
| BSA | $q_5$ | $m$ | $M$ | $M \leftarrow PC, PC \leftarrow m + 1$ |
| ISZ | $q_6$ | $m$ | $M$ | $M \leftarrow M + 1$, if $(M + 1 = 0)$ then $(PC \leftarrow PC + 1)$ |

tions. The $q_i$ variable in the operation decoder that belongs to each instruction is included in the table. The effective address of the instruction is designated by the letter $m$. This address specifies a word in memory (the operand) and this word is designated by the letter $M$. The symbolic function for each instruction is a *macro-operation* and not a micro-operation. It is not a micro-operation because the statement

$$AC \leftarrow AC + M$$

cannot be performed during one clock pulse. Remember that data stored in memory words cannot be processed directly with external registers. The data must be read out of memory into processor registers where their binary content can be operated on. To implement the above macro-operation we need the following *sequence* of micro-operations:

$$MAR \leftarrow m$$
$$MBR \leftarrow M$$
$$AC \leftarrow AC + MBR$$

The effective address must be placed in $MAR$. A memory read operation reads the operand into $MBR$. Only after the operand is in $MBR$ can the control initiate the ADD micro-operation between two processor registers.

When writing a statement in symbolic notation, one must distinguish between a macro-operation and a micro-operation. As long as this distinction is recognized, there is no reason why one cannot use a register transfer language to specify the macro-operations defined by computer instructions.

We now explain the function of each instruction separately and list the micro-operations and control functions associated with each.

### *AND to* AC

This is an instruction that performs the AND logic operation on pairs of bits in the *AC* and the memory word specified by the effective address. The result of the operation remains in the *AC*. The micro-operations that execute this instruction are:

| | | |
|---|---|---|
| $q_0c_2t_0$: | $MAR \leftarrow MBR(AD)$ | Transfer effective address |
| $q_0c_2t_1$: | $MBR \leftarrow M$ | Read operand |
| $q_0c_2t_2$: | $AC \leftarrow AC \wedge MBR$ | AND with *AC* |
| $c_2t_3$: | $F \leftarrow 0$ | Go to fetch cycle |

The control functions for this instruction need variables $q_0$ and $c_2$. The first recognizes the code of the AND operation and the second recognizes the execute cycle. Three of the timing variables that occur during the execute cycle initiate the micro-operations for reading the operand from memory and performing the AND micro-operation. At time $t_3$, $F$ is cleared to 0. The timing signal that occurs after $t_3$ is $t_0$, so this $t_0$ finds the computer in the fetch cycle. Note that $q_0$ is not used with $t_3$. The condition for returning to the fetch cycle is common to all instructions and belongs at the end of the execute cycle no matter what instruction has been processed. As a consequence, the last statement in the above sequence will not be repeated again in the list of statements for the other instructions.

The reader should be reminded that the program counter (*PC*) is incremented during the fetch cycle at the same time that the current instruction is read from memory. Therefore, when control returns to the fetch cycle after executing the current instruction, it finds in *PC* the address of the next instruction.

### *ADD to* AC

This operation adds the content of the memory word specified by the effective address to the present value of the *AC*. The sum is transferred into the *AC* and the end-carry into the *E* flip-flop (*EAC* represents a register that combines the *E* and *AC* registers). The sign bit in the left-most position is treated as any other bit according to the signed-2's complement addition rule stated in Sec. 3-2. The micro-operations that execute this instruction are:

| | | |
|---|---|---|
| $q_1c_2t_0$: | $MAR \leftarrow MBR(AD)$ | Transfer effective address |
| $q_1c_2t_1$: | $MBR \leftarrow M$ | Read operand |
| $q_1c_2t_2$: | $EAC \leftarrow AC + MBR$ | Add to *AC* and store carry in *E* |

### *LDA:* *Load to* AC

This instruction transfers the memory word (specified by the effective address) into the *AC*. The word read from memory into *MBR* can be transferred to the *AC* by the micro-operation $AC \leftarrow MBR$. Such a statement defines a direct path from *MBR* to *AC*. However, we can utilize the existing path through the parallel-adder that is provided for the implementation of the *add* micro-operation. This path can be used if the *AC* is cleared prior to the transfer. Using the adder path, we specify the micro-operations for the LDA instruction as follows:

| | | |
|---|---|---|
| $q_2c_2t_0$: | $MAR \leftarrow MBR(AD)$ | Transfer effective address |
| $q_2c_2t_1$: | $MBR \leftarrow M,\ AC \leftarrow 0$ | Read operand, clear *AC* |
| $q_2c_2t_2$: | $AC \leftarrow AC + MBR$ | Add to *AC* |

The operand is read into *MBR* and the *AC* is cleared. The addition of *MBR* to the zero content of the *AC* results in the transfer of the content of *MBR* into the *AC*. Note that the carry is not transferred to *E*. We do not want to disturb the value of *E* in a direct transfer.

### *STA:* *Store* AC

This instruction stores the present content of the *AC* in the memory word specified by the effective address. The micro-operations that execute this instruction are:

| | | |
|---|---|---|
| $q_3c_2t_0$: | $MAR \leftarrow MBR(AD)$ | Transfer effective address |
| $q_3c_2t_1$: | $MBR \leftarrow AC$ | Transfer data to *MBR* |
| $q_3c_2t_2$: | $M \leftarrow MBR$ | Store word in memory |

### *BUN:* *Branch Unconditionally*

This instruction transfers the program to the instruction specified by the effective address. The instruction is listed with the memory-reference instructions because it has an address part. However, it does not need a reference to memory to read an operand (it may need a reference to memory to read the effective address if $I = 1$). Remember that *PC* holds the address of the instruction to be read from memory at the next fetch cycle. Normally, the *PC* is incremented to give the address of the next instruction in sequence. The programmer has the prerogative of specifying any other instruction out of sequence by using the BUN instruction. This instruction informs the control to take the effective address and transfer it into *PC*. During the next fetch cycle, this address becomes the address of the instruction that is read from memory. The micro-operation that performs this function is:

$q_4 c_2 t_0$: $PC \leftarrow MBR(AD)$ Transfer effective address to $PC$

Timing variables $t_1$ and $t_2$ are not used for this instruction and will not initiate any micro-operations.

The instructions discussed thus far are not difficult to comprehend compared to the function of the next two instructions. The next two memory-reference instructions require a slightly more complicated sequence of micro-operations. The usefulness of these two instructions will be demonstrated by the programming examples in the next chapter.

### *BSA: Branch and Save Return Address*

This instruction is useful for branching to a portion of the program called a *subroutine*. When executed, the instruction stores the address of the next instruction held in $PC$ (called the *return address*) into the word specified by the effective address $m$. The content of $m$ plus 1 is transferred into $PC$ to serve as the address of the instruction for the next fetch cycle (the beginning of the subroutine). The return from the subroutine to the program at the saved address is accomplished by means of an indirect BUN instruction. This instruction, when placed at the end of the subroutine, causes the program to transfer back to the position it left when it branched to the subroutine.

This process is depicted in the example of Fig. 5-7. The BSA instruction performs the macro-operations (see Table 5-3)

$$M \leftarrow PC, \quad PC \leftarrow m + 1$$

Suppose that the BSA instruction read during the fetch cycle is at address 25. During the execute cycle, $PC$ contains 26, since it was incremented during the fetch cycle. The content of $PC$ is transferred into the memory word specified by address $m$, and $m + 1$ is placed in $PC$. The next fetch cycle finds $PC$ with the value $m + 1$, so control continues to execute the subroutine program. The last instruction in the subroutine is an indirect ($I = 1$) BUN instruction with an address $m$. When this instruction is executed, control goes to the indirect cycle to read the effective address at location $m$. It finds the previously saved address 26, and places it into $PC$. (Note that here the effective address is 26 and not $m$.) The next fetch cycle finds $PC$ with the value 26 so control continues to execute the instruction at the return address. The BSA instruction performs the function usually referred to as a subroutine *call*. The last instruction in the subroutine performs the function referred to as a subroutine *return*.

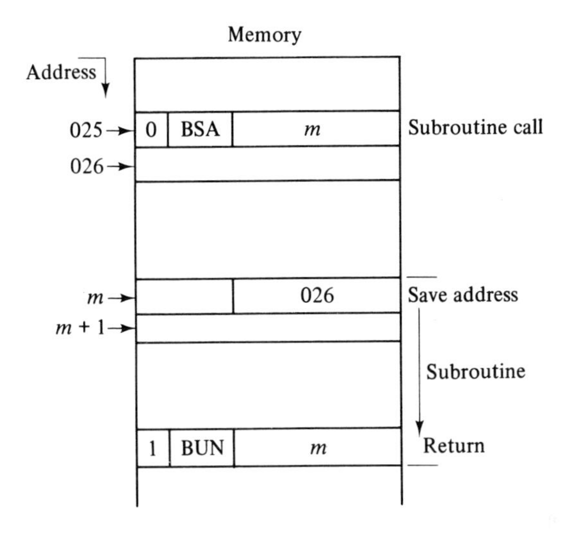


**Fig. 5-7** Demonstration of subroutine call and return.

The macro-operations for the BSA instruction are implemented in computer registers by a sequence of micro-operations as follows:

| | | |
|---|---|---|
| $q_5c_2t_0$: | $MAR \leftarrow MBR(AD)$, | Transfer $m$ to $MAR$ |
| | $MBR(AD) \leftarrow PC$, | Transfer $PC$ to be stored |
| | $PC \leftarrow MBR(AD)$ | Transfer $m$ to $PC$ |
| $q_5c_2t_1$: | $M \leftarrow MBR$ | Store previous content of $PC$ |
| $q_5c_2t_2$: | $PC \leftarrow PC + 1$ | Increment $m$ in $PC$ |

Three simultaneous micro-operations are performed during $t_0$. The contents of $PC$ and $MBR(AD)$ are swapped, and the effective address transferred to $MAR$. At this time, $m$ is in $MAR$ and the previous content of $PC$ in $MBR$. A memory write operation results in the implementation of $M \leftarrow PC$. The previous value of $m$, stored in $PC$, is incremented at time $t_2$ to implement $PC \leftarrow m + 1$.

### *ISZ: Increment and Skip-if-Zero*

The increment and skip instruction is useful for address modification and for counting the number of times a program loop is executed. A negative number previously stored in memory at address $m$ is read by the ISZ instruction. This number is incremented by 1 and stored back into memory. If, after it is incremented, the number reaches zero, the next instruction is skipped. Thus at the end of a program loop one inserts an ISZ instruction followed by a BUN instruction. If the stored number does not reach zero, the program returns to execute the loop again. If it reaches zero, the next instruction (BUN) is skipped and the program continues to execute instructions out of the loop.

The function of the ISZ instruction as stated in Table 5-3 is symbolized by the macro-statements:

$$M \leftarrow M + 1$$
$$\text{If } (M + 1 = 0) \text{ then } (PC \leftarrow PC + 1)$$

The sequence of micro-operations that implement the function are listed below:

| | | |
|---|---|---|
| $q_6c_2t_0$: | $MAR \leftarrow MBR(AD)$ | Transfer effective address |
| $q_6c_2t_1$: | $MBR \leftarrow M$ | Read memory word |
| $q_6c_2t_2$: | $MBR \leftarrow MBR + 1$ | Increment value |
| $q_6c_2t_3$: | $M \leftarrow MBR$, | Restore incremented word |
| | if $(MBR = 0)$ then $(PC \leftarrow PC + 1)$ | Skip if zero |

The memory word specified by the effective address is read from memory at time $t_1$. It is incremented in *MBR* at $t_2$. (Remember that no processing can be done with memory words; they must be read into a processor register such as *MBR* to be incremented.) At $t_3$, the incremented word is restored to memory, and *PC* is incremented if the word in *MBR* is zero. Incrementing *PC* during the execute cycle causes a skip of one instruction in the program because it is incremented during the fetch cycle also.

### *Register-Reference Instructions*

Register-reference instructions are recognized by the control when $q_7 = 1$ and $I = 0$. These instructions use the other 12 bits of the code to specify one of 12 different micro-operations. These 12 bits are available in *MBR*(5–16) during the execute cycle.

The micro-operation statements for the register-reference instructions are listed in Table 5-4. These instructions are executed with timing variable $t_3$, although any other timing variable could be used (except for the HLT instruction). Each control function needs the Boolean relation $q_7I'c_2t_3$ which we designate for convenience by the symbol $r$. The control function is distinguished by the one bit in *MBR*(5–16) which is equal to 1. By assigning the symbol $B_i$ to bit $i$ of *MBR*, all control functions can be simply denoted by $rB_i$. For example, the instruction CLA has the hexadecimal code 7800 which gives the binary equivalent 0111 1000 0000 0000. The first bit is a zero

**Table 5-4** *Register-reference instructions*

| Symbol | Hexadecimal Code | Control Function | Micro-Operation |
|---|---|---|---|
| | | $r = q_7 I' c_2 t_3$ | |
| | | $B_i = MBR(i)$ | |
| CLA | 7800 | $rB_5$: | $AC \leftarrow 0$ |
| CLE | 7400 | $rB_6$: | $E \leftarrow 0$ |
| CMA | 7200 | $rB_7$: | $AC \leftarrow \overline{AC}$ |
| CME | 7100 | $rB_8$: | $E \leftarrow \bar{E}$ |
| CIR | 7080 | $rB_9$: | cir $EAC$ |
| CIL | 7040 | $rB_{10}$: | cil $EAC$ |
| INC | 7020 | $rB_{11}$: | $EAC \leftarrow AC + 1$ |
| SPA | 7010 | $rB_{12}$: | If $(AC(1) = 0)$ then $(PC \leftarrow PC + 1)$ |
| SNA | 7008 | $rB_{13}$: | If $(AC(1) = 1)$ then $(PC \leftarrow PC + 1)$ |
| SZA | 7004 | $rB_{14}$: | If $(AC = 0)$ then $(PC \leftarrow PC + 1)$ |
| SZE | 7002 | $rB_{15}$: | If $(E = 0)$ then $(PC \leftarrow PC + 1)$ |
| HLT | 7001 | $rB_{16}$: | $S \leftarrow 0$ |

and is recognized from $I'$. The next three bits constitute the operation code and are recognized from decoder output $q_7$. Bit 5 in $MBR$ is 1 and is recognized from $B_5$. The control function that initiates the micro-operation for this instruction is $q_7 I' c_2 t_3 B_5 = rB_5$. Note that, since the register-reference instructions operate on a single register, they can be specified by micro-operation statements.

The first seven register-reference instructions perform clear, complement, circular shift, and increment micro-operations on the $AC$ and/or $E$ registers. The next four instructions cause a skip of the next instruction in sequence when a stated condition is satisfied. The skipping of the instruction is achieved by incrementing $PC$ once again (in addition to the incrementing during the fetch cycle). The condition control statements must be recognized as part of the control requirement. The $AC$ is positive when its sign bit $AC(1) = 0$; it is negative when $AC(1) = 1$. The content of $AC$ is zero $(AC = 0)$ if all cells of the register are zero. The HLT instruction clears the start-stop flip-flop $S$ and stops the timing sequences.

## 5-5 INPUT-OUTPUT AND INTERRUPT

A computer can serve no useful purpose unless it communicates with the external environment. Instructions and data stored in memory must come from some input device. Computational results must be transmitted to the user through some output device. Commerical computers include many different types of input and output devices. To demonstrate the most basic requirements for input and output communication, we will use as an illustration a teletypewriter unit for the basic computer. Further discussion of input-output organization can be found in Chap. 11.

A teletypewriter, also known by its trade name *Teletype*, has an electric typewriter keyboard, a printer, a paper-tape reader, and a paper-tape punch. The input device consists of either the typewriter keyboard or the paper-tape reader, with a manual switch available for selecting the one to be used. The output device consists of the typewriter printer or the paper-tape punch, with another switch available for selecting either device. The unit has a facility for producing a series of pulses equivalent to a binary code of the character whose key is struck. These pulses are transmitted into a shift register and constitute the input character. Serial pulses of an alphanumeric character code are sent to the printer where they are decoded to determine the character to be printed. The speed of the Teletype is very slow, usually about ten characters per second.

Instructions and data are transferred into the computer either in symbolic form through the keyboard or in binary form through the paper-tape reader. A 16-bit instruction or binary data word can be prepared on paper tape in two rows of eight bits each. The first punched row represents half of the word and the second row supplies the other half of the word. The two parts can be packed into one 16-bit computer word and stored in memory.

### *Input-Output Registers*

The teletypewriter sends and receives serial information. Each quantity of information has eight bits of an alphanumeric code. The serial information from the keyboard is shifted into an input register. The serial information for the printer is stored in an output register. These two registers communicate with the teletypewriter serially and with the *AC* in parallel. The register configuration is shown in Fig. 5-8.

The input register *INPR* consists of eight bits and holds an alphanumeric input information. The one-bit input flag *FGI* is a control flip-flop. The flag

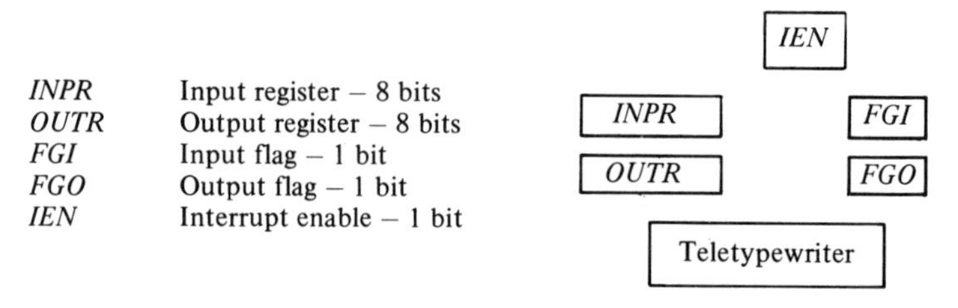


**Fig. 5-8** Registers for input, output, and interrupt.

bit is set when new information is available in the input device and cleared when the information is accepted by the computer. The flag is needed to synchronize the timing rate differential between the input device and the computer. The process of information transfer is as follows: Initially, the input flag *FGI* is cleared. When a key is struck, an eight-bit code is shifted into *INPR* and the input flag is set to 1. As long as the flag is set, the information in *INPR* cannot be changed by striking another key. The computer checks the flag bit; if it is 1, the information from *INPR* is transferred in parallel into the *AC* and *FGI* is cleared. Once the flag is cleared, new information can be shifted into *INPR* by striking another key.

The output register *OUTR* works similarly but the direction of information flow is reversed. Initially, the output flag (*FGO*) is set to 1. The computer checks the flag bit; if it is 1, the information from *AC* is transferred in parallel to *OUTR* and *FGO* is cleared. The output device accepts the coded information, prints the corresponding character, and when the operation is completed, it sets *FGO* to 1. The computer does not load a new character into *OUTR* when *FGO* is 0 because this condition indicates that the output device is in the process of printing the character.

The process of communication just described is sometimes called *hand-shaking*. The computer keeps checking the flag bit and when it finds it set, it initiates an information transfer. The difference of information flow rate between the processor unit and that of the input-output device makes this type of hand-shaking inefficient. To see why this is inefficient, consider a computer that can go through the fetch and execute cycles in 10 $\mu$sec. The input-output device can transfer information at a maximum rate of 10 characters per second. This is equivalent to one character every 100,000 $\mu$sec. Two instructions are executed when the computer checks the flag bit and decides not to transfer the information. This means that, at the maximum rate, the computer will check the flag 50,000 times between each transfer. The computer is wasting time while checking the flag instead of doing some other useful processing task.

An alternate hand-shaking procedure is to let the external device inform the computer when it is ready for the transfer. In the meantime the processor can be busy with other tasks. This type of hand-shaking is accomplished by means of an interrupt facility. While the computer is running a program, it does not check the flags. However, when a flag is set the computer is momentarily interrupted from proceeding with the current program and is informed of the fact that a flag has been set. The computer deviates momentarily from what it is doing to take care of the input or output transfer. It then returns to the current program to continue what it was doing before the interrupt. The hardware that takes care of this procedure is explained below. At this time we explain the function of the interrupt enable flip-flop shown in Fig. 5-8.

The interrupt enable flip-flop (*IEN*) can be set and cleared by two instructions. When it is cleared, the flags cannot interrupt the computer and are neglected. When *IEN* is set, the computer can be interrupted. This flip-flop provides the programmer with a capability for making a decision whether to use the interrupt facility or not. If he issues an instruction to clear *IEN*, then he is saying in effect that he does not want his program to be interrupted. If he sets it, he has available the interrupt facility at his disposal.

### *Input-Output Instructions*

Input and output instructions are needed for transferring information to and from the *AC* register, for checking the flag bits, and for controlling the interrupt enable flip-flop. These instructions are listed in Table 5-5. They have

**Table 5-5** *Input-output instructions*

| *Symbol* | *Hexadecimal Code* | *Description* | *Function* |
|---|---|---|---|
| INP | F800 | Input character to *AC* | $AC(9\text{–}16) \leftarrow INPR,\ FGI \leftarrow 0$ |
| OUT | F400 | Output character from *AC* | $OUTR \leftarrow AC(9\text{–}16),\ FGO \leftarrow 0$ |
| SKI | F200 | Skip on input flag | If $(FGI = 1)$ then $(PC \leftarrow PC + 1)$ |
| SKO | F100 | Skip on output flag | If $(FGO = 1)$ then $(PC \leftarrow PC + 1)$ |
| ION | F080 | Interrupt on | $IEN \leftarrow 1$ |
| IOF | F040 | Interrupt off | $IEN \leftarrow 0$ |

an operation code 111 with $I = 1$, which gives for the first digit of the instruction the hexadecimal digit F. The remaining 12 bits contain a single 1 and eleven 0's for each instruction. The INP instruction transfers the input information into the eight low-order bits of the *AC* and also clears the input flag. The OUT instruction transfers eight bits into the output registers and clears the flag. The next two instructions check the status of the flags and cause a skip of the next instruction if the flag is 1. The instruction that is skipped will normally be a branch instruction to return and check the flag again. This instuction is not skipped if the flag is 0. If the flag is 1, the branch instruction is skipped and an input or output instruction is executed. The last two instructions set and clear the interrupt enable bit, respectively.

The micro-operations needed to execute each instruction are listed under the function column in Table 5-5. They are executed by the control during the execute cycle $c_2$ at time $t_3$. The input-output instructions are recognized by variable $q_7I$ and the bit $B_i$ in *MBR* that is equal to 1. Thus, the INP instruction is executed with the following control function:

$$q_7Ic_2t_3B_5: \quad AC(9\text{–}16) \leftarrow INPR,\ FGI \leftarrow 0$$

The other instructions have a similar control function, except for the $B_i$ variable which is different in each.

*Interrupt Cycle*

So far we have shown three cycles for the computer: fetch, indirect, and execute. When the cycle control flip-flops $F$ and $R$ are both 1's, the computer goes to an interrupt cycle. This cycle is recognized by the cycle decoder output $c_3$ (see Table 5-2). It is initiated from the execute cycle after the current instruction is completed. Previously we have assumed that the last micro-operation in the execute cycle is:

$$c_2t_3: \quad F \leftarrow 0$$

which returns control to the fetch cycle. We now modify this condition as shown in the flow-chart of Fig. 5-9. *IEN* is checked at the end of each execute cycle. If it is 0, it indicates that the programmer does not want to use the interrupt, so control goes to the next fetch cycle by clearing $F$. If *IEN* is 1, control checks the flag bits. If both flags are 0, it indicates that neither the input nor the output registers are ready for transfer of information. In this case, control goes back to the fetch cycle. If any flag is set to 1, control goes to the interrupt cycle by setting $R$ to 1 ($F$ is already set to 1 during the execute cycle).

The interrupt cycle is a hardware implementation of a branch and save address operation. The current address in *PC* is stored in a specific location where it can be found later when the program returns to the instruction at which it was interrupted. This location may be a processor register or a memory location. We choose here the memory location at address 0 as the word for storing the return address. Control then inserts address 1 into *PC* and moves to the next fetch cycle. It also clears *IEN* so no more interruptions can occur until the interrupt request from the flag has been serviced.

At the beginning of the next fetch cycle, the instruction that is read from memory is in address 1 since this is the content of *PC*. At memory address 1, the programmer must store a branch instruction that sends the computer to a service program where it checks the flags, determines which flag is set and then transfers the required input or output information. Once this is done, the instruction ION is executed to set *IEN* to 1 (to enable other interrupts), and the next instruction executed returns the program to the location where it was interrupted. The instruction that returns the computer to the original program is:

| I | BUN | 0 |
|---|---|---|
| 1 | 100 | 0000 0000 0000 |

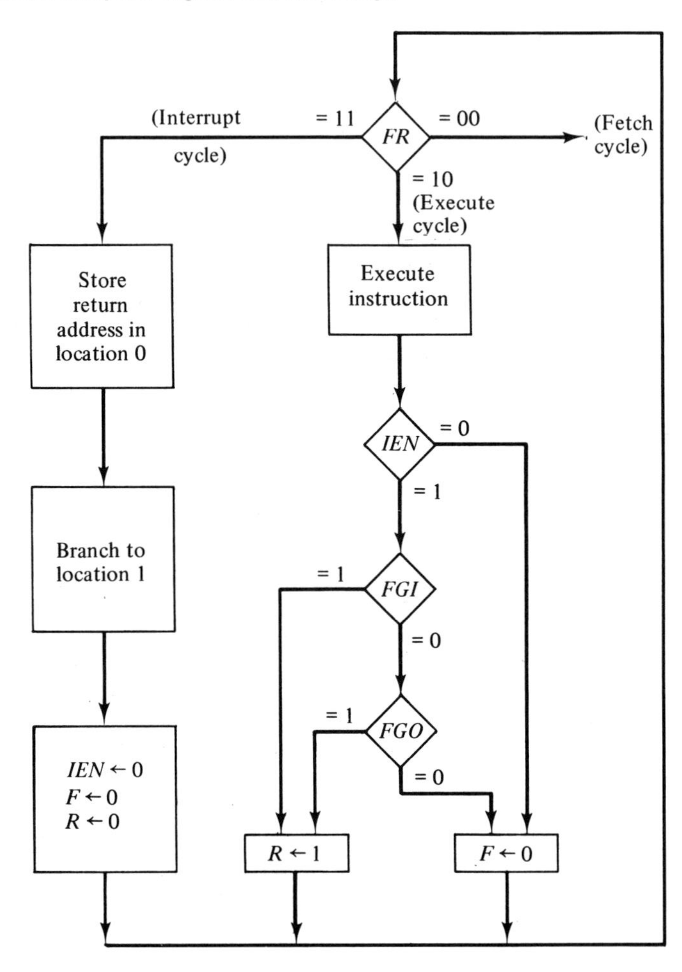


**Fig. 5-9** Flow chart for interrupt cycle.

This is a branch indirect instruction with an address part of 0. When this instruction is read during the fetch cycle, control goes to the indirect cycle (because $I = 1$) to read the effective address. But the effective address is in location 0 and is the return address that was stored there during the previous interrupt cycle. The execution of the above instruction results in placing into *PC* the return address from location 0.

We are now ready to list the register transfer relations for the interrupt cycle. The interrupt cycle is initiated at the end of each execute cycle by the following micro-operations:

$c_2 t_3$: If $[IEN \wedge (FGI \vee FGO) = 1]$ then $(R \leftarrow 1)$

If $[IEN \wedge (FGI \vee FGO) = 0]$ then $(F \leftarrow 0)$

The symbols $\wedge$ and $\vee$ stand for logic AND and OR, respectively. These conditional control statements replace the previously assumed micro-operation that cleared $F$ unconditionally. These statements are in accordance with the requirements specified in the flow chart of Fig. 5-9.

Note that when the ION (interrupt on) instruction is executed by control, it is done during time $t_3$ as follows:

$$q_7 I c_2 B_9 t_3: \qquad IEN \leftarrow 1$$

The micro-operation may be executed at the same time that the conditional micro-operation listed above is executed because they have common variables in their control functions. If this occurs, and $IEN = 0$ during $t_3$, the computer goes to the fetch cycle and $IEN$ does not become 1 until the next $t_0$ (in the fetch cycle). So an ION instruction would not cause an interrupt (if a flag is on) until the end of the *next* execute cycle. This insures that the return address is placed in $PC$ before another interrupt can occur.

The interrupt cycle occurs when $F = R = 1$ which makes variable $c_3 = 1$. The micro-operations for the interrupt cycle are:

| | | |
|---|---|---|
| $c_3 t_0$: | $MBR(AD) \leftarrow PC,\ PC \leftarrow 0$ | Transfer return address and clear $PC$ |
| $c_3 t_1$: | $MAR \leftarrow PC,\ PC \leftarrow PC + 1$ | Transfer 0 to $MAR$, set $PC$ to 1 |
| $c_3 t_2$: | $M \leftarrow MBR,\ IEN \leftarrow 0$ | Store return address and clear interrupt enable |
| $c_3 t_3$: | $F \leftarrow 0,\ R \leftarrow 0$ | Go to fetch cycle. |

The return address is in $PC$ and must be transferred to $MBR$ for storage in memory. The $PC$ is cleared and then transferred to $MAR$. At time $t_2$, $MAR$ contains 0 and $MBR$ has the return address. A memory-write operation stores the return address in location 0. $PC$ is incremented at $t_1$ so it will contain address 1 at the beginning of the next fetch cycle. $IEN$ is cleared and control returns to the fetch cycle.

## 5-6 DESIGN OF COMPUTER

The basic computer consists of a memory unit, a teletypewriter, a master clock generator, eight registers, eight flip-flops, three decoders, and a number of control logic gates. The memory and teletypewriter are standard units that can be purchased as finished products. The master clock generator is a common clock pulse source, usually an oscillator, that generates a periodic train of pulses. These pulses are fanned out by means of inverters and buffers and distributed over the entire system. Each pulse must reach every register and flip-flop at the same instant. Phasing delays are sometimes needed intermittently so that difference in transmission delays is uniform throughout.

The other components in the computer are decoders and registers which are available in standard MSI ICs. Flip-flops and gates are available in standard SSI ICs. From the list of register transfer statements developed for the computer, it is possible to determine the registers, flip-flops, and gates that are needed for the design of the computer. To illustrate with a specific example, consider the operation register *OPR* and its associated register transfer statement:

$$c_0t_2: \quad OPR \leftarrow MBR(OP)$$

**Table 5-6** *Control functions and micro-operations for the basic computer*

| | | |
|---|---|---|
| fetch | $c_0t_0$: | $MAR \leftarrow PC$ |
| | $c_0t_1$: | $MBR \leftarrow M, PC \leftarrow PC + 1$ |
| | $c_0t_2$: | $OPR \leftarrow MBR(OP), I \leftarrow MBR(I)$ |
| | $q_7'Ic_0t_3$: | $R \leftarrow 1$ |
| | $(q_7 + I')c_0t_3$: | $F \leftarrow 1$ |
| indirect | $c_1t_0$: | $MAR \leftarrow MBR(AD)$ |
| | $c_1t_1$: | $MBR \leftarrow M$ |
| | $c_1t_3$: | $F \leftarrow 1, R \leftarrow 0$ |
| interrupt | $c_3t_0$: | $MBR(AD) \leftarrow PC, PC \leftarrow 0$ |
| | $c_3t_1$: | $MAR \leftarrow PC, PC \leftarrow PC + 1$ |
| | $c_3t_2$: | $M \leftarrow MBR, IEN \leftarrow 0$ |
| | $c_3t_3$: | $F \leftarrow 0, R \leftarrow 0$ |
| execute | $c_2t_3$: | If $[IEN \wedge (FGI \vee FGO) = 1]$ then $(R \leftarrow 1)$,<br>If $[IEN \wedge (FGI \vee FGO) = 0]$ then $(F \leftarrow 0)$ |
| AND | $q_0c_2t_0$: | $MAR \leftarrow MBR(AD)$ |
| | $q_0c_2t_1$: | $MBR \leftarrow M$ |
| | $q_0c_2t_2$: | $AC \leftarrow AC \wedge MBR$ |
| ADD | $q_1c_2t_0$: | $MAR \leftarrow MBR(AD)$ |
| | $q_1c_2t_1$: | $MBR \leftarrow M$ |
| | $q_1c_2t_2$: | $EAC \leftarrow AC + MBR$ |
| LDA | $q_2c_2t_0$: | $MAR \leftarrow MBR(AD)$ |
| | $q_2c_2t_1$: | $MBR \leftarrow M, AC \leftarrow 0$ |
| | $q_2c_2t_2$: | $AC \leftarrow AC + MBR$ |
| STA | $q_3c_2t_0$: | $MAR \leftarrow MBR(AD)$ |
| | $q_3c_2t_1$: | $MBR \leftarrow AC$ |
| | $q_3c_2t_2$: | $M \leftarrow MBR$ |
| BUN | $q_4c_2t_0$: | $PC \leftarrow MBR(AD)$ |
| BSA | $q_5c_2t_0$: | $MAR \leftarrow MBR(AD), PC \leftarrow MBR(AD), MBR(AD) \leftarrow PC$ |
| | $q_5c_2t_1$: | $M \leftarrow MBR$ |
| | $q_5c_2t_2$: | $PC \leftarrow PC + 1$ |
| ISZ | $q_6c_2t_0$: | $MAR \leftarrow MBR(AD)$ |
| | $q_6c_2t_1$: | $MBR \leftarrow M$ |
| | $q_6c_2t_2$: | $MBR \leftarrow MBR + 1$ |
| | $q_6c_2t_3$: | $M \leftarrow MBR$, if $(MBR = 0)$ then $(PC \leftarrow PC + 1)$ |

***Table 5-6—Cont.***

| | | |
|---|---|---|
| | $q_7I'c_2t_3 = r$ | (common for all register-reference instructions) |
| | $MBR(i) = B_i$ | $i = 5, 6, \ldots, 16$ |
| CLA | $rB_5$: | $AC \leftarrow 0$ |
| CLE | $rB_6$: | $E \leftarrow 0$ |
| CMA | $rB_7$: | $AC \leftarrow \overline{AC}$ |
| CME | $rB_8$: | $E \leftarrow \bar{E}$ |
| CIR | $rB_9$: | cir $EAC$ |
| CIL | $rB_{10}$: | cil $EAC$ |
| INC | $rB_{11}$: | $EAC \leftarrow AC + 1$ |
| SPA | $rB_{12}$: | If $(AC(1) = 0)$ then $(PC \leftarrow PC + 1)$ |
| SNA | $rB_{13}$: | If $(AC(1) = 1)$ then $(PC \leftarrow PC + 1)$ |
| SZA | $rB_{14}$: | If $(AC = 0)$ then $(PC \leftarrow PC + 1)$ |
| SZE | $rB_{15}$: | If $(E = 0)$ then $(PC \leftarrow PC + 1)$ |
| HLT | $rB_{16}$: | $S \leftarrow 0$ |
| | $q_7Ic_2t_3 = p$ | (common for all input-output instructions) |
| | $MBR(i) = B_i$ | $i = 5, 6, \ldots, 10$ |
| INP | $pB_5$: | $AC(9\text{–}16) \leftarrow INPR$, $FGI \leftarrow 0$ |
| OUT | $pB_6$: | $OUTR \leftarrow AC(9\text{–}16)$, $FGO \leftarrow 0$ |
| SKI | $pB_7$: | If $(FGI = 1)$ then $(PC \leftarrow PC + 1)$ |
| SKO | $pB_8$: | If $(FGO = 1)$ then $(PC \leftarrow PC + 1)$ |
| ION | $pB_9$: | $IEN \leftarrow 1$ |
| IOF | $pB_{10}$: | $IEN \leftarrow 0$ |

This statement implies that the computer needs an AND gate with inputs $c_0$ and $t_2$ coming from the cycle decoder and timing decoder, respectively. The output of the gate must go to the load input of a 3-bit register with parallel-load capability. The data inputs to *OPR* are bits 2, 3, and 4 of *MBR*.

The control functions and micro-operations for the entire computer are summarized in Table 5-6. This table describes in a very concise form the internal organization of the basic computer. It also gives all the information that is needed for designing the logic circuits of the computer. The control functions and conditional control statements listed in the table formulate the Boolean functions for the gates in the control unit. The list of micro-operations specifies the type of control inputs needed for the registers. A register transfer language is useful not only for describing the internal organization of a digital system but also for specifying the logic circuits needed for its design.

### Accumulator Register

The design process will be illustrated by going through the procedure for designing the accumulator register (*AC*). This is the most complicated register in the computer because it serves as a processor register. The first step in the design is to scan the register transfer statements and retrieve all those statements that change the content of the *AC*. A micro-operation that changes the content of a register is recognized by the presence of its symbol on the left side of the arrow. To recognize the micro-operations belonging to the *AC* we scan Table 5-6 and retrieve all those statements that have the *AC* symbol on the left side of the arrow. The micro-operations for the other registers are obtained in a similar manner.

The register transfer statements that we find for the *AC* are listed below:

| | | |
|---|---|---|
| $q_0c_2t_2$: | $AC \leftarrow AC \wedge MBR$ | AND with *MBR* |
| $q_1c_2t_2 + q_2c_2t_2$: | $AC \leftarrow AC + MBR$ | Add |
| $q_2c_2t_1 + rB_5$: | $AC \leftarrow 0$ | Clear |
| $rB_7$: | $AC \leftarrow \overline{AC}$ | Complement |
| $rB_9$: | shr $AC$, $AC(1) \leftarrow E$ | Shift-right |
| $rB_{10}$: | shl $AC$, $AC(16) \leftarrow E$ | Shift-left |
| $rB_{11}$: | $AC \leftarrow AC + 1$ | Increment |
| $pB_5$: | $AC(9\text{–}16) \leftarrow INPR$ | Transfer *INPR* |

Note that the *add* micro-operation occurs twice, and the two control functions are combined by a Boolean OR operation. They are also combined for the *clear* micro-operation. The circular shifts are separated from *E* and converted to shift micro-operations with *E* entering the serial input of the *AC*. The transfer from *INPR* is to the eight low-order bits of the *AC*.

The control functions associated with the *AC* are generated by logic gates. The accumulator register itself is a general purpose register that requires eight different control inputs in addition to clock pulses. Such a register is available in integrated circuit form.†

Part of the hardware implementation for the *AC* is shown in Fig. 5-10. The rest of the implementation is illustrated in Fig. 5-11. Two diagrams are needed because of the large number of functions associated with this register. The total implementation is the combination of these two diagrams.

Figure 5-10 shows the gates that generate six of the control functions for the *AC*. They are derived directly from the control functions listed with the register transfer statements above. The outputs of *MBR* are needed for the AND micro-operation and for the control functions that generate the register-reference and input-output micro-operations. Note that the *E* variable is applied to the serial inputs of the *AC* register during the shift micro-operations.

Figure 5-11 shows the circuit that implements the *add* and *transfer* micro-operations. The *AC* and parallel-adder are divided into two parts with eight

†For example, Texas Instruments type SN74S281 or RCA type CD4057.

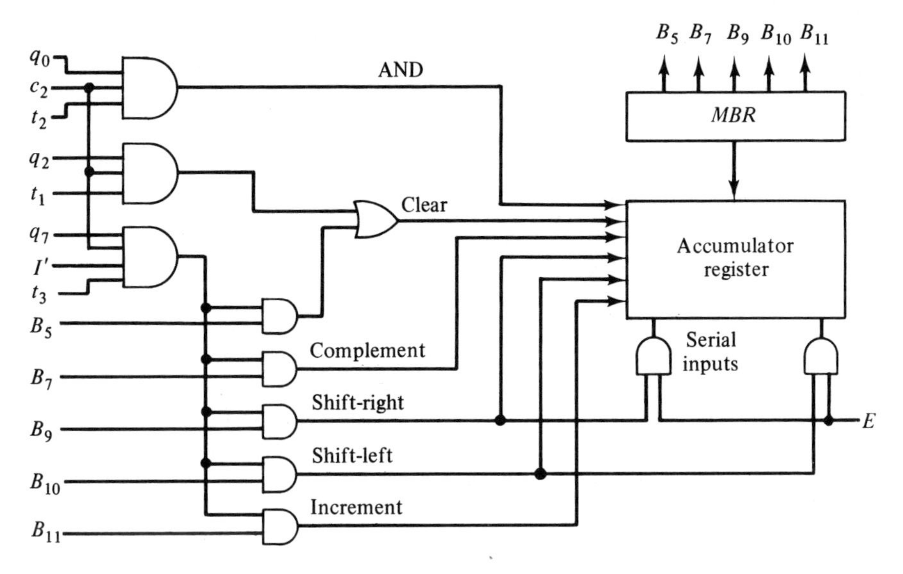


**Fig. 5-10** Block diagram of accumulator (See Fig. 5-11).

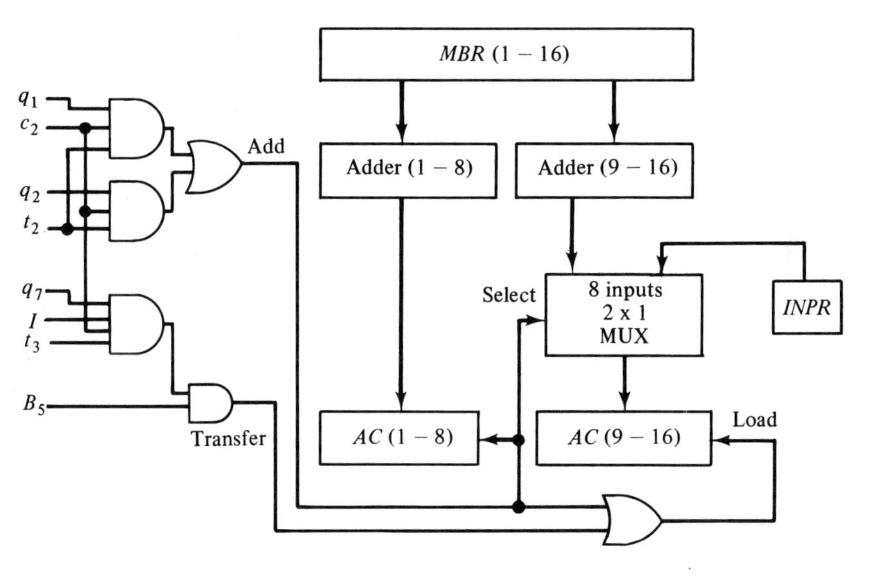


**Fig. 5-11** Block diagram of accumulator (See Fig. 5-10).

bits in each. An 8-input, 2 by 1 multiplexer is inserted at the inputs of the eight low-order bits of the *AC*. The multiplexer chooses the eight outputs of *INPR* when its single select line is 0, and the outputs of the parallel-adder when the select line is 1. An *add* micro-operation loads all 16 bits from the parallel-adder.

Note that the outputs of *MBR* for the AND micro-operation (shown in Fig. 5-10) do not have to go through the multiplexer if the AND micro-operation is implemented as in Fig. 4-14 (Sec. 4-4). This implementation requires that the complements of *MBR* be ANDed with the AND control function and then applied to the *K* inputs of each *JK* flip-flop in the *AC* register. Figure 4-14 also shows the internal implementation of the *clear* and *complement* micro-operations. The *shift* micro-operations dictate that the *AC* be a bidirectional shift-register. The *increment* micro-operation specifies that the *AC* acts also as a counter.

The other registers in the computer can be designed in a similar manner. The register transfer statements for a particular register are first retrieved from Table 5-6 and listed separately. The list of control functions so obtained specifies the logic gates that control the register. The list of micro-operations specifies the types of digital function that must be incorporated within the register.

### *Computer Console*

Any computer has a control panel or console with switches and indicator lights to allow manual and visual communication between an operator and the computer. The communication is needed for starting the operation of the computer and for maintenance purposes. The indicator lights inform the operator of the status of registers in the computer. An indicator light when connected to the output of a flip-flop will light when the flip-flop is set and turn off when the flip-flop is cleared. The purpose of the switches is to start, stop, and manually communicate with the computer.

The basic computer may need indicator lights for the eight registers in the system. These are: *PC*, *MAR*, *MBR*, *AC*, *OPR*, *SC*, *INPR*, and *OUTR*. The eight single flip-flops may have indicator lights as well: *I*, *E*, *S*, *F*, *R*, *IEN*, *FGI*, and *FGO*.

A set of switches for the basic computer may include: a start switch, a stop switch, a set of 16 switches for loading a number manually into the *AC*, and a set of 12 switches for loading an address into *PC*. A "memory-read" and a "memory-write" switch may be helpful for communicating manually with the memory unit.

## 5-7 CONCLUDING REMARKS

The basic computer, whose internal organization is described in this chapter, is a simplified version of the first minicomputer introduced in 1964.†

†The basic computer is similar but not identical to the PDP-8 computer manufactured by Digital Equipment Corp., Maynard, Massachusetts.

Although the basic computer is simple, it is far from useless. Its scope is quite limited when compared to commercial computer systems, yet it encompasses enough functional capabilities to demonstrate the power of a stored program, general purpose digital computer. It is suitable for construction in the laboratory with ICs, and the finished product can be a useful system capable of processing any type of binary data.

This chapter demonstrates that a register transfer language is a convenient tool when dealing with the architecture of computers. Specifically it can be used for the following tasks.

1. Defining computer instructions precisely by macro-operation statements.
2. Defining the internal organization of a computer by a sequence of micro-operations and control functions.
3. Designing a computer from a specified list of register transfer relations.

Each sequence of statements listed in this chapter is preceeded and followed by an explanation in words. The explanations are not necessary once a statement is written down because the statement itself tells the whole story. The explanations are included for those readers who are not thoroughly familiar with the register transfer symbology. In an industrial situation, the specifications for the basic computer could be condensed to a few pages. All that would be needed is to specify the registers, tabulate the instructions and their format, define the control network, and list the control functions and micro-operations as they appear in Table 5-6.

The architecture of a computer is influenced by its intended use, i.e., by the type of programs that are written for it. Knowing how the computer is used may help to understand its internal organization. For this reason, Chap. 6 is devoted to the study of the programming aspects of digital computers.

The computer introduced in this chapter provides the basic concepts from which one can proceed to study more advanced and complex computer systems. These advanced concepts are introduced in the chapters that follow.

Chapter 7 presents a more realistic organization of a processor unit in modern digital computers. The instruction formats for the basic computer are too simple and are oriented towards a processor unit with one accumulator register. Commerical computers have multiple processor registers and use more complicated instruction word formats.

The control unit of a computer is more efficiently implemented by means of a control memory and a microprogram. This type of control organization is presented in Chap. 8.

The only arithmetic instruction in the basic computer is the addition of two binary numbers. In Chap. 9 we show the procedure for including other arithmetic operations such as subtraction, multiplication, and division. In

Chap. 10 we show how to include arithmetic operations for floating-point and decimal data.

The input, output, and interrupt in the basic computer are very crude compared to what is available in commercial computers. Chapter 11 discusses a more realistic input-output organization and interrupt facility.

Finally, the memory unit in most computers communicates not only with the processor but also with other external devices. Large computer systems have a memory hierarchy that communicates with many processor units. Chapter 12 discusses the memory organization in large computer systems.

## REFERENCES

1. MANO, M. M., *Computer Logic Design*, Englewood Cliffs, N.J.: Prentice-Hall, Inc., 1972.
2. FOSTER, C. C., *Computer Architecture*, New York: Van Nostrand Reinhold Co., 1970.
3. SOUCEK, B., *Minicomputers in Data Processing and Simulation*, New York: John Wiley & Sons, Inc., 1972.
4. *Small Computer Handbook*, Maynard, Mass.: Digital Equipment Corp., 1973.
5. HILL, F. J., and G. R. PETERSON, *Digital Systems: Hardware Organization and Design*, New York: John Wiley & Sons, Inc., 1973.
6. BOOTH, T. L., *Digital Networks and Computer Systems*, New York: John Wiley & Sons, Inc., 1971.
7. SOBEL, H. S., *Introduction to Digital Computer Design*, Reading, Mass.: Addison Wesley Publishing Co., 1970.

## PROBLEMS

5-1 A memory unit has a capacity of 65,536 words of 25 bits each. It is used in conjunction with a general purpose computer. The instruction code is divided into four parts: an indirect mode bit, operation code, two bits that specify a processor register, and an address part.
(a) What is the maximum number of operations that can be incorporated in the computer if an instruction is stored in one memory word?
(b) Draw the instruction-word format indicating the number of bits and the function of each part.
(c) How many processor registers are there in the computer and how many bits in each?
(d) How many bits are there in *MBR*, *MAR*, and *PC*?

5-2 Suppose the word in address 14 of Fig. 5-2(c) is an instruction and the word at memory address 36 contains the binary equivalent of 9. What is the operand?

5-3 What is the difference between an immediate, a direct, and an indirect address instruction? How many references to memory are needed for each type of instruction to bring an operand into a processor register?

5-4 Show that the logic operations AND, complement, and clear are sufficient to implement the logic operations listed in Table 4-5.

5-5 Show that the instruction CIR (circulate right $E$ and $AC$) together with other instructions can be used to implement (a) a logic shift-right of the $AC$, (b) an arithmetic shift-right of the content of the $AC$ when negative numbers are in signed-2's complement representation (the sign bit is in bit 1 of $AC$ and the binary number may be positive or negative).

5-6 What are the two instructions needed in the basic computer in order to set the $E$ register to 1?

5-7 A digital computer has a memory unit with a capacity of 8,192 words, 36 bits per word. The instruction code format consists of 5 bits for the operation part and 13 bits for the address part (no indirect mode bit). Two instructions are packed in one memory word and a 36 bit instruction register $IR$ is available in the control unit. Formulate the fetch and execute cycles for the computer.

5-8 A computer is available *without* a program counter ($PC$). Instead, all instructions contain three parts: an operation code, an address of an operand, and the address of the next instruction. The operation code consists of 6 bits and the computer has a memory unit of 8,192 words.

(a) How many bits must be in a memory word if an instruction is stored in one word? Show the instruction word format.

(b) What other register is needed in the control unit besides an operation register?

(c) List the micro-operations for the instruction fetch cycle of this computer. Use any register specified in part (b).

5-9 List the eight registers and eight single flip-flops in the basic computer. Give their abbreviated name and full name. State the number of bits in each register. State, in one sentence for each, the function of each register and flip-flop.

5-10 An instruction in address $(021)_{16}$ in the basic computer has a mode bit $I = 0$, an operation code of the AND instruction, and an address part equal to $(083)_{16}$. The memory word at address $(083)_{16}$ contains the operand $(B8F2)_{16}$ and the content of the $AC$ is $(A937)_{16}$. Go over the fetch and execute cycles and determine the content of the following registers at the end of the execute cycle: $PC$, $MAR$, $MBR$, $AC$, and $OPR$. Repeat the problem six more times starting with the operation code of another memory reference instruction.

5-11 The content of the $AC$ in the basic computer is $(A937)_{16}$ and the content of $E$ is 1. Determine the content of the $AC$, $E$, $PC$, and $MBR$ after the execution of the CLA instruction. Repeat eleven more times starting from each one of the register-reference instruction. The initial value of $PC$ is $(021)_{16}$.

5-12 A computer similar to the basic computer has six timing signals $t_0$–$t_5$ and only one flip-flop $F$ for cycle control. When $F = 0$, control performs the fetch and indirect cycle (if necessary). When $F = 1$, it executes the instruction. List the control functions and micro-operation for the computer when $F = 0$.

5-13 Some of the instructions for the computer specified in Prob. 5-12 are listed below. List the control functions and micro-operations that execute these instructions. Use any convenient set of micro-operations that are known to be implemented by hardware.

| | *Operation Code* | *Symbolic Function* | *Description* |
|---|---|---|---|
| (a) | 000 | $AC \leftarrow AC \oplus M$ | Exclusive OR to $AC$. |
| (b) | 001 | If $(AC > 0)$ then $(PC \leftarrow m)$ | Branch if $AC$ positive and non-zero. |
| (c) | 010 | $M \leftarrow M + AC$ | Add $AC$ to memory. $AC$ doesn't change. |
| (d) | 011 | $AC \leftarrow AC - M$ | Subtract memory operand from $AC$. |
| (e) | 100 | $M \leftarrow AC, AC \leftarrow M$ | Swap $AC$ and memory word. |
| (f) | 101 | If $(M = AC)$ then $(PC \leftarrow PC + 1)$ | Skip next instruction if $AC$ is equal to $M$. $AC$ doesn't change. |

5-14 It is possible to reduce the time it takes the control to process a register-reference instruction in the basic computer. Show that if the register-reference instructions are executed with timing variable $t_3$ during the fetch cycle, the control will process them in half the time it now takes. Show the register transfer relations for the fetch cycle that will take care of this proposed change.

5-15 It is possible to combine two register-reference instruction codes to produce a new code for a different instruction. For example:
(a) A "2's complement $AC$" instruction can use the code 7220
(b) A "set $E$ to 1" instruction can use the code 7500
(c) A "set $AC$ to all 1's" instruction can use the code 7A00
What changes must be made in the control functions for realizing these additional capabilities?

5-16 Draw a diagram similar to Fig. 5-7 to demonstrate the interrupt cycle. What is the difference between the BSA instruction and the interrupt cycle? Explain why the BSA instruction cannot fulfill the function of the interrupt cycle.

5-17 Draw a flow chart showing all the paths control takes when executing an input-output instruction.

5-18 Draw the logic diagram of the gates that set and reset flip-flops $F$ and $R$ in the basic computer.

5-19 Obtain the list of register transfer statements that change the content of *MAR*. Show the hardware implementation of this register.

5-20 Repeat Prob. 5-19 for the *PC* register.

5-21 Suppose that you have an integrated circuit that includes an accumulator register together with all the control inputs required for the *AC* of the basic computer. However, only three terminals are available in the IC for the eight control functions. (a) List any convenient 3-bit code for the eight functions. (b) Design an encoder that accepts eight inputs from the control functions and generates the 3-bit code for the IC.

# 6

# COMPUTER SOFTWARE

## 6-1 INTRODUCTION

A total computer system includes both *hardware* and *software*. Hardware consists of the physical components and all associated equipment. Software refers to the programs that are written for the computer. It is possible to be familiar with various aspects of computer software without being concerned with details of how the computer hardware operates. It is also possible to design parts of the hardware without a knowledge of its software capabilities. However, those concerned with computer architecture should have a knowledge of both hardware and software because the two branches influence each other.

Writing a program for a computer consists of specifying, directly or indirectly, a sequence of machine instructions. Machine instructions inside the computer form a binary pattern which is difficult, if not impossible, for people to work with and understand. It is preferable to write programs with the more familiar symbols of the alphanumeric character set. As a consequence, there is a need for translating user-oriented symbolic programs into binary programs recognized by the hardware.

A program written by a user may be either dependent or independent of the physical computer that runs his program. For example, a program written in standard Fortran is machine independent because most computers provide a translator program that converts the standard Fortran program to the binary code of the computer available in the particular installation. But the translator program itself is machine dependent because it must translate the Fortran program to the binary code recognized by the hardware of the particular computer used.

This chapter introduces some elementary programming concepts and shows their relation to the hardware representation of instructions. The first part presents the basic operation and structure of a program that translates a user's symbolic program into an equivalent binary program. The discussion emphasizes the important concepts of the translator rather than the details of actually producing the program itself. The usefulness of various machine instructions is then demonstrated by means of several basic programming examples. The last section presents a brief discussion of the software components commonly found in computer systems.

The instruction set of the basic computer, whose hardware organization was explored in Chap. 5, will be used in this chapter to illustrate many of the techniques commonly used to program a computer. In this way, it will be possible to explore the relationship between a program and the hardware operations that execute the instructions.

The 25 instructions of the basic computer are repeated in Table 6-1 to provide an easy reference for the programming examples that follow. Each

**Table 6-1** *Computer instructions*

| *Symbol* | *Hexadecimal Code* | *Description* |
|---|---|---|
| AND | 0 $m$ | AND $M$ to $AC$ |
| ADD | 1 $m$ | Add $M$ to $AC$, carry to $E$ |
| LDA | 2 $m$ | Load $AC$ from $M$ |
| STA | 3 $m$ | Store $AC$ in $M$ |
| BUN | 4 $m$ | Branch unconditionally to $m$ |
| BSA | 5 $m$ | Branch to $m + 1$ and save return address in $M$ |
| ISZ | 6 $m$ | Increment $M$ and skip if zero |
| CLA | 7800 | Clear $AC$ |
| CLE | 7400 | Clear $E$ |
| CMA | 7200 | Complement $AC$ |
| CME | 7100 | Complement $E$ |
| CIR | 7080 | Circulate right $E$ and $AC$ |
| CIL | 7040 | Circulate left $E$ and $AC$ |
| INC | 7020 | Increment $AC$, carry to $E$ |
| SPA | 7010 | Skip if $AC$ is positive |
| SNA | 7008 | Skip if $AC$ is negative |
| SZA | 7004 | Skip if $AC$ is zero |
| SZE | 7002 | Skip if $E$ is zero |
| HLT | 7001 | Halt computer |
| INP | F800 | Input information and clear flag |
| OUT | F400 | Output information and clear flag |
| SKI | F200 | Skip if input flag is on |
| SKO | F100 | Skip if output flag is on |
| ION | F080 | Turn interrupt on |
| IOF | F040 | Turn interrupt off |

instruction is assigned a three-letter symbol to facilitate writing symbolic programs. The seven memory-reference instructions have three parts: a mode bit, an operation code and an address. The other eighteen instructions have a 16-bit operation code. The instructions are listed for convenience by a 4-digit hexadecimal number. The first hexadecimal digit of a memory-reference instruction includes the mode bit and the operation code. The other three digits specify the address. In an indirect address instruction the mode bit is 1 and the first hexadecimal digit of a memory-reference instruction ranges in value from 8 to E. The letter $M$ mentioned in the description column refers to the memory word (operand) found in the effective address. The first digit of a register-reference instruction is always 7. The first digit of an input-output instruction is always F.

## 6-2 PROGRAMMING LANGUAGES

A program is a list of instructions or statements for directing the computer to perform a required data processing task. There are various types of programming languages that one may *write* for a computer but the computer can *execute* programs only when they are represented internally in binary form. Programs written in any other language must be translated to the binary representation of instructions before they can be executed by the computer. Programs written for a computer may be in one of the following categories:

(a) *Binary code.* This is a sequence of instructions and operands in binary that list the exact representation of instructions as they appear in computer memory.

(b) *Octal or hexadecimal code.* This is an equivalent translation of the binary code to octal or hexadecimal representation.

(c) *Symbolic code.* The user employs symbols (letters, numerals, or special characters) for the operation part, the address part, and other parts of the instruction code. Each symbolic instruction can be translated into one binary coded instruction. This translation is done by a special program called an *assembler*. Because an assembler translates the symbols, this type of symbolic program is referred to as an *assembly-language* program.

(d) *High-level programming languages.* These are special languages developed to reflect the procedures used in the solution of a problem rather than be concerned with the computer hardware behavior. An example of a high-level programming language is *Fortran*. It employs problem-oriented symbols and formats. The program is written in a sequence of statements in a form that people prefer to think in when solving a problem. However, each statement must be translated into a sequence of binary instructions before the program can be executed in a computer. The program that translates a high-level language program to binary is called a *compiler*.

Strictly speaking, a *machine-language* program is a binary program of category (a). Because of the simple equivalency between binary and octal or hexadecimal representation, it is customary to refer to category (b) as machine language. Because of the one-to-one relationship between a symbolic instruction and its binary equivalent, an assembly language is considered to be a machine-level language.

In computer science, the term *programming languages* refers to the study of the structure of various high-level programming languages. This study is carried out independent of any particular computing device and its hardware. Since we are interested in the relation between software and hardware, the term as used here has a different connotation since it includes machine-level languages.

We now use the basic computer to illustrate the relation between the various programming languages. Consider the binary program listed in Table 6-2. The first column gives the memory location (in binary) of each instruction or operand. The second column lists the binary content of these memory locations. (The *location* is the address of the memory word where the instruction is stored. It is important to differentiate it from the address part of the instruction itself.) The program can be stored in the indicated portion of memory, and then executed by the computer starting from address 0. The hardware of the computer will execute these instructions and perform the intended task. However, a person looking at this program will have a difficult time understanding what is to be achieved when this program is executed. Nevertheless, the computer hardware recognizes *only* this type of instruction code.

**Table 6-2** *Binary program to add two numbers*

| *Location* | *Instruction Code* |
|---|---|
| 0 | 0010 0000 0000 0100 |
| 1 | 0001 0000 0000 0101 |
| 10 | 0011 0000 0000 0110 |
| 11 | 0111 0000 0000 0001 |
| 100 | 0000 0000 0101 0011 |
| 101 | 1111 1111 1110 1001 |
| 110 | 0000 0000 0000 0000 |

Writing 16 bits for each instruction is tedious because there are too many digits. We can reduce the number of digits per instruction if we write the octal equivalent of the binary code. This will require six digits per instruction. On the other hand, we can reduce each instruction to four digits if we write the equivalent hexadecimal code as shown in Table 6-3. The hexadecimal

**Table 6-3** *Hexadecimal program to add two numbers*

| *Location* | *Instruction* |
|---|---|
| 000 | 2004 |
| 001 | 1005 |
| 002 | 3006 |
| 003 | 7001 |
| 004 | 0053 |
| 005 | FFE9 |
| 006 | 0000 |

representation is convenient to use; however, one must realize that each hexadecimal digit must be converted to its equivalent 4-bit number when the program is entered into the computer. The advantage of writing binary programs in equivalent octal or hexadecimal form should be evident from this example.

The program in Table 6-4 uses the symbolic names of instructions (listed

**Table 6-4** *Program with symbolic operation codes*

| *Location* | *Instruction* | *Comments* |
|---|---|---|
| 000 | LDA 004 | Load first operand into $AC$ |
| 001 | ADD 005 | Add second operand to $AC$ |
| 002 | STA 006 | Store sum in location 006 |
| 003 | HLT | Halt computer |
| 004 | 0053 | First operand |
| 005 | FFE9 | Second operand (negative) |
| 006 | 0000 | Store sum here |

in Table 6-1) instead of their binary or hexadecimal equivalent. The address parts of memory-reference instructions, as well as operands, remain in their hexadecimal value. Note that location 005 has a negative operand because the sign bit in the left-most position is 1. The inclusion of a column for comments provides some means for explaining the function of each instruction. Symbolic programs are easier to handle and as a consequence, it is preferable to write programs with symbols. These symbols can be converted to their binary code equivalent to produce the binary program.

We can go one step further and replace each hexadecimal address by a symbolic address and each hexadecimal operand by a decimal operand. This is convenient because one usually does not know exactly the numeric memory location of operands while writing a program. If the operands are placed in memory following the instructions, and if the length of the program is not known in advance, the numerical location of operands is not known until the end of the program is reached. In addition, decimal numbers are more familiar than their hexadecimal equivalents.

The program in Table 6-5 is the assembly-language program for adding

**Table 6-5** *Assembly-language program to add two numbers*

| | | |
|---|---|---|
| | ORG 0 | /Origin of program is location 0 |
| | LDA A | /Load operand from location *A* |
| | ADD B | /Add operand from location *B* |
| | STA C | /Store sum in location *C* |
| | HLT | /Halt computer |
| A, | DEC 83 | /Decimal operand |
| B, | DEC −23 | /Decimal operand |
| C, | DEC 0 | /Sum stored in location *C* |
| | END | /End of symbolic program |

two numbers. The symbol ORG followed by a number is not a machine instruction. Its purpose is to specify an *origin*, i.e., the memory location of the next instruction below it. The next three lines have symbolic addresses. Their value is specified by their being present as a label in the first column. Decimal operands are specified following the symbol DEC. The numbers may be positive or negative, but if negative, they must be converted to binary in the signed-2's complement representation. The last line has the symbol END indicating the end of the program. The symbols ORG, DEC and END are called *pseudo-instructions* and will be defined in the next section. Note that all comments are preceded by a slash.

The equivalent Fortran program for adding two integer numbers is listed in Table 6-6. The two values for *A* and *B* may be specified by an input

**Table 6-6** *Fortran program to add two numbers*

```
INTEGER A, B, C
DATA A,83 / B,−23
C = A + B
END
```

statement or by a data statement. The arithmetic operation for the two numbers is specified by one simple statement. The translation of this Fortran program into a binary program consists of assigning three memory locations, one each for the augend, addend, and sum, and then deriving the sequence of binary instructions that form the sum. Thus, a compiler program translates the symbols of the Fortran program into the binary values listed in the program of Table 6-2.

## 6-3 ASSEMBLY LANGUAGE

A programming language is defined by a set of rules. The user must conform with all format rules of the language if he wants his program to be translated correctly. Almost every commercial computer has its own particular assembly language. The rules for writing assembly-language programs are documented and published in manuals which are usually available from the computer manufacturer.

The basic unit of an assembly-language program is a line of code (when the input is from a teletypewriter, although it could just as well be a punched card). The specific language is defined by a set of rules that specify the symbols that can be used and how they may be combined to form a line of code. We will now formulate the rules of an assembly language for writing symbolic programs for the basic computer.

### *Rules of the Language*

Each line of an assembly-language program is arranged in three columns called fields. The fields specify the following information.

1. The *label* field may be empty or it may specify a symbolic address.
2. The *instruction* field specifies a machine instruction or a pseudo-instruction.
3. The *comment* field may be empty or it may include a comment.

A symbolic address consists of one, two, or three, but not more than three alphanumeric characters. The first character must be a letter; the next two may be letters or numerals. The symbol can be chosen arbitrarily by the programmer. A symbolic address in the label field is terminated by a comma so it will be recognized as a label by the assembler.

The instruction field in an assembly-language program may specify one of the following items:

1. A memory-reference instruction (MRI).

2. A register-reference or input-output instruction (non-MRI).
3. A pseudo-instruction with or without an operand.

A memory-reference instruction occupies two or three symbols separated by spaces. The first must be a three-letter symbol defining an MRI operation code from Table 6-1. The second is a symbolic address. The third symbol, which may or may not be present, is the letter I. If I is missing, the line denotes a direct address instruction. The presence of the symbol I denotes an indirect address instruction.

A non-MRI is defined as an instruction that does not have an address part. A non-MRI is recognized in the instruction field of a program by any one of the three-letter symbols listed in Table 6-1 for the register-reference and input-output instructions.

The following is an illustration of the symbols that may be placed in the instruction field of a program.

```
CLA          non-MRI
ADD OPR      direct address MRI
ADD PTR I    indirect address MRI
```

The first three-letter symbol in each line must be one of the instruction symbols of the computer and must be listed in Table 6-1. A memory-reference instruction, such as ADD, must be followed by a symbolic address. The letter I may or may not be present.

A symbolic address in the instruction field specifies the memory location of an operand. This location must be defined somewhere in the program by appearing again as a label in the first column. In order to be able to translate an assembly-language program to a binary program, it is absolutely necessary that each symbolic address that is mentioned in the instruction field *must* occur again in the label field.

A pseudo-instruction is not a machine instruction but rather an instruction to the assembler giving information about some phase of the translation. Four pseudo-instructions that are recognized by the assembler are listed in Table 6-7. (Other assembly-language programs recognize many more pseudo-

**Table 6-7** *Definition of pseudo-instructions*

| *Symbol* | *Information for the Assembler* |
|---|---|
| ORG N | Hexadecimal number N is the memory location for the instruction or operand listed in the following line. |
| END | Denotes the end of symbolic program. |
| DEC N | Signed decimal number N to be converted to binary. |
| HEX N | Hexadecimal number N to be converted to binary. |

instructions.) The ORG (origin) pseudo-instruction informs the assembler that the instruction or operand in the following linc is to be placed in a memory location specified by the number next to ORG. It is possible to use ORG more than once in a program to specify more than one segment of memory. The END symbol is placed at the end of the program to inform the assembler that the program is terminated. The other two pseudo-instructions specify the radix of the operand and tell the assembler how to convert the listed number to a binary number.

The third field in a program is reserved for comments. A line of code may or may not have a comment, but if it has, it must be preceeded by a slash for the assembler to recognize the beginning of a comment field. Comments are useful for explaining the program and are helpful in understanding the step by step procedure taken by the program. Comments are inserted for explanation purposes only and are neglected during the binary translation process.

### *An Example*

The program of Table 6-8 is an example of an assembly-language program. The first line has the pseudo-instruction ORG to define the origin of the program at memory location $(100)_{16}$. The next six lines define machine instructions and the last four have pseudo-instructions. Three symbolic addresses have been used and each is listed in column one as a label and in column two as an address of a memory-reference instruction. Three of the pseudo-instructions specify operands and the last one signifies the END of the program.

When the program is translated into binary code and executed by the computer it will perform a subtraction between two numbers. The subtraction is performed by adding the minuend to the 2's complement of the subtrahend. The subtrahend is a negative number. It is converted into a binary number in signed-2's complement representation because we dictate that all negative numbers be in their 2's complement form. When the 2's complement of the subtrahend is taken (by complementing and incrementing the $AC$), $-23$ converts to $+23$ and the difference is $83 +$ (2's complement of $-23$) $= 83 + 23 = 106$.

### *Translation to Binary*

The translation of the symbolic program into binary is done by a special program we have called an *assembler*. The tasks performed by the assembler will be better understood if we first perform the translation on paper. The translation of the symbolic program of Table 6-8 into an equivalent binary code may be done by scanning the program and replacing the symbols by their machine code binary equivalent. Starting from the first line, we encoun-

**Table 6-8** *Assembly-language program to subtract two numbers*

| | | |
|---|---|---|
| | ORG 100 | /Origin of program is location 100. |
| | LDA SUB | /Load subtrahend to *AC*. |
| | CMA | /Complement *AC*. |
| | INC | /Increment *AC*. |
| | ADD MIN | /Add minuend to *AC*. |
| | STA DIF | /Store difference. |
| | HLT | /Halt computer. |
| MIN, | DEC 83 | /Minuend. |
| SUB, | DEC −23 | /Subtrahend. |
| DIF, | HEX 0 | /Difference stored here. |
| | END | /End of symbolic program. |

ter an ORG pseudo-instruction. This tells us to start the binary program from hexadecimal location 100. The second line has two symbols. It must be a memory-reference instruction to be placed in location 100. Since the letter I is missing, the first bit of the instruction code must be 0. The symbolic name of the operation is LDA. Checking Table 6-1 we find that the first hexadecimal digit of the instruction should be 2. The binary value of the address part must be obtained from the address symbol SUB. We scan the label column and find this symbol in line 9. To determine its hexadecimal value we note that line 2 contains an instruction for location 100 and every other line specifies a machine instruction or an operand for sequential memory locations. Counting lines, we find that label SUB in line 9 corresponds to memory location 107. So the hexadecimal address of the instruction LDA must be 107. When the two parts of the instruction are assembled, we obtain the hexadecimal code 2107. The other lines representing machine instructions are translated in a similar fashion and their hexadecimal code is listed in Table 6-9.

Two lines in the symbolic program specify decimal operands with the pseudo-instruction DEC. A third specifies a zero by means of a HEX pseudo-instruction (DEC could be used as well). Decimal 83 is converted to binary and placed in location 106 in its hexadecimal equivalent. Decimal −23 is a negative number and must be converted into binary in signed-2's complement form. The hexadecimal equivalent of the binary number is placed in location 107. The END symbol signals the end of the symbolic program telling us that there are no more lines to translate.

The translation process can be simplified if we scan the entire symbolic program twice. No translation is done during the first scan. We merely assign a memory location to each machine instruction and operand. The location assignment will define the address value of labels and facilitate the translation process during the second scan. Thus in Table 6-9, we assign location 100 to the first instruction after ORG. We then assign sequential locations for each

**Table 6-9** *Listing of translated program of Table 6-8*

| *Hexadecimal Code* | | *Symbolic Program* | |
|---|---|---|---|
| *Location* | *Content* | | |
| | | | ORG 100 |
| 100 | 2107 | | LDA SUB |
| 101 | 7200 | | CMA |
| 102 | 7020 | | INC |
| 103 | 1106 | | ADD MIN |
| 104 | 3108 | | STA DIF |
| 105 | 7001 | | HLT |
| 106 | 0053 | MIN, | DEC 83 |
| 107 | FFE9 | SUB, | DEC −23 |
| 108 | 0000 | DIF, | HEX 0 |
| | | | END |

line of code that has a machine instruction or operand up to the end of the program. (ORG and END are not assigned a numerical location because they do not represent an instruction or an operand.) When the first scan is completed, we associate with each label its location number and form a table that defines the hexadecimal value of each symbolic address. For this program, the address symbol table is as follows:

| *Address Symbol* | *Hexadecimal Address* |
|---|---|
| MIN | 106 |
| SUB | 107 |
| DIF | 108 |

During the second scan of the symbolic program we refer to the address-symbol table to determine the address value of a memory-reference instruction. For example, the line of code LDA SUB is translated during the second scan by getting the hexadecimal value of LDA from Table 6-1 and the hexadecimal value of SUB from the address-symbol table listed above. We then assemble the two parts into a 4-digit hexadecimal instruction. The hexadecimal code can be easily converted to binary if we wish to know exactly how this program resides in computer memory.

When the translation from symbols to binary is done by an assembler program, the first scan is called the *first pass*, and the second is called the *second pass*.

## 6-4 THE ASSEMBLER

An assembler is a program that accepts a symbolic-language program and produces its binary machine language equivalent. The input symbolic program is called the *source program* and the resulting binary program is called the *object program.* The assembler is a program that operates on character strings and produces an equivalent binary interpretation.

### *Representation of Symbolic Program in Memory*

Prior to starting the assembly process, the symbolic program must be stored in memory. The user types the symbolic program on a Teletype (or prepares it in punched cards). A loader program is used to input the characters of the symbolic program into memory. Since the program consists of symbols, its representation in memory must use an alphanumeric character code. In the basic computer, each character is represented by an 8-bit code. The high-order bit is always 0 and the other seven bits are as specified by ASCII. The hexadecimal equivalent of the character set is listed in Table 6-10. Each character is assigned two hexadecimal digits which can be easily converted to their equivalent 8-bit code. The last entry in the table does not

**Table 6-10** *Hexadecimal character code*

| *Character* | *Code* | *Character* | *Code* | *Character* | *Code* |
|---|---|---|---|---|---|
| A | 41 | Q | 51 | 6 | 36 |
| B | 42 | R | 52 | 7 | 37 |
| C | 43 | S | 53 | 8 | 38 |
| D | 44 | T | 54 | 9 | 39 |
| E | 45 | U | 55 | space | 20 |
| F | 46 | V | 56 | ( | 28 |
| G | 47 | W | 57 | ) | 29 |
| H | 48 | X | 58 | * | 2A |
| I | 49 | Y | 59 | + | 2B |
| J | 4A | Z | 5A | , | 2C |
| K | 4B | 0 | 30 | — | 2D |
| L | 4C | 1 | 31 | . | 2E |
| M | 4D | 2 | 32 | / | 2F |
| N | 4E | 3 | 33 | = | 3D |
| O | 4F | 4 | 34 | CR | 0D (carriage return) |
| P | 50 | 5 | 35 | | |

print a character but is associated with the physical movement of the carriage in the Teletype. The code for CR is produced when the "carriage-return" key is depressed. This causes the carriage to return to its initial position to start typing a new line. The assembler recognizes a CR code as the end of a line of code.

A line of code is stored in consecutive memory locations with two characters in each location. Two characters can be stored in each word since a memory word has a capacity of 16 bits. A label symbol is terminated with a comma. Operation and address symbols are terminated with a space and the end of the line is recognized by the CR code. For example, the following line of code:

PL3, LDA SUB I

is stored in seven consecutive memory locations as shown in Table 6-11. The

**Table 6-11** *Computer representation of the line of code: PL3, LDA SUB I*

| *Memory Word* | *Symbol* | *Hexadecimal Code* | *Binary Representation* |
|---|---|---|---|
| 1 | P L | 50 4C | 0101 0000 0100 1100 |
| 2 | 3 , | 33 2C | 0011 0011 0010 1100 |
| 3 | L D | 4C 44 | 0100 1100 0100 0100 |
| 4 | A | 41 20 | 0100 0001 0010 0000 |
| 5 | S U | 53 55 | 0101 0011 0101 0101 |
| 6 | B | 42 20 | 0100 0010 0010 0000 |
| 7 | I CR | 49 0D | 0100 1001 0000 1101 |

label PL3 occupies two words and is terminated by the code for comma (2C). The instruction field in the line of code may have one or more symbols. Each symbol is terminated by the code for space (20) except for the last symbol which is terminated by the code of carriage-return (0D). If the line of code has a comment, the assembler recognizes it by the code for a slash (2F). The assembler neglects all characters in the comment field and keeps checking for a CR code. When this code is encountered, it replaces the space code after the last symbol in the line of code.

An assembler must know the arrangement of the characters in memory so it can distinguish between symbols and lines. The memory space that stores the symbolic program constitutes the input data for the assembler. This input data is scanned by the assembler twice to produce the equivalent binary program. The binary program constitutes the output data generated by the assembler. We will now describe briefly the major tasks that must be performed by the assembler during the translation process.

*First Pass*

A two-pass assembler scans the entire symbolic program twice. During the first pass, it generates a table that correlates all user-defined address symbols with their binary equivalent value. The binary translation is done during the second pass. In order to keep track of the location of instructions, the assembler uses one memory word called a *location counter* (abbreviated LC). The content of LC stores the value of the memory location assigned to the instruction or operand presently being processed. The ORG pseudo-instruction initializes the location counter to the value of the first location. Since instructions are stored in sequential locations, the content of LC is incremented by 1 after processing each line of code. To avoid ambiguity in case ORG is missing, the assembler sets the location counter to 0 initially.

The tasks performed by the assembler during the first pass are described in the flow chart of Fig. 6-1. LC is initially set to 0. A line of symbolic code is analyzed to determine if it has a label (by the presence of a comma). If the line of code has no label, the assembler checks the symbol in the instruction field.

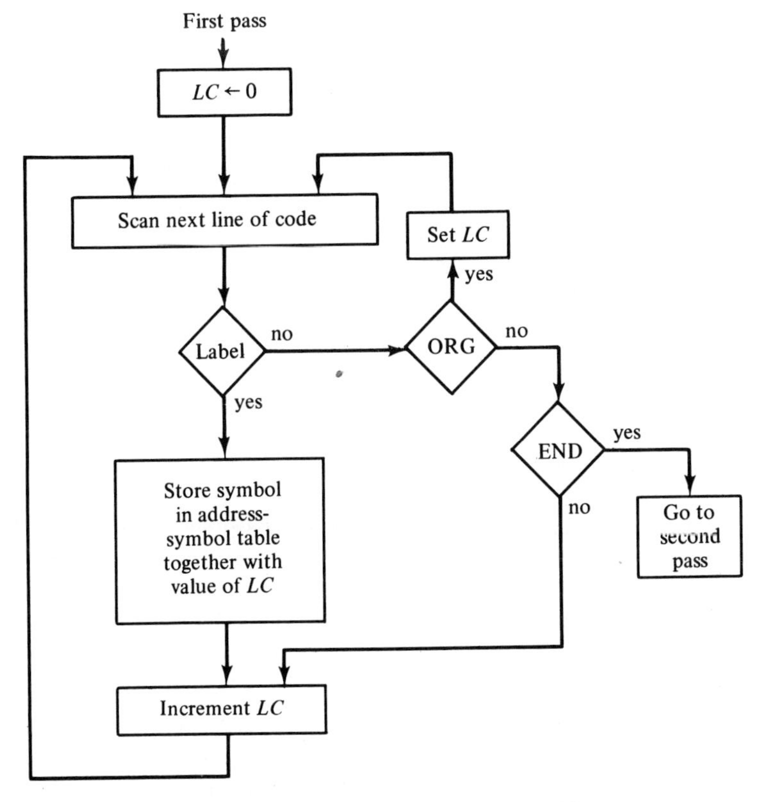


**Fig. 6-1** Flow chart for first pass of assembler.

If it contains an ORG pseudo-instruction, the assembler sets LC to the number that follows ORG and goes back to process the next line. If the line has an END pseudo-instruction, the assembler terminates the first pass and goes to the second pass. (Note that a line with ORG or END should not have a label.) If the line of code contains a label, it is stored in the address-symbol table together with its binary equivalent number specified by the content of LC. Nothing is stored in the table if no label is encountered. LC is then incremented by 1 and a new line of code is processed.

For the program of Table 6-8, the assembler generates the address-symbol table listed in Table 6-12. Each label symbol is stored in two memory loca-

**Table 6-12** *Address-symbol table for program in Table 6-8*

| *Memory Word* | *Symbol or* (LC)* | *Hexadecimal Code* | *Binary Representation* |
|---|---|---|---|
| 1 | M I | 4D 49 | 0100 1101 0100 1001 |
| 2 | N , | 4E 2C | 0100 1110 0010 1100 |
| 3 | (LC) | 01 06 | 0000 0001 0000 0110 |
| 4 | S U | 53 55 | 0101 0011 0101 0101 |
| 5 | B , | 42 2C | 0100 0010 0010 1100 |
| 6 | (LC) | 01 07 | 0000 0001 0000 0111 |
| 7 | D I | 44 49 | 0100 0100 0100 1001 |
| 8 | F , | 46 2C | 0100 0110 0010 1100 |
| 9 | (LC) | 01 08 | 0000 0001 0000 1000 |

*(LC) designates content of location counter.

tions and is terminated by a comma. If the label contains less than three characters, the memory locations are filled with the code for space. The value found in LC while the line was processed is stored in the next sequential memory location. The program has three symbolic addresses: MIN, SUB, and DIF. These symbols represent 12-bit addresses equivalent to hexadecimal 106, 107, and 108, respectively. The address-symbol table occupies three words for each label symbol encountered and constitutes the output data that the assembler generates during the first pass.

### *Second Pass*

Machine instructions are translated during the second pass by means of table-lookup procedures. A table-lookup procedure is a search of table entries to determine whether a specific item matches one of the items stored in the table. The assembler uses four tables. Any symbol that is encountered in the program must be available as an entry in one of these tables; otherwise the symbol cannot be interpreted. We assign the following names to the four tables:

1. Pseudo-instruction table.
2. MRI table.
3. Non-MRI table.
4. Address-symbol table.

The entries of the pseudo-instruction table are the four symbols ORG, END, DEC, and HEX. Each entry refers the assembler to a subroutine that processes the pseudo-instruction when encountered in the program. The MRI table contains the seven symbols of the memory-reference instructions and their 3-bit operation code equivalent. The non-MRI table contains the symbols for the 18 register-reference and input-output instructions and their 16-bit binary code equivalent. The address-symbol table is generated during the first pass of the assembly process. The assembler searches these tables to find the symbol that it is currently processing in order to determine its binary value.

The tasks performed by the assembler during the second pass are described in the flow chart of Fig. 6-2. LC is initially set to 0. Lines of code are then analyzed one at a time. Labels are neglected during the second pass so the assembler goes immediately to the instruction field and proceeds to check the first symbol encountered. It first checks the pseudo-instruction table. A match with ORG sends the assembler to a subroutine that sets LC to an initial value. A match with END terminates the translation process. An operand pseudo-instruction causes a conversion of the operand into binary. This operand is placed in the memory location specified by the content of LC. The location counter is then incremented by 1 and the assembler continues to analyze the next line of code.

If the symbol encountered is not a pseudo-instruction, the assembler refers to the MRI table. If the symbol is not found in this table, the assembler refers to the non-MRI table. A symbol found in the non-MRI table corresponds to a register reference or input-output instruction. The assembler stores the 16-bit instruction code into the memory word specified by LC. The location counter is incremented and a new line analyzed.

When a symbol is found in the MRI table, the assembler extracts its equivalent 3-bit code and inserts it in bits 2–4 of a word. A memory reference instruction is specified by two or three symbols. The second symbol is a symbolic address and the third, which may or may not be present, is the letter I. The symbolic address is converted to binary by searching the address symbol table. The first bit of the instruction is set to 0 or 1, depending on whether the letter I is absent or present. The three parts of the binary instruc-

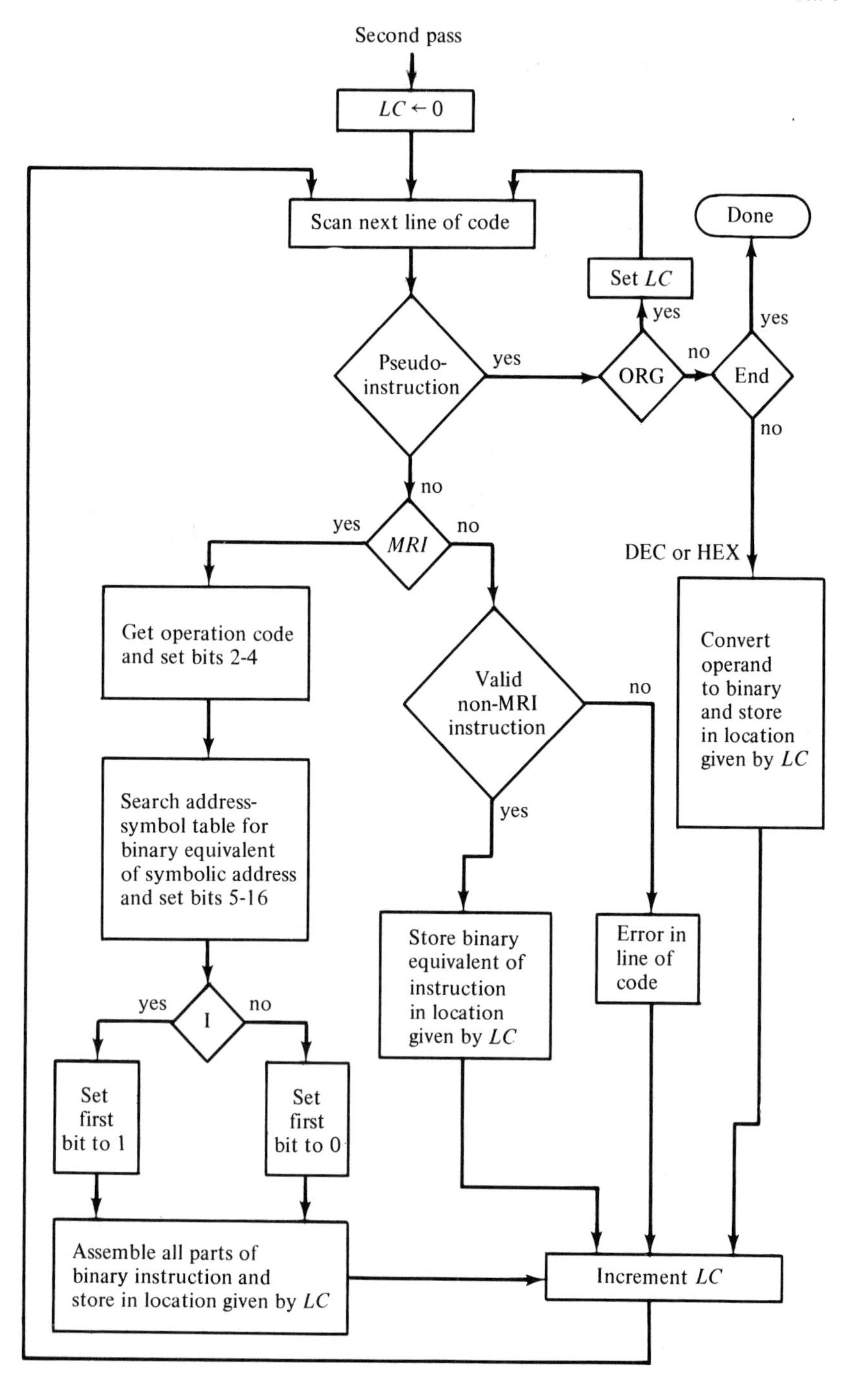


**Fig. 6-2** Flow chart for second pass of assembler.

tion code are assembled and then stored in the memory location specified by the content of LC. The location counter is incremented and the assembler continues to process the next line.

One important task of an assembler is to check for possible errors in the symbolic program. This is called *error diagnostics*. One such error may be an invalid machine-code symbol which is detected by its being absent in the MRI and non-MRI tables. The assembler cannot translate such a symbol because it does not know its binary equivalent value. In such a case, the assembler prints an error message to inform the programmer that his symbolic program has an error at a specific line of code. Another possible error may occur if the program has a symbolic address that did not appear also as a label. The assembler cannot translate the line of code properly because the binary equivalent of the symbol will not be found in the address-symbol table generated during the first pass. Other errors may occur and a practical assembler should detect all such errors and print an error message for each.

It should be emphasized that a practical assembler is much more complicated than the one explained here. Most computers give the programmer more flexibility in writing assembly-language programs. For example, the user may be allowed to use either a number or a symbol to specify an address. Many assemblers allow the user to specify an address by an arithmetic expression. Many more pseudo-instructions may be specified to facilitate the programming task. As the assembly language becomes more sophisticated, the assembler becomes more complicated.

## 6-5 PROGRAM LOOPS

A program loop is a sequence of instructions that are executed many times, each time with a different set of data. Program loops are specified in Fortran by a DO statement. The following is an example of a Fortran program that forms the sum of 100 integer numbers.

```
      DIMENSION A(100)
      INTEGER SUM, A
      SUM = 0
      DO 3 J = 1, 100
3     SUM = SUM + A(J)
```

Statement number 3 is executed 100 times, each time with a different operand A(J) for J = 1, 2, . . . , 100.

A system program that translates a program written in a high-level programming language such as the above to a machine-language program is called a *compiler*. A compiler is a more complicated program than an assembler and requires knowledge of systems programming to fully understand its operation. Nevertheless, we can demonstrate the basic functions of a compiler by going through the process of translating the above program to an assembly-language program. A compiler may use an assembly language as an intermediate step in the translation or may translate the program directly to binary.

The first statement in the Fortran program is a DIMENSION statement. This statement instructs the compiler to reserve 100 words of memory for 100 operands. The value of the operands is determined from an input statement (not listed in the program). The second statement informs the compiler that the numbers are integers. If they were of the *real* type, the compiler would have to reserve locations for floating-point numbers and generate instructions that perform the subsequent arithmetic with floating-point data. These two statements are nonexecutable and are similar to the pseudo-instructions in an assembly language. Suppose that the compiler reserves locations $(150)_{16}$ to $(1B3)_{16}$ for the 100 operands. These reserved memory words are listed in lines 19 to 118 in the translated program of Table 6-13. This is done by the ORG pseudo-instruction in line 18 which specifies the origin of the operands.

**Table 6-13** *Symbolic program to add 100 numbers*

| *Line* | | | |
|---|---|---|---|
| 1 | | ORG 100 | /Origin of program is HEX 100. |
| 2 | | LDA ADS | /Load first address of operands. |
| 3 | | STA PTR | /Store in pointer. |
| 4 | | LDA NBR | /Load minus 100. |
| 5 | | STA CTR | /Store in counter. |
| 6 | | CLA | /Clear accumulator. |
| 7 | LOP, | ADD PTR I | /Add an operand to *AC*. |
| 8 | | ISZ PTR | /Increment pointer. |
| 9 | | ISZ CTR | /Increment counter. |
| 10 | | BUN LOP | /Repeat loop again. |
| 11 | | STA SUM | /Store sum. |
| 12 | | HLT | /Halt. |
| 13 | ADS, | HEX 150 | /First address of operands. |
| 14 | PTR, | HEX 0 | /This location reserved for a pointer. |
| 15 | NBR, | DEC −100 | /Constant to initialized counter. |
| 16 | CTR, | HEX 0 | /This location reserved for a counter. |
| 17 | SUM, | HEX 0 | /Sum is stored here. |
| 18 | | ORG 150 | /Origin of operands is HEX 150. |
| 19 | | DEC 75 | /First operand. |
| · | | | |
| · | | | |
| · | | | |
| 118 | | DEC 23 | /Last operand. |
| 119 | | END | /End of symbolic program. |

The first and last operands are listed with a specific decimal number although these values are not known during compilation. The compiler just reserves the data space in memory and the values are inserted later when an input data statement is executed. The line numbers in the symbolic program are for reference only and are not part of the translated symbolic program.

The indexing of the DO statement is translated into the instructions in lines 2–5 and the constants in lines 13–16. The address of the first operand (150) is stored in location ADS in line 13. The number of times that Fortran statement number 3 must be executed is 100. So −100 is stored in location NBR. The compiler then generates the instructions in lines 2–5 to initialize the program loop. The address of the first operand is transferred to location PTR. This corresponds to setting A(J) to A(1). The number −100 is then transferred to location CTR. This location acts as a counter with its content incremented by one every time the program loop is executed. When the value of the counter reaches zero, the 100 operations will be completed and the program will exit from the loop.

Some compilers will translate the statement SUM = 0 into a machine instruction that initializes location SUM to zero. A reference to this location is then made every time Fortran statement number 3 is executed. A more intelligent compiler will realize that the sum can be formed in the accumulator and only the final result stored in location SUM. This compiler will produce an instruction in line 6 to clear the $AC$. It will also reserve a memory location symbolized by SUM (in line 17) for storing the value of this variable at the termination of the loop.

The program loop specified by the DO statement is translated to the sequence of instructions listed in lines 7–10. Line 7 specifies an indirect ADD instruction because it has the symbol I. The address of the current operand is stored in location PTR. When this location is addressed indirectly the computer takes the content of PTR to be the address of the operand. As a result, the operand in location 150 is added to the accumulator. Location PTR is then incremented with the ISZ instruction in line 8 so its value changes to the value of the address of the next sequential operand. Location CTR is incremented in line 9 and if it is not zero, the computer does not skip the next instruction. The next instruction is a branch (BUN) instruction to the beginning of the loop so the computer returns to repeat the loop once again. When location CTR reaches zero (after the loop is executed 100 times), the next instruction is skipped and the computer executes the instructions in lines 11 and 12. The sum formed in the accumulator is stored in SUM and the computer halts. The halt instruction is inserted here for clarity; actually, the program will branch to a location where it will continue to execute the rest of the program or branch to the beginning of another program. Note that ISZ in line 8 is used merely to add 1 to the address pointer PTR. Since the address is a positive number, a skip will never occur.

The program of Table 6-13 introduces the idea of a pointer and a counter which can be used, together with the indirect address operation, to form a program loop. The pointer points to the address of the current operand and the counter counts the number of times that the program loop is executed. In this example we use two memory locations for these functions. In computers with more than one processor register, it is possible to use one processor register as a pointer, another as a counter and a third as an accumulator. When processor registers are used as pointers and counters they are called *index registers*. Index registers are discussed in Sec. 7-5.

## 6-6 PROGRAMMING ARITHMETIC AND LOGIC OPERATIONS

The number of instructions available in a computer may be a few hundred in a large system or a few dozen in a small one. Some computers perform a given operation with one machine instruction; others may require a large number of machine instructions to perform the same operation. As an illustration, consider the four basic arithmetic operations. Some computers have machine instructions to add, subtract, multiply, and divide. Others, such as the basic computer, have only one arithmetic instruction such as ADD. Operations not included in the set of machine instructions must be implemented by a program. We have shown in Table 6-8 a program for subtracting two numbers. Programs for the other arithmetic operations can be developed in a similar fashion.

Operations that are implemented in a computer with one machine instruction are said to be implemented by hardware. Operations implemented by a set of instructions that constitute a program are said to be implemented by software. Some computers provide an extensive set of hardware instructions designed to speed up common tasks. Others contain a smaller set of hardware instructions and depend more heavily on the software implementation of many operations. Hardware implementation is more costly because of the additional circuits needed to implement the operation. Software implementation results in long programs both in number of instructions and in execution time.

This section demonstrates the software implementation of a few arithmetic and logic operations. Programs can be developed for any arithmetic operation and not only for fixed-point binary data but for decimal and floating-point data as well. The hardware implementation of arithmetic operations is carried out in Chaps. 9 and 10.

### *Multiplication Program*

We will now develop a program for multiplying two numbers. To simplify the program, we neglect the sign bit and assume positive numbers. We also assume that the two binary numbers have no more than eight significant bits so their product cannot exceed the word capacity of 16 bits. It is possible to modify the program to take care of the signs or use 16-bit numbers. However, the product may be up to 31 bits in length and will occupy two words of memory.

The program for multiplying two numbers is based on the procedure we use to multiply numbers with paper and pencil. As shown in the numerical example of Fig. 6-3, the multiplication process consists of checking the bits of the multiplier Y and adding the multiplicand X as many times as there are 1's in Y, provided the value of X is shifted left from one line to the next. Since the computer can add only two numbers at a time, we reserve a memory location, denoted by P, to store intermediate sums. The intermediate sums are called partial products since they hold a partial product until all numbers are added. As shown in the numerical example under P, the partial product starts with zero. The multiplicand X is added to the content of P for each bit of the multiplier Y that is 1. The value of X is shifted left after checking each bit of the multiplier. The final value in P forms the product. The numerical example has numbers with four significant bits. When multiplied, the product contains eight significant bits. The computer can use numbers with eight significant bits to produce a product of up to 16 bits.

The flow chart of Fig. 6-3 shows the step-by-step procedure for programming the multiplication operation. The program has a loop that is traversed eight times, once for each significant bit of the multiplier. Initially, location X holds the multiplicand and location Y holds the multiplier. A counter CTR is set to $-8$ and location P is cleared to zero.

The multiplier bit can be checked if it is transferred to the $E$ register. This is done by clearing $E$, loading the value of Y into the $AC$, circulating right $E$ and $AC$ and storing the shifted number back into location Y. This bit stored in $E$ is the low-order bit of the multiplier. We now check the value of $E$. If it is 1, the multiplicand X is added to the partial product P. If it is 0, the partial product does not change. We then shift the value of X once to the left by loading it into the $AC$ and circulating left $E$ and $AC$. The loop is repeated eight times by incrementing location CTR and checking when it reaches zero. When the counter reaches zero, the program exits from the loop with the product stored in location P.

The program in Table 6-14 lists the instructions for multiplying two unsigned numbers. The initialization is not listed but should be included when the program is loaded into the computer. The initialization consists of bringing the multiplicand and multiplier into locations X and Y, respectively; initializing the counter to $-8$; and initializing location P to zero. If these locations are not initialized, the program may run with incorrect data. The program itself is straightforward and follows the steps listed in the flow chart. The comments may help in following the step by step procedure.

This example has shown that if a computer does not have a machine

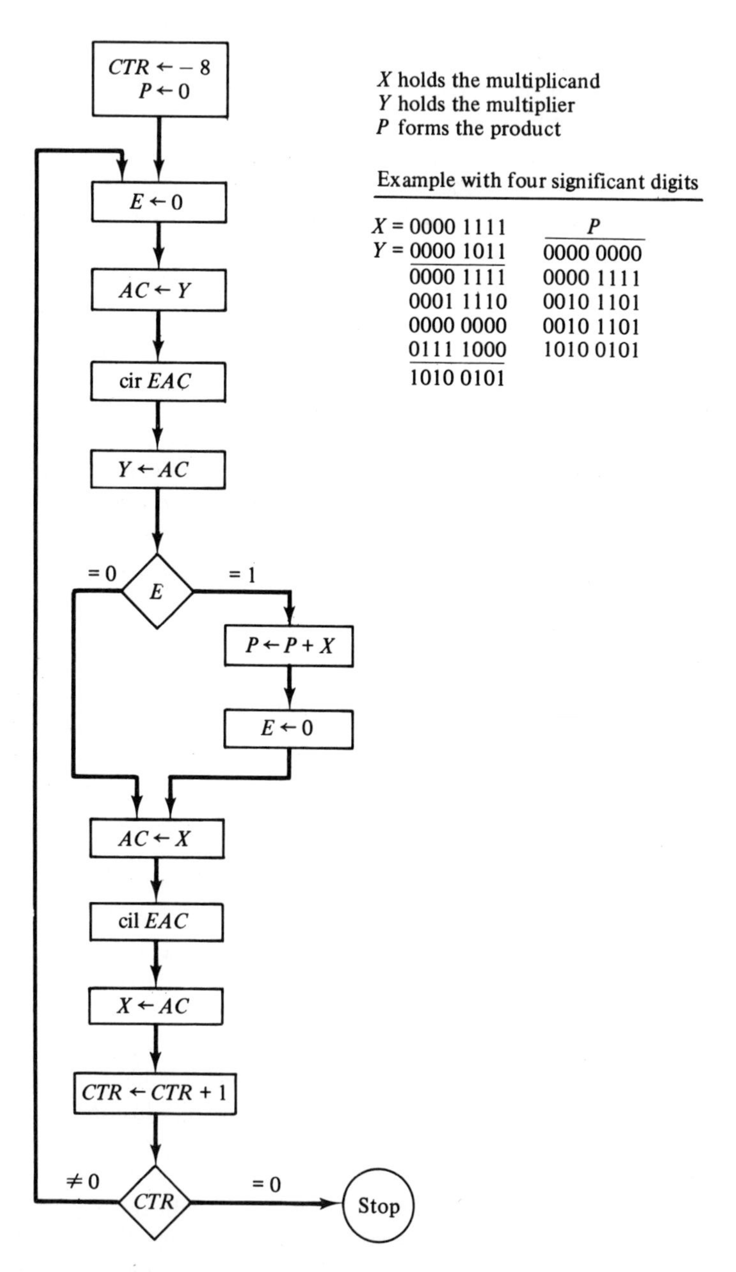


**Fig. 6-3** Flow chart for multiplication program.

**Table 6-14** *Program to multiply two positive numbers*

```
        ORG 100
LOP,    CLE             /Clear E
        LDA Y           /Load multiplier
        CIR             /Transfer multiplier bit to E
        STA Y           /Store shifted multiplier
        SZE             /Check if bit is zero
        BUN ONE         /Bit is one; go to ONE
        BUN ZRO         /Bit is zero; go to ZRO
ONE,    LDA X           /Load multiplicand
        ADD P           /Add to partial product
        STA P           /Store partial product
        CLE             /Clear E
ZRO,    LDA X           /Load multiplicand
        CIL             /Shift left
        STA X           /Store shifted multiplicand
        ISZ CTR         /Increment counter
        BUN LOP         /Counter not zero; repeat loop
        HLT             /Counter is zero; halt
CTR,    DEC -8          /This location serves as a counter
X,      HEX 000F        /Multiplicand stored here
Y,      HEX 000B        /Multiplier stored here
P,      HEX 0           /Product formed here
        END
```

instruction for a required operation, the operation can be programmed by a sequence of machine instructions. Thus, we have demonstrated the software implementation of the multiplication operation. The corresponding hardware implementation is presented in Sec. 9-4.

### *Double-Precision Addition*

When two 16-bit unsigned numbers are multiplied, the result is a 32-bit product that must be stored in two memory words. A number stored in two memory words is said to have double precision. When a partial product is computed, it is necessary that a double-precision number be added to the shifted multiplicand which is also a double-precision number. For greater accuracy, the programmer may wish to employ double-precision numbers and perform arithmetic with operands that occupy two memory words. We now develop a program that adds two double-precision numbers.

One of the double-precision numbers is placed in two consecutive memory locations, AL and AH, with AL holding the 16 low-order bits. The other number is placed in BL and BH. The program is listed in Table 6-15. The two low-order portions are added and the carry transferred into *E*. The

**Table 6-15** *Program to add two double-precision numbers*

```
        LDA AL      /Load A low
        ADD BL      /Add B low, carry in E
        STA CL      /Store in C low
        CLA         /Clear AC
        CIL         /Circulate to bring carry into AC(16)
        ADD AH      /Add A high and carry
        ADD BH      /Add B high
        STA CH      /Store in C high
        HLT
AL,     —           /Location of operands
AH,     —
BL,     —
BH,     —
CL,     —
CH,     —
```

$AC$ is cleared and the bit in $E$ is circulated into the least significant position of the $AC$. The two high-order portions are then added to the carry and the double-precision sum is stored in CL and CH.

### *Logic Operations*

The basic computer has three machine instructions that perform logic operations: AND, CMA, and CLA. The LDA instruction may be considered as a logic operation that transfers a logic operand into the $AC$. In Sec. 4-4 we listed 16 different logic operations. All 16 logic operations can be implemented by software means because any logic function can be implemented using the AND and complement operations. For example, the OR operation is not available as a machine instruction in the basic computer. From DeMorgan's theorem we recognize the relation $x + y = (x'y')'$. The second expression contains only AND and complement operations. A program that forms the OR operation of two logic operands $A$ and $B$ is listed below:

```
LDA A       /Load first operand A
CMA         /Complement to get Ā
STA TMP     /Store in a temporary location
LDA B       /Load second operand B
CMA         /Complement to get B̄
AND TMP     /AND with Ā to get Ā ∧ B̄
CMA         /Complement again to get A ∨ B
```

The other logic operations can be implemented by software in a similar fashion.

### *Shift Operations*

The circular-shift operations are machine instructions in the basic computer. The other shifts of interest are the logical shifts and arithmetic shifts. These two shifts can be programmed with a small number of instructions.

The logical shift requires that zeros be added to the extreme positions. This is easily accomplished by clearing $E$ and circulating the $AC$ and $E$. Thus for a logical shift-right operation we need the two instructions:

```
CLE
CIR
```

For a logical shift-left operation we need the two instructions:

```
CLE
CIL
```

The arithmetic shifts depend on the type of representation of negative numbers. For the basic computer we have adopted the signed-2's complement representation. The rules for arithmetic shifts are listed in Table 4-6 of Sec. 4-5. For an arithmetic right-shift it is necessary that the sign bit in the left-most position remain unchanged. But the sign bit itself is shifted into the high-order bit position of the number. The program for the arithmetic right-shift requires that we set $E$ to the same value as the sign bit and circulate right, thus:

```
CLE          /Clear E to 0
SPA          /Skip if AC is positive; E remains 0
CME          /AC is negative; set E to 1
CIR          /Circulate E and AC
```

For arithmetic shift-left it is necessary that the added bit in the least significant position be 0. This is easily done by clearing $E$ prior to the circulate-left operation. The sign bit must not change during this shift. With a circulate instruction, the sign bit moves into $E$. It is then necessary to compare the sign bit with the value of $E$ after the operation. If the two values are equal, the arithmetic shift has been correctly implemented. If they are not equal, an overflow occurs. An overflow indicates that the unshifted number was too large. When multiplied by 2 (by means of the shift), the number so obtained exceeds the capacity of the $AC$.

## 6-7 SUBROUTINES

Frequently the same piece of code must be written over again in many different parts of a program. Instead of repeating the code every time it is needed, there is an obvious advantage if the common instructions are written only once. A set of common instructions that can be used in a program many times is called a *subroutine*. Each time that a subroutine is used in the main part of the program, a branch is executed to the beginning of the subroutine. After the subroutine has been executed, a branch is made back to the main program.

A subroutine consists of a self-contained sequence of instructions that carries out a given task. A branch can be made to the subroutine from any part of the main program. This poses the problem of how the subroutine knows which location to return to, since many different locations in the main program may make branches to the same subroutine. It is therefore necessary to store the return address somewhere in the computer for the subroutine to know where to return. Because branching to a subroutine and returning to the main program is such a common operation, all computers provide special instructions to facilitate subroutine entry and return.

In the basic computer, the link between the main program and a subroutine is the BSA instruction (branch and save return address). To explain how this instruction is used, let us write a subroutine that shifts the content of the accumulator four times to the left. Shifting a word four times is a useful operation for processing binary-coded decimal numbers or alphanumeric characters. Such an operation could have been included as a machine instruction in the computer. Since it is not included, a subroutine is formed to accomplish this task. The program of Table 6-16 starts by loading the value

**Table 6-16** *Program to demonstrate the use of subroutines*

| *Location* | | | |
|---|---|---|---|
| | | ORG 100 | /Main program |
| 100 | | LDA X | /Load X |
| 101 | | BSA SH4 | /Branch to subroutine |
| 102 | | STA X | /Store shifted number |
| 103 | | LDA Y | /Load Y |
| 104 | | BSA SH4 | /Branch to subroutine again |
| 105 | | STA Y | /Store shifted number |
| 106 | | HLT | |
| 107 | X, | HEX 1234 | |
| 108 | Y, | HEX 4321 | |
| | | | /Subroutine to shift left 4 times |
| 109 | SH4, | HEX 0 | /Store return address here |
| 10A | | CIL | /Circulate left once |
| 10B | | CIL | |
| 10C | | CIL | |
| 10D | | CIL | /Circulate left fourth time |
| 10E | | AND MSK | /Set $AC(13\text{–}16)$ to zero |
| 10F | | BUN SH4 I | /Return to main program |
| 110 | MSK, | HEX FFF0 | /Mask operand |
| | | END | |

of X into the *AC*. The next instruction encountered is BSA SH4. The BSA instruction is in location 101. Subroutine SH4 must return to location 102 after it finishes its task. When the BSA instruction is executed, the control unit stores the return address 102 into the location defined by the symbolic address SH4 (which is 109). It also transfers the value of SH4 + 1 into the program counter. After this instruction is executed, memory location 109 contains the binary equivalent of hexadecimal 102 and the program counter contains the binary equivalent of hexadecimal 10A. This action has saved the return address and the subroutine is now executed starting from location 10A (since this is the content of *PC* in the next fetch cycle).

The computation in the subroutine circulates the content of *AC* four times to the left. In order to accomplish a logical shift operation, the four low-order bits must be set to zero. This is done by masking FFF0 with the content of *AC*. A mask operation is a logic AND operation that clears the bits of the *AC* where the mask operand is zero and leaves the bits of the *AC* unchanged where the mask operand bits are 1's.

The last instruction in the subroutine returns the computer to the main program. This is accomplished by the indirect branch instruction with an address symbol identical to the symbol used for the subroutine name. The address to which the computer branches is not SH4 but the value found in location SH4 because this is an indirect address instruction. What is found in location SH4 is the return address 102 which was previously stored there by the BSA instruction. The computer returns to execute the instruction in location 102. The main program continues by storing the shifted number into location X. A new number is then loaded into the *AC* from location Y, and another branch is made to the subroutine. This time location SH4 will contain the return address 105 since this is now the location of the next instruction after BSA. The new operand is shifted and the subroutine returns to the main program at location 105.

From this example we see that the first memory location of each subroutine serves as a link between the main program and the subroutine. The procedure for branching to a subroutine and returning to the main program is referred to as a subroutine *linkage*. The BSA instruction performs an operation commonly called subroutine *call*. The last instruction of the subroutine performs an operation commonly called subroutine *return*.

The procedure used in the basic computer for subroutine linkage is commonly found in computers with only one processor register. Many computers have multiple processor registers and some of them are assigned the name *index registers*. In such computers, an index register is usually employed to implement the subroutine linkage. A branch-to-subroutine instruction stores the return address in an index register. A return-from-subroutine instruction is effected by branching to the address presently stored in the index register.

*Subroutine Parameters and Data Linkage*

When a subroutine is called, the main program must transfer the data it wishes the subroutine to work with. In the previous example, the data was transferred through the accumulator. The operand was loaded into the *AC* prior to the branch. The subroutine shifted the number and left it there to be accepted by the main program. In general, it is necessary for the subroutine to have access to data from the calling program and to return results to that program. The accumulator can be used for a single input parameter and a single output parameter. In computers with multiple processor registers, more parameters can be transferred this way. Another way to transfer data to a subroutine is through the memory. Data are often placed in memory locations following the call. They can also be placed in a block of storage. The first address of the block is then placed in the memory location following the call. In any case, the return address always gives the link information for transferring data between the main program and the subroutine.

As an illustration, consider a subroutine that performs the logic OR operation. Two operands must be transferred to the subroutine and the subroutine must return the result of the operation. The accumulator can be used to transfer one operand and to receive the result. The other operand is inserted in the location following the BSA instruction. This is demonstrated in the program of Table 6-17. The first operand in location X is loaded into the *AC*. The second operand is stored in location 202 following the BSA instruction. After the branch, the first location in the subroutine holds the number 202. Note that in this case, 202 is not the return address but the address of the second operand. The subroutine starts performing the OR operation by complementing the first operand in the *AC* and storing it in a temporary location TMP. The second operand is loaded into the *AC* by an indirect instruction at location OR. Remember that location OR contains the number 202. When the instruction refers to it indirectly, the operand at location 202 is loaded into the *AC*. This operand is complemented and then ANDed with the operand stored in TMP. Complementing the result forms the OR operation.

The return from the subroutine must be manipulated so the main program continues from location 203 where the next instruction is located. This is accomplished by incrementing location OR with the ISZ instruction. Now location OR holds the number 203 and an indirect BUN instruction causes a return to the proper place.

It is possible to have more than one operand following the BSA instruction. The subroutine must increment the return address stored in its first location for each operand that it extracts from the calling program. Moreover, the calling program can reserve one or more locations for the subroutine to

**Table 6-17** *Program to demonstrate parameter linkage*

| *Location* | | | |
|---|---|---|---|
| | | ORG 200 | |
| 200 | | LDA X | /Load first operand into *AC* |
| 201 | | BSA OR | /Branch to subroutine OR |
| 202 | | HEX 3AF6 | /Second operand stored here |
| 203 | | STA Y | /Subroutine returns here |
| 204 | | HLT | |
| 205 | X, | HEX 7B95 | /First operand stored here |
| 206 | Y, | HEX 0 | /Result stored here |
| 207 | OR, | HEX 0 | /Subroutine OR |
| 208 | | CMA | /Complement first operand |
| 209 | | STA TMP | /Store in temporary location |
| 20A | | LDA OR I | /Load second operand |
| 20B | | CMA | /Complement second operand |
| 20C | | AND TMP | /AND complemented first operand |
| 20D | | CMA | /Complement again to get OR |
| 20E | | ISZ OR | /Increment return address |
| 20F | | BUN OR I | /Return to main program |
| 210 | TMP, | HEX 0 | /Temporary storage |
| | | END | |

return results that are computed. The first location in the subroutine must be incremented for these locations as well, before the return. If there is a large amount of data to be transferred, the data can be placed in a block of storage and the address of the first item in the block is then used as the linking parameter.

A subroutine that moves a block of data starting at address 100 into a block starting with address 200 is listed in Table 6-18. The length of the block is 16 words. The first instruction is a branch to subroutine MVE. The first part of the subroutine transfers the three parameters 100, 200 and −16 from the main program and places them in its own storage location. The items are retrieved from their blocks by the use of two pointers. The counter insures that only 16 items are moved. When the subroutine completes its operation, the required data is in the block starting from the location 200. The return to the main program is to the HLT instruction.

### *Fortran Subroutines*

The relation between machine language and a high-level programming language such as Fortran can be demonstrated by writing the equivalent Fortran program for the MVE subroutine. A subroutine is defined in Fortran by a SUBROUTINE statement. The last statement is always a

**Table 6-18** *Subroutine to move a block of data*

```
                            /Main program
          BSA MVE           /Branch to subroutine
          HEX 100           /First address of source data
          HEX 200           /First address of destination data
          DEC -16           /Number of items to move
          HLT
MVE,      HEX 0             /Subroutine MVE
          LDA MVE I         /Bring address of source
          STA PT1           /Store in first pointer
          ISZ MVE           /Increment return address
          LDA MVE I         /Bring address of destination
          STA PT2           /Store in second pointer
          ISZ MVE           /Increment return address
          LDA MVE I         /Bring number of items
          STA CTR           /Store in counter
          ISZ MVE           /Increment return address
LOP,      LDA PT1 I         /Load source item
          STA PT2 I         /Store in destination
          ISZ PT1           /Increment source pointer
          ISZ PT2           /Increment destination pointer
          ISZ CTR           /Increment counter
          BUN LOP           /Repeat 16 times
          BUN MVE I         /Return to main program
PT1,      —
PT2,      —
CTR,      —
```

RETURN statement. The MVE subroutine is written as follows:

```
      SUBROUTINE MOVE (SOURCE, DEST, N)
      DO 20 I = 1, N
20    DEST(I) = SOURCE(I)
      RETURN
```

The parameters are enclosed in parentheses after the name of the subroutine. When this subroutine is compiled, it produces a machine-language program similar to the one listed in Table 6-18.

The CALL statement is used to link the main program with the subroutine. It is equivalent to the BSA instruction. The CALL statement in this case is:

```
CALL MOVE (X, Y, 16)
```

X and Y are array identifiers whose dimension must be defined by a DIMENSION statement. Note that the names of the parameters in the CALL statement can be different from the names used in the SUBROUTINE statement. However, the compiler correlates X with SOURCE, Y with DEST, and 16 with N.

## 6-8 INPUT-OUTPUT PROGRAMMING

The user of the computer writes his program with symbols that are defined by the programming language he employs. The symbols are strings of characters and each character is assigned an 8-bit code so it can be stored in computer memory. A binary-coded character enters the computer when an INP (input) instruction is executed. A binary-coded character is transferred to the output device when an OUT (output) instruction is executed. The output device detects the binary code and types the corresponding character.

Table 6-19(a) lists the instructions needed to input a character and store

**Table 6-19** *Programs to input and output one character*

```
(a) Input a character:
    CIF,    SKI           /Check input flag
            BUN CIF       /Flag=0, branch to check again
            INP           /Flag=1, input character
            OUT           /Print character
            STA CHR       /Store character
            HLT
    CHR,    —             /Store character here
(b) Output one character:
            LDA CHR       /Load character into AC
    COF,    SKO           /Check output flag
            BUN COF       /Flag=0, branch to check again
            OUT           /Flag=1, output character
            HLT
    CHR,    HEX 0057      /Character is "W"
```

it in memory. The SKI instruction checks the input flag to see if a character is available for transfer. The next instruction is skipped if the input flag bit is 1. The INP instruction transfers the binary-coded character into $AC$(9–16). The character is then printed by means of the OUT instruction. A Teletype unit that communicates directly with a computer does not print the character when a key is depressed. To type it, it is necessary to send an OUT instruction for the printer. In this way, the user is insured that the correct transfer has occurred. If the SKI instruction finds the flag bit at 0, the next instruction in sequence is executed. This instruction is a branch to return and check the flag bit again. Because the input device is much slower than the computer, the two instructions in the loop will be executed many times before a character is transferred into the accumulator.

Table 6-19(b) lists the instructions needed to print a character initially stored in memory. The character is first loaded into the *AC*. The output flag is then checked. If it is 0, the computer remains in a two-instruction loop checking the flag bit. When the flag changes to 1, the character is transferred from the accumulator to the printer.

### *Character Manipulation*

A computer is not just a calculator but also a symbol manipulator. The binary-coded characters that represent symbols can be manipulated by computer instructions to achieve various data processing tasks. One such task may be to pack two characters in one word. This is convenient because each character occupies 8 bits and a memory word contains 16 bits. The program in Table 6-20 lists a subroutine named IN2 that inputs two characters and packs them into one 16-bit word. The packed word remains in the accumulator. Note that subroutine SH4 (Table 6-16) is called twice to shift the accumulator left eight times.

**Table 6-20** *Subroutine to input and pack two characters*

```
IN2,   —           /Subroutine entry
FST,   SKI
       BUN FST
       INP         /Input first character
       OUT
       BSA SH4     /Shift left four times
       BSA SH4     /Shift left four more times
SCD,   SKI
       BUN SCD
       INP         /Input second character
       OUT
       BUN IN2 I   /Return
```

In the discussion of the assembler it was assumed that the symbolic program is stored in a section of memory which is sometimes called a *buffer*. The symbolic program being typed enters through the input device and is stored in consecutive memory locations in the buffer. The program listed in Table 6-21 can be used to input a symbolic program from the teletypewriter, pack two characters in one word and store them in the buffer. The first address of the buffer is 500. The first double character is stored in location 500 and all characters are stored in sequential locations. The program uses a

**Table 6-21** *Program to store input characters in a buffer*

| | | |
|---|---|---|
| | LDA ADS | /Load first address of buffer |
| | STA PTR | /Initialize pointer |
| LOP, | BSA IN2 | /Go to subroutine IN2 (Table 6-20) |
| | STA PTR I | /Store double character word in buffer |
| | ISZ PTR | /Increment pointer |
| | BUN LOP | /Branch to input more characters |
| | HLT | |
| ADS, | HEX 500 | /First address of buffer |
| PTR, | HEX 0 | /Location for pointer |

pointer for keeping track of the current empty location in the buffer. No counter is used in the program so characters will be read as long as they are available, or until the buffer reaches location 0 (after location FFF). In a practical situation it may be necessary to limit the size of the buffer and a counter may be used for this purpose. Note that subroutine IN2 of Table 6-20 is called to input and pack the two characters.

In discussing the second pass of the assembler in Sec. 6-4 it was mentioned that one of the most common operations of an assembler is table lookup. This is an operation that searches a table to find out if it contains a given symbol. The search may be done by comparing the given symbol with each of the symbols stored in the table. The search terminates when a match occurs or if none of the symbols match. When a match occurs, the assembler retrieves the equivalent binary value. A program for comparing two words is listed in Table 6-22. The comparison is accomplished by forming the 2's complement

**Table 6-22** *Program to compare two words*

| | | |
|---|---|---|
| | LDA WD1 | /Load first word |
| | CMA | |
| | INC | /Form 2's complement |
| | ADD WD2 | /Add second word |
| | SZA | /Skip if *AC* is zero |
| | BUN UEQ | /Branch to "unequal" routine |
| | BUN EQL | /Branch to "equal" routine |
| WD1, | — | |
| WD2, | — | |

of a word (as if it were a number) and arithmetically adding it to the second word. If the result is zero, the two words are equal and a match occurs. If the result is not zero, the words are not the same. This program can serve as a subroutine in a table-lookup program.

### *Program Interrupt*

The running time of input and output programs is primarily made up of the time spent by the computer in waiting for the external device to set its flag. The waiting loop that checks the flag keeps the computer occupied with a task that wastes a large amount of time. This waiting time can be eliminated if the interrupt facility is used to notify the computer when a flag is set. The advantage of using the interrupt is that the information transfer is initiated upon request from the external device. In the meantime, the computer can be busy performing other useful tasks. Obviously, if no other program resides in memory, there is nothing for the computer to do so it might as well check for the flags. The interrupt facility is useful in a multiprogram environment when two or more programs reside in memory at the same time.

Only one program can be executed at any given time even though two or more programs may reside in memory. The program currently being executed is referred to as the running program. The other programs are usually waiting for input or output data. The function of the interrupt facility is to take care of the data transfer of one (or more) program while another program is currently being executed. The running program must include an ION instruction to turn the interrupt on. If the interrupt facility is not used, the program must include an IOF instruction to turn it off. (The *start* switch of the computer should also turn the interrupt off.)

The interrupt facility allows the running program to proceed until the input or output device sets its ready flag. Whenever a flag is set to 1, the computer completes the execution of the instruction in progress and then acknowledges the interrupt. The result of this action is that the return address is stored in location 0. The instruction in location 1 is then performed; this initiates a service routine for the input or output transfer. The service routine can be stored anywhere in memory provided a branch to the start of the routine is stored in location 1. The service routine must have instructions to perform the following tasks:

1. Save contents of processor registers.
2. Check which flag is set.
3. Service the device whose flag is set.
4. Restore contents of processor registers.
5. Turn the interrupt facility on.
6. Return to the running program.

The contents of processor registers before the interrupt and after the return to the running program must be the same; otherwise, the running program may be in error. Since the service routine may use these registers, it is necessary to save their contents at the beginning of the routine and restore them at the end. The sequence by which the flags are checked dictates the priority assigned to each device. Even though two or more flags may be set at the same time, the devices nevertheless are serviced one at a time. The device with higher priority is serviced first followed by the one with lower priority.

The occurrence of an interrupt disables the facility from further interrupts. The service routine must turn the interrupt on before the return to the running program. This will enable further interrupts while the computer is executing the running program. The interrupt facility should not be turned on until after the return address is inserted into the program counter.

An example of a program that services an interrupt is listed in Table 6-23. Location 0 is reserved for the return address. Location 1 has a branch

**Table 6-23** *Program to service an interrupt*

| *Location* | | | |
|---|---|---|---|
| 0 | ZRO, | — | /Return address stored here |
| 1 | | BUN SRV | /Branch to service routine |
| 100 | | CLA | /Portion of running program |
| 101 | | ION | /Turn on interrupt facility |
| 102 | | LDA X | |
| 103 | | ADD Y | /Interrupt occurs here |
| 104 | | STA Z | /Program returns here after interrupt |
| . | | . | |
| . | | . | |
| . | | | /Interrupt service routine |
| 200 | SRV, | STA SAC | /Store content of *AC* |
| | | CIR | /Move *E* into *AC*(1) |
| | | STA SE | /Store content of *E* |
| | | SKI | /Check input flag |
| | | BUN NXT | /Flag is off, check next flag |
| | | INP | /Flag is on, input character |
| | | OUT | /Print character |
| | | STA PT1 I | /Store it in input buffer |
| | | ISZ PT1 | /Increment input pointer |
| | NXT, | SKO | /Check output flag |
| | | BUN EXT | /Flag is off, exit |
| | | LDA PT2 I | /Load character from output buffer |
| | | OUT | /Output character |
| | | ISZ PT2 | /Increment output pointer |
| | EXT, | LDA SE | /Restore value of *AC*(1) |
| | | CIL | /Shift it to *E* |
| | | LDA SAC | /Restore content of *AC* |
| | | ION | /Turn interrupt on |
| | | BUN ZRO I | /Return to running program |
| | SAC, | — | /*AC* is stored here |
| | SE, | — | /*E* is stored here |
| | PT1, | — | /Pointer of input buffer |
| | PT2, | — | /Pointer of output buffer |

instruction to the beginning of the service routine SRV. The portion of the running program listed has an ION instruction that turns the interrupt on. Suppose that an interrupt occurs while the computer is executing the instruction in location 103. The interrupt cycle stores the binary equivalent of hexadecimal 104 in location 0 and branches to location 1. The branch instruction in location 1 sends the computer to the service routine SRV.

The service routine performs the six tasks mentioned above. The contents of $AC$ and $E$ are stored in special locations. (These are the only processor registers in the basic computer.) The flags are checked sequentially, the input flag first and the output flag second. If any or both flags are set, an item of data is transferred to or from the corresponding memory buffer. Before returning to the running program the previous contents of $E$ and $AC$ are restored and the interrupt facility is turned on. The last instruction causes a branch to the address stored in location 0. This is the return address previously stored there during the interrupt cycle. Hence the running program will continue from location 104 where it was interrupted.

A typical computer may have many more input and output devices connected to the interrupt facility. Furthermore, interrupt sources are not limited to input and output transfers. Interrupts can be used for other purposes such as internal processing errors or special alarm conditions. Further discussion of interrupts and some advanced concepts concerning this important subject can be found in Sec. 11-5.

## 6-9 SYSTEM SOFTWARE

A computer system is composed of its hardware components and the system software available for its use. The system software of a computer consists of a collection of operative programs whose purpose is to make the use of the computer more effective. The programs included in a system software package are called *system programs*. They are distinguished from *application programs* written by computer users for the purpose of solving particular problems. For example, a Fortran program written by a scientist to solve his particular research problem is an application program but the compiler that translates the Fortran program to a machine-language executable program is a system program. Most of the system programs are distributed by the computer manufacturer. The customer who buys or leases a computer system would usually receive, in addition to the hardware, any available software needed for the effective operation of his computer. The system software is an indispensable part of a total computer system. Its function is to compensate for the differences that exist between the user needs and the capabilities of the hardware. A computer without some kind of system software would be very ineffective and most likely impossible to operate.

The production of system programs is a complex undertaking requiring extensive knowledge and considerable specialized training in computer science. System programs offer several advantages and conveniences to application programmers and computer users in general. A brief summary of the major components that system programs offer is included in this section.

Software systems can be subdivided into six different categories as follows.

1. Language processors that convert programs from user-oriented languages to machine language.
2. Library programs that provide standard routines for the application programmer.
3. Utility programs to facilitate the communication among computer components and between computer and user.
4. Loader programs to facilitate the reading of various programs into memory.
5. Diagnostic programs to facilitate the maintenance of the computer.
6. An operating system that supervises all other programs and controls their execution.

### *Language Processors*

A language processor is a system program that translates a *source* program written by the user to an *object* program which is meaningful to the hardware of the computer. We have already discussed two language processors: assemblers and compilers. An *assembler* is a system program that translates an assembly-language program to an equivalent binary machine language program. A *compiler* is a system program that translates a high-level language program to machine language. Two other language processors widely used and worth mentioning are macro-assemblers and interpreters.

A *macro* is a pseudo-instruction that defines a group of machine instructions. A *macro-assembler* translates assembly-language programs with macro facility. When employing a macro, the programmer essentially defines a symbolic name to represent a sequence of instructions. For every occurrence of this macro, or symbolic name, the macro-assembler substitutes the defined sequence of instructions. For example, a program that computes the average value of two positive numbers consists of four machine instructions which can be defined by a macro routine as follows:

```
AVG,    MACRO  OP1  OP2
        LDA    OP1
        ADD    OP2
        CLE
        CIR
        END    MACRO
```

In the above program, a macro routine is defined by the symbolic name AVG. The instructions following the macro definition, when executed, will add two operands (OP1 and OP2) and divide their sum by 2 (by shifting right) to obtain the average value. Now, if we want to compute the average of two positive operands, say X and Y, it is not necessary to rewrite the four instructions again. We can use the macro symbol already defined and write only one line of code as follows:

```
AVG X Y
```

The macro-assembler will substitute the instructions defined by the macro routine but with the new specified operands. In other words, the macro-assembler will produce the binary code equivalent to the following instruction sequence:

```
LDA X
ADD Y
CLE
CIR
```

A macro is a special type of subroutine, usually with very few instructions, that is included in the main program whenever the instructions are needed. To differentiate between a macro and a normal subroutine, it is customary to refer to a macro as an *open* subroutine and to a normal subroutine as a *closed* subroutine. An open subroutine is different from a closed one in that all instructions defined by a macro name are inserted in the main program every time the macro symbolic name is encountered. Thus, if the same open subroutine were used four times, it would appear in four different places in the main program. A closed subroutine resides outside of the main program and control transfers to the subroutine by means of a *call* instruction. The closed subroutine uses less overall storage space for instructions but takes longer to execute because of the additional instructions for subroutine and parameter transfer.

An *interpreter* is a language processor that translates each statement of a high-level language program and then immediately executes it. Translation and execution alternate for each statement encountered. This differs from a compiler which merely translates the entire source program and is not involved in its execution. The advantage of the interpreter over a compiler is fast response to changes in the source program. This is useful in a time sharing environment where the user can type part of his program and ask the interpreter to execute it. He does not have to type the entire program first as required by a conventional compiler. The interpreter, however, is a time-consuming translation method because each statement must be translated every time it is executed from the source program.

### *Library Programs*

Library programs are available in a computer system for the purpose of simplifying the drudgery of repetitious programming. Routines that are repetitious and similar to previously written ones become standard routines and conventions are adopted for each computer so that any user has access to a library of routines. These routines are typically prepared by computer users and distributed by an association of computer users or by the manufacturer.

In the area of scientific applications, the usual types of library routines available are the mathematical functions such as square root and exponential functions. Other operations of various types are also encountered such as matrix inversion and statistical analysis. In the area of commercial data processing applications, the most widely used library routines are *sort* and *merge*. Sort programs are used to arrange data into a specified sequence. For example, business transactions may be stored in a computer in the order in which they occur. The transactions may be sorted by different items such as by account number to identify the customer or by salesman's name to calculate the commission to be paid. Merge programs are used to combine two or more sets of sorted data into one file containing all the items from both of the original sets. Sort and merge are sometimes categorized as utility programs.

### *Utility Programs*

Utility programs are a collection of commonly used routines that the programmer may use to perform specific tasks, thereby reducing his own programming effort. Each computer installation will have its own library of utility programs and a well-informed programmer would know how and when to use them. A few examples of utility programs commonly available in a computer system are text editors, debugging aids, and input-output routines.

A *text editor* is a program that facilitates the creation of corrected and well-organized text. The text being edited could be an English language letter, but most often, it is a symbolic-language program typed by the user. The text editor program does not interpret the meaning of the text but has the capability of changing it when special commands are issued by the user. For example, when a symbolic language program is being entered into a computer memory via a Teletype terminal, the programmer may use the facility of a text editor program to correct his typing errors by issuing commands to insert, delete, or replace characters in his source program. A time-sharing service which provides remote access to a computer via a typewriter terminal will have available a text editor system so that users can prepare programs and correct them with relative ease.

*Debugging aids* are programs that help the user correct logical mistakes in his program. Debugging is a process for locating and correcting logical mistakes in a program after it has been executed. These mistakes are called *bugs* and correcting them is referred to as debugging. Debugging procedures begin after the machine-language program is executed and results are not as expected.

A *dynamic debugging* program is a system program which allows the programmer to execute his binary program in the computer while using a Teletype keyboard to control program execution. He can examine contents of registers, change contents of registers and memory, make alterations to the binary program, and other similar functions. By using the facilities of a dynamic debugging program the user can detect and correct logical errors in his program.

A *memory dump* is a system program that selects specified locations in memory, taken at some particular point during the program execution, and prints their content. A memory dump typically shows both the program and operand data. By inspecting both program and data, and comparing it with what it should have been if the program had run correctly, the programmer is able to find his mistakes.

A *trace* is a system program that allows the user to trace the flow of his program while it is executed. He can request, for example, that the contents of certain registers or memory locations be printed every time a branch is executed or when certain memory locations are changed. This allows the user to get a picture of what his program is doing and thus be able to correct mistakes in his program.

In many computer systems, input and output procedures are quite complicated and writing effective input and output programs becomes a cumbersome process. For that reason, the computer manufacturer will provide ready made utility routines in the form of macros or subroutines to relieve the user of the drudgery of programming in detail his own input-output requirements. Other utility routines facilitate interchange among peripheral units. Peripheral transfer routines make possible the copying of data from one unit, for instance, magnetic tape, to another unit, for instance magnetic disk. This results in a more efficient utilization of the data preparation equipment. In a large computer system, all input-output and peripheral interchange is handled by the operating system.

### *Loaders*

A loader is a system program that places other programs into memory and prepares them for execution. The simplest type of loader is called an *absolute* loader. In this scheme the binary program produced by an assembler is punched on cards or paper tape instead of being placed directly in memory after translation. The function of the loader is to accept the machine-language program and place it in memory in the locations specified by the user by means of established pseudo-instructions such as ORG.

A more efficient scheme is to use a *relocating* loader. Such a loader does not allow the programmer to specify the memory space for his binary program. The task of a relocating loader is to adjust programs and subroutines so they can be placed in arbitrary memory locations in an efficient manner. A relocating loader performs four basic functions. It allocates space in memory for the binary program. It links symbolic references between the main program and its subroutines. It relocates memory addresses to correspond to the allocated memory space. And it places the program and data into the allocated memory space. An application program submitted by the user will be processed in a computer system by running it three times. In the first run the program will be translated to a binary program by means of a language processor. In the second run the binary program will be loaded into memory and prepared for execution by a relocating loader. Only in the third run will the program be executed.

A *bootstrap* loader is a program whose function is to start the computer when "cold," when nothing meaningful is in its memory. A bootstrap loader performs a process similar to the initial operation involved in starting an idle engine. To start the operation of a computer, it is not enough to turn the power on; it is necessary also that an initial program be resident in memory so it can be used to load other programs. Once the initial program is loaded in a nonvolatile magnetic core memory, it will stay there even after power is turned off and on again. But if this program is destroyed, or if a volatile memory is employed, or if the computer just came out of production, the bootstrap program must be loaded into memory to start the operation of the computer. Since initially no programs reside in memory, this process must be implemented by special hardware whose sole purpose is to transfer the bootstrap routine from an external source into memory. The bootstrap process is sometimes referred to as *initial program load* (IPL) or *cold start*.

In small computers, the binary instructions of the bootstrap routine are loaded into memory by means of console switches. A more practical method is to store the bootstrap routine in a read-only memory (ROM) where it can never be destroyed. A special switch can be used to initiate the transfer of the content of ROM into a predetermined space in main memory. In some systems, the binary bootstrap routine is punched on a single card which is then placed in a card reader. When the operator activates an IPL switch, the hardware of the computer reads the card and transfers its contents to a number of predetermined words in memory starting from location 0. Then, starting the computer from location 0 causes the execution of this program. The bootstrap program is then used to read other cards containing other programs. In large systems, the common procedure is to store the bootstrap routine together with the operating system in a peripheral unit such as a magnetic disk. A special switch in the computer console causes the transfer of an initial routine from disk to memory.

### *Diagnostic Programs*

The purpose of the diagnostic programs is to exercise selected parts of the hardware and check for malfunctions. A diagnostic program exercises a portion of the hardware and then checks the results obtained against known correct results. In this way, functional failures can be detected and failure messages printed out. Diagnostic programs assist field engineers in equipment maintenance work. They are useful for checking whether parts of the computer hardware are operating properly. In addition, diagnostic programs are frequently run at fixed intervals, usually at a time when the computer load is light, to make sure that the equipment is functioning correctly.

### *Operating System*

An operating system is a collection of programs that control the operation of the computer for the purpose of obtaining an efficient performance. It is basically a software control program which resides in memory at all times and supervises all other programs that run in the computer. An operating system places a considerable demand on the hardware available in the computer and the benefit derived from using it increases as the range and complexity of the hardware increases. For this reason, the most comprehensive and powerful operating systems are used with the largest computers. Smaller computers often run with a very rudimentary operating system which is referred to as a *monitor*, *supervisor*, or *executive* program.

An operating system includes all the systems programs mentioned previously as well as other programs that control and supervise the operations of all programs residing in the computer. The analysis and design of operating systems is a subject that by itself can fill an entire volume. All we can do in this section is justify its need.

A brief examination of some functions performed by an operating system may help clarify its usefulness. An operating system allocates memory space and loads programs for execution. It provides services for obtaining input data and producing output data. In addition, it provides automatic recovery from many types of errors, for example, input read error or arithmetic overflow. In a *multiprogram* system, many programs can reside simultaneously in the computer. The operating system allocates various computer resources to selected programs and keeps switching resources back and forth. For example, while one program is being executed in the central processor, another program may be receiving input data from a magnetic tape and a third may be in the process of printing its output. In a *time-sharing* system, many users communicate with the computer system via remote terminal devices. The operating system allocates to each job a time-slice on a priority basis. A *job* is a unit of specified work as applied to the execution of a data processing task. A *time-slice* is a given amount of time assigned to a job. In any given time-slice, the operating system causes the computer to process a job until one of the following four conditions occur:

(a) the job is completed;

(b) an error is detected;

(c) an input or output is required;

(d) the time-slice runs out.

In each case the processor is assigned to the job with the next highest priority. In the first two cases, the job may be removed from memory. In the last two, the job is only temporarily suspended.

The operating system contributes to a more efficient use of the hardware by managing memory resources. For example, if a program, because of its size, cannot be entirely accomodated in main memory, the operating system will partition the program into pieces called *pages* or *segments*. It then transfers segments back and forth between the main memory and an auxilliary memory such as magnetic drum. This gives the operating system further control over multiprogram and time-sharing operations.

The effect of the operating system on the management of the computer system is to improve its efficiency. Efficiency in computer systems is measured by throughput. *Throughput* is the amount of processing that the system accomplishes during a specified interval of time, such as an hour or a day. In general, throughput is a measure of both hardware speed and software facilities. Operating systems contribute to greater throughput by providing an efficient software facility.

In conclusion, it must be emphasized that computer software is a field of study in its own right. The presentation in this chapter was merely an overview of the subject. The introductory software concepts presented here constitute a bare minimum of knowledge necessary for understanding the concept of a total computer system.

## REFERENCES

1. Donovan, J. J., *System Programming*, New York: McGraw-Hill Book Co., 1972.
2. *Introduction to Programming*, Maynard, Mass.: Digital Equipment Corp., 1973.
3. Booth, T. L., *Digital Networks and Computer Systems*, New York: John Wiley & Sons, Inc., 1971.

4. GEAR, C. W., *Computer Organization and Programming*, 2nd ed., New York: McGraw-Hill Book Co., 1974.
5. CORBATO, F. J., J. W. PODUSKA and J. H. SALZER, *Advanced Computer Programming*, Cambridge, Mass.: The M.I.T. Press, 1963.
6. CHAPIN, N., *Computers—A System Approach*, New York: Van Nostrand Reinhold Co., 1971.
7. SOUCEK, B., *Minicomputers in Data Processing and Simulation*, New York: John Wiley & Sons, Inc., 1972.
8. MADNICK, S. E., and J. J. DONOVAN, *Operating Systems*, New York: McGraw-Hill Book Co., 1974.

## PROBLEMS

6-1 The following program is stored in the memory unit of the basic computer. Show the contents of the *AC*, *PC*, and *OPR* (in hexadecimal), at the end, after each instruction is executed. All numbers listed below are in hexadecimal.

| *Location* | *Instruction* |
|---|---|
| 010 | CLA |
| 011 | ADD 016 |
| 012 | BUN 014 |
| 013 | HLT |
| 014 | AND 017 |
| 015 | BUN 013 |
| 016 | C1A5 |
| 017 | 93C6 |

6-2 The following program is a list of instructions in hexadecimal code. The computer executes the instructions starting from address 100. What is the content of the *AC* and the memory word at address 103 when the computer halts?

| *Location* | *Instruction* |
|---|---|
| 100 | 5103 |
| 101 | 7200 |
| 102 | 7001 |
| 103 | 0000 |
| 104 | 7800 |
| 105 | 7020 |
| 106 | C103 |

6-3 List the assembly-language program (of the equivalent binary instructions) generated by a compiler from the following Fortran program. Assume integer variables.

SUM = 0
SUM = SUM + A + B
DIF = DIF − C
SUM = SUM + DIF

6-4 Can the letter I be used as a symbolic address in the assembly-language program defined for the basic computer? Justify the answer.

6-5 What happens during the first pass of the assembler (Fig. 6-1) if the line of code that has a pseudo-instruction ORG or END also has a label? Modify the flow chart to include an error message if this occurs.

6-6 A line of code in an assembly language program is as follows:

DEC −35

(a) Show that four memory words are required to store the line of code and give their binary content.
(b) Show that one memory word stores the binary translated code and give its binary content.

6-7 (a) Obtain the address symbol table generated for the program of Table 6-13 during the first pass of the assembler.
(b) List the translated program in hexadecimal.

6-8 The pseudo-instruction BSS N (block started by symbol) is sometimes employed to reserve $N$ memory words for a group of operands. For example, the line of code

A, BSS 10

informs the assembler that a block of 10 (decimal) locations is to be left free, starting from location A. This is similar to the Fortran statement DIMENSION A(10). Modify the flow chart of Fig. 6-1 to process this pseudo-instruction.

6-9 Modify the flow chart of Fig. 6-2 to include an error message when a symbolic address is not defined by a label.

6-10 Show how the MRI and non-MRI tables can be stored in memory.

6-11 List the assembly-language program (of the equivalent binary instructions) generated by a compiler for the following IF statement:

IF(A−B) 10, 20, 30

The program branches to statement 10 if $A - B < 0$; to statement 20 if $A - B = 0$; and to statement 30 if $A - B > 0$.

6-12 (a) Explain in words what the following program accomplishes when it is executed. What is the value of location CTR when the computer halts?
(b) List the address symbol table obtained during the first pass of the assembler.

(c) List the hexadecimal code of the translated program.

```
       ORG 100              BUN AGN
       CLE                  BUN ROT
       CLA           AGN,   CLE
       STA CTR              ISZ CTR
       LDA WRD              SZA
       SZA                  BUN ROT
       BUN ROT       STP,   HLT
       BUN STP       CTR,   HEX 0
ROT,   CIL           WRD,   HEX 62C1
       SZE                  END
```

6-13 Write a program loop, using a pointer and a counter, that clears to 0 the contents of hexadecimal locations 500 to 5FF.

6-14 Write a program to multiply two positive numbers by a repeated addition method. For example, to multiply $5 \times 4$, the program evaluates the product by adding 5 four times, or $5 + 5 + 5 + 5$.

6-15 The multiplication program of Table 6-14 is not initialized. After the program is executed once, location CTR will be left with zero. Show that if the program is executed again starting from location 100, the loop will be traversed 65536 times. Add the needed instructions to initialize the program.

6-16 Write a program to multiply two unsigned positive numbers, each with 16 significant bits, to produce an unsigned double-precision product.

6-17 Write a program to multiply two signed numbers with negative numbers being initially in signed-2's complement representation. The product should be single-precision and signed-2's complement representation if negative.

6-18 Write a program to subtract two double-precision numbers.

6-19 Write a program that evaluates the logic exclusive-OR of two logic operands.

6-20 Write a program for the arithmetic shift-left operation. Branch to OVF if an overflow occurs.

6-21 Write a subroutine to subtract two numbers. In the calling program, the BSA instruction is followed by the subtrahend and minuend. The difference is returned to the main program in the third location following the BSA instruction.

6-22 Write a subroutine to complement each word in a block of data. In the calling program, the BSA instruction is followed by two parameters: the starting address of the block and the number of words in the block.

6-23 Write a subroutine to circulate $E$ and $AC$ four times to the right. If $AC$ contains hexadecimal 079C and $E = 1$, what are the contents of $AC$ and $E$ after the subroutine is executed?

6-24 Write a program to accept input characters, pack two characters in one word and store them in consecutive locations in a memory buffer. The first address of the buffer is $(400)_{16}$. The size of the buffer is $(512)_{10}$ words. If the buffer overflows, the computer should halt.

6-25 Write a program to unpack two characters from location WRD and store them in bits 9–16 of locations CH1 and CH2. Bits 1–8 should contain zeros.

6-26 Obtain a flow chart for a program to check for a CR code (hexadecimal 0D) in a memory buffer. The buffer contains two characters per word. When the code for CR is encountered, the program transfers it to bits 9–16 of location LNE without disturbing bits 1–8.

6-27 Translate the service routine SRV from Table 6-23 to its equivalent hexadecimal code. Assume that the routine is stored starting from location 200.

6-28 Define a macro routine that subtracts two numbers and leaves the difference in the $AC$. Show how the macro can be used to perform $A - B$.

6-29 Write an interrupt service routine that performs all the required functions but the input device is serviced only if a special location, MOD, contains all 1's. The output device is serviced only if location MOD contains all 0's.

6-30 What is a bootstrap loader and why must every computer have one? List four ways for loading a bootstrap routine into a computer.

6-31 What is the difference between an application program and a system program? Can an application program run in a computer if the computer has no system programs? List about 10 different system programs and explain their usefulness.

# 7

# CENTRAL PROCESSOR ORGANIZATION

## 7-1 PROCESSOR BUS ORGANIZATION

The part of a computer that performs the bulk of data processing operations is called the *central processor unit* and is referred to as the CPU. The CPU contains the hardware components for processing instructions and data. It is comprised of a control unit and a processor unit which together supervise and implement the various data processing tasks in the central part of a computer system. If we remove the memory and Teletype units from the basic computer of Chap. 5, what remains can be classified as a CPU.

Computers with a limited number of registers in the CPU employ a single accumulator for implementing micro-operations. With the availability of integrated circuits, registers and other digital circuits are not as expensive as when constructed with discrete components. Consequently, most recent computers employ a large number of processor registers and route information among them through common buses.

In the programming examples of Chap. 6, we have shown that memory locations are needed for storing pointers, counters, return addresses, temporary results, and partial products during multiplication. Having to refer to memory locations for such applications is time consuming because memory access is the most time-consuming micro-operation in a CPU. It is more convenient and more efficient to store these intermediate values in processor registers. Registers that store values of pointers, counters, and return addresses are often called *index registers*. A register that stores the multiplier and partial product during multiplication is sometimes called an *MQ* (multiplier quotient) register. We will refer to such registers (including the accumulator) as *processor registers.*

In addition to processor registers, a CPU needs registers for information transfer between memory and processor and memory and control. Such registers were used in the basic computer and were designated by the names program counter (*PC*), memory address register (*MAR*), and memory buffer register (*MBR*). Another register commonly found in computers is an *instruction register* (*IR*). This is a control register that holds the instruction code extracted from memory after the fetch cycle. The instruction is transferred to *IR* so the control can check all the bits of the instruction (including the address part) without having to refer to any other register.

When a large number of registers are included in a CPU, it is most efficient to connect them through a common bus or arrange them as a small scratch-pad memory having a very fast access time. The registers communicate with each other not only for direct data transfers, but also while performing various micro-operations. Hence, it is necessary to provide a common unit that can perform arithmetic, logic, and shift micro-operations between any register and any other register.

A bus organization for eight CPU registers is shown in Fig. 7-1. The registers are labeled by one of the names mentioned previously. *PC*, *MAR*, and, in some cases, the index registers *XR*1 and *XR*2 have a number of bits equal to the memory address bits. The other registers need a number of bits equal to a memory word. *MAR* and *MBR* must be connected also to the memory unit for their usual memory functions. Some computers may employ two or more bus systems. One bus may be used for data transfers, another for memory address transfers and a third for input and output information transfers.

Each of the CPU registers is connected to two multiplexers to form the input busses *A* and *B*. The selection lines in each multiplexer select one register for the bus. The *A* and *B* busses go through a common arithmetic logic unit (ALU). The function select in the ALU determines the particular arithmetic or logic micro-operation that is to be implemented. The shift micro-operations are implemented in the shifter. The result of the micro-operation goes through the output bus *S* into the inputs of all registers. The destination register that receives the information from the output bus is selected by a decoder. This decoder, when enabled, activates one of the register load inputs, thus providing a transfer path between the data in the *S* bus and the flip-flop inputs of the selected destination register.

The operation of the multiplexers, the bus, and the destination decoder is explained in Sec. 4-2. The arithmetic logic unit and the shifter are discussed in the next section.

The logical construction of an ALU will be better understood if we first consider a binary parallel-adder connected to two common busses, as shown

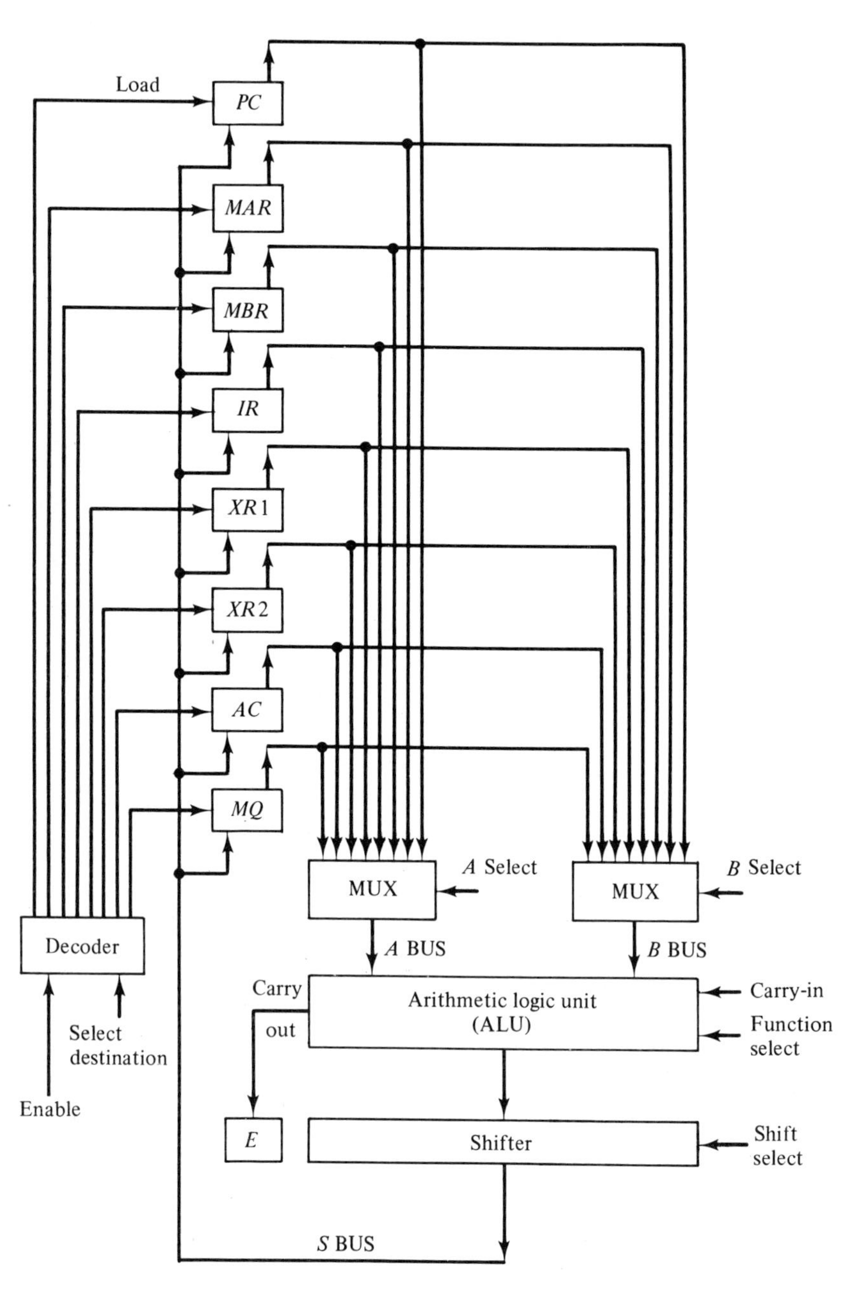


**Fig. 7-1** CPU registers connected by a common bus.

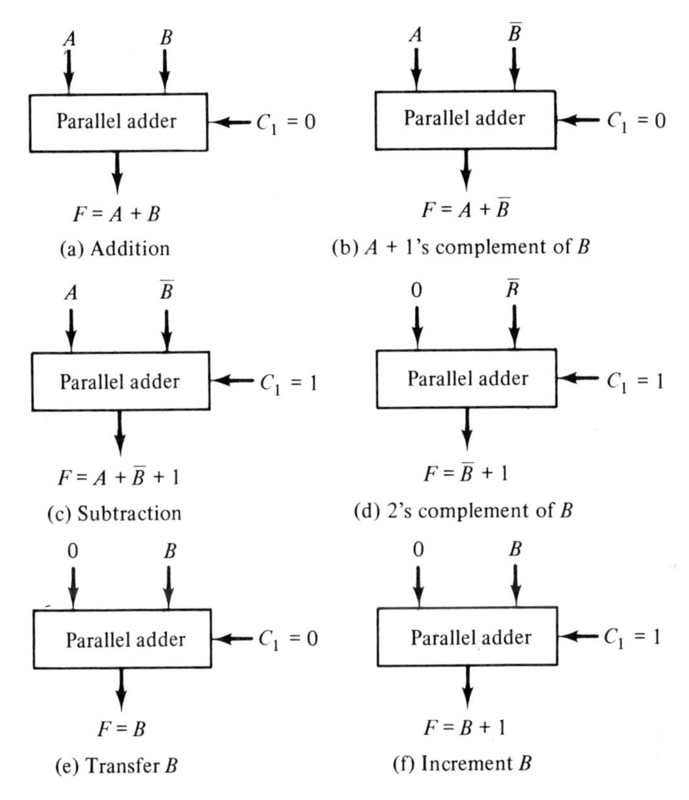


**Fig. 7-2** Arithmetic micro-operations obtained by controlling the inputs of a parallel-adder.

in Fig. 7-2. Different arithmetic micro-operations can be obtained by controlling the data input in busses $A$ and $B$ and the input carry $C_1$. With $C_1 = 0$, the $F$ outputs of the parallel-adder form the sum of $A$ and $B$. If all bits coming from bus $B$ are complemented, the result at output $F$ will be $A + \bar{B}$ which is equivalent to $A$ plus the 1's complement of $B$. By making the input carry $C_1 = 1$, a 1 is added to the sum and the result is $A + \bar{B} + 1$ which is equal to $A$ plus the 2's complement of $B$. This is equivalent to a subtraction operation. The 2's complement of $B$ is obtained by complementing the bits in bus $B$, forcing 0's into the inputs of $A$ and making $C_1 = 1$ to obtain $F = \bar{B} + 1$. A direct transfer from $B$ to $F$ is accomplished by making the $A$ inputs all zeros and $C_1$ a 0, to obtain $F = B$. The increment micro-operation is obtained by changing $C_1$ to 1 to obtain $F = B + 1$.

From this example we see that a binary arithmetic unit is basically a parallel-adder with additional circuits for controlling the bits entering the two input lines. The logic micro-operations can be similarly controlled. The carry is not used during the logic micro-operations since these operations are performed on pairs of bits irrespective of any carry from previous bits.

## 7-2 ARITHMETIC LOGIC UNIT (ALU)

Just as in a parallel-adder, an ALU can be partitioned into stages, one for each pair of bits of the input operands. For operands with $n$ bits, the ALU consists of $n$ identical stages. Figure 7-3 shows the block diagram of

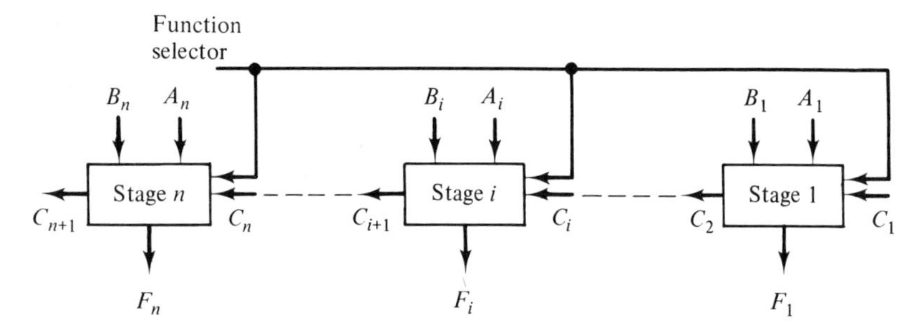


**Fig. 7-3** ALU partitioned into $n$ stages.

an ALU partitioned into $n$ identical stages. The bits of inputs $A$ and $B$ are designated by subscript numbers from right to left with subscript 1 denoting the low-order bit. The carries are connected in a chain through the ALU stages. The function selection lines select the arithmetic or logic micro-operation and the $F$ terminals generate the required output function. Most often, a 4-bit ALU is enclosed within one integrated circuit package. Such a package will contain four stages with four inputs for $A$, four inputs for $B$ and four outputs for $F$. The number of lines for the function selector determines the number of operations that the ALU can perform. An $n$-bit ALU can be constructed from 4-bit ALUs by cascading several packages. The output-carry from one IC package must be connected to the input-carry of the package with the next higher-order bits.

The internal construction of the ALU depends on the micro-operations that it implements. In any case, it always needs full-adders to perform the arithmetic operations. Additional gates are sometimes included for logic micro-operations. In order to minimize the number of terminals for the function selection, IC ALUs use $m$ selection lines to specify $2^m$ micro-operations. A typical logic diagram of a one-stage ALU is shown in Fig. 7-4. Selection line $S_2$ controls input $A_i$. Selection lines $S_1$ and $S_0$ control input $B_i$. The mode $M$ controls the input-carry $C_i$. When $S_2S_1S_0 = 101$ and $M = 1$, the terminals marked $x$, $y$, and $z$ have a binary value equal to $A_i$, $B_i$, and $C_i$, respectively. The exclusive-OR of the three variables provides the sum output

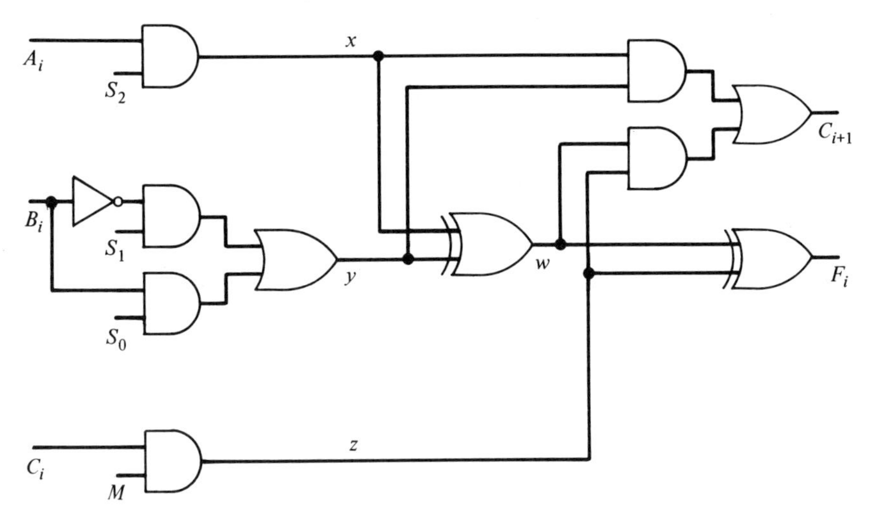


**Fig. 7-4** One stage ALU.

of a full-adder. The other circuit in the diagram provides the carry output for the next higher-order stage.

Selection lines $S_2S_1S_0$ may have eight possible bit combinations and each combination provides a different function for $F_i$ and $C_{i+1}$. The mode control $M$ enables the input-carry $C_i$ and is used to differentiate between an arithmetic and logic function. When $M = 1$, input carry $C_i$ propagates through the gate making $z = C_i$. This allows the propagation of the carry through all the ALU stages for an arithmetic micro-operation. When $M = 0$, thc input carry is inhibited, making $z = 0$. This is a necessary condition for a logic micro-operation. Hence, the ALU can provide up to eight arithmetic operations and eight logic operations.

Table 7-1 shows how the selection lines control inputs $A$, $B$, and $C$. The value of $x$ may be 0 or $A_i$ depending on whether $S_2$ is 0 or 1. Selection lines $S_1$ and $S_0$ control the value of $y$ which may be 0, 1, $B_i$ or $B_i'$. Terminal $z$ may be equal to 0 or $C_i$ depending on whether $M$ is 0 or 1.

In order to evaluate the Boolean functions for $w$ and $F_i$ of Fig. 7-4, we

**Table 7-1** *Effect of selection lines on ALU*

| $S_2$ | $x$ | $S_1$ | $S_0$ | $y$ | $M$ | $z$ |
|---|---|---|---|---|---|---|
| 0 | 0 | 0 | 0 | 0 | 0 | 0 |
| 1 | $A_i$ | 0 | 1 | $B_i$ | 1 | $C_i$ |
| | | 1 | 0 | $B_i'$ | | |
| | | 1 | 1 | 1 | | |

need certain Boolean relations for the exclusive-OR operation. These relations are listed in Table 7-2.

**Table 7-2** *Exclusive-OR relations*

| | | |
|---|---|---|
| $0 \oplus 0 = 0$ | $x \oplus 0 = x$ | $x \oplus y' = (x \oplus y)'$ |
| $0 \oplus 1 = 1$ | $x \oplus 1 = x'$ | $x' \oplus y = (x \oplus y)'$ |
| $1 \oplus 0 = 1$ | $x' \oplus 0 = x'$ | $x' \oplus y' = x \oplus y$ |
| $1 \oplus 1 = 0$ | $x' \oplus 1 = x$ | |

The Boolean functions for the two outputs of the one-stage ALU are:

$$F_i = x \oplus y \oplus z$$

$$C_{i+1} = xy + (x \oplus y)z = xy + xz + yz$$

and are identical to the full-adder circuit derived in Sec. 1-4 (Fig. 1-19).

For each binary combination of the selection lines, the one-stage ALU will have different values for $x$, $y$, and $z$. Table 7-3 gives a list of the Boolean functions for each of the eight possible combinations of the selection lines. The values of $x$ and $y$ for each combination are determined from Table 7-1. The function for $w$ is derived from the exclusive-OR relation of $x$ and $y$. When $M = 0$, output $F_i$ is the same as $w$ since $F_i = w \oplus 0 = w$. Output carry $C_{i+1} = xy$ since $z = 0$. However, this signal is not allowed to propagate to the $z$ terminal of the next higher stage when $M = 0$. The Boolean functions listed under $F_i$ (with $M = 0$) provide the eight logic functions of the ALU.

The arithmetic operations of the ALU are generated when $M = 1$. The Boolean functions of the eight arithmetic operations in the one-stage ALU

**Table 7-3** *Boolean functions for one stage of ALU*

| $S_2\ S_1\ S_0$ | $x$ | $y$ | $w$ | $F_i$ | | $C_{i+1}$ for $M = 1$ |
|---|---|---|---|---|---|---|
| | | | | $M = 0$ | $M = 1$ | |
| 0 0 0 | 0 | 0 | 0 | 0 | $C_i$ | 0 |
| 0 0 1 | 0 | $B_i$ | $B_i$ | $B_i$ | $B_i \oplus C_i$ | $B_iC_i$ |
| 0 1 0 | 0 | $B_i'$ | $B_i'$ | $B_i'$ | $B_i' \oplus C_i$ | $B_i'C_i$ |
| 0 1 1 | 0 | 1 | 1 | 1 | $C_i'$ | $C_i$ |
| 1 0 0 | $A_i$ | 0 | $A_i$ | $A_i$ | $A_i \oplus C_i$ | $A_iC_i$ |
| 1 0 1 | $A_i$ | $B_i$ | $A_i \oplus B_i$ | $A_i \oplus B_i$ | $A_i \oplus B_i \oplus C_i$ | $A_iB_i + A_iC_i + B_iC_i$ |
| 1 1 0 | $A_i$ | $B_i'$ | $A_i \oplus B_i'$ | $(A_i \oplus B_i)'$ | $A_i \oplus B_i' \oplus C_i$ | $A_iB_i' + A_iC_i + B_i'C_i$ |
| 1 1 1 | $A_i$ | 1 | $A_i'$ | $A_i'$ | $A_i' \oplus C_i$ | $A_i + C_i$ |

are listed in the last two columns of Table 7-3. They are derived from the following relations:

$$F_i = w \oplus C_i$$

$$C_{i+1} = xy + xC_i + yC_i$$

We now construct the ALU by connecting $n$ identical stages in cascade. Output-carry $C_{i+1}$ of one stage is connected to the input-carry $C_i$ of the next higher-order stage (as indicated in Fig. 7-3). From the fifth column of Table 7-3, we obtain the logic functions of the ALU. These micro-operations are listed in Table 7-4. Note that there are 16 possible micro-operations for two logic operands and only eight of them are available in this ALU. In fact, the two important logic operations AND and OR are not generated in this ALU. By providing a fourth selection line it is possible to include these functions (see Prob. 7-5).

**Table 7-4** *Logic micro-operations in ALU*

| $M$ | $S_2\ S_1\ S_0$ | *Micro-Operation* | *Description* |
|---|---|---|---|
| 0 | 0 0 0 | $F = 0$ | Clear all bits |
| 0 | 0 0 1 | $F = B$ | Transfer $B$ |
| 0 | 0 1 0 | $F = \bar{B}$ | Complement $B$ |
| 0 | 0 1 1 | $F = 1$ | Set all bits |
| 0 | 1 0 0 | $F = A$ | Transfer $A$ |
| 0 | 1 0 1 | $F = A \oplus B$ | Exclusive-OR |
| 0 | 1 1 0 | $F = \overline{A \oplus B}$ | Exclusive-NOR |
| 0 | 1 1 1 | $F = \bar{A}$ | Complement $A$ |

The arithmetic operations are derived from the last two columns of Table 7-3. These functions should be compared with the conditions listed in Fig. 7-2. In each case, a parallel binary adder composed of full-adder circuits is used, but some of the input lines are either missing or complemented. Thus, in row 001, input $A$ is missing because all the $x$ inputs of the full-adders change to zero by selection line $S_2$. The output function for this condition is $F = B$ when $C_1 = 0$ and $F = B + 1$ when $C_1 = 1$, as indicated in Fig. 7-2 parts (e) and (f), respectively. In row 010, input $A$ is changed to zero and all $B$ inputs are complemented so $F = \bar{B}$ when $C_1 = 0$ and $F = \bar{B} + 1$ when $C_1 = 1$. In row 110, all bits of input $B$ are complemented so that $F$ generates the arithmetic operation of $A$ plus the 1's complement of $B$. The Boolean function for row 111 represents one stage of a decrement micro-operation. The proof that this function decrements input $A$ is left for an exercise (see Prob. 7-6).

The useful arithmetic micro-operations are listed in Table 7-5. The input-carry $C_1$ that enters the first low-order stage of the ALU is employed for adding 1 to the sum in four micro-operations. Hence, arithmetic micro-operations require five control lines. $M$ must always be 1. The three selection lines specify an operation and input carry $C_1$ must be set to 0 or 1 for a particular micro-operation. Some of the arithmetic functions generate the same operation as the logic functions when $C_1 = 0$. Others have no useful application.

**Table 7-5** *Useful arithmetic micro-operations in ALU*

| $M$ | $S_2$ $S_1$ $S_0$ | $C_1$ | Micro-Operation | Description |
|---|---|---|---|---|
| 1 | 0 0 1 | 1 | $F = B + 1$ | Increment $B$ |
| 1 | 0 1 0 | 1 | $F = \bar{B} + 1$ | 2's complement $B$ |
| 1 | 1 0 0 | 1 | $F = A + 1$ | Increment $A$ |
| 1 | 1 0 1 | 0 | $F = A + B$ | Add $A$ and $B$ |
| 1 | 1 1 0 | 0 | $F = A + \bar{B}$ | $A$ plus 1's complement of $B$ |
| 1 | 1 1 0 | 1 | $F = A + \bar{B} + 1$ | $A$ plus 2's complement of $B$ |
| 1 | 1 1 1 | 0 | $F = A - 1$ | Decrement $A$ |

### *The Shifter*

The shifter attached to the bus system transfers the output of the ALU into the output bus. The shifter may transfer the information directly or may shift it to the right or left. Provision is sometimes available for no transfer from ALU to the output bus. The latter case is sometimes needed, for example, when two numbers are compared to determine their relative magnitude. This is done by placing one number in bus $A$, the other in bus $B$ and the selection lines of the ALU for $F = A + \bar{B}$. The output carry of the ALU gives the information concerning the relative magnitude. The result of the operation $A + \bar{B}$ need not be transferred anywhere if a comparison is all that is required.

The shifter provides the shift micro-operations commonly not available in an ALU. However, some IC ALUs are capable of shifting left and therefore, only a shift-right circuit is needed external to such ALUs. Other ALUs include the shifter within the IC package.

The most obvious circuit for a shifter is a bidirectional shift-register with parallel load (see Fig. 2-17). The control inputs in the register shift the content of the register to the left or right or not at all. Shifting by means of a register delays the information transfer from the ALU to the output bus by a number of clock pulse periods equal to the number of shifts executed. One additional clock pulse is needed for loading the outputs of the ALU into the register.

The transfer from the source registers to the destination register can be done with one clock pulse if the shifter is implemented with a *position scaler*. A position scaler is a shifter made up of gates without the use of flip-flops. It is classified as a combinational circuit since only gates are included in the digital function. In a combinational circuit shifter, the signals from the ALU terminals to the output bus propagate without a need of a clock pulse. Hence, the only clock pulse needed in the system is for loading the data from the output bus into the destination register.

Figure 7-5 shows the logic diagram of a combinational circuit shifter. It has two control lines $H_1$ and $H_0$ for selecting the type of operation. The control lines specify four different operations for the shifter. The diagram shows only the first and last stages and a typical stage. The shifter, of course, must consist of $n$ such identical stages.

Table 7-6 lists the four functions of the shifter selection control. When $H_1H_0 = 00$, no shift is executed and the signals from the $F$ lines go directly into the $S$ lines. Two control input combinations cause a shift-right and shift-left operation. When $H_1H_0 = 11$, all three decoder outputs are equal to zero.

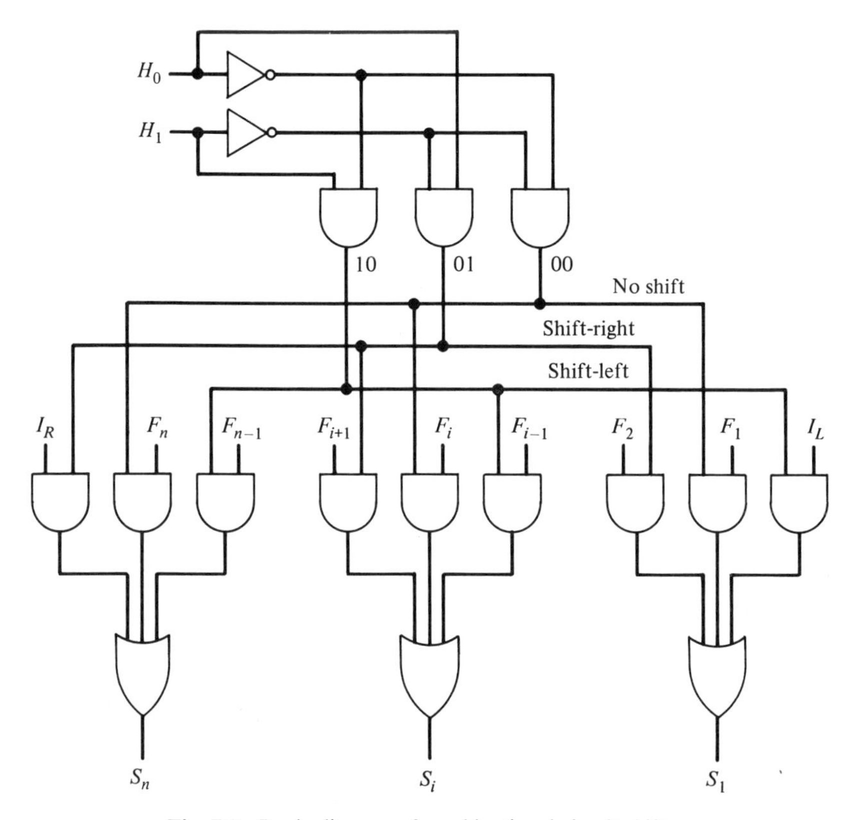


**Fig. 7-5** Logic diagram of combinational circuit shifter.

Table 7-6 *Shift selection control*

| $H_1$ | $H_0$ | *Function* |
|---|---|---|
| 0 | 0 | No shift, transfer $F$ to $S$ |
| 0 | 1 | Shift-right $F$ to $S$ |
| 1 | 0 | Shift-left $F$ to $S$ |
| 1 | 1 | No transfer from $F$ to $S$ |

As a consequence, the $S$ outputs are also equal to zero, blocking the transfer of information from the ALU to the output bus. The shifting to the right or left is for one bit position. Inputs $I_R$ and $I_L$ serve as serial inputs for the last and first stage during a shift-right or shift-left operation.

## 7-3 PROPAGATION DELAY

The control unit that operates the CPU bus system of Fig. 7-1 directs the information flow through the ALU by selecting the various components in the system. For example, to perform the micro-operation

$$AC \leftarrow AC + MBR$$

the control must provide binary variables to the following selector inputs.

1. MUX A selector: to transfer the content of $AC$ into bus $A$.
2. MUX B selector: to transfer the content of $MBR$ into bus $B$.
3. ALU function selector: to provide the function $F = A + B$.
4. Shift selector: for direct transfer from $F$ to bus $S$.
5. Decoder destination selector: to transfer the content of bus $S$ into the $AC$.

The five control functions must be generated simultaneously and be available during one common clock pulse interval. The binary information should propagate from the source registers to the two busses, through the ALU and shifter, to the output bus and into the inputs of the $AC$, all during one clock pulse interval. Then, when the next clock pulse arrives, the binary information in the output bus is transferred into the $AC$.

If the shifter is a shift-register, at least two clock pulses are needed to complete the operation. The first pulse loads the outputs of the ALU into the shift-register and another pulse transfers the content of the shift-register into the $AC$.

The gates that form the path between the outputs of the source registers and the inputs of the destination register determine the speed at which the micro-operation is executed. Each gate takes a certain amount of time to propagate the signals from its input terminals to its output terminal. This time interval is defined as the *propagation delay* time of the gate. For example, an OR gate with two inputs having the values of 0 and 1 will have in its output the value of 1. Now, if the 0 input is changed to 1, the output remains 1 and the propagation delay is zero. If, on the other hand, the 1 input changes to 0, the output will go through a transition from 1 to 0. The maximum time of this transition period is the maximum propagation delay of the OR gate. When logic gates are interconnected and the values of inputs cannot be predicted, the signal propagation delay between the inputs and the outputs cannot be predicted exactly. However, we can predict the maximum propagation delay by evaluating the longest possible transition through the various gates. The propagation delay time is variable and depends on the circuit components and on the input combination. In clocked systems, one must always wait for the maximum possible propagation time before the transfer of new information into a destination register.

There are other factors that delay the propagation of signals besides the delay through gates. When new information is triggered into a register, the flip-flops take a certain amount of time to change in value and to settle into a new steady-state condition. The propagation of the signal through wires and busses also takes a certain amount of time. Electronic signals propagate through wires at a speed close to the speed of light. But this speed is finite and produces an average delay in the signal of approximately 2 nsec for each foot of wire that it travels.

By far the longest delay in the ALU path is the carry propagation. From the logic diagram of a single-stage ALU we see that the signal from the input-carry to the output-carry must propagate through two AND gates and an OR gate. The output-carry in the last stage will be in its final steady-state value after the carry propagates through all $n$ stages of the ALU. Since each output $F_i$ depends on the value of the input-carry, the value of $F_i$ at any stage will be in its steady-state condition only after the input-carry to that stage has been propagated. Consider the output from a single stage, stage 15. Inputs $A_{15}$ and $B_{15}$ settle to their steady-state values as soon as their signals arrive from the input busses. After they propagate through the input gates of the ALU, the signal at terminal $w$ settles to a steady-state value. But input-carry $C_{15}$ will not settle to its final steady-state value unitl $C_{14}$ is available in its steady value. Similarly, $C_{14}$ has to wait for $C_{13}$ and so on down to $C_2$. Thus, only after the carry is propagated through all stages of the ALU will all the outputs settle to their final steady-state values.

The total propagation delay through the bus system is the sum total of the delays in the various paths from the source registers to the destination register. This total delay should be less than the time of one clock pulse interval if the micro-operation is finalized by the next clock pulse. This is demonstrated in the diagram of Fig. 7-6. The diagram shows two clock pulses. The pulse interval is the time from the falling edge of the first pulse to the falling edge of the second pulse. The frequency of the pulses is the reciprocal of this pulse interval. We assume that one of the source registers has been triggered with the first pulse (say the $AC$) for the execution of the previous micro-operation. To transfer the result of the current micro-operation with the next clock pulse, it is necessary that the signals propagate from the source registers to the destination register in less time than a clock pulse interval. The various delays in each section of the path are indicated in the diagram. The delay through the ALU is shown to be the longest because of its carry propagation time.

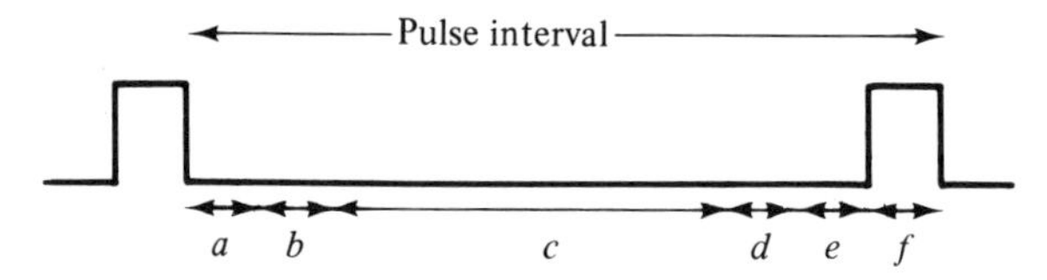


(a) Settling time of flip-flops in source registers.
(b) Propagation through multiplexers and input busses.
(c) Propagation through ALU.
(d) Propagation through shifter.
(e) Propagation through output bus and destination register.
(f) Pulse width.

**Fig. 7-6** Propagation delay through a CPU bus system.

The carry propagation time is a limiting factor on the speed by which two numbers are added in parallel. Since all other arithmetic operations are implemented by successive additions, the time consumed during the addition process is very critical. An obvious method for reducing the carry propagation delay time is to employ faster gates with reduced delays. But physical circuits have a limit to their capability. Another solution is to increase the equipment complexity in such a way as to reduce the carry delay time. There are several techniques for reducing the carry propagation time in a parallel-adder or the parallel-adder part of an ALU. The most widely used technique utilizes the principle of carry *look-ahead.* We will explain this principle in conjunction with a parallel-adder. The application to the ALU follows directly.

Consider the circuit of a full-adder as shown in Fig. 7-7. The output carry $C_{i+1}$ is implemented from the Boolean function

$$C_{i+1} = A_iB_i + (A_i \oplus B_i)C_i$$

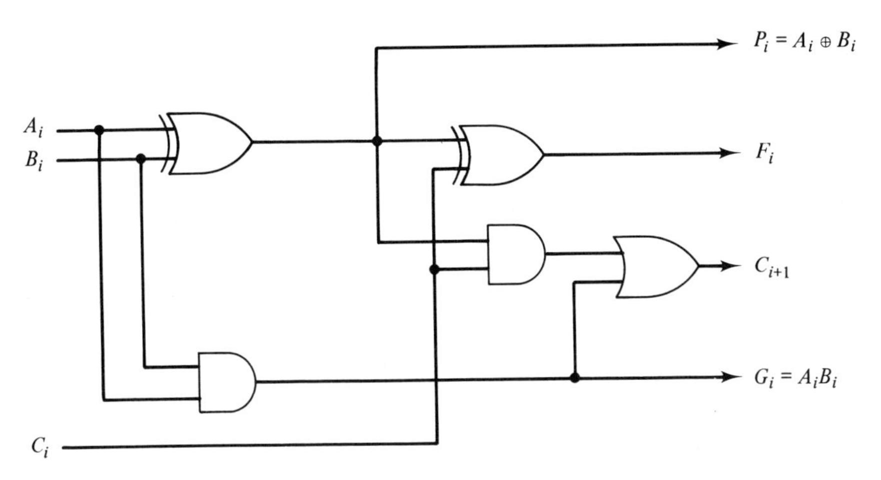


**Fig. 7-7** Full adder circuit with $G_i$ and $P_i$ outputs.

To facilitate the discussion, it is necessary to define two new binary variables:

$$G_i = A_iB_i$$
$$P_i = A_i \oplus B_i$$

The output carry can now be expressed as

$$C_{i+1} = G_i + P_iC_i$$

$G_i$ is called a *carry generate* and produces an output-carry when both $A_i$ and $B_i$ are 1's, irrespective of the input-carry. $P_i$ is called a *carry propagate* because it is the term associated with the propagation of the carry from $C_i$ to $C_{i+1}$.

We now write the Boolean functions for the carry output of each stage and substitute for each $C_i$ its value from the previous equation as shown below.

$$C_2 = G_1 + P_1C_1$$
$$C_3 = G_2 + P_2C_2 = G_2 + P_2(G_1 + P_1C_1) = G_2 + P_2G_1 + P_2P_1C_1$$
$$C_4 = G_3 + P_3C_3 = G_3 + P_3(G_2 + P_2G_1 + P_2P_1C_1)$$
$$= G_3 + P_3G_2 + P_3P_2G_1 + P_3P_2P_1C_1$$

Expressions for other output-carries may be obtained in a similar fashion. Any output-carry $C_n$ may be expressed as:

$$C_n = G_n + P_nC_1$$

where $G_n$ and $P_n$ are formed by the expressions:

$$G_n = G_{n-1} + P_{n-1}G_{n-2} + P_{n-1}P_{n-2}G_{n-3} + \cdots + P_{n-1}P_{n-2}\cdots P_2G_1$$
$$P_n = P_{n-1}P_{n-2}\cdots P_2P_1$$

The above carry functions define the following operation: A carry is formed at the output of a particular stage if the stage generates a carry, or if the previous stage generates a carry and the original stage propagates that carry, or if the second from the previous stage generates a carry and both the previous and original stages propagate that carry, etc. The final term shows that a carry will be propagated by the overall-adder if an initial carry-input is present and all stages propagate it.

Since the Boolean functions for each output-carry are expressed in a sum of products form, each function can be implemented with one level of AND gates followed by an OR gate (or by a two-level NAND gate circuit as in some ICs). The three Boolean functions for $C_2$, $C_3$ and $C_4$ are implemented in the carry look-ahead generator shown in Fig. 7-8. Note that $C_4$ does not have to wait for $C_3$ and $C_2$ to propagate; in fact, $C_4$ is propagated

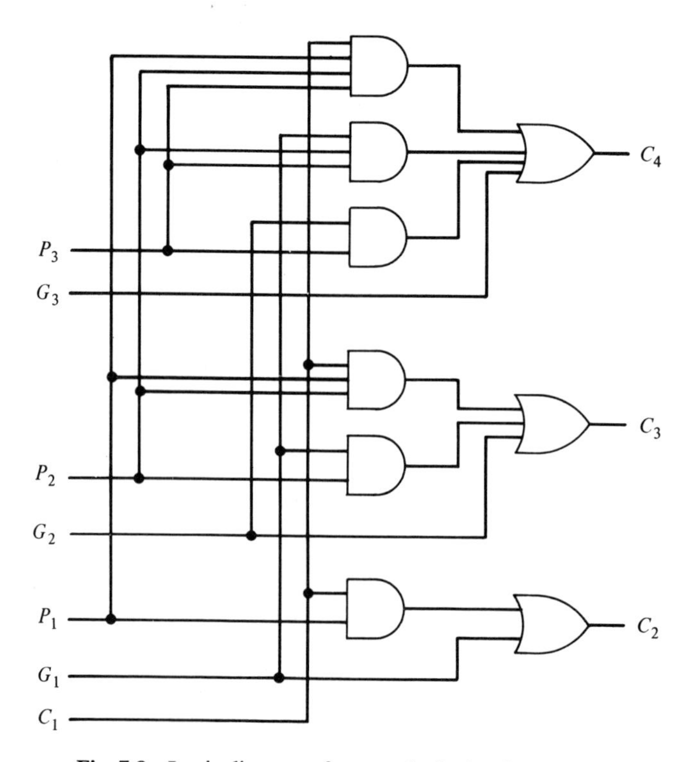


**Fig. 7-8** Logic diagram of a carry look-ahead generator.

at the same time as $C_2$ and $C_3$. The logic diagram may be used with any set of four consecutive bit-positions. The diagram is shown with subscripts 1, 2, 3, and 4, for convenience, but any four consecutive subscripts could have been used instead.

The construction of a 4-bit parallel-adder with a look-ahead carry scheme is shown in Fig. 7-9. Each sum output $F_i$ requires two exclusive-OR gates. The output of the first exclusive-OR gate supplies the $P_i$ variable and the AND gate supplies the $G_i$ variable. The carries are generated in a circuit similar to Fig. 7-8 and applied to the input of the second exclusive-OR. As soon as the $P$ and $G$ signals settle into their steady-state values, the output-carries are generated after a delay of two levels of gates. Thus, outputs $F_1$ through $F_4$ have equal propagation delay times.

Figure 7-9 shows two outputs, $G_5$ and $P_5$, not shown in Fig. 7-8. These outputs provide the carry generate and carry propagate for the next full-adder circuit. The Boolean functions for these binary variables are obtained from the general expressions for $G_n$ and $P_n$ defined previously. These variables are useful for expanding the 4-bit adder into a parallel-adder of more bits. When the 4-bit adder with carry look-ahead is enclosed in an IC package it has four inputs for the augend $A$, four inputs for the addend $B$, four outputs for the sum $F$, a carry-input, and two outputs $G_5$ and $P_5$. The output-carry $C_5$ is obtained from the relation:

$$C_5 = G_5 + P_5C_1$$

where $G_5$ and $P_5$ are derived from the general expressions given for $G_n$ and $P_n$, with $n = 5$.

An ALU can be constructed with a carry look-ahead in a similar fashion. It differs from a parallel-adder by the input control gates and selection lines. ALUs with carry look-ahead are available in integrated circuit form.

The IC package of a 4-bit parallel-adder (or ALU) can be expanded into a larger unit by means of an external look-ahead carry generator. The arrangement of a 16-bit parallel-adder is shown in Fig. 7-10. Each 4-bit adder package has an internal carry look-ahead circuit and provides a $G_5$ and $P_5$ output. These outputs are connected to an external look-ahead carry generated to provide a carry-output for each group of four bits. An investigation of the internal construction of each box in the diagram should convince the reader that this arrangement will reduce the carry propagation considerably.

To get an idea about the order of magnitudes in the delays encountered by various configurations, let us consider typical standard TTL ICs and their delay times. A typical 4-bit ALU without carry look-ahead has a propagation delay time from inputs to outputs of about 60 nsec. Using four such IC packages to construct a 16-bit ALU will result in a total delay of $60 \times 4 =$ 240 nsec. A 4-bit ALU with carry look-ahead reduces the propagation time

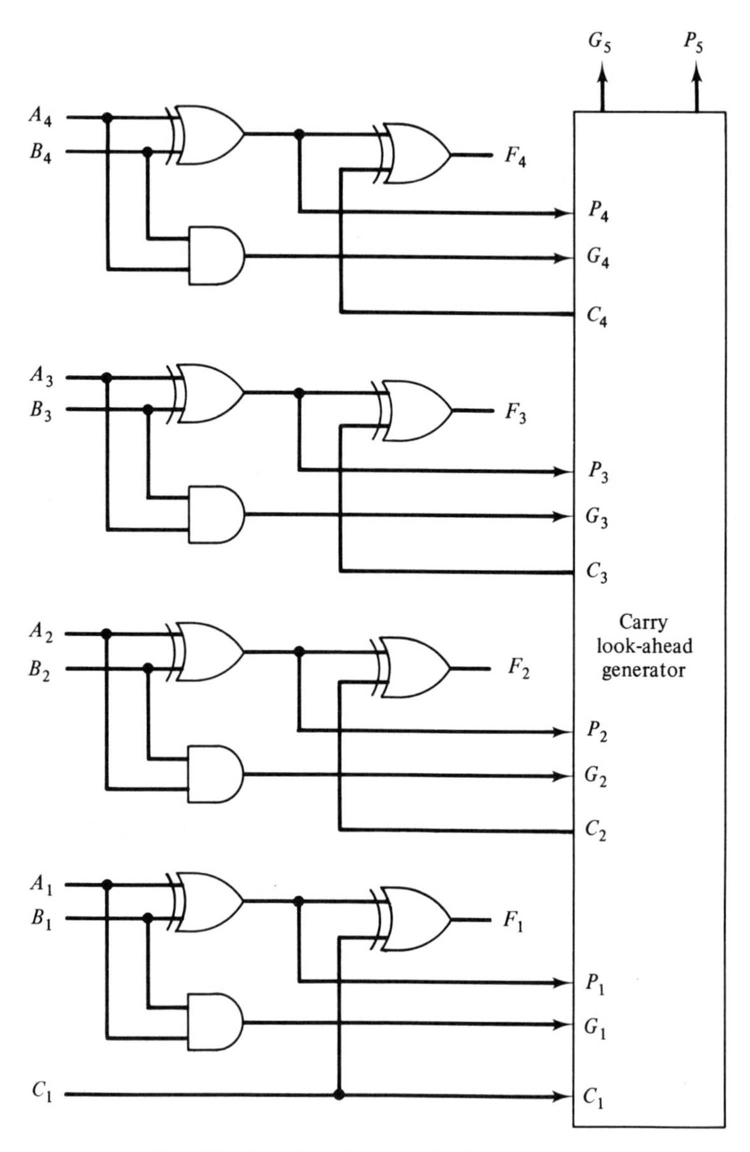


**Fig. 7-9** Four-bit adder with look-ahead carry.

to 25 nsec. Using four such ICs results in a total delay of 100 nsec for a 16-bit ALU. With an external look-ahead carry generator, connected as shown in Fig. 7-10, only 15 nsec are added to the 25 nsec delay for a total of 40 nsec in a 16-bit ALU. Thus the delay time is reduced to one sixth of what it was, from 240 to 40 nsec.

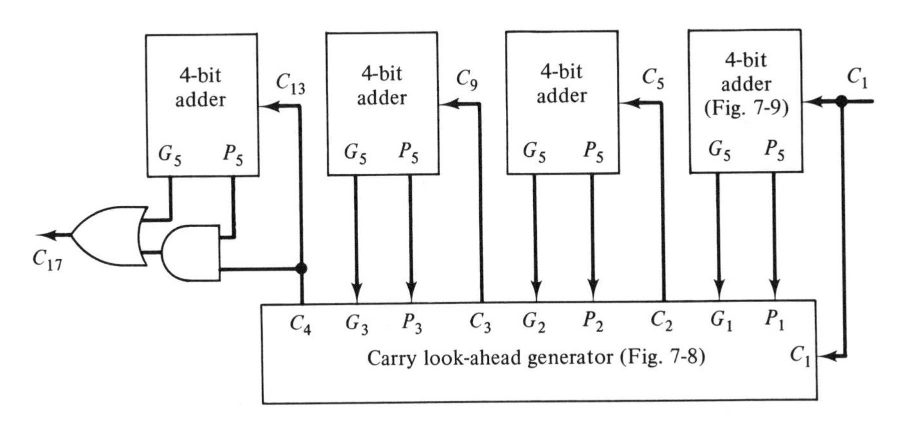


**Fig. 7-10** Sixteen-bit adder with group carry-look-ahead.

## 7-4 DECIMAL ARITHMETIC UNIT

The user of a computer prepares his data with decimal numbers and receives his results in decimal form. A CPU with an arithmetic logic unit can perform arithmetic micro-operations with binary data. To perform arithmetic operations with decimal data, it is necessary to convert the input decimal numbers to binary, to perform all calculations with binary numbers, and then to convert the results into decimal. This may be an efficient method in applications requiring a large number of calculations and a relatively smaller amount of input and output data. When the application calls for a large amount of input-output and a relatively smaller number of arithmetic calculations, it becomes convenient to do the internal arithmetic directly with the decimal numbers. Computers capable of performing decimal arithmetic must store the decimal data in binary-coded form. The decimal numbers are then applied to a decimal arithmetic unit capable of executing decimal arithmetic micro-operations.

Electronic calculators invariably use an internal decimal arithmetic unit since inputs and outputs are frequent. There does not seem to be a reason for converting the keyboard input numbers to binary and again converting the displayed results to decimal, since this process requires special circuits and also takes a longer time to execute. Many computers have hardware for arithmetic calculations with both binary and decimal data. The user can specify by programmed instructions whether he wants the computer to perform calculations with binary or decimal data.

A decimal arithmetic unit is a digital function that performs decimal micro-operations. It can add or subtract decimal numbers, usually by forming the 9's or 10's complement of the subtrahend. The unit accepts coded decimal numbers and generates results in the same adopted binary code. A single-stage decimal arithmetic unit consists of nine binary input variables and five binary output variables, since a minimum of four bits are required to represent each coded decimal digit. Each stage must have four inputs for the augend digit, four inputs for the addend digit and an input-carry. The outputs include four terminals for the sum digit and one for the output-carry. Of course, there is a wide variety of possible circuit configurations dependent upon the code used to represent the decimal digits.

### *BCD Adder*

Consider the arithmetic addition of two decimal digits in BCD, together with a possible carry from a previous stage. Since each input digit does not exceed 9, the output sum cannot be greater than $9 + 9 + 1 = 19$, the 1 in the sum being an input-carry. Suppose we apply two BCD digits to a 4-bit binary adder. The adder will form the sum in *binary* and produce a result which may range from 0 to 19. These binary numbers are listed in Table 7-7 and are labeled by symbols $K$, $Z_8$, $Z_4$, $Z_2$, and $Z_1$. $K$ is the carry and the sub-

**Table 7-7** *Derivation of BCD adder*

| *Binary Sum* $K\ Z_8\ Z_4\ Z_2\ Z_1$ | BCD *Sum* $C\ S_8\ S_4\ S_2\ S_1$ | *Decimal* |
|---|---|---|
| 0 0 0 0 0 | 0 0 0 0 0 | 0 |
| 0 0 0 0 1 | 0 0 0 0 1 | 1 |
| 0 0 0 1 0 | 0 0 0 1 0 | 2 |
| 0 0 0 1 1 | 0 0 0 1 1 | 3 |
| 0 0 1 0 0 | 0 0 1 0 0 | 4 |
| 0 0 1 0 1 | 0 0 1 0 1 | 5 |
| 0 0 1 1 0 | 0 0 1 1 0 | 6 |
| 0 0 1 1 1 | 0 0 1 1 1 | 7 |
| 0 1 0 0 0 | 0 1 0 0 0 | 8 |
| 0 1 0 0 1 | 0 1 0 0 1 | 9 |
| 0 1 0 1 0 | 1 0 0 0 0 | 10 |
| 0 1 0 1 1 | 1 0 0 0 1 | 11 |
| 0 1 1 0 0 | 1 0 0 1 0 | 12 |
| 0 1 1 0 1 | 1 0 0 1 1 | 13 |
| 0 1 1 1 0 | 1 0 1 0 0 | 14 |
| 0 1 1 1 1 | 1 0 1 0 1 | 15 |
| 1 0 0 0 0 | 1 0 1 1 0 | 16 |
| 1 0 0 0 1 | 1 0 1 1 1 | 17 |
| 1 0 0 1 0 | 1 1 0 0 0 | 18 |
| 1 0 0 1 1 | 1 1 0 0 1 | 19 |

scripts under the letter $Z$ represent the weights 8, 4, 2, and 1 that can be assigned to the four bits in the BCD code. The first column in the table lists the binary sums as they appear in the outputs of a 4-bit *binary* adder. The output sum of two *decimal* numbers must be represented in BCD and should appear in the form listed in the second column of the table. The problem is to find a simple rule by which the binary number in the first column can be converted to the correct BCD digit representation of the number in the second column.

In examining the contents of the table, it is apparent that when the binary sum is equal or less than 1001, the corresponding BCD number is identical and therefore no conversion is needed. When the binary sum is greater than 1001, we obtain a non-valid BCD representation. The addition of binary 6 (0110) to the binary sum converts it to the correct BCD representation and also produces an output-carry as required.

One method of adding decimal numbers in BCD would be to employ one 4-bit binary adder and perform the arithmetic operation one digit at a time. The low-order pair of BCD digits are first added to produce a binary sum. If the result is equal or greater than 1010, it is corrected by adding 0110 to the binary sum. This second operation will automatically produce an output-carry for the next pair of significant digits. The next higher-order pair of digits, together with the input-carry, are then added to produce their binary sum. If this result is equal or greater than 1010, it is corrected by adding 0110. The procedure is repeated again until all decimal digits are added.

The logic circuit that detects the necessary correction can be derived from the table entries. It is obvious that a correction is needed when the binary sum has an output carry $K = 1$. The other six combinations from 1010 to 1111 that need a correction have a 1 in position $Z_8$. To distinguish them from binary 1000 and 1001 which also have a 1 in position $Z_8$, we specify further that either $Z_4$ or $Z_2$ must have a 1. The condition for a correction and an output-carry can be expressed by the Boolean function

$$C = K + Z_8Z_4 + Z_8Z_2$$

When $C = 1$, it is necessary to add 0110 to the binary sum and provide an output-carry for the next stage.

A BCD adder is a circuit that adds two BCD digits in parallel and produces a sum digit also in BCD. A BCD adder must include the correction logic in its internal construction. To add 0110 to the binary sum, we use a second 4-bit binary adder as shown in Fig. 7-11. The two decimal digits, together with the input-carry, are first added in the top 4-bit binary adder to produce the binary sum. When the output-carry is equal to 0, nothing is added to the binary sum. When it is equal to 1, binary 0110 is added to the binary sum through the bottom 4-bit binary adder. The output-carry gener-

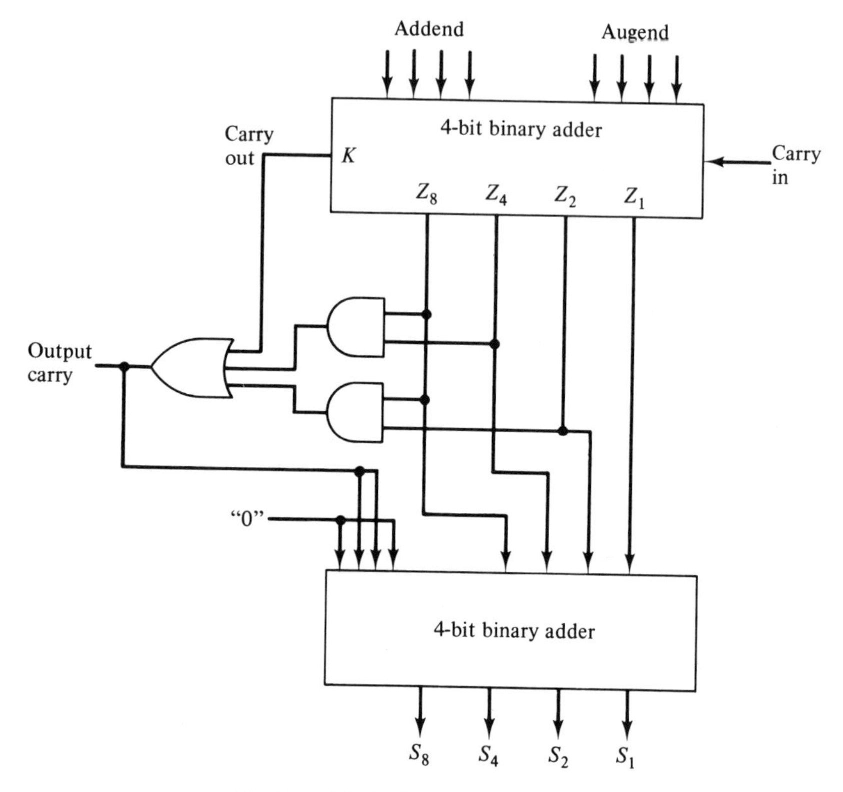


**Fig. 7-11** Block diagram of BCD adder.

ated from the bottom binary adder may be ignored, since it supplies information already available in the output-carry terminal.

A decimal parallel-adder that adds $n$ decimal digits needs $n$ BCD adder stages with the output-carry from one stage connected to the input-carry of the next higher-order stage. To achieve shorter propagation delays, IC BCD adders include the necessary circuits for carry look-ahead. Furthermore, the adder circuit for the correction does not need all four full-adders and this circuit can be optimized within the IC package.

### *BCD Subtraction*

A straight subtraction of two decimal numbers will require a subtractor circuit which will be somewhat different from a BCD adder. It is more economical to perform the subtraction by taking the 9's or 10's complement of the subtrahend and adding it to the minuend. Since the BCD is not a self-complementing code, the 9's complement cannot be obtained by complementing each bit in the code. It must be formed by a circuit that subtracts each BCD digit from 9.

The 9's complement of a decimal digit represented in BCD may be obtained by complementing the bits in the coded representation of the digit provided a correction is included. There are two possible correction methods. In the first method, binary 1010 (decimal 10) is added to each complemented digit and the carry discarded after each addition. In the second method, binary 0110 (decimal 6) is added before the digit is complemented. As a numerical illustration, the 9's complement of BCD 0111 (decimal 7) is computed by first complementing each bit to obtain 1000. Adding binary 1010 and discarding the carry, we obtain 0010 (decimal 2). By the second method, we add 0110 to 0111 to obtain 1101. Complementing each bit, we obtain the required result of 0010. Complementing each bit of a 4-bit binary number $N$ is identical to the subtraction of the number from 1111 (decimal 15). Adding the binary equivalent of decimal 10 gives $15 - N + 10 = 9 - N + 16$. But 16 signifies the carry that is discarded so the result is $9 - N$ as required. Adding the binary equivalent of decimal 6 and then complementing gives $15 - (N + 6) = 9 - N$ as required.

The subtraction of two decimal numbers employing only one 4-bit ALU can be accomplished by a sequence of micro-operations repeated for each pair of digits. The 9's complement of the subtrahend is first obtained. This is accomplished by complementing each bit in the digit and then adding 1010, or adding 0110 to each coded digit and then complementing the number. The two numbers are then added as described previously. If a carry occurs in the output of the highest-order digits, a 1 is added to the sum. This is a lengthy and time-consuming process but saves a considerable amount of equipment because only one 4-bit ALU is required. This is the usual procedure employed in electronic calculators since the response time of the user is on the order of seconds while each micro-operation can be executed in a few nanoseconds.

The 9's complement of a BCD digit can be obtained also through a combinational circuit. When this circuit is attached to a BCD adder, the result is a BCD adder/subtractor. Let the subtrahend (or addend) digit be denoted by the four binary variables $B_8$, $B_4$, $B_2$, and $B_1$. Let $M$ be a mode bit that controls the add/subtract operation. When $M = 0$, the two digits are added; when $M = 1$, the digits are subtracted. Let the binary variables $x_8, x_4, x_2$, and $x_1$ be the outputs of the 9's complementer circuit. By an examination of the truth table for the circuit, it may be observed (see Prob. 7-18) that $B_1$ should always be complemented; $B_2$ is always the same in the 9's complement as in the original digit; $x_4$ is 1 when the exclusive-OR of $B_2$ and $B_4$ is 1; and $x_8$ is 1 when $B_8B_4B_2 = 000$. The Boolean functions for the

9's complementer circuit are:

$$x_1 = B_1M' + B_1'M$$
$$x_2 = B_2$$
$$x_4 = B_4M' + (B_4'B_2 + B_4B_2')M$$
$$x_8 = B_8M' + B_8'B_4'B_2'M$$

From these equations we see that $x = B$ when $M = 0$. When $M = 1$, the $x$ outputs produce the 9's complement of $B$.

One stage of a decimal arithmetic unit that can add or subtract two BCD digits is shown in Fig. 7-12. It consists of a BCD adder and a 9's complementer. The mode $M$ controls the operation of the unit. With $M = 0$, the $S$ outputs form the sum of $A$ and $B$. With $M = 1$, the $S$ outputs form the sum of $A$ plus the 9's complement of $B$. For numbers with $n$ decimal digits we need $n$ such stages. The output-carry $C_{i+1}$ from one stage must be connected to the input-carry $C_i$ of the next higher order stage. The best way to subtract the two decimal numbers is to let $M = 1$ and apply a 1 to the input-carry $C_1$ of the first stage. The outputs will form the sum of $A$ plus the 10's complement of $B$, which is equivalent to a subtraction operation if the carry out of the last stage is discarded.

Other arithmetic micro-operations can be included in the decimal arithmetic unit. The increment micro-operation can be included by controlling the $B$ inputs to produce all 0's in the addend inputs of the BCD adder. The unit will produce the micro-operation $A + 1$ if 1 is applied to the input-carry $C_1$ of the first stage. Another method would be to use a decimal counter with parallel-load capability. This is a common digital function found in

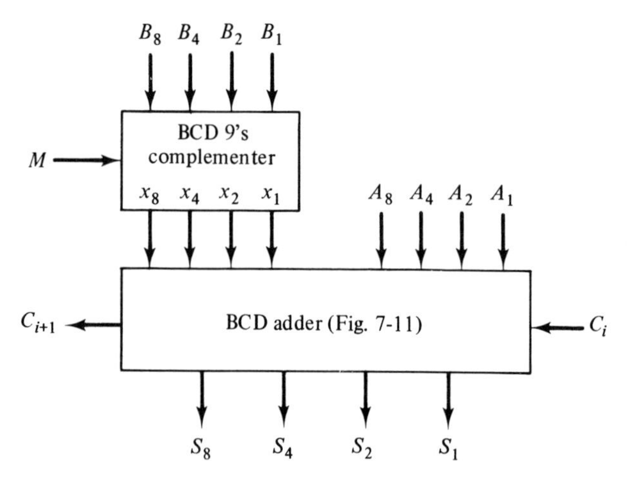


**Fig. 7-12** One stage of a decimal arithmetic unit.

integrated circuit form. The decimal number can be incremented in the counter by enabling the appropriate control input.

A shifter connected to a decimal arithmetic unit must shift the data four bits at a time, equivalent to one decimal digit. This is easily achieved by means of 4-bit registers with parallel load. To shift a decimal number left, it is necessary to load the four bits from each 4-bit register into the next higher order 4-bit register on its left.

## 7-5 CPU INSTRUCTIONS AND FORMATS

The physical and logical structure of computers is normally described in reference manuals provided with the systems. Such manuals explain the internal construction of the CPU, including the processor registers available and their logical capabilities. They list all hardware-implemented instructions, specify their binary code format and provide a precise definition of each instruction. A computer will usually have a variety of instruction code formats. It is the function of the control unit within the CPU to interpret each instruction code and provide the necessary control functions needed to process the instruction.

In some cases, an instruction code may not require as many bits as a memory word; in others, it may require more. If an instruction code is close to the length of a memory word, then one word may be used to store each instruction. If, however, the number of bits in an instruction is considerably less than the number of bits in a word, several instructions can be packed into one memory word. If the number of bits in an instruction is more than the length of a word, one instruction is stored in two or more consecutive words. With one instruction per word, the control reads one word for each instruction. With multiple instructions per word, the control reads a word and processes two or more instructions before a memory reference is made for the next fetch cycle. With an instruction occupying two or more words, the control reads two or more memory words to fetch one instruction.

The format of an instruction is usually depicted in a rectangular box symbolizing the bits of the instruction as they appear in memory words or in the instruction register of the control unit. The bits of the instruction are divided into groups called fields. Each field is assigned a symbolic name such as operation field or address field. The various fields specify different functions for the instruction and when shown together they constitute the instruction code format. In all the examples that follow except the last (Fig. 7-13), the rectangular box and the specific bits that each field occupies are omitted for convenience. The various fields of the instruction code format are specified by symbolic names only.

An instruction code specifies, through its various fields, one or more of the following functions:

1. An operation to be executed by the hardware.
2. The location of the data that are to be used in conjunction with the operation.
3. How to evaluate the address of the next instruction.

Each computer has a unique set of instructions and instruction code formats to accomplish the three tasks listed above. The following discussion presents the common properties of instruction codes and some variations for specifying operations, operands and the address of the next instruction.

### *Types of Operations*

Computers provide an extensive set of hardware instructions to speed up common tasks. The operation field of an instruction code format specifies the operation to be executed. The most familiar examples are the four arithmetic operations of addition, subtraction, multiplication, and division. These are the most basic arithmetic operations from which scientific problems can be formulated using numerical analysis methods. The data type assumed to be in processor registers during the execution of an arithmetic operation is included implicitly in the definition of the operation code. An arithmetic operation may specify fixed-point or floating-point data, binary or decimal data, single-precision or double-precision data. It is not uncommon to find computers with three or more types of ADD instructions: one for binary integers, one for floating-point operands, and one for decimal operands.

Fixed-point binary numbers are assumed to be either integers or fractions. Negative numbers may be represented either in signed-magnitude or signed-complement form. Floating-point arithmetic operations require special hardware implementation to take care of alignment of mantissas and scaling of exponents. Decimal data are represented by a binary code and manipulated through a decimal arithmetic unit. The number of bits in any register is of finite length and therefore, the results of arithmetic operations are of finite precision. Some computers provide hardware double-precision operations where the length of each operand is taken to be the length of two memory words.

Computers must provide a sufficient set of logic operations for bit manipulation and logical decisions. Other operations may be available which are concerned with format editing of data such as code translation, packing and unpacking of characters, and editing of data (for example, during the preparation of output characters for a printer).

Most computers have a multiple-field format for the shift instructions. One field contains the operation code and the others specify the type of shift and the number of times that an operand is to be shifted. A typical instruction code format of a shift instruction may include up to four fields:

OP TYPE LR COUNT

Here OP is a symbolic name for the operation code field; TYPE may be a 2-bit field specifying three different types of shifts (logical, circular, or arithmetic); LR is a 1-bit field specifying a left or right shift; and COUNT is a $k$-bit field specifying up to $2^k - 1$ shifts. With such a format, it is possible to specify the type of shift, the direction, and the number of shifts, all in one instruction.

Computers have an extensive set of operations that move data between registers without changing their information content. These operations move data among processor registers, between memory and CPU, and are essential for input and output movement of data. A *move* instruction usually has an instruction format with at least three fields. The first field specifies the type of operation. The second specifies the source register and the third specifies the destination register. The information at the source is invariably assumed to remain undisturbed. However, the previous information in the destination register will be destroyed once it receives the new information.

### *Determination of Next Instruction*

A rule must be set up to determine which location in memory is used to provide the next instruction. The most obvious rule is to use the next sequential location in memory. This is accomplished by storing the address of the current instruction in a program counter and incrementing it to provide the address of the next instruction. This type of instruction sequencing is done by an external counter so the next instruction address need not be specified in the instruction code itself. Although this method is used in the majority of computers, in some early machines the address of the next instruction is specified in a special field of the instruction code. By this method, a program counter is not used at all. Instead, the address of the next instruction is explicitly specified in the current instruction. As an illustration, consider the three-field format of the following instruction:

ADD $m_1$ $m_2$

The instruction format consists of an operation field and two address fields. ADD is a symbolic name for the operation code, $m_1$ specifies the address of the operand and $m_2$ specifies the address of the next instruction.

Instruction codes in computers that employ a program counter specify the address of the next instruction only when it is out of sequence. There are three types of instructions for specifying an out of sequence next instruction.

These are usually designated as a *skip*, *branch*, or *call* instruction. A skip instruction needs only an operation field. A branch or call instruction needs at least two fields, one for the operation code and one for the address of the next instruction.

The difference between a branch and a call instruction is that the latter branches to a new location and at the same time saves the return address. A branch instruction is sometimes called a *jump* instruction. A *call* instruction is sometimes called a *branch* or *jump to subroutine*. Either type of instruction may specify a condition or may be unconditional. An unconditional branch or call causes a branch to the specified address unconditionally. A conditional branch or call causes a branch only if a specified condition is satisfied; otherwise, the next instruction in sequence is executed. It is possible to have a branch instruction with three fields:

BRANCH $m_1$ $m_2$

where BRANCH is the symbolic name of a conditional branch operation code, $m_1$ is the address of the next instruction if the condition is satisfied and $m_2$ is the address of the next instruction if the condition is not satisfied.

Some computers have a *status* register that contains status bits indicating results from a previous operation. For example, a status register may have four bits. One bit is set if the output of the ALU is zero, a second bit is set if the ALU has an output-carry, a third if the result is negative, and a fourth if an overflow occurs. The computer will have a branch instruction code format with three fields:

BRANCH COND m

The BRANCH is the symbol for a general branch operation code. COND is a condition field containing two bits to specify one of the four bits in the status register, and m is the branch address if the specified bit is equal to 1. The condition field may contain $k$ bits to specify $2^k$ branch conditions.

### *Specifying Operands (Addressing Modes)*

The operation field of an instruction code specifies the operation to be performed. This operation must be executed on some data stored in computer registers or memory. An instruction code, therefore, must specify not only the operation but also the registers or memory words where the operands are to be found and where results are to be stored. An operand is said to be specified *explicitly* if the instruction code contains a field for its identification. For example, an address field specifies an *explicit* operand in memory. On the other hand, an operand is said to be specified *implicitly* if it is included as part of the definition of the operation. For example, an instruction *clear AC* needs only an operation field because the *AC* is *implied* in the definition of the operation.

Most computer code formats have special fields for evaluating the location of operands. These fields are called by various names such as *tag field*, *register field*, or *address mode field*. The interpretation of the bits in this field causes the control to compute an effective address for the operand in a variety of ways. To the inexperienced programmer, the variety of addressing modes in some computers may seem excessively complicated. However, the availability of different addressing schemes gives the experienced user a flexibility for writing programs that are more efficient with respect to the number of instructions and execution time.

We have already discussed in Chap. 5 three addressing modes: *immediate*, *direct* and *indirect*. An immediate instruction contains two fields:

OP OPERAND

The OP is the operation code field and the OPERAND field contains the actual operand to be used in conjunction with an implied processor register. The direct and indirect instructions are specified with three fields,

I OP m

I is a 1-bit field. When I = 0, m is the address of the operand. When I = 1, the address of the operand, called the *effective address*, is found in the memory word at address m. Some computers allow multiple-level indirect addressing. In this mode, the control checks the I bit of the memory word found in location m. If it is 0, the word contains the effective address; if it is 1, the memory is accessed again. This process is repeated until a word is found with a 0 in I. The address part of this word is then taken as the effective address of the operand.

An *index* field in an instruction code specifies a particular index register. The effective address is obtained by adding the content of the address field to the content of the specified index register. An instruction format with an index contains at least three fields:

OP X m

where X is a $k$-bit index field that specifies one of $2^k - 1$ index registers (when X = 0, none of the index registers are specified). The effective address is calculated by the control and placed in the memory-address register by the micro-operation:

$$MAR \leftarrow \text{m} + XR$$

where $XR$ is the index register specified in the instruction field X.

Computers with index registers contain a variety of instructions which manipulate the data in these registers. Instructions are usually available for transferring an initial number into the register, for incrementing or decrementing the register and for testing the value of the register and branching if its content is zero. In this way, the index-register can serve as a counter, as a pointer, or for storing temporary data and other useful functions.

Some computers use a *base* register to evaluate the effective address of the operand. The value in the base register is used in conjunction with a *relative* or *displacement* address field in the instruction. A relative address instruction format may be of the form:

OP *BR* mr

where the *BR* field specifies one register as the base register and mr is a relative address. The effective address is calculated and placed in *MAR* by the micro-operation:

$$MAR \leftarrow BR + \text{mr}$$

As a numerical example, consider a computer having a memory of $2^{14}$ words. A full address must be specified with 14 bits. Suppose that the instruction code has space for only 7 bits in its address field. The computer uses a 7-bit relative address field while the other 7 high-order address bits are stored in a base register. The effective address is computed by adding the low-order 7-bit relative address to the content of the base register, to obtain a 14-bit memory address for the operand.

Base registers and relative addresses facilitate the relocation of programs in memory space. When programs and data are moved from one segment of memory to another, as required in multiprogramming systems, the address values of instructions must reflect this change of position. With a base register, the relative address values of instructions do not have to change. Only the value of the base register requires updating to reflect the beginning of a new memory segment.

In some cases, the program counter is used as the base register. An address relative to *PC* is useful in small computers for increasing the range of memory addresses when only a limited number of bits are available for the address field of the instruction. When only the high-order bits of *PC* are used as the base value, the relative address scheme is referred to in some minicomputers as *paging*.

A *register* field in an instruction code specifies one particular processor register, among many, to act as an accumulator for the operation. An instruction with a register field needs the following format:

OP *R* m

where *R* is a $k$-bit field that specifies one of $2^k$ processor registers. The operation in the OP field is carried out between the content of the specified register and the content of the memory word found in address m.

To perform complicated operations, it is sometimes convenient to load the operands from memory into processor registers and then perform the operations among the numbers stored in the registers. This procedure saves computer time because intermediate results can remain in the registers, thus eliminating the need for referring to memory for storing temporary results. An instruction code format for a register-to-register operation needs at least three fields:

OP $SR$ $DR$

where $SR$ is a field that specifies a source register and $DR$ is another field that specifies a second source register which is also the destination register. A bit configuration for the above format may look like this:

1101 0011 0111

Assume that the content of the operation field 1101 specifies an ADD operation. The source and destination registers are $R3$ and $R7$, respectively. The above instruction specifies the operation:

$$R7 \leftarrow R3 + R7$$

So far, we have assumed that an address field refers to a single memory location. Some computers have instruction formats for specifying an entire block in memory. The address field usually gives the location of the first word within the block. When the block length is variable, it is further necessary to specify the total number of words or the last address of the block. An instruction code format that moves data between blocks may be specified by four fields:

MVE SA DA LENGTH

The operation field MVE specifies a *move* operation. The SA and DA fields specify the first address of the source and destination blocks, respectively. The LENGTH field gives the length or number of words in the blocks. This type of instruction will cause a transfer of words equal to the number specified by field LENGTH from the source block to the destination block. Block addressing can handle a large amount of information since an entire memory block can be specified with a single instruction.

We conclude this section by presenting a typical instruction code format to illustrate some of the addressing modes which have been discussed. The instruction code format shown in Fig. 7-13 contains four fields. The operation field specifies an operation; the register field specifies one of 16 processor registers to serve as the accumulator. The MOD field has three bits and specifies one of eight addressing modes. The address field $m$ contains 12 bits.

The eight address modes specified by the MOD field are listed in Table 7-8. An immediate mode considers the 12 bits of the $m$ field as the actual operand. The direct mode considers $m$ as the effective address. An indirect

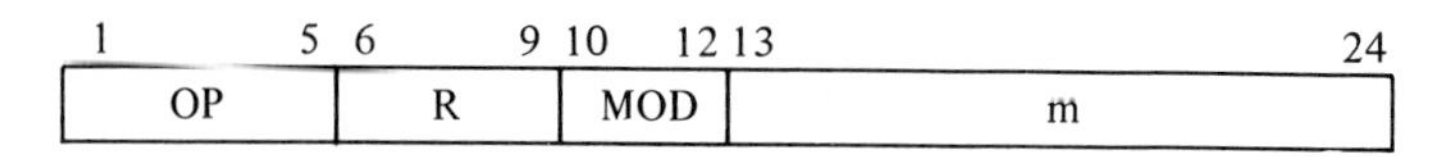


OP Operation field – 5 bits
R Register field – 4 bits
MOD Address mode field – 3 bits
m Address field – 12 bits

**Fig. 7-13** An example of an instruction code format.

**Table 7-8** *Code for mode field MOD of Fig. 7-13*

| *Bits* 10 11 12 | *Mode Name* | *Effective Address* |
|---|---|---|
| 0 0 0 | Immediate | $m$ field contains the operand |
| 0 0 1 | Direct | $m$ |
| 0 1 0 | Indirect | $M$ |
| 0 1 1 | Indexed | $m + XR$ |
| 1 0 0 | Indexed-increment | $m + XR$, $XR \leftarrow XR + 1$ |
| 1 0 1 | Indexed-indirect | $M + XR$ |
| 1 1 0 | Relative to $PC$ | $PC + m$ |
| 1 1 1 | Relative to $PC$ | $PC - m$ |

$M$ is the memory word specified by $m$.
$XR$ is the index register
$PC$ is the program counter

mode needs an access to memory to read the content of the word specified by $m$. The address part of this word becomes the effective address and is designated by $M$ in the table. An indexed mode specifies an effective address obtained from the sum of $m$ plus the content of the index register $XR$. The indexed-increment mode is similar to the indexed mode except that the index register is incremented by 1 after its value is used to find the effective address. An indexed-indirect mode uses the indirect address in $M$ plus the content of $XR$ for the effective address. The relative mode defines $m$ as a relative address with respect to $PC$. Since $PC$ holds the address of the present (or next) instruction, the calculated effective address finds the operand $m$ positions above or below the address of the instruction.

## 7-6 STACK ORGANIZATION

A very useful feature that is included in the CPU of some computers is a memory *stack* or *last-in-first-out* (LIFO) list. A stack is a storage device which stores information in such a manner that the item stored last is the first item retrieved. The operation of a stack can be compared to a stack of trays. The last tray placed on the stack is the first to be taken off.

The stack in digital computers is essentially a memory unit with an address register that can only count; no other value is ever loaded into the address register. This type of address register is called a *stack pointer* because its value always points to the address of the top word in the stack. Contrary to a stack of trays where the tray itself may be taken out or inserted, the physical registers of a memory stack are always available for visual inspection. It is the *item*, the content of the word, that is inserted or deleted. The stack pointer always holds the address of the last item inserted in the stack.

The two operations of a stack are the insertion and deletion of items. The operation of insertion is called *push* (or *push-down*) because it can be thought of as the result of pushing a new item on top. The operation of deletion is called *pop* (or *pop-up*) because it can be thought of as the result of moving each item up one register so that the top pops out. However, nothing is pushed or popped in a computer stack. These operations are simulated by incrementing or decrementing the stack pointer register.

Figure 7-14 shows the organization of a 64-word memory stack. The stack pointer register *SPR* contains a binary number whose value is equal to the address of the word which is currently on top of the stack. Three items are placed in the stack, *A*, *B*, and *C*, in that order. Item *C* is on top of the stack so that the content of *SPR* is now binary address 3. To remove the top item, the stack is popped by reading the memory word at address 3 and decrementing the content of *SPR*. Item *B* is now on top of the stack since *SPR* holds address 2. To insert a new item, the stack is pushed by incrementing *SPR* and writing a word in the next higher location in the stack.

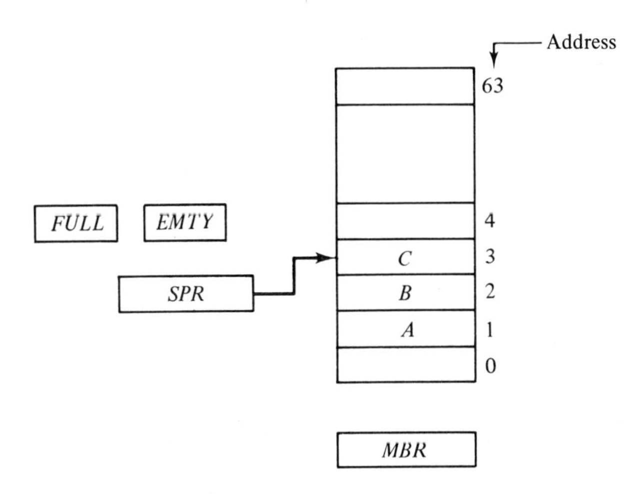


**Fig. 7-14** Block diagram of a memory stack.

Note that item $C$ has been read out but not physically removed. This does not matter because when the stack is pushed, a new item is written in its place.

In a 64-word memory stack, the stack pointer register contains 6 bits since $2^6 = 64$. The one-bit registers *FULL* and *EMTY* are set when the stack is full or empty of items, respectively. The *MBR* is the memory buffer register that holds the binary item to be written into or read out of the memory stack.

Initially, *SPR* is cleared and *EMTY* is set, so that *SPR* points to the word at address 0 and the stack is marked empty. If the stack is not full (if $FULL = 0$), a new item is inserted by a *push* operation. The push operation is implemented with the following sequence of micro-operations:

| | |
|---|---|
| $SPR \leftarrow SPR + 1$ | Increment stack pointer |
| $M \leftarrow MBR$ | Write item on top of the stack |
| If $(SPR = 0)$ then $(FULL \leftarrow 1)$ | Check if stack is full |
| $EMTY \leftarrow 0$ | Mark the stack not empty |

The stack pointer is incremented so it points to the address of the next higher word. A memory *write* micro-operation inserts the word from *MBR* into the top of the stack. If *SPR* becomes zero, the stack is full of items so *FULL* is set to 1. This condition is reached if the last item was in location 63 and by incrementing *SPR*, the new item is stored in location 0. Once an item is stored in location 0, there are no more empty registers in the stack. If an item is written in the stack, obviously the stack cannot be empty, so *EMTY* is cleared.

A new item is deleted from the stack if the stack is not empty (if $EMTY = 0$). The *pop* operation consists of the following sequence of micro-operations:

| | |
|---|---|
| $MBR \leftarrow M$ | Read item from the top of the stack |
| $SPR \leftarrow SPR - 1$ | Decrement stack pointer |
| If $(SPR = 0)$ then $(EMTY \leftarrow 1)$ | Check if stack is empty |
| $FULL \leftarrow 0$ | Mark the stack not full |

The top item is read from the stack into *MBR*. The stack pointer is then decremented. If its value reaches zero, the stack is empty so *EMTY* is set to 1. This condition is reached if the item read was in location 1. Once this item is read out, all the registers in the stack are empty. Note that if a pop operation reads the item from location 0 and then *SPR* is decremented, *SPR* changes to all 1's which is equivalent to binary 63. In this configuration, the word in address 0 receives the last item in the stack. Note also that an erroneous operation will result if the stack is pushed when $FULL = 1$ or popped when $EMTY = 1$.

A memory stack can exist as a stand-alone unit or can be simulated with a random-access memory. The simulation of a stack in the CPU is done by assigning a portion of the computer memory to a stack operation and using an index register as a stack pointer. This configuration is shown in Fig. 7-15. Here the random access memory is accessed through its memory address register *MAR* which can receive an address from many CPU registers. A segment of memory is assigned to operate as a stack. One index register holds the address of the bottom of the stack, another holds the address of the upper limit of the stack, and a third acts as a stack pointer. To pop the stack, the content of *XR* is transferred to *MAR* and the memory is accessed to read a word. *XR* is then decremented and checked if it reached the bottom stack limit. To push the stack, *XR* is incremented and its content transferred to *MAR*. The memory is then accessed to write a word. *XR* is then checked to see if its value reached the upper limit of the stack. In this configuration, the memory can perform random access operations as well as stack operations.

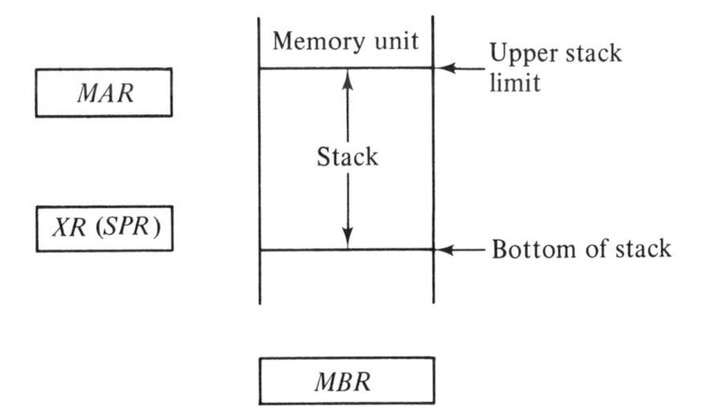


**Fig. 7-15** Simulation of stack in a random access memory.

A stack organization facilitates many data processing tasks. It is useful for storing the return address for subroutines and interrupts, for evaluating arithmetic expressions, for the construction of compiler programs and for many more applications. Some computers employ a CPU that is entirely organized with memory stacks. A number of electronic calculators use an internal stack for evaluating arithmetic expressions. The remainder of this section presents a few applications to illustrate the usefulness of a memory stack.

### *Subroutine Stack*

A branch to subroutine or *call* instruction stores the return address before branching to a subroutine. The return address can be stored in the first memory location of the subroutine, in an index register or in a memory stack. The advantage of using a stack for the return address is that when a succession of subroutines is called, the sequential return addresses can be pushed into the stack. The *return* from subroutine instruction causes the stack to pop and the contents of the top of the stack transferred to *PC*. In this way, the return is always to the program which last called a subroutine. Thus, a subroutine call is implemented by the micro-operations:

$MBR \leftarrow PC$

Push the stack

$PC \leftarrow$ Effective address

If another subroutine is called by the current subroutine, the new return address is pushed into the stack and so on. The instruction that returns from the last subroutine is implemented by the micro-operations:

Pop the stack

$PC \leftarrow MBR$

By using a subroutine stack, all return addresses are automatically stored by the hardware in one unit. The programmer does not have to be concerned or remember where the return address was stored.

A *recursive* subroutine is a subroutine that calls itself. If only one register is used to store the return address, and the recursive subroutine calls itself, it destroys the previous return address. This is undesirable because vital information is destroyed. For this reason, most computers forbid the use of recursive subroutines. This problem can be solved if different storage locations are employed for each use of the subroutine while another higher level use is still active. When a stack is used, each return address can be pushed into the stack without destroying any previous values. This solves the problem of recursive subroutines because the next subroutine to exit is always the last subroutine that was called.

### *Interrupt Stack*

When the CPU receives an interrupt request, the program currently under way is interrupted and a device service routine initiated. Once the device request has been satisfied, the processor returns to the interrupted program. If only one memory location or register is used to store the return address, the hardware must prevent any interrupts from occuring while the service routine is being executed. Otherwise, the previous return address will be destroyed. Some computers solve this problem by providing a different memory location for storing the return address of each interrupt request. The return address of the interrupted routine can also be stored in a stack, with the return address of the program last interrupted being on top of the stack. This has an advantage because the computer can be interrupted while servicing another interrupt. Since the top of the stack always contains the return address of the last interrupted program, popping the stack and placing its content into *PC* always causes a return to the program that was last interrupted.

The stack is also a convenient place for storing the contents of processor registers prior to servicing the interrupt request. In fact, many computers use a stack organization to facilitate the processing of interrupts by the hardware. The interrupt cycle automatically pushes the return address into the stack. The contents of processor registers are also pushed into the stack before the branch to the service routine. A return to the running program is effected by first popping the contents of registers out of the stack and then popping the return address and placing it into *PC*. Thus, a stack organization is a very efficient hardware method for handling interrupts.

### *Polish Notation*

A stack organization is very effective for evaluating arithmetic expressions. The common mathematical method of writing arithmetic expressions imposes difficulties when evaluated by a computer. The common arithmetic expressions are written in *infix* notation, with each operator written *between* the operands. Consider the simple arithmetic expression

$$A * B + C * D$$

The star (denoting multiplication) is placed between two operands $A$ and $B$ or $C$ and $D$. The plus is between the two products. To evaluate this arithmetic expression it is necessary to compute the product $A * B$, store this product while computing $C * D$ and then sum the two products. From this example we see that to evaluate arithmetic expressions in infix notation it is necessary to scan back and forth along the expression to determine the next operation to be performed.

The Polish mathematician Lukasiewicz showed that arithmetic expressions can be represented in *prefix* notation. This representation, often referred to as *Polish* notation, places the operator before the operands. The *suffix* notation, referred to as *reverse Polish* notation, places the operator after the operands. The following examples demonstrate the three representations:

| | |
|---|---|
| $A + B$ | Infix notation |
| $+AB$ | Prefix notation |
| $AB+$ | Suffix notation |

The suffix or reverse Polish notation is in a form suitable for stack manipulation. The expression

$$A * B + C * D$$

is written in reverse Polish notation as

$$AB * CD * +$$

and is evaluated as follows: Scan the expression from left to right. When an operator is reached, perform the operation with the two operands found on the left side of the operator. Remove the two operands and the operator and replace them by the number obtained from the result of the operation. Continue to scan the expression and repeat the procedure for every operator encountered until there are no more operators.

For the above expression we find the operator $*$ after $A$ and $B$. We perform the operation $A * B$ and replace $A$, $B$, and $*$ by the product to obtain:

$$(A * B)\ CD * +$$

where $(A * B)$ is a *single* quantity obtained from the product. The next operator is a $*$ and its previous two operands are $C$ and $D$ so we perform $C * D$ and obtain an expression with two operands and one operator:

$$(A * B)\ (C * D) +$$

The next operator is $+$ and the two operands to be added are the two products, so we add the two quantities to obtain the result.

The conversion from infix notation to reverse Polish notation must take into consideration the operational hierarchy adopted for infix notation. This hierarchy dictates that we first perform all arithmetic inside inner parentheses, then inside outer parentheses, and do multiplication and division operations before addition and subtraction operations. Consider the expression

$$(A + B) * [C * (D + E) + F]$$

To evaluate the expression we must first perform the arithmetic inside the parantheses $(A + B)$ and $(D + E)$. Next we must calculate the expression inside the square brackets. The multiplication of $C * (D + E)$ must be done prior to the addition of $F$ since multiplication has precedence over addition. The last operation is the multiplication of the two terms between the parentheses and brackets. The expression can be converted to reverse Polish notation, without the use of parentheses, by taking into consideration the operation hierarchy. The converted expression is

$$AB + DE + C * F + *$$

Proceeding from left to right, we first add $A$ and $B$, then add $D$ and $E$. At this point we are left with

$$(A + B)(D + E)C * F + *$$

where $(A + B)$ and $(D + E)$ are each a *single* number obtained from the sum. The two operands for the next $*$ are $C$ and $(D + E)$. These two numbers are multiplied and the product added to $F$. The final $*$ causes the multiplication of the two terms.

### *Evaluation of Arithmetic Expressions*

Reverse Polish notation, combined with a stack arrangement of registers, is the most efficient way known for evaluating arithmetic expressions. This procedure is employed in some electronic calculators and also in some computers. The stack is particularly useful for handling long, complex problems involving chain calculations. It is based on the fact that any arithmetic expression can be expressed in parentheses-free Polish notation.

The procedure consists of first converting the arithmetic expression into its equivalent reverse Polish notation. The operands are pushed into the stack in the order that they appear. The initiation of an operation depends on whether we have a calculator or a computer. In a calculator, the operators are entered through the keyboard. In a computer, they must be initiated by instructions that contain an operation field (no address field is required). The following micro-operations are executed with the stack when an operation is entered in a calculator or issued by the control in a computer: (a) the two top-most operands in the stack are used for the operation, and (b) the stack is popped and the result of the operation replaces the lower operand. By continuously pushing the operands into the stack and performing the operations as defined above, the expression is evaluated in the proper order and the final result remains on top of the stack.

The following numerical example may clarify this procedure. Consider the arithmetic expression

$$(3 * 4) + (5 * 6)$$

In reverse Polish notation, it is expressed as

$$3\,4 * 5\,6 * +$$

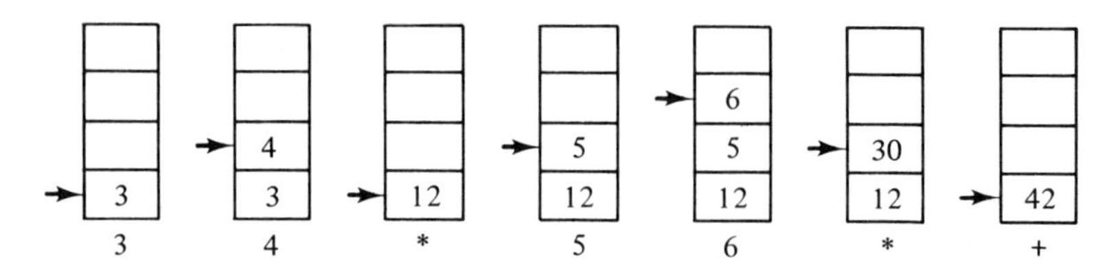


**Fig. 7-16** Stack operations to evaluate 3 * 4 + 5 * 6.

Now consider the stack operations shown in Fig. 7-16. Each box represents one stack operation and the arrow always points to the top of the stack. Scanning the expression from left to right, we encounter two operands. First the number 3 is pushed into the stack, then the number 4. The next symbol is the multiplication operator *. This causes a multiplication of the two top-most items in the stack. The stack is then popped and the product is placed on top of the stack, replacing the two original operands. Next we encounter the two operands 5 and 6, so they are pushed into the stack. The stack operation that results from the next * replaces these two numbers by their product. The last operation causes an arithmetic addition of the two top-most numbers in the stack to produce the final result of 42.

Scientific calculators that employ an internal stack require that the user convert the arithmetic expressions into reverse Polish notation. Computers that use a stack organized CPU provide a system program to perform the conversion for the user. Most compilers, irrespective of their CPU organization, convert all arithmetic expressions into Polish notation anyway because this is the most efficient method for translating arithmetic expressions into machine-language instructions. So in essence, a stack organized CPU may be more efficient in some applications than a CPU without a stack.

### *Stack Organized CPU*

In a stack organized CPU, the top two locations of the stack are processor registers. The rest of the stack is stored in the memory unit. In this way, the operations that must be performed with the top two items of the stack are available in processor registers for manipulation. If the top of the stack happens to be in the second register, the stack must be adjusted to bring an operand from memory into a processor register.

A stack organized CPU is depicted in Fig. 7-17(a). The two processor registers are labeled $A$ and $B$. The rest of the stack remains in memory with the memory stack pointer MSPR pointing to the top item in memory, not to the top of the entire stack which is at register $A$. Consider the case depicted in the fifth box of Fig. 7-16 and repeated in Fig. 7-17(b). Since register $A$ is the top of the stack, it contains the number 6. Register $B$ holds the next item which is number 5. The third number (12) is stored in the memory stack

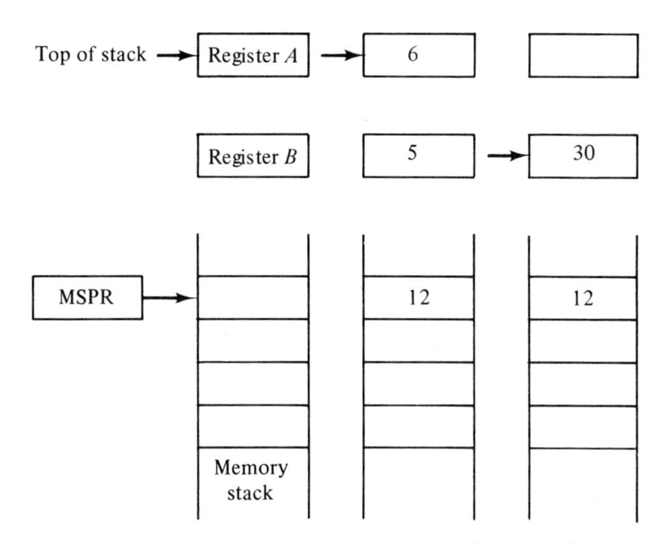


(a) General configuration (b) Need for stack adjustment

**Fig. 7-17** Stack organized CPU.

where MSPR is currently pointing. A multiply operation multiplies the two numbers in $A$ and $B$, places the product in register $B$ and pops the stack so that register $B$ is now the top of the stack. In order to perform the arithmetic addition of the two remaining numbers, 30 and 12, it is necessary that the stack be adjusted. This adjustment consists of popping the memory stack so that the number 30 moves into register $A$ and 12 into register $B$ (see Prob. 7-25). Now that the two operands are in processor registers, they can be arithmetically added to provide the final result in register $B$. A stack adjustment operation is automatically carried out by the hardware in a stack organized CPU.

## 7-7 LSI MICROPROCESSOR

A CPU can be designed and constructed by utilizing various MSI functions such as registers, ALUs, multiplexers, and decoders. A CPU constructed with MSI functions will require tens and sometimes hundreds of IC packages but has the advantage that the unit can be tailored to the needs of the particular application. However, because a CPU is a widely used digital function, it is also available in LSI form. A *microprocessor*, also called a *processor-on-a-chip*, is a central processor unit enclosed in one or two LSI circuits. Unlike the custom designed CPU, the functional characteristics of a microprocessor are fixed by the internal architecture of the device. The only access available to a microprocessor is through the terminals of the package—no direct connection can be made to the registers, the ALU, or any other internal component. Microprocessors have many of the features introduced in this chapter. The characteristic that makes the microprocessor unique is that the CPU is enclosed entirely in one or two very small packages.

Because of their small size and low cost, microprocessors are used in an increasing range of applications. They can function as a CPU in a general purpose computer or as a processor unit in a special purpose digital system. Microprocessor applications extend across a wide product line such as special purpose controllers, electronic calculators, keyboard terminals for data entry, traffic control, and biomedical instrumentation.

Standard LSI microprocessors come in various configurations and word lengths. Typical word lengths are 4, 8, or 16 bits. Some units have a modular construction (referred to as *bit-slice*) to facilitate the expansion to units of longer word lengths. Most microprocessors come with a fixed instruction set around which software must be developed for an application. Some units, however, provide microprogramming ability to allow the development of any convenient instruction set suitable for the particular application.

In order to guarantee a wide range of acceptability, most microprocessors provide an internal organization suited for a wide range of applications. Microprocessors have some properties in common, although every unit differs from all others in its internal architecture. The basic function of a microprocessor is to interpret instruction codes received from an external source such as a memory unit, or an input-output device, and perform arithmetic, logic, and control operations on data stored in internal registers. A microprocessor usually includes a number of registers, an ALU, a bus system, and timing and control logic. Externally, it provides a bus system for transferring instructions, addresses, and data between the CPU and the other modules connected to it.

The characteristics of particular microprocessors are described in reference manuals published by the manufacturers. These manuals invariably assume that the reader is familiar with the basic concepts of computer hardware and software architecture. There is a wide variety of microprocessor units available commercially. Although the architectures are different, all microprocessors have one property in common: they are organized as a central processor unit. This means that the CPU components introduced in this chapter are also found in microprocessors. The control logic of a microprocessor may be organized through a sequence of timing signals and control functions as described in Chap. 5 or by means of a microprogram as explained in Chap. 8. The communication with the external environment is implemented by means of interface logic as presented in Chap. 11.

An LSI system organized around a microprocessor must be programmed to perform a specific function and this is usually done by employing an assembly language similar to the one introduced in Chap. 6. Many of the programming techniques discussed in Chap. 6 also apply to microprocessor programs. In many instances, the programs are permanent and do not alter, especially when the microprocessor is used to perform a special dedicated application. For this reason, the fixed programs are stored in a read-only memory (ROM) and become part of the total design effort. The programs written for a particular system must be derived from a set of algorithms that specify the sequence of operations that the system must undergo. These algorithms can be derived by the methods introduced in Chaps. 9 and 10.

### *Microcomputer*

A microprocessor combined with memory and input-output capabilities becomes a *microcomputer*. The word *micro* is used to indicate the small physical size of the components involved. The second half of the word in microprocessor and microcomputer is what really sets them apart. The word *processor* is used to indicate that section of the system which performs the basic system control for executing operations and processing data as specified by the program. This part is usually referred to as the CPU. The term *microcomputer* is used to indicate a complete computer system consisting of the three basic units: processor, memory, and input-output.

A block diagram of a typical microcomputer is shown in Fig. 7-18. The microprocessor has a bidirectional data bus for data transfer in both directions. A separate address bus transfers the memory address, although sometimes the address is also transferred through the data bus. Each control line usually has a separate function although control information may also be transferred through a bus. The ROM (read-only memory) is used for storing fixed programs for special applications or a microprogram to control the micro-operations in the CPU. The size of the ROM varies according to the

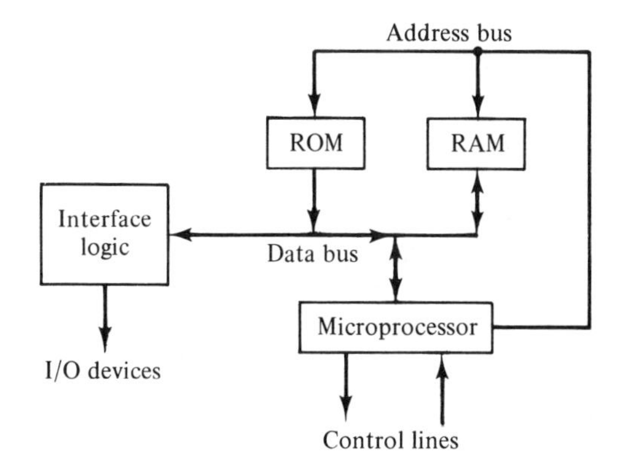


**Fig. 7-18** Typical microcomputer block diagram.

application but is limited by the allowable capacity dictated by the addressing capability of the microprocessor. The RAM (random-access memory) consists of a number of LSI units and is used to store programs and data that need changing and updating. The input-output section consists of the necessary interface logic for connecting the data bus to input-output devices such as teletypewriters, terminals, and other peripheral devices.

The development of a microcomputer unit requires detailed knowledge of the microprocessor operation. To facilitate the development of microcomputer and microcontroller systems, many manufacturers offer complete microcomputer units mounted on a single printed circuit (PC) board. The LSI components and interface logic circuits are internally connected within the PC board giving the user access to the I/O interface through the PC board connector. Besides providing the necessary components for a host of applications, these products quite often include special circuits that help extend the capabilities of the internal LSI microprocessor.

### *A Typical Microprocessor*

A microprocessor must provide a sufficient amount of internal hardware in order to qualify as a general purpose CPU. The following components are included in most microprocessors:

An instruction register and decoder

A number of internal registers

An arithmetic logic unit and shifter

Temporary storage for status conditions

A register stack

Timing and control logic

An internal bus structure

Facility for communicating with the external environment

Figure 7-19 shows a block diagram of a typical microprocessor with all the components listed above.

The instruction register receives instructions from memory through the data bus. The instruction code is decoded and interpreted by the control. The control then generates a sequence of signals to initiate the required micro-operations. The data arriving in the data bus are stored in internal registers. These registers may be connected through a bus system or may be grouped within a small scratch-pad memory. The scratch-pad memory contains a small number of words (eight words is typical) and each word functions as a register. The individual words are selected by an address register.

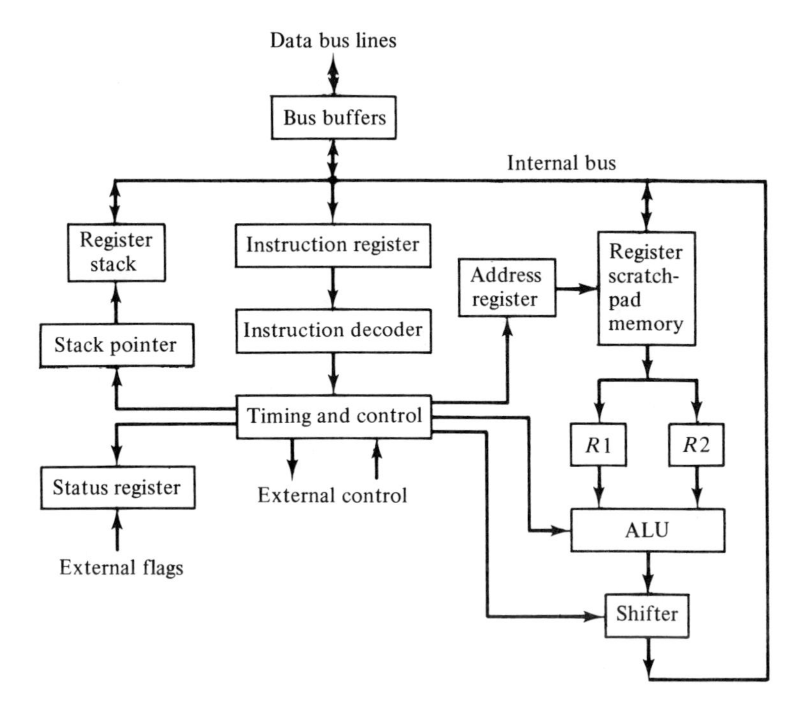


**Fig. 7-19** Block diagram of a typical microprocessor.

The content of the selected scratch-pad memory word is transferred into one of two external registers that communicate with the ALU. The CPU registers in the scratch-pad memory store temporary data and act as accumulators, index registers, memory address registers, memory buffer registers, and program counters.

The arithmetic logic unit (ALU) performs various arithmetic, logic, and shift micro-operations. Microprocessors oriented towards calculator applications provide a decimal arithmetic unit instead of an ALU. Others may provide both binary and decimal arithmetic units.

The status register consists of a number of flip-flops that store status conditions such as output-carry from ALU, contents of accumulator equal zero, and status of external input and output flags. The status flip-flops are set when the corresponding conditions occur and are later tested by special instructions to provide decision making capabilities.

Microprocessors employ stack-oriented registers that can be accessed only on a last-in-first-out basis. These are used for subroutine nesting, for interrupts, and for temporary storage of contents of processor registers. The stack automatically stores the content of the program counter upon execution of a *call* instruction and automatically restores the program counter upon the execution of a *return* instruction. The stack pointer is used to designate the present top of the stack location. Some microprocessors use a portion of the external memory for the stack but include the stack pointer within the microprocessor. In this way, the stack can be extended to any number of words desired. The memory stack is addressed by the stack pointer upon the execution of a *call* or *return* instruction.

The timing and control logic controls the sequence of micro-operations within the microprocessor. It controls the various cycles of the computer, the data transfers through the internal bus system, the ALU and shifter, and the scratch-pad memory. The control also provides external signals to let all other modules know the status in which the microprocessor is at any particular time. During the fetch cycle, the control generates a fetch status signal to request an instruction from memory. During the execute cycle the control may be in a memory-read status or a memory-write status or in an input-output status. The bidirectional bus buffers are controlled by the control status request. When the microprocessor is requesting information from the external environment, the bidirectional bus is placed in the input mode. When it sends information out to the external environment, the bus buffers are placed in the output mode and the information placed in the data bus. The external modules connected to the microprocessor detect the control status condition generated by the microprocessor control. Proper communication is achieved by conforming with the status request and the direction of information flow in the data bus.

When only one external data bus is available in the microprocessor, it must be used alternately for data, addresses, and instructions. A double bus system uses one separate bus for data and instructions and another for addresses. Control information may or may not have a special bus. By using a double bus system, data and addresses can be transferred back and forth simultaneously in the same cycle without waiting for a sequential usage of a common bus. A multiple bus requires a larger number of pins in the IC microprocessor package.

A bidirectional data bus system is used in most microprocessors because

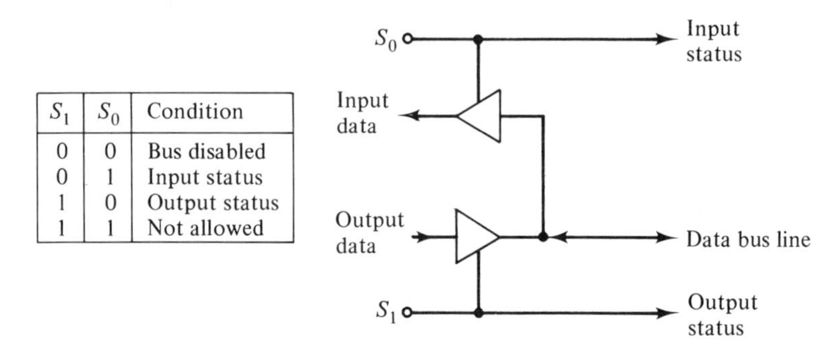

| $S_1$ | $S_0$ | Condition |
|---|---|---|
| 0 | 0 | Bus disabled |
| 0 | 1 | Input status |
| 1 | 0 | Output status |
| 1 | 1 | Not allowed |



**Fig. 7-20** Bidirectional bus line with tri-stage buffers.

it reduces the number of pins in the package. The bus buffers that control the direction of information flow are usually constructed with tri-state gates as shown in Fig. 7-20. The control input of each tri-state buffer controls its output. When the control input is enabled, the output of the gate is equal to its input value. When the control input is disabled, the output of the buffer is disabled irrespective of its input condition (see also Fig. 2-2). By controlling selection lines $S_0$ and $S_1$, the data bus lines may be placed in an input or output status. The two selection lines are used also to inform all external modules of the status condition in which the bidirectional data bus is at any particular time.

### *Software Consideration*

A microprocessor is a CPU and as such, it has a set of instructions and instruction code formats just as any other CPU. When used with other components to design a digital system, the microprocessor must be programmed to provide the special functions required by the particular application. In addition to the obvious application that it can be used as a component in a general purpose microcomputer, the microprocessor is quite often employed as a processor unit in special-purpose controllers. The use of a microprocessor as a component in a special purpose digital system has the advantage that one LSI unit replaces a large number of MSI packages that would have been needed otherwise. The fixed repetitive functions needed for the special purpose application are implemented by programming the microprocessor. Unalterable programs for the microcontroller are stored in the ROM part of the system. Once a program is frozen into a custom mask set of ROMs, there is no difference between a microprocessor-controlled system and a custom hardware design. If the system must be updated or changed, it is not necessary to change any hardware logic; the change can be implemented by reprogramming the ROM. Thus, the design of a special-purpose controller with a microprocessor requires that special routines be generated as part of the design. The relevant properties of a microprocessor that are important for developing special programs are:

1. The instruction repertoire of the microprocessor, including execution time and the number of words occupied by each instruction.
2. The data formats available (e.g., does the unit employ 2's complement representation, binary coded decimal numbers, etc.?).
3. The programmed controlled registers available.
4. The function of the flags and status bits under program control.
5. Program storage and memory space available.
6. The nature of the interface through programmed instructions.

Much of the development effort in the design of a digital system with a microcomputer is linked to the programming phase. For this reason, vendors of microprocessors provide software design aids to facilitate the design effort. The software design aids are system programs that generally require the use of other computers or a time-sharing service. Assemblers are usually available to convert symbolic programs into binary machine-language instructions. Editors available in time-sharing services allow designers to prepare assembly language programs and change or correct them with simple commands. Several microprocessors have compilers which allow programs to be written in a high-level language. In addition, test programs such as simulators are available to check the hardware prototype unit prior to its final production.

Once the hardware configuration of a microcomputer system has been established, the designer must determine the binary configuration of the ROM where a fixed program for the dedicated application is to be stored. The flow chart in Fig. 7-21 enumerates the procedural steps for obtaining the ROM binary program. It is convenient to use a host computer, preferably in a time-sharing mode, to facilitate the software design effort. The designer specifies the repetitive operations which must be performed in the microcomputer system. The designer then writes a symbolic program that implements the required function. The symbolic program may be written in assembly language or in a high-level programming language, depending on the software aids available for the microprocessor. The program can be edited, using the time-sharing facility, while it is being entered via the teletypewriter keyboard. The translation to binary is done by a cross assembler or cross compiler. These are special systems programs available in the host computer that translate the user's symbolic program into a binary program which is recognized by the particular microprocessor used. If the cross assembler finds errors in the symbolic program, the designer must modify his program and assemble again.

The binary program obtained from the cross assembler is then used to simulate the operation of the microprocessor system. The software simulator residing in the host computer simulates the microcomputer system performance. The user provides input information to the simulator and checks the simulated output listings. The output listings of the simulator are checked with expected values of performance. Logical errors which may have been overlooked during the initial specification can be detected in this manner. Any errors detected during the simulation run are corrected by changing the symbolic program. The assembly and simulation processes are repeated again until a good simulation run is achieved.

Once the designer is satisfied with his program, he directs the time-sharing computer to output the binary program on paper tape, punch cards or any other convenient output medium. The binary program so obtained is then used to mask the system ROMs by a computerized procedure.

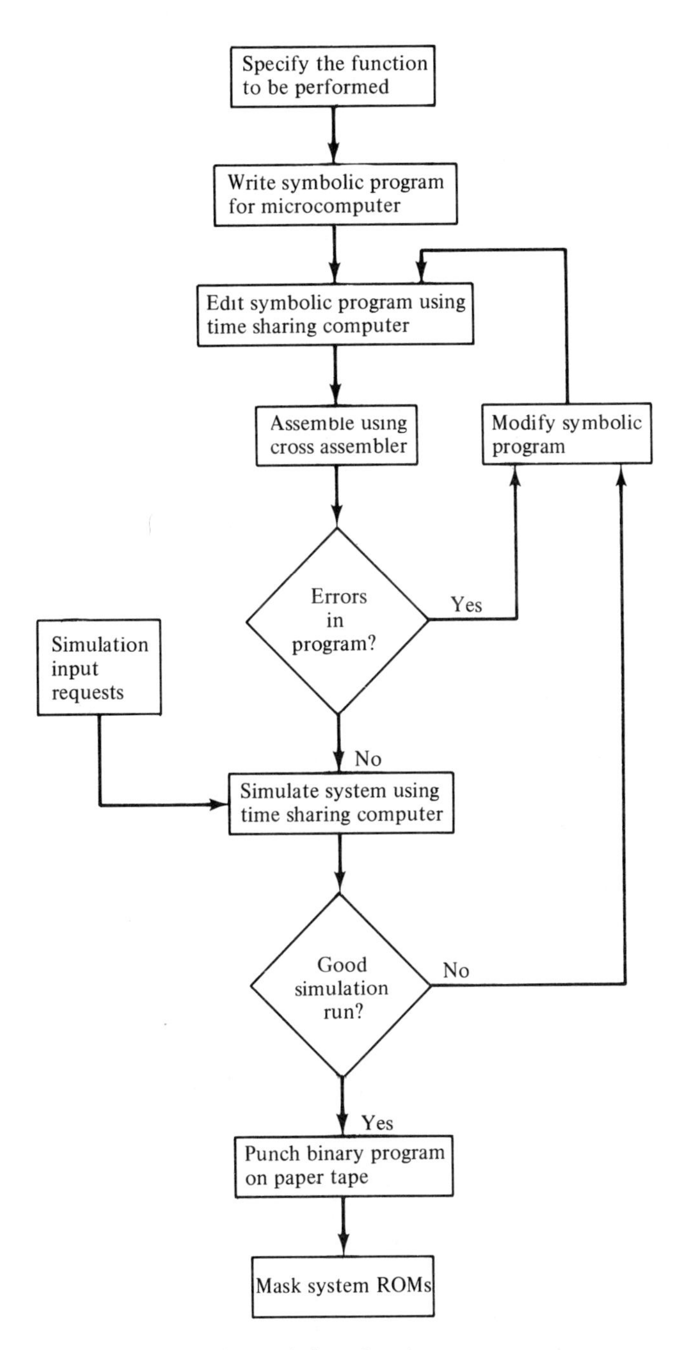


**Fig. 7-21** Software design of a microcomputer system.

The differences between programming a large computer and programming a microcomputer or microcontroller are not fundamental, but rather differences in emphasis. Microcomputer applications are mostly concerned with hardware systems for some special use and must take into consideration the problems associated with the particular application.

## REFERENCES


1. Sobel, H. S., *Introduction to Digital Computer Design*, Reading, Mass.: Addison-Wesley Publishing Co., 1970.
2. Morris, R. L., and J. R. Miller, *Designing with TTL Integrated Circuits*, New York: McGraw-Hill Book Co., 1971.
3. "Arithmetic Logic Unit/Function Generator" and "Look-Ahead Carry Generators," in *The TTL Data Book for Design Engineers*, Dallas, Texas: Texas Instruments, Inc. 1973, pp. 381–395.
4. DeLaune, J. M., "High-Speed Addition Using Lookahead Carry Techniques," Motorola Semiconductor Products, Inc., Application note AN-488. Phoenix Ariz.: 1971.
5. MacSorley, O. L., "High-Speed Arithmetic in Binary Computers," *Proc. of the IRE*, Vol. 49 (January, 1961), pp. 67–91.
6. Gschwind, H. W., *Design of Digital Computers*, New York: Springer-Verlag, 1967.
7. Hauck, E. A., and B. A. Dent, "Burrough's B6500/B7500 Stack Mechanism," *AFIPS Conf. Proc.*, Vol. 32 (1968), pp. 245–251.
8. *HP-45 Owner's Handbook*, Hewlett Packard Co., Cupertino, Cal., 1973.
9. Lapidus, G., "MOS/LSI Launches the Low-Cost Processor," *IEEE Spectrum*, Vol. 9 (November, 1972), pp. 33–40.
10. Ward, A. R., "LSI Microprocessor and Microcomputers: A Bibliography," *Computer*, Vol. 7 (July, 1974), pp. 35–39.
11. *8008 8-bit Parallel Central Processor Unit—User's Manual*, Intel Corp., Santa Clara, Cal., 1973.


## PROBLEMS

7-1 The control unit that operates the CPU bus system of Fig. 7-1 provides the binary variables to select the various components in the system. The eight registers are encoded in a straight binary sequence starting with 000 for *PC*. The ALU and shifter selection are as specified in Sec. 7-2. List the binary variables that must be generated by the control and applied to the five select inputs in the system in order to initiate the following micro-operations:

$$AC \leftarrow AC + MBR$$

$$PC \leftarrow PC + 1$$

$$MAR \leftarrow IR + XR1$$

$$\text{shl } AC$$

7-2 What control input in the bus system of Fig. 7-1 will prevent the transfer of information into any destination register?

7-3 Prove the Boolean relations listed in Table 7-2.

7-4 There are 16 logic functions for two Boolean variables. Table 7-4 lists eight of these functions. List the remaining eight functions.

7-5 The OR and AND logic functions can be included in the ALU of Sec. 7-2 by modifying the output circuit and using a fourth selection line $S_3$ as shown in the diagram below.

(a) Using the following two *Boolean* identities:

$$A + B = A \oplus B + AB$$

$$AB = 0 + AB$$

determine the values of $S_3S_2S_1S_0$ and $M$ for the OR and AND logic functions.

(b) Show that when $S_3 = 0$, none of the other operations of the ALU are altered.

(c) What other logic operations can be implemented with this modification and what are their selection values?

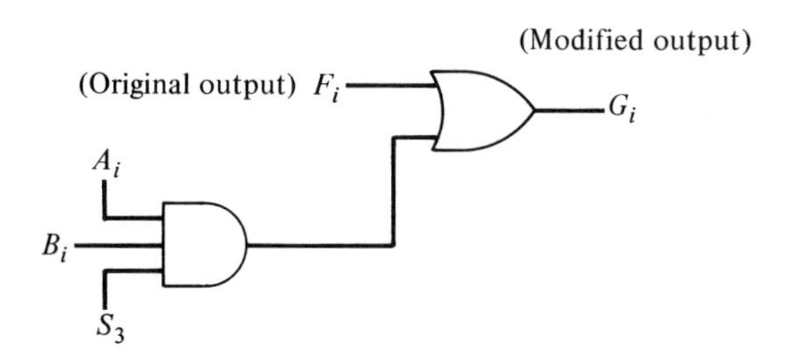


**Fig. P7-5**

7-6 (a) Design a combinational circuit with four inputs $A_4A_3A_2A_1$ and four outputs $F_4F_3F_2F_1$. The output binary number should be equal to the input binary number minus 1 (decrement operation).

(b) Show that the output Boolean functions of the circuit can be expressed in the following form:

$$F_1 = A_1' \oplus 0$$

$$F_2 = A_2' \oplus A_1$$

$$F_3 = A_3' \oplus (A_1 + A_2)$$

$$F_4 = A_4' \oplus (A_1 + A_2 + A_3)$$

(c) From the above result, verify the decrement operation in the ALU of Sec. 7-2.

• 7-7 The logic diagram of the first stage of the integrated circuit ALU type 74181 is shown below. Note that an inverted carry input is used, $C_1'$.

(a) Obtain a table for $x$, $y$, and $z$ as a function of the four selection lines $S_3S_2S_1S_0$ and the mode control $M$ (similar to Table 7-1).

(b) Show that logic functions are generated when $M = 1$ and arithmetic functions when $M = 0$.

(c) Obtain the simplified Boolean functions for $F_1$ and $C_2$ for both $M = 1$ and $M = 0$ as a function of $x$, $y$, and $C_1$.

(d) Show that $F$ produces the AND operation when $S = 1011$ and $M = 1$.

(e) Show that $F$ produces the add micro-operation when $S = 1001$ and $M = 0$.

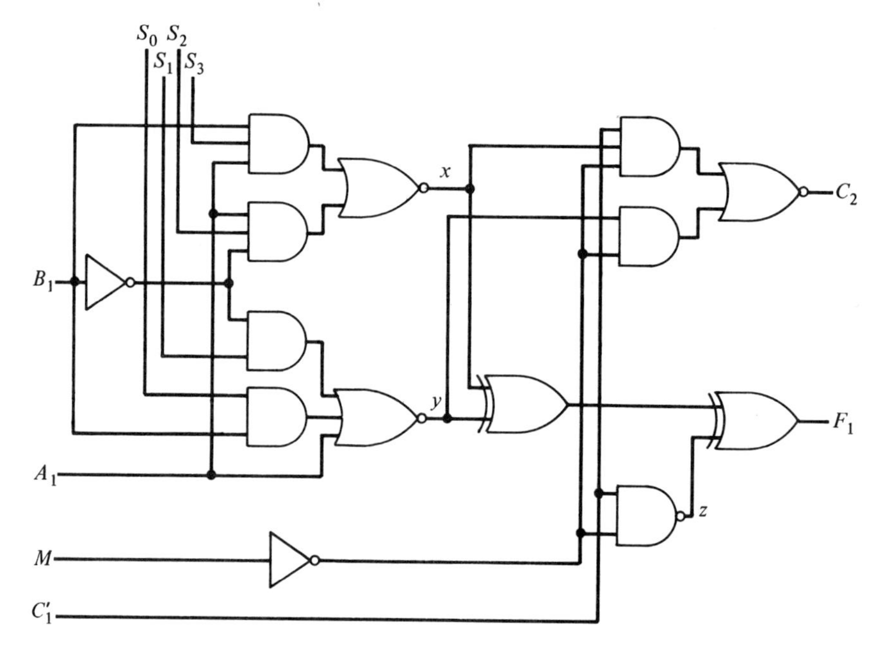


**Fig. P7-7**

7-8 A control unit generates seven control functions $P_1, P_2, \ldots, P_7$. Each control function specifies one of the micro-operations listed in Table 7-5. Design an encoder circuit that accepts the seven control functions and generates the five binary variables required for the ALU function.

7-9 Design a shifter with combinational circuits that can shift-right one position, or two positions, or none at all.

7-10 A 24-bit parallel-adder is partitioned into six groups of four stages each. A carry look-ahead circuit, with propagation delay of 10 nsec, is available in each group for the input-carry to the next group. The internal carry in each stage ripples through with 8 nsec per stage. Determine the total propagation delay time in the parallel-adder.

7-11 The 4-bit binary counter of Fig. 2-14 has a carry-output that ripples through four AND gates. Show that the output-carry can be generated with one 5-input AND gate to produce a carry look-ahead for the next high-order 4-bit counter. Now use 10 such circuits to produce a 40-bit binary counter. Calculate the carry propagation delay time through the 40-bit counter assuming that each gate has a maximum delay of 20 nsec.

7-12 List the Boolean functions and draw the logic diagram for outputs $G_5$ and $P_5$ of the carry look-ahead generator of Fig. 7-9.

7-13 How many levels of gates are there between $C_1$ and $C_{17}$ in the parallel-adder of Fig. 7-10?

7-14 (a) Show that the carry propagate $P_i$ in a full-adder can be expressed by the Boolean function:

$$P_i = A_i + B_i$$

(b) The logic diagram of one stage of a binary parallel-adder as implemented in some ICs is shown below. Show that the circuit implements a full-adder and identify the $P_i'$ and $G_i'$ terminals.

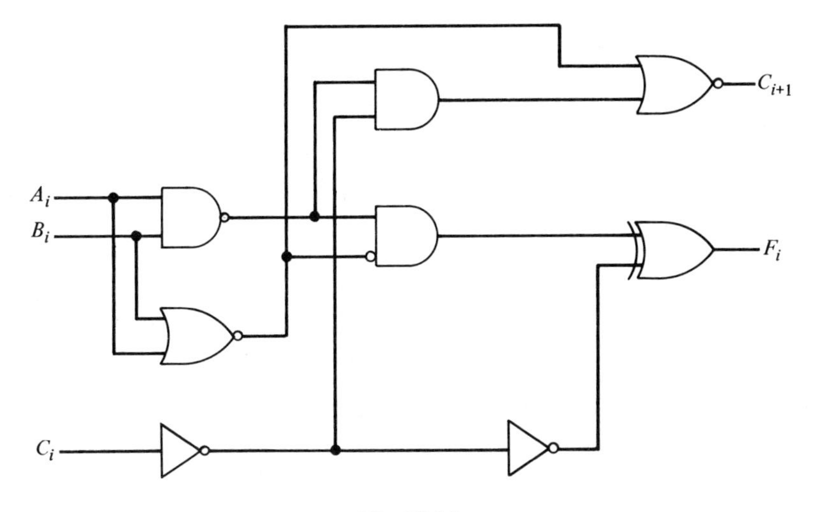


Fig. P7-14

7-15 Show the subtraction of BCD 356 from BCD 673 digit by digit. Use 9's complement method of adding 6 before complementing each bit and correct each addition by adding 6 when necessary.

7-16 Show that 673 − 356 can be computed by adding 673 to the 10's complement of 356 and discarding the end carry. Draw the block diagram of a three-stage decimal arithmetic unit and show how this operation is implemented. List all input bits and output bits of the unit.

7-17 Show that the lower 4-bit binary adder in Fig. 7-11 can be replaced by one full-adder and two half-adders.

7-18 Using combinational circuit design techniques (Sec. 1-4), derive the Boolean functions for the BCD 9's complementer of Fig. 7-12. Draw the logic diagram.

7-19 It is necessary to design an adder for two decimal digits represented in the excess-3 code (Table 3-6). Show that the correction after adding two digits with a 4-bit binary adder is as follows:
(a) The output-carry is equal to the uncorrected carry.
(b) If output-carry = 1, add 0011.
(c) If output-carry = 0, add 1101 and ignore the carry from this addition.
Show that the excess-3 adder can be constructed with seven full-adders and two inverters.

7-20 Derive the circuit for a 9's complementer when decimal digits are represented in the excess-3 code (Table 3-6). A mode control input determines whether the digit is complemented or not. What is the advantage of using this code over BCD?

7-21 A computer has 16 processor registers and instructions with four bits in the operation field.
(a) Show a possible instruction code format for an operation with the content of any register with any other register and the result placed in any third register. How many bits are there in the instruction?
(b) Give a possible binary value for an instruction that specifies the operation $R13 \longleftarrow R6 + R9$.

7-22 (a) Explain how index registers can be used as pointers and counters.
(b) What is the difference between an index register and a base register?

7-23 Consider a computer having the instruction code format shown in Fig. 7-13. Assume that the control unit has a decoder with outputs $a_0$ to $a_7$ for the eight modes in the MOD field as specified in Table 7-8. Define a set of registers and timing signals for the computer. List the sequence of micro-operations and control functions needed to read an instruction from memory and place the operand into the memory buffer register.

7-24 List the micro-operations for popping and pushing a stack simulated with a random access memory (see Fig. 7-15).

7-25 Two operations of a stack organized CPU (Fig. 7-17) are concerned with stack adjustments. A *pop-stack adjustment* brings the top element of the stack to register $A$. A *push-stack adjustment* pushes the contents of $A$ and $B$ into the memory stack. Let the $B$ register be the memory buffer register and use two flip-flops, $YA$ and $YB$, so that when $YA = 1$, register $A$ is full and is on top of the stack. If $YA = 0$ and $YB = 1$, register $B$ is the top of the stack. When both are 0, the top of the stack is in the memory part. Draw a flow chart showing the micro-operations needed for the two stack adjustment operations as a function of the values of $YA$ and $YB$. Neglect any overflow.

7-26 Convert the following arithmetic expressions into reverse Polish notation:
(a) $A + B + C$
(b) $A * B + A * (B * D + C * E)$
(c) $A * B/C + D$

7-27 Give the infix notation of the following reverse Polish expressions:
(a) $ABCDE * / - +$
(b) $AB * CD * + EF * +$
(c) $AB + C * D +$

7-28 Convert the following numerical expression into reverse Polish notation and show the stack operations for evaluating the numerical result.

$$(3 + 4)[10(2 + 6) + 8]$$

7-29 A *first-in-first-out* (FIFO) is a memory unit that stores information in such a manner that the item first in is the item first out. Show how a FIFO memory operates with three counters: a write counter $WC$ that holds the address for the memory write operation; a read counter $RC$ that holds the address for the read operation; and an available storage counter $ASC$ that indicates the number of items stored. $ASC$ is incremented for every item stored and decremented for every item that is retrieved. The memory unit communicates with $MAR$ and $MBR$.

7-30 An 8-bit microprocessor can communicate with up to $2^{16}$ words of memory. It has an 8-line bidirectional data bus for transfer of instructions, data and addresses. One type of instruction format consists of three 8-bit words: the first word contains the operation field and the other two, the address field. Give the type of information (instruction, data, or address), the direction of transfer (to or from the microprocessor) and the number of times that the data bus is used in order to fetch and execute the following instructions:
(a) Load from memory to $AC$.
(b) Store content of $AC$ in memory.

# 8

# MICROPROGRAM CONTROL ORGANIZATION

## 8-1 CONTROL MEMORY

The function of the control unit in a digital system is to initiate sequences of micro-operations. The number of different micro-operations available in a given system is finite. The complexity of the digital system is derived from the fact that a large number of micro-operations are performed in a given time sequence. When the control functions are generated by hardware using conventional logic design techniques, the control unit is said to be *hard-wired.* Microprogramming is a second alternative for designing the control unit of a digital computer. The principle of microprogramming is an elegant and systematic method for generating the micro-operation sequences in a digital system.

The control signal that specifies a micro-operation is a binary variable. When it is in the 1 state, the corresponding micro-operation is executed. A control variable in its 0 state does not affect the state of the registers in the system. There are occasions when the state of control variables are defined in reverse with the 0 state initiating the micro-operation and the 1 state being the idle state. However, in order not to complicate the discussion we will adopt the convention that a control variable is active only when it is in the 1 state.

As already mentioned, the control unit initiates a series of sequential steps of micro-operations. During any given time interval, certain micro-operations are to be initiated while all others remain idle. Thus the micro-operation steps in each time interval can be represented by a string of 1's and 0's called a *control word.* As such, control words can be programmed to initiate the various components of the system in a prescribed fashion. A control unit whose micro-operation steps are stored in a memory is called a *microprogrammed control unit.* Each control word of memory is called a *microinstruction* and a sequence of words is called a *microprogram.* Since alterations of the microprogram are seldom needed, the memory can be a read-only memory (ROM). The concept of microprogramming was not practical to implement until fast read-only memories became available commercially. The utilization of a microprogram involves placing all micro-operation steps in words of ROM for use by the control unit through successive read operations. The content of the words in ROM are fixed and cannot be altered by simple programming since no writing capability is available in the ROM. ROM words are made permanent during the hardware production of the unit. Although sometimes programmable read-only memories (PROM) are used, the programming procedure is a hardware process requiring the opening of fused links. Once a PROM is programmed it cannot be altered by simple programming.

A more advanced development known as *dynamic* microprogramming permits a prescribed microprogram to be loaded initially from either the computer console or from an auxiliary memory. Control units that use dynamic microprogramming employ a *writable control memory* (WCM). This memory has the capability of writing (to change the microprogram) but is used mostly for reading. A read-only memory or a writable control memory when used in the control unit of a computer is referred to as a *control memory.*

A computer that employs a microprogrammed control unit will have two separate memories: a main memory and a control memory. The main memory is available to the user for storing his programs. The contents of main memory may alter when the program is executed and every time the program is changed. The user's program in main memory consists of machine instructions and data. The control memory holds a fixed microprogram that cannot be altered by the occasional user. The microprogram consists of microinstructions that specify various internal control signals for execution of register micro-operations. Each machine instruction initiates a series of microinstructions in control memory. These microinstructions generate the micro-operations to (a) fetch the instruction from main memory; (b) evaluate the effective address of the operand; (c) execute the operation specified by the instruction; and (d) return control to the beginning of the fetch cycle to repeat the sequence again for the next instruction.

Figure 8-1 illustrates the major components of a microprogrammed control unit. The ROM address register specifies the word read from control memory. It must be realized that a ROM operates as a combinational circuit with the address value as the input and the corresponding word as the output.

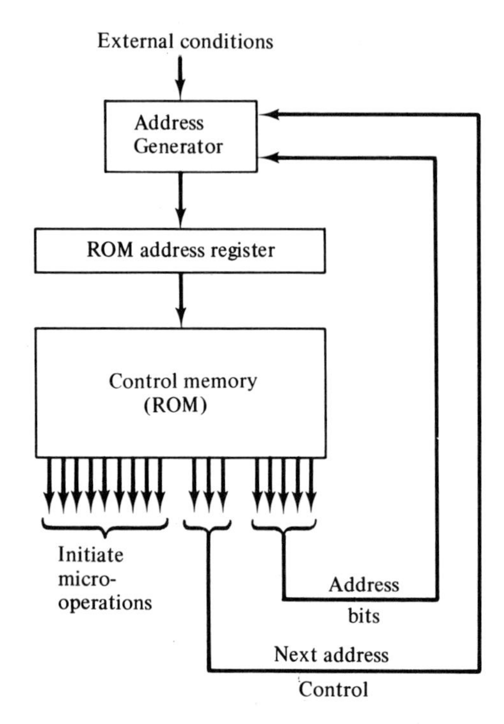


**Fig. 8-1** Block diagram of a microprogrammed control unit.

The content of the specified word remains in the output wires as long as the address value remains in the address register. No *read* signal is needed as in a random access memory. The word content of ROM should be transferred to a buffer register if the address register changes while the ROM word is still in use. If the change in address and ROM word can occur simultaneously, no buffer register is needed.

The word read from control memory represents a microinstruction. The microinstruction specifies one or more micro-operations for the components in the computer. Once these micro-operations are executed, the control unit must determine its next address. The location of the next microinstruction may be the one next in sequence or, it may be located somewhere else in the control memory. For this reason, it is necessary to use a few bits of the microinstruction to control the generation of the address for the next microinstruction. A given microinstruction may also have special bits that specify explicitly the address of the next microinstruction. Thus, control words contain bits for controlling the micro-operations in the digital system and bits that determine the address sequence of the control memory itself. We shall consider the problem of address sequencing first and then discuss possible variations of control word formats.

## 8-2 ADDRESS SEQUENCING

Microinstructions are stored in control memory in groups, with each group specifying a *routine*. Each computer instruction has its own routine in control memory to generate the micro-operations that execute the instruction. The hardware that controls the address sequencing of the control memory must be capable of sequencing the microinstructions within a routine and be able to branch from one routine to another.

Figure 8-2 shows a block digram of a control memory and the associated hardware needed for selecting the next microinstruction address. The micro-

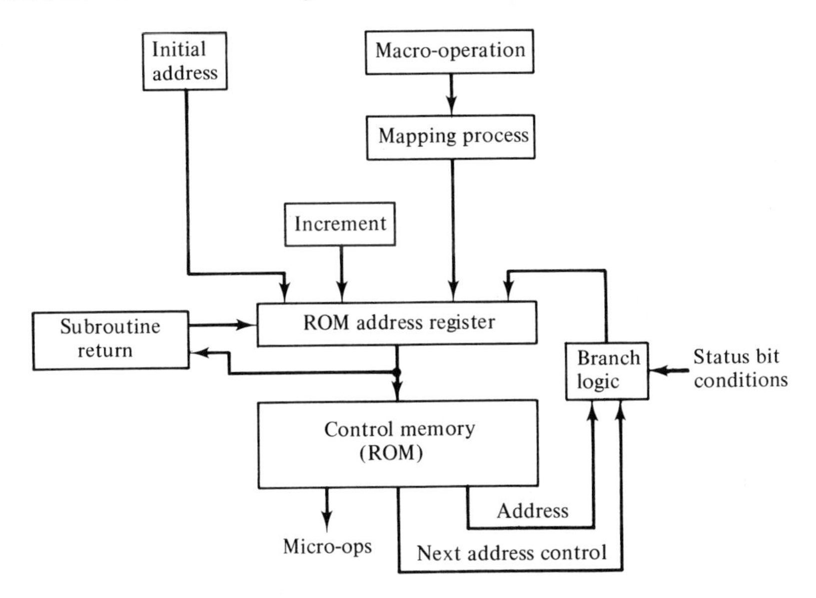


**Fig. 8-2** Selection of next address in a control memory.

instruction in control memory contains a set of control bits to specify the method by which the next ROM address is obtained. It may also contain an address field to specify the next address explicitly. The diagram shows five different paths from which the ROM address register can receive the next address. In order to appreciate the address sequencing in a microprogram control unit, let us enumerate the steps that the control must undergo during the execution of a single computer instruction.

An initial address is loaded into the ROM address register when a start switch is activated in the computer console. This address is usually the address of the first microinstruction that activates the instruction fetch routine. The fetch cycle routine may be sequenced by incrementing the ROM address register through the rest of its microinstructions. At the end of the fetch routine, the machine instruction would be in the instruction register of the computer.

The control memory next must go through the routine that determines the effective address of the operand. A machine instruction may have bits that specify various addressing modes such as indirect address and index registers. The effective address computation routine in control memory can be reached through a branch microinstruction which is conditioned upon the status of the mode bits of the instruction. When the effective address computation routine is completed, the address of the operand is available in the memory address register.

The next step is to generate the micro-operations that execute the instruction fetched from memory. The micro-operation steps to be generated in processor registers depend on the operation code part of the instruction, the macro-operation. Each macro-operation has its own routine stored in a given space of control memory. The transformation from the macro-operation bits to the bits of the first ROM address where the routine is stored is referred to as a *mapping* process. A mapping procedure is a rule that transforms the macro-operation into a ROM address. Once the required routine is reached, the microinstructions that execute the macro-operation may be sequenced by incrementing the ROM address register but sometimes the sequence of micro-operations will depend on values of certain status bits in processor registers. Microprograms that employ subroutines will require an external register for storing the return address. Return addresses cannot be stored in ROM because the unit has no writing capability.

When the execution of the instruction is completed, control must return to the fetch routine. This is accomplished by executing an unconditional branch microinstruction to the first address of the fetch routine.

In summary, the address sequencing capabilities required in a control memory are:

1. Incrementing of the ROM address register.
2. Unconditional branch as specified by the address field of the microinstruction.
3. Conditional branch depending on status bits in the registers of the computer.
4. A mapping process from the bits of the macro-operation to the required bits of a ROM address.
5. An address transfer from an external source, such as a subroutine return-register, or from an initial address source during start-up conditions.

In a microprogrammed device with short ROM words, a program counter can be used to select the next sequential address by incrementing it by 1 just as the program counter is incremented in a typical computer. However, it is not necessary to provide a separate register for this function since the ROM address register itself can be incremented. The existence of an increment operation in the address register carries with it the implication that the next address will be selected automatically by counting, unless something is done to override this procedure. This saves bits of ROM because there is no need to have the address bits presented at the output of the control memory except when an out-of-sequence address is desired.

In microprogram devices with longer ROM words, each microinstruction contains the address of the next microinstruction, even for sequential addresses. This eliminates the need for incrementing the ROM address register because the address field available in each microinstruction specifies the address of the next microinstruction.

### *Conditional Branch*

The branch logic of Fig. 8-2 provides decision making capabilities in the control unit. The status conditions are special bits in the system that provide parameter information such as overflow indication, adder carry out, the sign bit of a register, the mode bits of an instruction, and input or output status conditions. Information in these bits can be tested and actions initiated based on their condition, i.e., whether their value is 1 or 0. The status bits, together with the bits in the microinstruction devoted to determining the next address, control the conditional branch decisions generated in the branch logic. The branch logic hardware may be implemented in a variety of ways. The simplest way is to test the specified condition and branch to the indicated address if the condition is met; otherwise, the address register is incremented. This can be inplemented with a multiplexer as shown in Fig. 8-3. Suppose we have eight status bit conditions to consider. Three bits in the microinstruction are used to specify any one of eight conditions. These three bits provide the selection logic for a multiplexer. If the selected status bit is in the 1 state, the output of the multiplexer is a 1; otherwise it is a 0. A 1 output in the multiplexer generates a control signal to load the address bits of the microinstruction into the address register. A 0 output in the multiplexer causes the address register to be incremented by 1. In this configuration, the ROM address register acts as a counter with parallel-load capability.

The address bits in the microinstruction can be eliminated if a skip condition is used. If the ROM address register is permitted to count up in steps of one or two, a skip microinstruction will increment the address register by 1 if the condition is not satisfied and by 2 if it is satisfied. An unconditional branch microinstruction in the next word will transfer control to any address if the condition is not satisfied. A similar but different scheme may be used that eliminates the need for incrementing the address register by 2. In this scheme, the skip microinstruction sets a special flip-flop to 1 if the

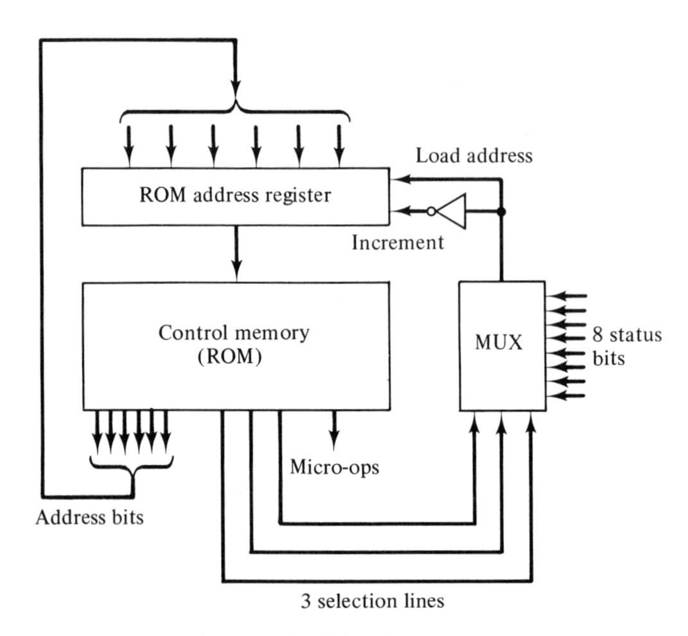


**Fig. 8-3** Conditional branch logic.

condition is satisfied. The address register is incremented by 1 irrespective of the value of the status bit. If the flip-flop is set, the next microinstruction is not executed. A branch microinstruction is placed in the word following the skip. The branch is executed only if the flip-flop is not set. Thus control is transferred to the branch address if the condition is not satisfied.

Control memories that do not increment the ROM address register include the address of the next microinstruction in the bits of the current microinstruction. This provides a capability for specifying a sequential address or an address for an unconditional branch. In a conditional branch microinstruction it is necessary to specify two branch locations, one for when the condition is satisfied and the other when it is not. One possibility would be to include two addresses in the branch microinstruction, but this requires an excessive number of control word bits. The second address can be avoided if the conditional branch microinstruction employs an address field with a 0 in the least significant bit position. The branch logic transfers the status bit tested into the last bit of the address register, causing a two way branch. This two-way branch is similar to a skip condition and is explained further by means of Fig. 8-4. For an unconditional branch, the address control bit in ROM is set to 0. This prevents the status bit from changing the value of the address bits that are transferred into the ROM address register. A conditional branch microinstruction will have a 1 in the address control bit and a 0 in the low-order position of the address bits. If the status bit is 0,

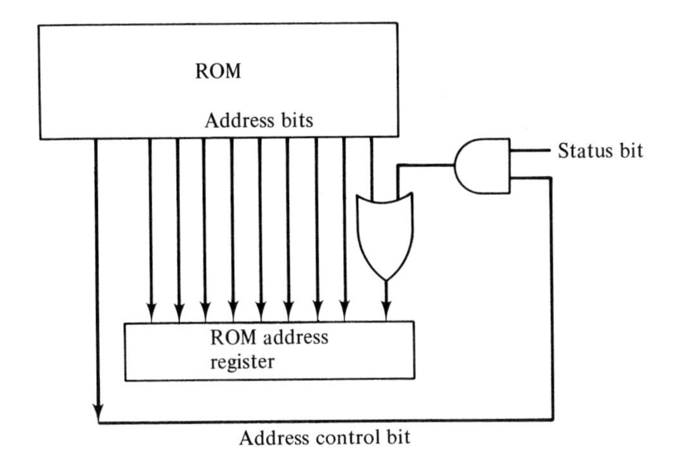


**Fig. 8-4** Two-way branch in a control memory.

the ROM address register receives an even-number address with zero in the last position. If the status bit is 1, a branch to the odd-numbered location would be forced, because the last bit would be a 1. It is possible to have a four-way branch if the last two bits of the address field in the microinstruction contain zeros. Two status bits can be tested simultaneously and forced into the address register. The result is a branch to an address ending with bits 00, 01, 10, or 11, depending on the two status bits tested. Saving ROM bits to specify addresses in this fashion can be accomplished by truncating the address field in the microinstruction. Most microprograms are usually short and involve routines of less than 8 or 16 words. This means that the selection of the next microinstruction can be specified by a relatively few bits, the rest of the bits already being present in the address register. Therefore, it is possible to specify a conditional branch with an address field three or four bits in length. Obviously other microinstructions are required to branch outside the restricted range.

### *Mapping of Macro-Operation*

A special type of branch exists when a microinstruction specifies a branch to the first word in ROM where a routine for a macro-operation is located. The address bits for this type of branch are a function of the bits used in the operation part of the machine instruction. For example, a computer with a simple instruction format as shown in Fig. 8-5 has an operation code of four bits which can specify up to 16 distinct macro-operations. Assume further that the control memory has 128 words requiring an address of seven bits. For each macro-operation there exists a routine in ROM of the microinstructions that execute the macro-operation. One specific mapping process that

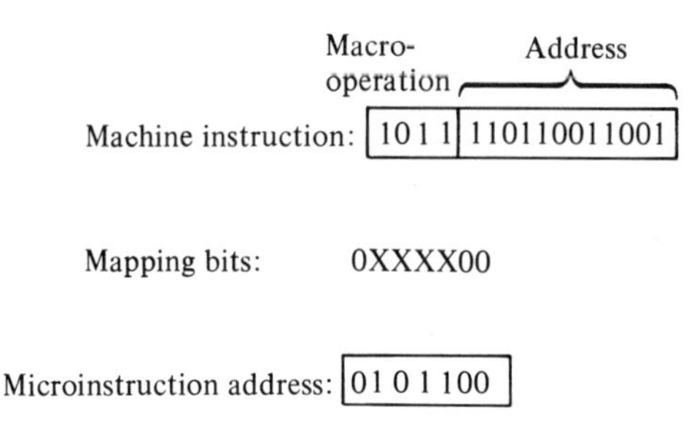


**Fig. 8-5** A mapping process from macro-operation to ROM address.

converts the 4-bit operation-code to a 7-bit ROM address is shown in Fig. 8-5. This mapping consists of clearing the most significant ROM address bit to 0, transferring the operation-code bits, and clearing the last two bits of the address register. This gives each macro-operation routine a capacity of four microinstructions. If the routine needs more space, it can use ROM addresses 10000000 to 1111111. If it needs less space, the unused locations would be available for other routines.

One can extend this concept to a more general mapping rule by having the mapping information stored in the microinstruction that specifies the branch. A totally flexible scheme is one that uses a second ROM to specify the mapping bits as shown in Fig. 8-6. In this configuration, the bits in the macro-operation specify the address of a second ROM (the mapping memory). The content of the second ROM at this address maps the macro-operation bits to a control memory address. In this way, the routine that executes the macro-operation can be placed in any desired location in control memory.

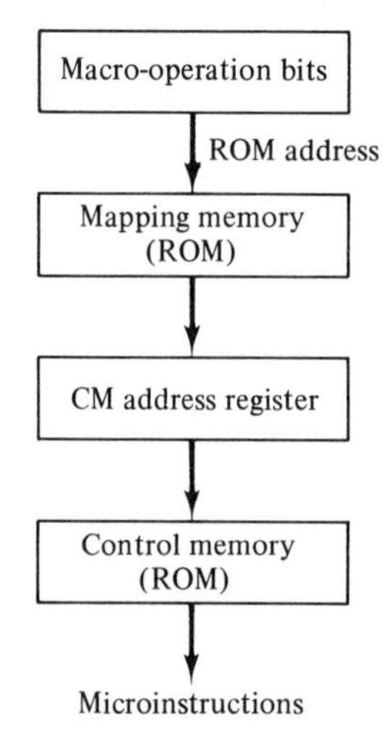


**Fig. 8-6** Use of a second ROM to map a macro-operation to a control memory address.

### *Subroutines*

Subroutines are programs to be used by other routines to accomplish a particular task. These routines can be called from any point within the main body of the microprogram. Frequently, many microprograms contain identical sections of code. Microinstructions can be saved by employing subroutines which use common sections of microcode. For example, the sequence of micro-operations needed to generate the effective address of the operand for a machine-instruction is common to all memory reference instructions. This sequence could be a subroutine which is called from within many other routines to execute the effective address computation. Microprograms that use subroutines must have a provision for storing and restoring the return address of ROM. This may be accomplished by placing the output from the address register into a special register and branching to the beginning of the subroutine. This temporary storage register can then become the address source for setting the ROM address register for the return to the main routine.

From the above discussion it is evident that the designer has many alternatives to choose from when considering the address sequencing formats of microinstructions. The criteria one must consider when choosing among the alternatives are the effects of cost, speed, and flexibility. The cost is determined by the size of the ROM and the amount of hardware needed external to the control memory. The speed is a function of how many microinstructions must be executed to reach the next address. The flexibility is a function of how easy it is to generate a microprogram by utilizing the branch capabilities built into the control memory.

## 8-3 MICROPROGRAM EXAMPLE

Once the configuration of a computer and its microprogrammed control unit is established, the designer's task is to generate the microcode for the control memory. This code generation is called microprogramming and is a process very similar to conventional machine-language programming. In order to appreciate this process, we present here a simple general-purpose computer and show how it is microprogrammed.

### *Computer Configuration*

The block diagram of the computer is shown in Fig. 8-7. It consists of two memory units: a main memory for storing instructions and data; and a control memory for storing the microprogram. Four of the registers are associated with the processor unit and two with the control unit. The processor

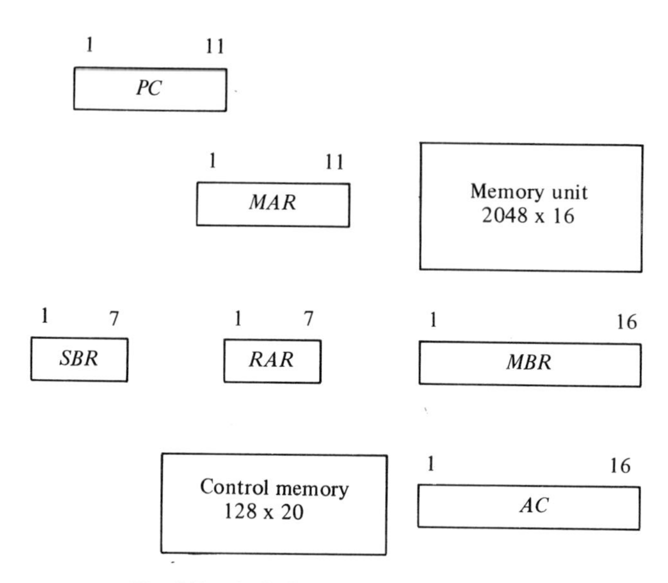


**Fig. 8-7** Block diagram of the computer.

registers are: program counter *PC*, memory address register *MAR*, memory buffer register *MBR*, and accumulator register *AC*. The function of these registers is similar to the basic computer introduced in Chap. 5. The control unit has a ROM address register *RAR* and a subroutine return register *SBR*. The control memory and its registers are organized as a microprogrammed control unit similar to Fig. 8-2.

The computer instruction format is depicted in Fig. 8-8(a). It consists of

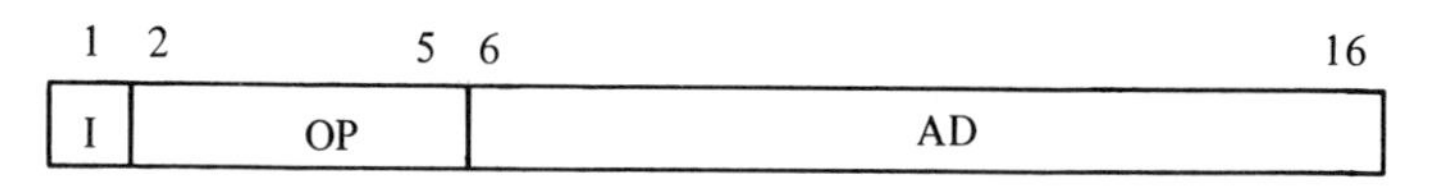


(a) Instruction code format

| Symbol | Op-code | Function |
|---|---|---|
| ADD | 0000 | $AC \leftarrow AC + M$ |
| BRANCH | 0001 | if $(AC < 0)$ then $(PC \leftarrow \text{m})$ |
| STORE | 0010 | $M \leftarrow AC$ |

m is the effective address.
*M* is the memory word specified by m.

(b) Operation code (macro-operation)

**Fig. 8-8** Computer instructions.

three fields: a 1-bit field for indirect addressing symbolized by I, a 4-bit operation code symbolized by OP, and an 11-bit address field AD. Figure 8-8(b) lists three of sixteen possible memory-reference instructions. The ADD instruction adds the content of the operand found in the effective address to the content of the *AC*. The BRANCH instruction causes a branch to the effective address if the operand in the *AC* is negative. Control goes to the next consecutive address if the *AC* is not negative. The *AC* is negative if its sign bit (the bit in the left-most position of the register) is a 1. The STORE instruction transfers the content of the *AC* into the memory word specified by the effective address.

It will be shown subsequently that each machine instruction must be microprogrammed. In order not to complicate the microprogramming example, only three computer instructions are considered here. It should be realized that thirteen other instructions can be included and each instruction must be microprogrammed by the procedure outlined below.

### *Microinstruction Format*

The microinstruction format for the control memory is shown in Fig. 8-9(a). The 20 bits of the microinstruction are subdivided into four fields. The *micro-ops* field consists of nine bits with each bit specifying one micro-operation as listed in the table of Fig. 8-9(b). In order to simplify the example, we have chosen only nine micro-operations. Obviously, many more would be needed in a typical computer.

The *condition field* (CD) consists of two bits which are encoded to specify four status conditions listed in the table of Fig. 8-9(c). The first condition is always a 1 so that a reference to this condition will always cause a branch. This is equivalent to an unconditional branch operation. The indirect bit *I* is available from bit 1 of *MBR* after an instruction is read from memory. The sign bit of the accumulator, denoted by *AC*(*S*), provides the next status bit. The $AC = 0$ condition is a binary variable whose value is equal to 1 if all the flip-flops in the *AC* are equal to zero.

The branch (BR) field consists of two bits and is used, in conjunction with the address field ADF, to choose the address of the next microinstruction. The address field is seven bits long since the control memory has $128 = 2^7$ words. As shown in the table of Fig. 8-9(d), when BR = 00, the control memory recognizes a branch condition and when BR = 01, it recognizes a call to subroutine. These two conditions are similar except that a call microinstruction stores the return address in *SBR*. The branch and call conditions depend on the value of the CD field. If the specified status bit in the CD field is equal to 1, a branch to the address specified by the ADF field occurs. Otherwise, the *RAR* is incremented by 1.

The return from subroutine is accomplished when the BR field is equal

(a) Control word format:

| 1–9 | 10 11 | 12 13 | 14–20 |
|---|---|---|---|
| Micro-ops | CD | BR | ADF |

(b) Micro-operations field bit assignment:

| Bit | Micro-operation | Description |
|---|---|---|
| 1 | $MBR \leftarrow M$ | Memory read |
| 2 | $M \leftarrow MBR$ | Memory write |
| 3 | $MAR \leftarrow PC$ | Transfer address of instruction |
| 4 | $PC \leftarrow PC + 1$ | Increment Program Counter |
| 5 | $MAR \leftarrow MBR(AD)$ | Transfer address part |
| 6 | $PC \leftarrow MBR(AD)$ | Transfer address part |
| 7 | $MBR \leftarrow AC$ | Transfer *AC* into *MBR* |
| 8 | $AC \leftarrow MBR$ | Transfer *MBR* into *AC* |
| 9 | $AC \leftarrow AC + MBR$ | Add *MBR* to *AC* |

(c) CD (condition) field bit assignment:

| Bits 10 11 | Condition | Comments |
|---|---|---|
| 0 0 | always 1 | Unconditional branch |
| 0 1 | I = 1 | Branch if I = 1 |
| 1 0 | $AC(S) = 1$ | Branch if *AC* is negative |
| 1 1 | $AC = 0$ | Branch if *AC* is zero |

(d) BR (branch) field bit assignment:

| Bits 12 13 | Function | Type of branch |
|---|---|---|
| 0 0 | If (condition = 1) then ($RAR \leftarrow ADF$)<br>If (condition = 0) then ($RAR \leftarrow RAR + 1$) | Branch |
| 0 1 | If (condition = 1) then ($RAR \leftarrow ADF, SBR \leftarrow RAR + 1$)<br>If (condition = 0) then ($RAR \leftarrow RAR + 1$) | Call subroutine |
| 1 0 | $RAR \leftarrow SBR$ | return from subroutine |
| 1 1 | $RAR$ (2-5) $\leftarrow MBR$ ($OP$), $RAR$ (1,6,7) $\leftarrow 0$ | Macro-op mapping |

**Fig. 8-9** Microinstruction format and field assignment.

to 10. This causes a transfer of the return address from *SBR* to *RAR*. The mapping from the macro-operation bits to the *RAR* is implemented when the BR field is equal to 11. This mapping is as depicted in Fig. 8-5. The macro-operation is specified by the operation code bits of the instruction. These bits are in *MBR*(2–5) after an instruction is read from memory. Note that the last two branch conditions are independent of the values in the CD and ADF fields.

### *Microprogramming the Control Memory*

The control memory has 128 words, and each word contains 20 bits. To microprogram the control memory, it is necessary to determine the bit values of each of the 128 words. The first 64 words (addresses 0 to 63) are to be occupied by the routines for the 16 macro-operations. The last 64 words may be used for any other purpose. A convenient starting location for the fetch cycle routine is address 64. The microinstructions needed for the fetch routine are:

$$MAR \leftarrow PC$$

$$MBR \leftarrow M,\ PC \leftarrow PC + 1$$

$$MAR \leftarrow MBR(AD),\ RAR(2\text{–}5) \leftarrow MBR(OP),\ RAR(1, 6, 7) \leftarrow 0$$

The address of the instruction is transferred from *PC* to *MAR* and the instruction is then read from memory into *MBR*. Since no instruction register is available, the instruction code remains in *MBR*. The address part is transferred to *MAR* and then control is transferred to one of 16 micro-routines by mapping the operation code part of the instruction from *MBR*(*OP*) into *RAR*.

The fetch cycle routine in control memory uses three microinstructions. This part of the microprogram is listed in Table 8-1 and occupies the control words at addresses 64, 65, and 66. The bit values of the control words at these addresses are obtained from the tables of Fig. 8-9.

The execution of the microinstruction at address 66 results in a branch to address 0xxxx00 where xxxx are the four bits of the macro-operation. For example, if *MBR* has an ADD instruction whose operation code is 0000, the microinstruction at address 66 will transfer to *RAR* the adress 0000000 which is the start address for the ADD routine. The first ROM address for the BRANCH and STORE routines are 0 0001 00 (decimal 4) and 0 0010 00 (decimal 8) respectively. The first ROM address for the other thirteen routines are at address values 12, 16, 20, . . . , 60. This gives four ROM words for each routine.

In each routine we must provide microinstructions for fetching the operand and for execution of the instruction. The indirect address condition

**Table 8-1** *Partial microprogram for control memory*

| Micro Routine | Address Decimal | Address Binary | Microinstruction Micro-ops | CD | BR | ADF | Micro-Operations and Next Address |
|---|---|---|---|---|---|---|---|
| ADD | 0 | 0000000 | 000000000 | 01 | 01 | 1000011 | If $I = 1$ go to 67, $SBR \leftarrow 1$ If $I = 0$ go to 1 |
| | 1 | 0000001 | 100000000 | 00 | 00 | 0000010 | $MBR \leftarrow M$, go to 2 |
| | 2 | 0000010 | 000000001 | 00 | 00 | 1000000 | $AC \leftarrow AC + MBR$, go to 64 |
| | 3 | 0000011 | 000000000 | 00 | 00 | 1000000 | Nothing, go to 64 |
| BRANCH | 4 | 0000100 | 000000000 | 10 | 00 | 0000110 | If $AC(S) = 1$ go to 6 If $AC(S) = 0$ go to 5 |
| | 5 | 0000101 | 000000000 | 00 | 00 | 1000000 | Go to 64 |
| | 6 | 0000110 | 000000000 | 01 | 01 | 1000011 | If $I = 1$ go to 67, $SBR \leftarrow 7$ If $I = 0$ go to 7 |
| | 7 | 0000111 | 000001000 | 00 | 00 | 1000000 | $PC \leftarrow MBR(AD)$, go to 64 |
| STORE | 8 | 0001000 | 000000000 | 01 | 01 | 1000011 | If $I = 1$ go to 67, $SBR \leftarrow 9$ If $I = 0$ go to 9 |
| | 9 | 0001001 | 000000100 | 00 | 00 | 0001010 | $MBR \leftarrow AC$, go to 10 |
| | 10 | 0001010 | 010000000 | 00 | 00 | 1000000 | $M \leftarrow MBR$, go to 64 |
| | ⋮ | ⋮ | ⋮ | | | | ⋮ |
| FETCH | 64 | 1000000 | 001000000 | 00 | 00 | 1000001 | $MAR \leftarrow PC$, go to 65 |
| | 65 | 1000001 | 100100000 | 00 | 00 | 1000010 | $MBR \leftarrow M$, $PC \leftarrow PC + 1$, go to 66 |
| | 66 | 1000010 | 000010000 | 00 | 11 | 0000000 | $MAR \leftarrow MBR(AD)$, go to specified routine |
| INDIRECT | 67 | 1000011 | 100000000 | 00 | 00 | 1000100 | $MBR \leftarrow M$, go to 68 |
| | 68 | 1000100 | 000010000 | 00 | 10 | 0000000 | $MAR \leftarrow MBR(AD)$, $RAR \leftarrow SBR$ |

may occur with any memory-reference instruction. A saving of ROM words may be achieved if the microinstructions for the indirect address are stored as a subroutine. This subroutine is located in addresses 67 and 68. To see how the transfer and return from this subroutine occurs, let us assume that address 66 caused a branch to address 0 (ADD routine). The first microinstruction in address 0 is a branch, conditioned on bit $I$. If $I = 1$, a branch to address 67 occurs and the subroutine return register ($SBR$) is set to the value of 1 (the address of the next microinstruction). At address 67 and 68 we have the following microinstructions:

$$MBR \leftarrow M$$

$$MAR \leftarrow MBR(AD), \quad RAR \leftarrow SBR$$

Remember that an indirect address considers the address part of the instruction as an address where the address of the operand is to be found. Therefore, the memory has to be accessed once more to get the address of the operand. The return from subroutine (BR = 10) transfers address 1 to *RAR* thus returning to the second microinstruction of the ADD routine. The execution of the ADD instruction is carried out by the microinstructions at addresses 1 and 2. These microinstructions read the operand from memory into *MBR*, perform an add micro-operation with the content of *AC* and then cause a branch back to the beginning of the fetch routine. Address 3 is not used in this routine but something must be specified for each word in ROM. We could have specified all 0's in the word since this location will never be used. However, if some unforeseen error occurs, or if a noise signal sets *RAR* to the value of 3, it will be wise to branch to address 64 which is the beginning of the fetch routine.

Table 8-1 lists the microprogram for the control memory of the computer. This is only a partial list since only 3 out of 16 machine instructions have been used. Also ROM words at locations 69–127 have not been used. Normally a computer will have *multiply* and *divide* instructions that will require more than four microinstructions for their execution. ROM words 69–127 could be used for this purpose.

The BRANCH routine starts by checking the value of *AC*(*S*). If it is 0, the content of the *AC* is positive or zero so the computer proceeds with the next instruction in sequence. Since the address of this instruction is in *PC*, control returns to the fetch cycle without doing anything. If $AC(S) = 1$, the content of the *AC* is negative so it is necessary to branch by transferring the effective address into *PC*. If $I = 1$, the effective address is read by the INDIRECT subroutine; otherwise, the effective address is already in *MBR*(*AD*). This address is then transferred into *PC* and control goes back to the fetch cycle.

The STORE routine again uses the INDIRECT subroutine of $I = 1$. The content of the *AC* is transferred into *MBR* and a memory-write operation is initiated to store the content of *MBR* in a location specified by the effective address.

### *Implementation*

The microprogram listed in Table 8-1 specifies the word content of the control memory. When a ROM is used for the control memory, the microprogram binary list provides the truth table for fabricating the unit. This fabrication is a hardware process and consists of creating a mask for the ROM so as to produce the 1's and 0's for each word. The bits of ROM are fixed once the links are fused during the hardware production. The ROM is made of IC packages that can be removed if necessary and replaced by other packages. To modify the instruction set of the computer, it is necessary to generate a new microprogram and mask a new ROM. The old one can be removed and the new one inserted in its place.

If a writable control memory is employed, the ROM is replaced by a RAM. The advantage of employing a RAM for the control memory is that the microprogram can be altered by simply writing a new pattern of 1's and 0's without resorting to hardware procedures. A writable control memory possesses the flexibility of choosing the instruction set of a computer dynamically, i.e., by changing the microprogram under processor control. However, most microprogrammed systems use a ROM for the control memory because it is cheaper and faster than a RAM and also to prevent the occasional user from changing the architecture of the system.

The example has shown that the microprogram stored in a control memory contains the binary variables that control the hardware components of the system. The control information is stored in a memory and executed as a stored program. This gives microprogramming a software as well as a hardware flavor, so the term *firmware* is sometimes used.

## 8-4 CONTROL WORD FORMATS

A microinstruction stored in control memory is called a *control word* because the bits in each microinstruction word are used to specify control signals. A control word is usually subdivided into groups of bits called *fields*. Each field provides a distinct separate function. The bits encountered in control words provide one or more of the following functions:

1. Micro-operations for the registers and memory in the system. These micro-operations are sometimes divided into separate fields.
2. Micro-operations for the control unit itself to specify the way the next microinstruction address is determined.
3. An address field for branch microinstructions.
4. Other special fields containing data for transfer to a given destination.

The micro-operation fields in the control word initiate signals for the various registers and components in the system. The address and data fields contain bits that are transferred into a register or other destination.

In the previous section we have shown an example of a control word employing the first three types of fields listed above. The process of introducing data into the system from the output of the control memory is a frequently used technique in many microprogrammed systems. The field in the control word that does this is called *emit* field or a *literal*. Output from the emit field may be used to set up control registers and introduce data into processor registers. For example, a constant in the emit field may be added to a register to increment its content by a specified value. Another use of the emit field is in setting a sequence counter to a constant value. The sequence counter is then used to count the number of times a microprogram loop is traversed, as is usually required in a *multiply* or *divide* routine.

The designer who is assigned the task of formulating the control-word format for a control memory must be thoroughly familiar with the total system operation and have an insight for any future developments. He must provide control bits for all conceivable micro-operations using a minimum number of bits in the control word, a minimum of words in the control memory, a minimum of external hardware in the control unit, all while trying to achieve a minimum time for the execution of the microprogram. There are many techniques which are useful in formulating the control word and some of these techniques are discussed below. Usually, a combination of techniques is employed to formulate microinstructions; the ones used depend on the particular application.

### *Horizontal Microinstructions*

The simplest configuration is to use one bit of the microinstruction to control each micro-operation. This was done in the micro-ops field in the example of the previous section. The technique concentrates on the individual control variables that are required in the system and is concerned with the optimum generation of these variables. There can be as many as fifty or more different micro-operations in a computer which may result in an excessively long control word. Horizontal microinstructions with 64 bits or more are common. The term horizontal implies the existence of a long control word that produces a horizontal pattern of 1's and 0's.

Horizontal microinstructions are able to control a variety of components operating in parallel. A horizontal microinstruction may initiate the simultaneous and independent micro-operations for many registers, for a memory-read or memory-write operation and for the generation of the next address, all in one microinstruction. Horizontal microprogramming has the potential advantage of efficient hardware utilization. However, the bits in the control word are not fully utilized and the fact that long words are used makes the control memory very expensive.

## *Multiphase Clock*

Multiphase refers to the number of clock cycles used to execute each microinstruction. In a monophase implementation, there are no distinct subcycles of the basic clock cycle; each microinstruction is effected by a single simultaneous issue of a clock pulse. In a multiphase implementation, each major clock cycle is subdivided into multiple minor clock cycles. The microinstruction is read from control memory with a major clock pulse but control signals are generated with the minor clock pulses. Multiphase operations allow interaction among the components of the system at the expense of more complicated control.

The following example illustrates the multiphase operation. Consider the microprogram for the fetch routine in Table 8-1. The three microinstructions in locations 64–66 use three control words. The system employs a monophase clock; all micro-operations are generated during the occurrence of one common clock pulse. The three control words can be combined into one control word with a three-phase clock system as shown in Fig. 8-10. All micro-

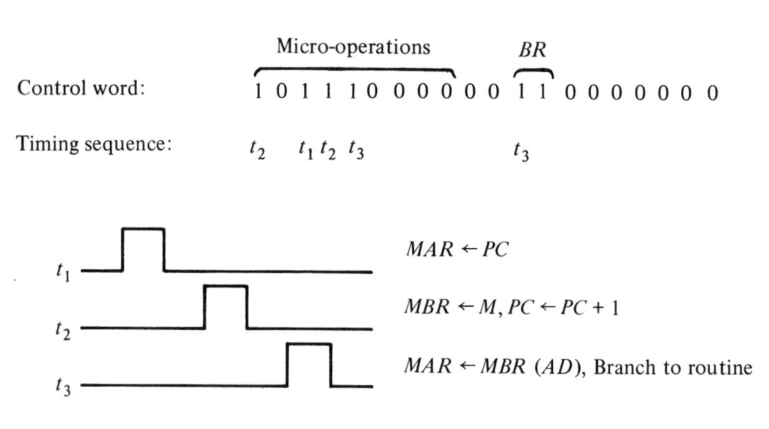


**Fig. 8-10** Fetch cycle in a three-phase system.

operations for the fetch routine are combined in one word but the three-phase clock system controls the sequence in which the control signals are generated. It is obvious that the multiphase system minimizes the number of control words in a control memory but requires a considerable amount of external hardware to control the timing process.

## *Encoding of Control Bits*

The number of control bits in a control word can be reduced by grouping mutually exclusive variables into fields and encoding the $k$ bits in each field to provide $2^k$ micro-operations. Each field requires a hardware decoder to produce the corresponding control signals. This method reduces the size of the control word but requires additional hardware external to the control memory. It also increases the generation time of the control signals because the bits of the microinstruction must propagate through the decoder circuits. The designer must select mutually exclusive operations when grouping control bits into fields.

The encoding of control bits was demonstrated in the programming example of the previous section. Both the condition (CD) and branch (BR) fields are encoded to give four functions with two bits. The micro-ops field could be encoded to provide more micro-operations. The nine bits in this field can be encoded to supply up to 512 micro-operations. However, a computer would not have that many distinct micro-operations and a 9 by 512 decoder would require an excessive number of gates. Moreover, only one micro-operation could be specified in each microinstruction. A more efficient method is to divide the nine bits into a number of fields. For example, they can be divided into three fields F1, F2, and F3, each having three bits, as shown in Fig. 8-11. Each field can be encoded to generate one of eight micro-

| 1 3 | 4 6 | 7 9 | 10 | 12 | 14 20 |
|---|---|---|---|---|---|
| F1 | F2 | F3 | CD | BR | ADF |

**Fig. 8-11** Modified microinstruction format for Fig. 8-9(a).

operations. A possible set of micro-operations for each field is listed in Table 8-2. This gives a total of 21 micro-operations as compared to 9 for the control word format used without encoding. However, while the horizontal format can generate nine micro-operations simultaneously, the encoded format can generate only three micro-operations simultaneously. As an illustration, one

**Table 8-2** *Encoding the three fields of Fig. 8-11*

| *Bits* | F1 | F2 | F3 |
|---|---|---|---|
| 000 | None | None | None |
| 001 | $AC \leftarrow AC + MBR$ | $AC \leftarrow AC - MBR$ | $AC \leftarrow AC \oplus MBR$ |
| 010 | $AC \leftarrow 0$ | $AC \leftarrow AC \vee MBR$ | $AC \leftarrow \overline{AC}$ |
| 011 | $AC \leftarrow AC + 1$ | $AC \leftarrow AC \wedge MBR$ | shl $AC$ |
| 100 | $AC \leftarrow MBR$ | $MBR \leftarrow M$ | shr $AC$ |
| 101 | $MAR \leftarrow MBR(AD)$ | $MBR \leftarrow AC$ | $PC \leftarrow PC + 1$ |
| 110 | $MAR \leftarrow PC$ | $MBR \leftarrow MBR + 1$ | $PC \leftarrow MBR(AD)$ |
| 111 | $M \leftarrow MBR$ | $MBR(AD) \leftarrow PC$ | halt |

microinstruction can specify the following micro-operations simultaneously:

| | |
|---|---|
| $MBR \leftarrow M$ | Memory read |
| $PC \leftarrow PC + 1$ | Increment $PC$ |
| $AC \leftarrow 0$ | Clear $AC$ |
| $RAR \leftarrow ADF$ | Branch unconditionally |

The microinstruction bit configuration will be:

| $F1$ | $F2$ | $F3$ | $CD$ | $BR$ | $ADF$ |
|---|---|---|---|---|---|
| 010 | 100 | 101 | 00 | 00 | 1100000 |

when the branch is to location 96.

### *Multiple Word Format*

In large computers, speed is attained by allowing many operations to proceed simultaneously. The greater the simultaneity, the longer the control word becomes. In slow computers, control decisions are made sequentially and therefore shorter control words can be used. One frequently used technique in small systems is to have a number of different control word formats. Each of these formats will generally be dedicated to one type of major operation. This greatly reduces the length of the control words but also slows down the system performance. For example, in short word-length microprogrammed devices, one microinstruction will be used to add two registers, a second to test the result and a third to branch to an address based on the result of the test. Each of these microinstructions might have a different format, whereas in a longer control word this would be accomplished in one microinstruction word.

A method by which a multiple control word format may be achieved is by encoding the meaning of some fields according to the value of the bits in another field. Thus, one field can specify the way the other fields are interpreted. The use of multiple-bit format can save a significant number of control bits at the expense of more complex decoding circuitry.

An example of a multiple word format is shown in Table 8-3 where an eight-bit control word is used to give five different formats. Bits 1 and 2 provide a field whose purpose is to specify the meaning of the other six bits. When bits 1 and 2 are 00, the other six bits specify one of 64 micro-operations; when 01, the other bits specify the address for an unconditional branch. When 10, the other bits specify an ALU function and when 11, bits 3 and 4 are further used to specify two possible configurations. When bits 3 and 4 are 00, the remaining bits specify one of 16 possible status conditions for a

**Table 8-3** *Mutliple-bit format for an eight-bit control word*

| 12 3 4 5 6 7 8 | *Control Word Bits* |
|---|---|
| 00 X X X X X X | 64 micro-operations specified by XXXXXX bits |
| 01 Y Y Y Y Y Y | Branch to address YYYYYY |
| 10 Z Z Z Z Z Z | Perform ALU function specified by ZZZZZZ bits |
| 11 0 0 C C C C | Skip next microinstruction on status condition CCCC |
| 11 1 1 S S S S | Transfer SSSS to sequence counter |

skip microinstruction. When 11, the remaining four bits are interpreted as an emit field whose value is transferred to a sequence counter.

### *Vertical Microinstructions*

A microinstruction format that is not horizontal is commonly classified as a vertical microinstruction. This is a term given to a microinstruction that needs decoding circuits external to the control memory. As such, it encompasses the last two techniques discussed above. In the horizontal configuration, there is usually no decoding of control bits since each bit controls one micro-operation. The term vertical is derived from the fact that the encoding of fields necessitates decoding circuits that form a vertical pattern. This pattern may consist of one or two levels of decoding.

A *direct* encoding of bits results in a single level of decoding as shown in Fig. 8-12(a). The bits that control the mutually exclusive operations are combined into fields. The circuits that decode the bits in each field form a single level of decoders.

An *indirect* encoding results in a multiple word format with the meaning of the fields made to depend on the value of a control field in the micro-

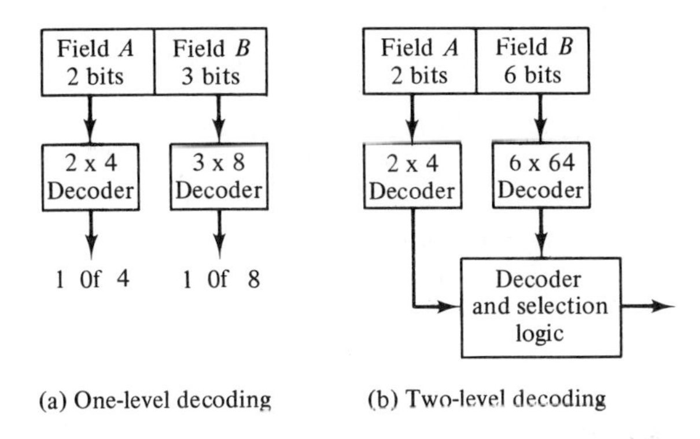


**Fig. 8-12** Decoding pattern of vertical microinstructions.

instruction. The circuits that decode this type of control word require two levels of decoding. As shown in Fig. 8-12(b), the two bits of field $A$ control the function of the six bits in field $B$. Both fields are decoded in the first level. The second level combines each of the four output lines from decoder $A$ with the outputs of decoder $B$ to supply the control signals.

Vertical microinstructions have a slight resemblance to machine-language instructions. Instructions are usually divided into fields with an operation field always present. The operation field of an instruction resembles the control field of a microinstruction as far as they both specify the meaning of the other fields.

### *Direct Control of Bus System*

A CPU is quite often organized around a bus system. A microinstruction that controls a bus organized CPU may be classified as a vertical microinstruction with the decoders for the various fields being placed in the bus system itself. A block diagram of a CPU bus system was presented in Sec. 7-1. From Fig. 7-1 we note that the control selection inputs to each of the five components in the system are already decoded within the components. The microinstruction that controls this bus system can be divided into five fields, with each field providing the control bits to select the function in each component.

A control-word format for controlling a bus system is depicted in Fig. 8-13. Two fields LB and RB specify the source registers for the input busses

| LB | RB | DB | FU | SH |
|---|---|---|---|---|

LB Specifies the register to be connected to the left bus of ALU
RB Specifies the register to be connected to the right bus of ALU
DB Specifies the register where the result is to be transferred
FU Specifies an ALU function
SH Specifies a shift function

**Fig. 8-13** Control word format for a bus organized CPU.

and the ALU. If there are eight registers in the system, each of these fields must contain three bits. These bits are applied directly to the selection inputs of the multiplexer that controls the input bus. The FU field specifies the ALU function and the SH field, the type of shift. The numbers of bits in these fields are dependent on the number of decoded functions that the units provide. The DB field specifies the destination register for storing the result. In addition to these fields, the control word must have fields for determining the address sequence of microinstructions.

We have discussed here a few methods commonly employed to formulate the control word formats for a control memory. In a practical situation, a combination of techniques is used, taking into consideration the particular application and economic factors.

## 8-5 TIMING CONSIDERATIONS

In every microprogrammed system there must be some logic which controls the ROM and does the basic system timing. The complexity of this logic depends on the microprogrammed implementation. In the simple microprogram example of Sec. 8-3, the timing is controlled entirely by the clock pulses. This can be done if it is assumed that one clock pulse interval is long enough to provide the time for the propagation delay to access the ROM and the delay that occurs during the propagation of micro-operation signals. At the same time, the next ROM address propagates to the inputs of the ROM address register. The next clock pulse initiates the micro-operations and simultaneously transfers a new address for the ROM to start a new cycle.

In higher-speed systems there may exist a ROM output buffer register if it desirable to overlap the access time of the next microinstruction with the execution of the current one. With such a register, one timing pulse will transfer the ROM output to the buffer register and a second timing pulse will sample the outputs of the buffer register to initiate the required micro-operations.

Many computers use magnetic cores for the main memory. This type of memory is slower than a semiconductor ROM. As a result, microinstructions may have to be delayed after an access to main memory. For example, a core memory may have an access time of 500 nsec as compared with a control memory cycle time of 200 nsec. This time differential can be taken care of by setting an interlock flip-flop when a main memory *read* micro-operation is issued by a microinstruction. The content of main memory in *MBR* cannot be used by the microprogram until the interlock flip-flop is cleared at the end of the main memory-read cycle. Moreover, during the time that the word is being restored to the core memory, the contents of *MBR* should not be altered by the microprogram.

Figure 8-14 shows the timing required for the control memory in a typical microprogrammed system. The first timing pulse loads the output from the ROM into the buffer register. This register will exist in high-speed systems. In slower systems, the output of ROM can fulfill this function. As soon as the outputs of the buffer register reach their steady state level, the control bits cause the signals to propagate through the combinational circuits that will execute the micro-operations. This time should be long enough to permit each micro-operation to be propagated to a destination register prior to its execution. However, some of the longer micro-operations might take two or more control-memory cycles to propagate. For example, suppose that the

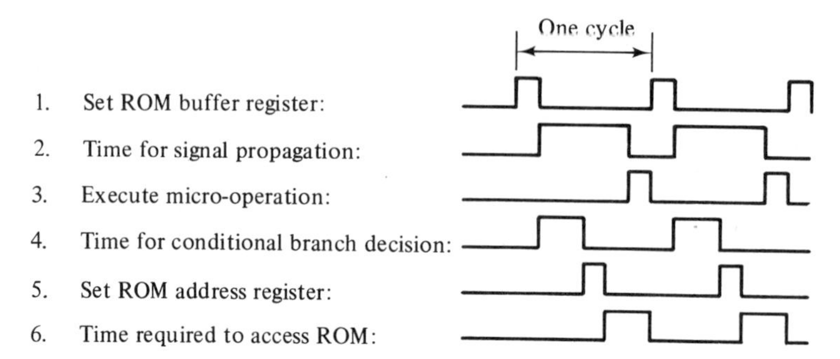


**Fig. 8-14** Time required for making the logical decision for a conditional branch microinstruction.

time for data to propagate from source registers to the output of an adder is 300 nsec. If the control-memory cycle is 200 nsec, then an add micro-operation will require two control-memory cycles. This could be accomplished by executing the same microinstruction twice with the one exception being that data would not be transferred to the destination register until the second microinstruction is executed. Another way to handle operations that take a long time to propagate is to let the microinstruction have a bit which is used to extend the microinstruction execution time. Still another way for simpler systems is to merely let the longest micro-operation dominate the timing. For example, if 300 nsec is the longest register-to-register propagation time, the basic cycle for the control memory could be selected as 300 nsec.

The fourth line in Fig. 8-14 shows the time required for making the logical decision for a conditional branch microinstruction. The fifth line shows the timing pulse that will clock the next address into the ROM address register. For an unconditional branch, or when the ROM address register is incremented, the pulse in line five may occur sooner. A conditional branch to be executed in the current microinstruction must use status bits which have resulted from previous microinstructions. If the conditional branch is dependent on a status bit resulting from a micro-operation in the current microinstruction, then the micro-operation must be executed before a decision is made. This requires that the times shown in lines four and five be moved to the right of the pulse in line three. Obviously, this requirement will produce a longer control memory cycle.

The sixth line in the timing diagram shows the time required to access the ROM. As soon as the control word is available at the output of the ROM, it can be transferred into the buffer register to start a new cycle.

There are obviously many variations of the timing scheme shown here. The particular timing technique selected by the designer depends on the particular application and the objectives of the system being designed.

## 8-6 SOFTWARE AIDS

Microprograms are considered to be one level lower than machine-language programs. Machine-language programs deal with instructions that specify macro-operations between memory and processor registers. The programmer does not have to be concerned with micro-operations or other control details involved in the execution of the instructions. Microprograms for a control memory deal with the hardware resources of the system and require a familiarity with and knowledge of the hardware organization of components and how they react to each microinstruction. Nevertheless, the two types of programming are conceptually similar and knowledge of one provides valuable experience for working with the other.

Just as in machine language, microprograms can be written in straight binary or in symbolic form. The binary procedure is tedious and error prone. However, for a small control memory to be used in a particular system only once, this would be the most economical method because there is no way to justify the development costs of a symbolic translator program such as an assembler. A simple register transfer language may help in the process of writing binary programs. The microprogram is first written in symbolic form by means of register transfer statements. The translation to binary can be carried out by the programmer himself by inspection without resorting to an automatic translator.

When a large microprogram has to be developed, or when the same system is used to implement various different configurations, the cost of developing an assembler or even a compiler is justified. Programming with familiar symbols is much less tedious and produces microcodes more quickly and with fewer errors. The translation to binary is done by a system program so the programmer does not have to be concerned with strings of 1's and 0's.

When a microprogram is developed for a new system, it is necessary to produce the ROM with the appropriate 1's and 0's and exercise the system to check for errors and to make sure that the system works properly. This is an expensive procedure because the hardware production of ROMs is costly and time-consuming. Everytime a 1 has to be changed to a 0 or vice-versa, a new ROM must be produced. The best way to check a microprogram is to use a ROM simulator. A ROM simulator is a high-speed special random-access memory that can be operated in a read-only mode to simulate the operation of a ROM. A pattern of 1's and 0's is entered into the simulator RAM by placing the unit in an off-line position and a write mode. Simulation is achieved by placing the unit in an on-line position which extends control of only the read function to the user's equipment. The cables in the simulator have special connectors designed to plug directly into the ROM sockets of the system being checked. The simulator performs under actual working conditions and is used to exercise the system. Changes can be effected by placing the simulator in an off-line position and writing a new pattern. When the design has been proved to work correctly, error-free ROM masks can be generated from the content of the simulator memory.

Simulators facilitate microprogram checkout, but do not simplify the writing of microprograms. They are useful in determining alternate machine architectures and in developing new and experimental systems. To facilitate microprogram preparation, most manufacturers of microprogramable machines develop suitable support software such as assemblers and compilers.

An assembler is a computer program which translates symbolic code into an equivalent binary pattern. Assemblers can be used to translate symbolic microprograms just as they are used to translate machine-language programs. Symbolic microprograms can be written either in a register transfer language or in a conventional assembly language. A register transfer language for writing microprograms would be similar to the one used in this book except that it must be defined precisely. The exact rules for writing symbolic statements must be formulated so one can write a symbolic program that can be translated correctly without any ambiguity. Each register transfer statement would have an equivalent bit or a group of bits in a microinstruction that defines the relation between the symbolic statement and its equivalent binary pattern. Any special character employed in the register transfer language (such as an arrow) must be available in the input device used to prepare the program (such as a teletypewriter or punch cards). If not available, it would be necessary to replace it by another available character. An example of a register transfer microprograming language is presented in Sec. 9-8.

An assembly microprogramming language provides the capability to express microinstructions in symbolic form similar to a machine-language assembler. A fixed format in which certain columns are reserved for each field is characteristic of such languages. The symbols for each field are defined and the assembler translates each symbol to an equivalent binary field. The microinstruction is assembled from the binary fields so obtained.

The microprogramming example of Sec. 8-3 will be used to illustrate an assembly microprogramming language. We specify three fields for writing programs in this language. The *label* field designates symbolic addresses. The *micro-op* field may be empty or include up to nine micro-operation symbols, separated by commas. The *address* field specifies the next address in symbolic form including the branch condition. Table 8-4 shows a specific example of how the ADD routine from Table 8-1 can be programmed in this language. The first line has the symbolic address ADD in the label field. No symbols are in the micro-ops field so the first nine bits of the micro-

**Table 8-4** *Assembly language microprogram*

| *Label* | *Micro-ops* | *Address* |
|---|---|---|
| ADD | | CALL INDIRECT, I |
| | READ | NEXT |
| | ADDAC | BRANCH FETCH |

instruction are set to all 0's. The address field specifies a call to subroutine INDIRECT, conditioned on the value of I. These symbols produce 01 for the CD field, 01 for the BR field, and 67 for the ADF field.

The second line of the symbolic program has a READ in the micro-ops field. We define this symbol to designate a memory read micro-operation which is symbolized by $MBR \leftarrow M$ in the register transfer language. The address field has a NEXT symbol designating an unconditional branch to the next address in sequence.

The third line has the symbolic micro-op ADDAC used to denote $AC \leftarrow AC + MBR$. The address field specifies an unconditional branch to the beginning of the fetch routine.

To define the microprogramming language in its entirety, it is necessary to define symbols for the nine micro-operations, for the three status conditions, and the four branch conditions, defined in Fig. 8-9.

The translation of an assembly language program to binary is often performed on a separate computer and the resulting microcode is then used for the system that executes the microprogram. This is especially necessary when the development of the hardware and the microprogram is done concurrently. A host computer is employed to translate the microprogram while the hardware of the system that will use the microprogram is being developed.

The use of high-level languages for microprogramming is, at the time of this writing, in its infancy. The development and use of such languages has been restricted due to the scarcity of user microprogrammable computers and the inefficiency of compiled microcodes. The adoption of microprogramming for the control section of microprocessors and the use of this technique by developers of microcomputer systems will most likely stimulate the development of efficient high-level microprogramming languages.

## 8-7 ADVANTAGES AND APPLICATIONS

It was shown in the previous sections that microprogramming is a method for implementing the control unit of a digital computer. A second alternative is to employ a hard-wired control implementation and design it entirely with hardware, without the use of a control memory. There are many advantages and a few disadvantages to using a microprogrammed control unit as opposed to a hard-wired configuration. Moreover, the microprogramming concept is not unique to a digital computer. There are many other digital systems that can use this concept to obtain an efficient control implementation.

The design of a control unit with a control memory, as opposed to a hard-wired inplementation, may, sometimes, be too costly. This is especially true when the digital system is very simple and does not require many micro-operations or many control decisions. If only a few identical units are to be produced, the cost of the ROM may be higher than the few gates and flip-flops that a hard-wired control may require. One must realize that the price to be paid for a control memory is not only the cost of the ROM itself but also the time and cost involved in the hardware production for masking the microprogram bits. In other words, the vendor will usually add on an extra charge for every new ROM configured by the customer, in addition to the price of each IC package. However, for a system with a rather complex set of instructions, the investment in the control memory is often justified.

The use of a control memory may decrease the speed of the computer if the access time of the ROM is longer than the time that signals would take to propagate if a hard-wired control were used. Control decisions in a hard-wired implementation are available as soon as the control signals propagate. In a microprogrammed control unit, the time it takes to execute a micro-operation includes the access time of ROM. However, if the access time of ROM is relatively short, a control memory may not markedly affect the speed of the computer.

The most important advantage of microprogramming is that it provides a well-structured control organization. A hard-wired control unit is generally quite random. It contains counters, special flip-flops, decoders, and assorted combinational circuits. In microprogramming, control functions are systematized into a kind of programming discipline and a regular memory replaces most of the random combinational circuits. The more regular a machine organization, the fewer miscellaneous parts must be implemented with small-scale integration, low density, logic circuits.

A microprogrammed control unit is more adaptable to changes. During the design of a system, new ideas always come up to improve it and frequently one discovers that some portions have been left out. With microprogramming, many additions and changes can be made by changing the microprogram in control memory. Final system definition can be postponed to a later time in the design cycle since it is possible to alter the instruction set without affecting the hardware design. Because of the nature of the control memory organization, it is possible to introduce rather complex instructions into the instruction set with no additional hardware. The required micro-operation steps can be provided by simply using additional locations in the control memory.

Microprogramming has many economic advantages. Although hard-wired logic is a more economical way of implementing very simple systems, as the complexity of the system increases, the cost of the control logic increases at a fairly rapid rate. In microprogrammed implementations, the cost of the simplest system is somewhat higher, but adding new features only requires additional control memory. In general, replacing most of the control logic with a ROM affords substantial hardware savings because of the high-density packaging of ROM arrays. It is estimated that about 16 bits of ROM can be used to replace a gate in the control logic. Thus a 4096 bit ROM organized as a 256 by 16 array is capable of replacing 256 gates connected randomly.

The problem of servicing and maintaining a computer system is facilitated when microprogramming is used. Every computer system requires a diagnostic package of routines for checking, locating, and isolating hardware malfunctions. These software routines are supplied by the manufacturer for each specific system to help maintenance personnel repair malfunctions in the equipment. If the system does not employ microprogramming, these routines would be written in machine language and use the main memory for their execution. With microprogramming, it is possible to use routines which reside in control memory. They are usually called microdiagnostic routines and their purpose is to provide the necessary diagnostic procedures for checking malfunctions in the system. A given data path is diagnosed by forcing a sequence of micro-operations by means of predetermined bit test patterns stored in control memory. The output from the data path is analyzed in order to select a finer set of test patterns to isolate an error in a particular unit. The control memory that contains microdiagnostics may employ a ROM or a writable control memory. In the former case, special ROM units containing the microdiagnostic routines must be inserted manually. With a writable control memory, the microdiagnostic routines may be loaded in small segments with each segment being able to check a different portion of the hardware.

Because of the regularity of the control memory, computer-aided methods can be utilized to reduce the design cost of the system. The designer can specify the microprogram in symbolic language and employ a computer to translate it into the binary configuration of each control word. Microprogramming also simplifies the documentation and service training of the system, resulting in reduced total system cost.

By changing the content of control memory it is possible to change the meaning of the coded bits of computer instructions. The simulation of the instruction set of one computer in another computer is called *emulation.*

By changing the microprogram it is possible to emulate one computer in another. Microprogrammable machines have been used to emulate a variety of computers so that one host computer with several emulators can economically replace several different target computers. Also, emulation provides a research facility to experiment with different computer architectures.

Implementing commonly used routines directly in microcode can result in significant performance improvement. Microprogramming simple routines such as multiply, square root, matrix inversion, and table look-up saves the hardware which would be required in a hard-wired implementation or the memory space that will be occupied by a software implementation. Microprogramming is typically more efficient than software and more flexible than hardware in many applications.

Not only a central processor may be controlled by a microprogram, but also other parts of a general-purpose computer. An example would be an input-output processor whose function is to control the transfer of data between a number of specialized devices and main memory. A data communication processor supervises the transfer of information between a computer and many remote terminals. Microprogramming data communication processors provides efficiency and flexibility of implementation because they can be microprogrammed to suit the particular needs of each terminal.

For some time, special, dedicated digital systems have been implemented by hard-wired methods. Because microprogramming offers direct low-level control over the hardware components, as well as the flexibility to alter the design, it is replacing the hard-wired configurations of many special purpose systems. System efficiency is achieved by using instructions which are particularly suited to the specific application. A significant impact on consumer electronics has been the application of microprogramming to the implementation of electronic calculators. Microprogrammed calculator ICs can be modified in function by changes in the content of the read-only memory in the chip.

The use of a writable control memory whose microprogram content can be changed by conventional programming procedures under processor control offers a number of advantages. Multiple sets of microprograms can make the same computer appear at different times as a different logical machine. It can increase performance for certain specialized functions in such areas as scientific applications and compilers. In many scientific applications, a computer may spend the major portion of its processing time executing a given function. Savings in speed may be achieved if a special microprogram is used to execute the repetitive function.

Efficient language translation and compilation can be achieved through microprogramming, as opposed to conventional software compilers. Writable control memory can support a multiplicity of architectures within a single computer. A computer may have a number of different machine codes, say one suitable for scientific calculations and another for commercial use. It can also include different specialized instructions that are efficient for the process of compilation. In a dynamic microprogrammed computer, the microprogram can be changed by the operating system. One microprogram may be used to compile a Fortran program, and another for executing machine instructions. When a Fortran program is to be compiled, the operating system would load into control memory a microprogram which is efficient for compilation. A different microprogram would be loaded during the machine-language program execution.

Many of the functions once performed by hardware are shifting into the domain of microprogramming. The development of integrated circuit memories, both ROM and RAM, is encouraging this trend since these units provide a satisfactory component for the control memory.

## REFERENCES


1. HUSSON, S. S., *Microprogramming Principles and Practices*, Englewood Cliffs, N.J.: Prentice-Hall Inc., 1970.
2. ROSIN, R. F., "Contemporary Concepts of Microprogramming and Emulation," *Computing Surveys*, Vol. 1 (December, 1969), pp. 197–212.
3. WILKES, M. V., "The Growth of Interest in Microprogramming: A Literature Survey," *Computing Surveys*, Vol. 1 (September, 1969), pp. 139–145.
4. REDFIELD, S. R., "A Study in Microprogrammed Processor: A Medium Sized Microprogrammed Processor," *IEEE Trans. on Computers*, Vol. C-20 (July, 1971), pp. 743–750.
5. AGRAWALA, A. K., and T. G. RAUSCHER, "Microprogramming: Perspective and Status," *IEEE Trans. on Computers*, Vol. C-23 (August, 1974), pp. 817–837.
6. "Design of Microprogrammable Systems," Signetics Memory Systems, Application Note SMS 0052 AN, Sunnyvale, Cal., 1970.
7. "IMP MM5751 MOS/LSI Control and Read Only Memory Unit (CROM)," Preliminary Data; National Semiconductor Corp., Santa Clara, Cal., January, 1974.
8. "Microprogramming Guide for Hewlett Packard 2100 Computer," Hewlett Packard Co., Cupertino, Cal., November, 1971.
9. "Microprogramming Handbook," Microdata Corp., Santa Ana, Cal., 1971.


## PROBLEMS

8-1 Define the following terms in your own words: (1) control memory; (2) hard-wired control; (3) dynamic microprogramming; (4) control word; (5) microinstruction; (6) microprogram; (7) microcode; (8) micro-operation; (9) macro-operation.

8-2 What are the two main functions that are specified in a micro-instruction? What is a third function usually specified in instructions but not in micro-instructions?

8-3 The microprogramming method is claimed to be superior for implementing the control unit of digital computers. Yet this method was not used in earlier computers. Explain why.

8-4 Why is it that the main memory must use both a program counter and a memory address register while a control memory can increment its address register without a need of a separate program counter?

8-5 List four alternatives for achieving a conditional branch operation in a control memory.

8-6 Expand the two-way branch method depicted in Fig. 8-4 from one status bit to eight status bits.

8-7 Show a block diagram similar to Fig. 8-4 for a four-way branch.

8-8 Using the mapping process defined in Fig. 8-5, give the first microinstruction address for the following macro-operation codes: (a) 0001; (b) 1110; (c) 1010.

8-9 Formulate a mapping process that will provide eight control words for each macro-operation routine. The macro-operation code has five bits and the control memory has 1024 words.

8-10 Suppose we want to achieve the mapping specified in Fig. 8-5 by means of a mapping memory as described in Fig. 8-6.
(a) What is the size of the mapping memory, i.e., how many words and how many bits per word?
(b) Tabulate the bits of each word in each address.
(c) Show how any routine may be assigned any number of words.

8-11 Add the following instructions to the computer defined in Sec. 8-3. Obtain the microprogram for each routine and include it in Table 8-1.
(a) Load from memory to $AC$. Operation code 0011.
(b) Swap content of $AC$ and memory word. Operation code 0100.
(c) Branch if $AC = 0$, Operation code 0101.
(d) Branch if $AC > 0$ ($AC$ positive and non-zero). Operation code 0110.

8-12 Change the INDIRECT subroutine in Table 8-1 to a multiple level indirect address. In multiple level indirect addressing, bit $I$ must be successively checked in all words read from memory and every time it is a 1, a new operand address is read. Memory access terminates and the address of the operand is available when $I = 0$.

8-13 The first microinstruction in the ADD routine of Table 8-1 has no micro-operations. The routine can be reduced to two words if the first microinstruction includes the micro-operation $MBR \leftarrow M$. Follow this suggestion and show all necessary changes in the ADD and INDIRECT routines. Can the modified INDIRECT subroutine be called by the BRANCH routine?

8-14 Microprogram the seven memory-reference instructions of the basic computer listed in Table 5-3 of Sec. 5-4. Use the control word format of Fig. 8-11 with the encoding of the micro-ops into three fields as shown in Table 8-2. Use the indirect and fetch routines from Table 8-1. Redefine the CD field and the mapping process to suit the problem.

8-15 What is the difference between hardware, software and firmware implementation? Consider the multiplication of two binary numbers and explain how this operation is implemented in each of the three methods. Discuss the advantages and disadvantages between the three implementations.

8-16 How many control words are needed for the ADD routine of Table 8-1 if a three-phase clock is used? Specify the bit values and the time sequence of execution.

8-17 What is the difference between a horizontal and vertical microinstruction?

8-18 Using the encoded micro-operation fields from Table 8-2, reassign the first nine bits in the microprogram of Table 8-1.

8-19 Show how the micro-operation bits in the control-word format of Fig. 8-9(a) can be divided into fields to supply 46 micro-operations. How many micro-operations can be specified in one microinstruction?

8-20 Refer to Sec. 7-5 to study the various instruction formats and compare them with the microinstruction formats presented in Sec. 8-4. List a few similarities and differences between the two formats.

8-21 Show how a conditional branch operation is to be handled by the multiple control-word format of Table 8-3.

8-22 A CPU has 16 registers, an ALU with 16 logic and 16 arithmetic functions and a shifter with 8 operations, all connected with a common bus system.

(a) Formulate a control word to specify the various micro-operations for the CPU.

(b) Specify the number of bits for each field and give a general encoding scheme for each.

(c) Show the bits of a control word that specify the micro-operation $R7 \leftarrow R1 + R14$.

8-23 Define symbols similar to the ones used in Table 8-4 for each of the fields of Fig. 8-9. Using these symbols, write the microprogram of Table 8-1 in assembly language.

8-24 Formulate an assembly language for writing microprograms for a control memory whose microinstruction formats are as specified in Table 8-3.

8-25 Show a control memory timing diagram similar to Fig. 8-14 but with conditional branch decisions made on status bits from the micro-operations in the current microinstruction.

8-26 Under what conditions would it be more feasible to use a hard-wired control than a microprogrammed control unit?

8-27 State five advantages of the microprogrammed control unit over hard-wired implementation.

8-28 The basic computer of Chap. 5 uses a hard-wired control unit. It is necessary to redesign it with a microprogrammed control unit. Define a control memory and any suitable control word format and then write the microprogram for the control memory. You may find it convenient to leave the register-reference and input-output instructions in their hard-wired form.

# 9

# ARITHMETIC PROCESSOR DESIGN

## 9-1 INTRODUCTION

Arithmetic instructions in digital computers manipulate data to produce results necessary for the solution of computational problems. These instructions perform arithmetic calculations and are responsible for the bulk of activity involved in processing data in a computer. The four basic arithmetic operations are: addition, subtraction, multiplication, and division. From these four basic operations, it is possible to formulate other arithmetic functions and solve scientific problems by means of numerical analysis methods.

An arithmetic processor is the part of a processor unit that executes arithmetic operations. The data type assumed to reside in processor registers during the execution of an arithmetic instruction is specified in the definition of the instruction. An arithmetic instruction may specify binary or decimal data and in each case the data may be in fixed-point or floating-point form. Fixed-point numbers may represent integers or fractions. Negative numbers may be in signed-magnitude or signed-complement representation. The arithmetic processor is very simple if only a binary fixed-point *add* instruction is included. It would be more complicated if it includes all four arithmetic operations for binary and decimal data in fixed-point and floating-point representation.

At an early age we are taught how to perform the basic arithmetic operations in signed-magnitude representation. This knowledge is valuable when the operations are to be implemented by hardware. However, the designer must be thoroughly familiar with the sequence of steps to be followed in order to carry out the operation and achieve a correct result. The solution to any problem which is stated by a finite number of well defined procedural steps is called an *algorithm.* An algorithm was stated in Sec. 3-2 for the addition of two fixed-point binary numbers when negative numbers are in signed-2's complement representation. This is a simple algorithm since all it needs for its implementation is a parallel binary adder. When negative numbers are in signed-magnitude representation, the algorithm is slightly more complicated and its implementation requires circuits to add and subtract, and to compare the signs and the magnitudes of the numbers. Usually, an algorithm will contain a number of procedural steps which are dependent on results of previous steps. A convenient method for presenting algorithms is a flow chart. The computational steps are specified in the flow chart inside rectangular boxes. The decision steps are indicated inside diamond-shaped boxes from which two or more alternate paths emerge.

The purpose of this chapter is to develop the algorithms and show a procedure for the design of an arithmetic processor. The arithmetic processor performs the four basic operations of addition, subtraction, multiplication, and division. The type of data to be employed is *binary, fixed-point*, *signed-magnitude*, *integer* numbers. Algorithms for signed-complement representation and floating-point or decimal data are presented in the following chapter.

Each of the three representations for negative numbers (signed-magnitude, signed-1's complement and signed-2's complement) produce a different set of steps for carrying out the various arithmetic operations. A different algorithm will require a different sequence of micro-operations when the operation is implemented with hardware. The designer must adopt one, and only one, representation and design the hardware according to the algorithm of the adopted representation. The hardware will produce correct results if, and only if, negative numbers are stored in memory and processor registers in the adopted representation. Results generated by the hardware will also be in the adopted representation.

It is important to realize that the adopted representation for negative numbers refers to the representation of numbers in the registers before and after the execution of the arithmetic operation. It does not mean that complement arithmetic is used as an intermediate step. For example, it is convenient to employ complement arithmetic when performing a subtraction operation with numbers in signed-magnitude representation. As long as the initial minuend and subtrahend, as well as the final difference, are in signed-magnitude form the fact that complements have been used in an intermediate step does not alter the fact that the representation is in signed-magnitude.

## 9-2 COMPARISON AND SUBTRACTION OF UNSIGNED BINARY NUMBERS

The algorithms for addition and subtraction of binary numbers in signed-complement representation treat the sign bit as an extended bit of the number. In contrast, the arithmetic algorithms for numbers in signed-magnitude representation treat the sign bit and the magnitude of the numbers separately. For this reason, it is convenient to consider the magnitude part alone as being an unsigned binary number. The operations performed with the magnitude of the numbers are comparison, subtraction, and addition. In this section we consider a few alternatives for comparing and subtracting unsigned binary numbers. These procedures are useful for deriving the arithmetic algorithms for numbers in signed-magnitude representation.

### *Magnitude Comparator*

The comparison of two numbers is an operation that determines if one number is greater than, less than, or equal to the other number. A magnitude comparator is a combinational circuit that compares two numbers $A$ and $B$ and determines their relative magnitude. The outcome of the comparison is specified by three binary variables that indicate whether $A > B$, $A = B$, or $A < B$.

The circuit of a magnitude comparator can be derived from the procedure most commonly used to compare the relative magnitude of numbers. Consider two numbers $A$ and $B$ with four digits in each. Let $A = A_3A_2A_1A_0$ and $B = B_3B_2B_1B_0$ where each subscripted letter represents one of the digits in the number. The two numbers are equal if all pairs of significant digits are equal, that is, if $A_3 = B_3$ and $A_2 = B_2$ and $A_1 = B_1$ and $A_0 = B_0$. When the numbers are binary, the digits are either 1 or 0 and the equality relation of the individual bits can be expressed by the following Boolean function:

$$x_i = A_iB_i + A_i'B_i' \qquad i = 0, 1, 2, 3$$

where $x_i = 1$ if the pair of bits in position $i$ are equal, that is, if both are 1's or both are 0's.

The equality of numbers $A$ and $B$ is specified by a binary variable which we designate by the symbol $(A = B)$. This binary variable is equal to 1 if $A$ is arithmetically equal to $B$ and is 0 otherwise. For the *binary* variable $(A = B)$ to be equal to 1 we must have all $x_i$ variables equal to 1. This dictates an AND Boolean function as follows:

$$(A = B) = x_3x_2x_1x_0$$

To determine if $A$ is greater than or less than $B$, we inspect the relative magnitude of pairs of significant digits starting from the most significant position. If the two digits are equal, we compare the next lower significant pair of digits. This comparison is continued until a pair of unequal digits is reached. If the corresponding digit of $A$ is greater than that of $B$ we have $A > B$. If the corresponding digit of $B$ is greater, we have $A < B$. In the case of binary digits, the sequential comparison can be expressed by the following Boolean functions:

$$(A > B) = A_3B'_3 + x_3A_2B'_2 + x_3x_2A_1B'_1 + x_3x_2x_1A_0B'_0$$
$$(A < B) = A'_3B_3 + x_3A'_2B_2 + x_3x_2A'_1B_1 + x_3x_2x_1A'_0B_0$$

The symbols $(A > B)$ and $(A < B)$ are *binary* output variables which are equal to 1 when $A > B$ or $A < B$, respectively.

The logic diagram of a 4-bit magnitude comparator is shown in Fig. 9-1. The $x$ outputs are generated by an exclusive-NOR circuit and applied to a 4-input AND gate to produce the binary output variable $(A = B)$. The other two outputs are generated according to the Boolean functions listed above. The procedure for obtaining magnitude comparator circuits for binary numbers with more than four bits is obvious. Four-bit magnitude comparators are available in integrated circuit packages.

### *Complements*

Complements were introduced in Sec. 3-2. We review here some of the properties of complements and extend the discussion to obtain additional properties that will be useful in the development of comparison and subtraction algorithms.

In the following discussion, $A$ and $B$ refer to unsigned binary numbers and $n$ refers to the number of bits in the registers that store their equivalent binary value. It is important to realize that $2^n$ is equal in binary to a number consisting of a 1 followed by $n$ zeros. $2^n - 1$ is represented in binary as $n$ 1's. The 2's complement of an unsigned integer $B$ is defined as $2^n - B$. The 1's complement is defined as $2^n - 1 - B$. These definitions are convenient for proving arithmetic algorithms involving complement arithmetic.

As a numerical example, consider a number $B = 20$. For $n = 6$, the binary equivalents of the various quantities are:

$$B = 010100$$

$$2^6 = 1000000$$

$$2^6 - 1 = 111111$$

$$2^6 - B = 101100 = \text{2's complement of } B$$

$$2^6 - 1 - B = 101011 = \text{1's complement of } B$$

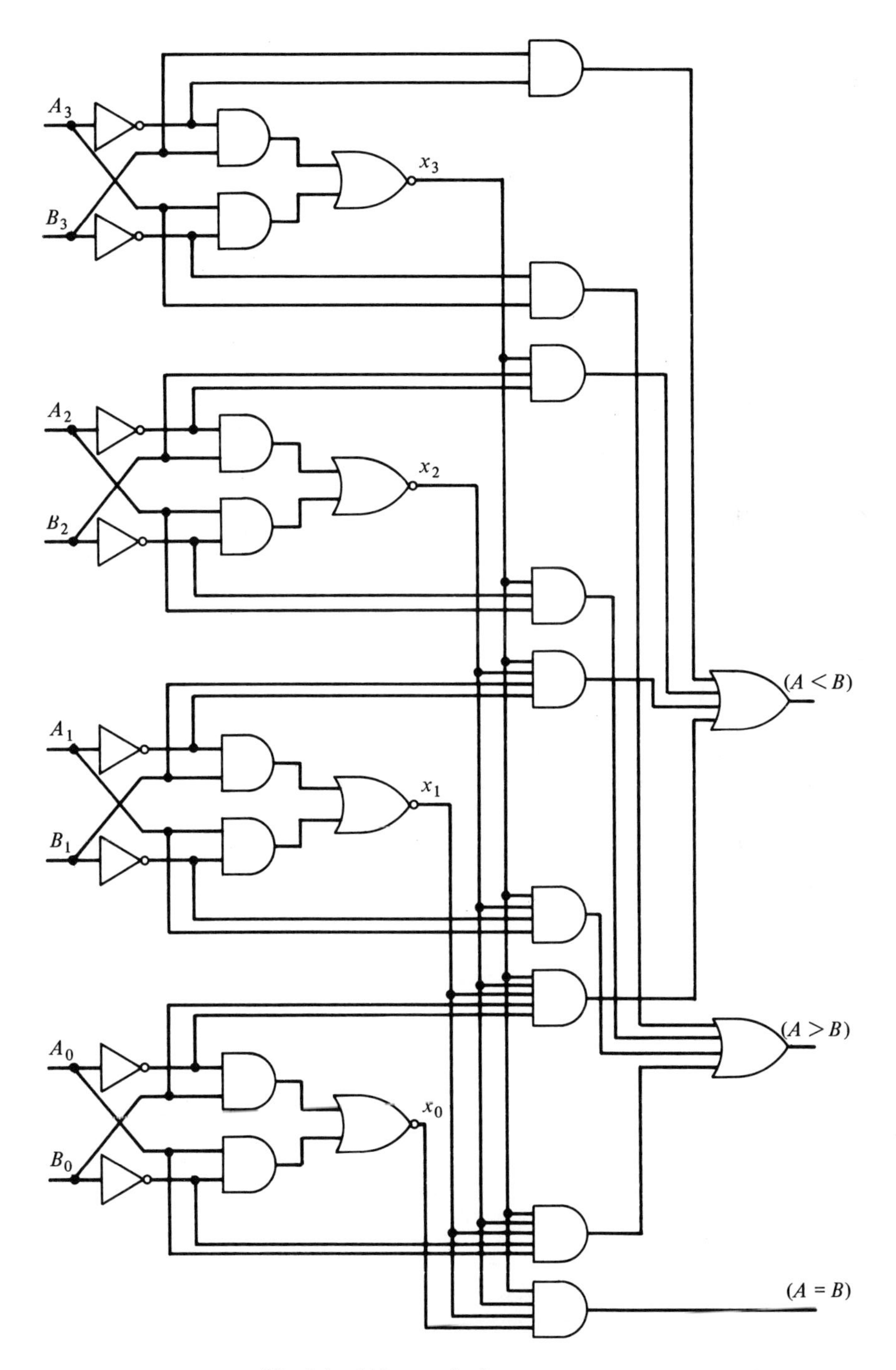


**Fig. 9-1** 4-bit magnitude comparator.

From the above definitions it is easily shown that the 1's complement is obtained by complementing each bit. The 2's complement is obtained by either one of the following simple procedures: (a) take the 1's complement of the number and add 1; or (b) leave all least significant 0's and the first 1 unchanged and then complement the remaining bits.

### *Straight Subtraction*

The subtraction of two unsigned binary numbers may be implemented by means of hardware with $n$ full-subtractors in cascade. The output-borrow of each full-subtractor is connected to the input-borrow of the full-subtractor on its left. The output-borrow of the most significant stage will be referred to as the end-borrow. When an unsigned number $B$ is subtracted from another unsigned number $A$, the difference $A - B$ will appear at the $D$ (difference) outputs of the full-subtractors. If the end-borrow is a 0, it means that $A \geq B$ and the difference is the correct number. The difference is equal to zero if $A = B$. If the end-borrow is a 1, it signifies that $2^n$ has been borrowed to form the difference $2^n + A - B$. This will occur if $A < B$. The result of this operation can be represented as $2^n - (B - A)$ which, by definition, is the 2's complement of $(B - A)$. To obtain the correct difference, we take the 2's complement again and obtain: $2^n - (2^n + A - B) = B - A$. A negative sign must be transferred to the sign flip-flop when the number is represented in sign-magnitude. The results of the above discussion are tabulated in the first entry of Table 9-1.

The relative magnitude of two unsigned numbers $A$ and $B$ may be determined from the subtraction of $B$ from $A$ and a check of the end-borrow. If the end-borrow is 0, the difference $A - B$ is positive and $A \geq B$. If it is 1, the difference is negative and $A < B$. The two numbers are equal if the end-

**Table 9-1** *Subtraction and comparison of unsigned binary numbers*

| *Operation* | *if* | *E is* | *Result is* | *if* | *E is* | *Result is* | *If $A = B$ result contains* |
|---|---|---|---|---|---|---|---|
| $A - B$ | $A \geq B$ | 0 | $A - B$ | $A < B$ | 1 | 2's complement of $(B - A)$ | All 0's |
| $A + \bar{B}$ | $A \leq B$ | 0 | 1's complement of $(B - A)$ | $A > B$ | 1 | $A - B - 1$ | All 1's |
| $A + \bar{B} + 1$ | $A < B$ | 0 | 2's complement of $(B - A)$ | $A \geq B$ | 1 | $A - B$ | All 0's |

$E$ is the end-carry for addition or end-borrow for subtraction.

borrow is 0 and the difference is also 0. This comparison algorithm follows from the previous discussion.

### *Subtraction with Complements*

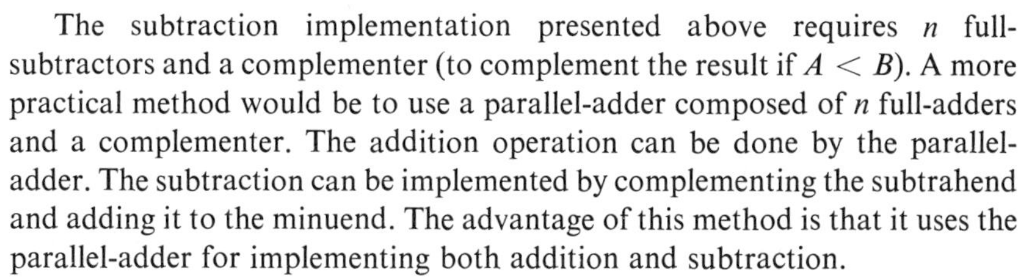

The subtraction implementation presented above requires $n$ full-subtractors and a complementer (to complement the result if $A < B$). A more practical method would be to use a parallel-adder composed of $n$ full-adders and a complementer. The addition operation can be done by the parallel-adder. The subtraction can be implemented by complementing the subtrahend and adding it to the minuend. The advantage of this method is that it uses the parallel-adder for implementing both addition and subtraction.

The subtraction of two unsigned binary numbers by means of 2's complements or 1's complements is summarized in Table 9-1. The operation $A + \bar{B}$ designates the addition of $A$ to the 1's complement of $B$. The operation $A + \bar{B} + 1$ designates the addition of $A$ to the 2's complement of $B$. In each case, $E$ designates the end-carry out of the last, most significant, stage.

The proof for the 1's complement subtraction will be left as an exercise. The proof for the 2's complement subtraction follows. The addition of $A + \bar{B} + 1$ is equivalent to $A + (2^n - B) = 2^n + (A - B)$. When the end-carry $E$ is equal to 1, it means that a 1 is available in the $n + 1$ position of the result. This value is equal to $2^n$ because it represents a number consisting of a 1 followed by $n$ zeros. Now, if $A \geq B$ then $(A - B)$ must be a positive number and $2^n + (A - B) \geq 2^n$. If we remove the end-carry we obtain $A - B$. Note also that when $A = B$ the result of the operation gives $2^n$ which indicates that $E = 1$ and the remaining bits consist of all zeros.

If $A < B$, then $(A - B)$ must be a negative number. Therefore, $2^n + (A - B) < 2^n$ and $E$ must be 0. The result of this operation can be written as $2^n - (B - A)$, where $B - A$ is a positive number. This is equivalent to the 2's complement of $(B - A)$. To obtain the magnitude of the difference we must complement again to obtain $2^n - (2^n + A - B) = B - A$, and the result is negative.

The relative magnitude of $A$ and $B$ can be determined from the above operation. If $E = 1$, the difference $A - B$ is positive and $A \geq B$. If $E = 0$, the difference is negative and $A < B$. The two numbers are equal if $E = 1$ and all the bits of the result are zeros.

It is worth emphasizing again that the above algorithms are for unsigned binary numbers. These algorithms are useful for implementing the subtraction and comparison operations with the magnitude part of binary numbers when they are in signed-magnitude representation. When the numbers are represented in signed-complement form, the addition and subtraction algorithms treat the sign bit as an extended bit of the number.

## 9-3 ADDITION AND SUBTRACTION ALGORITHMS

The representation of numbers in signed-magnitude is familiar because it is used in every day arithmetic calculations. The procedure for adding or subtracting two signed binary numbers with paper and pencil is simple and straightforward. A review of this procedure will be helpful for deriving the hardware algorithm.

We designate the magnitude of the two numbers by $A$ and $B$. When the signed numbers are added or subtracted, we find that there are eight different conditions to consider, depending on the sign of the numbers and the operation performed. These conditions are listed in the first column of Table 9-2.

**Table 9-2** *Addition and subtraction of signed-magnitude numbers*

| Operation | Add Magnitudes | *Subtract Magnitudes* | | |
|---|---|---|---|---|
| | | When $A > B$ | When $A < B$ | When $A = B$ |
| $(+A) + (+B)$ | $+(A + B)$ | | | |
| $(+A) + (-B)$ | | $+(A - B)$ | $-(B - A)$ | $+(A - B)$ |
| $(-A) + (+B)$ | | $-(A - B)$ | $+(B - A)$ | $+(A - B)$ |
| $(-A) + (-B)$ | $-(A + B)$ | | | |
| $(+A) - (+B)$ | | $+(A - B)$ | $-(B - A)$ | $+(A - B)$ |
| $(+A) - (-B)$ | $+(A + B)$ | | | |
| $(-A) - (+B)$ | $-(A + B)$ | | | |
| $(-A) - (-B)$ | | $-(A - B)$ | $+(B - A)$ | $+(A - B)$ |

The other columns in the table show the actual operation to be performed with the *magnitude* of the numbers. The last column is needed to prevent a negative zero. In other words, when two equal numbers are subtracted, the result should be $+0$ not $-0$.

The algorithms for addition and subtraction are derived from the table and can be stated as follows (the words inside parentheses should be used for the subtraction algorithm):

*Addition* (*subtraction*) *algorithm*: when the signs of $A$ and $B$ are identical (different) add the two magnitudes and attach the sign of $A$ to the result. When the signs of $A$ and $B$ are different (identical), compare the magnitudes and subtract the smaller number from the larger. Choose the sign of the result to be the same as $A$ if $A > B$ or the complement of the sign of $A$ if $A < B$. If the two magnitudes are equal, subtract $B$ from $A$ and make the sign of the result a plus.

The two algorithms are similar except for the sign comparison. The procedure to be followed for identical signs in the addition algorithm is the same as for different signs in the subtraction algorithm, and vice-versa.

### *Hardware Implementation*

To implement the two arithmetic operations with hardware, it is first necessary that the two numbers be stored in registers. Let $A$ and $B$ be two registers that hold the magnitudes of the numbers, and $A_s$ and $B_s$ be two flip-flops that hold the corresponding signs. The result of the operation may be transferred to a third register; however, a saving is achieved if the result is transferred into $A$ and $A_s$. Thus $A$ and $A_s$ together form an accumulator register.

Consider now the hardware implementation of the above algorithms. First, a parallel-adder is needed to perform the micro-operation $A + B$. Second, a comparator circuit is needed to establish if $A > B$, $A = B$, or $A < B$. Third, two parallel-subtractor circuits are needed to perform the micro-operations $A - B$ and $B - A$. The sign relationship can be determined from an exclusive-OR gate with $A_s$ and $B_s$ as inputs.

This procedure requires a magnitude comparator, an adder and two subtractors. However, from the discussion of the previous section we know that a different procedure can be found that requires less equipment. First of all, we know that subtraction can be accomplished by means of complement and add. Second, the result of a comparison can be determined from the end-carry after the subtraction. Careful investigation of the alternatives reveals that the use of 2's complement for subtraction and comparison is an efficient procedure that requires only an adder and a complementer.

Figure 9-2 shows a block diagram of the hardware for implementing the addition and subtraction operations. It consists of registers $A$ and $B$ and sign flip-flops $A_s$ and $B_s$. Subtraction is done by adding $A$ to the 2's complement of $B$. The end-carry is transferred to flip-flop $E$ where it can be checked to determine the relative magnitudes of the two numbers. The add-overflow

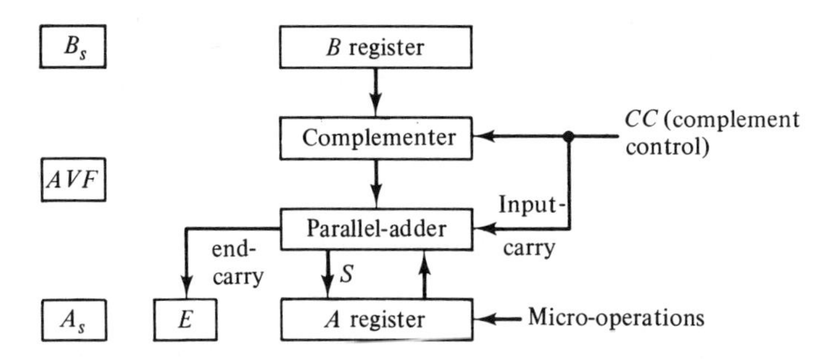


**Fig. 9-2** Block diagram of hardware for addition and subtraction.

flip-flop *AVF* holds the overflow bit when *A* and *B* are added. The *A* register provides other micro-operations that may be needed when we specify the sequence of steps in the algorithm.

The addition of *A* and *B* is done through a binary parallel-adder. The *S* outputs of the adder are applied to the inputs of the *A* register for their transfer with a parallel-load micro-operation. The complementer provides an output of *B* or $\bar{B}$ depending on the state of the binary variable *CC* (complement control). The complementer consists of exclusive-OR gates and the parallel-adder of full-adder (FA) circuits. One typical stage of the complementer and adder is shown in Fig. 9-3. From the truth table of the exclusive-OR gate it is clear that input $y_i$ to the full-adder is equal to $B_i$ when $CC = 0$. But $y_i = B_i'$ if $CC = 1$. The *CC* variable also supplies the input carry to the binary parallel-adder. When $CC = 0$, *B* is applied to the adder, the input-carry is 0, and the output of the parallel-adder is equal to $A + B$. When $CC = 1$, $\bar{B}$ is applied to the adder, the input-carry is 1, and $S = A + \bar{B} + 1$. This is equal to *A* plus the 2's complement of *B*.

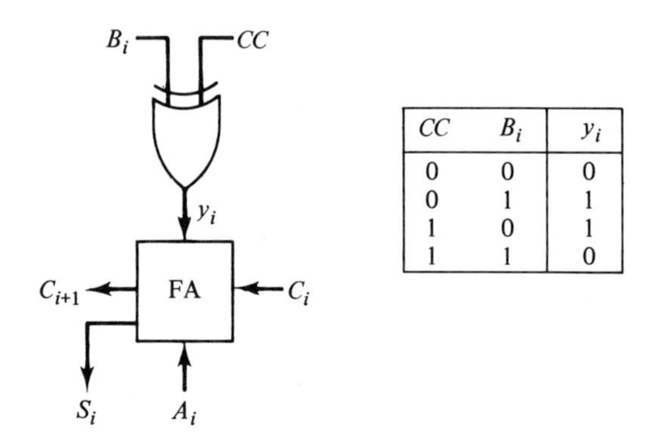


| $CC$ | $B_i$ | $y_i$ |
|---|---|---|
| 0 | 0 | 0 |
| 0 | 1 | 1 |
| 1 | 0 | 1 |
| 1 | 1 | 0 |

**Fig. 9-3** One stage of complementer and parallel-adder.

### *Hardware Algorithm*

The flow chart for the hardware algorithm is presented in Fig. 9-4. The two signs $A_s$ and $B_s$ are compared by an exclusive-OR gate. If the output of the gate is 0, the signs are identical; if it is 1, the signs are different. For an *add* operation, identical signs dictate that the magnitudes be added. For a *subtract* operation, different signs dictate that the magnitudes be added. The magnitudes are added with a micro-operation $EA \leftarrow A + B$, where *EA* is a register that combines *E* and *A*. The carry in *E* after the addition constitutes an overflow if it is equal to 1. The value of *E* is transferred into the add-overflow flip-flop *AVF*.

The two magnitudes are subtracted if the signs are different for an *add* operation or identical for a *subtract* operation. The magnitudes are sub-

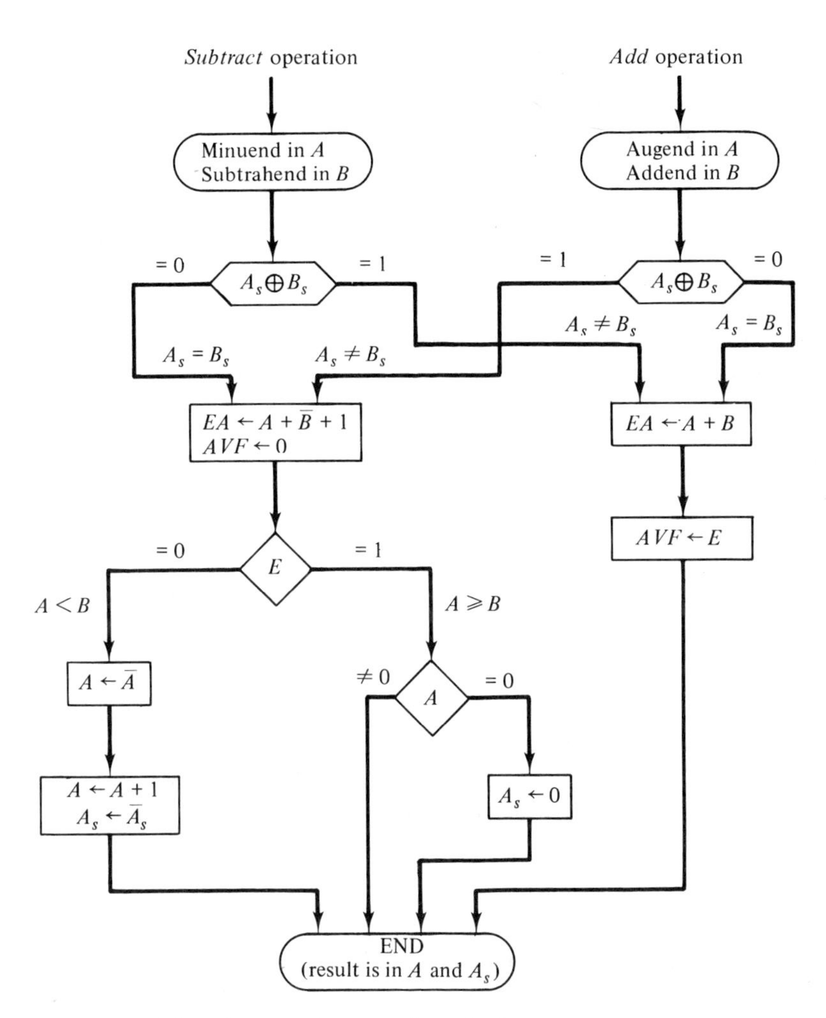


**Fig. 9-4** Flow chart for add and subtract operations.

tracted by adding $A$ to the 2's complement of $B$. No overflow can occur if the numbers are subtracted so $AVF$ is cleared to 0. A 1 in $E$ indicates that $A \geq B$ and the number in $A$ is the correct result. If this number is zero, the sign $A_s$ must be made positive to avoid a negative zero. A 0 in $E$ indicates that $A < B$. For this case, it is necessary to take the 2's complement of the value in $A$. This operation can be done with one micro-operation $A \leftarrow \bar{A} + 1$. However, we assume that the $A$ register has circuits for micro-operations *complement* and *increment*, so the 2's complement is obtained from these two micro-operations. In other paths of the flow chart, the sign of the result is the same as the sign of $A$, so no change in $A_s$ is required. However, when $A < B$, the sign of the result is the complement of the original sign of $A$. It is then necessary to complement $A_s$ in order to obtain the correct sign. The final result is found in register $A$ and its sign in $A_s$. The value in $AVF$ provides an overflow indication. The final value of $E$ is immaterial.

## 9-4 MULTIPLICATION ALGORITHM

Multiplication of two fixed-point binary numbers in signed-magnitude representation is done with paper and pencil by a process of successive shift and add operations. This process is best illustrated with a numerical example as shown in Fig. 9-5. The process consists of looking at successive bits of the

```
 23          10111     Multiplicand
 19        x 10011     Multiplier
             10111
            10111
           00000    +
          00000
         10111
437      110110101     Product
```

**Fig. 9-5** Example of binary multiplication.

multiplier, least significant bit first. If the multiplier bit is a 1, the multiplicand is copied down; otherwise, zeros are copied down. The numbers copied down in successive lines are shifted one position to the left from the previous number. Finally, the numbers are added and their sum forms the product.

The sign of the product is determined from the signs of the multiplicand and multiplier. If they are alike, the sign of the product is plus. If they are unlike, the sign of the product is minus.

### *Hardware Implementation*

When multiplication is implemented in a digital computer, it is convenient to change the process slightly. First, instead of providing registers to store and add simultaneously as many binary numbers as there are bits in the multiplier, it is convenient to provide an adder for the summation of only two binary numbers and successively accumulate the partial products in a register. Second, instead of shifting the multiplicand to the left, the partial product is shifted to the right, which results in leaving the partial product and the multiplicand in the required relative positions. Third, when the corresponding bit of the multiplier is 0, there is no need to add all zeros to the partial product since it will not alter its value.

The hardware for multiplication consists of the equipment shown in Fig. 9-2 plus two more registers. These registers together with registers $A$ and $B$ are shown in Fig. 9-6. The multiplier is stored in the $Q$ register and its sign in $Q_s$. The sequence counter SC is initially set to a number equal to the number

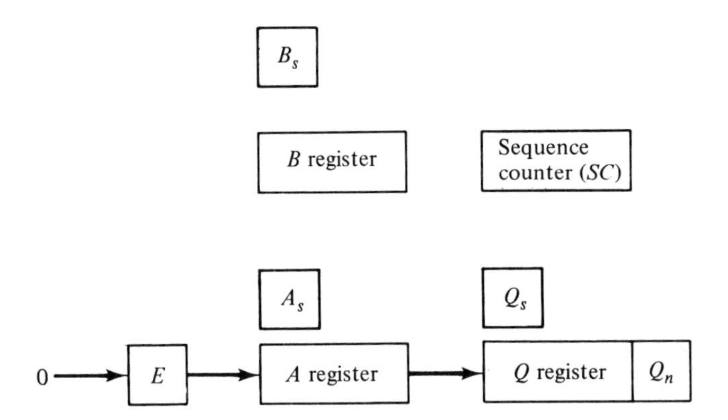


**Fig. 9-6** Register *EAQ* and sequence counter needed for multiplication and division.

of bits in the multiplier. The counter is decremented by 1 after forming each partial product. When the content of the counter reaches zero, the product is formed and the process stops.

Initially, the multiplicand is in register *B* and the multiplier in *Q*. The sum of *A* and *B* forms a partial product which is transferred to the *EA* register. Both partial product and multiplier are shifted to the right. This shift will be denoted by the statement shr *EAQ* to designate the right shift depicted in Fig. 9-6. The least significant bit of *A* is shifted into the most significant position of *Q*; the bit from *E* is shifted into the most significant position of *A*; and 0 is shifted into *E*. After the shift, one bit of the partial product is shifted into *Q*, pushing the multiplier bits one position to the right. In this manner, the right-most flip-flop in register *Q*, designated by $Q_n$, will hold the bit of the multiplier which must be inspected next.

### *Hardware Algorithm*

Figure 9-7 is a flow chart of the hardware multiply algorithm. Initially, the multiplicand is in *B* and the multiplier in *Q*. Their corresponding signs are in $B_s$ and $Q_s$, respectively. The signs are compared, and both *A* and *Q* are set to correspond to the sign of the product since a double-length product will be stored in registers *A* and *Q*. Registers *A* and *E* are cleared and the sequence counter SC is set to a number equal to the number of bits of the multiplier. We are assuming here that operands are transferred to registers from a memory unit that has words of *n* bits. Since an operand must be stored with its sign, one bit of the word will be occupied by the sign and the magnitude will consist of $n - 1$ bits.

After the initialization, the low-order bit of the multiplier in $Q_n$ is tested. If it is a 1, the multiplicand in *B* is added to the present partial product in *A*.

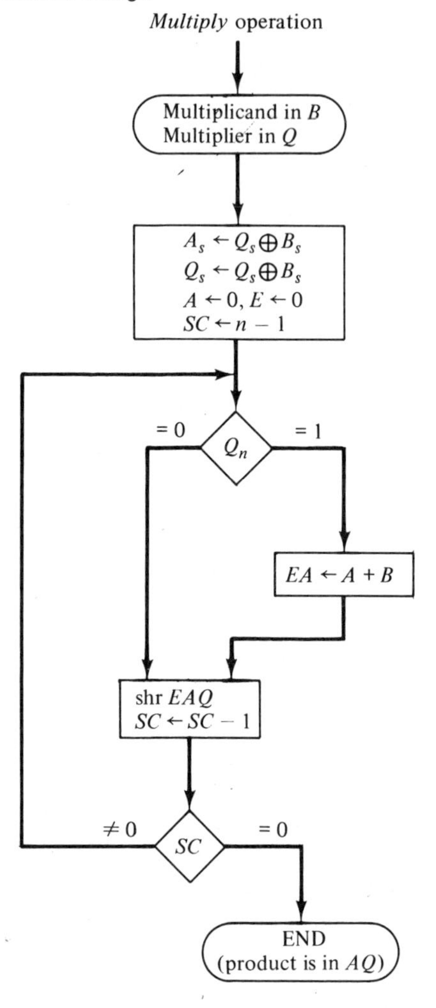


**Fig. 9-7** Flow chart for multiply operation.

If it is a 0, nothing is done. Register $EAQ$ is then shifted once to the right to form the new partial product. The sequence counter is decremented by 1 and its new value checked. If it is not equal to zero, the process is repeated and a new partial product is formed. The process stops when SC = 0. Note that the partial product formed in $A$ is shifted into $Q$ one bit at a time and eventually replaces the multiplier. The final product is available in both $A$ and $Q$, with $A$ holding the most significant bits and $Q$ holding the least significant bits.

The previous numerical example is repeated in Fig. 9-8 in order to clarify the hardware multiplication process. The procedure follows the steps outlined in the flow chart.

| Multiplicand: $B = 10111$ | $E$ | $A$ | $Q$ | $SC$ |
|---|---|---|---|---|
| Multiplier in $Q$: | | 00000 | 10011 | 5 |
| $Q_n = 1$; add $B$ | | 10111 | | |
| First partial product | 0 | 10111 | | |
| shr $EAQ$ | 0 | 01011 | 11001 | 4 |
| $Q_n = 1$; add $B$ | | 10111 | | |
| Second partial product | 1 | 00010 | | |
| shr $EAQ$ | 0 | 10001 | 01100 | 3 |
| $Q_n = 0$; shr $EAQ$ | 0 | 01000 | 10110 | 2 |
| $Q_n = 0$; shr $EAQ$ | 0 | 00100 | 01011 | 1 |
| $Q_n = 1$; add $B$ | | 10111 | | |
| Fifth partial product | 0 | 11011 | | |
| shr $EAQ$; final product: | | 01101 | 10101 | 0 |

**Fig. 9-8** Example of binary multiplication with digital hardware.

## 9-5 DIVISION ALGORITHM

Division of two fixed-point binary numbers in signed-magnitude representation is done with paper and pencil by a process of successive compare, shift, and subtract operations. Binary division is simpler than decimal division because the quotient digits are either 0 or 1 and there is no need to estimate how many times the dividend or partial remainder fits into the divisor. The division process is illustrated by a numerical example in Fig. 9-9. The divisor $B$ consists of five bits and the dividend $A$, of ten bits. The five most significant bits of the dividend are compared with the divisor. Since the 5-bit number is smaller than $B$, we try again by taking the six most significant bits of $A$ and compare this number with $B$. The 6-bit number is greater than $B$ so we place a 1 for the quotient bit in the sixth position above the dividend. The divisor is then shifted once to the right and subtracted from the dividend. The difference is called a *partial remainder* because the division could have

| Divisor: | | |
|---|---|---|
| | 11010 | Quotient = $Q$ |
| $B = 10001$ | )0111000000 | Dividend = $A$ |
| | 01110 | 5 bits of $A < B$, quotient has 5 bits |
| | 011100 | 6 bits of $A \geq B$ |
| | -10001 | Shift right $B$ and subtract; enter 1 in $Q$ |
| | -010110 | 7 bits of remainder $\geq B$ |
| | --10001 | Shift right $B$ and subtract; enter 1 in $Q$ |
| | --001010 | Remainder $< B$; enter 0 in $Q$; shift right $B$ |
| | ---010100 | Remainder $\geq B$ |
| | ----10001 | Shift right $B$ and subtract; enter 1 in $Q$ |
| | ----000110 | Remainder $< B$; enter 0 in $Q$ |
| | -----00110 | Final remainder |

**Fig. 9-9** Example of binary division.

stopped here to obtain a quotient of 1 and a remainder equal to the partial remainder. The process is continued by comparing a partial remainder with the divisor. If the partial remainder is greater than or equal to the divisor, the quotient bit is equal to 1. The divisor is then shifted right and subtracted from the partial remainder. If the partial remainder is smaller than the divisor, the quotient bit is 0 and no subtraction is needed. The divisor is shifted once to the right in any case. Note that the result gives both a quotient and a remainder.

### *Hardware Implementation*

When the division is implemented in a digital computer, it is convenient to change the process slightly. Instead of shifting the divisor to the right, the dividend, or partial remainder, is shifted to the left, thus leaving the two

Divisor $B = 10001$, $\overline{B} + 1 = 01111$

| | $E$ | $A$ | $Q$ | $SC$ |
|---|---|---|---|---|
| Dividend: | | 01110 | 00000 | 5 |
| shl $EAQ$ | 0 | 11100 | 00000 | |
| add $\overline{B} + 1$ | | 01111 | | |
| $E = 1$ | 1 | 01011 | | |
| Set $Q_n = 1$ | 1 | 01011 | 00001 | 4 |
| shl $EAQ$ | 0 | 10110 | 00010 | |
| Add $\overline{B} + 1$ | | 01111 | | |
| $E = 1$ | 1 | 00101 | | |
| Set $Q_n = 1$ | 1 | 00101 | 00011 | 3 |
| shl $EAQ$ | 0 | 01010 | 00110 | |
| Add $\overline{B} + 1$ | | 01111 | | |
| $E = 0$; leave $Q_n = 0$ | 0 | 11001 | 00110 | |
| Add $B$ | | 10001 | | |
| | | | | 2 |
| Restore remainder | 1 | 01010 | | |
| shl $EAQ$ | 0 | 10100 | 01100 | |
| Add $\overline{B} + 1$ | | 01111 | | |
| $E = 1$ | 1 | 00011 | | |
| Set $Q_n = 1$ | 1 | 00011 | 01101 | 1 |
| shl $EAQ$ | 0 | 00110 | 11010 | |
| Add $\overline{B} + 1$ | | 01111 | | |
| $E = 0$; leave $Q_n = 0$ | 0 | 10101 | 11010 | |
| Add $B$ | | 10001 | | |
| Restore remainder | 1 | 00110 | 11010 | 0 |
| Neglect $E$ | | | | |
| Remainder in $A$: | | 00110 | | |
| Quotient in $Q$: | | | 11010 | |

**Fig. 9-10** Example of binary division with digital hardware.

numbers in the required relative position. Subtraction may be achieved by adding $A$ to the 2's complement of $B$. The information about the relative magnitudes is then available from the end-carry.

The hardware for implementing the division operation is identical to that required for multiplication and consists of the components shown in Fig. 9-6. Register $EAQ$ is now shifted to the left with 0 inserted into $Q_n$ and the previous value of $E$ lost. The numerical example is repeated in Fig. 9-10 in order to clarify the proposed division process. The divisor is stored in the $B$ register and the double-length dividend is stored in registers $A$ and $Q$. The dividend is shifted to the left and the divisor is subtracted by adding its 2's complement value. The information about the relative magnitude is available in $E$. If $E = 1$, it signifies that $A \geq B$. A quotient bit 1 is inserted into $Q_n$ and the partial remainder is shifted to the left to repeat the process. If $E = 0$, it signifies that $A < B$ so the quotient in $Q_n$ remains a 0 (inserted during the shift). The value of $B$ is then added to restore the partial remainder in $A$ to its previous value. The partial remainder is shifted to the left and the process is repeated again until all five quotient bits are formed. Note that while the partial remainder is shifted left, the quotient bits are shifted also and after five shifts, the quotient is in $Q$ and the final remainder is in $A$.

Before showing the algorithm in flow chart form, we have to consider the sign of the result and a possible overflow condition. The sign of the quotient is determined from the signs of the dividend and the divisor. If the two signs are alike, the sign of the quotient is plus. If they are unlike, the sign is minus. The sign of the remainder is the same as the sign of the dividend.

### *Divide Overflow*

The division operation may result in a quotient with an overflow. This is not a problem when working with paper and pencil, but is critical when the operation is implemented with hardware. This is because the length of registers is finite and will not hold a number that exceeds the standard length. To see this, consider a system that has 5-bit registers. We use one register to hold the divisor and two registers to hold the dividend. From the example of Fig. 9-9 we note that the quotient will consist of six bits if the five most significant bits of the dividend constitute a number greater than the divisor. The quotient is to be stored in a standard 5-bit register so the overflow bit will require one more flip-flop for storing the sixth bit. This divide overflow condition must be avoided in normal computer operations because the entire quotient will be too long for transfer into a memory unit which has words of standard length, i.e., the same as the length of registers. Provisions to insure that this condition is detected must be included in either the hardware or software of the computer, or in a combination of the two.

When the dividend is twice as long as the divisor, the condition for overflow can be stated as follows:

*A divide-overflow condition occurs if the high-order half bits of the dividend constitute a number greater than or equal to the divisor.*

Another problem associated with division is the fact that a division by zero must be avoided. The divide-overflow condition stated above takes care of this condition as well. This occurs because any dividend will be greater than or equal to a divisor which is equal to zero. Overflow condition is usually detected when a special flip-flop is set. We will call it a divide-overflow flip-flop and label it $DVF$.

The occurrence of a divide overflow can be handled in a variety of ways. In some computers it is the responsibility of the programmer to check if $DVF$ is set after each divide instruction. He then branches to a subroutine that takes a corrective measure such as rescaling the data to avoid overflow. In some older computers, the occurrence of a divide overflow stopped the computer and this condition was referred to as a *divide stop*. Stopping the operation of the computer is not recommended because it is time-consuming. The procedure employed in most computers is to provide an interrupt request when $DVF$ is set. The interrupt causes the computer to suspend the current program and branch to a service routine to take a corrective measure. The most common corrective measure is to remove the program and type an error message explaining the reason why the program could not be completed. It is then the responsibility of the user who wrote the program to rescale his data or take any other corrective measure. The best way to avoid a divide overflow is to use floating-point data. We will see in the next chapter that a divide overflow can be handled very simply if numbers are in floating-point representation.

### *Hardware Algorithm*

The hardware divide algorithm is shown in the flow chart of Fig. 9-11. The dividend is in $A$ and $Q$ and the divisor in $B$. The sign of the result is transferred into $Q_s$ to be part of the quotient. A constant is set into the sequence counter $SC$ to specify the number of bits in the quotient. As in multiplication, we assume that operands are transferred to registers from a memory unit that has words of $n$ bits. Since an operand must be stored with its sign, one bit of the word will be occupied by the sign and the magnitude will consists of $n - 1$ bits.

A divide-overflow condition is tested by subtracting the divisor in $B$ from half of the bits of the dividend stored in $A$. If $A \geq B$, the divide-overflow flip-flop $DVF$ is set and the operation is terminated prematurely. If $A < B$,

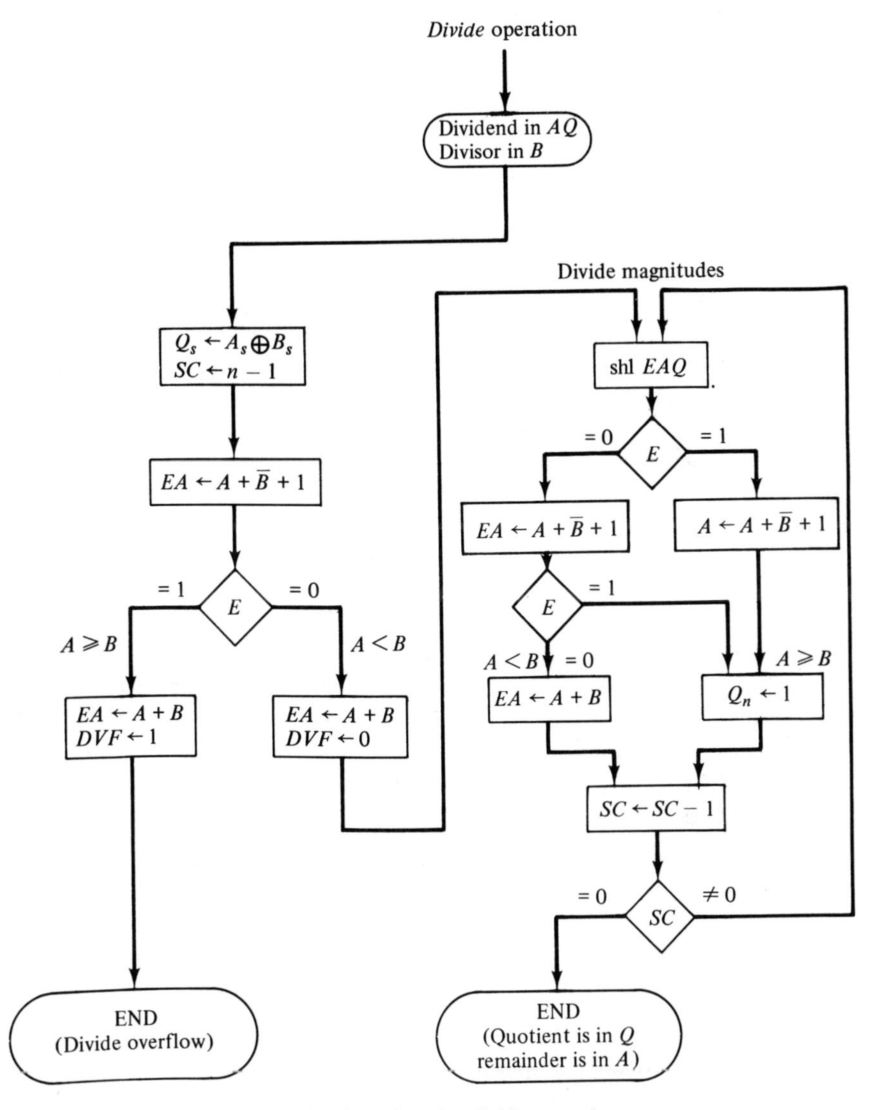


**Fig. 9-11** Flow chart for divide operation.

no divide overflow occurs, so the value of the dividend is restored by adding $B$ to $A$.

The division of the magnitudes starts by shifting the dividend in $AQ$ to the left with the high-order bit shifted into $E$. If the bit shifted into $E$ is 1, we know that $EA > B$ because $EA$ consists of a 1 followed by $n-1$ bits while $B$ consists of only $n-1$ bits. In this case, $B$ must be substracted from $A$ and a 1 inserted into $Q_n$ for the quotient bit. Since register $A$ is missing the high-order bit of the dividend (which is in $E$), its value is $A - 2^{n-1}$. Adding to this value the 2's complement of $B$ results in

$$(A - 2^{n-1}) + (2^{n-1} - B) = A - B$$

The carry from this addition is not transferred to $E$ if we want $E$ to remain a 1.

If the shift-left operation inserts a 0 into $E$, the divisor is subtracted by adding its 2's complement value and the carry is transferred into $E$. If $E = 1$, it signifies that $A \geq B$, therefore, $Q_n$ is set to 1. If $E = 0$, it signifies that $A < B$ and the original number is restored by adding $B$ to $A$. In the latter case, we leave a 0 in $Q_n$ (0 was inserted during the shift).

This process is repeated again with register $A$ holding the partial remainder. After $n - 1$ times, the quotient magnitude is formed in register $Q$ and the remainder is found in register $A$. The quotient sign is in $Q_s$ and the sign of the remainder in $A_s$ is the same as the original sign of the dividend.

### *Other Algorithms*

The hardware method just described is called the *restoring method.* The reason for this name is that the partial remainder is restored by adding the divisor to the negative difference. Two other methods are available for dividing numbers, the *comparison* method and the *non-restoring* method. In the comparison method $A$ and $B$ are compared *prior* to the subtraction operation. Then, if $A \geq B$, $B$ is subtracted from $A$. If $A < B$ nothing is done. The partial remainder is shifted left and the numbers are compared again. The comparison can be determined prior to the subtraction by inspecting the end-carry out of the parallel-adder prior to its transfer to register $E$.

In the non-restoring method, $B$ is not added if the difference is negative but instead, the negative difference is shifted left and then $B$ is added. To see why this is possible consider the case when $A < B$. From the flow chart in Fig. 9-11 we note that the operations performed are $A - B + B$, i.e., $B$ is subtracted and then added to restore $A$. The next time around the loop, this number is shifted left (or multiplied by 2) and $B$ subtracted again. This gives: $2(A - B + B) - B = 2A - B$. This result is obtained in the non-restoring method by leaving $A - B$ as is. The next time around the loop, the number is shifted left and $B$ *added* to give: $2(A - B) + B = 2A - B$ which is the same as before. Thus, in the non-restoring method, $B$ is subtracted if the previous value of $Q_n$ was a 1 but $B$ is added if the previous value of $Q_n$ was a 0 and no restoring of the partial remainder is required. This process saves the step of adding the divisor if $A$ is less than $B$ but it requires special control logic to remember the previous result. The first time the dividend is shifted, $B$ must be subtracted. Also, if the last bit of the quotient is 0, the partial remainder must be restored to obtain the correct final remainder.

## 9-6 PROCESSOR CONFIGURATION

The part of a digital computer devoted to processing arithmetic operations is identified as an arithmetic processor. A stand-alone arithmetic processor is called a calculator. The difference between an electronic calculator and a digital computer lies in their overall capability: a calculator is a dedicated device that performs arithmetic operations only; a general purpose computer can perform other data processing functions as well. Input data and arithmetic operations in a calculator are entered through a keyboard and output data are displayed visually. Some expensive calculators come close to resembling a digital computer by having printing capabilities and programmable facilities, but all programs are concerned with arithmetic functions. Calculators use decimal arithmetic with floating-point numbers to facilitate the communication with the user. General purpose computers may, sometimes, have hardware for processing decimal floating-point numbers. However, if a computer has hardware for fixed-point binary arithmetic operations only, it can be programmed to do calculations with floating-point binary or decimal numbers.

This section introduces a computer configuration for processing fixed-point arithmetic operations. In the next section we will show a method for the design of a hard-wired control for this processor. Section 9-8 demonstrates a procedure for the design of a microprogram controlled arithmetic processor. Although the microprogrammed version is used to describe a binary calculator, it can be easily applied to a general purpose computer.

The position of the arithmetic processor among other computer components is shown in the block diagram of Fig. 9-12. The arithmetic processor consists of four registers: $BR$, $AC$, $QR$, and $SC$, and three flip-flops: $E$, $AVF$, and $DVF$. It also has combinational circuits for implementing various micro-operations. The $AC$ register consists of 16 bits with the high-order bit designated by $A_s$ and the other 15 bits by $A$. Thus, $A_s$ and $A$ together constitute the $AC$. Similarly, the memory buffer register $BR$ is subdivided into $B_s$ and $B$ and register $QR$ into $Q_s$ and $Q$. A 16-bit operand read from memory is transferred into $BR$ with the high-order bit going to $B_s$ and the other 15 bits to $B$. A word in $BR$ is stored in memory from $B_s$ (one bit) and $B$ (15 bits). Transfers between $BR$ and $AC$ or $QR$ are 16-bit transfers and include both the magnitude and sign.

The other components of the computer are: a memory unit; a program counter $PC$; an address register $MAR$; and an operation register $OPR$ to hold the operation code of the instruction. The hard-wired control consists of two

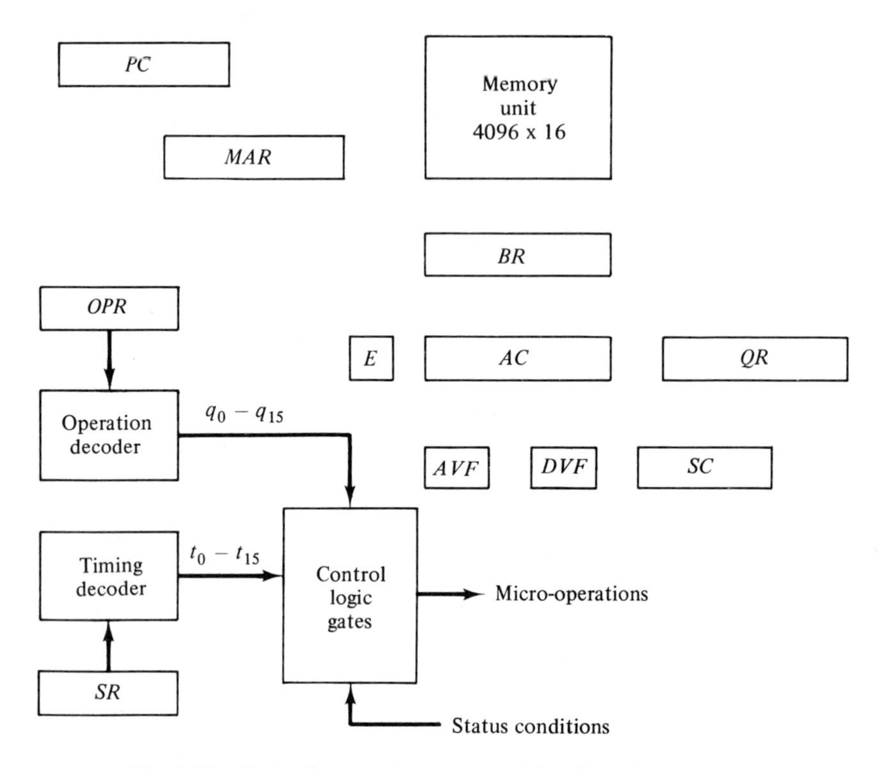


**Fig. 9-12** Block diagram of computer with arithmetic processor.

decoders, control logic gates and a sequence register *SR*. The design of the control unit is discussed in the next section.

The instruction format is chosen to be as simple as possible in order not to complicate the example. It consists of four bits for the operation code and 12 bits for the address. This computer uses the same instructions as the basic computer of Chap. 5 with additional arithmetic instructions. The 16 instructions are listed in Table 9-3. The symbol *m* designates a 12-bit address field. *M* is the memory word specified by the address *m*. The first four instructions are arithmetic instructions for fixed-point signed-magnitude binary numbers. The next four are needed for transfer of operands to and from memory and processor registers. The next two are branch instructions to special routines that take care of overflow conditions. The last six instructions are the same as the basic computer of Chap. 5.

The operands must be available in processor registers before an arithmetic instruction is executed. The following instructions add two operands from memory and transfer the result back to memory:

| | |
|---|---|
| LDA X | Transfer augend to *AC* |
| ADD Y | Transfer addend to *BR* and add to *AC* |

**Table 9-3** *Computer instructions*

| *Symbol* | *Instruction Code* | *Discription* | *Function* |
|---|---|---|---|
| ADD | 0000 $m$ | Add | $AC \leftarrow AC + M$ |
| SUB | 0001 $m$ | Subtract | $AC \leftarrow AC - M$ |
| MUL | 0010 $m$ | Multiply | $AC\&QR \leftarrow QR * M$ |
| DIV | 0011 $m$ | Divide | $QR \leftarrow AC\&QR/M$, $AC \leftarrow$ remainder |
| LDA | 0100 $m$ | Load $AC$ | $AC \leftarrow M$ |
| LDQ | 0101 $m$ | Load $QR$ | $QR \leftarrow M$ |
| STA | 0110 $m$ | Store $AC$ | $M \leftarrow AC$ |
| STQ | 0111 $m$ | Store $QR$ | $M \leftarrow QR$ |
| BAF | 1000 $m$ | Branch on $AVF$ | If $(AVF = 1)$ then $(PC \leftarrow m)$ |
| BDF | 1001 $m$ | Branch on $DVF$ | If $(DVF = 1)$ then $(PC \leftarrow m)$ |
| AND | 1010 $m$ | Logical AND | $AC \leftarrow AC \wedge M$ |
| ISZ | 1011 $m$ | Increment and skip if 0 | $M \leftarrow M + 1$, if $(M + 1 = 0)$ then $(PC \leftarrow PC + 1)$ |
| BSA | 1100 $m$ | Branch and save address | $M \leftarrow PC$, $PC \leftarrow m + 1$ |
| BUN | 1101 $m$ | Branch unconditionally | $PC \leftarrow m$ |
| | 1110 | Register reference instructions | |
| | 1111 | Input-output instructions | |

| | |
|---|---|
| STA Z | Transfer result back to memory |
| BAF AF | Branch to routine $AF$ if overflow occurs |

Operand transfers to and from registers and memory are 16-bit transfers and include both sign and magnitude. Although the processor manipulates the signs and magnitudes separately, the initial operands and final results are always transferred as signed numbers with the most significant bit representing the sign and the other 15 bits representing the magnitude.

To subtract two numbers stored in memory and transfer the result back to memory we need the following instructions:

| | | |
|---|---|---|
| LDA | X | Transfer minuend to $AC$ |
| SUB | Y | Transfer subtrahend to $BR$ and subtract from $AC$ |
| STA | Z | Store result back in memory |
| BAF | AF | Branch to a program that takes care of overflow |

In this example, and all others listed here, it is assumed that the operands are in memory. If the augend in the previous example or the minuend in this example is already in the $AC$ (from a previous operation), it is not necessary to use the instructions that load them into the $AC$.

After two numbers are multiplied, the product is of double length with both $A_s$ and $Q_s$ holding the sign, and $A$ and $Q$ holding the magnitude. The double length product in *AC* and *QR* must be stored in memory in two words. The following is a program that multiplies two operands and stores their product in memory:

```
LDQ   X    Transfer multiplier to QR
MUL   Y    Transfer multiplicand to BR and multiply
STA   Z1   Store most significant bits of product
STQ   Z2   Store least significant bits of product
```

To divide two numbers, we must transfer the double length dividend into *AC* and *QR* and then store both the quotient from *QR* and the remainder from *AC*:

```
LDA   X1   Transfer high-order bits of dividend to AC
LDQ   X2   Transfer low-order bits of dividend to QR
DIV   Y    Transfer divisor to BR and divide
BDF   DF   Branch to DF if overflow occurs
STQ   ZQ   Store quotient in memory
STA   ZR   Store remainder in memory
```

If the dividend has only one memory word, it must be placed in *QR* and the *AC* must be cleared. The sign of the dividend must be placed in the sign bit of the *AC*. This can be accomplished by the following instructions:

```
        LDQ   X       Transfer dividend to QR
        LDA   X       Transfer dividend to AC
        AND   MASK    Mask the magnitude but leave the sign
        DIV   Y       Transfer divisor to BR and divide
         .
         .
         .
MASK,   HEX   8000    Operand for clearing magnitude of AC
```

The mask operand does not change the sign bit in the high-order position of the *AC* but clears the magnitude bits to all zeros.

## 9-7 DESIGN OF CONTROL

The basic computer of Chap. 5 is controlled by four cycles with four timing sequences in each cycle. A short timing sequence in the execute cycle may not be sufficient for executing complicated operations such as the arithmetic operations considered here. The longest sequence of timing signals for a computer is determined from the instruction with the most time-consuming sequence of micro-operations. Moreover, it is not mandatory for the control to distinguish between the fetch and execute cycles. The timing signals for executing the instruction can follow the fetch micro-operations as soon as they are completed. A careful investigation reveals that the most time-consuming instruction in the arithmetic processor requires more than eight but less than sixteen timing sequences to fetch the instruction from memory and execute it.

The control unit of the arithmetic processor employs a sequence generator *SR* as shown in Fig. 9-12. This register has four flip-flops that can be in any one of 16 possible states. The timing decoder attached to this register provides outputs for 16 distinct timing signals. The sequence register functions as a binary counter most of the time to produce an orderly numerical sequence of timing signals. Once in awhile, the content of *SR* is forced out of sequence by a parallel transfer of a constant value. Moreover, *SR* is cleared as soon as the execution of an instruction is completed causing a return to the beginning of the fetch cycle. In this manner, the control has a maximum of 16 timing signals $t_0$–$t_{15}$ for each instruction, but the normal sequence can be altered or terminated at any time.

The instruction fetch cycle is common to all instructions and is activated during timing sequences $t_0$–$t_2$ as shown in Table 9-4. Note that *SR* is incre-

**Table 9-4** *Register transfer statements for fetch cycle*

$$
\begin{aligned}
t_0&: MAR \leftarrow PC, && && SR \leftarrow SR + 1\\
t_1&: BR \leftarrow M, && PC \leftarrow PC + 1, && SR \leftarrow SR + 1\\
t_2&: MAR \leftarrow BR(AD), && OPR \leftarrow BR(OP), && SR \leftarrow SR + 1
\end{aligned}
$$

mented at the same time that the other micro-operations are executed and causes control to go to the next timing sequence. After time $t_2$, the operation code of the instruction is available in *OPR*. This register is decoded to provide 16 outputs $q_0$–$q_{15}$, one for each of the operation codes in the computer.

Each instruction has its own set of control gates that generate the control functions for its micro-operations. Each control function receives one input from the operation decoder (to specify the operation), one input from the timing decoder (to specify the timing sequence) and, sometimes, inputs from other registers in the processor (to specify a status condition). The gates generate the control functions for the micro-operations and for *SR* as well. The control functions are determined from the list of register transfer statements that are written for each instruction.

The list of all control functions for the computer is too lengthy and will not be undertaken here. A few examples will be presented to show how they can be derived.

The register transfer statements for the ADD and SUB instructions are listed in Table 9-5. The operations decoded are either $q_0$ for ADD or $q_1$ for

**Table 9-5** *Register transfer statements for ADD and SUB*

| | | | |
|---|---|---|---|
| $(q_0 + q_1)t_3$: | $BR \leftarrow M$, | $SR \leftarrow SR + 1$ | Read operand |
| $(x'q_0 + xq_1)t_4$:† | | $SR \leftarrow SR + 1$ | Go to $t_5$ to add |
| $(xq_0 + x'q_1)t_4$: | | $SR \leftarrow 0111$ | Go to $t_7$ to subtract |
| $(q_0 + q_1)t_5$: | $EA \leftarrow A + B$, | $SR \leftarrow SR + 1$ | Add magnitudes |
| $(q_0 + q_1)t_6$: | $AVF \leftarrow E$, | $SR \leftarrow 0$ | Set overflow and return |
| $(q_0 + q_1)t_7$: | $EA \leftarrow A + \bar{B} + 1$, $AVF \leftarrow 0$, | $SR \leftarrow SR + 1$ | Subtract magnitudes |
| $E(q_0 + q_1)t_8$: | If $(A = 0)$ then $(A_s \leftarrow 0)$, | $SR \leftarrow 0$ | Set sign and return |
| $E'(q_0 + q_1)t_8$: | $A \leftarrow \bar{A}$, | $SR \leftarrow SR + 1$ | Complement $A$ |
| $(q_0 + q_1)t_9$: | $A \leftarrow A + 1$, $A_s \leftarrow \bar{A}_s$, | $SR \leftarrow 0$ | Increment $A$ and return |

†$x = A_s \oplus B_s$

SUB. The signs of the two operands are compared by an exclusive-OR gate whose function is $x = A_s \oplus B_s$. The conditions for adding or subtracting the magnitudes is determined by the control functions at time $t_4$. $SR$ is incremented if the magnitudes are to be added and is set to a constant value of 7 (binary 0111) if the magnitudes are to be subtracted. In this way, the present control function can determine the next timing sequence. The control functions at time $t_4$ implement the conditional transfers specified at the beginning of the flow chart of Fig. 9-4. Following the flow chart one can develop the register transfer statements for the execution of the two instructions.

Incrementing $SR$ at $t_4$ gives $t_5$ as the next timing sequence. The contol functions at $t_5$ and $t_6$ add the two magnitudes and set the add-overflow flip-flop $AVF$. The execution of the instruction is completed at $t_6$ and therefore, $SR$ is set to 0. The next timing sequence becomes $t_0$ and control returns to the beginning of the fetch cycle. If control moved from $t_4$ to $t_7$, the magnitudes are subtracted during time $t_7$, $t_8$, and $t_9$. Control returns back to the beginning of the fetch cycle after $SR$ is set to 0.

Table 9-6 lists the register transfer statements needed to execute the multiply operation. The steps follow the algorithm developed in Fig. 9-7. The initialization is done during $t_4$. A partial product is formed during $t_5$ and $t_6$ and the sequence counter $SC$ is decremented. At $t_6$ control goes back to $t_5$ if

**Table 9-6** *Register transfer statements for MUL*

| | |
|---|---|
| $q_2t_3$: | $BR \leftarrow M$, $SR \leftarrow SR + 1$ |
| $q_2t_4$: | $A_s \leftarrow Q_s \oplus B_s$, $Q_s \leftarrow Q_s \oplus B_s$, $A \leftarrow 0$, $E \leftarrow 0$, $SC \leftarrow 15$, $SR \leftarrow SR + 1$ |
| $Q_nq_2t_5$: | $EA \leftarrow A + B$ |
| $q_2t_5$: | $SC \leftarrow SC - 1$, $SR \leftarrow SR + 1$ |
| $q_2t_6$: | shr $EAQ$, if $(SC = 0)$ then $(SR \leftarrow 0)$, if $(SC \neq 0)$ then $(SR \leftarrow 0101)$ |

$SC \neq 0$ to form a new partial product. The execution terminates and $SR$ is set to 0 when $SC = 0$.

The register transfer statements for the other 14 instructions of the computer may be derived in a similar manner. The set of control functions thus obtained gives the Boolean functions for the gates in the control logic network. All those control functions that activate an identical micro-operation are ORed together and the output is applied to the corresponding register. It is obvious that this type of control requires a multitude of gates forming a most irregular logic network. Because of its irregular pattern, the hard-wired control is said to have "random logic." Irregular logic is usually implemented with SSI (small-scale integration), low-density integrated circuits.

## 9-8 MICROPROGRAMMED CALCULATOR

Chapter 8 presents a procedure for implementing a microprogrammed control unit in a digital computer. It was also mentioned there that the microprogram concept is not unique to a digital computer. Any special purpose digital system can be microprogrammed for a dedicated application. An electronic calculator is a special-purpose digital system controlled by a microprogram and devoted to the calculation of arithmetic functions. The microprogram controls the arithmetic operations as well as the input data and arithmetic functions entered through the keyboard. In this section we discuss the microprogram aspect of calculators and present a few microprogram routines. The arithmetic routines for the calculator are applicable for use in a digital computer and they can be easily incorporated into the control memory of a general-purpose computer.

A commercial calculator has a keyboard with keys for the ten decimal digits and a decimal point, and for a certain number of arithmetic operations and functions. Signed decimal numbers are displayed with a moving decimal point indicator. When the number of digits exceeds the capacity of the display, some calculators display an overflow symbol and others change the display to a floating-point representation. Internally, the calculator has one or more LSI circuits commonly referred to as *chips*. Within the chips are the electronic circuits for processor registers, a decimal arithmetic unit, and a ROM control memory. In order to manipulate decimal numbers with decimal points, the processor must employ floating-point data and the control memory must be microprogrammed to implement decimal floating-point arithmetic operations.

A discussion of the internal operation of commercial calculators would take us too far afield. We may simplify the presentation by considering instead a binary calculator that performs arithmetic operations with fixed-point binary numbers. Obviously, this is not a practical device, but because it is a simplified version, the basic functions of a microprogrammed calculator will be easier to demonstrate. The extension of the principle to a practical decimal calculator should be apparent from this example and after studying the decimal algorithms in the next chapter.

### *Calculator Configuration*

The arithmetic processor for the binary calculator is similar to the one used for the computer in the previous section. As shown in the block diagram of Fig. 9-13, the arithmetic processor consists of registers *BR*, *AC*, *QR*, *SC*, and flip-flops *E*, *AVF*, *DVF* as before. The keyboard is very simple and consists of eight keys. Since the calculator processes binary numbers in fixed-point integer representation, data entry consists of the digits 0 and 1 only (instead of the ten decimal digits and decimal point in a commercial calculator). There is a key for each of the four arithmetic operations. The "equals" key functions as a command for executing and displaying the result of the calculation. The key marked C is used for clearing the display.

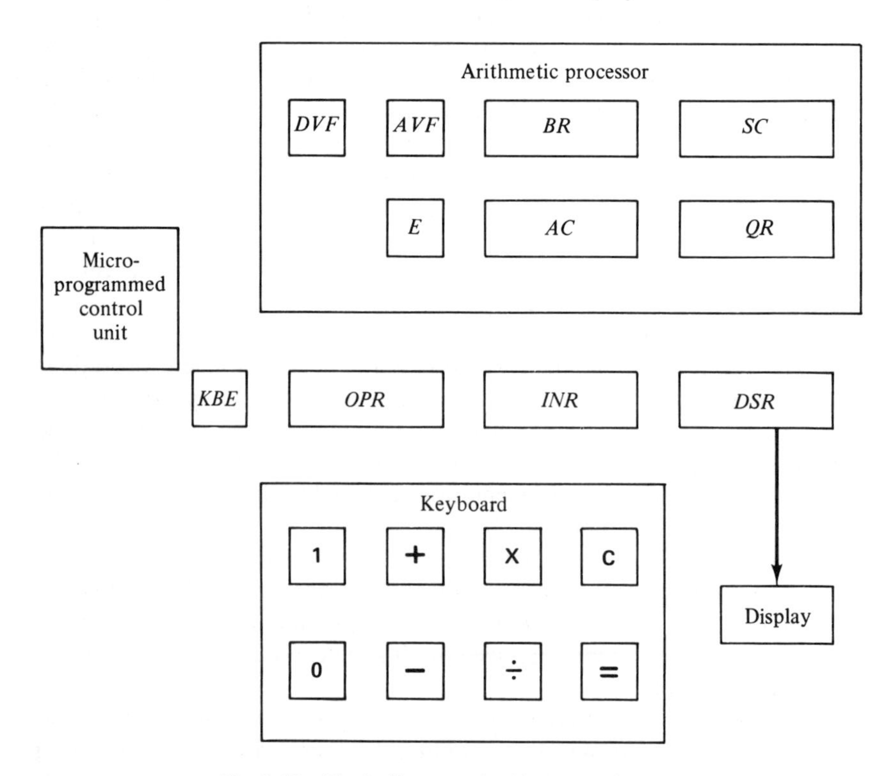


**Fig. 9-13** Block diagram of a binary calculator.

Four registers are needed for communicating with the keyboard and display:

| | |
|---|---|
| *DSR* | A display register of 16 bits |
| *INR* | An input register of 3 bits |
| *OPR* | An operation register of 3 bits |
| *KBE* | A keyboard entry flip-flop of 1 bit |

*DSR* holds the binary number presently being displayed. *INR* holds a 3-bit code of the last item entered from the keyboard. The binary code for each item is listed in Table 9-7. The conversion of a keyboard entry to its 3-bit code representation in *INR* is accomplished by means of a combinational circuit. The *KBE* flip-flop is set to 1 every time a key is depressed. It is cleared to 0 after the keyboard entry in *INR* is processed by the control. *OPR* holds the binary code of the last operation entered. This code is the same as the one used for *INR*.

**Table 9-7** *Bit assignment for INR and OPR*

| *Key Depressed* | *Content of INR or OPR* |
|---|---|
| C | 000 |
| + | 001 |
| − | 010 |
| × | 011 |
| ÷ | 100 |
| = | 101 |
| 0 | 110 |
| 1 | 111 |

The numbers entered from the keyboard are first displayed in *DSR*. When an operation is executed, the numbers are transferred to processor registers. Results are transferred back to *DSR* for display. The registers in the arithmetic processor that hold the various operands are listed in Table 9-8. The registers employed are as specified by the algorithms developed in previous sections except that single precision (16 bits) is used. For multiplication, the result may be up to 31 bits and sign but only the least 15 significant bits and the sign are displayed. If the product exceeds 16 bits, an overflow symbol is displayed. The dividend has only 16 bits when entered from the keyboard and is placed in *QR*. The *AC* must be cleared at the beginning of the division operation. This must be done because the calculator cannot enter or display numbers that exceed 16 bits.

**Table 9-8** *Registers for operands and results*

| | First Operand | | Second Operand | | Answer | |
|---|---|---|---|---|---|---|
| *Operation* | *Register* | *Operand* | *Register* | *Operand* | *Register* | *Result* |
| + | *AC* | Augend | *BR* | Addend | *AC* | Sum |
| − | *AC* | Minuend | *BR* | Subtrahend | *AC* | Difference |
| × | *QR* | Multiplier | *BR* | Multiplicand | *QR* | Product |
| ÷ | *QR* | Dividend | *BR* | Divisor | *QR* | Quotient |

### *Keyboard Entry*

A keyboard entry sets *KBE* to 1 and transfers a binary code into *INR*. The control unit processes each entry as shown in Table 9-9. Pressing the C key

**Table 9-9** *Micro-operations for keyboard entry*

| *Key Depressed* | *Micro-Operations* |
|---|---|
| C | $DSR \leftarrow 0$ |
| + *or* − | $OPR \leftarrow INR$, $AC \leftarrow DSR$, $DSR \leftarrow 0$ |
| × *or* ÷ | $OPR \leftarrow INR$, $QR \leftarrow DSR$, $AC \leftarrow 0$, $DSR \leftarrow 0$ |
| = | $BR \leftarrow DSR$, perform operation and display result |
| 0 *or* 1 | shl *DSR*, $DSR(16) \leftarrow INR(3)$ |

clears the display register. When one of the operation keys is depressed, the operation code entered in *INR* is transferred to *OPR*. For plus and minus, the number in *DSR* is transferred to the *AC*. For times and divide, the number in *DSR* is transferred to *QR*, and the *AC* is cleared. *DSR* is cleared to prepare it for the next data entry. Depressing the equals key causes a transfer of the binary number from *DSR* to *BR* and the last operation stored in *OPR* is then executed. The result of the operation is transferred to *DSR* for display. Binary digits entered through the keyboard are shifted into *DSR* one at a time. This is done by shifting *DSR* left and entering the least significant bit in *INR* into the least significant bit of *DSR*. Depressing the 0 or 1 key at the beginning of data entry will insert a sign bit into the high-order position of *DSR*. If more than 16 bits are entered, the display shows an overflow symbol and further entry is inhibited.

The keyboard entry must follow the following sequence.

1. Depress C to clear display.
2. Enter first operand.

3. Depress an operation key.
4. Enter second operand.
5. Depress the equals key.

For example, to multiply 9 by 6 the keyboard entry would be:

$$C\ 1001 \times 110 =$$

and the result $54 = (110110)_2$ will be transferred to *DSR* and displayed. For chain operations, the user will then enter a new operation followed by the next operand. For example, to add 8 to 54 which is presently displayed, the user will enter:

$$+\ 1000 =$$

and binary 62 will be displayed.

The first operand in *DSR* may come from the keyboard (after Clear) or from the result of a previous operation (after =). When an operation key is depressed, the number in *DSR* is taken as the first operand and is transferred to *AC* (if + or −) or to *QR* (if × or ÷). When the equals key is depressed, the number in *DSR* is taken as the second operand and is transferred to *BR*. The operation is executed and displayed. If an overflow occurs in any calculation, the overflow flip-flop sets the overflow symbol in the display.

### *The Control Unit*

The various micro-operations and branch decisions are controlled by a microprogram residing in a read-only memory. The microprogram must include microinstructions for the execution of arithmetic operations as well as for controlling the flow of information from keyboard and display. A microprogram must be capable of sequencing its own next address and specifying the sequence of micro-operations in the system. A multiple control word format that provides these capabilities is shown in Table 9-10. We are assuming a control memory of 128 words, 8 bits per word. If bit 1 of the word is a 1, the other seven bits are taken as the address for an uncondi-

**Table 9-10** *Control word format for binary calculator*

| 1 2 3 4 5 6 7 8 | 8 bits of control word |
|---|---|
| 1 X X X X X X X | Branch to address XXXXXXX |
| 0 1 Y Y Y Y Y Y | Skip next microinstruction if condition YYYYYY is met |
| 0 0 Z Z Z Z Z Z | Perform micro-operation specified by ZZZZZZ |

tional *branch* microinstruction. If bit 1 of the word is 0, bit 2 specifies either a *skip* microinstruction or a *micro-operation* microinstruction. In both cases, bits 3 to 8 are encoded to give up to 64 different conditions. The skip microinstruction is similar to a skip instruction in a computer, but is implemented differently. In a skip instruction, the program counter is incremented to cause a skip of the next instruction. The skip microinstruction in control memory is accomplished by inhibiting all outputs from ROM on the next clock pulse (if the condition is met). This causes the next microinstruction to be ignored and have no effect.

A partial encoding of the skip microinstructions is shown in Table 9-11.

**Table 9-11** *Partial encoding of skip microinstructions*

| *Control Word* | *Skip Next Microinstruction If:* |
|---|---|
| 01 000001 | $E = 1$ |
| 01 000010 | $E = 0$ |
| 01 000011 | $A_s \oplus B_s = 0$ |
| 01 000100 | $A \neq 0$ |
| 01 000101 | $SC = 0$ |
| 01 000110 | $Q_n = 0$ |
| 01 000111 | $KBE = 1$ |
| 01 001000 | $INR \neq 000$ |
| 01 001111 | $INR \neq 111$ |
| 01 010001 | $OPR \neq 001$ |
| 01 010100 | $OPR \neq 100$ |

The last 6 bits of the control word can be encoded to specify 64 different conditions. The conditions used in the succeeding microprogram examples have been listed in the table but other conditions can be added to the list. A table for encoding the 64 micro-operations is not provided but the reader can very easily formulate such a table.

A block diagram of the control memory and its associated logic is shown in Fig. 9-14. The skip microinstruction is applied to a multiplexer to select one of 64 conditions. If the condition is met (if it is equal to 1) the output of the multiplexer is 1, so on the next clock pulse the flip-flop is set making $Q' = 0$ and all microinstructions are disabled causing the next microinstruction to be inhibited during the next clock pulse. The same next clock pulse clears the flip-flop since the output of the multiplexer is 0. The flip-flop remains cleared (with $Q' = 1$) at all times except during one clock pulse interval after the skip microinstruction is executed and only if the specified condition has been met. The ROM address register is incremented with every clock pulse except during a branch condition, provided it is enabled by the flip-flop. When

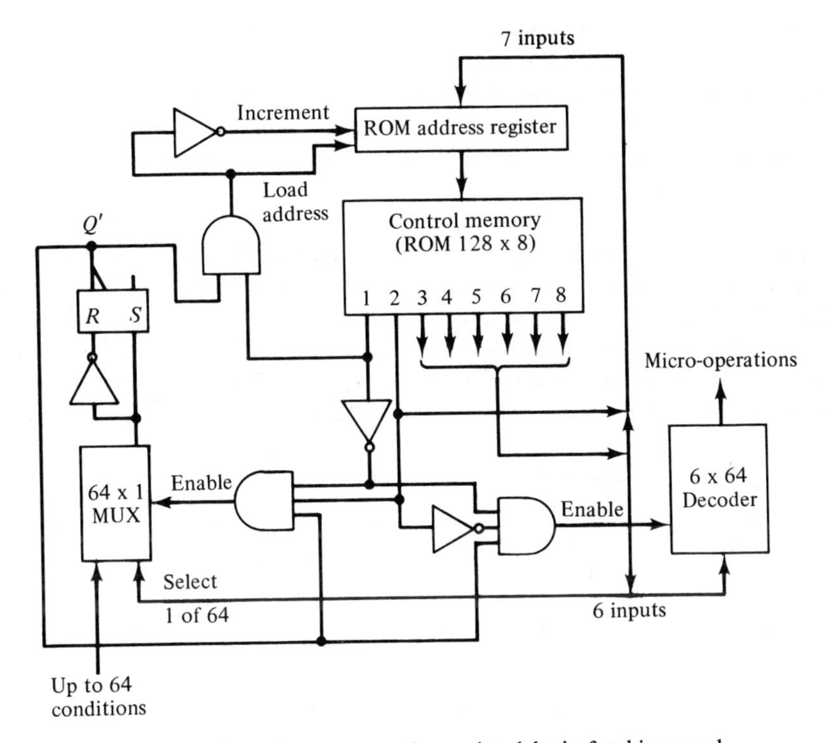


**Fig. 9-14** Control memory and associated logic for binary calculator.

ROM bits 1 and 2 are both 0 and $Q' = 1$, a 6 by 64 decoder is enabled to provide one of 64 different micro-operations.

### *The Microprogram*

We are now ready to write the microprogram for the calculator. To facilitate the writing of the microprogram we will employ symbolic names for the microinstructions. Each line of microcode may have a symbolic address in a label field. The second field in the microcode must contain a symbol which specifies one of the following types of microinstructions:

*branch to* address

*skip if* condition

*micro-operation*

The *branch to* symbol is translated to an 8-bit control word 1XXXXXXX where the bits designated by X specify a binary address. The symbolic address after *branch to* must also occur in the label field to specify its binary value. A *skip if* symbol designates a skip microinstruction and is translated to an 8-bit word 01YYYYYY where the bits designated by Y are determined from Table 9-11 for each specified condition. A *micro-operation* microinstruction is specified by a register transfer statement and is translated into binary as 00ZZZZZZ where the bits designated by Z must be encoded in some convenient manner.

When power is turned on in the binary calculator, the display register *DSR* and the operation register *OPR* are cleared. Control branches to a routine that scans the keyboard for an entry. This routine, called KBRD, is listed in Table 9-12. The first micro-instruction clears *KBE* to 0. Remember that every time a key is depressed, *KBE* is set to 1 and the 3-bit code specified in Table 9-7 enters the input register *INR*. The second microinstruction checks if $KBE = 1$, and if not, control returns to KD to check *KBE* again. If *KBE*

**Table 9-12** *Microprogram for keyboard entry*

| | | |
|---|---|---|
| KBRD | $KBE \leftarrow 0$ | Clear *KBE* |
| KD | Skip if $KBE = 1$ | Check keyboard entry |
| | branch to KD | $KBE = 0$, go to check again |
| | Skip if $INR \neq 000$ | $KBE = 1$, check entry |
| | Branch to CLEAR | Go to service C entry |
| | Skip if $INR \neq 001$ | |
| | Branch to POM | Go to service "plus" entry |
| | Skip if $INR \neq 010$ | |
| | Branch to POM | Go to service "minus" entry |
| | Skip if $INR \neq 011$ | |
| | Branch to TOD | Go to service "times" entry |
| | Skip if $INR \neq 100$ | |
| | Branch to TOD | Go to service "divide" entry |
| | Skip if $INR \neq 101$ | |
| | Branch to EQUALS | Go to service an "equals" entry |
| | Branch to ONZ | Go to service a numeric entry |
| CLEAR | $DSR \leftarrow 0$ | |
| | Branch to KBRD | |
| POM | $OPR \leftarrow INR$ | |
| | $AC \leftarrow DSR$ | |
| | $DSR \leftarrow 0$ | |
| | Branch to KBRD | |
| TOD | $OPR \leftarrow INR$ | |
| | $QR \leftarrow DSR$ | |
| | $AC \leftarrow 0$ | |
| | $DSR \leftarrow 0$ | |
| | Branch to KBRD | |
| ONZ | shl *DSR* | |
| | $DSR(16) \leftarrow INR(3)$ | |
| | Branch to KBRD | |

= 1, the next microinstruction is skipped and *INR* is scanned for the keyboard entry. If key C was depressed, control branches to routine CLEAR. If the plus or minus keys are depressed, control branches to routine POM. The KBRD routine continues to scan all eight entries and branches to one of five routines.

Four of the routines that process the keyboard entry are listed next. The micro-operations for each routine are as specified in Table 9-9. The CLEAR routine clears the display. POM (Plus Or Minus) transfers the first operand from *DSR* to *AC*. TOD (Times Or Divide) transfers the first operand from *DSR* to *QR* and clears the *AC*. In each case, the 3-bit code from *INR* is transferred to *OPR*. ONZ (One or Zero) causes a left shift of *DSR* and a transfer of the input bit from *INR* into the least significant position of *DSR*. When the processing of the keyboard is terminated, control goes back to the KBRD routine to process the next entry.

Assume now that two binary operands have been entered, together with an operation in between. Depressing the equals key should cause the execution of the operation and display of the result. This routine, called EQUALS, is listed in Table 9-13. The first microinstruction is a micro-operation that

**Table 9-13** *Microprogram for routine EQUALS*

| | | |
|---|---|---|
| EQUALS | $BR \leftarrow DSR$ | Transfer second operand to *BR* |
| | Skip if $OPR \neq 001$ | Check if plus operation |
| | Branch to ADD | Go to ADD routine |
| | Skip if $OPR \neq 010$ | Check if minus operation |
| | Branch to SUB | Go to SUB routine |
| | Skip if $OPR \neq 011$ | Check if times operation |
| | Branch to MUL | Go to MUL routine |
| | Skip if $OPR \neq 100$ | Check if divide operation |
| | Branch to DIV | Go to DIV routine |
| | $DSR \leftarrow 0$ | Clear display |
| | Branch to KBRD | Branch to scan keyboard |

transfers the second operand from *DSR* into *BR*. The routine then scans the *OPR* register for the operation and branches to one of four arithmetic routines. If *OPR* holds an unacceptable code, *DSR* is cleared and no operation is executed.

The four arithmetic routines ADD, SUB, MUL, and DIV are derived from the algorithms for addition, subtraction, multiplication, and division given in flow chart form in previous sections. The ADD and SUB routines are listed in Table 9-14; the other two are left for exercises. The microprogram follows the algorithm of Fig. 9-4 and should be self-explanatory. Note that at

**Table 9-14** *Microprogram routine for ADD and SUB*

| | | |
|---|---|---|
| ADD | Skip if $A_s \oplus B_s = 0$ | Check signs |
| | branch to SB1 | Go to SB1 if signs unlike |
| AD1 | $EA \leftarrow A + B$ | Add magnitudes |
| | $AVF \leftarrow E$ | Set overflow |
| | Branch to COMP | Operation completed |
| SUB | Skip if $A_s \oplus B_s = 0$ | Check signs |
| | Branch to AD1 | Go to AD1 if signs unlike |
| SB1 | $EA \leftarrow A + \bar{B} + 1$ | Subtract magnitudes |
| | Skip if $E = 0$ | Check end-carry |
| | Branch to SB2 | Go to SB2 if $E = 1$ |
| | $A \leftarrow \bar{A}$ | Complement $A$ |
| | $A \leftarrow A + 1$ | Increment $A$ |
| | $A_s \leftarrow \bar{A}_s$ | Complement sign |
| | Branch to COMP | Operation completed |
| SB2 | Skip if $A \neq 0$ | Check for zero content |
| | $A_s \leftarrow 0$ | Make sign plus if $A = 0$ |
| COMP | $DSR \leftarrow AC$ | Display result |
| | $DSR(OVF) \leftarrow AVF$ | Display overflow |
| | Branch to KBRD | Go to scan keyboard |

the end, control returns to routine KBRD to scan the next entry from the keyboard.

## REFERENCES

1. Chu, Y., *Digital Computer Design Fundamentals*, New York: McGraw-Hill Book Co., 1962.
2. Chu, Y., *Computer Organization and Microprogramming*, Englewood Cliffs, N.J.: Prentice-Hall, Inc., 1972.
3. Gschwind, H. W., *Design of Digital Computers*, New York: Springer-Verlag, 1967.
4. Sobel, H. S., *Introduction to Digital Computer Design*, Reading, Mass.: Addison-Wesley Publishing Co., 1970.
5. Flores, I., *The Logic of Computer Arithmetic*, Englewood Cliffs. N.J.: Prentice-Hall, Inc., 1963.
6. Hill, F. J., and G. R. Peterson, *Digital Systems: Hardware Organization and Design*, New York: John Wiley & Sons, 1973.
7. Brown, E. L., *Digital Computer Design*, New York: Academic Press, 1963.
8. Richards, R. K., *Arithmetic Operations in Digital Computers*, Princeton, N.J.: D. Van-Nostrand Co., Inc., 1955.
9. Mano, M. M., *Computer Logic Design*, Englewood Cliffs, N.J.: Prentice-Hall, Inc., 1972.

## PROBLEMS

9-1 The magnitude comparator of Fig. 9-1 does not have the facility for expansion to numbers of more than 4 bits. Modify the circuit by using three more inputs that will indicate the status of any external lower-significance bits and show how the three inputs are to be connected internally to provide an expansion capability. Draw a block diagram showing how several modified 4-bit comparator packages can be connected to produce a comparator for numbers of eight or more bits.

9-2 Prove the comparison and subtraction relations listed in Table 9-1 for $A + \bar{B}$.

9-3 Consider the following pairs of unsigned *binary* numbers:
(a) $A = 25, B = 18$
(b) $A = 15, B = 22$
(c) $A = 20, B = 20$
For each pair, perform the operation $A + \bar{B}$ and justify the result obtained.

9-4 Derive an algorithm in flow-chart form for the addition and subtraction of fixed-point binary numbers in signed-magnitude representation with subtraction done by a parallel-subtractor ($EA \leftarrow A - B$). Show one stage of the adder-subtractor circuit with an add-subtract control (ASC).

9-5 The complementer shown in Fig. 9-2 is not needed if instead of performing $A + \bar{B} + 1$ we perform $B + \bar{A}$ ($B$ plus the 1's complement of $A$). Derive an algorithm in flow chart form for addition and subtraction of fixed-point binary numbers in signed-magnitude representation with the magnitudes subtracted by the two micro-operations $A \leftarrow \bar{A}$ and $EA \leftarrow A + B$.

9-6 Mark each individual path in the flow chart of Fig. 9-4 by a number and then indicate the overall path that the algorithm takes when the following numbers are computed. In each case give the value of $AVF$. The left-most bit denotes the sign. A seventh bit in the magnitude constitutes an overflow.
(a) 0 101101 + 0 011111
(b) 1 011111 + 1 101101
(c) 0 101101 − 0 011111
(d) 0 101101 − 0 101101
(e) 1 011111 − 0 101101

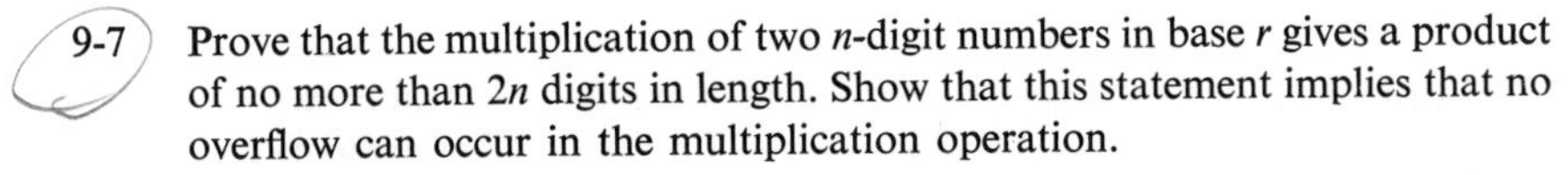

9-7 Prove that the multiplication of two $n$-digit numbers in base $r$ gives a product of no more than $2n$ digits in length. Show that this statement implies that no overflow can occur in the multiplication operation.

9-8 Show the contents of registers $A$, $E$, $Q$, and $SC$ (See Fig. 9-8) after each clock pulse during the process of multiplication of two binary numbers, 10111 (multiplicand) and 10011 (multiplier). The signs are not included.

9-9 Show the contents of registers $A$, $E$, $Q$, and $SC$ (See Fig. 9-10) after each clock pulse during the process of division of (a) 10100011 by 1011 and (b) 1111 by 0011.

9-10 Show that adding $B$ after the operation $A + \bar{B} + 1$ restores the original value of $A$. What should be done with the end-carry?

9-11 Why should the sign of the remainder after a division be the same as the sign of the dividend?

9-12 The algorithms for the four arithmetic operations presented in this chapter assume integer representation. List all changes necessary in the algorithms (if any) when the fixed-point numbers are assumed to be fractions.

9-13 In the comparison method of binary division the partial remainder in $EA$ is compared with the divisor in $B$ prior to the subtract operation. Then if $A \geq B$, $B$ is subtracted from $A$; but if $A < B$ nothing is done. Derive the flow chart for binary division by the comparison method.

9-14 Derive an algorithm in flow chart form for the non-restoring method of fixed-point binary division.

9-15 Derive an algorithm for evaluating the square root of a binary fixed-point number.

9-16 Write a program using the computer instructions of Table 9-3 that calculates: (a) $\frac{X*Y}{Z}$ (b) $\frac{X-Y}{Z}$ (c) $\frac{W+X}{Y-Z}$

9-17 From Tables 9-4, 9-5, and 9-6, determine the time it takes to process the ADD, SUB, and MUL instructions (including the fetch cycle). Assume that each timing signal is $T$ sec long.

9-18 Explain why the sequence counter $SC$ is decremented at time $t_5$ (Table 9-6) and not at time $t_6$ together with the shift as indicated in the flow chart of Fig. 9-7.

9-19 List the register transfer statements for the divide instruction (similar to Table 9-6). Determine the time it takes to process this instruction. Assume that each timing signal is $T$ sec long.

9-20 List the register transfer statements (similar to Table 9-5) for the following four instructions listed in Table 9-3: (a) LDA, (b) LDQ, (c) STA, and (d) STQ.

9-21 List the register transfer statements (similar to Table 9-5) for the following two instructions listed in Table 9-3: (a) ISZ; (b) BSA.

9-22 List all micro-operations executed in the $Q$ register. What kind of register is needed for $Q$?

9-23 List all the control functions that execute the micro-operations $EA \leftarrow A + B$ and $EA \leftarrow A + \bar{B} + 1$. Show how these control functions are to be connected to the $CC$ (complement control) and to the load function: $A \leftarrow S$, $E \leftarrow$ carry, shown in Fig. 9-2.

9-24 Show that the $BR$ register in the calculator of Sec. 9-8 can function as the display register and that $DSR$ can be removed. Modify the necessary micro-operations to take care of this change.

9-25 Design a combinational circuit that accepts eight inputs from the keyboard of Fig. 9-13 and generates a 3-bit code for *INR* as specified in Table 9-7. Generate also the signal for flip-flop *KBE.*

9-26 Write the microprogram for the MUL routine in symbolic form, for the calculator of Sec. 9-8.

9-27 Write the microprogram for the DIV routine in symbolic form, for the calculator of Sec. 9-8.

9-28 (a) List all micro-operations used in the examples of Table 9-14. Encode these micro-operations and assign a control word for each.

(b) Translate the symbolic microprogram of Table 9-14 to its equivalent binary form. Assume that the ROM location for ADD is binary 32 and that of KBRD, binary 0.

9-29 Formulate a microprogram control unit for the computer specified in Sec. 9-6 and write the microprogram for the fetch cycle and a few typical instructions.

# 10

# ARITHMETIC ALGORITHMS

## 10-1 INTRODUCTION

The design and analysis of digital systems is a complex undertaking especially since the development of IC technology. Many installations develop special software automation techniques to facilitate the design process. Design-automation programs are extensively used to perform such tasks as logic minimization and simplification; assignment of logic circuits from a list of register transfer statements; generation of wiring lists; simulation of the system prior to construction; and generation of documents for manufacturing and maintenance.

However, the specifications for a system and the development of algorithmic procedures for achieving the various data processing tasks cannot be automated and require the reasoning of a human designer. The most challenging and creative part of the design is the establishment of objectives and the formulation of algorithms and procedures for achieving these objectives. This task requires a considerable amount of experience and ingenuity on the part of the designer.

An algorithm is a procedure for obtaining a solution to a problem. A design algorithm is an algorithm for implementing the procedure with a given piece of equipment. The development of a design algorithm cannot start unless the designer has knowledge of two things. First, the problem at hand must be thoroughly understood and fully defined. Second, the designer must be familiar with the tools and methods available for expressing algorithms such as Boolean algebra, flow charts, register transfer languages and programming languages. The particular method employed would depend on the way the algorithm is to be expressed for its implementation.

Arithmetic algorithms are not difficult to define because we are all familiar with arithmetic operations. On the other hand, to define a procedure for an interface between a computer and an input device would be more complicated because one must be thoroughly familiar with the terminal behavior of the components. Nevertheless, the design procedure in each case is similar. Starting from the problem requirements and equipment availability, a solution must be found and an algorithm formed. The algorithm is stated by a finite number of well-defined procedural steps.

Because arithmetic algorithms are simpler to define, we use them here to demonstrate the procedures for deriving design algorithms. Other digital design algorithms will require a similar creative endeavor and reasoning ability. However, they may be more difficult to design because of the additional effort involved in formulating the exact specifications.

Many algorithms and especially arithmetic algorithms may be implemented in a computer by means of software, hardware, firmware, or a combination of the three methods. Some small computers have only one hardware arithmetic operation such as addition of two fixed-point binary numbers. The *add* instruction, together with *complement*, *shift*, and other instructions, is then used to generate subroutines for other arithmetic operations. These subroutines constitute a software implementation for the arithmetic operations. A subroutine occupies memory space for storing its instructions and the computational process is time-consuming because many instructions have to be executed for one operation. Software implementation saves hardware at the expense of memory space and time of execution.

An arithmetic operation is implemented by hardware if the computer has an instruction for the operation. In hardware implementation, the registers receive control signals from the control unit and generate a sequence of micro-operations for executing the operation specified by the instruction. Hardware implementation requires special circuits which would not be needed if the operation were to be implemented by software. On the other hand, hardware methods provide higher computation speed and occupy memory space for only one instruction.

The control unit in a hardware implementation may be either hard-wired or microprogrammed. In the latter case, the micro-operations are programmed in a control memory and constitute a microprogram for the instruction. Operations that are implemented by means of a microprogram are said to be implemented by firmware.

Algorithms for arithmetic operations are very important for the design of the arithmetic unit of a digital computer or for the development of arithmetic software routines. Some algorithms for fixed-point signed-2's complement data were presented in Sec. 3-2. Software implementation of arithmetic operations was discussed in Sec. 6-6. Algorithms for fixed-point signed-magnitude data were introduced in Chap. 9. This chapter presents arithmetic algorithms for the following types of data.

1. Fixed-point binary data in signed-2's complement representation.
2. Floating-point binary data.
3. Binary-coded decimal data.

The algorithms presented here assume the availability of a parallel arithmetic unit capable of performing addition and subtraction of numbers in parallel. The same algorithms can be easily adapted for serial operations. They can also be used as a basis for software subroutines or for a microprogram. The method by which an algorithm is implemented in a particular situation depends on the equipment availability and on the particular application.

## 10-2 ADDITION OVERFLOW

When two numbers in signed-magnitude representation are added, the overflow can be easily detected from the end-carry. When two numbers in signed-complement representation are added, the sign bit is treated as part of the number and the end-carry does not indicate an overflow. The algorithms for addition and subtraction of two binary fixed-point numbers with signed-2's complement representation are stated in Sec. 3-2, without including the condition for an overflow. The two algorithms are restated here and extended to include the detection of an overflow.

The addition of two binary numbers in signed-2's complement representation is done by adding the two numbers, including their sign bits and neglecting the end-carry. The subtraction is done by taking the 2's complement of the subtrahend (including the sign bit) and adding it to the minuend. An overflow cannot occur during the addition if one number is positive and the other is negative since adding a positive number to a negative number produces a number (positive or negative) which is smaller than the larger of the two original numbers.

An overflow may occur if the two numbers added are both positive or both negative. An overflow out of the magnitude part will tend to change the sign of the result. To see how this happens, consider the parallel addition of two numbers as shown in Fig. 10-1(a). The augend is in $AC$ and its sign is in the left-most bit position denoted by the symbol $A_s$. The addend is in $BR$ with its sign bit in $B_s$. A parallel-adder adds the two numbers, including their sign bits. The full-adder used for the sign bits has been separated from

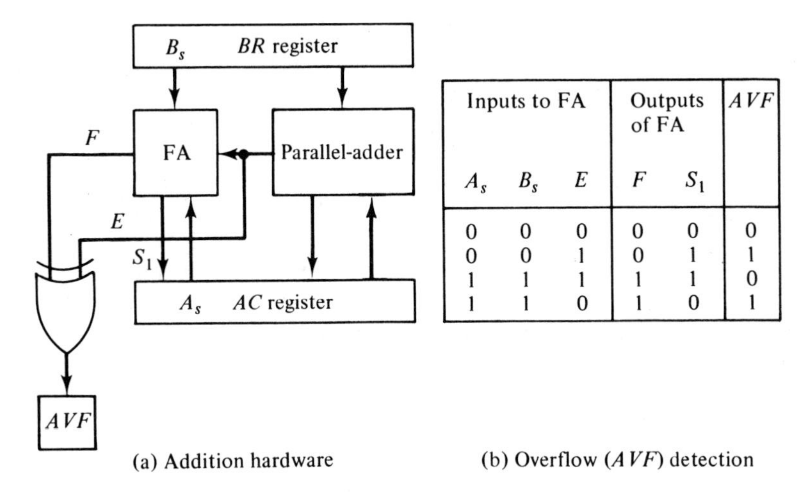


| Inputs to FA | | | Outputs of FA | | AVF |
|---|---|---|---|---|---|
| $A_s$ | $B_s$ | $E$ | $F$ | $S_1$ | |
| 0 | 0 | 0 | 0 | 0 | 0 |
| 0 | 0 | 1 | 0 | 1 | 1 |
| 1 | 1 | 1 | 1 | 1 | 0 |
| 1 | 1 | 0 | 1 | 0 | 1 |

(a) Addition hardware (b) Overflow (*AVF*) detection

**Fig. 10-1** Overflow detection in signed-2's complement numbers.

all other full-adders to show its effect. The carry into the sign position is designated by $E$ and the carry out of the sign position by $F$. The output of the full-adder in the sign position is designated by $S_1$.

Consider first the case when two positive numbers are added through the parallel-adder. Both $A_s$ and $B_s$ are equal to 0. The binary sum is positive, so the sign bit of the sum should be 0. If $E = 0$, the $S_1$ output of FA will produce a 0 as required. If there is an overflow out of the magnitude part, $E$ will be equal to 1. The $S_1$ output of FA will produce a 1 (minus) for the sign of the sum. The output-carry $F$ is 0 in any case. These results are tabulated in the first two rows of Fig. 10-1(b).

When the two numbers are negative, both $A_s$ and $B_s$ are equal to 1. The binary sum is negative so the sign bit of the result should be 1. If $E = 1$, the FA will produce a 1 output in $S_1$ and the sign of the result will be minus as required. The output-carry $F$ will also be a 1 in this case. However, if $E = 0$, the $S_1$ output will produce a 0 (plus) for the sign bit and output-carry $F$ will be a 1. This can occur only if there is an overflow during the addition of the two negative numbers because a 0 for negative numbers corresponds to a 1 for positive numbers.

From the above discussion we conclude that an overflow occurs if the two numbers are positive and the sum contains a negative sign or if the two numbers are negative and the sum contains a positive sign. In other words, an overflow produces an erroneous sign reversal. This is an algorithm that is commonly employed to detect an overflow by a software method. An overflow can be detected by a hardware method by means of an exclusive-OR gate with inputs $E$ and $F$ as shown in the diagram. From the table of Fig. 10-1(b) we note that an overflow occurs if $E \oplus F = 1$, i.e., when one carry is 1 and the other is 0. The output of the exclusive-OR gate is now applied to the overflow flip-flop *AVF*. *AVF* is set at the same time that the sum is transferred into the *AC*.

### *Addition and Subtraction with Signed-2's Complement Numbers*

The algorithm for adding and subtracting two binary numbers in signed-2's complement representation is shown in the flow chart of Fig. 10-2. The sum is obtained by adding the content of *AC* and *BR* (including the sign

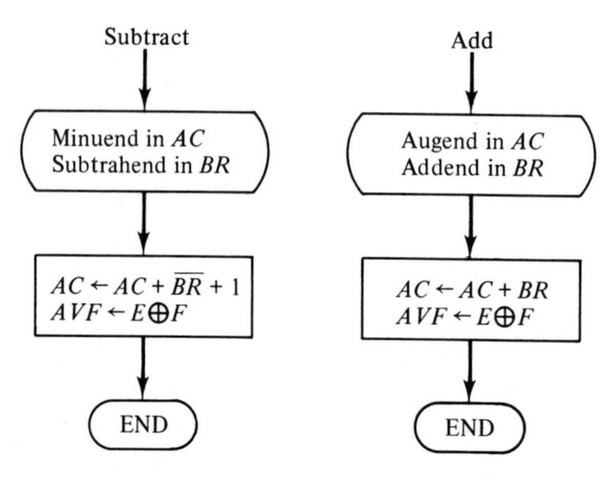


**Fig. 10-2** Algorithm for adding and subtracting numbers in signed-2's complement representation.

bits). *AVF* is set if there is an overflow. The subtraction operation is accomplished by adding the content of *AC* to the 2's complement of *BR*. Taking the 2's complement of *BR* has the effect of changing a positive number to negative or vice-versa. An overflow must be checked during this operation because the two numbers added could have the same sign. Obviously, if an overflow occurs, the *AC* has an erroneous result and something must be done if $AVF = 1$.

Comparing this algorithm with its signed-magnitude counterpart, we note that it is much simpler to add and subtract numbers if negative numbers are maintained in signed-2's complement representation. For this reason many computers adopt this representation over the more familiar signed-magnitude. However, we will see in the next section that multiplication and division have a reverse property. It is simpler to multiply and divide numbers in signed-magnitude than it is in signed-2's complement representation.

## 10-3 MULTIPLICATION AND DIVISION

In Chap. 9 we presented algorithms for multiplying and dividing binary numbers in signed-magnitude representation. This section presents some alternatives for multiplying and dividing fixed-point binary numbers.

### *Array Multiplier*

Checking the bits of the multiplier one at a time and forming partial products is a sequential operation that requires a sequence of add and shift micro-operations. The multiplication of two binary numbers can be done with one micro-operation by means of a combinational circuit that forms the product bits all at once. This is a fast way of multiplying two numbers since all it takes is the time for the signals to propagate through the gates that form the multiplication array. However, an array multiplier requires a large number of gates and for this reason it was not economical until the development of integrated circuits. Combinational circuit binary multipliers are available in IC packages.

To get an idea how an array binary multiplier is formed, consider the multiplication of two 2-bit numbers as shown in Fig. 10-3. The multiplicand bits are $b_1$ and $b_0$, the multiplier bits are $a_1$ and $a_0$ and the product is $c_3c_2c_1c_0$. The first partial product is formed by multiplying $a_0$ by $b_1b_0$. The multiplication of two bits such as $a_0$ and $b_0$ produces a 1 if both bits are 1; otherwise

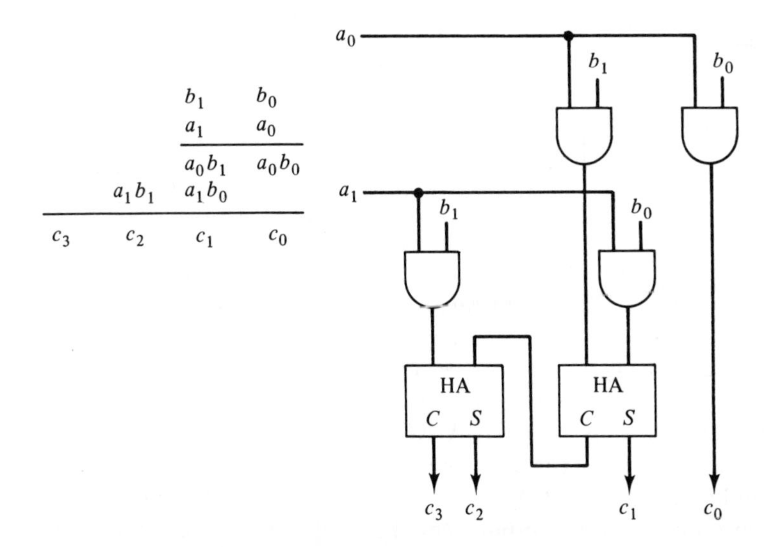


**Fig. 10-3** 2 by 2 binary array multiplier.

it produces a 0. This is identical to an AND operation and can be implemented by hardware with an AND gate. As shown in the diagram, the first partial product is formed by means of two AND gates. The second partial product is formed by multiplying $a_1$ by $b_1b_0$ and adding this product to the first partial product. This is achieved by two more AND gates and a parallel binary adder. The binary adder in this case consists of two half-adders (HA) since only two bits are added in each circuit. If more partial products are needed, we will have to use full-adder circuits to add two bits and a previous carry. Note that the least significant bit does not have to go through an adder since it is formed by the output of the first AND gate.

An array binary multiplier with more bits can be constructed in a similar fashion. A bit of the multiplier is ANDed with each bit of the multiplicand in as many levels as there are bits in the multiplier. The binary output in each level of AND gates is added in parallel to the partial product of the previous level to form a new partial product. For $j$ multiplier bits and $k$ multiplicand bits we need $jk$ AND gates and $(j - 1)$ parallel-adders.

The multiplication of two binary numbers in signed-magnitude representation can be implemented with one micro-operation as shown in Fig. 10-4.

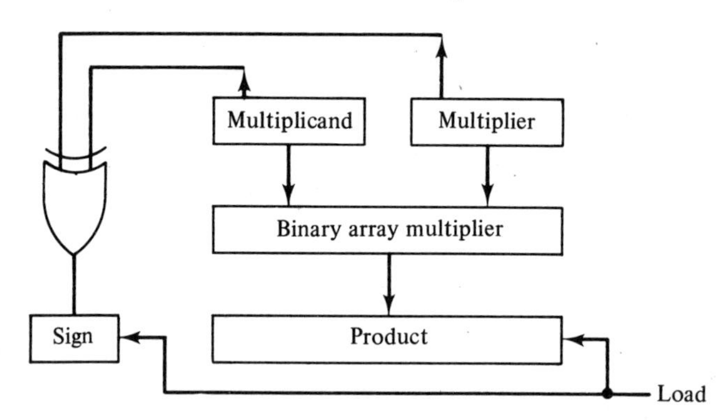


**Fig. 10-4** Block diagram for the multiplication micro-operation.

The absolute value of the product is available from the array multiplier. The sign of the product is generated by an exclusive-OR gate. A *load* control signal transfers the product and its sign into a register with one clock pulse.

Instead of using a large number of AND gates and a number of parallel adders, the array multiplier can be more conveniently implemented by means of a read-only memory. A ROM can implement any combinational circuit and as such it can implement a binary multiplier circuit. Thus, a 4 by 3 multiplier requires 7 inputs and 12 outputs. A 128 by 12 ROM will have 7 address lines and 12 output lines. Four of the address lines receive the multiplicand bits and the other three receive the multiplier bits. The multiplication truth table for each of the 128 words is then used to mask the required bits in the ROM. It may be worth noting that the least significant product bit can be obtained from one AND gate. This fact can be utilized to reduce the number of ROM outputs by one.

### *Multiplication with Signed-2's Complement Numbers*

The multiplication of two binary numbers when negative numbers are in signed-2's complement representation is complicated by the fact that the function of the multiplier bits is not always the same when forming partial products. The bits are treated as in signed-magnitude when the multiplier is positive. When it is negative, the multiplier is in its 2's complement form. Any least significant zeros and the first 1 must be considered as in a positive multiplier but the rest of the bits have an opposite effect because they are complemented. Although it is possible to formulate a multiplication algorithm that operates with 2's complement numbers directly, most of these algorithms require special control functions that sense the sign bits to determine how the partial products are to be formed.

The simplest way to solve this complication would be to employ an algorithm which complements a negative multiplier or multiplicand prior to the operation. Thus only positive numbers would be multiplied just as in the sign-magnitude case. The positive product obtained would then be complemented only if the product is to be negative. The correct sign can be determined as simply as in the sign-magnitude case.

A more convenient procedure is to change only the multiplier to a positive number and leave the multiplicand either positive or negative. If the original multiplier and multiplicand are both positive, no complementing is required. If the multiplier is positive but the multiplicand is negative, the product should be negative. If we add a negative multiplicand in the proper complement form to a negative partial product in the proper complement form, the result will be a negative product in the proper complement form. So it makes no difference whether the multiplicand is positive or negative. In the first case we form positive partial products and in the second case we form negative partial products.

The multiplier, however, must always be positive. If it is negative, both the multiplier and multiplicand are complemented. This is equivalent to multiplying both numbers by minus one which does not change the product but makes the multiplier positive.

The algorithm that follows this procedure is shown in Fig. 10-5. The multiplicand is in *BR* and the multiplier in *QR*. The sign bit of *QR* is designated by $Q_s$, the magnitude bits by $Q$ and the least significant bit by $Q_n$ (See Fig. 9-6). The partial products are formed in the *AC* and if negative, they are in signed-2's complement representation. The *AC* is first cleared to hold a zero

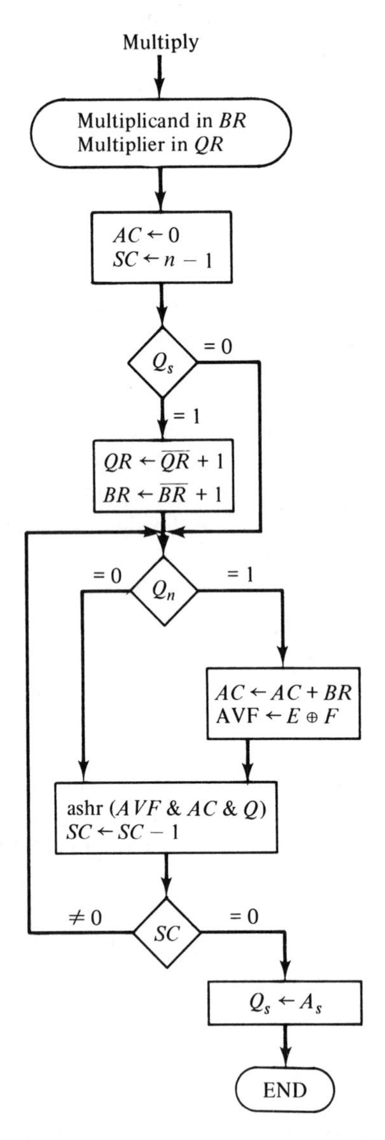


**Fig. 10-5** Multiply algorithm for binary numbers in signed-2's complement representation.

partial product and the sequence counter *SC* is set to a number equal to the number of bits in the magnitude part of the multiplier. If the multiplier sign is negative, both *QR* and *BR* are complemented. This insures that the multiplier is always positive at the start of the operation. If the least significant bit of the multiplier is 1, the multiplicand in *BR* is added to the present partial product in the *AC*. The partial product in *AC* and *Q* is shifted once to the right. Since the partial product may be either positive or negative it is necessary to perform an arithmetic shift appropriate for numbers in signed-2's complement representation with a possible overflow (see Prob. 10-11). The least significant bit of *AC* is shifted into *Q*, bypassing the sign bit in *QR*. The double-length product is formed in the *AC* and *Q*. The sign of the product is already available in the first bit of the *AC* (designated by $A_s$). The sign of *QR* must have the same sign as the product. The last operation in the flow chart transfers the sign bit from *AC* into *QR*.

### *Division with Signed-2's Complement Numbers*

The division of two binary numbers when negative numbers are in signed-2's complement representation is more complicated than multiplication. This is because the quotient bits must be generated in the adopted representation and the dividend may be either added or subtracted from the partial remainder, depending on the relative signs of the dividend and divisor. It is sometimes convenient to convert the negative numbers to positive, divide the two positive numbers as in signed-magnitude, and then complement the result if it is negative.

An algorithm that performs the division with converted positive numbers is shown in Fig. 10-6. The double length dividend is in *AC* and *QR* and the divisor in *BR*. The sign of the quotient is first determined from the signs of the dividend and divisor. The sign of the dividend in $A_s$ is checked and if it is negative, the dividend in *A* and *Q* is changed to positive by complementing the number. Similarly, the divisor in *BR* is complemented if it is negative. In this way, both numbers become positive but the sign bit in $Q_s$ is the correct sign of the quotient. The two positive magnitudes are then divided as in the signed-magnitude case. When the divide operation is terminated, the positive remainder is in *A* and the positive quotient in *Q*. The sign in $Q_s$ is checked and if negative, the quotient in *Q* is complemented. The original sign of the dividend in $A_s$ is checked and if negative, the remainder in *A* is complemented.

The algorithm requires that all three registers have a 2's complement capability. This is not a problem if the processor has a common ALU with all registers connected to it by a common bus system. Each complement micro-operation can be executed in the common ALU. There is no need to provide individual complement circuits for each register.

The algorithms presented in this and the previous section are for signed-2's complement representation. They can be easily modified to provide algorithms for performing arithmetic operations with numbers in signed-1's complement representation. When numbers in signed-1's complement representation are added, it is necessary to check the end-carry out of the sign position. The result in the *AC* must be incremented if the end-carry is a 1.

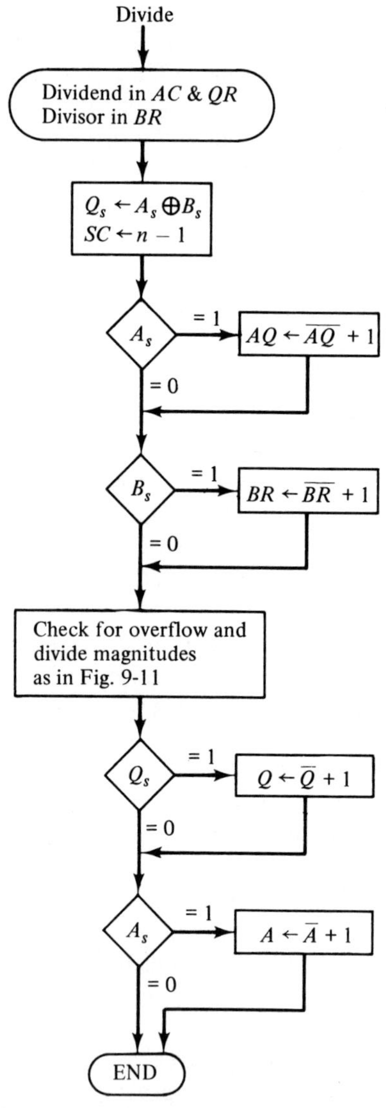


**Fig. 10-6** Division with binary numbers in signed-2's complement representation.

## 10-4 FLOATING-POINT ARITHMETIC OPERATIONS

Many high-level programming languages have a facility for specifying floating-point numbers. The most common way is to specify them by a *real* declaration statement as opposed to fixed-point numbers which are specified by an *integer* declaration statement. Any computer that has a compiler for such high-level programming language must have a provision for handling floating-point arithmetic operations. The operations are quite often included in the internal hardware. If no hardware is available for the operations, the compiler must be designed with a package of floating-point software subroutines. Although the hardware method is more expensive, it is so much more efficient than the software method that floating-point hardware is included in most computers and is omitted only in very small ones.

### *Basic Considerations*

Floating-point representation of data was introduced in Sec. 3-3. A floating-point number in computer registers consists of two parts: a mantissa $m$ and an exponent $e$. The two parts represent a number obtained from multiplying $m$ times a radix $r$ raised to the value of $e$, thus:

$$m \times r^e$$

The mantissa may be a fraction or an integer. The location of the radix point and the value of the radix $r$ are assumed and are not included in the registers. For example, assume a fraction representation and a radix 10. The decimal number 537.25 is represented in a register with $m = 53725$ and $e = 3$ and is interpreted to represent the floating-point number

$$.53725 \times 10^3$$

A floating-point number is normalized if the most significant digit of the mantissa is non-zero. In this way, the mantissa contains the maximum possible number of significant digits. A zero cannot be normalized because it does not have a non-zero digit. It is represented in floating-point by all 0's in the mantissa and exponent.

Floating-point representation increases the range of numbers that can be accomodated in a given register. Consider a computer with 48-bit words. Since one bit must be reserved for the sign, the range of a fixed-point integer number will be $\pm(2^{47} - 1)$ which is approximately $\pm 10^{14}$. The 48 bits can be used to represent a floating-point number with 36 bits for the mantissa and 12 bits for the exponent. Assuming fraction representation for the mantissa and taking the two sign bits into consideration, the range of numbers that can be accomodated is:

$$\pm(1 - 2^{-35}) \times 2^{2048}$$

This number is derived from a fraction that contains 35 1's, an exponent of eleven bits (excluding its sign), and the fact that $2^{11} = 2048$. The largest number that can be accomodated is approximately $10^{615}$ which is an astronomical number. The mantissa can accomodate 35 bits (excluding the sign) and if considered as an integer it can store a number as large as $(2^{35} - 1)$. This is approximately equal to $10^{10}$ which is equivalent to a decimal number of ten digits.

Computers with shorter word lengths use two or more words to represent a floating-point number. An 8-bit microcomputer may use four words to represent one floating-point number. One word of 8 bits is reserved for the exponent and the 24 bits of the other three words are used for the mantissa.

Arithmetic operations with floating-point numbers are more complicated than with fixed-point numbers and their execution takes longer and requires more complex hardware. Adding or subtracting two numbers requires first an alignment of the radix point since the exponent parts must be made equal before adding or subtracting the mantissas. The alignment is done by shifting one mantissa while its exponent is adjusted until it is equal to the other exponent. Consider the sum of the following floating-point numbers.

$$
\begin{array}{r}
.5372400 \times 10^{2} \\
+\ .1580000 \times 10^{-1}
\end{array}
$$

It is necessary that the two exponents be equal before the mantissas can be added. We can either shift the first number three positions to the left, or shift the second number three positions to the right. When the mantissas are stored in registers, shifting to the left causes a loss of most significant digits. Shifting to the right causes a loss of least significant digits. The second method is preferable because it only reduces the accuracy while the first method may cause an error. The usual alignment procedure is to shift the mantissa that has the smaller exponent to the right by a number of places equal to the difference between the exponents. After this is done, the mantissas can be added:

$$
\begin{array}{r}
.5372400 \times 10^{2} \\
+\ .0001580 \times 10^{2} \\
\hline
.5373980 \times 10^{2}
\end{array}
$$

When two normalized mantissas are added, the sum may contain an overflow digit. An overflow can be corrected easily by shifting the sum once to the right and incrementing the exponent. When two numbers are subtracted, the result may contain most significant zeros as shown in the following example.

$$
\begin{array}{r}
.56780 \times 10^{5} \\
-\ .56430 \times 10^{5} \\
\hline
.00350 \times 10^{5}
\end{array}
$$

A floating-point number that has a 0 in the most significant position of the mantissa is said to have an *underflow*. To normalize a number that contains an underflow, it is necessary to shift the mantissa to the left and decrement the exponent until a non-zero digit appears in the first position. In the above example, it is necessary to shift left twice to obtain $.35000 \times 10^3$. In most computers, a normalization procedure is performed after each operation to ensure that all results are in a normalized form.

Floating-point multiplication and division do not require an alignment of the mantissas. The product can be formed by multiplying the two mantissas and adding the exponents. Division is accomplished by dividing the mantissas and subtracting the exponents.

The operations performed with the mantissas are the same as in fixed-point numbers so the two can share the same registers and circuits. The operations performed with the exponents are compare and increment (for aligning the mantissas), add and subtract (for multiplication and division), and decrement (to normalize the result). The exponent may be represented in any one of the three representations: signed-magnitude, signed-2's complement, or signed-1's complement.

A fourth representation employed in many computers is known as a *biased* exponent. In this representation, the sign bit is removed from being a separate entity. The bias is a positive number which is added to each exponent as the floating-point number is formed, so that internally all exponents are positive. The following example may clarify this type of representation. Consider an exponent that ranges from $-50$ to 49. Internally it is represented by two digits (without a sign) by adding to it a bias of 50. The exponent register contains the number $e + 50$ where $e$ is the actual exponent. This way, the exponents are represented in registers as positive numbers in the range of 00 to 99. Positive exponents in registers have the range of numbers from 99 to 50. The subtraction of 50 gives the positive values from 49 to 0. Negative exponents are represented in registers in the range from 49 to 00. The subtraction of 50 gives the negative values in the range of $-1$ to $-50$.

The advantage of biased exponents is that they contain only positive numbers. It is then simpler to compare their relative magnitude without being concerned with their signs. As a consequence, an IC magnitude comparator (Fig. 9-1) can be used to compare their relative magnitude during the alignment of the mantissa. Another advantage is that the smallest possible biased exponent contains all zeros. The floating-point representation of zero is then a zero mantissa and the smallest possible exponent.

In the above examples, we used decimal numbers to demonstrate some of the concepts that must be understood when dealing with floating-point numbers. Obviously, the same concepts apply to binary numbers as well.

The algorithms developed in this section are for binary numbers. Decimal computer arithmetic is discussed in the next section.

### *Register Configuration*

The register configuration for floating-point operations is quite similar to the layout for fixed-point operations. As a general rule, the same registers and adder used for fixed-point arithmetic are used for processing the mantissas. The difference lies in the way the exponents are handled.

The register organization for floating-point operations is shown in Fig. 10-7. There are three registers *BR*, *AC*, and *QR*. Each register is subdivided into two parts. The mantissa part has the same upper case letter symbols as in fixed-point representation. The exponent part uses the corresponding lower case letter symbol.

It is assumed that each floating-point number has a mantissa in signed-magnitude representation and a biased exponent. Thus the *AC* has a mantissa whose sign is in $A_s$ and a magnitude which is in $A$. The exponent is in the part of the register denoted by the lower case letter symbol $a$. The diagram shows explicitly the most significant bit of $A$, labeled by $A_1$. The bit in this position must be a 1 for the number to be normalized. Note that the symbol *AC* represents the entire register, i.e., the concatenation of $A_s$, $A$, and $a$.

Similarly, register *BR* is subdivided into $B_s$, $B$, and $b$, and *QR* into $Q_s$, $Q$, and $q$. A parallel-adder adds the two mantissas and transfers the sum into $A$ and the carry into $E$. A separate parallel-adder is used for the exponents. Since the exponents are biased, they do not have a distinct sign bit but are represented as a biased positive quantity. It is assumed that the floating-point numbers are so large that the chance of an exponent overflow is very remote and for this reason the exponent overflow will be neglected (see Prob. 10-25). The exponents are connected also to a magnitude comparator that provides three binary outputs to indicate their relative magnitude.

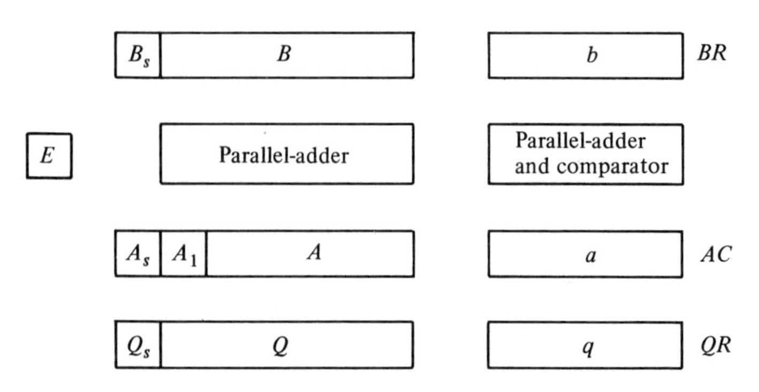


**Fig. 10-7** Registers for floating-point arithmetic operations.

The number in the mantissa will be taken as a *fraction* so the binary point is assumed to reside to the left of the magnitude part. Integer representation for floating-point causes certain scaling problems during multiplication and division. To avoid these problems, we adopt a fraction representation (see Prob. 10-26).

The numbers in the registers are assumed to be initially normalized. After each arithmetic operation, the result will be normalized. Thus all floating-point operands coming from and going to the memory unit are always normalized.

### *Addition and Subtraction*

During addition or subtraction, the two floating-point operands are in *AC* and *BR*. The sum or difference is formed in the *AC*. The algorithm can be divided into four consecutive parts.

1. Check for zeros.
2. Align the mantissas.
3. Add or subtract the mantissas.
4. Normalize the result.

A floating-point number that is zero cannot be normalized. If this number is used during the computation, the result may also be zero. Instead of checking for zeros during the normalization process we check for zeros at the beginning and terminate the process if necessary. The alignment of the mantissas must be carried out prior to their operation. After the mantissas are added or subtracted, the result may be un-normalized. The normalization procedure insures that the result is normalized prior to its transfer to memory.

The flow chart for adding or subtracting two floating-point binary numbers is shown in Fig. 10-8. If *BR* is equal to zero, the operation is terminated with the value in the *AC* being the result. If *AC* is equal to zero, we transfer the content of *BR* into *AC* and also complement its sign if the numbers are to be subtracted. If neither number is equal to zero, we proceed to align the mantissas.

The magnitude comparator attached to exponents $a$ and $b$ provides three outputs that indicate their relative magnitude. If the two exponents are equal, we go to perform the arithmetic operation. If the exponents are not equal, the mantissa having the smaller exponent is shifted to the right and its exponent incremented. This process is repeated until the two exponents are equal.

The addition and subtraction of the two mantissas is identical to the fixed-point addition and subtraction algorithm presented in Sec. 9-3. The mag-

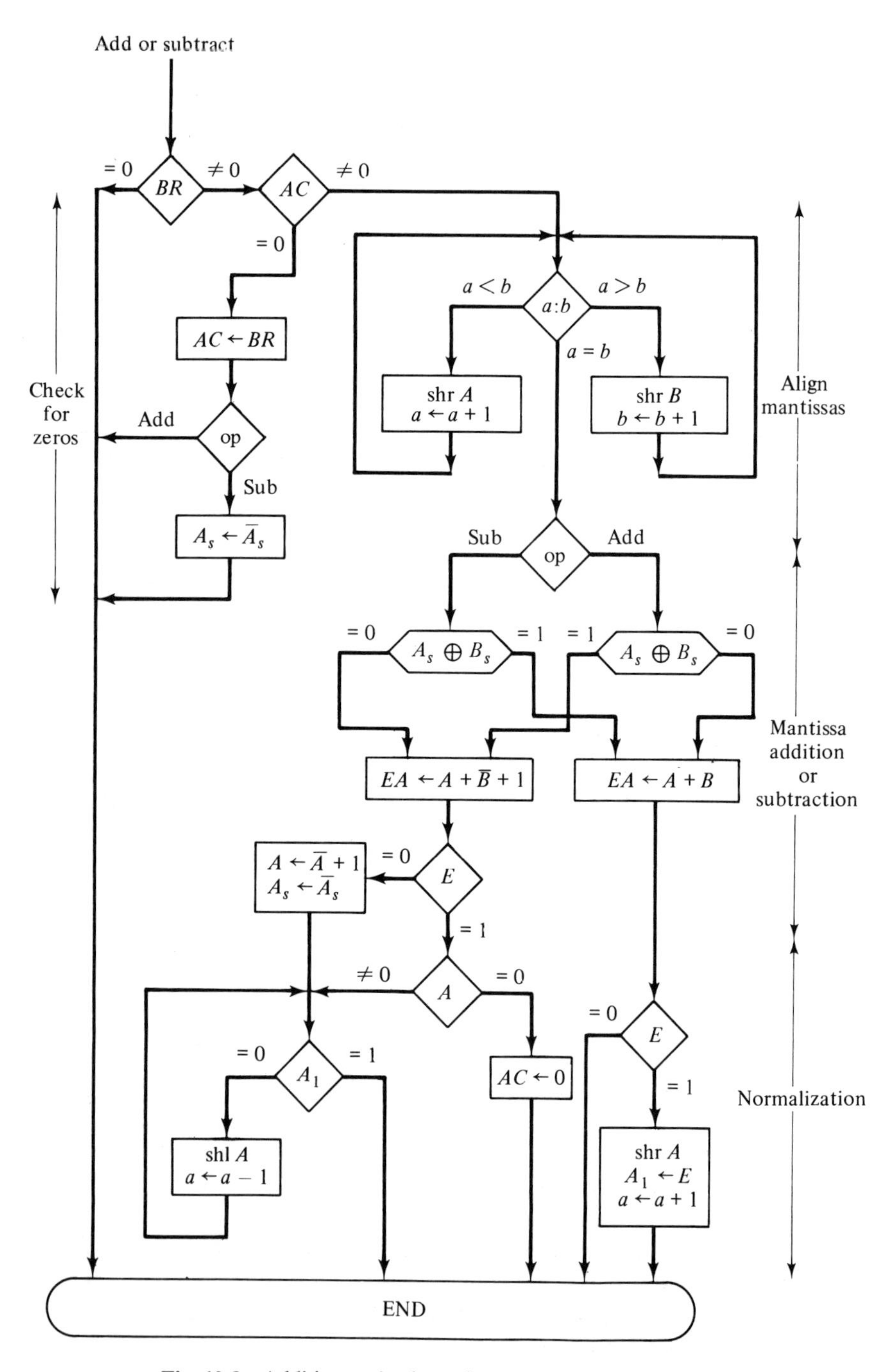


**Fig. 10-8** Addition and subtraction of floating-point numbers.

nitude part is added or subtracted depending on the operation and the signs of the two mantissas. If an overflow occurs when the magnitudes are added it is transferred into flip-flop $E$. If $E$ is equal to 1, the bit is transferred into $A_1$ and all other bits of $A$ are shifted right. The exponent must be incremented to maintain the correct number. No underflow may occur in this case because the original mantissa that was not shifted during the alignment was already in a normalized position.

If the magnitudes were subtracted, the result may be zero or may have an underflow. If the mantissa is zero, the entire floating-point number in the $AC$ is made zero. Otherwise, the mantissa must have at least one bit that is equal to 1. The mantissa has an underflow if the most significant bit in position $A_1$ is 0. In that case, the mantissa is shifted left and the exponent decremented. The bit in $A_1$ is checked again and the process is repeated until it is equal to 1. When $A_1 = 1$, the mantissa is normalized and the operation is completed.

### *Multiplication*

The multiplication of two floating-point numbers requires that we multiply the mantissas and add the exponents. No comparison of exponents or alignment of mantissas is necessary. The multiplication of the mantissas is performed in the same way as in fixed-point to provide a double-precision product. The double-precision answer is used in fixed-point numbers to increase the accuracy of the product. In floating-point, the range of a single-precision mantissa combined with the exponent is usually accurate enough so that only single precision numbers are maintained. Thus, the half most significant bits of the mantissa product and the exponent will be taken together to form a single-precision floating-point product.

The multiplication algorithm can be subdivided into four parts.

1. Check for zeros.
2. Add the exponents.
3. Multiply the mantissas.
4. Normalize the product.

Steps 2 and 3 can be done simultaneously if separate adders are available for the mantissas and exponents.

The flow chart for floating-point multiplication is shown in Fig. 10-9. The two operands are checked to determine if they contain a zero. If either operand is equal to zero, the product in the $AC$ is set to zero and the operation is terminated. If none of the operands are equal to zero, the process continues with the exponent addition.

The exponent of the multiplier is in $q$ and the adder is between exponents

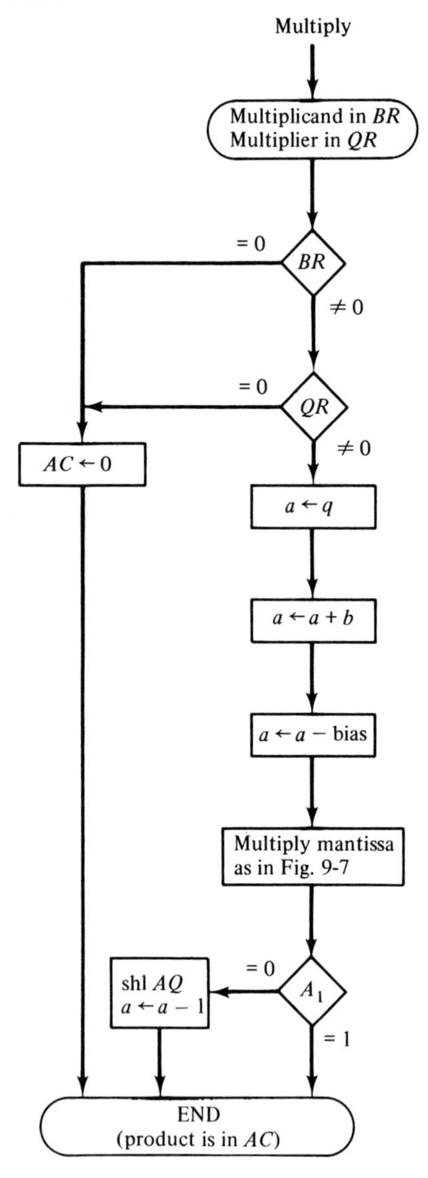


**Fig. 10-9** Multiplication of floating-point numbers.

$a$ and $b$. It is necessary to transfer the exponents from $q$ to $a$, add the two exponents and transfer the sum into $a$. Since both exponents are biased by the addition of a constant, the exponent sum will have double this bias. The correct biased exponent for the product is obtained by subtracting the bias number from the sum.

The multiplication of the mantissas is done as in the fixed-point case with the product residing in $A$ and $Q$. Overflow cannot occur during multiplication so there is no need to check for it.

The product may have an underflow so the most significant bit in $A$ is checked. If it is a 1, the product is already normalized. If it is a 0, the mantissa in $AQ$ is shifted left and the exponent decremented. Note that only one normalization shift is necessary. The multiplier and multiplicand were originally normalized and contained fractions. The smallest normalized operand is 0.1 so the smallest possible product is 0.01. Therefore, only one leading zero may occur.

Although the low-order half of the mantissa is in $Q$, we do not use it for the floating-point product. Only the value in the $AC$ is taken as the product.

### *Division*

Floating-point division requires that the exponents be subtracted and the mantissas divided. The mantissa division is done as in fixed-point except that the dividend has a single precision mantissa which is placed in the $AC$. Remember that the mantissa dividend is a fraction and not an integer. For integer representation, a single precision dividend must be placed in register $Q$ and register $A$ must be cleared. The zeros in $A$ are to the left of the binary point and have no significance. In fraction representation, a single precision dividend is placed in register $A$ and register $Q$ is cleared. The zeros in $Q$ are to the right of the binary point and have no significance.

The check for divide-overflow is the same as in fixed-point representation. However, with floating-point numbers the divide-overflow imposes no problems. If the dividend is greater than or equal to the divisor, the dividend fraction is shifted to the right and its exponent incremented by 1. For normalized operands this is a sufficient operation to insure that no mantissa divide-overflow will occur. The above operation is referred to as a *dividend alignment*.

The division of two normalized floating-point numbers will always result in a normalized quotient provided a dividend alignment is carried out before the division (see Prob. 10-23). Therefore, unlike the other operations, the quotient obtained after the division does not require a normalization.

The division algorithm can be subdivided into five parts.

1. Check for zeros.
2. Initialize registers and evaluate the sign.
3. Align the dividend.
4. Subtract the exponents.
5. Divide the mantissas.

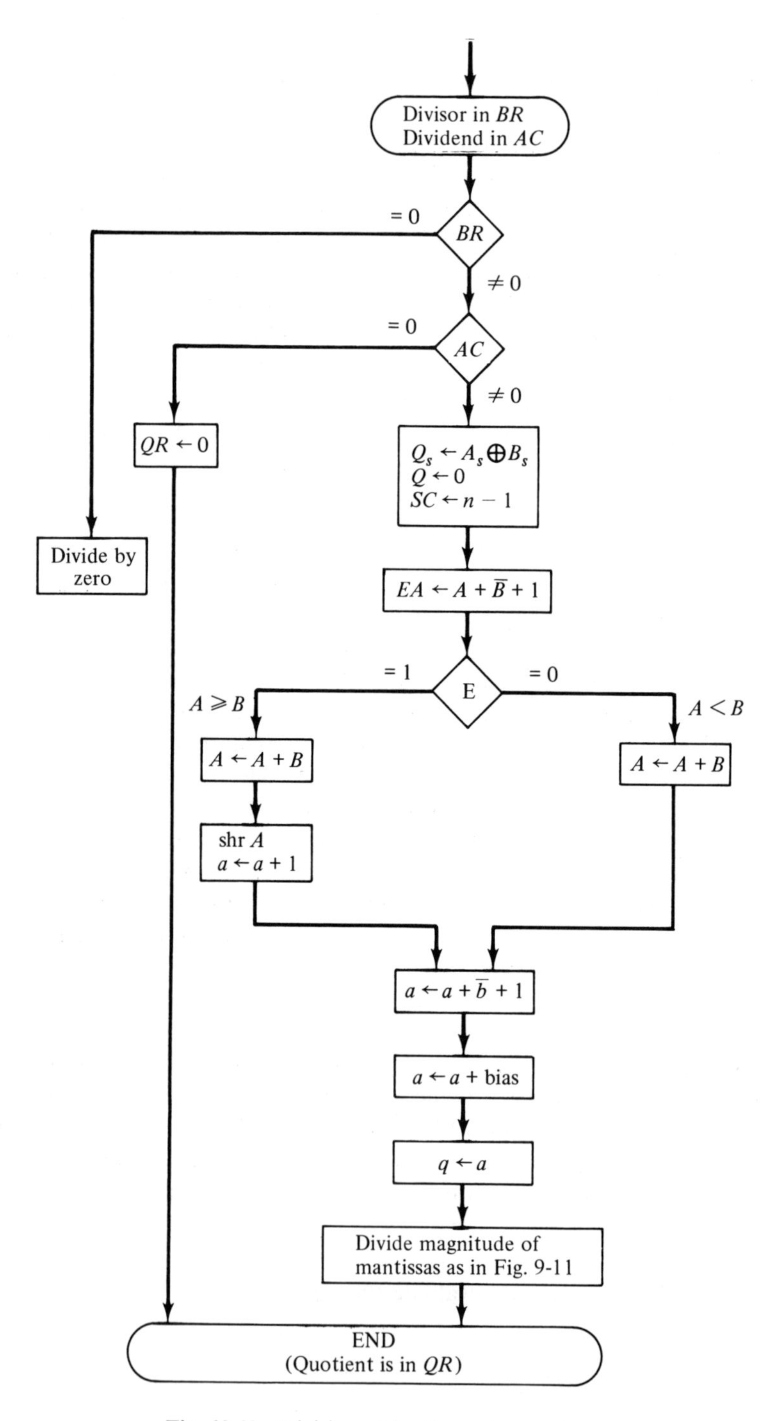


**Fig. 10-10** Division of floating-point numbers.

The flow chart for floating-point division is shown in Fig. 10-10. The two operands are checked for zero. If the divisor is zero, it indicates an attempt to divide by zero, which is an illegal operation. The operation is terminated with an error message. An alternative procedure would be to set the quotient in $QR$ to the most positive number possible (if the dividend is positive) or to the most negative possible (if the dividend is negative). If the dividend in $AC$ is zero, the quotient in $QR$ is made zero and the operation terminates.

If the operands are not zero, we proceed to determine the sign of the quotient and store it in $Q_s$. The sign of the dividend in $A_s$ is left unchanged to be the sign of the remainder. The $Q$ register is cleared and the sequence counter $SC$ is set to a number equal to the number of bits in the quotient.

The dividend alignment is similar to the divide-overflow check in the fixed-point operation. The proper alignment requires that the fraction dividend be smaller than the divisor. The two fractions are compared by a subtraction test. The carry in $E$ determines their relative magnitude. The dividend fraction is restored to its original value by adding the divisor. If $A \geq B$, it is necessary to shift $A$ once to the right and increment the dividend exponent. Since both operands are normalized, this alignment insures that $A < B$.

Next, the divisor exponent is subtracted from the dividend exponent. Since both exponents were originally biased, the subtraction operation gives the difference without the bias. The bias is then added and the result transferred into $q$ because the quotient is formed in $QR$.

The magnitudes of the mantissas are divided as in the fixed-point case. After the operation, the mantissa quotient resides in $Q$ and the remainder in $A$. The floating-point quotient is already normalized and resides in $QR$. The exponent of the remainder should be the same as the exponent of the dividend. The binary point for the remainder mantissa lies $(n - 1)$ positions to the left of $A_1$. The remainder can be converted to a normalized fraction by subtracting $n - 1$ from the dividend exponent and by shift and decrement until the bit in $A_1$ is equal to 1. This is not shown in the flow chart and is left as an exercise (see Prob. 10-24).

## 10-5 DECIMAL ARITHMETIC OPERATIONS

The algorithms for arithmetic operations with decimal data are similar to the algorithms for the corresponding operations with binary data. In fact, except for a slight modification in the multiplication and division algorithms, the same flow charts can be used for both types of data provided we interpret the micro-operation symbols properly. Decimal numbers in BCD are stored in computer registers in groups of four bits. Each 4-bit group represents a decimal digit and must be taken as a unit when performing decimal micro-operations.

For convenience, we will use the same symbols for binary and decimal arithmetic micro-operations but give them a different interpretation. As shown in Table 10-1, a bar over the register letter symbol denotes the 9's complement of the decimal number stored in the register. Adding 1 to the 9's complement produces the 10's complement. Thus for decimal numbers, the symbol $A \leftarrow A + \bar{B} + 1$ denotes a transfer of the decimal sum formed by adding the original content $A$ to the 10's complement of $B$. The use of identical symbols for the 9's complement and the 1's complement may be confusing if both types of data are employed in the same system. If this is the case, it may be better to adopt a different symbol for the 9's complement. If only one type of data is being considered, then the symbol would apply to the type of data used.

**Table 10-1** *Decimal arithmetic micro-operation symbols*

| *Symbolic Designation* | *Description* |
|---|---|
| $A \leftarrow A + B$ | Add decimal numbers and transfer sum into $A$ |
| $\bar{B}$ | 9's complement of $B$ |
| $A \leftarrow A + \bar{B} + 1$ | Content of $A$ plus 10's complement of $B$ into $A$ |
| $Q_L \leftarrow Q_L + 1$ | Increment BCD number in $Q_L$ |
| dshr $A$ | Decimal shift-right register $A$ |
| dshl $A$ | Decimal shift-left register $A$ |

Incrementing or decrementing a register is the same for binary and decimal except for the number of states that the register is allowed to have. A binary counter goes through 16 states, from 0000 to 1111, when incremented. A decimal counter goes through ten states from 0000 to 1001 and back to 0000, since 9 is the last count. Similarly, a binary counter sequences from 1111 to 0000 when decremented. A decimal counter goes from 1001 to 0000.

A decimal shift right or left is preceeded by the letter $d$ to indicate a shift over the four bits that hold the decimal digits. As a numerical illustration consider a register $A$ holding decimal 7860 in BCD. The bit pattern of the 12 flip-flops is:

0111 1000 0110 0000

The micro-operation *dshr A* shifts the decimal number one digit to the right to give 0786. This shift is over the four bits and changes the content of the register into

0000 0111 1000 0110

### *Addition and Subtraction*

The algorithm for addition and subtraction of binary signed-magnitude numbers applies also to decimal signed-magnitude numbers provided we interpret the micro-operation symbols in the proper manner. Similarly, the algorithm for binary signed-2's complement numbers applies to decimal signed-10's complement numbers. The binary data must employ a binary adder and a complementer. The decimal data must employ a decimal arithmetic unit capable of adding two BCD numbers and forming the 9's complement of the subtrahend. Such a decimal arithmetic unit was introduced in Sec. 7-4.

Decimal data can be added in three different ways as shown in Fig. 10-11. The parallel method uses a decimal arithmetic unit composed of as many BCD adders as there are digits in the number. The sum is formed in parallel and requires only one micro-operation. In the digit-serial bit-parallel method, the digits are applied to a single BCD adder serially while the bits of each coded digit are transferred in parallel. The sum is formed by shifting the decimal numbers through the BCD adder one at a time. For $k$ decimal digits, this configuration requires $k$ micro-operations, one for each decimal shift. In the all serial adder, the bits are shifted one at a time through a full-adder. The binary sum formed after four shifts must be corrected into a valid BCD digit. This correction, discussed in Sec. 7-4, consists of checking the binary sum. If it is greater than or equal to 1010, the binary sum is corrected by adding to it 0110 and generating a carry for the next pair of digits.

The parallel method is fast but requires a large number of adders. The digit-serial bit-parallel method requires only one BCD adder which is shared by all the digits. It is slower than the parallel method because of the time required to shift the digits. The all serial method requires a minimum amount of equipment but is very slow.

### *Multiplication*

The multiplication of fixed-point decimal numbers is similar to binary except for the way the partial products are formed. A decimal multiplier has digits that range in value from 0 to 9 whereas a binary multiplier has only 0 and 1 digits. In the binary case, the multiplicand is added to the partial product if the multiplier bit is 1. In the decimal case, the multiplicand must be multiplied by the digit multiplier and the result added to the partial product. This operation can be accomplished by adding the multiplicand to the partial product a number of times equal to the value of the multiplier digit.

The registers organization for the decimal multiplication is shown in Fig. 10-12. We are assuming here four-digit numbers with each digit occupy-

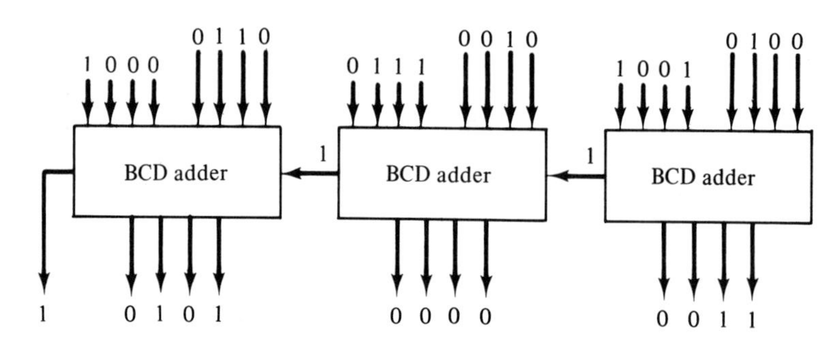


(a) Parallel decimal addition: 624 + 879 = 1503

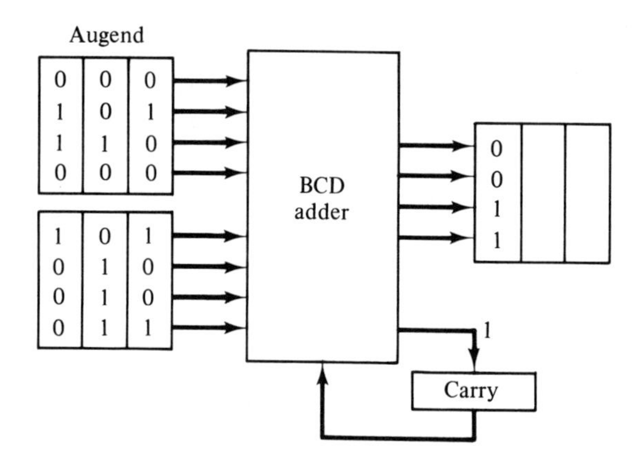


(b) Digit-serial, bit-parallel decimal addition

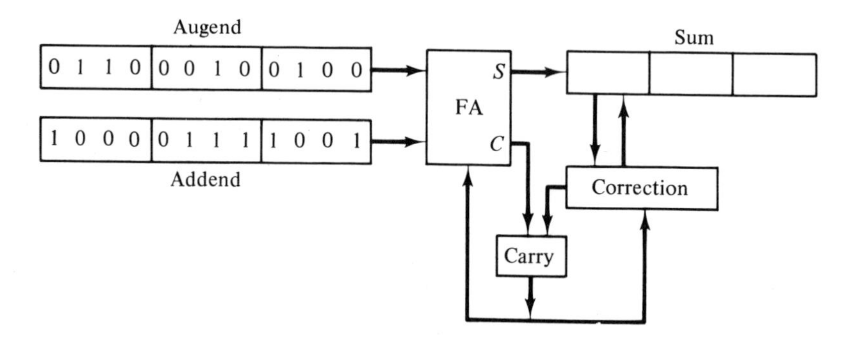


(c) All serial decimal addition

**Fig. 10-11** Three ways of adding decimal numbers.

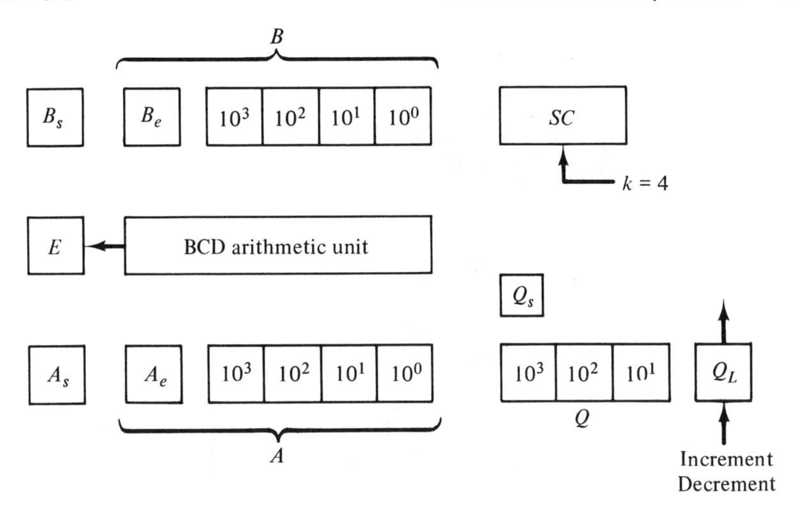


**Fig. 10-12** Registers for decimal arithmetic multiplication and division.

ing four bits for a total of 16 bits for each number. There are three registers, $A$, $B$, and $Q$, each having a corresponding sign flip-flop $A_s$, $B_s$, and $Q_s$. Registers $A$ and $B$ have four more bits designated by $A_e$ and $B_e$ that provide an extension of one more digit to the registers. The BCD arithmetic unit adds the five digits in parallel and places the sum in the 5-digit $A$ register. The end-carry goes to flip-flop $E$. The purpose of digit $A_e$ is to accomodate an overflow while adding the multiplicand to the partial product during multiplication. The purpose of digit $B_e$ is to form the 9's complement of the divisor when subtracted from the partial remainder during the division operation. The least significant digit in register $Q$ is denoted by $Q_L$. This digit can be incremented or decremented.

A decimal operand coming from memory consists of 17 bits. One bit (the sign) is transferred to $B_s$ and the magnitude of the operand is placed in the lower 16 bits of $B$. Both $B_e$ and $A_e$ are cleared initially. The result of the operation is also 17 bits long and does not use the $A_e$ part of the $A$ register.

The decimal multiplication algorithm is shown in Fig. 10-13. Initially, the entire $A$ register and $B_e$ are cleared and the sequence counter $SC$ is set to a number $k$ equal to the number of digits in the multiplier. The low-order digit of the multiplier in $Q_L$ is checked. If it is not equal to 0, the multiplicand in $B$ is added to the partial product in $A$ once and $Q_L$ is decremented. $Q_L$ is checked again and the process is repeated until it is equal to 0. In this way, the multiplicand in $B$ is added to the partial product a number of times equal to the multiplier digit. Any temporary overflow digit will reside in $A_e$ and can range in value from 0 to 9.

Next, the partial product and the multiplier are shifted once to the right.

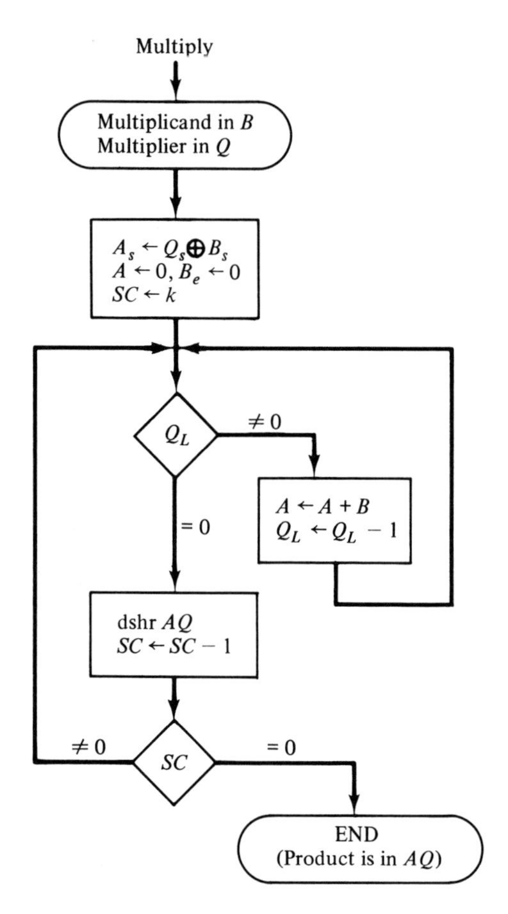


**Fig. 10-13** Flow chart for decimal multiplication.

This places zero in $A_e$ and transfers the next multiplier quotient into $Q_L$. The process is then repeated $k$ times to form a double-length product in $AQ$.

### *Division*

Decimal division is similar to binary division except of course that the quotient digits may have any of the ten values from 0 to 9. In the restoring division method, the divisor is subtracted from the dividend or partial remainder as many times as necessary until a negative remainder results. The correct remainder is then restored by adding the divisor. The digit in the quotient reflects the number of subtractions up to but excluding the one that caused the negative difference.

The decimal division algorithm is shown in Fig. 10-14. It is similar to the algorithm with binary data except for the way the quotient bits are

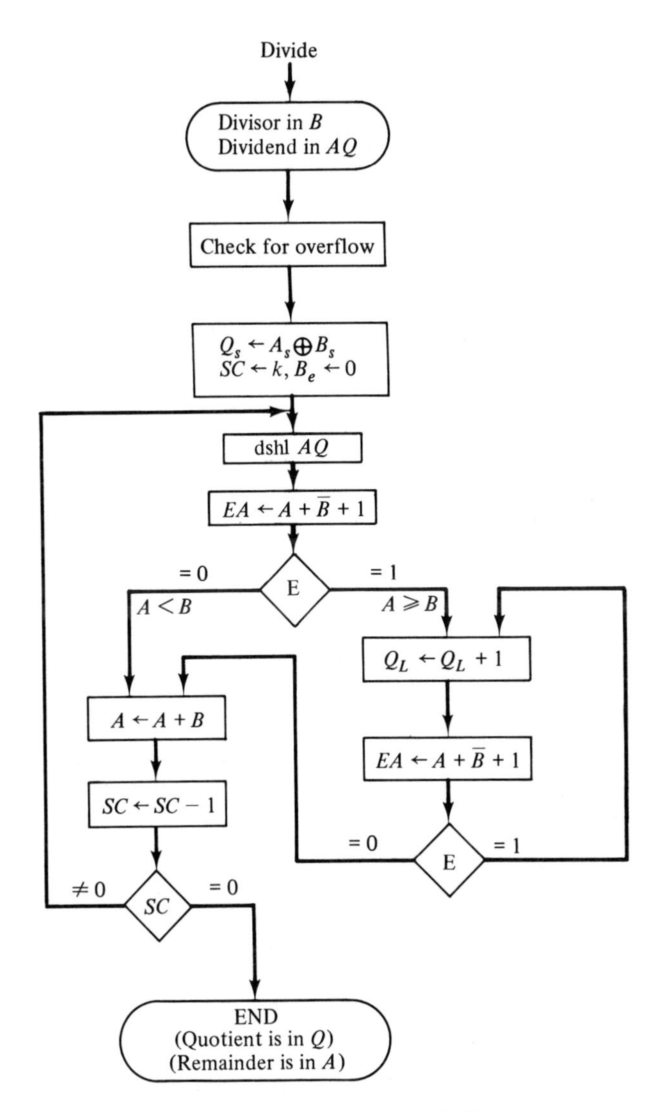


**Fig. 10-14** Flow chart for decimal division.

formed. The dividend (or partial remainder) is shifted to the left with its most significant digit placed in $A_e$. The divisor is then subtracted by adding its 10's complement value. Since $B_e$ is initially cleared, its complement value is 9 as required. The carry in $E$ determines the relative magnitude of $A$ and $B$. If $E = 0$, it signifies that $A < B$. In this case, the divisor is added to restore the partial remainder and $Q_L$ stays at 0 (inserted there during the shift). If $E = 1$, it signifies that $A \geq B$. The quotient digit in $Q_L$ is incremented once and the divisor subtracted again. This process is repeated until the subtraction results in a negative difference which is recognized by $E$ being 0. When this occurs, the quotient digit is not incremented but the divisor is added to restore the positive remainder. In this way, the quotient digit is made equal to the number of times that the partial remainder "goes" into the divisor.

The partial remainder and the quotient bits are shifted once to the right and the process is repeated $k$ times to form $k$ quotient digits. The remainder is then found in register $A$ and the quotient is in register $Q$. The value of $E$ is neglected.

### *Floating-Point Operations*

Decimal floating-point arithmetic operations follow the same procedures as binary operations. The algorithms in Sec. 10-4 can be adopted for decimal data provided the micro-operation symbols are interpreted correctly. The multiplication and division of the mantissas must be done by the methods described above.

## 10-6 DECIMAL–BINARY CONVERSION

Conversion between decimal and binary numbers is common in many digital computers. Data prepared by people are invariably in decimal. A computer without a decimal arithmetic unit must convert the decimal numbers to binary. Binary results must be converted to decimal to be understood by the user. Since decimal numbers are represented in computer registers with a binary code, the conversion between BCD numbers and binary numbers is essentially a code conversion problem. In this section we present algorithms for converting BCD numbers to binary and binary numbers to BCD.

### *BCD-to-Binary Conversion*

The conversion of a decimal number to binary is done by repeated divisions by 2 and accumulation of the remainders. For example, decimal 19 is converted to binary as shown below.

$$\frac{19}{2} = 9 + 1$$

$$\frac{9}{2} = 4 + 1$$

$$\frac{4}{2} = 2 + 0$$

$$\frac{2}{2} = 1 + 0$$

$$\frac{1}{2} = 0 + 1$$

19 is divided by 2 to give a quotient of 9 and a remainder of 1. The quotient is divided by 2 to give a new quotient 4 and a remainder of 1. This process is repeated until the quotient becomes 0. The coefficients of the binary number are obtained from the remainders with the first remainder giving the low-order bit. The equivalent binary number of decimal 19 is 10011.

For decimal numbers in BCD, the division by 2 can be done by a right shift provided all BCD digits are corrected after the shift. The bit that is shifted out will automatically give the remainder. To illustrate, consider decimal 19 in BCD. Since the number is odd, it has a 1 in the least significant bit position. Shifting to the right should divide the number by 2 and provide a remainder of 1. However, the shifted number must be corrected by subtracting 3 as shown below.

| | | | |
|---|---|---|---|
| BCD 19: | 0001 | 1001 | |
| shift right: | 0000 | 1100 | 1(remainder) |
| subtract 3: | | 0011 | |
| BCD 9: | 0000 | 1001 | |

BCD 19 shifted one bit to the right results in a non-valid BCD code in the unit decade. The least significant bit in the tens decade provides a value of 10 before shifting. Since a shift to the right represents a division by 2, we expect the shifted bit to carry a value of 5 into the units decade. However, the shifted bit gives a value of 8 since it is placed in the most significant bit position of the units decade. A subtraction by 3 is then required to correct the BCD number.

The procedure for dividing a BCD number by 2 is as follows: shift the number once to the right and inspect each decade; if the most significant bit of any decade is a 1, the decade is corrected by subtracting 3 from its value.

The hardware for the BCD-to-binary conversion consists of two shift registers as shown in Fig. 10-15. Register $A$ holds the BCD number with four flip-flops per decade. The converted binary number is formed in register $B$. The procedure is to shift both $A$ and $B$ once to the right and correct any BCD decade if its value is equal to or greater than 8. In this way, the BCD number is divided by 2 and the remainder is accumulated in register $B$. This

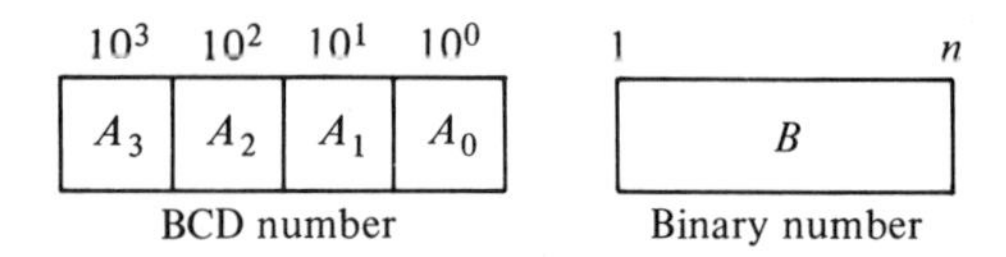


**Fig. 10-15** Registers for BCD-to-binary conversion.

process is repeated $n$ times, where $n$ is the number of bits of the binary number.

The flow chart algorithm for BCD-to-binary conversion is shown in Fig. 10-16. The BCD number is in register $A$ and register $B$ is cleared. A sequence counter $SC$ is set to a number equal to the number of bits of the desired binary value. Both registers $A$ and $B$ are shifted once to the right with the right-most bit from $A$ going into the left-most bit of $B$. Each decade is then inspected to see if it has a 1 in its most significant bit position. If it does, the decade is subtracted by 3. The process is repeated $n$ times to pro-

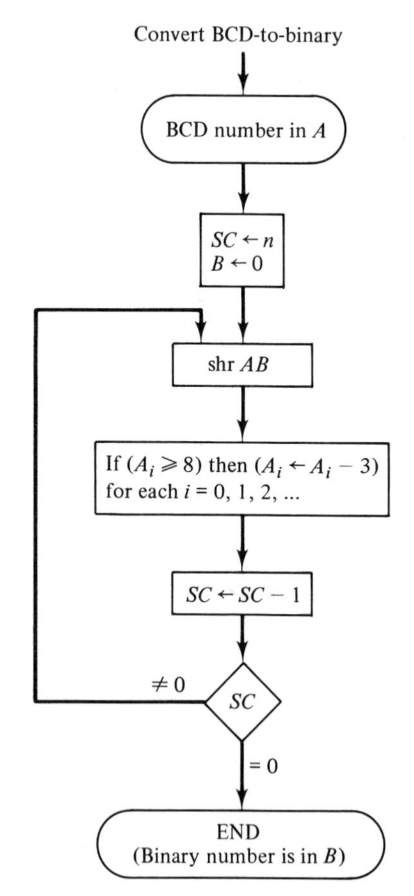


**Fig. 10-16** BCD-to-binary conversion algorithm.

vide an $n$-bit binary number in register $B$. Note that the correction is done only once after the shift. In other words, if after subtracting 3 the decade holds a number equal to 8 or 9, the corrected decade is left as is; a second subtraction is not allowed.

A numerical example that illustrates the BCD-to-binary conversion algorithm is shown in Table 10-2. BCD 249 is converted to binary by repeated shifts and corrections (when necessary). Note that the sequence counter is set to 10 because a 3-digit decimal number, when converted to binary, may produce a binary number of up to 10 bits.

**Table 10-2** *Example of BCD-to-binary conversion*

$(249)_{10} = (0010\ 0100\ 1001)_{BCD} = (11111001)_2$

| *Micro-Operation* | $A_2$ | $A_1$ | $A_0$ | *B (binary)* | *SC* |
|---|---|---|---|---|---|
| initial | 0010 | 0100 | 1001 | 00000000 | 10 |
| shr | 0001 | 0010 | 0100 | 1 | 9 |
| shr | 0000 | 1001 | 0010 | 01 | |
| sub 3 from $A_1$ | 0000 | 0110 | 0010 | 01 | 8 |
| shr | 0000 | 0011 | 0001 | 001 | 7 |
| shr | 0000 | 0001 | 1000 | 1001 | |
| sub 3 from $A_0$ | 0000 | 0001 | 0101 | 1001 | 6 |
| shr | 0000 | 0000 | 1010 | 11001 | |
| sub 3 from $A_0$ | 0000 | 0000 | 0111 | 11001 | 5 |
| shr | 0000 | 0000 | 0011 | 111001 | 4 |
| shr | 0000 | 0000 | 0001 | 1111001 | 3 |
| shr | 0000 | 0000 | 0000 | 11111001 | 2 |
| shr | 0000 | 0000 | 0000 | 011111001 | 1 |
| shr | 0000 | 0000 | 0000 | 0011111001 | 0 |

### *Binary-to-BCD Conversion*

Consider a 4-bit binary number given by the following expression:

$$N = a_3 2^3 + a_2 2^2 + a_1 2 + a_0$$

This can be expressed in a different form to show a repeated multiplication by 2:

$$N = ((2a_3 + a_2)2 + a_1)2 + a_0$$

This form suggests a procedure for converting the binary number $a_3 a_2 a_1 a_0$ into decimal. The procedure consists of multiplying $a_3$ by 2 and adding $a_2$. The result is multiplied by 2 and then $a_1$ is added. The new result is multiplied by 2 and $a_0$ added. As a numerical illustration, let the binary number be 10011 (decimal 19). The conversion which begins with the most significant bit is shown below.

$$1 = 1$$
$$1 \times 2 + 0 = 2$$
$$2 \times 2 + 0 = 4$$
$$4 \times 2 + 1 = 9$$
$$9 \times 2 + 1 = 19$$

This process requires that the partially formed decimal number be multiplied by 2 and one bit from the binary number added to the product.

For decimal numbers in BCD, the multiplication by 2 can be done by a left shift provided the BCD digits are corrected. The bit from the binary number can be added by shifting it into the least significant position. This suggests the use of the two shift registers of Fig. 10-15. The binary number is initially stored in $B$ and both registers $A$ and $B$ are shifted to the left. The binary bit from $B$ goes into $A$ and the BCD number in $A$ is multiplied by 2.

Shifting of a BCD number to the left will multiply the number by 2 provided it is corrected properly. Consider for example BCD 9. When 1001 is shifted left, it produces 1 0010 which is 18 in binary but is 12 in BCD. Adding 0110 to the number produces 1 1000 which is 18 as required. Thus, the bit shifted from one decade to the next has the value of 16 when considered as binary but gives a value of 10 for BCD representation. The difference, 6, is lost and must be restored by adding it to the decade that generated the carry. Another approach that can be used to obtain the same result is to add 3 before shifting. The shift-left operation, being equivalent to multiplication by 2, will result in a correction having a numerical value of 6. The correction must be applied if the decade is in the range of 5 to 9 since these are the numbers that produce a carry when multiplied by 2.

The algorithm for binary-to-BCD conversion is shown in the flow chart of Fig. 10-17. We use the two registers $A$ and $B$ as before, but now the binary number is in $B$ and the BCD number is formed in $A$. The number of shifts is equal to the number of bits in the binary number. The correction is done *before* the shift by inspecting each decade. If it is equal to or greater than 5, we add 3 to the decade and then shift left. This multiplies the BCD number by two and brings one bit of the binary number into $A$. The process is repeated $n$ times and the required BCD number is then found in $A$.

A numerical example that illustrates the binary-to-BCD conversion is presented in Table 10-3. Note that contrary to the previous algorithm, the correction is done *before* the shift and the sequence counter is decremented after the shift.

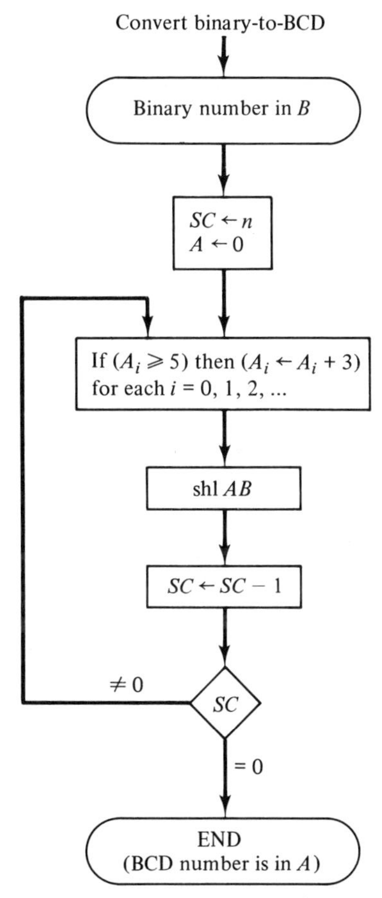


**Fig. 10-17** Binary-to-BCD conversion algorithm.

### *ROM Converters*

We have already mentioned that a read-only memory (ROM) can implement any combinational circuit. As such, it can implement any code conversion scheme. The binary code to be converted is applied to the input address lines of ROM and the converted code is made available at the outputs of the ROM. To construct such a function, we need to list the truth table that shows the binary relations between the two codes. The truth table is then used to mask the 1's and 0's in each word of ROM.

A 32 by 5 ROM that can be used as a BCD-to-binary converter is shown in Fig. 10-18(a). 32 words require five address lines. We utilize the fact that the least significant bit of the BCD number is equal to the least significant bit of the binary number. Therefore, the low-order bit does not have to be applied to the converter. The largest BCD number that can be used is 39. This

**Table 10-3** *Example of binary-to-BCD conversion*

$(11111001)_2 = (0010\ 0100\ 1001)_{BCD} = (249)_{10}$

| *Micro-Operation* | $A_2$ | $A_1$ | $A_0$ | *B (binary)* | *SC* |
|---|---|---|---|---|---|
| initial | 0000 | 0000 | 0000 | 11111001 | 8 |
| shl | | | 0001 | 1111001 | 7 |
| shl | | | 0011 | 111001 | 6 |
| shl | | | 0111 | 11001 | 5 |
| add 3 to $A_0$ | | | 1010 | 11001 | |
| shl | | 0001 | 0101 | 1001 | 4 |
| add 3 to $A_0$ | | 0001 | 1000 | 1001 | |
| shl | | 0011 | 0001 | 001 | 3 |
| shl | | 0110 | 0010 | 01 | 2 |
| add 3 to $A_1$ | | 1001 | 0010 | 01 | |
| shl | 0001 | 0010 | 0100 | 1 | 1 |
| shl | 0010 | 0100 | 1001 | 00000000 | 0 |

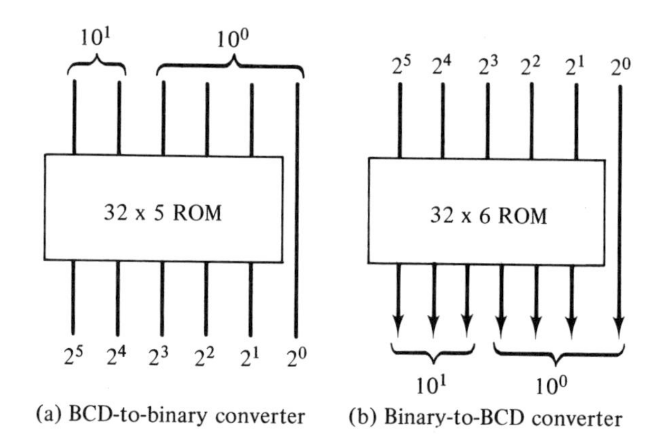


(a) BCD-to-binary converter (b) Binary-to-BCD converter

**Fig. 10-18** ROM converters.

gives a binary number of six bits. However, only five outputs are needed because the low-order bit is generated externally. The ROM can be easily specified by a truth table. Note that with five address lines it is possible to specify 32 inputs. However, only 20 of them have a meaning in BCD. The other 12 input combinations can be specified to give an all 0's output.

A 32 by 6 ROM is shown in Fig. 10-18(b) to provide a binary-to-BCD conversion. Again the low-order bit is the same for binary and BCD so it does not have to go through the converter. Since six bits can represent a number as large as 63, it is necessary to provide seven outputs for the BCD equivalent. One of these outputs is external so the ROM needs six output lines. ROMs that provide various types of code conversions are available in integrated circuit packages.

## 10-7 CONCLUDING REMARKS

The purpose of this chapter has been to suggest typical algorithms for implementing various arithmetic operations. Considering the complexity of the arithmetic processes, it should be evident that there can be many different algorithms for each one of the operations considered. Among the variety of algorithms, the ones presented here were chosen to have the simplest possible procedure for implementing the stated operation with the type of data considered. The reader should realize that many other arithmetic algorithms have been developed and many more will be developed. Although two algorithms may accomplish the same result, one may be better than the other depending on the particular application.

Some arithmetic algorithms are more suitable for minimizing the amount of equipment as would be required if the operations are implemented in a pocket calculator. Other algorithms have been developed so as to minimize the execution time by employing various short cut techniques. High-speed arithmetic algorithms are frequently used in large scale, high-speed computer systems. Algorithms used for software implementation may require that a limited number of processor registers be shared. While some operands (or parts of floating-point operands) are being processed, other operands (or parts of operands) are held temporarily in memory. Software algorithms must consider the time lost during the transfer of operands between memory and processor and an attempt must be made to minimize these transfers.

Many different arithmetic algorithms can be found in computer design books and in computer professional journals. The list of references at the end of Chap. 9 can serve also as a reference for this chapter and for further investigation of this subject.

## PROBLEMS

10-1 Perform the arithmetic operations below with binary numbers and with negative numbers in signed-2's complement representation. Use seven bits to accomodate each number together with its sign. In each case, determine if there is an overflow by checking the carries into and out of the sign bit position.

(a) $(+35) + (+40)$

(b) $(-35) + (-40)$

(c) $(-35) - (+40)$

10-2 Consider the binary numbers when they are in signed-2's complement representation. Each number has $n$ bits: one for the sign and $k = n - 1$ for the magnitude. A negative number $-X$ is represented as $2^k + (2^k - X)$, where the first $2^k$ designates the sign bit and $(2^k - X)$ is the 2's complement of $X$. A positive number is represented as $0 + X$, where the 0 designates the sign bit, and $X$, the $k$-bit magnitude. Using these generalized symbols, prove that the sum $(\pm X) + (\pm Y)$ can be formed by adding the numbers including their sign bits and discarding the carry out of the sign-bit position. In other words, prove the algorithm for adding two binary numbers in signed-2's complement representation.

10-3 Formulate a hardware procedure for detecting an overflow by comparing the sign of the sum with the signs of the augend and addend. The numbers are in signed-2's complement representation.

10-4 (a) Perform the operation $(-9) + (-6) = -15$ with binary numbers in signed-1's complement representation using only five bits to represent each number (including the sign). Show that the overflow detection procedure presented in Fig. 10-1 fails for this case.
(b) How should the procedure $AVF \leftarrow E \oplus F$ be modified for detecting an overflow when signed-1's complement numbers are used?
(c) Is the procedure suggested in Prob. 10-3 valid for signed-1's complement numbers?

10-5 Derive an algorithm in flow chart form for adding and subtracting two fixed-point binary numbers when negative numbers are in signed-1's complement representation.

10-6 Extend the table in Fig. 10-1 by including the other four possible inputs to FA. From the value of $S_1$ obtained, determine the relative magnitudes of the two numbers.

10-7 Show the diagram of a 3 by 3 array multiplier using nine AND gates, three full-adders and three half-adders.

10-8 Obtain the diagram of a 4 by 3 array multiplier using 12 AND gates and two 4-bit binary parallel adders.

10-9 List a few typical entries of the truth table for a 64 by 5 ROM that implements a 3 by 3 array multiplier. The least significant bit of the product is formed by an AND gate without using the ROM.

10-10 An array multiplier can be used to multiply two binary numbers in signed-2's complement representation if the sign bit is determined separately and the other bits are multiplied through an array multiplier. However, the product out of the array multiplier must be corrected. The correction algorithm depends on whether $X$ (multiplicand) or $Y$ (multiplier) or both are negative: If $X$ is negative, add the 2's complement of $Y$ to the most significant half of the product. If $Y$ is negative, add the 2's complement of $X$ to the most significant half of the product. If both $X$ and $Y$ are negative, add $X$ plus $Y$ to the most significant half of the product and discard the carry.

(a) Show that this procedure is valid by performing the multiplication of binary ($\pm 101$) by ($\pm 110$) four times, each time with a different set of signs and with negative numbers being in their 2's complement form.
(b) Prove that the stated corrections will produce the correct product for any two numbers of $n$ bits each.

10-11 A momentary overflow may occur while forming a partial product during multiplication with signed-2's complement numbers. Show that the arithmetic shift right symbolized by ashr ($AVF$ & $AC$ & $Q$) in Fig. 10-5 should be implemented as follows:
(a) If $AVF = 0$, shift $AC$ & $Q$ without changing $A_s$.
(b) If $AVF = 1$, shift $AC$ & $Q$, complement $A_s$ and clear $AVF$.

10-12 Derive a flow chart algorithm for multiplying two binary numbers in signed-2's complement representation. Both multiplier and multiplicand are changed to positive numbers at the beginning. The positive product is 2's complemented if it is to be negative.

10-13 Show the step-by-step multiplication process as given in the flow chart of Fig. 10-5 when the following numbers are multiplied. Assume 5-bit registers that hold both sign and magnitude. The multiplicand in each case is $+15$.
(a) $(+15) \times (+13)$
(b) $(+15) \times (-13)$

10-14 The following operation is encountered in the flow chart of Fig. 10-6:

$$AQ \leftarrow \overline{AQ} + 1$$

where $AQ$ is a combined register made up of registers $A$ and $Q$. Assume that only one register at a time can be 1's complemented or incremented. Specify the sequence of micro-operations in flow chart form for implementing the above operation.

10-15 Show the step-by-step division process as given in the flow chart of Fig. 10-6 when $(-160)/(+12)$ is computed. Assume 5-bit registers that hold both sign and magnitude.

10-16 (a) Prove that if $2^x$ is equal to $10^y$ then $y = 0.3x$.
(b) Using this relation, show that a 36-bit register can accomodate an integer signed binary number equivalent to 11 decimal digits.
(c) What would be the largest positive number that can be accomodated if the 36-bit register holds a floating-point number with eight exponent bits and integer representation for the mantissa?

10-17 A binary floating point number has seven bits for a biased exponent. The constant used for the bias is 64.
(a) List the biased representation of all exponents from $-64$ to $+63$.
(b) Show that a 7-bit magnitude comparator can be used to compare the relative magnitude of the two exponents.
(c) Show that after the addition of two biased exponents it is necessary to subtract 64 in order to have a biased exponent sum. How would you subtract 64 by adding its 2's complement value?

(d) Show that after the subtraction of two biased exponents it is necessary to add 64 in order to have a biased exponent difference.

10-18 Derive an algorithm in flow chart form for the comparison of two signed binary numbers when negative numbers are in signed-2's complement representation

(a) by means of a subtraction operation with the signed-2's complement numbers.

(b) by scanning and comparing pairs of bits from left to right.

10-19 Repeat Prob. 10-18 for signed-magnitude binary numbers.

10-20 Let $n$ be the number of bits of the mantissa in a binary floating-point number. When the mantissas are aligned during the addition or subtraction, the exponent difference may be greater than $n - 1$. If this occurs, the mantissa with the smaller exponent is shifted entirely out of the register. Modify the mantissa alignment in Fig. 10-8 by including a sequence counter $SC$ that counts the number of shifts. If the number of shifts is greater than $n - 1$, the larger number is then used to determine the result.

10-21 The procedure for aligning mantissas during addition or subtraction of floating-point numbers can be stated as follows:

Subtract the smaller exponent from the larger and shift the mantissa having the smaller exponent right a number of places equal to the difference between the exponents. The exponent of the sum (or difference) is equal to the larger exponents.

Without using a magnitude comparator, assuming biased exponents, and taking into account that only the $AC$ can be shifted, derive an algorithm in flow-chart form for aligning the mantissas and placing the larger exponent in the $AC$.

10-22 Show that there can be no mantissa overflow after a multiplication operation.

10-23 Show that the division of two normalized floating-point numbers with fractional mantissas will always result in a normalized quotient provided a dividend alignment is carried out prior to the division operation.

10-24 Extend the flow chart of Fig. 10-10 to provide a normalized floating-point remainder in the $AC$. The mantissa should be a fraction.

10-25 The algorithms for the floating-point arithmetic operations in Sec. 10-4 neglect the possibility of exponent overflow or underflow.

(a) Go over the three flow charts and find where an exponent overflow may occur.

(b) Repeat (a) for exponent underflow. An exponent underflow occurs if the exponent is more negative than the smallest number that can be accomodated in the register.

(c) Show how an exponent overflow or underflow can be detected by the hardware.

10-26 If we assume integer representation for the mantissa of floating-point numbers, we encounter certain scaling problems during mulitplication and division. Let the number of bits in the magnitude part of the mantissa be $(n - .1)$. For integer representation:

(a) Show that if a single-precision product is used, then $(n - 1)$ must be added to the exponent product in the $AC$.

(b) Show that if a single precision mantissa dividend is used then $(n - 1)$ must be subtracted from the exponent dividend when $Q$ is cleared.

10-27 Show the hardware to be used for the addition and subtraction of two decimal numbers in signed-magnitude representation. Indicate how an overflow is detected.

10-28 Show the hardware to be used for the addition and subtraction of two decimal numbers with negative numbers in signed-10's complement representation. Indicate how an overflow is detected. Derive the flow chart algorithm and try a few numbers to convince yourself that the algorithm produces correct results.

10-29 Show the content of registers $A$, $B$, $Q$, and $SC$ during the decimal multiplication (Fig. 10-13) of (a) $470 \times 152$ and (b) $999 \times 199$. Assume 3-digit registers and take the second number as the multiplier.

10-30 Show the content of registers $A$, $E$, $Q$, and $SC$ during the decimal division (Fig. 10-14) of 1680/32. Assume 2-digit registers.

10-31 Show that sub-register $A_e$ in Fig. 10-12 is zero at the termination of (a) the decimal multiplication as specified in Fig. 10-13 and (b) the decimal division as specified in Fig. 10-14.

10-32 Change the floating-point arithmetic algorithms in Sec. 10-4 from binary to decimal data. In a table, list how each micro-operation symbol should be interpreted.

10-33 Show the step by step procedure as specified by the algorithm in Fig. 10-16 for converting BCD 999 into binary.

10-34 Show the step by step procedure as specified by the algorithm in Fig. 10-17 for converting binary 99 into BCD.

10-35 List the truth tables for the two ROM converters specified in Fig. 10-18.

# 11

# INPUT-OUTPUT ORGANIZATION

## 11-1 PERIPHERAL DEVICES

The input-output subsystem of a computer provides an efficient mode of communication between the central system and the outside environment. Programs and data must be entered into computer memory for processing and results obtained from computations must be recorded or displayed for the user. A computer serves no useful purpose without the ability to receive information from an outside source and to transmit results in a meaningful form. The simplest and cheapest way to communicate with a computer is by means of a typewriter keyboard and printer. However, this is a very slow process and wastes computer time. A central processor is an extremely fast device capable of performing operations at very high speed. When input and output information are transferred to the processor via a slow terminal, the processor will be idle most of the time while waiting for the information to arrive. To use a computer efficiently, a large amount of programs and data must be prepared in advance and entered into a storage medium such as magnetic tapes or disks. The information in the disk is then transferred into computer memory at a rapid rate. Results of programs should also be transferred into a high-speed storage, such as disks, from which they can be transferred later into a printer to provide a printed output of results.

Devices that are under the direct control of the processor are said to be connected *on-line*. These devices are designed to read information into or out of the memory unit upon command from the CPU and are considered to be part of the computer system. A device is *off-line* when it is operated independently of the computer. Off-line equipment devices are useful for preparing programs and data. For example, a key-punch is an off-line device where the operator prepares his program and data on punched cards. A line printer may be operated off-line to print results of programs from a magnetic tape. Input or output devices attached to the computer on-line or available off-line are called *peripherals.*

Among the most common peripherals are card readers and punches, paper-tape readers and punches, keyboards, printers, plotters, and display devices. Peripherals that provide auxiliary storage for the system are magnetic tapes, disks and drums. Peripherals are electromechanical and electromagnetic devices of some complexity. Only a very brief discussion of their function will be given here without going into detail of their internal construction.

*Magnetic tapes* are used mostly for storing files of data, for example, a company's payroll record. Access is sequential and consists of records which can be accessed one after another as the tape moves along a stationary read-write mechanism. It is one of the cheapest and slowest methods for storage and has the advantage that tapes can be removed when not in use. *Magnetic disks* and *drums* have high-speed rotational surfaces coated with magnetic material. Access is achieved by moving a read-write mechanism to a track in the magnetized surface. Disks and drums are used mostly for bulk storage of programs and data. Tapes, disks and drums are discussed further in Sec. 12-2 in conjunction with their role as auxiliary memory.

Programs and data are often prepared on punched cards for input to a computer. Of the different cards that are in use, the Hollerith card is the most common. A punched card consists of 80 columns of 12 rows each. Each column represents an alphanumeric character of 12 bits by punching holes in the appropriate rows. A hole is sensed as a 1 and the absence of a hole as a 0. Punched cards offer a great convenience because they carry a complete record in a single separable card. The deletion of unwanted cards or the insertion of new cards in a card deck is a very simple process. For this reason, punched cards are very convenient for correcting errors in a program or for using different data for the same program. The 12-bit character code employed in punched cards is inefficient with respect to the number of bits used. Most computers convert the card code into an internal 6-bit code to conserve bits of storage.

A *card reader* is an electromechanical input device that senses holes in cards and produces electrical signals. The sensing is done by brush contacts which develop signals as they detect holes in the card that slides over them. The cards can be moved past the brushes to sense one column at a time or one row at a time. Cards can be read in this manner at speeds of a few hundred per minute. Higher reading speeds are attainable by using photoelectric sensing cells. Holes in the cards allow light to pass through to energize the photo cell that, in response to the light, produces electrical signals. Cards can be read in this manner at speeds of 1000 to 2000 per minute.

A *card-punch* is an electromechanical output device that punches holes in cards. The holes in each column are specified by the alphanumeric binary code presented to a buffer register. Cards are seldom used for output since people prefer to obtain results in printed form. They are sometimes used to punch a binary program after it is translated by a compiler. The binary program can then be used again without the need of a repeated compilation.

A *paper-tape reader and punch* provide a relatively inexpensive method of input and output for a computer. The paper tape commonly used is a one-inch wide strip of paper with eight hole positions along the tape width. In addition, a single strip of small holes along the paper provides sprockets that are used to hold the paper properly in place and to sense when the tape is in a reading position. Binary information is punched in the eight information channels in each row with a hole representing a 1 and no hole a 0. Each row of eight bits may represent the code of one alphanumeric character or part of a binary program. Paper tapes are also available with five, six, or seven hole positions per row. Often a paper-tape reader and punch are mounted on a teletypwriter. As the operator types characters on the keyboard, the unit can be made to punch the character on paper tape. When the computer prints results on the typewriter, the paper punch may be turned on to punch the characters being printed. In this way, a permanent record is produced and the paper tape can be used off-line to type a duplicate record.

Paper tape is subject to tear and is more awkward to handle than punched cards. The only reason that paper tape is used is its relatively low cost. An alternative to the paper-tape reader and punch is the digital *cassette recorder*. The cassette tape can be prepared off-line using a keyboard coupled with a cassette recorder. The advantage of cassette over paper tape is its compact size and ease of loading. Digital *cartridge recorders* are similar to cassettes except that they have more reliable reel-mounted performance and provide greater transfer rates than the lower-cost cassette units.

A *teletypewriter* is basically an electric typewriter which, in addition, has a capability of sending keyboard information and receiving printed information remotely via electric wires. The information is transmitted by a series of pulses representing the binary code of the character whose key is struck or the character that is printed. A teletypewriter is sometimes called a *teleprinter* or *Teletype*. The keyboard is used as an input terminal and the printer as an output terminal. The transfer rate of teletypewriters is very low, ranging from 10 to 100 characters per second. They are sometimes used in very small computers as a primary input and output device. In many computers, they are used as an operator's console or as remote terminals for time-sharing systems.

An *interactive display* device is similar to a teletypewriter except that characters are displayed on a cathode-ray tube instead of being printed. These devices commonly offer editing capabilities and a local storage. The text entered from the keyboard is stored in the local memory for later transmission to the computer. A characteristic feature of display devices is a cursor which marks the position in the screen where the next character will be inserted. The cursor can be moved to any position in the screen, to a single character, the beginning of a word, or to any line. Edit keys add or delete information based on the cursor position. The display terminal can operate in a Teletype mode where each character entered on the screen through the keyboard is simultaneously transmitted to the computer. In the block mode, the edited text is first stored off-line in the local memory and when ready, it is transferred to the computer as a block of information.

Teletypewriters and display devices can print or display one character at a time across a line. For faster printing, a high-speed *line printer* is commonly employed. This type of printer can print entire lines of up to 120 characters at a rate of up to 1000 lines per minute. All characters for a line are transferred to the printer at electronic speed and stored in a buffer memory until a complete line is assembled. The characters for the line stored in the buffer memory are then printed with one mechanical operation. The paper moves at a uniform speed so that when the next set of characters are assembled, they are printed in the next line. Mechanical printers are limited in their speed by the mechanical motion of the parts. When multiple copies are not required, an electrostatic printer can be used to print lines at a speed of thousands of lines per minute. Electrostatic printers require special paper with electrical conductive material. The characters are produced by charging the special paper with small dot patterns by means of electrodes.

Other input and output devices encountered in computer systems are digital incremental plotters, optical and magnetic character readers, analog to digital converters and various data acquisition equipment. Computers can be used to control various processes in real time such as machine tooling, assembly line procedures and chemical and industrial processes. For such applications, a method must be provided for sensing status conditions in the process and sending control signals to the process being controlled.

The input-output organization of a computer is a function of the size of the computer and the devices connected to it. The difference between a small and large system is largely dependent on the amount of hardware the computer has available for communicating with peripheral units and the number of peripherals connected to the system. Since each peripheral behaves differently from any other, it would be prohibitive to dwell on the detailed interconnections needed between the computer and each peripheral. Certain techniques common to most peripherals are presented in this chapter.

## 11-2 I/O INTERFACE

Input-output (I/O) interface provides a method for transferring binary information between internal storage, such as memory and CPU registers, and external I/O devices. Peripherals connected on-line to a computer need special communication links for interfacing them with the central processor. The purpose of the communication link is to resolve the differences that exist between the central computer and each peripheral. The major differences are:

1. Peripherals are electromechanical devices and their manner of operation is different from the operation of the CPU and memory which are electronic devices.
2. The data transfer rate of peripherals is much slower than the transfer rate in the central computer.
3. The operation of the peripherals must be synchronized with the operation of the CPU and memory unit.
4. Data formats in peripherals differ from the word format in the central processor.
5. The operation of each peripheral must be controlled so as not to disturb the operation of the central computer and other peripherals connected to the system.

To resolve these differences, computer systems invariably include special hardware components between the central computer and peripherals to supervise all input and output transfers. Large computers include an I/O processor in the system to provide a pathway for the transfer of information passing between input and output devices and internal memory. The I/O processor is sometimes called a *data channel controller*, since it controls and regulates the flow of data to and from the internal and external parts of the computer. To keep the price low, small computers come without an I/O processor but instead, an interface module is provided for each peripheral that is attached to the computer.

### *I/O Bus and Interface Module*

A typical communication link between a computer and several peripherals is shown in Fig. 11-1. The computer has an I/O control that supervises the flow of information in the I/O bus. The computer I/O control receives instructions from the CPU and proceeds to execute them by communicating with the peripheral through its interface. Each peripheral has associated with it

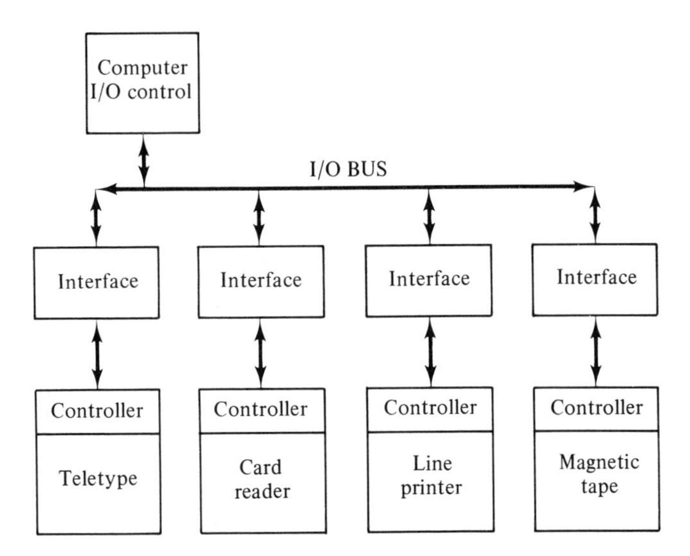


**Fig. 11-1** I/O communication link.

an interface module. The interface logic decodes the commands received from the I/O bus, interprets them for the peripheral and provides signals for the peripheral controller. It also synchronizes the data flow and supervises the transfer rate between peripheral and computer. Each peripheral has its own controller that operates and controls the particular electromechanical device. For example, a line-printer controller controls the paper motion, the print timing, and the selection of printing characters. A controller may be housed separately or may be physically integrated with the peripheral. Several peripherals of the same type may sometimes share a common controller.

The I/O bus of most computers is a common bus attached to all peripheral interfaces. To communicate with a particular device, the I/O control places a device address on a set of lines in the bus. Each interface attached to the common bus contains an address decoder which monitors continuously the address lines. When the interface detects its own address code, it activates the paths between the I/O bus lines and the peripheral controller. All peripherals whose code does not correspond to the address code in the bus are disabled by their interface.

At the same time that the address is made available in the address lines, the computer I/O control provides a function code on another set of lines in the bus. The selected interface decodes the function code and proceeds to execute it. The function code is often called a *command* and is in essence an instruction that is executed in the interface module.

To see how the computer generates commands for the peripheral, consider an I/O instruction format in a typical minicomputer as shown in Fig. 11-2.

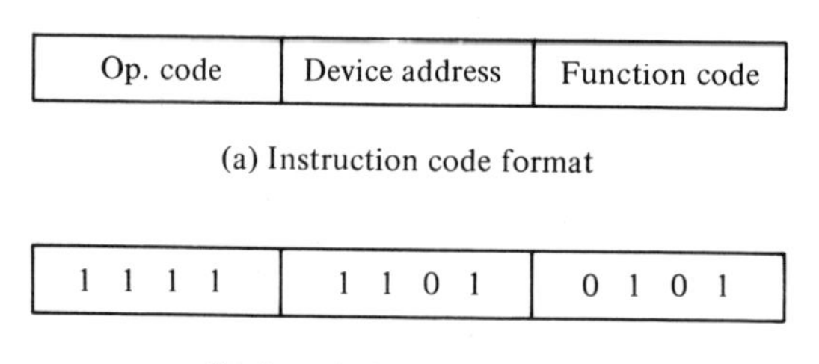


(a) Instruction code format

(b) A typical instruction code

**Fig. 11-2** Typical I/O instruction.

The instruction is read from memory during the fetch cycle and placed in an instruction register. The instruction has three fields. The operation code field distinguishes the instruction as an I/O type. The device address field can specify up to 16 peripherals. The function code specifies the command for the I/O interface. In this example, we assume that all I/O instructions have an operation code 1111. The instruction specifies the peripheral with assigned address 1101 and the function code is a command for this peripheral.

The connection of the I/O bus to the computer is shown in Fig. 11-3. It consists of the address lines, the function code lines and bidirectional data lines for data transfer to and from the accumulator register and the interface. The sense lines detect the status of the peripheral as for example, the status of the flag that indicates the readiness of the peripheral for data transfer.

The connection of the I/O bus to an interface is shown in Fig. 11-4. The address bits are decoded through an AND gate and the output of the gate enables the control section of the interface. It is assumed that the assigned

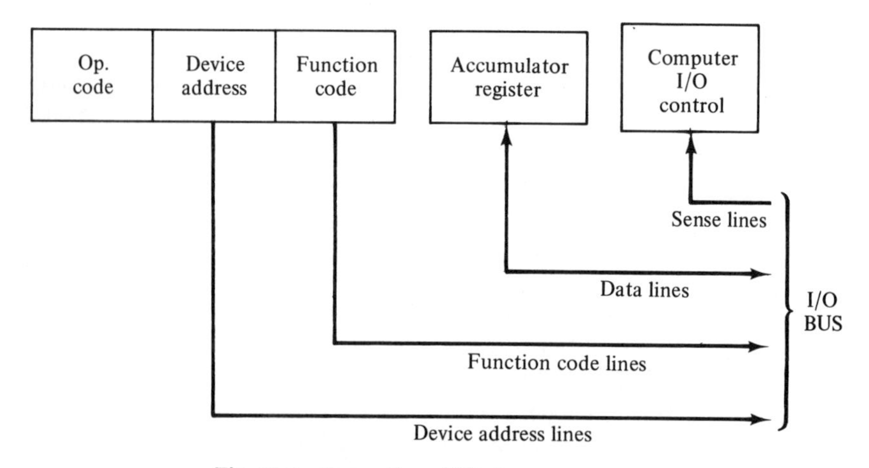


**Fig. 11-3** Connection of I/O bus to computer.

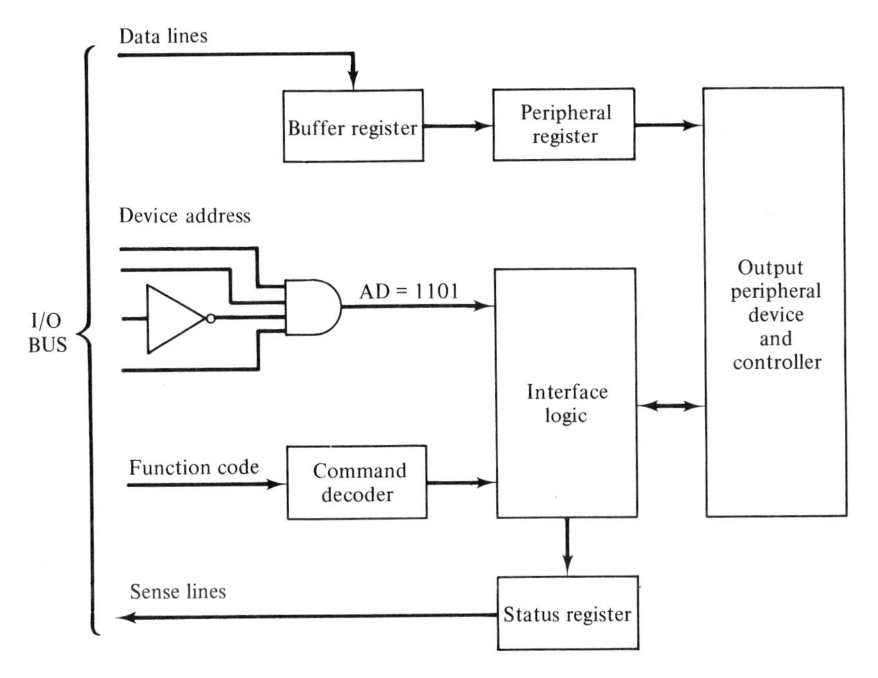


**Fig. 11-4** Connection of I/O bus to one interface.

device address for this peripheral is 1101 so the output of the gate is 1 only when the address lines contain these bits; otherwise, the output of the gate is 0. The function code bits are decoded in the command decoder. The decoded function is then applied to the interface control to activate the specified command. The interface has a buffer register for holding the data being transferred through the I/O bus. A second register is used to transfer data to the output peripheral device. The status register stores the flags that notify the computer of important conditions in the interface. These include conditions that data has been received from the peripheral, that the interface is ready to receive data from the computer, as well as error indications such as parity error, or device power being off.

An interface is assigned the task of synchronizing the data flow between computer and peripheral. For data input synchronization the interface receives an item of data at the rate that the peripheral can provide and transfers it to the computer through the I/O bus whenever it is available. For output synchronization, the interface receives an item of data from the I/O bus and holds it in its buffer register. It is then transferred to the peripheral at the rate it can be accepted. The interface must have specialized control signals to communicate with the particular peripheral to which it is attached.

### *Types of Commands*

The computer issues commands through its function code bits. The interpretation of the command depends on the peripheral that it is addressing. There are four types of commands that an interface may receive when it is addressed by the computer. They are classified as *control*, *sense*, *data-output*, and *data-input*.

A *control* command is issued to activate the peripheral and to inform it what to do. For example, a magnetic-tape unit may be instructed to backspace the tape by one record, to rewind the tape, or to start the tape moving in the forward direction. The particular control command issued depends upon the peripheral and each peripheral receives its own distinguished sequence of control commands dependent on its own mode of operation.

A *sense* command is used to test various status conditions in the interface, the controller, or the peripheral. Before a transfer of data is made, the computer may want to test the path to the peripheral to see if power is on and if the selected peripheral is connected on-line to the computer. The command decoder in the interface recognizes the conditions being tested, checks these conditions and transfers a response back to the computer via the sense lines in the I/O bus. The binary response in the sense lines is checked by the computer to determine what to do next. For example, if the status report indicates that the peripheral is available and ready, the computer then initiates a data transfer. If the device is not ready, the computer may either remain in a program loop checking the status of the peripheral or branch to some other program. A status response does not necessarily need special sense lines. The status bits may be transferred by the interface to the accumulator via the data lines. After issuing a sense command, the computer checks the bits of the accumulator and interprets the status bits according to some adopted convention.

A *data-output* command causes the interface to respond by taking an item of data, say one character, from the data lines in the I/O bus. Consider an example with a tape unit: the computer starts the tape moving by issuing a control command. The processor then monitors the status of the tape by means of sense commands. When the tape is in the correct position, the computer issues a data-output command. The interface responds to the address and command lines and transfers the data from the I/O bus data lines to its buffer register. The interface then communicates with the peripheral controller to accept a new item of data to be stored on tape.

A *data-input* command is just the opposite of a data-output. In this case, the interface receives an item of data from the peripheral and places it in its buffer register. The processor checks if data is available by means of a sense command and then issues a data-input command. The interface puts the data into the I/O data bus where it is accepted by the computer through its I/O control and placed in the accumulator register.

At some point during the bus transfer, the computer I/O control generates a strobe pulse to synchronize the transfer into the interface. This pulse occurs after all propagation delays are accounted for and when all signals are assumed to be stable. The strobe pulse is used to transfer the information from the bus to the appropriate register in the interface. The I/O control terminates the transfer by removing the strobe pulse together with the address and function code signals.

### *Modes of Transfer*

Data transfer between the central computer and peripherals is handled in one of three possible modes:

1. Data transfer under program control.
2. Interrupt initiated data transfer.
3. Direct memory access (DMA) transfer.

Program-controlled operations are the result of I/O instructions written in the computer program. Each data item transfer is initiated by an instruction in the program. Usually the transfer is to and from a processor register such as accumulator and peripheral. Another instruction is needed to transfer the data to and from accumulator and memory. Transferring data under program control requires constant monitoring of the peripheral by the processor. Once a data transfer is initiated, the processor is required to monitor the peripheral flag to see when a transfer can again be made. It is up to the processor to keep close tabs on everything that is taking place in the interface unit. Examples of program controlled input-output operations can be found in Sec. 6-8.

In the program controlled transfer, the processor stays in a program loop until the I/O unit indicates that it is ready. This is a time-consuming process since it keeps the processor busy needlessly. It can be avoided by using an interrupt facility and special commands to inform the interface to issue an interrupt request when the peripheral becomes available. The processor then goes to execute another program. The interface meanwhile keeps monitoring the peripheral. When the interface determines that the peripheral is ready for data transfer, it generates an interrupt request to the processor. Upon detecting an interrupt, the processor stops momentarily the task it is doing, branches to a service routine to process the data transfer, and then returns to the task it was performing. Interrupt initiated I/O transfers are discussed in more detail in Sec. 11-5.

Transfer of data under program control is through the I/O bus and between processor and peripheral. In direct memory access (DMA), the interface transfers data into and out of the memory unit through the memory bus. The CPU initiates this type of transfer by supplying the interface with a starting memory address and the number of words and then proceeds to other tasks. When a transfer is made, the interface requests a memory cycle through the memory bus. When the request is granted by the memory controller, the interface transfers a data word directly into memory. Such a transfer is said to *steal* a memory cycle from the processor. The processor merely delays its operation for one memory cycle to allow the direct memory I/O transfer. Since peripheral speed is much slower then processor speed, I/O memory transfers are infrequent compared to processor access to memory. An example of a direct memory access is presented in Sec. 11-4.

Many computers combine the interface logic with the requirements for a direct memory access into one unit and call it a data channel. A data channel is an I/O processor that can handle many peripherals through a DMA and interrupt facility. In such a system, the central computer can be divided into three separate modules: the memory unit, the CPU and the I/O processor. I/O processors are discussed in Secs. 11-6 and 11-7.

### *Software Considerations*

The previous discussion was concerned with the basic hardware needed to interface peripherals to a computer system. A computer must also have software routines for controlling peripherals and for transfer of data between the processor and peripherals. I/O routines must issue control commands to activate the peripheral and to check the device status to determine when it is ready for data transfer. Once ready, information is transferred item by item until all the data are transferred. In some cases, a control command is then given to execute a device function such as stop tape or print characters. Error checking and other useful steps often accompany the transfers. In interrupt controlled transfers, the I/O software must issue commands to the peripheral to interrupt when ready and to service the interrupt when it occurs. In DMA transfer, the I/O software must initiate the DMA channel to start its operation.

Software control of input-output equipment is a complex undertaking. For this reason I/O routines for standard peripherals are provided by the manufacturer as part of the computer system. Quite often they are included within the operating system. Most operating systems are supplied with a variety of I/O programs to support the particular line of peripherals offerred for a computer. I/O routines are usually available as macros or subroutines and the programmer uses the established routines to specify the type of transfer required without going into detailed machine language programs.

## 11-3 ASYNCHRONOUS SERIAL INTERFACE

The transfer of data between two units may be done in parallel or serial. In parallel data transmission, each bit of the message has its own path and the total message is transmitted at the same time. This means that an $n$-bit message must be transmitted through $n$ separate conductor paths. In serial data transmission, each bit in the message is sent in sequence one at a time. This method requires the use of one pair of conductors or one conductor and a common ground. Parallel transmission is faster but requires many wires. It is used for short distances and where speed is important. Serial transmission is slower but is less expensive since it requires only one pair of conductors.

The transfer of information between computer and interface is usually done in parallel, especially when the interface is in close proximity. The transfer between a peripheral and its interface may be in parallel or serial depending on the type of peripheral used.

The transfer of information between two independent units is asynchronous unless they share a common clock. The transfer between a computer and interface is usually asynchronous. One way of synchronizing the transfer is by means of a strobe pulse that the computer provides in the I/O bus. The transfer of information between a peripheral and its interface may be synchronous or asynchronous. In synchronous transmission, both units share a common clock. Bits are sent from one unit to another at equal intervals of time determined by the clock pulses which are available in both units. In asynchronous transfer, there is no clock that informs one unit when the other is sending the information. Control signals similar to a strobe may be employed to synchronize the two units. Sometimes, other techniques are used to inform the receiver when the transmitter is sending information.

A serial asynchronous data transmission technique used in most interactive terminals, such as Teletypes, employs special bits which are inserted at both ends of the character code. With this technique, each character consists of three parts: a start bit, the data bits, and stop bits. An example of this format is shown in Fig. 11-5. The convention in these terminals is that the transmitter rests at the 1-state when no message is transmitted. The first bit, called the start bit, is always a 0 and is used to indicate the beginning of a character. A character can be detected by the receiver from knowledge of four rules:

1. When data are not being sent, the line is kept in the 1 state.
2. The initiation of a character transmission is detected by a start bit which is always a 0.
3. The character bits always follow the start bit.

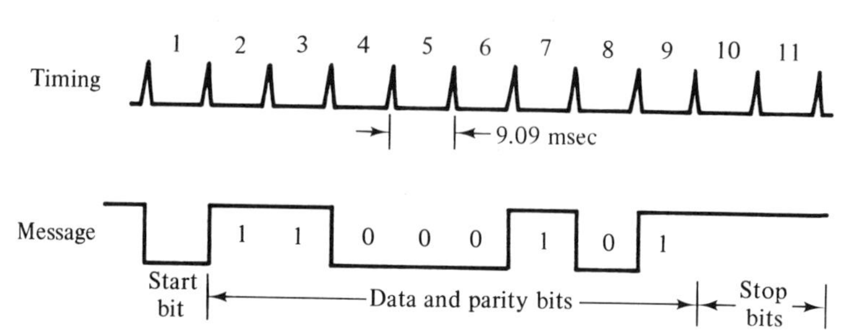


**Fig. 11-5** Asychronous serial transmission.

4. After the last character bit is transmitted, a stop bit is detected when the line returns to the 1-state for at least 1 bit time.

Using these rules, the interface can detect the start bit when the line goes from 1 to 0. A clock in the receiver interface then allows examination of the line at proper bit times. The receiver knows the transfer rate of the bits and the number of information bits to expect. After the character bits are transmitted, one or two stop bits are sent. The stop bits are always in the 1-state and frame the end of character to signify the idle or wait state.

At the end of the message the line is held at the 1-state for a period of at least 1 or 2 bit times so that both the transmit and receive terminals can resynchronize. The length of time that the line stays in this state depends on the amount of time required for the equipment to resynchronize. Most electromechanical equipment uses 2 stop bits. (Some newer terminals use 1 stop bit.) The line will remain in the 1-state until another character is transmitted. The stop time insures that a new character will not follow for at least 2 bit times.

As an illustration, let us consider the serial transmission in the Model 33 Teletype. This unit is very popular because of its low cost compared to other interactive terminals. The transfer rate is 10 characters per second. Each transmitted character consists of a start bit, seven information bits, a parity bit, and 2 stop bits, a total of 11 bits. The information bits specify a character according to the ASCII code.

Ten characters per second means that each character takes 0.1 second for transfer. Since there are eleven bits to be transmitted, it follows that the bit time is 9.09 msec. The receiver that accepts the message must have an internal clock that produces pulses at this interval. This is shown in Fig. 11-5 where the beginning of each pulse determines the next bit time of the message.

A Teletype has a keyboard and a printer. Every time a key is depressed, the Teletype sends an 11-bit message along a wire. To print a character in the Teletype, an 11-bit message must be received along another wire. The Teletype interface consists of a transmitter and a receiver. The transmitter accepts a character from the computer and proceeds to send a serial 11-bit message into the printer line. The recevier accepts a serial 11-bit message from the keyboard line and forwards the 8-bit character code to the computer. An integrated circuit is available which is specifically designed to provide the interface between computer and a Teletype or any other similar interactive terminal. This integrated circuit is called *asynchrouous data interface* or *universal asynchronous receiver-transmitter* and is abbreviated UART.

### *Interface Example*

We will now investigate an interface for the Teletype printer for the purpose of illustrating the internal operation of a typical interface module. The block diagram of the interface is shown in Fig. 11-6. The interface is connected to the computer on one side and to the Teletype printer on the other. The lines to and from the computer include:

1. A sense line from the output flag flip-flop *FGO*.

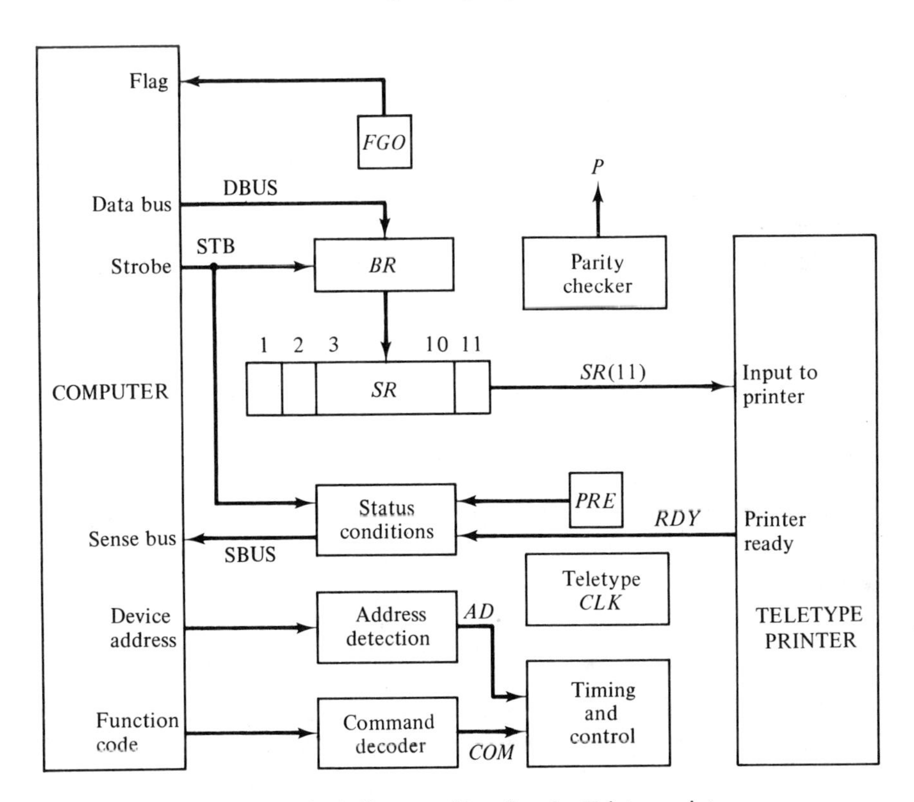


**Fig. 11-6** Block diagram of interface for Teletype printer.

2. An 8-bit data bus DBUS.
3. A strobe pulse STB.
4. A sense bus SBUS with two lines.
5. Address lines.
6. Function code lines.

The interface consists of the following registers and functional units:

1. An output flag flip-flop *FGO*.
2. An 8-bit buffer register *BR*.
3. An 11-bit shift-register *SR*.
4. A parity checker circuit whose output *P* is 1 if a parity error is detected.
5. A parity-error flip-flop *PRE* which is set to 1 if $P = 1$.
6. An address detection gate whose output *AD* is 1 if the interface detects its own address.
7. A command decoder that decodes two possible commands.
8. Timing and control for the interface.
9. A clock generator CLK that produces pulses at a rate of one every 9.09 msec.

The right-most bit of *SR* is connected to the printer intput wire through a buffer. The printer ready (*RDY*) line indicates whether power is turned on in the Teletype. The two status error conditions that are sent to the computer are *RDY* and *PRE*.

The function code can specify two commands. The *data-output* command informs the interface that an 8-bit character is available in the data bus. A *test* sense command informs the interface to transfer to the computer the status of *RDY* and *PRE*.

A flow chart that specifies the sequence of micro-operations and control decisions for the interface is shown in Fig. 11-7. Initially, *SR*(11) is set to 1 and *PRE* to 0. This provides a stop condition to the printer and clears the parity-error flip-flop. If the printer power is turned on, the *RDY* signal allows the interface to set its flag, indicating to the computer that it is ready to accept information. When the interface detects its own address, it checks the command (COM) in the command decoder. A *test* command causes the interface to transfer the status conditions *RDY* and *PRE* into the sense bus. The strobe pulse transfers this information to the computer through the SBUS. The interface then clears *PRE* and returns to check the address lines again.

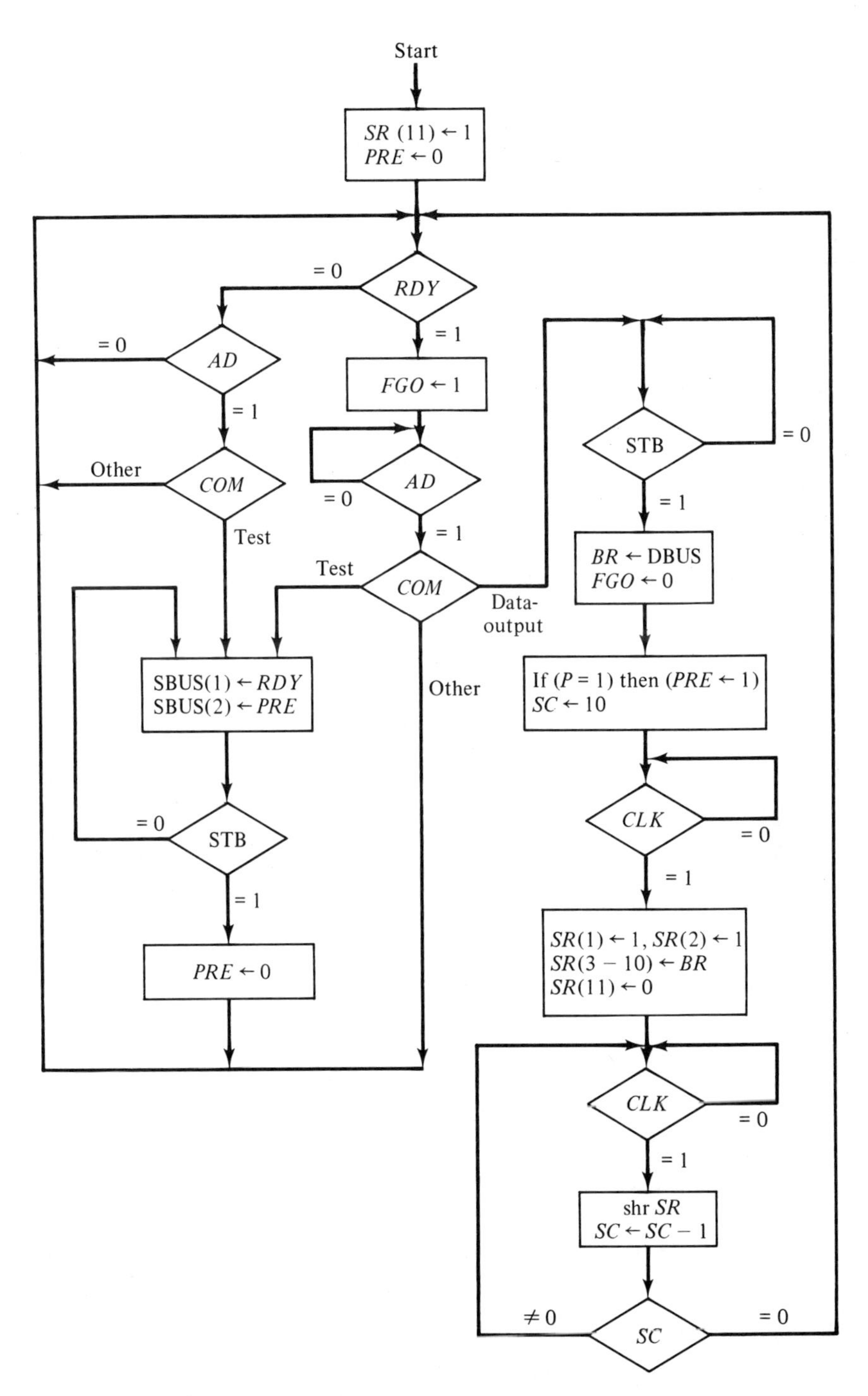


**Fig. 11-7** Flow chart for interface with Teletype printer.

If the Teletype power is off, the *RDY* signal will be 0. The interface will accept a test command under this condition and send a status report to the computer. When the computer detects that *RDY* is 0, it realizes that the printer is not operative. The computer can print a message in the operator's console telling the operator to manually turn on the inoperative printer. Alternatively, a control command could be included with the interface. The response of the interface to this type of command would be to send a signal that will turn the power on in the printer.

When a *data-output* command is detected by the interface, it transfers the 8-bit character code presently in the data bus into its buffer register *BR*. The flag is then cleared and the parity of the 8 bits is checked. If a parity error occurs, the PRE flip-flop is set to 1. A sequence counter *SC* is set to 10 to count the number of shifts in *SR*. By shifting *SR*, the 11 bits will be transmitted serially to the printer.

The interface waits for the next Teletype clock generated internally. When the next clock is detected, the *SR* register is prepared for transmitting the required 11 bits. *SR*(11) is set to 0 to provide the start bit. *SR*(3–10) receive the 8-bit character from *BR*, and *SR*(1, 2) are set to 1 to provide the two stop bits. For every occurrence of a clock pulse, the *SR* register is shifted right once. This places the next bit into *SR*(11) and into the input-printer line. After ten shifts, the second stop bit, originally in *SR*(1), will be available in *SR*(11). At this time, the interface sets its flag waiting for the next character from the computer. If the computer does not respond immediately, the input line to the printer remains in the 1 state which is the idle state. If the computer responds as soon as the flag is set, the interface inserts a start bit into *SR*(11) with the next clock pulse, and the new character is transmitted. In any case, the teletype receives at least two stop bits as required.

## 11-4 DIRECT MEMORY ACCESS

Direct memory access (DMA), as the name implies, is an interface that provides I/O transfer of data directly to and from the memory unit and peripheral. The CPU initializes the DMA by sending a memory address and the number of words to be transferred. The actual transfer of data is done directly between peripheral and the memory unit through the DMA, freeing the CPU for other tasks. The major difference between an I/O program controlled transfer and DMA is that data transfer does not employ the registers of the CPU. The transfer is done in the DMA interface by first checking if the memory unit is not used by the CPU and then the DMA *steals* one memory cycle to access a word in memory. DMA is the preferred form of data transfer for use with high-speed peripheral devices such as magnetic disks or tapes. An entire record is usually transferred between memory and peripheral.

This is stored in memory as a block of consecutive locations in a reserved space. The position of a DMA interface with other components of the computer is illustrated in Fig. 11-8.

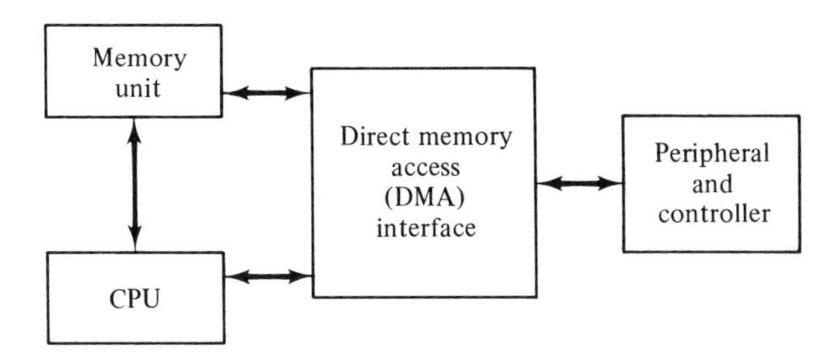


**Fig. 11-8** Block diagram of computer with DMA.

A DMA system needs the usual circuits of an interface such as a device address decoder, a command decoder, and special control logic. In addition, it needs a separate memory address register, a memory buffer register and a word count register. The address and buffer registers are used for direct communication with the memory unit. The word-count register specifies the number of words to be transferred. A computer with a DMA facility must include a special control section for the memory unit to communicate with both the CPU and DMA on a prority basis.

The DMA interface is first initialized by the CPU. After that, the DMA starts and continues to transfer data between memory and peripheral until an entire block is transferred. When the transfer is completed, the DMA prepares for the CPU a status report and then sends an interrupt request. When the CPU services the interrupt, it receives the status message and checks if the transfer was satisfactory.

The initialization process is essentially a program consisting of I/O instructions that include the device address and command codes for the DMA interface. The CPU checks the status of the peripheral and DMA and if all is in order, it sends the following information through the I/O communication lines:

1. The starting address of the memory block where data are available (for output) or where data are to be stored (for input).
2. The word count, which is the number of words in the memory block.
3. One bit specifying an input or output transfer.
4. A command to start the DMA.

The starting address, word count, and the bit specifying the direction of transfer are stored in designated registers in the DMA. The CPU then stops communicating with the DMA. The DMA does all the housekeeping operations such as packing characters into words (for input) or unpacking words into characters (for output) and checks the status of the peripheral. When a word is ready to be read or written in memory, the DMA communicates directly with the memory and receives a memory cycle for a word access.

The memory components for a system with DMA transfer are shown in the block diagram of Fig. 11-9. Both the CPU and DMA can communicate with the memory unit (MU), but DMA has priority over the CPU. Each of the three units have an address register (*AR*) and a buffer register (*BR*). A request flip-flop *RF*, one in the CPU and one in the DMA is set when the

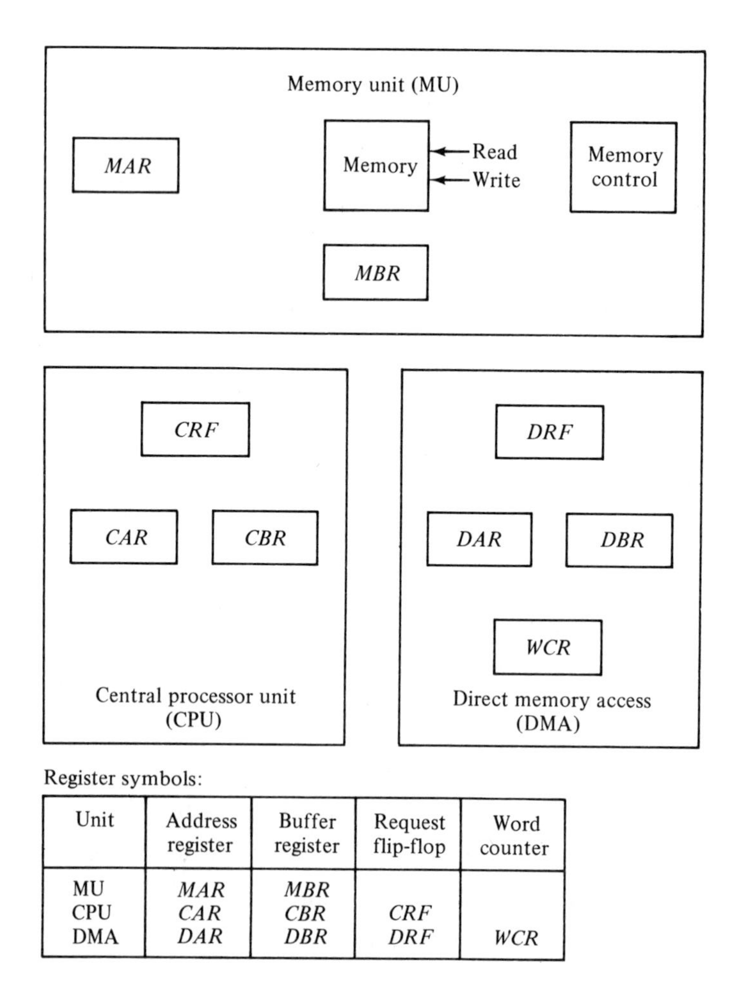


Register symbols:

| Unit | Address register | Buffer register | Request flip-flop | Word counter |
|---|---|---|---|---|
| MU | *MAR* | *MBR* | | |
| CPU | *CAR* | *CBR* | *CRF* | |
| DMA | *DAR* | *DBR* | *DRF* | *WCR* |

**Fig. 11-9** Memory configuration for DMA transfer.

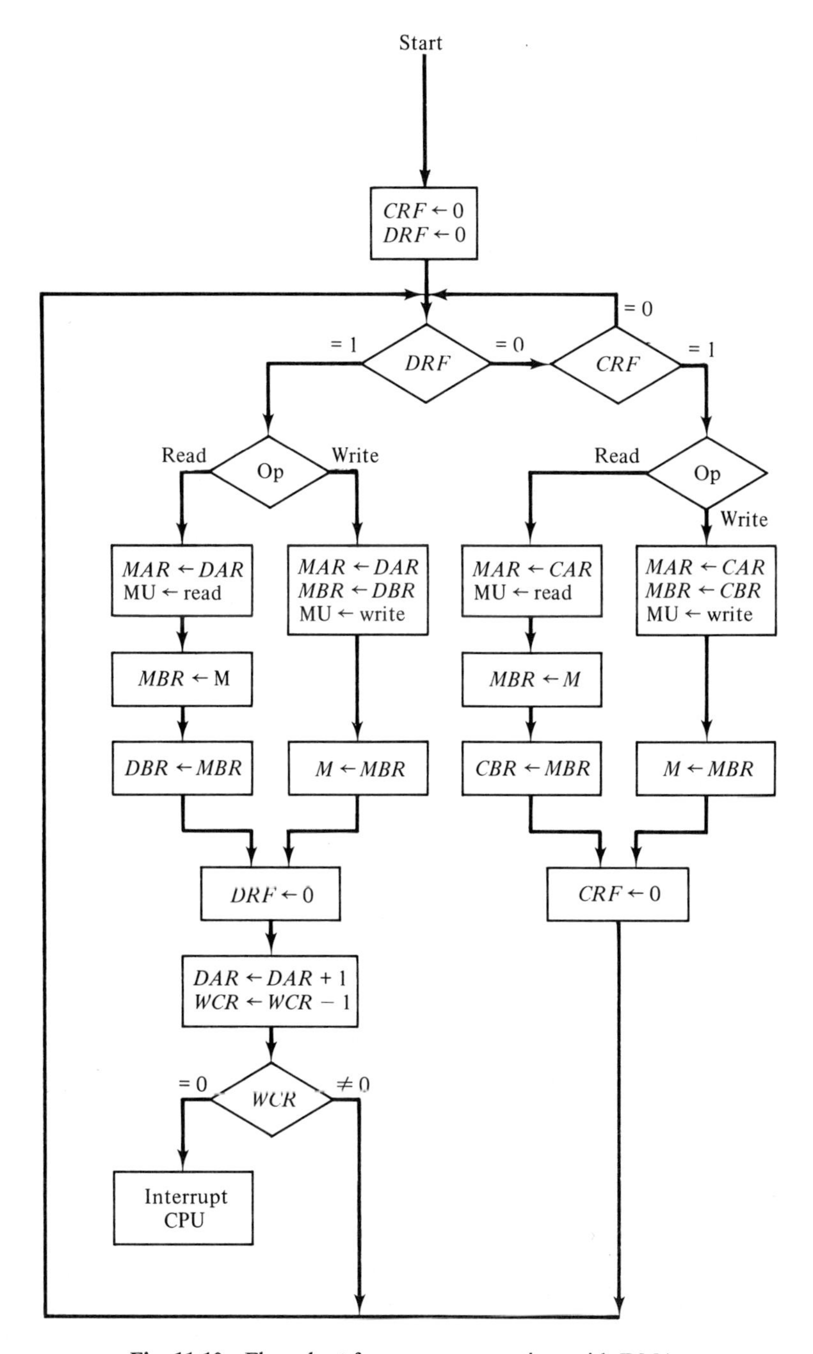


**Fig. 11-10** Flow chart for memory operations with DMA.

corresponding unit requests a memory cycle. The memory control services both units and resolves conflicts between the two requests. When a memory cycle request is terminated, the memory control clears the corresponding request flip-flop and the unit waits until a new memory cycle is requested.

A flow chart for the memory operations with DMA is shown in Fig. 11-10. Initially, both request flip-flops are cleared. The DMA request flip-flop *DRF* is checked first because the DMA has higher priority. If $DRF = 0$, the CPU request flip-flop *CRF* is checked. If it is 0, the memory control continues to check the request flip-flops until one of them is set. When the CPU requests a memory access (during the fetch or execute cycle), it sets *CRF* to 1. The memory control checks the operation requested by the CPU. For a write operation, the address and data from CPU registers are transferred to memory registers and the word is stored in memory. For a read operation, the address is transferred from *CAR* to *MAR*, the word is read into MBR and then transferred to the CPU register *CBR*. At the completion of the operation, the request bit is cleared and the memory control goes back to check for further requests.

When the DMA request flip-flop *DRF* is set, the memory control communicates with the DMA registers in the same manner to write or read a word from memory. After each DMA transfer, the DMA address register is incremented and the word count decremented simultaneously (this is done by the DMA control, not the memory control). When the word count reaches zero, the DMA stops the transfer and informs the CPU of the termination by means of an interrupt request.

## 11-5 PRIORITY INTERRUPT

The concept of program interrupt is used to handle a variety of problems which arise out of normal program sequence. Program interrupt refers to the transfer of control from the *currently* running program to another *service* program as a result of an external or internal generated request. Control returns to the original program after the service program is executed.

Program interrupts are initiated when internal processing errors occur, or when an external unit demands attention or when various alarm conditions occur. Examples of interrupts caused by internal error conditions are: register overflow; attempt to divide by zero; an invalid operation code; or an invalid address. These error conditions usually occur as a result of a premature termination of the instruction execution. The service program determines the corrective measures to be taken.

Examples of external request interrupts are I/O device ready and I/O device finished transfer of data. These interrupt conditions inform the system of some change in the external environment. They normally result in a momentary interruption of the normal program process which is continued after servicing or recording the interrupt condition.

Interrupts caused by special alarm conditions inform the system of some detrimental change in environment. They normally result from either a programming error or hardware failure. Examples of alarm condition interrupts are: running program is in an endless loop; running progam tries to change a system program; or power failure. Alarm conditions due to programming error result in a rejection of the program that causes the error. Power failure might have as its service routine the storing of all the information from processor registers into a magnetic core memory in the few milliseconds before power ceases.

Each of the contingencies that demand the attention of the computer may cause a program interrupt by setting a particular bit of an *interrupt register*. The control checks the interrupt register prior to going into the next instruction fetch cycle to determine if a situation exists which calls for an interrupt. If none of the bits of the interrupt register are set, the computer goes to fetch and execute the next instruction. If any bit of the interrupt register is set, the control goes to an interrupt cycle. This cycle consists of hardware microoperations that store the address of the next instruction in a predetermined memory location, usually location 0, and transfers control to a routine that services the interrupt. Return to the original program is achieved by an instruction that transfers the previously stored address in location 0 into the program counter.

To determine the cause of an interrupt, the interrupt service routine examines the bits of the interrupt register. The order in which the bits of the interrupt register are tested determines the priority of each interrupt request. The interrupt bit corresponding to the condition with the highest priority is tested first. Then, the bits of lower priority are tested sequentially. Once an interrupt is identified, all interrupts are disabled until the service routine is executed. Disabling of all interrupt requests while servicing a particular interrupt must be adopted in computers that have only a single fixed location in memory to store the return address. This is because if another interrupt is allowed while the computer is in an interrupt service program, a new address will replace the previous address at location 0 and the service program will lose the address of the instruction to which it is supposed to return.

In many situations, the computer must be interrupted while it is servicing another interrupt. This is necessary when an interrupt request must be serviced within a given interval of time. For example, a high-speed device asking for a data transfer may have to be serviced within the next 10 $\mu$sec, otherwise the data may be lost. On the other hand, a Teletype unit with a transfer rate of 10 characters per second is serviced at intervals of 0.1 sec. If the computer is servicing a Teletype unit with a relatively long program, and if the interrupt facility is disabled, the high-speed device interrupt request may not get attention and its data may be lost. In such a case, it is necessary to allow the device to interrupt while the computer is servicing an interrupt from the Teletype.

### *Hardware Interrupt*

A priority interrupt is an interrupt system that establishes a priority over the various sources to determine which condition is to be serviced first when two or more requests arrive simultaneously. It can be designed to determine also which conditions are permitted to interrupt the computer while another interrupt is being serviced. An interrupt source which is assigned a high-priority level can interrupt requests from sources assigned a lower priority level. High-priority interrupt levels are assigned to requests which, if delayed or interrupted, could have serious consequences. Interrupts of special alarm conditions are usually given the highest priority level. I/O devices with high-speed transfers such as magnetic disks are given a high priority and slow-speed I/O devices receive a lower priority. Internal program error interrupts are usually given a low priority because they can wait to be serviced without having detrimental consequences.

A priority interrupt system is a combination of hardware and software techniques. A block diagram of the hardware for a priority interrupt system is shown in Fig. 11-11. It consists of an interrupt register whose individual bits are set by external conditions and cleared by program instructions. To provide program control over various interrupt levels, the hardware includes a mask register that has the same number of bits as the interrupt register. By means of special instructions, the program can set or clear any bit in the mask register. If a bit position in the mask register is set to 1, the corresponding

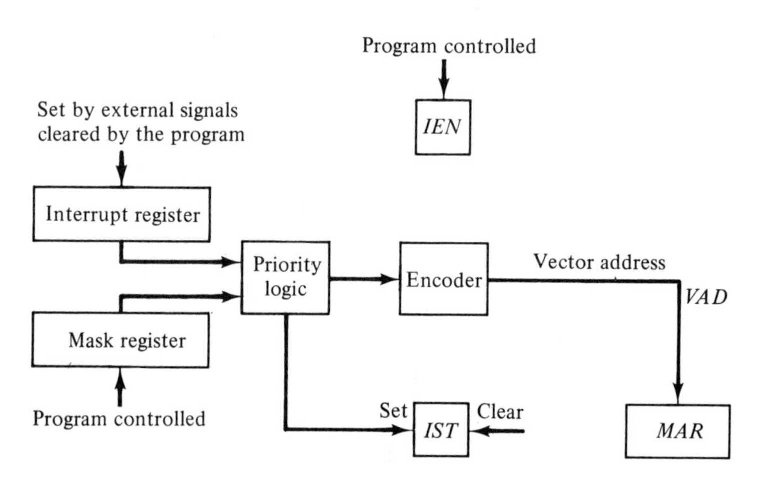


**Fig. 11-11** Priority interrupt block diagram.

bit in the interrupt register is recognized as an interrupt; otherwise it is neglected by the control. The priority logic checks the various interrupt levels and provides a signal for the highest level. The encoder generates a *vector* address *VAD* for the memory address register *MAR*. The content of *MAR* determines where the return address will be stored in memory. Two other flip-flops are used. The interrupt status *IST* is set if a masked interrupt request occurs. The interrupt enable *IEN* can be set or cleared by the program to provide overall control over the interrupt system. A vector address is transferred to *MAR* only if both *IST* and *IEN* are set to 1.

The priority logic for a system with four interrupt sources is shown in Fig. 11-12. The magnetic disk, being a high-speed I/O device, is given the highest priority. A memory parity error has the next priority followed by the Teletype keyboard and an overflow which may result from an *add* instruction. Each interrupt bit and its corresponding mask are applied to an AND gate to produce the four outputs, designated $N_1$ to $N_4$. In this way, an interrupt is enabled only if its corresponding mask bit is set to 1 by the program. The priority logic takes the $N$ variables and generates the four $P$ outputs. The priority logic is derived from the truth table listed in Table 11-1. $P_1$ has the highest priority so it is equal to 1 when $N_1$ is equal to 1, irrespective of the

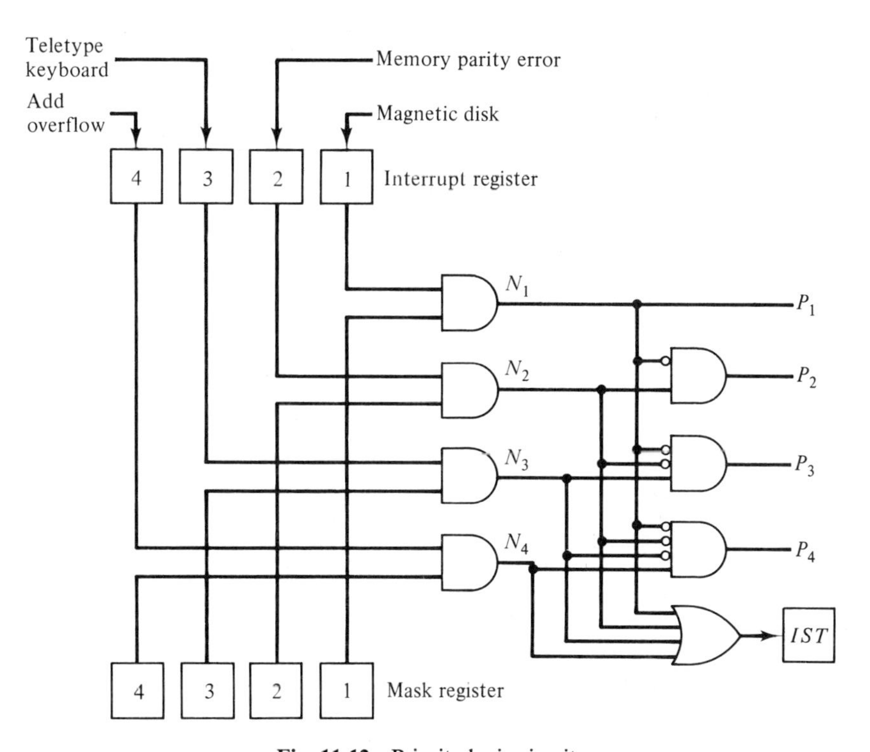


**Fig. 11-12** Priority logic circuit.

**Table 11-1** *Truth table for priority logic*

| *Masked Interrupt Bits* | | | | *Priority Logic Outputs* | | | | *Boolean Functions* |
|---|---|---|---|---|---|---|---|---|
| $N_1$ | $N_2$ | $N_3$ | $N_4$ | $P_1$ | $P_2$ | $P_3$ | $P_4$ | |
| 1 | X | X | X | 1 | 0 | 0 | 0 | $P_1 = N_1$ |
| 0 | 1 | X | X | 0 | 1 | 0 | 0 | $P_2 = N'_1 N_2$ |
| 0 | 0 | 1 | X | 0 | 0 | 1 | 0 | $P_3 = N'_1 N'_2 N_3$ |
| 0 | 0 | 0 | 1 | 0 | 0 | 0 | 1 | $P_4 = N'_1 N'_2 N'_3 N_4$ |

other $N$ values. $P_2$ has the next priority and it is equal to 1 if $N_2 = 1$ provided $N_1 = 0$. Thus, the priority levels dictate that a low-level interrupt be recognized only if all higher level interrupts are not asking for service. The priority is implemented in Fig. 11-12 by complementing the interrupt signal at a given priority level and applying it to the inputs of the AND gates at all lower priority levels, thus blocking any lower priority interrupt. Note that the interrupt status *IST* is set if any interrupt request is enabled. If two or more sources interrupt the computer at the same time, the computer services first the one with highest priority.

The computer interrupt cycle stores the content of the program counter (which holds the return address) in memory at the specified vector address *VAD*. The value of $VAD + 1$ is then transferred into *PC*. A branch instruction in location $VAD + 1$ sends the program to the beginning of the service routine. Thus, contrary to the simple interrupt scheme where the return address is always stored in the same location, the vector address technique allows the hardware to determine the memory location for storing the return address and/or the memory location for the beginning of the service routine. The circuit that generates the vector address in this particular case is the encoder. Let us assume that the vector address for the various interrupt sources is as listed in Table 11-2. *VAD* in the table specifies the address for storing the return address. The first address of the service routine is one greater than the corresponding *VAD*.

**Table 11-2** *Interrupt priority address assignment*

| *Priority* | *Source* | *Vector Address VAD* | *First Address of Service Program* |
|---|---|---|---|
| 1 | Magnetic disk | 0 0 0 | 0 0 1 |
| 2 | Parity error | 0 1 0 | 0 1 1 |
| 3 | Teletype keyboard | 1 0 0 | 1 0 1 |
| 4 | Add overflow | 1 1 0 | 1 1 1 |

The encoder circuit is derived from the truth table of Table 11-3. The low-order bit of *VAD* is always 0 and so are all high-order bits except the second (designated by $y$) and the third (designated by $x$). The Boolean functions specify an OR gate for generating $x$ and $y$. The encoder circuit is shown in Fig. 11-13. Usually, a computer will have more than four interrupt sources and the encoder will consist of more than two OR gates.

**Table 11-3** *Truth table for encoder*

| *Priority Output* $P_1$ | $P_2$ | $P_3$ | $P_4$ | *VAD* 00000. . . . $xy$ 0 | *Boolean Functions* |
|---|---|---|---|---|---|
| 1 | 0 | 0 | 0 | 00 | $x = P_3 + P_4$ |
| 0 | 1 | 0 | 0 | 01 | $y = P_2 + P_4$ |
| 0 | 0 | 1 | 0 | 10 | |
| 0 | 0 | 0 | 1 | 11 | |

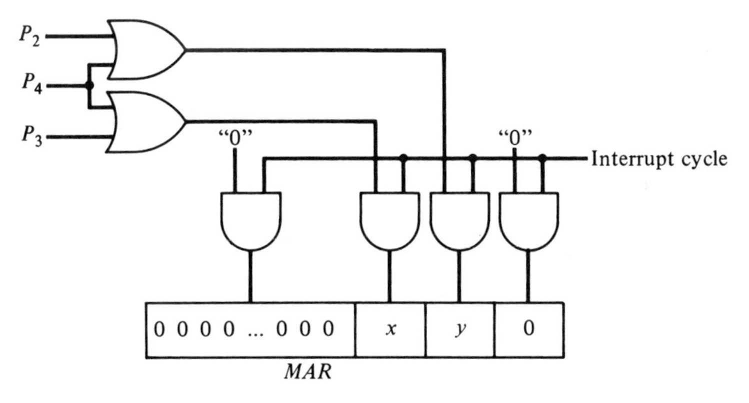


**Fig. 11-13** Priority encoder circuit.

At the end of each execute cycle, the computer goes to an interrupt cycle if both *IEN* and *IST* are set. The interrupt cycle generates the following sequence of micro-operations:

$t_0$: $MAR \leftarrow VAD$, $MBR \leftarrow PC$

$t_1$: $M \leftarrow MBR$, $PC \leftarrow MAR$

$t_2$: $PC \leftarrow PC + 1$, $IEN \leftarrow 0$

$t_3$: Go to the fetch cycle.

At $t_0$, the vector address is transferred into *MAR* and the contents of *PC* into *MBR*. At $t_1$, the return address (originally in *PC*) is stored in a memory location specified by $VAD$ and the program counter receives the value of $VAD$. At $t_2$, $PC$ is incremented so it will contain the value of $VAD + 1$. At the same time, the interrupt enable bit $IEN$ is cleared to prevent an interrupt cycle again until the service program clears appropriate mask bits. During the next fetch cycle, the instruction at location $VAD + 1$ will be executed.

Some computers do not have a fixed vector address for each interrupt source. Instead, they allow the peripheral interface to determine its own vector address. This is done by responding to an interrupt request with an interrupt acknowledge signal if conditions are such that the interrupt can be processed. When the interface receives the interrupt acknowledge signal from the processor, it responds by placing a vector address in the I/O bus. The processor accepts this address and uses it as the first address of the service routine while the return address is pushed into a memory stack.

### *Software Routines*

So far we have discussed the hardware aspects of a priority interrupt system. The computer must also have software routines for servicing the interrupt requests and for controlling the interrupt hardware registers. Figure 11-14 shows the programs that must reside in memory for handling the interrupt system. Binary locations 0, 10, 100, and 110 are reserved for storing the return address and binary locations 01, 011, 101, and 111 have an unconditional branch instruction (BUN) to the routines that service the interrupt source.

To illustrate with a specific example, assume that the teletype keyboard

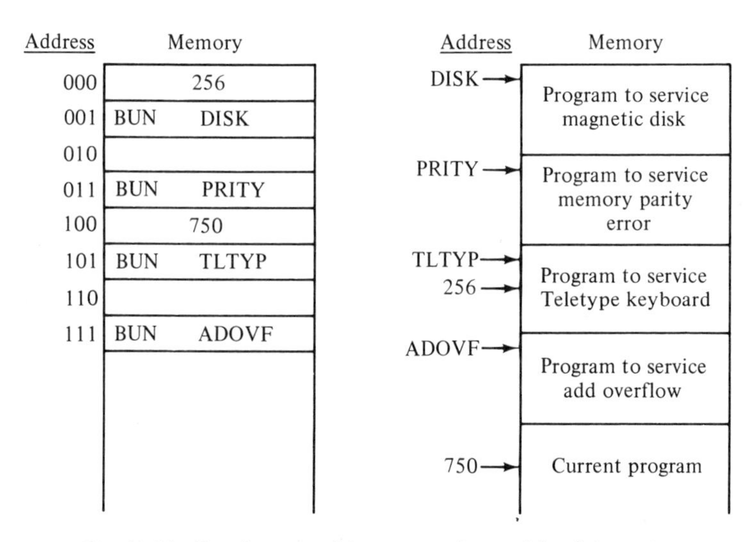


**Fig. 11-14** Routines stored in memory for servicing interrupts.

sets its interrupt bit while the computer is executing the instruction in location 749 of the current program. At the end of the execute cycle, the computer goes to an interrupt cycle and stores the return address 750 in location $(100)_2$. It also inserts $(101)_2$ into *PC*. The instruction in location $(101)_2$ is executed next resulting in a transfer of control to the TLTYP routine. Now suppose that the disk sets its interrupt bit when the computer is executing the instruction at address 255 in the Teletype service routine. Address 256 is then stored in location 0 and control transferred to the DISK service routine. When the disk service routine is completed, the last instruction causes a branch to the address in location 0, where the return address has been stored. This returns control to the TLTYP routine at address 256 to continue servicing the Teletype. At the end of the Teletype routine, the last instruction returns control to the current program at address 750. Thus, a higher priority source can interrupt a lower priority source. It is assumed that the time spent in servicing the high-priority interrupt is short compared to the transfer rate of the low-priority source so that no loss of information takes place.

### *Initial and Final Operations*

Each interrupt service routine must have an initial and final set of operations for controlling the registers in the hardware interrupt system. Remember that the interrupt enable *IEN* is cleared at the end of an interrupt cycle. This flip-flop must be set again to enable higher priority interrupt requests, but not before lower priority interrupts are disabled. The initial sequence of each interrupt service routine must have instructions to control the interrupt hardware in the following manner.

1. Clear lower level mask register bits.
2. Clear interrupt status bit *IST*.
3. Save contents of processor registers.
4. Set interrupt enable bit *IEN*.
5. Proceed with service routine.

The lower level mask register bits (including the bit of the source being interrupted) are cleared to prevent these conditions from enabling the interrupt. Although lower priority interrupt sources are assigned to higher numbered bits in the mask register, priority can be changed if desired since the programmer can use any bit configuration he wishes for the mask register. The interrupt status bit must be cleared so it can be set again when a higher priority interrupt occurs. The contents of processor registers are saved because they may be needed by the program which has been interrupted after control returns to it. The interrupt enable *IEN* is then set to allow other (higher priority) interrupts and the computer proceeds to service the interrupt request.

The final sequence in each interrupt service routine must have instructions to control the interrupt hardware in the following manner:

1. Clear interrupt enable bit *IEN*.
2. Restore contents of processor registers.
3. Clear the bit in the interrupt register belonging to the source that has been serviced.
4. Set lower level priority bits in the mask register.
5. Restore return address into *PC* and set *IEN*.

The bit in the interrupt register belonging to the source of the interrupt must be cleared so it will be available again for the source to interrupt. The lower priority bits in the mask register (including the bit of the source being interrupted) are set so they can enable the interrupt. The return to the interrupted program can be accomplished by an indirect branch instruction to the location where the return address has been originally stored. Note that the hardware must be designed so that no interrupts occur while executing steps 2–5; otherwise the return address may be lost and the information in the mask and processor registers may be ambiguous if an interrupt is acknowledged while executing the operations in these steps. For this reason *IEN* is initially cleared and then set after the return address is transferred into *PC*.

The initial and final operations listed above are referred to as *overhead* operations or *housekeeping* chores. They are not part of the service program proper but are essential for processing interrupts. All overhead operations can be implemented by software. This is done by inserting the proper instructions at the beginning and at the end of each service routine. Some of the overhead operations can be done automatically by the hardware. The contents of processor registers can be pushed into a stack by the hardware before branching to the service routine. Other initial and final operations can be assigned to the hardware. In this way, it is possible to reduce the time between receipt of an interrupt and the execution of the first instruction that services the interrupt source.

## 11-6 PERIPHERAL PROCESSOR

Instead of having each interface communicate with the CPU, a computer may incorporate one or more I/O processors and assign to them the task of communicating directly with all I/O devices. An I/O processor may be classified as an interface with direct memory access that can communicate not only with one but with many I/O devices simultaneously. In this configuration, the computer system can be divided into a memory unit and a number of processors comprised of the CPU and one or more I/O processors. The I/O processors take care of all input-output tasks, relieving the CPU from the housekeeping chores involved in I/O transfers. Processors that communicate directly with I/O devices are also called *data channels.*

It is sometimes convenient to distinguish between two types of I/O processors. A processor that communicates with high-speed peripherals is called a *peripheral processor* and sometimes a *selector channel.* A processor that communicates with slower remote terminals over telephone wires and other communication media is called a *data communication processor* and sometimes a *multiplexor channel.*

The block diagram of a computer with three different types of processors is shown in Fig. 11-15. The memory unit occupies a central position and can communicate with each processor by means of direct memory access. The CPU is responsible for processing data needed in the solution of computational tasks. The peripheral processor provides a path for transfer of data between various input devices, output devices, auxiliary storage, and the memory unit. Computers with time-sharing capabilities must provide communication with many remote terminals via communication lines. The data communication processor handles data transfers between the computer and many terminals operating concurrently. The CPU is usually assigned the task of initiating the I/O processors. Once an I/O processor is initiated, it

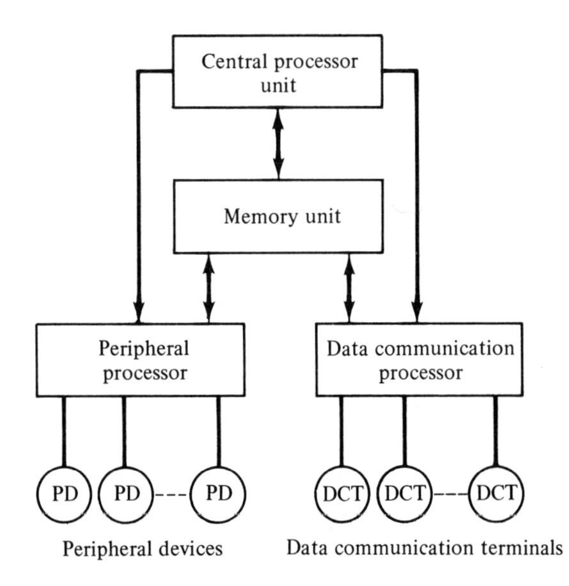


**Fig. 11-15** Block diagram of a computer with I/O processors.

operates independently of the CPU and continues to transfer data to and from external devices and memory.

The data format of peripheral devices differs from the memory and CPU data formats, so the peripheral processor must structure data words from many different sources. For example, it may be necessary to take four 8-bit characters from an input device and pack them into one 32-bit word before the transfer to memory. Each peripheral device has a different information interchange rate. In the interest of efficiency, it is inadvisable to devote CPU time to waiting for peripheral devices to transfer information. Instead data are gathered in the peripheral processor while the CPU is executing another program. After the input data is assembled into a memory word, it is transferred from the peripheral processor directly into memory by *stealing* one memory cycle from the CPU. Similarly, an output word transferred from memory to the peripheral processor is transferred from the latter to the output device at the device rate and bit capacity. Thus a peripheral processor acts as a transfer-rate buffer.

Data become available in the peripheral processor from many sources operating concurrently. The peripheral processor must assign priorities to different devices. This assignment may be on a simple first-come, first-serve basis. However, devices with higher transfer rates are usually given higher priority.

The communication between a peripheral processor and the devices attached to it is similar to an I/O interface except that the peripheral processor performs all the I/O tasks instead of the CPU. Communication with the memory unit is by direct memory access. The method by which the CPU and peripheral processor communicate depends on the level of sophistication included in the system. In a few very large computers, each processor is independent of all others and either one can initiate an operation. In most computer systems, the CPU is assigned the task of initiating all operations but I/O instructions initiated in the CPU are executed in the peripheral processor. CPU instructions provide operations to start an I/O transfer and also to test I/O status conditions to aid in making decisions on various I/O activities. The peripheral processor in turn typically asks for CPU attention by means of an interrupt. It also responds to CPU requests by placing a status word in a prescribed memory location which can be examined by a CPU instruction. When an I/O operation is desired, the CPU transfers one instruction to the peripheral processor indicating which peripheral is to be used and the location in memory where to find further instructions, and then leaves the transfer details to the peripheral processor.

Instructions that are read from memory by an I/O processor are called *commands*, to distinguish them from instructions that are read by the CPU. Otherwise an instruction and a command have similar functions. Command words are prepared by the CPU and stored in memory. When the CPU sends a *start I/O* instruction, it informs the peripheral processor where to find the command words in memory. The peripheral processor refers to its own program in memory by *stealing* a memory cycle from the CPU. The command words fetched from memory constitute the program for the peripheral processor.

In order to appreciate the function of a peripheral processor, we will illustrate by a specific example the method by which the CPU and peripheral processor communicate. The CPU initiates an I/O operation by transferring an I/O instruction to the peripheral processor. A possible format for this instruction is shown in Fig. 11-16. The peripheral processor receives the

| Device address | Memory address | Function code |
|---|---|---|

| Function code | Operation |
|---|---|
| 001 | Test peripheral device |
| 010 | Start I/O transfer |
| 011 | Read interrupt register |
| 100 | Read status word |

**Fig. 11-16** Example of I/O instructions for peripheral processor.

instruction word and proceeds to execute it. The instruction code has three fields:

1. The *device address* field specifies the address of a particular I/O device attached to the peripheral processor.
2. The *memory address* field specifies a memory address for the peripheral processor to use when it responds to the CPU instruction.
3. The *function code* field specifies an operation. Some typical operations are listed in Fig. 11-16.

The sequence of operations may be carried out in the following manner. The CPU sends the instruction *test peripheral device*. The peripheral processor responds by inserting a status word in memory at the location specified by the memory address field of the instruction. Each bit in the status word indicates a specific condition, such as device ready, peripheral processor overloaded, or device is busy with another transfer.

The CPU refers to the status word in memory to decide what to do next. If all is in order, the CPU then sends the instruction *start I/O transfer*. The memory address received with this instruction tells the peripheral processor where to find the first command word for the I/O operation. The command words constitute a program for the peripheral processor. This program may consist of one word or of many words.

The peripheral processor refers to the memory address which it receives with the start I/O transfer instruction and proceeds to execute the I/O program. When the execution of the program is terminated, the peripheral processor sends an interrupt request to the CPU. It is assumed that the peripheral processor has its own interrupt register. In a system with many processors, it is advisable to include an interrupt register in each processor in order not to bother the CPU unless necessary. When the CPU receives an interrupt request from the peripheral processor it sends the instruction *read interrupt register.* The peripheral processor responds to this instruction by placing the contents of its interrupt register into the memory location specified by the memory address field of the instruction.

The CPU checks the bits of the interrupt register, and if it finds a bit that indicates that the previously initiated I/O transfer is completed, it sends an instruction to the peripheral processor to *read status word.* This status word would indicate if the transfer has been completed satisfactorily or if any errors occured during the transfer. From inspection of the bits in the status word, the CPU determines if the I/O operation was completed satisfactorily without any errors.

The command words specify the program that is executed in the peripheral processor. The address of the command word is given to the peripheral processor by the CPU with a *start I/O transfer* instruction. A command-word format usually specifies the memory buffer area associated with the operation and the actions to be taken during the transfer. A typical command-word format is illustrated in Fig. 11-17. This command may be placed in one memory word (if all its bits fit into one word) or in two or more words. The command word has four fields:

1. The *buffer address* field specifies a memory address for the beginning of a buffer area in memory.

| Buffer address | Word count | Operation code | Special code |
|---|---|---|---|

| Operation code | Operation |
|---|---|
| 001 | Read (input from device) |
| 010 | Write (output to device) |
| 011 | Read backwards (for tapes) |

| Special code | Operation |
|---|---|
| 00001010 | Translate from 12-bit to 6-bit code (for card reader) |
| 01110010 | Address of a record in magnetic tape |

**Fig. 11-17** Example of a command word for peripheral processor.

2. The *word count* field indicates the length of the buffer, i.e., the number of words it contains.
3. The *operation* field specifies the operation to be performed.
4. The *special* field specifies a particular function and is different for each I/O device.

The memory buffer is an area in memory where data from an input device are to be stored or where data are available for transfer to an output device. The operation field specifies an input, output, or other operations. The special field is unique for each device and may specify a variety of functions, a few of which are listed in the Fig. 11-17.

To continue with a specific example, assume that a CPU *start I/O transfer* instruction specifies a device address of a card reader. The control word in the specified memory address contains a buffer address, a word count, a read operation code, and the special code for translating the 12-bit card code to an internal 6-bit code. The peripheral processor first activates the card reader and goes to fulfil other I/O tasks while waiting for a signal from the card reader to indicate that it is ready to transfer information. When the ready signal is received, the peripheral processor starts receiving data from cards. The 12-bit character code from each card column is converted to an internal 6-bit code by the peripheral processor. Characters are then packed into a word length suitable for memory storage. When a word is ready to be stored, the peripheral processor *steals* a memory cycle and stores the word in the assigned buffer. The buffer address is then incremented and the word count decremented, preparing the next word for storage. If the count reaches 0, the peripheral processor stops receiving data; otherwise, data transfer continues until the card reader has no more cards.

While data are being transferred, the peripheral processor prepares a status word that indicates all error conditions that occur. The status word may also contain the number of words in the buffer that have been used since there may not have been enough cards to fill the buffer. When the transfer terminates, the peripheral processor sets the card reader interrupt bit in its interrupt register and then interrupts the CPU. The CPU then asks for the status word and examines it to determine if the transfer was satisfactory.

When the peripheral processor is reading information from a low-speed unit such as a card reader, the actual data transfer does not take much processor time. If it has several registers for addresses and counters, it can handle several units simultaneously. These units would actually be staggered in their transmission times. Several card readers and printers, for example, could each be transmitting characters at the same time.

A peripheral processor provides the transfer of data between several I/O units and the memory while the CPU is processing its own program.

The peripheral processor and CPU are competing for the use of memory so the number of units that can be in operation is limited by the access time of the memory. It is not possible to saturate the memory by I/O devices on most systems, as the speed of most devices is much slower than memory. However, some very fast units, such as magnetic disks, can use an appreciable number of the available memory cycles. In that case, the speed of the CPU is decreased because it will often have to wait for the peripheral processor to finish a memory reference before it can use the memory.

## 11-7 DATA COMMUNICATION PROCESSOR

A data communication processor is an I/O processor that distributes and collects data from many remote terminals connected through telephone and other communication lines. It is a specialized I/O processor designed to communicate directly with data communication networks. A communication network may consist of any of a wide variety of devices such as teletypewriters, printers, interactive display devices, digital sensors, or a remote computing facility. With the use of a data communication processor, the computer can service fragments of each network demand in an interspersed manner and thus have the apparent behavior of serving many users at once. In this way the computer is able to operate efficiently in a time-sharing environment.

The most striking difference between a peripheral processor and a data communication processor is in the way the processor communicates with the I/O devices. A peripheral processor communicates with the peripherals through a common I/O bus which is comprised of many data and control lines. All peripherals share the common bus and use it to transfer information to and from the peripheral processor. A data communication processor communicates with each terminal through a single pair of wires. Both data and control information are transferred in a serial fashion with the result that the transfer rate is much slower. The task of the data communication processor is to transmit and collect digital information to and from each terminal, determine if the information is data or control and respond to all requests according to predetermined established procedures. The processor, obviously, must also communicate with the CPU and memory in the same manner as any I/O processor.

The way that remote terminals are connected to a data communication processor is via telephone lines or other public or private communication facilities. Since telephone lines were originally designed for voice communication and computers communicate in terms of digital signals, some form of conversion must be used. The converters are called *data sets*, *acoustic couplers*, or *modems* (from modulator-demodulator). A modem converts digital signals into audio tones to be transmitted over telephone lines and also converts audio tones from the line to digital signals for machine use. Various modulation schemes as well as different grades of communication media and transmission speeds are used.

A block diagram showing the various units that are connected to a data communication processor is presented in Fig. 11-18. Each remote terminal (or a group of terminals) is connected to the communication line via a modem. The other side of the line is also connected to a modem. The two modems receive and transmit audio tones along the line but convert them to digital signals for the terminal and adapter. The adapter is a special interface that converts characters from serial to parallel and vice-versa as they are transferred to and from the processor. The data communication processor scans the adapters in sequence to receive or send characters. This scan is called *multiplexing* and is analogous to a rotary switch rotating at high speed

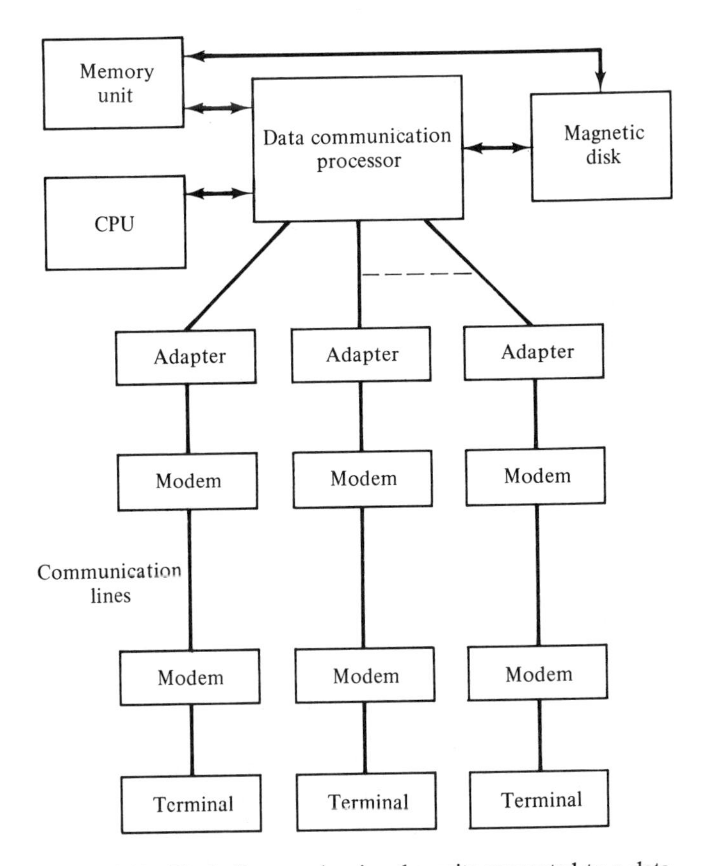


**Fig. 11-18** Block diagram showing the units connected to a data communication processor.

while sampling each adapter in sequence. The data communication processor comes with an extensive character comparison logic which is activated during input operations to examine the incoming character stream from each adapter. Special control characters activate the processor according to specific line procedures. The actual data received by the processor, referred to as *text*, are assembled into words and transferred into a memory unit. A data communication processor may have its own memory unit for storing incoming and outgoing information. It could also communicate directly with a magnetic disk storage.

A line may be connected to a synchronous or asynchronous adapter, depending on the transmission method of the remote terminal. An asynchronous adapter receives serial data with start-stop bits in each character. This type of adapter would be similar to the asynchronous serial interface presented in Sec. 10-3.

A synchronous adapter receives synchronous serial bits from the line in the same manner as the asynchronous serial bit stream except that there are no start-stop bits. In this technique a clock signal is transmitted to the receiver terminal along with the serial data. The message usually consists of a group of characters transmitted sequentially as a block of data. The entire block is transmitted with special control characters at the beginning and at the end of the block. The control characters cause the receiver to lock in and count the incoming bits and assemble them into characters. As in the asynchronous technique, the receiver must know the number of bits in each character.

One of the functions of the data communication processor is to check for transmission errors. An error can be detected by checking the parity in each received character. Another procedure used in asynchronous terminals involving a human operator is to *echo* the character. The character transmitted from the keyboard to the computer is recognized by the processor and retransmitted to the terminal printer. The operator would realize that an error occured during transmission if the character printed is not the same as the character whose key he has struck.

In synchronous transmission, where an entire block of characters is transmitted, each character has a parity bit for the receiver to check. After the entire block is sent, the transmitter sends one more character that constitutes a parity over the length of the message. This character is called a longitudinal redundancy check (LRC) and is the accumulation of the exclusive-OR of all transmitted characters. The receiving station calculates the LRC as it receives characters and compares it with the transmitted LRC. The calculated and received LRC should be equal for error free messages.

Data can be transmitted between two points in three different modes: simplex, half-duplex, or full-duplex. A simplex line carries information in one direction only. A half-duplex transmission system is one that is capable of transmission in both directions but data are transmitted in one direction at any given time. A pair of wires is needed for this mode of transmission. The full-duplex transmission requires two pairs of wires and data can be transmitted in both directions simultaneously. The simplex mode is seldom used because the receiver cannot communicate with the transmitter to indicate the occurrence of errors. Half-duplex is used with a dial-up line supplied by the common carriers (telephone service). Full-duplex requires two dial-up lines or a leased line with a four-line link.

There are many binary codes used in data communication. The code most commonly employed is ASCII (American Standard Code for Information Interchange). It is a 7-bit code with an eighth bit used for parity. The code has 128 characters. There are 95 *graphic characters* that include upper and lower case letters, the numerals from 0 to 9 and special symbols. A partial list of the ASCII graphic characters can be found in Table 3-4. The other 33 characters are *control characters* whose function is to route data properly and put it into a specific format. Some of these characters control the layout of printing and display devices. Others are used to separate a text into pages, paragraphs, and sentences. The characters that control the transmission are called *communication control* characters. Some of these characters are listed in Table 11-4. Each character has a 7-bit code and is commonly referred to by a three-letter symbol. The meaning and function of each character are explained further in the example presented below.

**Table 11-4** *ASCII communication control characters*

| *Code* | *Symbol* | *Meaning* | *Function* |
|---|---|---|---|
| 0010110 | SYN | Synchronous idle | Establishes synchronism |
| 0000001 | SOH | Start of heading | Heading of block message |
| 0000010 | STX | Start of text | Precedes block of text |
| 0000011 | ETX | End of text | Terminates block of text |
| 0000100 | EOT | End of transmission | Concludes transmission |
| 0000110 | ACK | Acknowledge | Affirmative acknowledgement |
| 0010101 | NAK | Negative acknowledge | Negative acknowledgement |
| 0000101 | ENQ | Inquiry | Inquire if terminal is on |

In order to appreciate the function of a data communication processor, let us illustrate by a specific example the method by which a terminal and the processor communicate. The communication with the memory unit and CPU is similar to any I/O processor.

A typical message that might be sent from a terminal to the processor is listed in Table 11-5. A look at this message reveals that there are a number of control characters used for message formation. Each character, including the control characters, is transmitted serially as an 8-bit binary code which

**Table 11-5** *A typical transmission from a terminal to processor*

| *Code* | *Symbol* | *Comments* |
|---|---|---|
| 0001 0110 | SYN | Line is idling |
| 0001 0110 | SYN | Line is idling |
| 0000 0001 | SOH | Start of heading |
| 0101 0100 | T | Address of terminal is T4 |
| 0011 0100 | 4 | |
| 0000 0010 | STX | Start of text transmission |
| 0101 0010 | | |
| 0100 0101 | request | Text sent is a request to respond with the balance of account number 1234 |
| . | balance | |
| . | of account | |
| . | No. 1234 | |
| 1011 0011 | | |
| 0011 0100 | | |
| 1000 0011 | ETX | End of text transmission |
| 0111 0000 | LRC | Longitudinal parity character |
| 0000 0100 | EOT | End of transmission |
| 0001 0110 | SYN | Line is idling |
| 0001 0110 | SYN | Line is idling |

consists of the seven ASCII bits plus an odd parity bit in the eighth most significant position. In a synchronous system, the SYN characters are used to synchronize the receiver and transmitter in the absence of any other character. They are continuously transmitted while the line is idling.

The message starts with the SOH character and continues with two characters that specify the address of the terminal. In this particular example, the address is T4, but in general it can have any set of two or three graphic characters. The STX character terminates the heading and signifies the beginning of the text transmission. The text data that is of concern here is "Request balance of account number 1234." The individual characters for this message are not listed in the table because they will take too much space. It must be realized, however, that each character in the message has an 8-bit code and that each bit is transmitted serially. The ETX control character signifies the termination of the text characters.

The next character following ETX is a longitudinal redundancy check (LRC). Each bit in this character is a parity bit along the longitudinal or vertical column of the characters. The last character in the message is EOT which indicates the conclusion of the message. The line then continues to transmit SYN characters while idling.

The data communication processor receives this message and proceeds to analyze it. It recognizes terminal T4 and stores the text associated with the message. While receiving the characters, the processor checks the parity in each character and also computes the longitudinal parity. The computed

LRC is compared with the LRC character received. If the two match, a positive acknowledgment (ACK) is sent back to the terminal. If a mismatch exists, a negative acknowledgement (NAK) is returned to the terminal which would initiate a retransmission of the same block. If the processor finds the message without errors, it transfers the message into memory and interrupts the CPU. When the CPU acknowledges the interrupt, it analyzes the message and prepares a text message for responding to the request. The CPU sends an instruction to the data communication processor to send the message to the terminal.

A typical transmission from processor to terminal is listed in Table 11-6. The SYN characters are sent while the line is idling. The processor acknowledges the previously sent message with the ACK character and continues to idle. The message received from the CPU is arranged in the proper format in the processor by inserting the proper control characters in the block. The message has a heading SOH and the address of the terminal T4. The text message informs the terminal that the balance is $100. An LRC character is computed and sent to the terminal. The transmission terminates with an EOT and the line goes back to transmit SYN characters. If the terminal responds with a NAK character, the processor retransmits the message.

**Table 11-6** *A typical transmission from processor to terminal*

| *Code* | *Symbol* | *Comments* |
|---|---|---|
| 0001 0110 | SYN | Line is idling |
| 0001 0110 | SYN | Line is idling |
| 1000 0110 | ACK | Processor acknowledges previous message |
| 0001 0110 | SYN | Line is idling |
| · | · | |
| · | · | |
| · | · | |
| 0001 0110 | SYN | Line is idling |
| 0000 0001 | SOH | Start of heading |
| 0101 0100 | T | Address of terminal is T4 |
| 0011 0100 | 4 | |
| 0000 0010 | STX | Start of text transmission |
| 1100 0010 | | |
| 1100 0001 | balance | Text sent is a response from the computer giving the |
| · | is | balance of account |
| · | $100.00 | |
| · | | |
| · | | |
| 1011 0000 | | |
| 1000 0011 | ETX | End of text transmission |
| 1101 0101 | LRC | Longitudinal parity character |
| 0000 0100 | EOT | End of transmission |
| 0001 0110 | SYN | Line is idling |
| 0001 0110 | SYN | Line is idling |

While the processor is taking care of this terminal it is also busy processing other terminals as well. Since the characters are received in a serial fashion, it takes a certain amount of time to receive and collect an 8-bit character. During this time the processor is multiplexing all other communication lines and services each one in turn. The speed of most remote terminals is extremely slow compared to the processor speed. This property allows multiplexing of many users to achieve greater efficiency in a time-sharing system. This also allows many users to operate simultaneously while each is being sampled at speeds comparable to speeds of a computer system.

## REFERENCES

1. SOUCEK, B., *Minicomputers in Data Processing and Simulation*, New York: John Wiley & Sons, Inc., 1972.
2. HOFFMAN, A. A. J., R. L. FRENCH, and G. M. LANG, "Minicomputer Interfaces: Know More, Save More," *IEEE Spectrum*, Vol. 11 (February, 1974), pp. 64–68.
3. FALK, H., "Linking Microprocessors to the Real World," *IEEE Spectrum*, Vol. 11 (September, 1974), pp. 59–67.
4. AMDAHL, G. M., G. A. BLAAUW, and F. P. BROOKS, Jr., "Architecture of the IBM System/360," *IBM Journal of Research and Development*, Vol. 8 (April, 1964), pp. 87–101.
5. WEITZMAN, C., *Minicomputer Systems*, Englewood Cliffs, N.J.: Prentice-Hall, Inc., 1974.
6. GEAR, C. W., *Computer Organization and Programming*, New York: McGraw-Hill Book Co., 1974.
7. "Data Sheet S-1757 UART-Universal Asynchronous Receiver/Transmitter," American Microsystems, Inc., Santa Clara, Cal., 1971.
8. HILL, F. J., and G. R. PETERSON, *Digital Systems: Hardware Organization and Design*, New York: John Wiley & Sons, 1973.
9. CHU, Y., *Computer Organization and Microprogramming*, Englewood Cliffs, N.J.: Prentice Hall, Inc., 1972.
10. MURPHY, D. E., and S. A. KALLIS, JR., *Introduction to Data Communication*, Maynard Mass.: Digital Equipment Corp., 1971.
11. STEELE, J. M., and R. C. MATTSON, "Architecture of a Universal Communication Processor," *Computer Design*, Vol. 12 (November, 1973), pp. 63–68.

## PROBLEMS

11-1 Discuss three different ways for preparing programs and data off-line. What peripherals will be used?

11-2 List four peripheral devices that produce an acceptable output for a person to understand.

11-3 A Fortran program is punched on cards. The computer accepts the Hollerith code and translates the program by means of a compiler into binary. The binary program is given back to the user on punched cards. Devise a card format for binary programs.

11-4 What is the difference between I/O program control transfer and DMA transfer?

11-5 Why is it that I/O interrupts make a more efficient use of the CPU?

11-6 (a) What is the difference between an instruction and a command?
(b) What is the difference between a control and a sense command?
(c) Show how the accumulator register can be used to specify a number of control functions with one control command.
(d) Show how the accumulator can be used to receive sense information.

11-7 The sequence of steps required to read 8-bit characters from a paper tape reader is as follows:

1. Make sure that the unit is turned on.
2. Start tape moving.
3. Wait until sprocket hole is sensed.
4. Read the character.
5. Repeat steps 3 and 4 until all characters are read, then stop the unit.

Specify function codes for the tape reader and a device address. Draw a block diagram of the interface for a paper tape reader.

11-8 In the flow chart of Fig. 11-7, the interface neglects any command code that does not specify a data-output or test command. Include a command error flip-flop (*CER*) with the interface to be set to 1 when an invalid function code is detected. Modify the flow chart to show when *CER* is set or cleared. Include this condition with the status report when the interface responds to the test command.

11-9 Add a control command to the interface of Fig. 11-6 that informs the interface to turn the printer power on. Modify the flow chart of Fig. 11-7 showing the response to this command.

11-10 A Teletype receiver interface accepts bits from the keyboard line at an interval of 9.09 msec. To insure that the bit in the line is not in a transition but in a steady-state condition, the line is sampled by the receiver at a time midway between two intervals. Show how this can be done by using a clock 16 times faster and a 4-bit counter.

11-11 Draw a block diagram of an asynchronous interface that receives serial asynchronous characters from a Teletype keyboard and transfers them to the computer in parallel. Obtain the flow chart showing the micro-operations and control decisions for this interface.

11-12 A DMA interface receives characters of 8 bits from a peripheral, packs four characters in a 32-bit word and then stores words of 32 bits in memory.

Draw a block diagram of the DMA registers and list the sequence of microoperations for the DMA.

11-13 Design a priority logic and encoder for an interrupt system with eight interrupt sources.

11-14 The two boxes labeled "priority logic" and "encoder" in Fig. 11-11 are sometimes combined into one combinational circuit and the overall circuit is called a "4 to 2 line priority encoder."
(a) Obtain the truth table of a 4 to 2 line priority encoder.
(b) Derive the simplified Boolean functions for the combined circuit and draw the logic diagram.

11-15 What is the basic advantage of priority interrupt over a non-priority system? Is it possible to have a priority interrupt without a mask register?

11-16 What programming steps are required in order to check when a source interrupts the computer while it is still being serviced by a previous interrupt request from the same source?

11-17 Consider a computer without priority interrupt hardware. Any interrupt request results in storing the return address in memory location 0 and branching to location 1. Explain how a priority can be established by software means.

11-18 A program for a peripheral processor may consist of a variable number of command words. How would you design the control word format so the peripheral processor knows if there are more command words in its program?

11-19 The peripheral processor responds to three of the CPU instructions listed in Fig. 11-16 by placing a word in a specified memory location. Devise a method by which the CPU will know that the word in that memory location is indeed the one requested.

11-20 Formulate a command word (Fig. 11-17) when the I/O device is a magnetic tape. It is necessary to specify the number of blocks to be read or written on tape, the address of the first block and the number of characters in each block. What should be done if all the bits of the command code do not fit in one memory word?

11-21 List a possible line procedure and the character sequence for the communication between a data communication processor and a remote terminal. The processor inquires if the terminal is operative. The terminal responds with yes or no. If the response is yes, the processor sends a block of text.

11-22 The address of a terminal connected to a data communication processor consists of two letters of the alphabet or a letter followed by one of the 10 numerals. How many different addresses can be formulated?

11-23 The longitudinal redundancy check (LRC) character is computed by the exclusive-OR of the bits along the longitudinal (vertical) bits of a block. Show that the total bits in a column including the LRC bit has an even parity.

# 12

# MEMORY ORGANIZATION

## 12-1 MEMORY HIERARCHY

The memory unit is an essential component in any digital computer since it is needed for storing the programs that are executed by the CPU. A very small computer with a limited application may be able to fulfil its intended task without the need of additional storage capacity. However, most computers would run more efficiently if they are supplied with additional storage beyond the capacity of the main memory. There is just not enough space in one memory unit to accomodate all the systems programs written for a typical computer. Moreover, most computer installations accumulate and continue to accumulate large amounts of information. Not all accumulated information is needed by the processor at the same time. Therefore, it is more economical to use lower cost storage devices to serve as a backup for storing the information that is not currently used by the CPU. The memory unit that communicates directly with the CPU is called the *main memory*. Devices that provide backup storage are called *auxiliary memory*. Examples of auxiliary memory devices are magnetic disks, drums, and tapes. Only programs and data currently used by the processor reside in main memory. All other information is stored in auxiliary memory and is transferred to main memory on a demand basis.

The total memory capacity of a computer can be visualized as being a hierarchy of components. The memory hierarchy system consists of all storage devices employed by a computer system from the slow but high-capacity auxiliary memory devices, to a relatively faster main memory, to an even smaller and very fast buffer memory accessible to the high-speed processing logic. Figure 12-1 illustrates the components in a typical memory hierarchy. On top of the hierarchy are the relatively slow magnetic tapes used to store removable files. Below it are the magnetic disks or drums used as backup storage. The main memory occupies a central position by being able to communicate directly with the CPU and with auxiliary devices through an I/O processor. When programs not residing in main memory are needed by the CPU, they are brought in from auxiliary memory. Programs not currently needed in main memory are transferred into auxiliary memory to provide space for currently used programs and data.

A special very high-speed memory is sometimes used to increase the speed of processing by making current programs and data available to the CPU at a rapid rate. The buffer memory shown in Fig. 12-1 is sometimes employed in large computer systems to compensate for the speed differential between main memory access time and processor logic. Processor logic is usually faster than main memory access time with the result that processing speed is mostly limited by the speed of the main memory. A technique used to compensate for the mismatch in operating speeds is to employ an extremely fast, small memory between CPU and main memory whose access time is close to processor logic propagation delays. This type of memory is called a *buffer* and sometimes a *cache* memory. It is used to store segments of programs currently being executed in the CPU and/or temporary data frequently

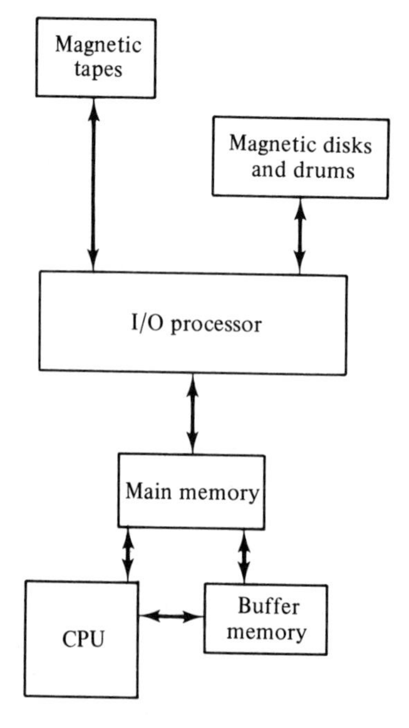


**Fig. 12-1** Storage hierarchy in a large computer system.

needed in the present calculations. By making programs and data available at a rapid rate, it is possible to increase the performance rate of the processor.

In a computer system where the demand for service is high, it is customary to run all programs in one of two possible modes: a *batch* mode or a *time-sharing* mode (some computers are capable of operating in both modes). In a batch mode, each user prepares his program off-line and submits it to the computer center. An operator loads all programs into the computer where they are executed. The operator retrieves the printed output and returns it to the user. What makes the batch mode efficient is the fact that programs can be fed into the computer as fast as they can be processed. In this way it is insured that the computer is busy processing information most of the time.

In a *time-sharing* mode, many users communicate with the computer via remote terminals. Because of slow human response compared to computer speeds, the computer can respond to multiple users at, seemingly, the same time. This is accomplished by having many programs reside in memory while the system allocates a time-slice to each program for execution in the CPU.

A major concept common to both batch and time-sharing modes is their use of *multiprogramming*. Multiprogramming refers to the existence of many programs in different parts of main memory at the same time. In this way, it is possible to keep all parts of the computer busy by working with several programs in sequence. For example, suppose a program is being executed in the CPU and an I/O transfer is required. The CPU initiates the I/O processor to start executing the transfer. This leaves the CPU free to execute another program. In a multiprogramming system, when one program is waiting for input or output transfer, there is another program ready to utilize the CPU.

With multiprogramming systems the need arises for running partial programs, for varying the amount of main memory in use by a given program, and for moving programs around in the memory hierarchy. Application programs are sometimes too long to be accomodated in the total space available in main memory. Bearing in mind that a computer system uses not only application programs but also many system programs, it becomes apparent that all programs cannot reside in main memory at all times. A program with its data normally resides in auxiliary memory. When the program or a segment of the program is to be executed, it is transferred to main memory to be executed by the CPU. Thus, one may think of auxiliary memory as containing the totality of information stored in a computer system. It is the task of the operating system to maintain in main memory a portion of this information that is currently active. The part of the operating system that supervises the flow of information between all storage devices is called the *memory management* system.

The most important reason for a memory hierarchy is economic. The cost per bit of storage is roughly proportional to the memory's level in the hierarchy. It would be prohibitively expensive to maintain all programs and data in main memory especially during a time when they are not needed by the processor. The memory management system distributes programs and data to various levels in the memory hierarchy according to their expected frequency of usage. The objective of the memory management system is to adjust the frequency with which the various memories are referrenced to provide an efficient method of transfers between levels so as to maximize the utilization of all computer components.

## 12-2 AUXILIARY MEMORY

The most common auxiliary memory devices used in computer systems are magnetic drums, magnetic disks, and magnetic tapes. Other components used, but not as frequently, are large capacity core memories, plated wire, and laser memories. To understand fully the physical mechanism of auxiliary memory devices one must have a knowledge of magnetics, electronics, and electro-mechanical systems. Although the physical properties of these storage devices can be quite complex, their logical properties can be characterized and compared by a few parameters. The important characteristics of any device are its access mode, access time, transfer rate, capacity, and cost.

The average time required to reach a storage location in memory for the purpose of reading or writing is called the access time. In electromechanical devices with moving parts such as drums, disks and tapes, the access time consists of a *seek* time required to position the read-write head to a location and a *transfer* time required to transfer data to or from the device. Because the seek time is usually much longer than the transfer time, auxiliary storage is organized in records or blocks. A record is a specified number of characters or words. Reading or writing is always done on entire records. The transfer rate is the number of characters or words that the device can transfer per second, after it has been positioned at the beginning of the record.

Magnetic drums and disks are quite similar in operation. Both consist of high-speed rotating surfaces coated with a magnetic recording medium. The rotating surface of the drum is a cylinder and that of the disk, a round flat plate. The recording surface rotates at uniform speed and is not started or stopped during access operations. Bits are recorded as magnetic spots on the surface as it passes a stationary mechanism called a *write-head.* Stored bits are detected by a change in magnetic field produced by a recorded spot on the surface as it passes through a *read-head.* The amount of surface available for recording in a disk is greater than in a drum of equal physical size. Therefore, more information can be stored on a disk than on a drum of comparable size. For this reason, disks are employed more frequently than drums.

*Magnetic Drum*

The cylindrical surface of a drum is divided into tracks as shown in Fig. 12-2. Each track can accomodate a large number of magnetized spots. The read-write head is mounted on a movable arm near the surface of the cylinder. A drum may have one head which can be moved mechanically to any one track position, or may have several heads over several tracks for simultaneous access to a number of bits at one time. The bit timing track has permanent bits recorded in its surface at equal intervals. These bits are used to generate clock pulses and to synchronize the bits in each track. A typical drum may have as many as 500 tracks with 30,000 magnetized spots or bits around each track.

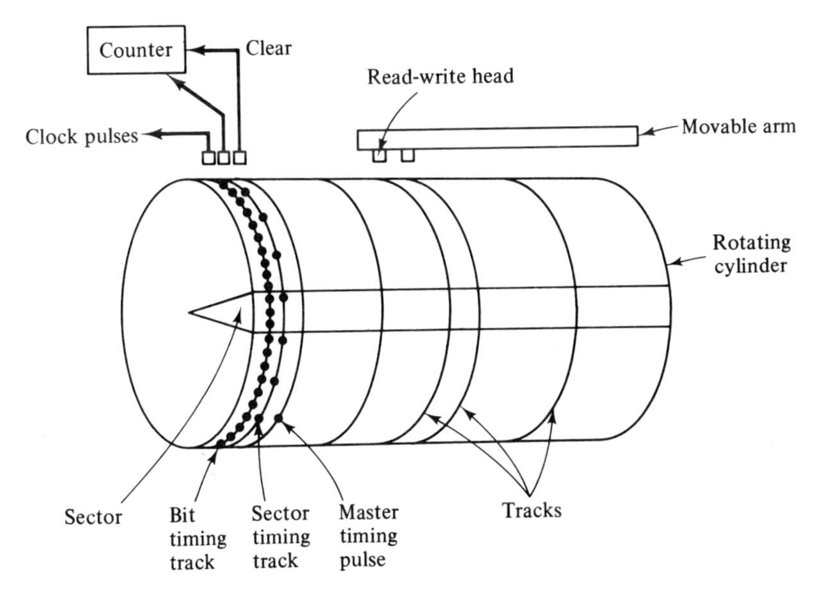


**Fig. 12-2** Magnetic drum.

Each track is divided into sectors with each sector specifying a given number of bits. A typical sector may have 32 bits. The sectors are identified by counting permanent stored bits in the sector timing track. This track has one bit at the end of each sector. These permanently recorded bits are applied to a counter to provide the address of the sector presently being scanned by the read-write heads. A master timing pulse on a separate track is used to clear the counter once every revolution.

A drum is addressed by specifying a track and sector number. For example, 512 tracks can be specified with 8 bits and 1024 sectors with 10 bits. An address of 18 bits is needed to specify a particular sector (of 32 bits) in a particular track. The high-order 8 bits of the address go to a control mechanism that physically moves the read-write head to the specified track. The 10 low-order bits of the address are compared with the content of the counter that counts the pulses coming out of the sector timing track. When the count is equal to the desired sector address, the bits from the specified track are read and transferred to a shift register one after another until the whole sector is assembled. The 32 bit sector is then ready to be transferred to main memory.

### *Magnetic Disk*

The storage organization of a magnetic disk is similar to that of a drum except that a flat surface is used instead of a cylinder. A disk unit is an electromechanical assembly, containing a flat disk coated with magnetic material. Often both sides of the disk are used and several disks may be stacked on one spindle with read-write heads available in each surface. All disks rotate together at high speed and are not stopped or started for access purposes. Bits are stored in the magnetized surface in spots along concentric circles called tracks. The tracks are commonly divided into sections called sectors. In most systems, the minimum quantity of information which can be transferred is a sector. The subdivision of one disk surface into tracks and sectors is shown in Fig. 12-3.

Some units use a single read-write head for each disk surface. In this type of unit, the track address bits are used by a mechanical assembly to move the head into the specified track position before reading or writing. In other disk systems, separate read-write heads are provided for each track in each surface. The address bits can then select a particular track electronically through a decoder circuit. This type of unit is more expensive and is found only in very large computer systems.

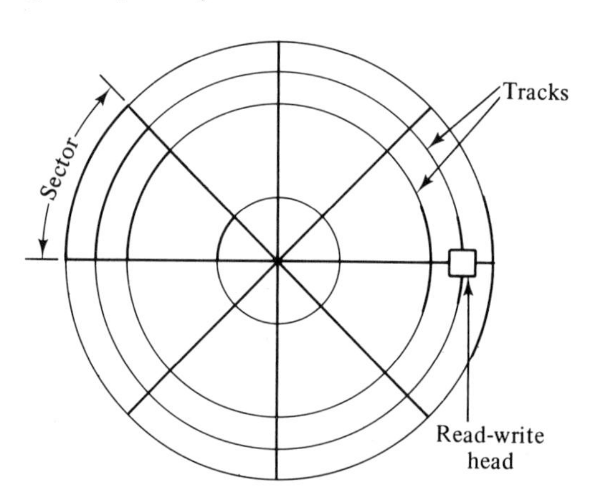


**Fig. 12-3** Magnetic disk.

Permanent timing tracks are used in disks as in drums to synchronize the bits and recognize the sectors. A disk system is addressed by address bits that specify the disk number, the disk surface, the sector number and the track within the sector. After the read-write heads are positioned in the specified track, the system has to wait until the rotating disk reaches the specified sector under the read-write head. Information transfer is very fast once the beginning of a sector has been reached. Both drums and disks may have multiple heads and simultaneous transfer of bits from several tracks at the same time.

A track in a given sector near the circumference is longer than a track near the center of the disk. If bits are recorded with equal density, some tracks will contain more recorded bits than others. To make all the records in a sector of equal length, some disks use a variable recording density with higher density on tracks near the center than on tracks near the circumference. This equalizes the number of bits on all tracks of a given sector.

Very often, the disks are permanently attached to the unit assembly and cannot be removed by the occasional user. A different type of unit called a *disk-pack* is also available which allows the disk to be removed easily. A relatively recent innovation in disk storage is the *flexible* or *floppy* disk that replaces the more conventional rigid disk. The flexible disk is made of plastic coated with a magnetic recording medium and is approximately the size and shape of a 45-rpm record. The flexible disk can be inserted and removed about as easily as a tape cartridge.

### *Magnetic Tape*

A magnetic tape transport consists of the electrical, mechanical, and electronic components to provide the parts and control mechanism for a magnetic-tape unit. The tape itself is a strip of plastic coated with a magnetic recording medium. Bits are recorded as magnetic spots on the tape along several tracks. Usually 7 or 9 bits are recorded simultaneously to form a character together with a parity bit. Read-write heads are mounted one in each track so that data can be recorded and read as a sequence of characters.

Magnetic-tape units can be stopped, started to move forward or in reverse, or can be rewound. However, they cannot be started or stopped fast enough between individual characters. For this reason, information is recorded in blocks referred to as records. Gaps of unrecorded tape are inserted between records where the tape can be stopped. The tape starts moving while in a gap and attains its constant speed by the time it reaches the next record. Each record on tape has an identification bit pattern at the beginning and end. By reading the bit pattern at the beginning, the tape control identifies the record number. By reading the bit pattern at the end of the record, the control recognizes the beginning of a gap. A tape unit is addressed by specifying the record number and the number of characters in the record. Records may be of fixed or variable length.

## 12-3 MEMORY BUS ORGANIZATION

The main memory in a computer system occupies a central position through which information passes to and from peripheral units and CPU. A large computer system may have several CPUs and several I/O processors communicating with the memory through a bus system. The rate at which information can be transferred between various units and main memory is limited by the transfer capabilities of the memory itself and the memory bus. The transfer rate is often referred to as the memory *bandwidth* measured in words or bits per second.

The functional organization of the main memory is shown in Fig. 12-4. The memory consists of an array of cells for storing the information, an address register, and a buffer register. The data and address busses are controlled by the memory controller. In small systems the controller may just initiate a read or write operation. In more sophisticated systems, the memory control logic permits all processors to operate at full speed with minimal interference. Note that the address bus is unidirectional and the data bus

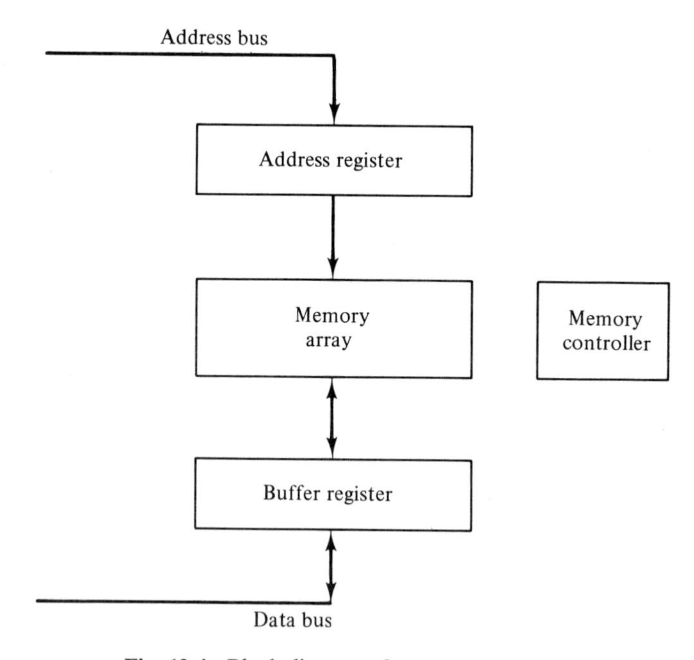


**Fig. 12-4** Block diagram of a memory module.

bidirectional. A memory must receive an address but may either receive data (for a *write* operation) or transmit data (after a *read* operation).

A memory *module* is defined as a memory array together with a single address register and a single buffer register. Figure 12-4 shows a block diagram of one memory module. A single module is used in small systems for economic reasons. In large systems or where speed is of the utmost importance, it is more convenient to use a multiple module memory system. Figure 12-5

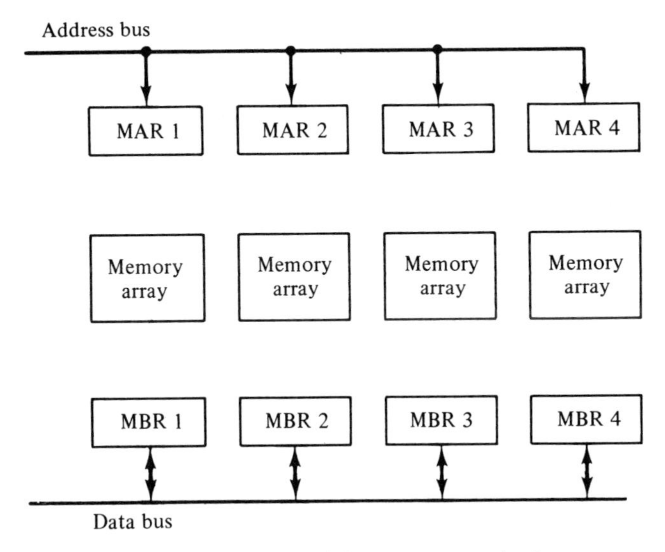


**Fig. 12-5** Multiple module memory organization.

shows a memory unit organized in four modules. Each module has its own address register and buffer register. The two most significant bits of the address in the bus distinguish between the four modules. It is the job of the memory controller to route the address from the bus to the specified module and transfer the data to and from the specified module and the data bus. The multiple-module system is more expensive but can provide a higher speed of operation than the single-module system. The modular system permits one module to be accessed while other modules are in a process of reading or writing a word since each module can honor a memory request independently of the state of other modules. Thus, if an I/O processor and CPU request data from different modules, both can be serviced as soon as the bus is available without having to wait for the memory access time in the other module.

Another advantage of a modular memory is that it allows the use of the technique called *interleaving*. In an interleaved memory, consecutive addresses are in different memory modules. For example, in a two-module memory system, all the even addresses would be in one module and all odd addresses in the other. By staggering the memory access, it is possible to reduce the effective memory cycle time by one half. If instructions and operands are placed in two different modules, the instruction fetch cycle and reading of the operand many be interleaved. This allows the initiation of the fetch cycle while the operand for the previous instruction is being read from another memory module.

The main memory can be organized with a multiple bus structure so that any memory module can send information to or receive information from a number of processors operating concurrently. Figure 12-6 shows the interconnection between two CPUs, two I/O processors and four memory modules. This type of interconnection is called an electronic crossbar switch. The small squares are switch-points that determine the path from each processor to each memory module. Each switch-point has control logic to set up the transfer path between a processor and a memory module. The switch-point examines the word that is placed in the bus to determine whether its particular module is being addressed. This eliminates the need for a central

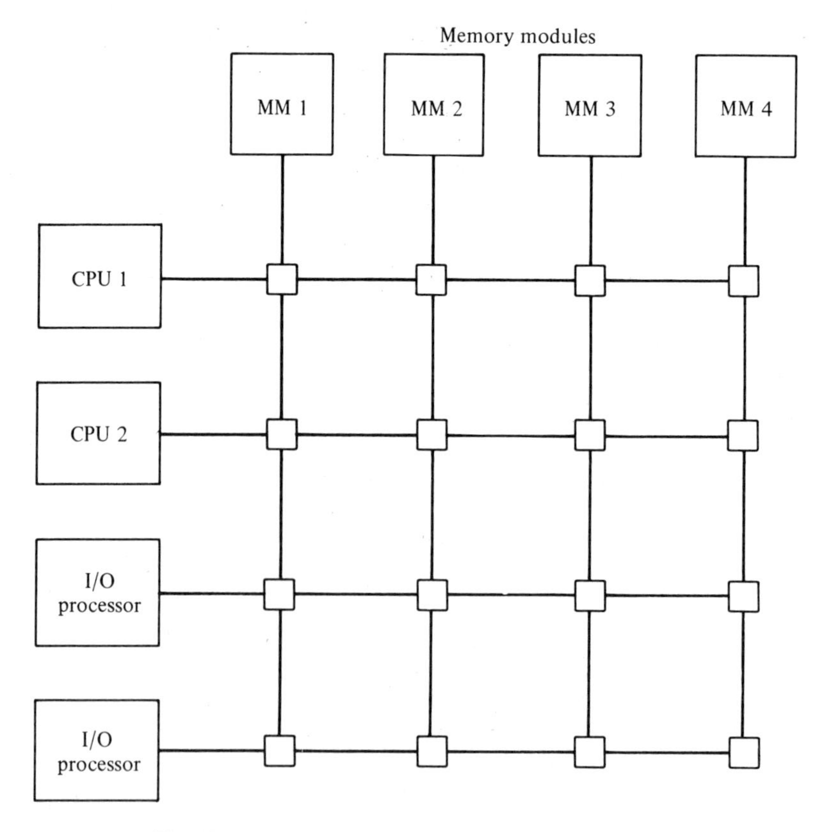


**Fig. 12-6** A crossbar switch memory bus organization.

control to establish a linkage directing the word to the proper module. The operation of each memory module is independent of the operation of any other memory module and memory cycles can occur simultaneously within all four modules.

## 12-4 ASSOCIATIVE MEMORY

Many data processing applications require the search of items in a table stored in memory. An assembler program searches the symbol address table in order to extract the symbol's binary equivalent. An account number may be searched in a file to determine the holder's name and account status. The established way to search a table is to store all items where they can be addressed in sequence. The search procedure is a strategy for choosing a sequence of addresses, reading the content of memory at each address, and comparing the information read with the item being searched until a match occurs. The number of accesses to memory depends on the location of the item and the efficiency of the search algorithm. Many search algorithms have been developed to minimize the number of accesses while searching for an item in a random or sequential access memory.

The time required to find an item stored in memory can be reduced considerably if stored data can be identified for access by the content of the data itself rather than by an address. A memory unit accessed by content is called an *associative memory* or *content addressable memory* (CAM). This type of memory is accessed simultaneously and in parallel on the basis of data content rather than by specific address or location. When a word is written in an associative memory, no address is given. The memory is capable of finding an empty unused location to store the word. When a word is to be read from an associative memory, the content of the word, or part of the word, is specified. The memory locates all words which match the specified content and marks them for reading.

Because of its organization, the associative memory is uniquely suited to do parallel searches by data association. Moreover, searches can be done on an entire word or on a specific field within a word. An associative memory is more expensive than a random access memory because each cell must have storage capability as well as logic circuits for matching its content with an external argument. For this reason, associative memories are used in applications where the search time is very critical and must be very short.

### *Hardware Organization*

The block diagram of an associative memory is shown in Fig. 12-7. It consists of a memory array and logic for $m$ words with $n$ bits per word.

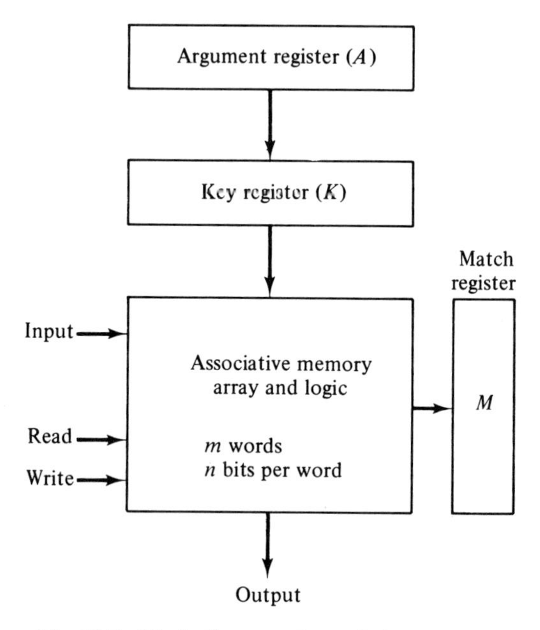


**Fig. 12-7** Block diagram of associative memory.

The argument register $A$ and key register $K$ each have $n$ bits, one for each bit of a word. The match register $M$ has $m$ bits, one for each memory word. Each word in memory is compared in parallel with the content of the argument register. The words that match the bits of the argument register set a corresponding bit in the match register. After the matching process, those bits in the match register that have been set indicate the fact that their corresponding words have been matched. Reading is accomplished by a sequential access to memory for those words whose corresponding bits in the match register have been set.

The key register provides a mask for choosing a particular field or key in the argument word. The entire argument is compared with each memory word if the key register contains all 1's. Otherwise, only those bits in the argument that have 1's in their corresponding position of the key register are compared. Thus, the key provides a mask or identifying piece of information which specifies how the reference to memory is made. To illustrate with a numerical example, suppose that the argument register $A$ and the key register $K$ have the bit configuration shown below. Only the three left-most bits of $A$ are compared with memory words because $K$ has 1's in these positions.

| | |
|---|---|
| $A$ | 101 111100 |
| $K$ | 111 000000 |

| | | |
|---|---|---|
| word 1 | 100 111100 | no match |
| word 2 | 101 000001 | match |

Word 2 matches the unmasked argument field because the three left-most bits of the argument and the word are equal.

The relation between the memory array and external registers in an associative memory is shown in Fig. 12-8. The cells in the array are marked by the

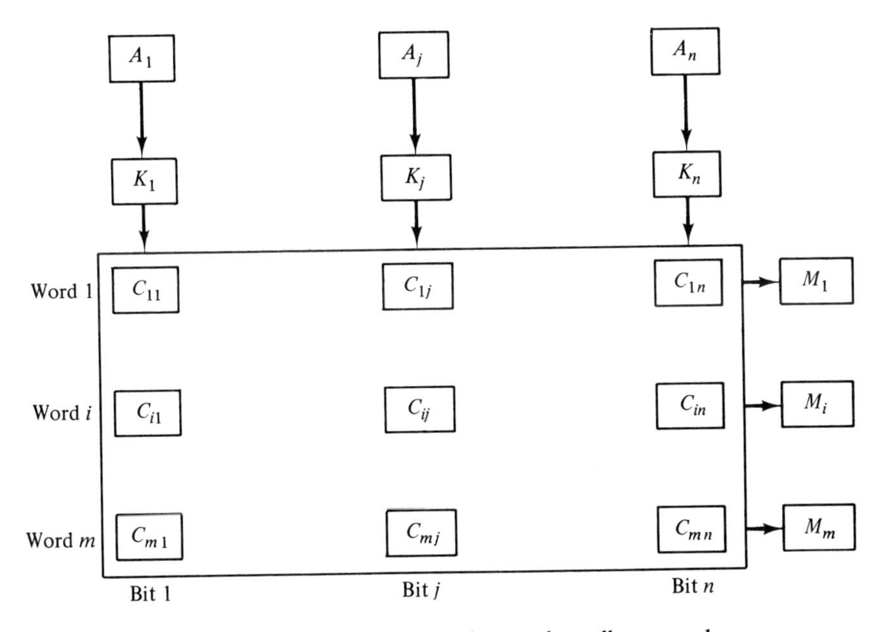


**Fig. 12-8** Associative memory of $m$ word, $n$ cells per word.

letter $C$ with two subscripts. The first subscript gives the word number and the second specifies the bit position in the word. Thus, cell $C_{ij}$ is the cell for bit $j$ in word $i$. A bit $A_j$ in the argument register is compared with all the bits in column $j$ of the array provided $K_j = 1$. This is done for all columns $j = 1, 2, \ldots, n$. If a match occurs between all the unmasked bits of the argument and the bits in word $i$, the corresponding bit $M_i$ in the match register is set to 1. If one or more unmasked bit of the argument and the word do not match, $M_i$ is cleared to 0.

The internal organization of a typical cell $C_{ij}$ is shown in Fig. 12-9. It consists of a flip-flop storage element $F_{ij}$ and the circuits for reading, writing, and matching the cell. The input bit is transferred into the storage cell during a write operation. The bit stored is read out during a read operation. The match logic compares the content of the storage cell with the correspond-

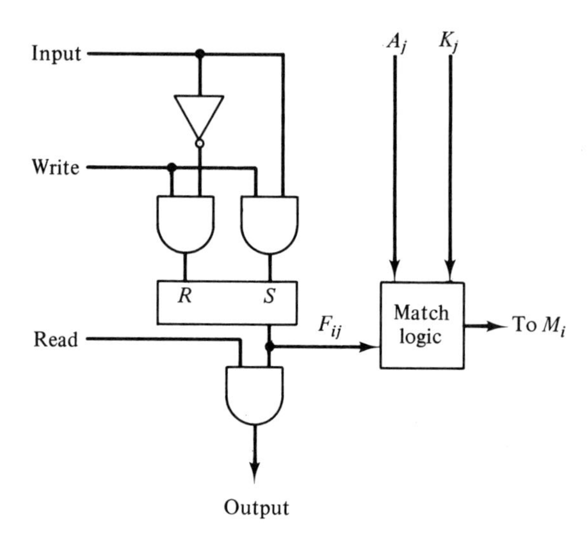


**Fig. 12-9** One cell of associative memory.

ing unmasked bit of the argument and provides an output for the decision logic that sets the bit in $M_i$.

### *Match Logic*

The match logic for each word can be derived from the comparison algorithm for two binary numbers. First, we *neglect* the key bits and compare the argument in $A$ with the bits stored in the cells of the words. Word $i$ is equal to the argument in $A$ if $A_j = F_{ij}$ for $j = 1, 2, \ldots, n$. Two bits are equal if they are both 1 or both 0. The equality of two bits can be expressed logically by the Boolean function:

$$x_j = A_j F_{ij} + A'_j F'_{ij}$$

where $x_j = 1$ if the pair of bits in position $j$ are equal, otherwise $x_j = 0$.

For a word $i$ to be equal to the argument in $A$ we must have all $x_j$ variables equal to 1. This is the condition for setting the corresponding match bit $M_i$ to 1. The Boolean function for this condition is

$$M_i = x_1 x_2 x_3 \ldots x_n$$

and constitutes the AND operation of all pairs of matched bits in a word.

We now include the key bit $K_j$ in the comparison logic. The requirement is that if $K_j = 0$, the corresponding bits of $A_j$ and $F_{ij}$ need no comparison. Only when $K_j = 1$ must they be compared. This requirement is achieved by

ORing each term with $K'_j$, thus:

$$x_j + K'_j = \begin{cases} x_j \text{ if } K_j = 1 \\ 1 \text{ if } K_j = 0 \end{cases}$$

When $K_j = 1$, we have $K'_j = 0$ and $x_j + 0 = x_j$. When $K_j = 0$, then $K'_j = 1$ and $x_j + 1 = 1$. A term $(x_j + K'_j)$ will be in the 1 state if its pair of bits are not compared. This is necessary because each term is ANDed with all other terms so that an output of 1 will have no effect. The comparison of the bits has an effect only when $K_j = 1$.

The match logic for word $i$ in an associative memory can be now expressed by the following Boolean function:

$$M_i = (x_1 + K'_1)(x_2 + K'_2)(x_3 + K'_3) \ldots (x_n + K'_n)$$

Each term in the expression will be equal to 1 if its corresponding $K_j = 0$. If $K_j = 1$, the term will be either 0 or 1 depending on the value of $x_j$. A match will occur and $M_i$ will be equal to 1 if all terms are equal to 1.

If we substitute the original definition of $x_j$, the above Boolean function can be expressed as follows:

$$M_i = \prod_{j=1}^{n} (A_j F_{ij} + A'_j F'_{ij} + K'_j)$$

where $\prod$ is a product symbol designating the AND operation of all $n$ terms. We need $m$ such functions, one for each word $i = 1, 2, 3, \ldots, m$.

The circuit for matching one word is shown in Fig. 12-10. Each cell requires two AND gates and one OR gate. The inverters for $A_j$ and $K_j$ are needed once for each column and are used for all bits in the column. The output of all OR gates in the cells of the same word go to the input of a common AND gate to generate the match signal for $M_i$. $M_i$ will be logic 1 if a match occurs and 0 if no match occurs. Note that if the key register contains all 0's, output $M_i$ will be a 1 irrespective of the value of $A$ or the word. This occurrence must be avoided during normal operation.

### *Read Operation*

If more than one word in memory matches the unmasked argument field, all the matched words will have 1's in the corresponding bit position of the match register. It is then necessary to scan the bits of the match register one at a time. The matched words are read in sequence by applying a read signal to each word line whose corresponding $M_i$ bit is a 1.

In most applications, the associative memory stores a table with no two identical items under a given key. In this case, only one word may match the

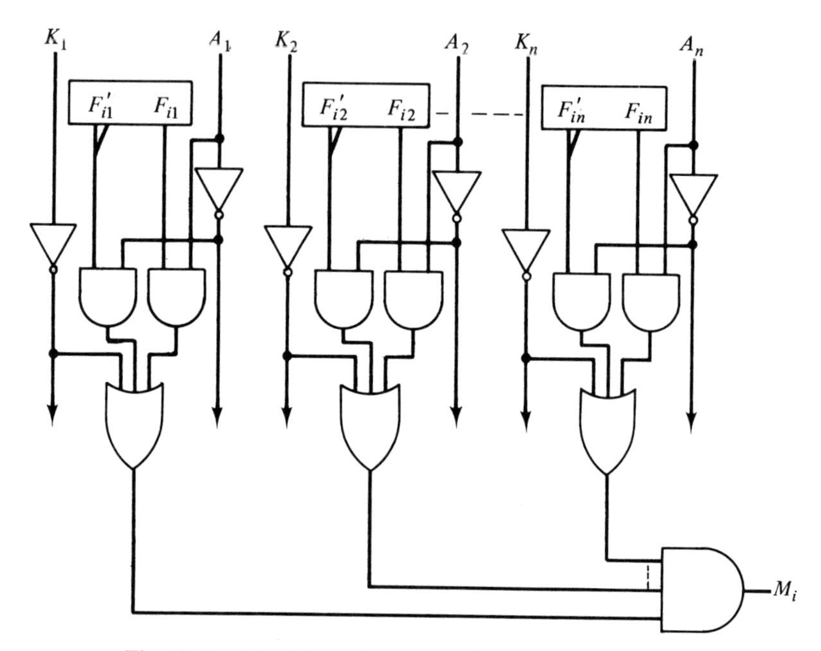


**Fig. 12-10** Match logic for one word of associative memory.

unmasked argument field. By connecting output $M_i$ directly to the read line in the same word position (instead of the $M$ register), the content of the matched word will be presented automatically at the output lines and no special read command signal is needed. Furthermore, if we exclude words having a zero content, then an all zero output will indicate that no match occurred and that the searched item is not available in memory.

### *Write Operation*

An associative memory must have a write capability for storing the information to be searched. Writing in an associative memory can take different forms, depending on the application. If the entire memory is loaded with new information at once prior to a search operation then the writing can be done by addressing each location in sequence. This will make the device a random-access memory for writing and a content addressable memory for reading. The advantage here is that the address for input can be decoded as in a random access memory. Thus, instead of having $m$ address lines, one for each word in memory, the number of address lines can be reduced by the decoder to $d$ lines where $m = 2^d$.

If unwanted words have to be deleted and new words inserted one at a time, there is a need for a special register to distinguish between active and inactive words. This register, sometimes called a *tag* register, would have as many bits as there are words in the memory. For every active word stored in memory, the corresponding bit in the tag register is set to 1. A word is deleted from memory by clearing its tag bit to 0. Words are stored in memory by scanning the tag register until the first 0 bit is encountered. This gives the first available inactive word and a position for writing a new word. After the new word is stored in memory it is made active by setting its tag bit to 1. An unwanted word when deleted from memory can be cleared to all 0's if this value is used to specify an empty location. Moreover, the words that have a tag bit of 0 must be masked (together with the $K_j$ bits) with the argument word so that only active words are compared.

### *Associative Processor*

The advantages of associative memories are numerous and many applications have been found for their use. A considerable amount of research activity has been conducted to include such a memory in the design of general-purpose computers. A computer with an associative memory (instead of a random-access memory) is called an *associative processor*. In an associative processor each cell is "associated" with its neighboring cells for handling the usual arithmetic, logic, and shift operations. The operations are performed in parallel instead of having to bring the operands one by one to the CPU for processing. A group of operations that would be programmed as a routine in a conventional computer can be executed in parallel in an associative processor. However, as may be evident from the previous discussion, an associative memory requires a considerable number of logic circuits within its individual cells and in its environment. Because of economic reasons, associative memories have been used mostly in specialized applications.

## 12-5 VIRTUAL MEMORY

In a memory hierarchy system, programs and data are first stored in auxiliary memory. Portions of a program or data are brought into main memory as they are needed by the CPU. *Virtual memory* is a concept used in some large computer systems that permit the user to construct his programs as though he had a large memory space, equal to the totality of auxiliary memory. Each address which is referenced by the CPU goes through an address mapping from the so-called virtual address to an actual address in main memory. Virtual memory is used to give the programmer the illusion that he has a very large memory at his disposal, even though the computer actually has a relatively small main memory. A virtual memory system provides a mechanism for translating program-generated addresses into correct main memory locations. This is done dynamically, while programs are being executed in the

CPU. The translation or mapping is handled automatically by the hardware by means of a mapping table.

### *Address Space and Memory Space*

An address used by a programmer will be called a *virtual* address, and the set of such addresses the *address space*. An address in main memory is called a *location* or *physical address*. The set of such locations is called the *memory space*. Thus, the address space is the set of addresses generated by programs as they reference instructions and data; the memory space consists of the actual main memory locations directly addressable for processing. In most computers the address and memory spaces are identical. The address space is allowed to be larger than the memory space in computers with virtual memory.

As an illustration, consider a computer with a main-memory capacity of $32K$ words ($K = 1024$). Fifteen bits are needed to specify a physical address in memory since $32K = 2^{15}$. Suppose that the computer has available auxiliary memory for storing $2^{20} = 1024K$ words. Thus, auxiliary memory has a capacity for storing information equivalent to the capacity of 32 main memories. Denoting the address space by $N$ and the memory space by $M$ we then have for this example $N = 1024K$ and $M = 32K$.

In a multiprogram computer system, programs and data are transferred to and from auxiliary memory and main memory based on demands imposed

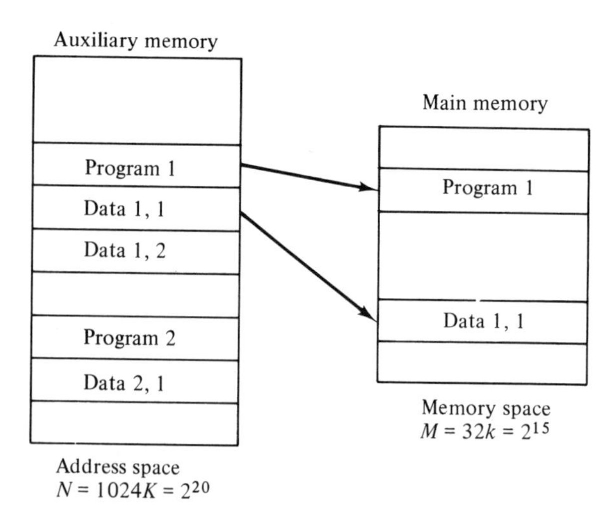


**Fig. 12-11** Relation between address and memory space in a virtual memory system.

by the CPU. Suppose that program 1 is currently being executed in the CPU. Program 1 and a portion of its associated data are moved from auxiliary memory into main memory as shown in Fig. 12-11. Portions of programs and data need not be in contiguous locations in memory since information is being moved in and out, and empty spaces may be available in scattered locations in memory.

In a virtual memory system, the programmer is told that he has the total address space at his disposal. Moreover, the address field of the instruction code has a sufficient number of bits to specify all virtual addresses. In our example, the address field of an instruction code will consist of 20 bits but physical memory addresses must be specified with only 15 bits. Thus CPU will reference instructions and data with a 20 bit address but the information at this address must be taken from physical memory because access to auxiliary storage for individual words will be prohibitively long. (Remember that for efficient transfers, auxiliary storage moves an entire record to the main memory.) A table is then needed, as shown in Fig. 12-12, to map a virtual address of 20 bits to a physical address of 15 bits. The mapping is a dynamic operation which means that every address is translated immediately as a word is referenced by CPU.

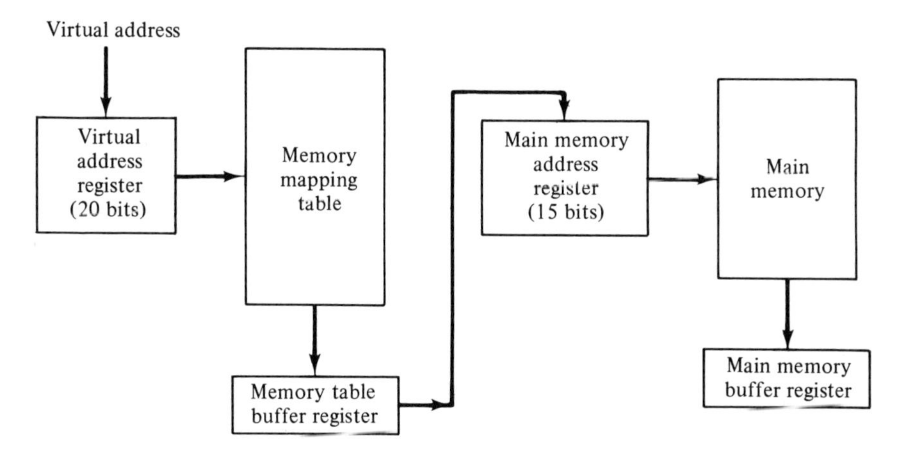


**Fig. 12-12** Memory table for mapping a virtual address.

The mapping table may be stored in a separate memory as shown in Fig. 12-12 or in main memory. In the first case, an additional memory unit is required as well as one extra memory access time. In the second case, the table takes space from main memory and two accesses to memory are required with the program running at half speed. A third alternative is to use an associative memory as explained below.

### *Address Mapping*

The table implementation of the address mapping is simplified if the information in the address space and the memory space are each divided into groups of fixed size. The physical memory is broken down into groups of equal size called *blocks*, which may range from 64 to 1024 words each. The term *page* refers to groups of address space of the same size. For example, if a page or block consists of $1K$ words then, using the previous example, address space is divided into 1024 pages and main memory is divided into 32 blocks. Although both a page and a block are split into groups of $1K$ words, a page refers to the organization of address space, while a block refers to the organization of memory space. The programs are also considered to be split into pages. Portions of programs are moved from auxiliary memory to main memory in records equal to the size of a page.

Consider a computer with an address space of $8K$ and a memory space of $4K$. If we split each into groups of $1K$ words we obtain 8 pages and 4 blocks as shown in Fig. 12-13. At any given time, up to four pages of address space may reside in main memory in any one of thւ four blocks.

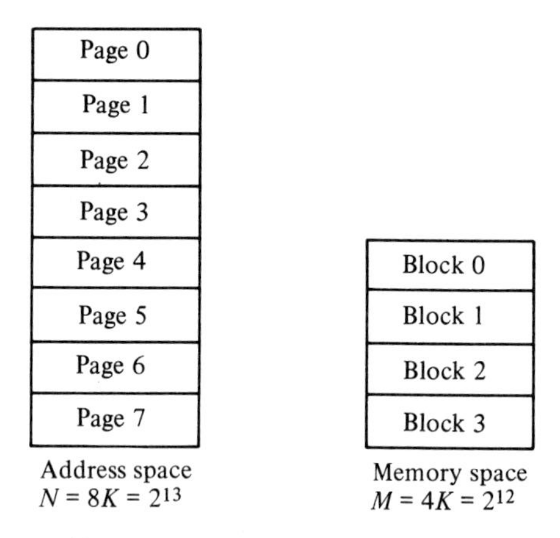


**Fig. 12-13** Address space and memory space split into groups of $1K$ words.

The mapping from address space to memory space is facilitated if each virtual address is considered to be represented by two numbers: a page number address and a line within the page. In a computer with $2^p$ words per page, $p$ bits are used to specify a line address and the remaining high-order bits of the virtual address specify the page number. In the example of Fig. 12-13, a virtual address has 13 bits. Since each page consists of $2^{10} = 1024$ words, the high-order three bits of a virtual address will specify one of the eight pages and the low-order 10 bits give the line address within the page. Note that the line address in address space and memory space is the same; the only mapping required is from a page number to a block number.

The organization of the memory mapping table in a paged system is shown in Fig. 12-14. The memory-page table consists of eight words, one for each page. The address in the page table denotes the page number and the content of the word gives the block number where that page is stored in main memory. The table shows that pages 1, 2, 5, and 6 are now available in main memory in blocks 3, 0, 1, and 2, respectively. A presence bit in each location indicates whether the page has been transferred from auxiliary memory into main memory. A 0 in the presence bit indicates that this page is not available in main memory. The CPU references a word in memory with a virtual address of 13 bits. The three high-order bits of the virtual address specify a page number and also an address for the memory-page table. The content of the word in the memory-page table at the page number address is read out into the memory table buffer register. If the presence bit is a 1, the block number thus read is transferred to the two high-order bits of the main memory address register. The line number from the virtual address is transferred into the 10 low-order bits of the memory address register. A read signal to main memory transfers the content of the word to the main memory buffer register ready to be used by the CPU. If the presence bit in the word read from the page table is 0, it signifies that the content of the word referenced by the virtual

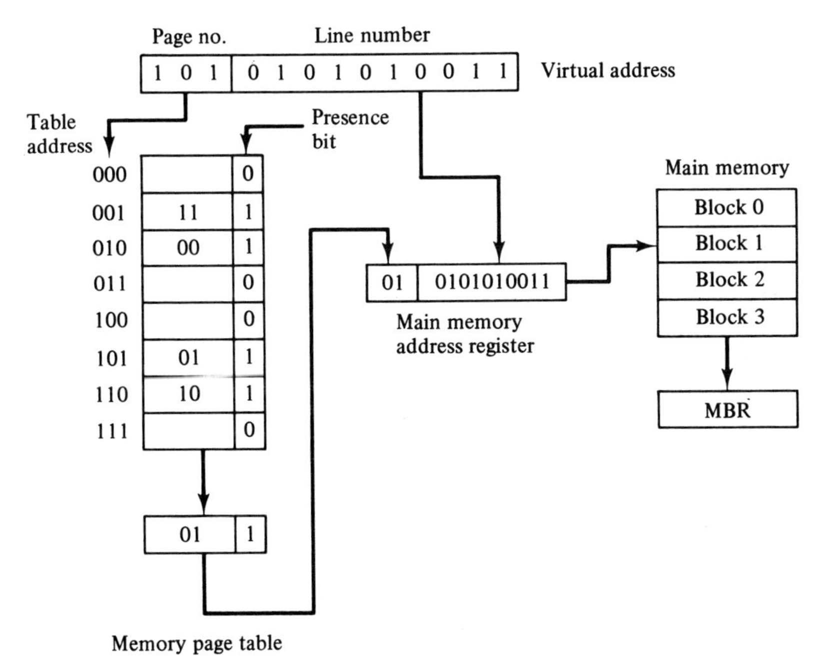


**Fig. 12-14** Memory table in a paged system.

address does not reside in main memory. A call to the operating system is then generated to fetch the required page from auxiliary memory and place it into main memory before resuming computation.

### *Associative Memory-Page Table*

A random access memory-page table is inefficient with respect to storage utilization. In the example of Fig. 12-14 we observe that eight words of memory are needed, one for each page, but at least four words will always be marked empty because main memory cannot accomodate more than four blocks. In general, a system with $n$ pages and $m$ blocks would require a memory-page table of $n$ locations of which up to $m$ blocks will be marked with block numbers and all others will be empty. As a second numerical example, consider an address space of $1024K$ words and memory space of $32K$ words. If each page or block contains $1K$ words then the number of pages is 1024 and the number of blocks 32. The capacity of the memory-page table must be 1024 words and only 32 locations may have a presence bit equal to 1. At any given time, at least 992 locations will be empty and not in use.

A more efficient way to organize the page table would be to construct it with a number of words equal to the number of blocks in main memory. In this way, the size of the memory is reduced and each location is fully utilized. This method can be implemented by means of an associative memory with each word in memory containing a page number together with its corresponding block number. The page field in each word is compared with the page number in the virtual address. If a match occurs, the word is read from memory and its corresponding block number is extracted.

Consider again the case of eight pages and four blocks as in the example of Fig. 12-14. We replace the random access memory-page table with an associative memory of four words as shown in Fig. 12-15. Each entry in the associative memory array consists of two fields. The first three bits specify a field for storing the page number. The last two bits constitute a field for storing the block number. The virtual address is placed in the argument register. The page number bits in the argument register are compared with all page numbers in the page field of the associative memory. If the page number is found, the 5-bit word is read out from memory. The corresponding block number, being in the same word, is transferred to the main memory address register. If no match occurs, a call to the operating system is generated to bring the required page from auxiliary memory.

### *Page Allocation*

A virtual memory system is a combination of hardware and software techniques. The memory management software system handles all the software operations for the efficient utilization of memory space. It must decide:

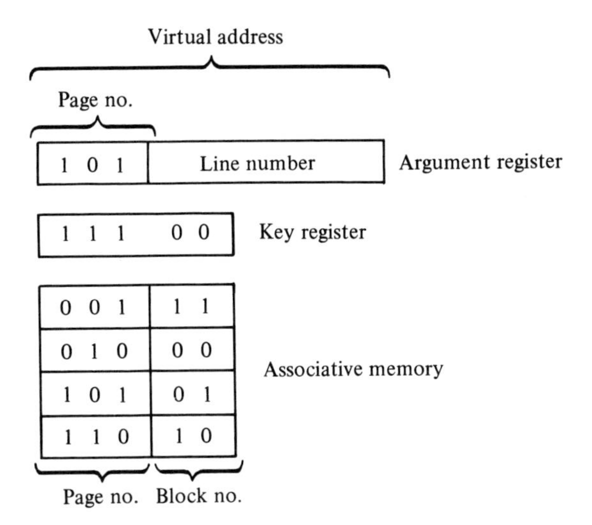


**Fig. 12-15** An associative memory page table.

(a) which page in main memory ought to be removed to make room for a new page; (b) when a new page is to be transferred from auxiliary memory to main memory; and (c) where the page is to be placed in main memory. The hardware mapping mechanism and the memory management software together constitute the architecture of a virtual memory.

When a program starts execution, one or more pages are transferred into main memory and the page table is set to indicate their position. The program is executed from main memory until it attempts to reference a location that is still in auxiliary memory. A call to the operating system is then generated to fetch the required page from auxiliary memory into main memory. In the meantime, control is transferred to the next program in memory that is waiting to be processed in the CPU. The memory management software system decides what page to remove from main memory (if any) and what page to bring in its place. Later, when the memory block has been assigned and the transfer completed, the original program can resume.

Since the software system cannot rely on memory being freed by terminating programs, it must use a scheduling algorithm to take memory pages away from programs that are currently residing in main memory. The scheduling algorithm directs the transfer of pages in and out of main memory and auxiliary memory according to the needs of the programs being executed while attempting to maximize the processing efficiency of the total computer system.

### *Memory Protection*

Computers designed for multiprogramming must provide a memory protection mechanism to prevent one program from changing another program. One way of implementing a memory protection procedure is by placing additional bits in each word of the memory page table to indicate whether the corresponding block in main memory can be accessed for reading, writing, or not at all. The decision is made in the memory controller by matching the protection bits in the page table with a *key* code in the program being executed. The CPU may be allowed to access main memory depending on the program currently in execution and the protection code bits in the page table. The protection bits specify whether the page is available to the current program

(a) for reading and writing, or

(b) for reading only (write protection), or

(c) is not accessible at all (full protection).

Full read and write privileges are given to a program when it is executing its own instructions. This privilege is also given to the operating system that supervises all other programs in the computer.

Write protection is useful for sharing system programs such as text editors, utility programs, and other common subroutines. These system programs are stored in an area of memory where they can be shared by many users. They can be read by many programs but no writing is allowed. This protects them from being changed by other programs.

Full protection is necessary to prevent one program from changing another program. Portions of the operating system will reside in main memory at any given time. These system programs must be fully protected by making them inaccessible to other programs. Only the operating system can change its own or other programs. All other programs must be protected from each other.

## 12-6 CONCLUDING REMARKS

Computers are sometimes classified by categories to reflect their relative size and cost. The smallest and least expensive computers are the microcomputers. They are constructed from a number of LSI circuits and they are usually employed in dedicated and special-purpose applications. Next in complexity are the minicomputers which are somewhat more expensive but are still relatively small in size. Minicomputers are used in general purpose applications and are one step higher than microcomputers. With the development of microprocessors and other LSI circuits, the distinction between microcomputers and minicomputers is gradually fading away. Medium-scale and large-scale computer systems are large computer systems with the former being somewhat smaller and cheaper than the latter.

The memory organization of a computer is directly related to its category. Microcomputers would usually have a main memory made up of LSI RAMs and ROMs. The memory is attached to a common bus that communicates directly with the CPU and all I/O interfaces. A memory transfer involves the recognition of a special code that signifies a request to access the memory. The task of the memory controller is to provide a path between memory and the common bus.

A minicomputer would most likely have a magnetic core memory of basic configuration plus an option to expand it with additional memory arrays as needed by a particular application. It would include a number of low-cost auxiliary memory devices such as floppy disks and tape-cartridge recorders. One or more DMA channels may be provided for direct transfer between auxiliary memory and main memory. The memory controller in most minicomputers is therefore a DMA controller.

In medium-scale and especially large-scale computers, the memory organization is a major design project. The memory communicates with a number of processors simultaneously so it must resolve conflicts and establish priorities among many sources operating concurrently. The computer would most likely have a virtual memory configuration and possibly a buffer memory between CPU and main memory. The operation of the memory is very closely related to the way the operating system is designed and therefore, the two cannot be separated but must be designed concurrently. Operating systems place a considerable demand on the hardware of a memory system and the benefits derived from using them increase as the range and complexity of the hardware increases. For this reason, the most complicated memory control systems and the most powerful operating systems are used with the largest computers.

## REFERENCES

1. WATSON, R. W., *Timesharing System Design Concepts*, New York: McGraw-Hill Book Co., 1970.
2. CHU, Y., *Computer Organization and Microprogramming*, Englewood Cliffs, N.J.: Prentice-Hall, Inc., 1972.
3. HELLERMAN, H., *Digital Computer System Principles*, New York: McGraw-Hill Book Co., 1973.
4. HANLON, A. G., "Content-Addressable and Associative Memory Systems—A Survey," *IEEE Trans. on Electronic Computers*, Vol. EC-15 (August, 1966), pp. 509–521.
5. THURBER, K. J., and R. O. BERG, "Application of Associative Processors," *Computer Design*, Vol. 10 (November, 1971), pp. 103–110.
6. "Content Addressable Memory Element," Applications Memo No. 103, Signetics Corp., Sunnyvale, Cal., June, 1970.

7. FOSTER, C. C., *Computer Architecture*, New York: Van Nostrand Reinhold Co., 1970.

8. DENNING, P. J., "Virtual Memory," Tech. Rept. No. 81, Dept. of Electrical Engineering, Princeton Univ., January, 1970.

9. GLORIOSO, R. M., and T. D. CLOSE, "Design of Virtual Memory for Small Computers," *Computer Design*, Vol. 12 (December, 1973).

10. DONOVAN, J. J., *Systems Programming*, New York: McGraw-Hill Book Co., 1972.

## PROBLEMS

12-1 Explain the need for auxiliary memory devices. How are they different from main memory and from other peripheral devices?

12-2 Explain the need for memory hierarchy. What is the main reason for not having a large enough main memory for storing the totality of information in a computer system?

12-3 Give at least four differences between a magnetic-drum and a magnetic-tape unit.

12-4 Why is it that more binary information can be stored in a disk unit than a drum unit of comparable size?

12-5 A magnetic disk unit has eight disks with recording on both surfaces of each disk. Each surface has 16 tracks and 8 sectors. Each sector in a track contains one record. How many bits are needed to address a record in the disk?

12-6 Draw a block diagram for the address selection logic of a drum unit.

12-7 Show how a memory controller in a multiple module system can determine the memory module specified by the incoming address bits.

12-8 Obtain the complement function for the match logic of one word in an associative memory. In other words show that $M_i'$ is the sum of exclusive-OR functions. Draw the logic diagram for $M_i'$ and terminate it with an inverter to obtain $M_i$.

12-9 Obtain the Boolean function for the match logic of one word in an associative memory taking into consideration a tag bit that indicates whether the word is active or inactive.

12-10 What additional logic is required to give a no-match result for a word in an associative memory when all key bits are zeros?

12-11 (a) Draw the logic diagram of all the cells of one word in an associative memory. Include the read and write logic of Fig. 12-9 and the match logic of Fig. 12-10.

(b) Draw the logic diagram of all cells along one vertical column (column $j$) in an associative memory. Include a common output line for all bits in the same column.

(c) From the diagrams in (a) and (b) show that if output $M_i$ is connected to the *read* line of the same word, then the matched word will be read out, provided only one word matches the masked argument.

12-12 Describe in words and by means of a block diagram how multiple matched words can be read out from an associative memory.

12-13 Derive the logic of one cell and of an entire word for an associative memory that has an output indicator when the unmasked argument is greater than (but not equal to) the word in the associative memory.

12-14 An address space is specified by 16 bits and the corresponding memory space by 12 bits.
(a) How many words are there in the address space?
(b) How many words in the memory space?
(c) If a page consists of 256 words, how many pages and blocks are there in the system?

12-15 Assign symbolic names to the registers in Fig. 12-14 and list the sequence of micro-operations for reading or writing a word in main memory from a given virtual address.

12-16 Define multiprogramming and time-sharing and explain the necessity of a virtual memory in such systems.

12-17 Formulate a binary code to be placed in a memory-page table for the purpose of memory protection. Formulate a corresponding "key" code to accompany every program when it is executed in the CPU. The memory controller compares the memory protection code with the key code to determine what kind of access to main memory (if any) is allowed by the program.

# INDEX

**C**

**D**



**E**



**F**

**M**